CIM
TUTORIAL TEXT

Diploma

Strategic Marketing Management: Analysis and Decision

by Juanita Cockton
and Angela Hatton

New in this September 2002 Tutorial Text

This text contains:
- Revision and self-testing material
- A teaching case covering a variety of areas
- Interactive action programmes to build skills
- Analyses of two recent cases

BPP Publishing
September 2002

First edition 1999
Fourth edition September 2002

ISBN 0 7517 4875 7 (Previous edition 0 7517 4123 X)

British Library Cataloguing-in-Publication Data
A catalogue record for this book
is available from the British Library

Published by

BPP Publishing Limited
Aldine House, Aldine Place
London W12 8AW

www.bpp.com

Printed in Great Britain by W M Print
45-47 Frederick Street
Walsall, West Midlands
WS2 9NE

We are grateful to the Chartered Institute of Marketing for permission to reproduce in this text the syllabus, tutor's guidance notes, past cases, examination questions and extracts from the examiner's reports.

We are grateful to Dr Ashok Ranchhold, the examiner, for his contribution to this tutorial text.

BPP
PUBLISHING

PREFACE

The exam

The Diploma awarded by the Chartered Institute of Marketing is a management qualification which puts a major emphasis on the practical understanding of marketing activities. At the same time, the Institute's examinations recognise that the marketing professional works in a fast changing organisational, economic and social environment.

Strategic Marketing Management: Analysis and Decision is one of the two compulsory CIM Diploma papers. It is compulsory as the marketing professional is expected to be a **manager**. Knowledge and skills in analysis and decision, together with an appreciation of the role of marketing in the corporate structure, are essential ingredients of managerial competence in this field.

This BPP Tutorial Text (September 2002 edition)

The secret of exam success is effective study material which is focused and relevant to the exam *you* will be sitting. This is the philosophy underpinning this *Tutorial Text*, which has been especially written for candidates sitting this case study examination. It is divided into five parts.

This *Tutorial Text* starts in Part A with a description of the case study and a health-check to cover your knowledge of planning and control. We apply a detailed 10 step process to a 'teaching case', *Biocatalysts*, selected as it is good example of the processes you have to go through. We then apply this approach to *City of Daugavpils*, the December 2001 case. Further guidance is offered on the June 2002 Case, *World Class International,* with an extra contribution from the examiner.

Help us to help you

Your feedback will help us improve this *Tutorial Text*, so please complete and return the Review Form at the end of this *Tutorial Text;* you will be entered automatically in a free prize draw.

A final word

This *Tutorial Text* offers a professional solution to your needs in preparing for this challenging exam.

BPP Publishing
September 2002

Other elements in the BPP study package for CIM exams are listed on the Order Form at the back of this *Tutorial Text*.

For information about all the products and services offered by the BPP Holdings plc group, visit our website. The address is: *www.bpp.com*

HOW TO USE THIS TUTORIAL TEXT

1 **What is the CIM case study?**

There is no formal syllabus for the CIM's examination *Strategic Marketing Management: Analysis and Decision*. Instead the examination is based on a case study normally comprising 30 to 40 pages of narrative, charts and tables and issued to examinees by post about **four weeks in advance of the examination.**

The issue of the case study some four weeks in advance allows time for considerable analysis and discussion.

The case study is a **practical** test of the candidates' knowledge of marketing (gained in Certificate and Diploma, or equivalent, studies) and their ability to apply it. Normally candidates will also have some practical experience in marketing to bring to bear.

At the same time, some background knowledge is necessary. Those who are coming to the case study 'cold' will find the theoretical revision a useful complement to their practical experience. This is provided in Part A of this *Tutorial Text.*

Whilst case study methods vary according to the institution and lecturer concerned, a particular model embodying a comprehensive approach is detailed in this *Tutorial Text.*

2 **Discussing the case study**

Students are strongly advised to conduct in-depth discussion with colleagues on the case study analysis and its issues. This is often accomplished at colleges by the forming of **syndicate groups** of four to six people and the holding of frequent **plenary sessions** where all candidates gather together. In this way, a syndicate member not only hears the view of his or her syndicate, but also those of other syndicates. In this way a much more balanced, integrated and secure approach can be developed. Of course, whilst classroom discussion may be the best for obtaining this sort of feedback, you may benefit from using the Internet if you cannot attend class. How about conducting a discussion with another person using instant messenger?

Having said this, candidates should not copy out **group answers** word for word: these will be failed. Candidates must offer their own **individual** work on the day of the examination.

3 **Practice**

There are a number of different methods of dealing with case studies. In Part B, we explore a practice case, Biocatalysts, for teaching purposes. This is supplemented in Part C by the December 2001 practice case, City of Daugavpils, and some notes on World Class International (June 2002) with the examiner's answers.

One of the key success factors in case study examination (apart from being thoroughly prepared) is to be well organised in the exam room itself, freeing the mind to think more calmly and clearly about the exam questions.

A note on pronouns

On occasions in this *Tutorial Text*, 'he' is used for 'he or she', 'him' for 'him or her' and so forth. Whilst we try to avoid this practice, it is sometimes necessary for reasons of style. No prejudice or stereotyping according to sex is intended or assumed.

SYLLABUS OVERVIEW

Analysis and Decision

This Analysis and Decision paper tests a potential candidate's ability to demonstrate knowledge from different areas of marketing in order to develop appropriate strategies plans and innovative solutions for organisations. Many of the cases presented will draw from all areas of marketing from the CIM syllabuses up to and including Diploma level.

As each case is different, candidates should possess the capability to draw upon some of the key topic areas from across the CIM syllabus that will need to be refreshed in order to tackle case studies effectively. There will be a heavier emphasis on the syllabi for Integrated Marketing Communications, Planning and Control, and International Marketing Strategy.

Strategic thinking ability, coherence of argument, absorption of detail and clear justification of any solutions offered will be measured outcomes of the effective understanding of the case studies.

Aims and objectives

Objectives of the Analysis and Decision module are outlined below and students will be expected:

- To utilise the practical and marketing skills which are pre-requisites for analysis of the case and engage students in justifying their strategic recommendations.

- To analyse the case within given constraints and understand possible barriers to implementation.

- To apply the marketing processes within a wide variety of market sectors.

- To develop the ability to cross reference knowledge from other Diploma subjects.

- To develop creative and innovative applications of knowledge of strategic marketing.

- To be able to apply relevant marketing planning models and display critical analytical and decision-making skills within the Case Study examination.

- To comprehend and resolve a wide variety of marketing problems and provide realistic and innovative solutions.

Learning outcomes

Students will be able to:

- Demonstrate an in-depth understanding of the strategic marketing planning process and to develop a creative and innovative strategic marketing plan.

- Critically evaluate case studies using a wide variety of marketing techniques, concepts and models and an understanding of contemporary marketing issues.

- Understand and apply competitive positioning strategies within a given case study.

- Critically evaluate various options available within given constraints and justify any decisions taken.

- Demonstrate the ability to analyse numerical data and management information and utilise it to make decisions about key underlying issues within the Case Study.

- Synthesise various strands of knowledge from the different Diploma subjects effectively in the context of the Case Study examination.

- Apply both practical and academic marketing knowledge within a given Case Study.

- Comprehend and resolve a wide variety of marketing problems.

- Develop appropriate control aspects and contingency plans.

SENIOR EXAMINER'S VIEW OF THE PAPER

1   Overview of the area

The Analysis and Decision paper is the culmination of all the marketing subjects covered at all levels, but especially the Diploma and the Advanced Diploma. For this reason, there is no specific syllabus for this paper. The new Planning and Control syllabus now gives a clear strategic focus. This type of expertise will be needed to tackle the Case Study paper. It is also clear that it will not be possible to tackle the Case Study without a clear grasp of the fundamentals of Marketing Communications and International Marketing. In this sense, for all students, the Case Study is a culmination of the application of all the marketing knowledge they have gained over several years.

The title of the paper 'Analysis and Decision' implies that the candidates are competent enough to analyse problems within a marketing context and subsequently take appropriate decisions to implement marketing strategies for an organisation. In order to achieve competence in this area, prospective candidates will need to be conversant with all aspects of marketing, as strategic marketing problems do not come in neat packages. A comprehensive grasp of the basic subjects at the Certificate and Advanced Certificate level together with the key subjects of International Marketing and Marketing Communications is needed. The Planning and Control paper is an integral part of the preparation for this paper.

2   The changing focus of the paper

- Marketing as a subject area is undergoing major changes. These changes are taking place as a result of dramatic shifts in technology, demographics, globalisation, systems of production, logistics and ecological issues. In future, therefore, the paper will be designed to reflect more of these contemporary issues in addition to the knowledge base mentioned above.

- The case studies will also be designed to develop strategic marketing issues which can be operationalised and implemented within realistic constraints (June 1998 case). It is often forgotten that marketing is not just about positioning and growth, but also about **effectiveness** within **given constraints** within most organisations. These constraints mean that strategies have to be sensibly evaluated and chosen, with hard decisions being made. When particular strategies are chosen, it is clear that the constraints could be many and varied. Constraints, for instance could be financial, organisational (both employee and culture related), marketing (image, size of markets, branding, distribution systems, networks) and, if the organisation is a division of a large entity, headquarter-imposed constraints.

Globalisation

- The rapid changes in technology are far reaching as they are changing the normal paradigms of marketing. The four P's cannot be discussed with certainty. The nature and direction of marketing strategies, necessarily have to take into account the massive computing power available and the advent of business on the Internet. Many multi-nationals have operated globally for decades, but technology is changing the patterns of production and consumption.

- For instance, global brands are available anywhere and production facilities may be located in a myriad of different countries (December 1998 case). For smaller companies, the Internet holds the promises and pitfalls of operating in a global arena.

- The introduction of the Euro means that Pan-European marketing strategies have to be thought through in a different manner. The changing nature and the growth of south Asian markets has an enormous impact on the marketing strategies of organisations. The nature and strength of the American market is often forgotten in many marketing cases. The case studies will reflect these changes and will embrace many different sectors of industry.

Organisational issues

- When developing marketing strategies it is important that the culture and nature of the organisation is taken into account. Marketing strategies often succeed and fail as a result of inappropriate personnel, inappropriate structures or climates within organisations. Organisations are therefore always striving to create the appropriate structures and develop appropriate cultures to meet the demands of the market place.

- The customer is king and marketing strategists have to place the level of market orientation at the centre of their thinking.

Sustainability

- Marketing literature has for long been concerned with growth and market share. It is important that issues surrounding the constraints imposed by the environment are taken into account. The world is facing an enormous challenge in terms of the availability of resources and the needs of the population. In some respects a challenge posed to marketing strategists is the need to consider constraints and responsibility.

Financial issues

- Financial issues will also play a key role in developing strategies.

- A good knowledge of basic financial statements such as profit and loss accounts, balance sheets and cashflow statements is required.

Knowledge of contemporary marketing issues

- Each case is different and will therefore test some knowledge of contemporary issues. Students need to be encouraged to read journal articles pertaining to the case study.

Application of previous knowledge

- The need to apply models for analysis will continue. However, a more critical approach in applying these techniques will be needed. The paper will reflect the need for both academic and practical knowledge as a true marketer needs to have experience of both areas for developing sensible strategies.

Issues of implementation and control

- An awareness of the clear decision-making and implementation strategies will be tested. As will be strategic positioning, innovation and branding in the context of implementation and control

3 Links with other papers

This paper deliberately has no syllabus. The paper is the culmination of all the knowledge gained at the Advanced Diploma and Diploma levels. The foundations laid by the Marketing Communications Strategy, International Marketing Strategy and Planning and Control syllabuses underpin the Analysis and Decision paper. In addition to this, the Planning and Control syllabus offers the fundamental underpinning knowledge needed to undertake strategic analysis. In tutoring and preparing students for this paper, tutors need to be aware of the linkages with other areas and they need to be able to draw from a variety of literature sources in order to enhance and improve their analytic and decision-making skills. This is particularly important for both large and small organisations as amply demonstrated by the **Philips** and **Biocatalysts** case studies. In each case there is an emphasis on understanding international issues as well as communications issues thoroughly.

The examiners are looking for candidates to demonstrate analytical ability, interpretive skills, insight, innovation and creativity in answering questions. They are also looking for candidates to take clear and sensible decisions within the context of the case study. A critical awareness of the specific issues involved, relevant theoretical underpinning, attention to detail, coherence and justification of strategies adopted will also be assessed.

To perform well on the paper, candidates will have to exhibit the following.

- A need to concentrate on the strategic aspects of marketing underpinned by the necessary detail

- The ability to identify 'gaps' in the case study and to outline the assumptions made

- The ability to critically apply relevant models for case analysis

- The ability to draw and synthesise from any of the diploma subject areas as relevant

- Concentration on the question set rather than the pre-prepared answer

- The ability to answer in the report format with comprehensive sentences rather than providing simplistic lists

- The judicious use of diagrams for illustrative purposes

- The ability to draw disparate links together and give coherent answers

- The use of interesting an useful articles from journals in their answers

- Innovation and creativity in answering the questions

- Demonstration of practical applications of marketing knowledge

- Sensible use of time and an ability to plan the answer within the set time

- A good understanding of the cases study set

- The ability to draw up a comprehensive and convincing marketing plan with accompany costs and schedules

- The ability to suggest appropriate control mechanisms and contingency plans

Part A
Introducing case study

1

Why a Case Study?

Chapter Topic List

1	What the Case Study is and how it differs from other CIM papers
2	The value of Case Study in the work place
3	The challenges of a Case Study approach, the problems people face and how to overcome them
4	How to get the most from this Tutorial Text
5	What CIM expect
6	The characteristics of an excellent case candidate and the secret of winning examiner support

1 WHAT THE CASE STUDY IS AND HOW IT DIFFERS FROM OTHER CIM PAPERS

1.1 The final paper for the CIM Diploma is Strategic *Marketing Management: Analysis and Decision,* commonly referred to as the Case Study. *Planning and Control* and *Analysis and Decision* are the two compulsory CIM papers. No-one is exempt and both are without doubt very demanding examinations. The Case Study paper requires that you **integrate** all your previous studies and it provides a realistic assessment of whether you have acquired the knowledge and skills to tackle a practical marketing challenge in a commercially credible way.

1.2 This subject, *Analysis and Decision* is distinctly different from other CIM exams, both in terms of its assessment and its syllabus.

1.3 There is in fact **no** formal syllabus for this paper. Instead the examiner can call upon any aspect of the eleven CIM subjects. CIM expects you to be conversant with the breadth and depth of these other papers either through previous studies or on the basis of the exemptions you have been awarded.

Valuable information

1.4 You should **not** attempt to tackle this Analysis and Decision paper until you have studied the other three Diploma papers.

(a) **Strategic Marketing Management: Planning and Control** – which provides the tools and frameworks used to tackle a case study.

(b) **Integrated Marketing Communications Strategy** – which is often a strong theme in case studies and the questions set for it.

BPP PUBLISHING

(c) **International Marketing Strategy** – because the majority of cases represent international organisations, the examiner will expect to see evidence that you appreciate the implications of planning and operating in an international environment.

1.5 Case studies represent **real organisations** and describe the marketing challenges they face. Often, cases are also set in real time and so you may well be faced with a very topical issue. In the sample case we are using in the first part of this manual, **Biocatalysts**, the issue was GM products and biotechnology. At the time of the case, GM crop trials were headline news. You will be given management and marketing data in the form of a narrative with various appendices. This may well include financial data.

1.6 The case study assessment method is currently by open book examination. This means you are sent a copy of the exam case study four weeks prior to the exam date. You then have time to complete your analysis of the case data and to think through your strategic recommendations.

1.7 In the exam room, you will be faced with specific questions and some additional data and, having taken account of this, you will be expected to present and justify your decisions.

1.8 You are able to take some pre-prepared work into the exam with you and currently CIM are operating **two approaches** to this.

(a) You may be allowed to take in a limited number of pre-prepared appendices which you can attach to your exam script and refer to in your answers.

(b) You may be allowed to take unlimited notes for reference into the exam room, but in this case all work submitted must be written up in the exam room.

We will say more about these options and how to prepare for them later in this manual, but the basic approach, case technique and requirements for exam success remain the same.

1.9. There are few short cuts when it comes to tackling a case study and it is a time-consuming exercise, but you will find the process extends your knowledge and improves skills which have immediate relevance to your work.

2 THE VALUE OF CASE STUDY IN THE WORK PLACE

2.1 Case Study is a very **practical** examination. A knowledge of marketing theory on its own will not be sufficient to gain you an exam pass. You have to be able to apply that theory in the context of a real business issue and situation. This means that you must:

(a) Know the framework for developing both strategic marketing and operational marketing plans

(b) Be able to apply the various tools of analysis, recognising and acknowledging the limitations of these where appropriate

(c) Be able to make decisions, in a way which reflects customer needs and be able to justify those decisions

(d) Have the skills to present your views and ideas in a convincing way

2.2 This demanding test of a marketer's capabilities and competencies goes to the heart of the skills the professional marketer needs in the workplace. For most students, this is the paper which pulls together all they have learnt and enables them to see how they can really make a **difference** in their own organisations.

2.3   Even experienced marketers often pay little more than lip service to the marketing planning process. Faced with the pressure of an impending examination, many candidates are amazed at the depth and quality of strategic thinking possible, even with the limited information supplied in a case. This experience can be a useful **benchmark for marketing planning in your own business.**

2.4   Some students get concerned about not being expert in the sector of the featured case study. It can seem daunting if you have B2C experience and are suddenly faced with a B2B challenge, like Biocatalysts. This may seem unrealistic and less representative of life in the business world. However, in our experience as consultants, it is a very real reflection of the situations we face. Our expertise is marketing, and the disciplines and concepts of marketing travel well between sectors. If anything, **lack of detailed industry or product knowledge makes it easier to avoid the myopia so often characteristic of those who are product focused.**

2.5   Besides the chance to practise analysis and decision-making skills, the case study also provides the opportunity further to develop **team-work skills**. Unless you are studying independently, you will probably be tackling the case as part of a formal syndicate or study group. This is an excellent idea as it provides a time efficient way of tackling analysis as well as providing a forum for brainstorming and creative thinking. However, to make a syndicate work, you need to have and use team working skills and be disciplined in how you communicate with other members. Again, these are practical skills highly valued in the workplace.

3   THE CHALLENGES OF A CASE STUDY APPROACH, THE PROBLEMS PEOPLE FACE AND HOW TO OVERCOME THEM

3.1   Open book examinations may at first sight seem very easy. Certainly you do not have to worry about learning facts or remembering examples. However case study brings with it its own set of problems and challenges which you need to be aware of before beginning your studies.

3.2   In practice, relatively few candidates fail examinations because of lack of knowledge. **Much more common is a lack of exam technique.** This results in any one of a number of common problems including failing to **manage time** or answer the question set. Similarly, with the Case Study exam, it is often a failure of technique not knowledge which causes exam failure. Exam technique is rather different for a case exam, but none the less requires practice and the development of a wide range of skills already alluded to, from analysis to persuasive communication, skills which you would expect to find in a **competent, practising marketing manager.**

3.3   Exam technique for the case study starts when the exam case is **issued**. Finding enough time for preparation and using that time effectively is all part of case technique. The seeds of success or failure are sown during this important preparation time, so **preparation is key.**

Valuable information

3.4   The exams may seem like a long way off, but it is never too early to start planning for them. Check out the date of your Case Study exam. This will be on the first or second Friday of December or June, but the **exact date should be available on the CIM** website. Calculate back four weeks from this date. This is the latest date the case should be issued to you. By this date, you want to have broadly completed any work on other examination subjects, so you have the maximum time available for the case study. You will need to find about 40 hours preparation time during these weeks. Where will it come from?

- Avoid planning too many events for those pre-exam weekends
- Talk to your employer about taking some study leave
- Book holiday time for study if necessary

3.5 **Using your preparation time well** is the next case challenge. **Sharing the workload** by being part of a study group is to be advised whenever possible. There is no doubt that cracking a case study alone is hard and lonely work, but, whether working alone or as part of a group, you need a timetable and plan of action. In this Tutorial Text, we are going to work through a sample case in detail, showing you what must be done and providing you with a recommended framework, but you will need the self-discipline to apply that to the exam case.

3.6 Some candidates fail to meet the challenge of analysis. They do too little or too much. Both are recipes for failure. Watch out for indications of which trap you are most likely to fall into.

The Too Little Analysis Candidate	The Too Much Analysis Candidate
The Reader. Confuses reading the case with analysis of it. Does not see the importance of analysing appendices and cross referencing findings.	**The Analysis Addict.** Suffers from the complaint we know as **Analysis Paralysis**. The symptoms are fear of decision-making and finding comfort in the safe activity of analysis.
The Juggler. Typically puts off tackling the analysis till the week before the exam. With so many other things to do, it is easy to not take this paper seriously. Sadly what might seem straightforward and obvious at the first read often proves much more complex after detailed analysis.	**The Detail Fanatic.** It is easy to get hung upon calculations to the third decimal place, or be brought to a halt by inconsistencies in a case. There will be inconsistencies and discrepancies but successful candidates do not let this distract them. They keep focused on the bigger picture, and where necessary, they make assumptions and move on.

3.7   Adequate analysis will ensure you have a sound grasp of the case issues and have the facts and figures needed to support your recommendations and convince the examiner of their commercial credibility.

3.8   **Moving on from analysis to decision-making** is another exam challenge for case students. Analysis **can be comforting**; you are busy doing something and there is almost always something else that could be done. Case tutors tend to despair when, despite all our warnings, a student phones the week of the exam and says 'you know the figures in table 3...'. This candidate has been paralysed by analysis and is unlikely to do very well in the exam. They have failed to move on. **Decisions and recommendations need to be made**.

   (a)   The examiner does **not** want to be told to 'choose a profitable segment.' What he/she does want is to be told how to go about choosing a profitable segment, specific advice on the criteria to be applied and the decision framework to be used. If **enough data exists, the examiner wants you to apply the criteria and come up with the recommendation of which segment to target.**

   (b)   Advice which is a generality will not gain marks. 'Set a quantified objective' will not do. You need to set detailed objectives which are underpinned by quantitative measures.

   > 'I recommend that an ambitious growth objective is set, with profit reaching £10 million by 2005 (a £4 million increase). I believe this is achievable because:
   >
   > (i)   The key competitor is tied up in merger talks.
   > (ii)   The overall market is forecast to grow by 20% pa.
   > (iii) Our new service level package will provide us a strong competitive advantage'

   It is this clarity of advice and strong justification which the examiner will be looking for. You can see how a grasp of the facts and figures can help you.

3.9   Before the examination day, you will need to have a broad picture of the strategic options open to the business and which options you would support in what circumstances. **At this stage you must not over prepare**. This is the final pre-exam trap. The candidate who wants to pre-write a strategic marketing plan with the i's dotted and the t's crossed, feels perfectly prepared, but in fact has committed a cardinal marketing and exam sin – the product oriented answer.

   > Essentially he/she is saying to the examiner 'here is the answer I want to give you, irrespective of your needs and:
   >
   > (a)   The extra information you have given me
   >
   > (b)   The detail of the question you have set
   >
   > (c)   The importance you want me to attach to this part of the exam as indicated by the marks you have allocated for this question

   Irrespective of all these clues which allow well prepared candidates to 'customise' their answers, our over prepared student has a **'one size answer'** which has to fit all questions – another recipe for failure.

3.10   The focus and level for this paper can also cause problems. It is a **strategic** level focus, where the emphasis is on helping the organisation to decide :

   (a)   Which products and markets to serve

   (b)   The competitive strategy likely to be most effective in winning business from these markets

(c) Which segments of the selected markets to target

(d) How best to deploy the marketing mix to gain a competitive advantage within these segments

It is easy to end up working with the detail and not the big picture. The colour for staff uniforms or the design for the new logo are only important when the strategy has been agreed and your job in the case is to convince the examiner about the **strategic level. This will not be achieved with ad hoc tactical ideas, no matter how creative they are.**

3.11 The Case Study exam is **not** simply an exercise in writing out pre-prepared work. It is a tough, thinking paper, where you will need to have your wits about you to adapt and rethink in line with the specifics of the exam paper. The secret of success lies in a well managed decision file or clearly thought through prepared appendices.

3.12 On the exam day itself, exam technique for the case is not much different than for other subjects. **Questions for this paper must be answered in the order set**. Consider mark allocation to ensure you manage your time effectively. Remember that **how** you communicate our answer is critical and that there are two aspects to this.

(a) **Presentation**, report formats and clear lay out play a key role and make an important first impression.

(b) The **style and tone** of your work needs to be appropriate to the case role you have been allocated and your arguments need to be persuasive.

3.13 As you work through this Tutorial Text, we will help you improve your exam technique and case skills, but it is helpful if you have an honest evaluation of your likely strengths and weaknesses in terms of case exam skills and techniques. Once you have identified your weaknesses, you will be able to take positive steps to tackle them.

3.14 Take time now to identify your strengths and weaknesses against the following.

	Strengths	Weaknesses
Prioritising case and managing the 4 weeks prior to the exam		
Handling the analysis: • Quantifying data • Qualitative data		
Focusing at strategic not tactical level		
Moving on to decision-making		
Making clear decisions		
Organising your exam file or prepared appendices		
Presentation and communication		
Managing time in the exam		
Being flexible in the light of additional information		
Using data to justify decisions		

4   HOW TO GET THE MOST FROM THIS TUTORIAL TEXT

4.1   Objectives of this Tutorial Text

(a)   Provide you with a simple to follow case process

(b)   Ensure you are familiar with the expectations of the CIM examiner in terms of level, tone and focus

(c)   Demonstrate a sample case analysed in a step by step process

(d)   Give you the opportunity to practise case technique in the context of past cases prior to the exam to help you build skills and confidence

(e)   Make you aware of the most common pitfalls and mistakes made by unsuccessful case students

(f)   Help you review your knowledge of planning and control communications, and of international differences and develop the skills needed to apply these tools and frameworks to deliver a coherent and integrated set of plans from the strategic to the operational

(g)   Encourage you to review your presentation and communication skills so that your work has maximum impact

4.2   What this *Tutorial Text* will not do is teach you the tools and frameworks of the other CIM subjects – we assume you have studied these, but in the next chapter we will help you audit that knowledge and identify any gaps.

4.3   This Tutorial Text has been developed in three sections

(a)   Introducing Case Study
(b)   A sample case
(c)   Two further practice cases

4.4   It is tempting to try and speed up the process by missing out sections, in particular the practice cases in section C. We strongly advise you **not** to do this. You cannot pass a case exam simply by reading about the process; you **must** give yourself some hands on practice.

4.5   To get the most out of this Tutorial Text, you should use it as a guide through your preparation. We will provide you with signposts to help you assess your progress and will identify places where you might do additional work and practice. It is, however, important to recognise you are learning about the case process. Every case study is different and, like you, we will not know about the sector or industry of the case until the exam month.

4.6   In Section A, we will show you a generic process for tackling a case study. In Section B, we will apply that process to a past CIM Case. In section C, you will have two more recent CIM exams on which to build your own skills in applying the process.

Files

4.7   We would recommend you set up two working files for this subject.

(a)   Keep any notes, frameworks and advice for tackling case studies in general: this will be a master reference file for you.

(b)   Keep specific work related to practice cases: this will be of no real value to you after that case is complete.

Time

4.8 Remember when planning your case study preparation that the exam case will be issued four weeks in advance, so you need to have completed your work through this study manual by then. We recommend you allow:

	Minimum	*Maximum*	
Part A of this Tutorial Text	2 hours	4 hours	Introduction to the subject
Part B	20 hours	40 hours	Guided tour of the case process
Part C	40 per case	60 per case	Individual practice cases: time varies according to the depth you work these
Exam Case preparation	40 hours	60 hours	

5 WHAT CIM EXPECT

5.1 You will perhaps have already gathered that the case study is treated as something of a jewel in the crown. This final paper is the **last hurdle** to your official recognition as a professionally qualified marketer and it is seen as being the acid test of your commercial credibility.

5.2 In fact **commercial credibility** has, for a number of years, been one of the **key measures** the **examiners have used in assessing case candidates.**

(a) Does the proposed strategy make sense – can it be substantiated from the analysis?

(b) Is the proposal convincing?

5.3 Remember that, for the CIM examiner, the case study is simply a vehicle for assessing your commercial competence. Every six months the scenario changes but the **characteristics CIM are looking for in a successful candidate remain the same.**

(a) Does the candidate **appreciate the context** of the case scenario? Is the strategy realistic in terms of the available resources and are constraints such as time frames recognised?

(b) Is there evidence of an appreciation of the **broader business implications** of proposals in terms of the impact on profitability, the resources and budgets needed for implementation and the effect of any proposed changes on people within the organisation?

(c) Are **plans supported by specific strategies** to ensure implementation and do they incorporate proposals for **measuring performance** and progress.

Action Programme 1

If you have the opportunity, take time to review a marketing plan you have worked on or which has been developed within your organisation. How would you implement it based on the comments above?

5.4 **CIM expect you to spend up to 60 hours preparing for a case examination.** You have plenty of time to present well-thought out and sensible arguments. If you worked for the company in question, would your script be taken seriously?

Action Programme 2

In the *Sunday Times Business News* there is usually a featured company – their situation described and a number of experts asked their views. This is essentially a case study in action. Make a point of looking at these and in particular assess the experts. Who impresses you and why? Which of them would you be prepared to pay as a consultant?

What advice could you give to the business?

5.5 It is easy to get so involved in the case scenario that you forget that the real challenge is to **pass the exam**. You must make certain that you make the right impression. Irrespective of the quality of your strategy your paper tells the examiner a lot about you.

What it says about you	Symptom
Failure to finish the questions	A poor resource manager the exam task was clear and the resource available predicted
Poor presentation	A careless, unprofessional approach
Lack of quantification in the form of objectives, budgets etc	A fear of financial aspects
Unconvincing arguments	A poor communicator
Too much attention to the detail	A lack of strategic overview

5.6 The examiners are looking only for evidence of the characteristics you would expect in a competent marketing professional. We will be considering these required skills in detail in Chapter 2. Before you move on you might like to spend five minutes thinking through what you would expect these to be.

6 THE CHARACTERISTICS OF AN EXCELLENT CASE CANDIDATE AND THE SECRET OF WINNING EXAMINER SUPPORT

6.1 The excellent candidate is well prepared. Case study is a long process and careful preparation helps ensure precious study time is used both efficiently and effectively.

6.2 The best candidates are well organised. They have an action plan which they keep to and where possible they involve other people in the process.

6.3 Their analysis is thorough and is used as a basis for strategy and decision-making, not as an end in its own right.

BPP PUBLISHING

6.4   The successful candidate presents a script that wins examiner support.

Presentation

Well written in report format with clear structure. Lots of white space, diagrams and use of colour help to present information quickly and effectively.

✗

The Wall of Words Examiners do not want to be confronted by whole pages of written narrative, unbroken and unstructured – the horror of a wall of words

✓

Successful scripts **Structure** Clear headings and sub headings make structure clear **White space & colour** Presentation is easier with use of colour to highlight and lots of white space

Perspective is incorporated to ensure the audience is convinced you have thought about the commercial realise

A major above the line communication strategy for a small regional player	✗
Acknowledgement of the profit pressure and likely demands of the shareholders	✓
Product development suggested for the firm with limited time or money	✗
Product development for the cash-rich player with a dated portfolio	✓

Persuasion is incorporated to ensure the audience is convinced.

✗

I recommend we adopt a differentiated strategy and target European customers first.

✓

In this highly competitive sector a differentiated strategy rolled out across Europe would give us the opportunity to: • Win a premium price • Reflect the very real buyer behaviour – differences evidenced by our research • Learn from each successive launch

6.5 The best candidates know the case well enough to be able to respond flexibly in the exam room changing emphasis, and even strategy, in light of the questions and extra information.

Chapter Round-up

- This chapter has tried to provide the context for your case study preparations

    You should now be aware of the characteristics of a good candidate and understand how CIM has positioned the case study examination.

- You should be able to explain to others the value of the case process and identify a list of skills which both the successful case candidate and the experienced marketing practitioner need to demonstrate.

Quick Quiz

1   Case study differs from other CIM exams in two significant ways. What are they? (see para 1.3 and 1.6)

2   How long before the exam day can you expect to receive your case study? (1.6)

3   Case study is a very practical examination. Identify how the examiners might test whether you have the ability to apply the theory in the context of a case study. (2.1)

4   What do we mean if we described a case candidate as suffering from Analysis paralysis? (3.6)

5   Why do students sometimes find it difficult to move on from analysis to decisions? (3.8)

6   How would you describe to someone the focus and level which characterise how CIM has positioned this paper? (3.10)

7   Why is it important for candidates *not* to go to the exam with fully prepared answers? (3.9)

8   What are the two levels of communication which are critical to the successful case candidate? (3.12)

9   Where will you get a knowledge of the planning tools essential for this paper? (4.2)

10   Identify four ways in which an examiner might assess the commercial credibility of a case candidate. (5.3)

11   How much should you be prepared to invoice the case client for at the end of the examination? (5.4)

12   Identify four ways in which your approach to the exam paper gives the examiner an insight into your performance as a manager. (5.5)

13   What characteristics would you look for in a successful marketer? (5.6)

14   Three P's are important in a successful script. What are they? (6.4)

15   Why is flexibility an important characteristic for the case student and the practising manager? (6.5)

2 The tools and planning skills needed: a healthcheck

Introduction

A thorough knowledge of the planning and control, communications and international diploma subjects is essential for Analysis and Decision. Analysis and Decision provides you with the opportunity to demonstrate your ability to apply this knowledge by using your marketing management skills to solve the problems of a real case.

If you take the opportunity to do at least one practice case study, as well as preparing you for the examination, it has the added benefit of allowing you to improve existing marketing management skills and develop new skills that should help you improve your performance at work (or for a new job).

1 KEY SKILLS

1.1 You have already considered the key skills a marketing manager should have. Our list includes:

Characteristic	Evidence
1 Structured	Uses P&C frameworks and presents in clear report format
2 Knowledgeable	Working command of the marketer's tools, the confidence to adapt them and an appreciation of their limitations
3 Financially aware	Confident to use and include numbers, and a clear appreciation that marketing decisions will impact on profitability
4 Analytical	Decisions made on the basis of analysis not hunch
5 Creative	Able to look at problems in a different way, innovative ideas and approaches encouraged
6 Decisive	Criteria for decisions laid out but clear decisions then made – no procrastination: in today's fast moving markets, speed is often of the essence.
7 An Implementer	Anyone can write plans, but it takes real skill to implement them from internal marketing plans to contingency plans and timetables. The examiners will be looking for evidence that you can go from paper to action.
8 A Resource Manager	Budgets and appreciation of costs is key here. Control measures demonstrate your understanding of the value of resources... and remember the evidence of time management.

2 KNOWLEDGE CHECK

Checking your knowledge and assessing your knowledge gaps

2.1 Now is a good time to remind yourself of the other diploma subjects and establish your strengths and weaknesses in each of these subjects in preparation for the case study. Amongst other skills, the case study will provide you with the opportunity to develop your analytical and decision-making skills. It is not the intention to check comprehensively your knowledge of the diploma subjects in this chapter, but rather to prompt and remind you of some of the theory. Remember, the practice case studies are a test of your knowledge as well as your skills.

2.2 Please check the subject syllabus for more detail if you are not familiar with the current CIM syllabuses.

2.3 The key aims and objectives of each of these subjects will be covered briefly as a reminder of what the subject involved, followed by knowledge checks. Answers to these knowledge checks can be found at the end of the chapter.

Tutor Tip

Do take some time to test yourself on the knowledge check questions. Try to do them without referring to notes or books and see how you get on. If you have not studied the subjects for some time, it may be difficult to start with but worth the effort as it gets you back into study mode.

Make sure as you work your way through this manual that you identify and address knowledge gaps. Keep 'Notes to Self' as a way of ensuring that anything you are unfamiliar with, or need to check your understanding of, is dealt with. You do not want to be doing this with the exam case study.

BPP PUBLISHING

Planning and control

2.4 Aims and objectives

- Enable students to understand the theoretical concepts, techniques and models that underpin the marketing planning process.

- Build practical skills associated with the management of the planning process

- Enable students to justify their strategic decisions and recommendations

- Develop an understanding of the barriers that exist to effective implementation of strategy

- Appreciate the need to tailor marketing plans and process to allow for the specific sector and situational factors that apply to any given organisation

- Develop an awareness of the techniques that underpin innovation and creativity in organisations

Action Programme 1

Planning and Control knowledge check

1   What is the purpose of analysis, and what is the desired outcome?

2   What are the key components of an internal and external corporate or business audit?

3   Name four models the marketer can use during the analysis process and explain briefly their purpose.

4   What is the role of the vision and mission statements? How would you distinguish between the two?

5   What is planning gap analysis?

6   What are strategic options/business strategies and how might they be evaluated?

7   What competitive positions might a business adopt and what would be the implications of adopting these positions?

8   What common methods of consumer and business to business segmentation are available to the marketer?

9   What is the Decision Making Unit (DMU) and why is it important to marketers?

10   How can marketing research help in the analysis, planning and control processes?

11   What does the term 'Balanced Scorecard' mean?

12   What are the key components of a marketing information system (MKIS)?

Check your answers with ours at the end of the chapter.

Integrated Marketing Communications

2.5 Aims and objectives

- To enable students to develop a sound understanding of the formulation and implementation of integrated marketing communications plans and associated activities

- To enable students to appreciate and manage marketing communications within a variety of different contexts

- To encourage students to recognise, appreciate and contribute fully to the totality of an organisation's systems of communications with both internal and external audiences

- To enable students to be aware of the processes, issues and vocabulary associated with integrated marketing communications in order that they can make an effective contribution to their working environment

Action Programme 2

Integrated Marketing Communications knowledge check

1   What contexts affect marketing communications?

2   What factors affect customers' purchase decision making?

3   What is the decision making process (DMP)?

4   What types of perceived risk are involved in purchase decisions and how can marketers reduce perceived risk?

5   What internal factors affect communications with an organisation's external audiences?

6   What internal factors influence corporate image and reputation?

7   What models are there for establishing communication objectives?

8   A brand is made up of many parts, both tangible and intangible. What are the components of a brand?

9   How can a brand help to build loyalty?

10   Briefly define the meaning of push, pull and profile communication strategies.

11   How can marketers change attitudes?

12   What does 'share of voice' (SOV) mean?

Check your answers with ours at the end of the chapter.

BPP PUBLISHING

International Marketing Strategy

2.6 Aims and objectives

- To enable students to develop a thorough understanding of international marketing theory and key concepts

- To develop a knowledge and understanding of vocabulary associated with international/global marketing strategy in different types of economies, organisations and market situations

- To appreciate the complexities of international and global marketing in a mix of economies

- To create an awareness of processes, context and influences associated with international and global marketing strategies in a range of economies

- To develop students, appreciation of the implications for implementation, monitoring and control of the international marketing planning process

Action Programme 3

International marketing strategy knowledge check

1   Name three World Institutions that have helped to promote world trade.

2   What are market agreements and what types of agreements are there?

3   What is an economic trading bloc and name three?

4   What do NIC and LDC stand for?

5   What are the currents and cross currents referred to by Porter?

6   What are tariffs?

7   What are Harmonised Tariff System (HTS)?

8   What does high context and low context culture mean?

9   What is critical dissonance, often found in international marketing?

10   What is the process of internationalisation?

11   What direct methods of entry are available to exporters?

12   What are the four dimensions Hofstede uses to describe different national cultural characteristics?

Check your answers with our feedback at the end of the chapter.

How did you get on?

2.7 Make sure you take the time to review your answers thoroughly and honestly. The run up to a case exam is the wrong time to discover knowledge gaps. None of us knows it all, so don't be surprised if you have identified content you need to brush up on.

2.8 **Make a list of topics for review or revision.** Tick off one or two a week until you are confident with your underpinning knowledge.

Notes to Self

Topics for Review	Deadline date
1	
2	
3	
4	
5	
6	
7	
8	
9	
10	

3 INTEGRATING THE DIPLOMA SUBJECTS

3.1 The aims and objectives of Analysis and Decision are to convert theory and knowledge into practice. Throughout this workbook and the practice case studies you will have the opportunity to test your knowledge further and to practise your marketing skills.

At each stage of the analysis and decision process, you will be encouraged to use models and techniques on the case study to help you establish the current situation and develop credible solutions.

Introduction to the case study

3.2 The **Analysis & Decision** paper has always been a compulsory paper and is intended to assess not just knowledge and understanding of marketing planning, but that candidates have the ability to tackle real issues in a commercially credible way.

3.3 Your practical experience will be immensely important in this exercise. If you **treat the case study** as though it was **another project at work** and your **exam preparation** as though you were getting ready for a **presentation to senior management**, then you will have an idea of the level, depth and degree of detail which is needed.

3.4 As we have already indicated, the case study is a vehicle for the examiners to assess your marketing management competence. It is critical to your success in this paper that you remember that the **problems of the case are not the central focus for the examiner**. Your skills, the processes you go through, and the tools and techniques you use are what are being assessed.

3.5 The emphasis of the case study syllabus is on strategy not tactics. It is easy to get side tracked producing lots of tactical detail which detracts from the strategic issues. The examination is called Analysis and Decision – both dimensions are tested.

A typical case study

3.6 It is standard practice for the CIM to supply the examination case in the form of an A4 booklet, printed on both sides of the page. There is not much room therefore for making notes in the booklet and you may prefer to **copy single sides for this purpose**. You should always make a working copy of the exam case.

3.7 For those students working towards an exam where an appendix can be taken into the exam, this advice is critical. You will only be allowed to take the original case study into the exam with you and this may be notated. You will want to leave it to the end of your preparation to add the most useful notes to your case study – so **work on a copy**.

3.8 Typically, the CIM diploma case will be 35 to 60 pages long. It will consist of 5 to 10 pages of text followed by a number of appendices. The information contained in the case study will most likely include some or all of the following.

- Background and historical data on the company featured
- Corporate and group organisation
- Marketing and sales operations
- Strengths, weaknesses, opportunities and threats (indicative only)
- Market size, segments, competitors, trends
- Environmental factors
- Marketing mix
- Marketing research
- Consolidated accounts (profit and loss, balance sheet)

3.9 As is usual in most management case studies, the CIM case will:

- Include information which is not particularly useful
- Exclude data which you might feel is essential

3.10 This is to test your **ability to discern information needs** and also to design a marketing research plan and/or improvements to the marketing information system. You are likely to find some anomalies and contradictions in the case study, obliging you to make assumptions. Do not be distracted by these. This is usual and has never caused problems. In reality often it is difficult to obtain information, check its validity or comparability.

3.11 On the inside front cover of the case you will find **important notes** for candidates, followed by a page **candidates brief**, which you must of course read thoroughly and have in mind when interpreting the subsequent data in the case itself.

4 CASE STUDY: TECHNIQUE AND PITFALLS

Practising case study technique

4.1 Nowhere is a lack of technique more likely to result in exam failure than when tackling case studies. The aim of a **practice case** is to give you:

(a) The opportunity to see the **whole process** of case study from beginning to end

(b) The chance to **analyse that process** and **identify strengths and weaknesses** in your approach which can be taken into account with the exam case

(c) The opportunity to consolidate your knowledge and understanding of the other diploma syllabuses and practical marketing skills

Pitfalls to avoid

4.2 Avoid 'Analysis Paralysis'

In Chapter 1, we warned of the dangers of too much or too little analysis. We now want you to think about some other potential pitfalls.

4.3 Avoid 'wobbly' decisions

Remember the paper is strategic and the expectations are that managers can be focused on both the broader picture and implementation. Plans must be **integrated** and **consistent** to ensure that objectives and **recommendations do not conflict** with each other.

4.4 Avoid being a 'type'

(a) **The jumper** – knows the best solutions instantly and feels that developing and evaluating alternative solutions before making a choice menial and unnecessary. 'It's obvious' is the catch-phrase (delivered with thinly disguised scorn for those people who cannot see the obvious). Can tend towards impatience and is keen to finish the job in half the time.

(b) **The sitter** – finds it difficult to come to a decision and sits on the fence equivocating brilliantly on both sides. There is a tendency to forget that the subject they are being examined in is analysis and **decision.**

(c) **The Xerox** – with no strong views of his/her own and no real inclination to hard work, this person copies other people's ideas – unfortunately often those of the **jumper**. The Xerox is caught out by the exam question, that puts a slightly different slant on the matter and blindly copies out his/her pre-prepared answer regardless.

(d) **The tree** – never sees the wood. Tends to receive the case and plunge into analysis of all tables etc with calculator smoking. Works hard and is extremely difficult to beat in discussion since he/she can bring more and more data to bear on the question, endlessly splitting hairs, crossing t's and dotting i's.

(e) **Blinkers** – sees things only from his/her narrow experience. Tends to have one textbook approach for each situation and will not listen to the views of others or any evidence that indicates a contrary view.

Recognise any traits? We all have our weaknesses: being able to recognise them is a great strength and can help you avoid some of the pitfalls of working the case study.

5 EXAM TECHNIQUE

Additional information

5.1 Additional information is presented to students in the examination room. This is usually in the form of a memo or letter and usually gives information about either developments in the market place eg competitive information, or may inform you of a decision by management.

5.2 Sometimes the information decides a course of action for you, in which case you must be prepared to develop appropriate plans to deliver what has been decided. On other occasions the additional information leaves you to decide what course of action to take in light of the information.

BPP PUBLISHING

Questions

5.3 Typically there have been three or four questions of unequal marks, requiring you to calculate how much time to allocate to each question. You must answer all questions and in sequence. In the past questions have included:

- Strategic marketing plans
- Promotional plans
- Recommendations on implementing a marketing orientation
- Segmentation
- Brand values and positioning
- International strategy development
- E-strategy development

Case study examination rules

Tutor Tip

There are currently two forms of case study examination. One is completely open book and one is a modified version.

Open book exam

5.4 The completely open book exam means you can take as much pre-prepared material in as you like and reference books. However, unless you are planning to spend the three hours searching through this information, we recommend your pre-prepared material is kept to a minimum and **must** be in **outline only**. There are a number of reasons for this which are worth repeating:

(a) You do not know the mark allocation of each question so do not know how much to prepare.

(b) You do not know the precise wording and emphasis of the questions so do not know the slant you will be required to take.

(c) You do not know the mark allocation for additional information so you need to be discerning about which material you take in.

We would recommend you take in one good reference book. You cannot submit pre-prepared pages and material, as this will be treated as invalid.

5.5 In the **modified open book** exam you are permitted to take into the exam:

- Six A4 pages of pre-prepared analysis
- Your case study which you can have annotated

No other materials or textbooks are permitted.

Your six pre-prepared analysis pages can be attached to your script and need to be referred to where appropriate. The rest of your answers must be written in the examination room and only be submitted on CIM script and/or paper supplied by the invigilator.

Any pages you write in addition to the one script must be securely fastened to the script booklet.

5.6 Space will be at a premium, the desks are usually very small and wobbly!

5.7 Time allocation

This table shows how many minutes to allocate to each question in a three hour exam based on the number of marks per question. The time allocated marks **includes** planning and checking time. You will not be spending all this time writing.

Marks	Minutes
5	9
10	18
15	27
20	36
25	45
30	54
35	63
40	72
45	81
50	90
55	99
60	108
65	117
70	126
75	135
80	144
85	153
90	162
95	171
100	180

Going forward

5.8 In this *Tutorial Text* we are going to show you three case studies.

(a) Firstly, **Biocatalysts,** where we will take you step by step through the process of analysing case material and developing decisions. Biocatalysts is a particularly good teaching case as it **remains current** and stretches the **marketers who think they can throw money at problems**. The case will be used to introduce principal concepts and demonstrate key aspects of analysis. Remember the analysis given in examples is not exhaustive and is not the only way to conduct analysis.

(b) The second and third cases will bring you up to date with the latest case studies, provide further examples, give you the opportunity to practise further and allow you to see the variety of industries, companies and problems you will encounter. These cases also provide a reminder that in some industries short, medium and long term can be a matter of months while in others it can be years and that some companies have immediate short term problems while others face the challenge of a longer term vision for the future.

5.9 There are a number of ways you can use the material in this Tutorial Text. The **least** effective is to simply turn the pages – reading other people's analysis will not give you the experience and practice you need when it comes to the exam.

You can work all the cases completely, using our analysis or comments as prompts and feedback: to do this thoroughly will take time and effort, but your reward will be increasing confidence and valuable marketing skills.

Between these two extremes are many variations. You can use Biocatalysts as a guided tour for you to see what is expected and then work the next case in depth.

Think about the time you have available and then use the material in the most appropriate way for you.

BPP PUBLISHING

Action Programme review_____

1   **Planning and Control knowledge check answers**

1.1   The purpose of analysis is to establish the effectiveness of business performance in the environment in which it operates and the business's position in the market. This includes establishing internal strengths and weaknesses of the business and external opportunities and threats offered by market conditions, competition and customer behaviour.

1.2   The internal audit identifies the strengths and weaknesses of business activities. The components of the internal audit include evaluating the effectiveness of the business's structure, culture, financial performance, people (and management), business operations (processes and technology used), strategic purpose and planning and its market position. The external audit identifies the opportunities and threats in the business environment. The components of the external audit includes evaluating macro factors (PEST) and micro factors (competition, customers, suppliers, distribution etc).

1.3   Examples of models the marketer can use during the analysis process include:

- Product life cycle (PLC) – used to establish the stage of the product (eg introduction, growth, maturity, decline) and to provide indicators of investment needs and how the marketer should manage the product (eg heavy competition likely during maturity so differentiation important)

- Boston matrix (BCG) – used to evaluate products (and SBUs) for their cash generation and cash requirements. Helps the marketer make decisions about investing, harvesting

- Multifactor matrices – GE matrix used to evaluate business strengths and market attractiveness

- Porter's Five Forces – provides a framework for identifying the forces that affect the competitive structure of an industry and potential sources of profitability. The marketer is encouraged to consider new entrants into the market and barriers to entry, suppliers and supplier power, buyers and buyer power, potential or actual substitute products and possible unsatisfied needs.

1.4   The vision and mission statements are important communication statements that inform stakeholders of future intentions and the purpose of the business. The mission clarifies the purpose of the business by communicating what the business does, who for and how. The vision signals future aspirations, for example a future desired position in the market.

1.5   Planning gap analysis establishes the gap between the forecast of what the business can achieve if it carries on with its current strategies and performance in the predicted market conditions, and its desired corporate goals. The gap is the financial shortfall between forecast and target that will need to be filled by new and/or different strategies and performance.

1.6   The Ansoff matrix is a very useful model for identifying strategic options/business strategies. These are the broad product market opportunities identified during analysis. The GE matrix is one of the models that might be used to evaluate which options to select.

1.7   The best known theory on competitive position is Porter's generic competitive strategies. The positions are:

Cost leadership advantage: aims to achieve overall cost leadership being low cost provider requires:

- Cost and efficient objectives
- Tight cost and overhead control
- Pursuit of high value customers only
- Cost minimisation in all areas
- Achieving critical mass
- Achieving economies of scale

Implications

Usually requires high relative market share certainly requires volume
Possibly favourable access to raw materials
Investment up front and heavy investment in latest technology
Continued re-investment to maintain low cost leadership position

Differentiation advantage: aims to create unique offering (something perceived as different from rest) and requires:

- Design or brand image
- Technology
- Features
- Customer service
- Dealer network
- Combination of these to differentiate

Implications

Can preclude high market share if differentiation built on exclusivity
Balance between high costs of providing differentiation and profits
Need for professional marketing skills and ability to attract skilled people
Product engineering and capability in R and D, creativity/innovation
Needs corporate reputation for quality or technological expertise
Needs strong co-operation from channels
Needs strong co-ordination of R & D, marketing
Qualitative measurements

Focus advantage: aims to focus on needs of a particular buyer group, area of product line or geographic market and to do so more efficiently/effectively than competition. Requires:

- Cost leadership
- Differentiation, or
- Both the above

Implications

Vulnerability of niche approach
Doubts regarding profit potential
Implications as covered in cost and differentiation

1.8 Segmentation methods available to the marketer include:

Geographic: postcode, city, town, village, rural, coastal, county, region, country, continent, climate

Demographic: age, sex, family life cycle, family size, religion, income, occupation, ethnic origin, socio economic group

Behavioural: benefits sought, purchase behaviour, purchase occasion, usage

Psychographic: personality, attitude, lifestyle

Geodemographic: combines geographic and demographic **plus** overlay of psychographic **and** patterns of purchasing behaviour

Business to business: SIC codes, process or product, geographic, size of company, operating variables, circumstances, purchase methods; increasingly DMUs and behavioural factors are used

1.9 The Decision Making Unit (DMU) is the unit made of those people involved in the decision to buy. It is a model that has become most helpful in organisation buying (although also relevant in some consumer markets). It is important to marketers because it is a useful framework for ensuring that all members of the buying process are identified and their needs addressed.

1.10 Marketing research can help throughout the analysis, planning and control process.

Marketing research can help during **analysis** by gathering information that establishes the current situation. The business can establish its current position against competitors, customer perceptions and the likely impact of market forces.

Marketing research can help the **planning process** by ensuring decisions are informed. Decisions can be made on customer groups to serve, positioning and the development and design of the marketing mix to ensure efficient and effective use of resources.

Marketing research can help the **control process** in measuring business and marketing effectiveness and performance. This can be done using questionnaires, focus groups etc to ask customers, distribution channels and other stakeholders for their assessment of the business and its marketing mix.

1.11 The balanced scorecard refers to the linking of objective-setting to measuring performance and is a balance of both quantitative and qualitative measures. Customer feedback and input is an important part of measuring effectiveness as well as measuring business operations at a broader level. Measuring the effectiveness of the organisation in terms of its learning, innovation and continuous improvement is also important.

1.12 The key components of a marketing information systems are:

Marketing Information System MKIS

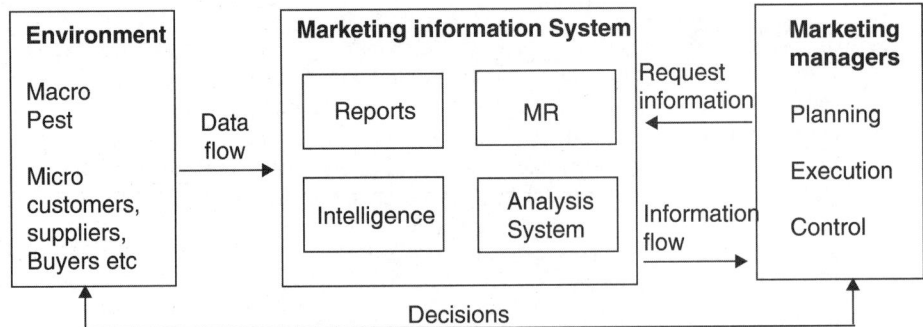

2 **Integrated Marketing Communications knowledge check answers**

2.1 The external contexts that affect marketing communications include legislative, economic, societal, corporate responsibility, technology (information and communications)

2.2 Factors that affect customers' purchase decision making include segmentation factors (eg geographic, demographic, behavioural, psychographic), involvement with purchase (high or low involvement), decision making process, wants, needs and motives, attitudes and beliefs

2.3 The decision making process (DMP) refers to the process consumers go through when deciding to buy. This process most typically, but not always, is:

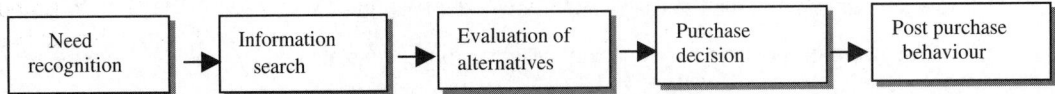

2.4 Perceived risk involved in purchase decisions include performance, financial, physical, social, ego and time. Marketers can try to reduce perceived risk by providing information, building brand loyalty, guarantees, endorsements, money back/exchange and samples.

2.5 Internal factors that affect communications with an organisation's external audiences include corporate vision, mission and strategy, culture and ethics, management and leadership style, employee attitudes and behaviour.

2.6 Internal factors that influence corporate image and reputation include corporate personality (culture, attitudes, values and beliefs) and corporate identity (cues and signals that are real indicators evident in product, place, communications and behaviour).

2.7 Some of the better known models for establishing communication objectives include:

STAGE	AIDA	ADOPTION	DAGMAR
			Unaware
COGNITIVE		Awareness	Awareness
	Attention		[Comprehension]
	Interest	Interest	
			Conviction
AFFECTIVE	Desire	Evaluation	
		Trial	
CONATIVE	Action	Adoption	Action

2.8 A brand is made up of tangible attributes: product components eg reliability, durability and measurable business and marketing mix, and performance e.g. accessibility of place, timeliness of messages. It is also made up of intangible attributes: the emotional values customers associate with the brand such as perceptions of reputation and trust, friendly and helpful staff. Brands are affected by corporate culture and behaviour, people's attitudes and behaviour as well as marketing mix performance.

2.9 Every purchase is a risk for the customer and they are looking for clues of what they can expect. A successful brand is a very effective way of reassuring customers of quality and reliability and of reducing risk. Providing the organisation continues to deliver what the customer wants and achieve high satisfaction levels, the brand can be very effective in building loyalty.

2.10 A push strategy is designed to encourage the organisation's channels or outlets to take products. A pull strategy is designed to attract customers into the organisation's channels or outlets. A profile strategy deals with the overall image and positioning of the company.

2.11 Marketers can change attitudes by changing beliefs, changing order of importance, changing attributes of product or service, changing associations, changing attitudes to comparable products.

2.12 Share of voice (SOV) refers to the total advertising spend in the market by all advertisers.

3 International marketing strategy knowledge check answers

3.1 World Institutions that have helped to promote world trade are the World Trade Organisation, WTO; International Monetary Fund, IMF: World Bank, IBRD: United Nations Conference on Trade & Development, UNCTAD; Group of 8, G8; OECD

3.2 A market agreement is a trading agreement between countries on the exchange goods and broader business operations. The types of agreements are free trade area, customs union, common market, economic union and political union.

3.3 An economic trading bloc is a group of countries that come together to form a trading area offering favourable conditions to member countries. Examples include APEC (Australia, Brunei, Canada, Chile, China, HK, Indonesia, Japan, South Korea, Malaysia, Mexico, New Zealand, Papua New Guinea, Philippines, Singapore, Taiwan, Thailand, US), Southern Common Market MerCoSur (Argentina, Brazil, Paraguay, Uruguay) as well as NAFTA, EU and ASEAN.

3.4 NIC stands for Newly Industrialised Country; LDC for Less Developed Country. They are examples of economic stages of development. Other terms include Advanced Industrialised Countries, Newly Emerging Economies, Big Emerging Economies.

3.5 Currents are primary macro forces affecting competition; cross currents are evolving trends driving international competition to behave differently

3.6 Tariffs are rules, duties, rate schedules, regulations of trade. Examples include customs duties (% value of goods), preferential tariff (in certain circumstances eg historical preference arrangements), specific duty (amount per weight, volume etc), countervailing (additional duties levied to offset subsidies granted in exporting country) variable import levies (levies on imported goods costing less than domestic}, temporary surcharges) anti dumping regulations

3.7 Harmonised tariff system (HTS) has been developed by importers and exporters to determine the correct classification number for product/service that will cross borders. With HT Schedule B export classification number is same as import number.

3.8 Extent to which language and communication is diffuse/implicit - high context [culture depends heavily on external environment, situation, non verbal behaviour in creating and interpreting communications] specific/explicit - low context [environment less important, non verbal behaviour often ignored, directness/bluntness valued, ambiguity disliked]). Example of a country with a high context culture is Japan and of a country with a low context culture is Switzerland.

3.9 Criticality dissonance refers to respondents transforming/disguising responses for fear of how responses will be used.

3.10 The process of internationalisation is when an organisation moves from indirect exporting to a global business, from being uninterested in exporting through to formulating long term strategies for international markets. An organisation might move through various stages including domestic marketing, experimental involvement, active involvement and finally to committed involvement.

3.11 Direct methods of entry include agents, distributors, licensing, franchise, JVs, SBAs, wholly owned subsidiaries.

3.12 Hofstede's four dimensions used to describe different national cultural characteristics are:

- Power distance – the extent of equality between management and subordinates
- Uncertainty avoidance – attitudes to risk and change
- Masculinity – traditional definition of sex roles
- Individualism – extent of recognition of the individual or the group

Part B

The sample case: Biocatalysts

3

The process case: the ten steps

1   THE CASE STUDY PROCESS

1.1   Tackling a major case study can be a daunting prospect. It is a very different method of assessment and one you may have little experience of. It can be quite off-putting for the unprepared student. However, case technique is, in fact, a method of management skill development which has proved to be very effective over a number of years. You will find that the process of undertaking this case will give you a deeper insight into the whole process of strategic marketing and much more confidence in using the planning and control tools and frameworks when tackling work related projects and planning activities.

1.2   In the previous chapter, you took the time to check out your underpinning knowledge from the other diploma papers. This provides you with critical foundations which you can build your case skills.

1.3   However, **knowledge** of planning and control is not enough to ensure a pass in this paper. You must **understand** the **process and techniques of case study** and have the practical **skills** to apply those recognised frameworks to the case scenario in a commercially credible way.

1.4   It is important that you recognise there are two aspects to the case or planning process:

(a)   The stages that make up the process

(b)   The outcomes of those stages recorded as decisions and actions in the planning document

1.5   The stages you will go through will be familiar to you from your Planning and Control studies.

- Where are we now? analysis and auditing

- Where do we want to be? corporate decisions
- How are we going to get there? marketing decisions
- How do we ensure we arrive? control decisions

Tutor Tip

Planning to pass

Students reading this Tutorial Text will already have made the decision that they want to pass, and have taken a step in planning to do so. This is an important decision and while it may seem obvious, it is surprising how many students fail to acknowledge that passing the case study requires personal planning and considerable effort. The CIM diploma is not handed out to marketers who cannot demonstrate their marketing knowledge and skills.

We have already identified for you the type of student that puts in lots of effort, working non stop up to the exam, developing detailed and fully written out plans in anticipation of the questions on the exam paper. These students are planning to fail.

The diligent student must remember **not** to plan to fail.

---

2   WHAT ARE WE TRYING TO ACHIEVE? THE OUTPUT OF THE CASE PROCESS

2.1   Professionally qualified and trained marketing managers can make a significant difference to an organisation, given a chance! In today's competitive environment, few organisations have the luxury of not needing marketing. Marketing is not just a matter of survival, and the challenge for marketers is to ensure their organisations are successful.

2.2   To do this requires using the analytical and decision making skills we have been discussing to the organisation's advantage.

2.3   Too often business success is measured by the bottom line: 'how much profit did we make this quarter'. It is short sighted, often short-term, and usually tactical. Sooner or later the lack of strategic perspective and customer focus will result in the organisation failing.

2.4   The desired outcome for business is success and this can be measured as profitability (in the broader sense if a non profit making organisation shareholder aspirations).

2.5   Success can be short-term survival, medium-term market development and/or long-term achievement of the vision. It should also be measured as:

- High customer satisfaction, value and loyalty
- High employee morale, productivity and loyalty
- Excellent and strong working partnerships with other stakeholders
- A strong and powerful brand
- A strong and distinct competitive position in the market
- Continued sustainable growth

2.6   The desired outcome of the case study process is the same but with an important additional goal, that of passing the exam.

2.7   Your goal is therefore to ensure you add value by **providing insights** into the current situation through your analysis and, through **effective decision making**, develop **credible** plans that will ensure organisation success. As has already been mentioned, exam technique is as important as your analysis and decision skills. The exam is your opportunity to demonstrate to the examiner your ability to communicate convincingly and persuasively.

2.8 To ensure you adopt a professional approach to working the case study process the following steps are recommended.

3   WORKING THE MAXI CASE

3.1 Tackling the case study requires a systematic and methodical approach. The amount of data you will be presented with provides you with ample opportunity to get lost. The skill you are required to demonstrate is that you can **sort, organise** and **analyse** this data, **disregarding** data that cannot help in the planning process and converting the rest into marketing intelligence that is useful for decision making purposes. (In other words. what good marketing professionals should be doing for their organisations.) One of the factors that separates successful managers and companies from the mediocre is their ability to gather, analyse and use information to inform decision making.

3.2 The case is first analysed to determine the **current situation**. Decisions that will solve problems and ensure success can then be made. Each stage of the Planning and Control process is covered by working the case study. You will also draw on your Integrated Marketing Communications and International Marketing Strategy knowledge and skills.

(a) **Where are we now?** analysis tools and models are used to help establish current business performance and market conditions

(b) **Where do we want to be?** – corporate decisions: tools and models are used to help determine future direction

(c) **How can we get there?** marketing decisions: further planning techniques and frameworks help to formulate marketing plans

(d) **How can we ensure we arrive?** control models and techniques are used to establish standards and measure and evaluate performance

3.3 One of the difficulties experienced by many students, and by many marketing managers in their jobs, is that of knowing where to start and how to proceed. The following framework has proved to be a successful way of working the case study and ensuring a methodical and systematic approach that delivers results.

3.4 It is worth remembering that in reality a company does not stop what it is doing to start an audit. There is often a logical sequence of events but **many activities can and would be carried out simultaneously.** However, for simplicity, we will be describing the auditing process step by step.

3.5 We will give guidelines on how long each stage may take. These are guidelines only as everyone works at a different pace and each case study is different, but the guidelines will help give you some idea of the time you should allocate.

4 INTRODUCING THE TEN-STEP PROCESS

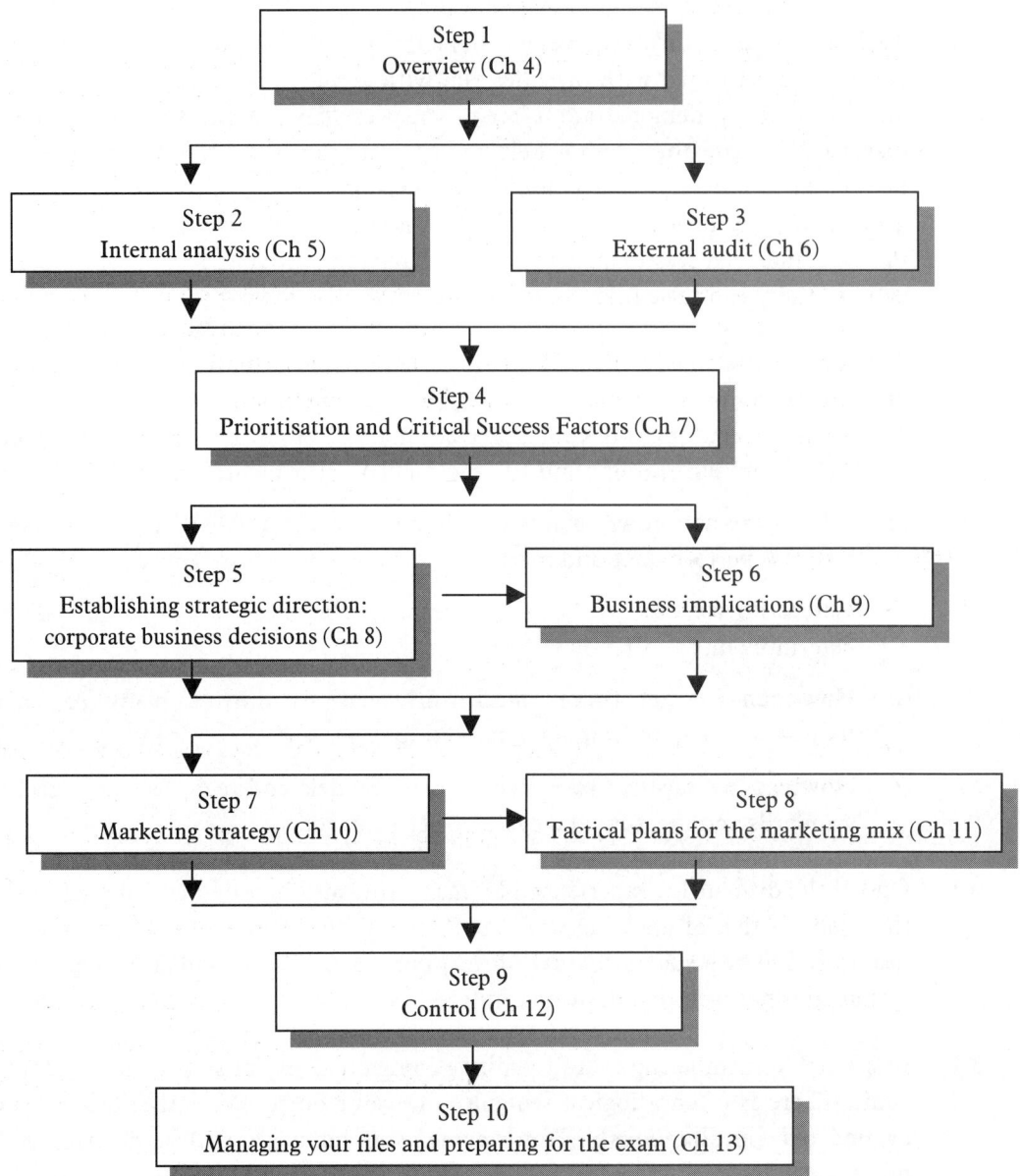

Ten-step process

```
                    ┌─────────────────────────────┐
                    │           Step 1            │
                    │      Overview (Ch 4)        │
                    └─────────────────────────────┘
                                  │
          ┌───────────────────────┴───────────────────────┐
          ▼                                                ▼
┌──────────────────────────┐              ┌──────────────────────────┐
│         Step 2           │              │         Step 3           │
│  Internal analysis (Ch 5)│              │  External audit (Ch 6)   │
└──────────────────────────┘              └──────────────────────────┘
          │                                                │
          └───────────────────────┬───────────────────────┘
                                  ▼
              ┌────────────────────────────────────────┐
              │                Step 4                  │
              │ Prioritisation and Critical Success    │
              │          Factors (Ch 7)                │
              └────────────────────────────────────────┘
                                  │
          ┌───────────────────────┴───────────────────────┐
          ▼                                                ▼
┌──────────────────────────┐   ──▶   ┌──────────────────────────┐
│         Step 5           │         │         Step 6           │
│ Establishing strategic   │         │ Business implications    │
│ direction: corporate     │         │        (Ch 9)            │
│ business decisions (Ch 8)│         │                          │
└──────────────────────────┘         └──────────────────────────┘
          │                                                │
          └────┐               ┌───────────────────────────┘
               ▼               ▼
┌──────────────────────────┐   ──▶   ┌──────────────────────────┐
│         Step 7           │         │         Step 8           │
│ Marketing strategy(Ch 10)│         │ Tactical plans for the   │
│                          │         │ marketing mix (Ch 11)    │
└──────────────────────────┘         └──────────────────────────┘
          │                                                │
          └───────────────────────┬───────────────────────┘
                                  ▼
              ┌────────────────────────────────────────┐
              │                Step 9                  │
              │          Control (Ch 12)               │
              └────────────────────────────────────────┘
                                  │
                                  ▼
      ┌────────────────────────────────────────────────────┐
      │                    Step 10                         │
      │ Managing your files and preparing for the exam(Ch 13)│
      └────────────────────────────────────────────────────┘
```

© Juanita Cockton

Step 1. Overview

4.1 When you are ready to start work on the practice case study, wait until you have a quiet hour or two and **read it through once and put aside.** When you have more time, read through again and this time begin making notes.

   (a) **Consider your focus: who are you, (position, responsibility) and what have you been asked to do?** You are getting into **role** and tackling the case study from the perspective of either an employee of the company or an external consultant to the company. This initial acknowledgement of your task is important. From time to time, when perhaps you are in one of those phases when you are overwhelmed by the case, you can return to your initial thoughts to focus you on the important issues.

(b) **Begin your marketing research shopping list** – start identifying information gaps. **Identifying information needs from the start is important.** You will add to this list throughout your working of the case study, but sometimes the obvious gaps you notice at the beginning can be forgotten as you start thinking of your information gaps in terms of the strategies you are developing.

(c) **Establish an overview of the industry you are operating in.** You may not work in this industry, and need to get a sense of what is going on. Experience shows that those who do work in the industry that the case study is set in are often more disadvantaged than those who do not because of the wealth of information they have. These people have to be very disciplined at staying within the case study and not allowing their knowledge to distract them from the scenario set.

(d) **Establish, broadly, the challenges facing the organisation.** At this stage you are not trying to identify every problem and challenge but rather impressions of what this organisation is doing. You will sort out the available information into themes or functional areas like sales information or competitor data.

> Step 1 will take you approximately 3 - 6 hours.

Step 2. Analysis: internal audit

4.2 Now the real work starts.

(a) From this point on, your analysis will be in **depth** and needs to produce results of value.

(b) The intention, during Step 2, is to establish the **organisation's strengths and weaknesses**.

(i) The case material and appendices are analysed to determine, where possible, what the organisation is doing well and where it is under performing.

(ii) A structured approach ensures we do not miss anything out that could impact on current and future performance.

(iii) We will need to do this in detail for the marketing activity and then for the whole business. This requires the marketer to put on the hats of others in the organisation to review the financial, HR or operational dimensions of the business.

Step 3. Analysis: external audit

4.3 This step requires analysis of both the micro and macro external environments.

(a) The market, its dynamics, customers and competitors are all included in the micro analysis.

(b) Analysis of the external environment provides insights into the macro factors affecting the business (eg PEST). We may have information on market conditions such as value of markets, stage of growth, maturity or decline or be left with no more than assumptions and impressions.

> Steps 2 and 3 will take you approximately 23 – 33 hours. (It is difficult to break up the hours between the steps sometimes because of a lot of the information on the organisation is required for two or more steps. You may break some of this work down by sharing analysis with others if you are working in syndicate groups.

BPP
PUBLISHING

Step 4. Critical Success Factors (CSFs)

4.4 The danger of the analysis process is that you end up with long lists of strengths, weaknesses, opportunities and threats which, while useful, will not focus management on what needs to be done. Before moving on to decisions, the final stage of analysis is to **prioritise our findings**. There are models and techniques to help do this.

The conclusion of analysis will be to prioritise the factors that are critical to the organisation's success and implementation of plans. Each CSF will have key issues associated with it. Terminology varies between companies. You may have your own terminology.

> Step 4, a review of your analysis, prioritising and reaching conclusions, will take you approximately 1 – 2 hours. In case study, this step is particularly important as the case questions are often drawn from these critical success factors.

Step 5. Corporate/business decisions

4.5 We now move into the decision stage. From this point on, you are generating alternative solutions/ideas in **outline only**. You will not be developing fully written out plans.

(a) The future desired, and/or necessary, direction of the organisation is determined and expressed through a **vision** (if applicable) and the **mission statements**. **Corporate objectives** are set if none exist or clarified, and the planning gap established. These will have to be quantified.

(b) **Strategic options**, identified during analysis, are reviewed and criteria to evaluate them are developed. **Selected strategies must be able** to fill the identified gap.

(c) The strategic role of the **brand** and **competitive positioning** will need to be agreed.

> Step 5 will take you approximately 4 - 5 hours.

Step 6. Business implications

4.6 Often an important aspect of developing and implementing a new strategic direction is the organisation's **current business operations**. The plans may require a **change in, for example, organisational culture or structure.** There may be implications for managing the brand strategically or improving international management.

Your internal analysis will have established what changes need to take place if the business is to succeed, for example adopting a marketing orientation, and at this stage you need to consider the issues.

> Step 6 will take you approximately 2 - 3 hours.

Step 7. Marketing strategy

4.7 When decisions on strategic direction have been finalised, and product market opportunities and competitive positioning have been agreed, decisions on **marketing objectives and strategy** can be agreed and developed. These decisions include **translating the business objective** into a **marketing objective**, segmenting markets identified, and selecting those segments the organisation should target, the positioning statement and targeting strategy. This work needs to be done for every selected business strategy.

> Step 7 will take you approximately 4 – 5 hours.

Step 8. Tactical plans

4.8 Outline marketing mix plans (the 7Ps) are developed to implement marketing strategies. These plans must be consistent with the organisation's overall competitive positioning and help to differentiate the business in a meaningful way.

Marketing research needs are identified and an outline plan prepared. Again this is needed for each selected segment.

> Step 8 will take you approximately 2 – 3 hours.

Step 9. Implementation and control

4.9 Plans are only of value if they are implemented, and thoughts about not only who must do what but how you will sell the strategy to senior manager colleagues and teams will earn you credit with the examiners.

Control is an important factor in successful marketing planning. It ensures we use our resources effectively and that plans will be delivered on time. Budgets, timetable of activities, targets and measurement all need to be considered and agreed.

> Step 9 will take you approximately 1 – 3 hours.

Step 10. Review and file management

4.10 Review plan for consistency. Have the business, financial and human resource implications been considered and included? Is the plan consistent and integrated?

Organise your file in preparation for the exam to ensure it aids rather than hinders progress in the examination room.

> Step 10 will take you approximately 1-2 hours.

Action Programme 1

Look ahead to when you are taking the exam. During the four weeks leading up to the exam, where are you going to find those 40 – 60 hours? Do a timetable and identify who you need to negotiate time with (employer, partner, friends etc). Log that time and protect it; it will be essential to passing. As you work through the practice cases, note how long each step takes and amend your time planner as appropriate.

---

5 TEAMWORK AND THE IMPORTANCE OF YOUR OWN WORK

5.1 All students of analysis and decision are required to work the case study individually and 'own' the analysis and decision. There are of course tempting short cuts 'a quick read through will do it', someone else's analysis etc and these are usually a short cut to failure.

5.2 There are a number of problems in working the case study alone, all of which can be overcome. It is important to acknowledge these early on and have strategies for overcoming them. For example, a lack of confidence that you are interpreting material correctly or a personal weakness in some area - for marketers the favourite is financial! – are problems that can be resolved, and any good marketing professional will review and utilise appropriate resources available.

BPP
PUBLISHING

5.3   Some students of case study work in groups, either in colleges or companies.

(a)   There are obvious advantages of group work, particularly that of dealing with the quantity of work that will be generated. More importantly, if you have the advantage of working in a team, make sure you recognise and play to each others' strengths. In particular try not to duplicate effort. Work can be broken down between team members to make the most of the limited time available. Good communications, participation and support are vital ingredients for effective teams.

(b)   However you cannot abdicate responsibility for the analysis. You need to review work generated by others, understand it and agree with it. You cannot simply **use** it, as you will not be able to adapt your thinking in the light of extra information in the exam room.

5.4   Whilst it is perfectly acceptable to share analysis in this way, you cannot work together after you move onto decision making. The examiner does **not** want group answers, each student repeating the same mission and strategy.

5.5   If you do not have the advantage of a case study group, you can still 'recruit' help in the form of, for example, a marketing manager who develops marketing plans, a financial manager who understands ratios. Do not expect these people to do the job for you. The intention is to gain their support in helping you understand and interpret, or develop a new skill that will enable you to analyse the case material and arrive at credible solutions.

5.6   Particularly during the practice case, there will never be a better opportunity for you to experiment and learn by applying the theory in a practice case scenario.

6   INTRODUCING THE BIOCATALYSTS CASE

Action Programme 2

To finish this chapter, we would like you to familiarise yourself with a typical CIM case – Biocatalysts.

You will need to find half an hour and some peace and quiet. You need to read through the narrative to get a feel for the case. This can be quite a quick read through, rather as you would a magazine article. **Do not** at this stage try and do anything with the material you are certainly not about to make any decisions at this stage. Treat it like a story. What is the setting, the business context? Who are the key players and what is happening?

Only read to page 16, the end of the narrative.

Tutor Tip

To make it easier for your to refer to the case material as we work though the next section, you may find it helpful to copy or remove the case pages so you have a separate case document to work on.

The Chartered
Institute of marketing

Case Study
December 1999

Strategic Marketing Management: Analysis & Decision

Biocatalysts Ltd.

BPP PUBLISHING

Case Study – June 1999

Strategic Marketing Management: Analysis & Decision

Important Notes

The examiners will be marking your scripts on the basis of questions put to you in the examination room. Candidates are advised to pay particular attention to the *mark allocation on the examination paper and budget their time accordingly.*

Your role is outlined in the candidate's brief and you will be required to recommend clear courses of action.

You WILL NOT be awarded marks merely for analysis. This should have been undertaken before the examination day in preparation for meeting the specific tasks which will be specified in the examination paper.

Candidates are advised not to waste valuable time collecting unnecessary data. Although cases are based upon real world situations, facts have been deliberately altered or omitted. No useful purpose will therefore be served by contacting companies in this industry and candidates *are strictly instructed not to do so* as it would simply cause unnecessary confusion.

As in real life, anomalies will be found in this case situation. Please simply state your assumptions where necessary when answering questions. The CIM is not in a position to answer queries on case data. Candidates are tested on their overall understanding of the case and its key issues, not on minor details. There are no catch questions or hidden agendas. In addition, for this particular case, the CIM is not prepared to answer any scientific queries.

Additional information will be introduced in the examination paper itself which candidates must take into account when answering the questions set.

Acquaint yourself thoroughly with the Case Study and be prepared to follow closely the instructions given to you on the examination day. To answer examination questions effectively, candidates must adopt report format.

The copying of pre-prepared 'group' answers written by consultants/tutors is strictly forbidden and will be penalised by failure. The questions will demand analysis in the examination itself and individually composed answers are required in order to pass.

Candidate's Brief

You are Joseph Mendes, a Marketing Consultant of some repute, who has been appointed by Biocatalysts Ltd. to undertake the development of a marketing report, prior to undertaking a strategic exercise. Joseph's previous work ranged across many industry sectors, but he had not undertaken any work in the biotechnology sector. He is keen to understand the sector and the company profile before he develops any plans. As part of his internal and external research he has prepared the following report. At the end of this report are appendices relating to the main body of the text. Joseph has prepared this report for the Managing Director, Stewart North, ready for the next Board Meeting.

BPP PUBLISHING

Report by Joseph Mendes
Private and Confidential

Biocatalysts Ltd.

Background Information

Biocatalysts Ltd. is an independent speciality enzyme company operating in the low-volume high-value end of the industrial enzyme market. Biocatalysts Ltd. started trading in 1986 as a wholly owned subsidiary of Grand Metropolitan. It occupies a large factory unit in Wales. Following a management buyout from Shell Ventures in 1991 it is now a totally independent company.

The company is one of the UK's leading developers and producers of speciality enzymes (natural proteins which act as catalysts). It produces enzymes in one of two ways. For the food and textile industries it produces speciality enzyme complexes complete with additional chemicals which are sold for moderate margins; for the diagnostic and pharmaceutical industries it has developed its own unique enzymes which it manufactures and sells at higher margins. The development costs of these higher margin manufactured enzymes are paid for by the profit and from Government/European grants which the company has so far been successful in obtaining.

Biocatalysts' customers use enzymes to improve the efficiency and convenience of processes in a wide range of industries, including flavour production, brewing, fruit processing, baking and textiles (enzyme fading of denim jeans). In addition, some of the higher value enzymes currently available and under development are used in diagnostic kits, used for testing for abnormalities in humans and pharmaceutical manufacturing. This broad spread of markets and wide geographical sales gives the company a balanced portfolio with steady, profitable income streams.

Enzyme Technology

Enzymes are nature's biological catalysts. They accelerate rates of reaction, helping the conversion of substances into other types of chemicals more useful for industrial processes. In the commercial arena, enzymes have two broad kinds of use: process aids and active ingredients. Enzymes have been used by mankind for at least 4,000 years in the form of natural microbial fermentations for making beer, wine, cheese and many other products. However, the recognition of enzymes as entities only began 170 years ago. In Germany, in 1830, a paper was first published which discussed the isolation of an enzyme which could convert starch to sugar. The substance is now known as amylase. By 1860, many other enzymes were recognised and isolated. Among these were pepsin, polyphenol oxidase, peroxidase and invertase.

Refined enzymes were first commercialised by a Danish chemist, Christian Hansen, who produced the first isolated preparation of rennet from dried calf stomach. It was primarily used for cheesemaking and the original company Danisco is currently a major supplier of enzymes for the dairy industry. In 1900, a Japanese scientist, Takamine, developed a fermentation for the industrial production of a fungal amylase for making soy sauce and other oriental seasonings. The Takamine laboratories are now part of CPC International. The early 1900s saw the development of a heat stable bacterial amylase in textile production, used for 'desizing', a process used to remove starch from fibres after completion of the weaving process. The use of this enzyme stopped the use of dilute acid in water which often damaged the textiles. Otto Rohm, a German chemist, developed the use of digestive enzymes for leather curing. Before this, dog and pigeon excrement was used for curing leather. The Rohm company is now a significant player in the enzyme business (see Appendix 1.).

After the Second World War, enzyme technology received a boost from developments which were taking place in the antibiotic field. The method of growing cultures in liquid media was adopted by the enzyme industry, increasing yields and lowering costs.

In essence, enzymes can be described as the catalysts of the living world. For example, enzymes are responsible for nearly all the metabolic processes taking place in the human body. These processes have been harnessed by industry so that a small amount of enzyme can enable a large scale chemical reaction to take place under very mild conditions. This increases the cost effectiveness of the production of a number of food and other products (see Appendix 2.). The enzymes are highly specific in their catalytic power and their ability to transform chemicals.

BPP PUBLISHING

World Market

The estimated sales of value of the sales of industrial enzymes was estimated to be in excess of $1 billion in 1994 – Figure 1. (about $1.3 billion in 1997). Sales growth is increasing in the more speciality applications sectors ('other' in pie chart) and tending to level out in the commodity sectors (Figure 2.). Technical research, however, continues to develop large volume enzymes for existing applications such as paper and pulp, textiles and in the longer term, waste treatment and environmental maintenance. Industry analysts (Enzymology, 1998), see the market for enzymes expanding from $1.7 billion to $2 billion by 2005. The Russian market is as yet undeveloped, owing to economic pressures, but could be large. The Chinese market is quite large, especially for food enzymes, but again this market is relatively 'closed' and full scale Western style processes have yet to be adopted.

Distribution of Enzyme Sales (1994)

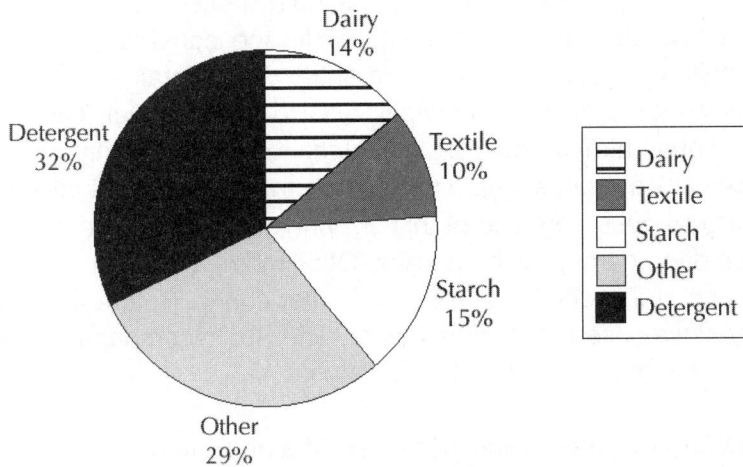

Figure 1.

Forecast Distribution of Enzyme Sales (2005)

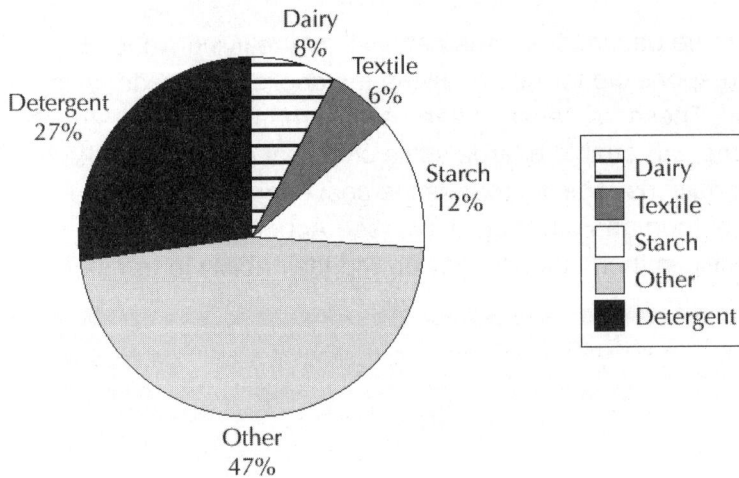

Figure 2.

There are now approximately 12 major global producers, with increasingly distinct separate product ranges between them. This number of key producers helps to reduce total domination by any one of them. At the same time, it shows a trend towards a reduction in customer choice of producer for a particular enzyme type. Approximately another 60 companies produce substantial amounts of a smaller range, and there are around 400 companies producing industrial quantities of a very limited range of enzyme types. Essentially all these companies are selling into a global market. For many companies that are producing enzymes in 15-40m^3 fermenters, difficult decisions have to be made regarding economies of scale. For them it is a classic case of 'being stuck in the middle'. They will either have to expand their facilities (costly) to compete with the market leaders or specialise in niche markets where they may not have the requisite expertise (see Figure 3.).

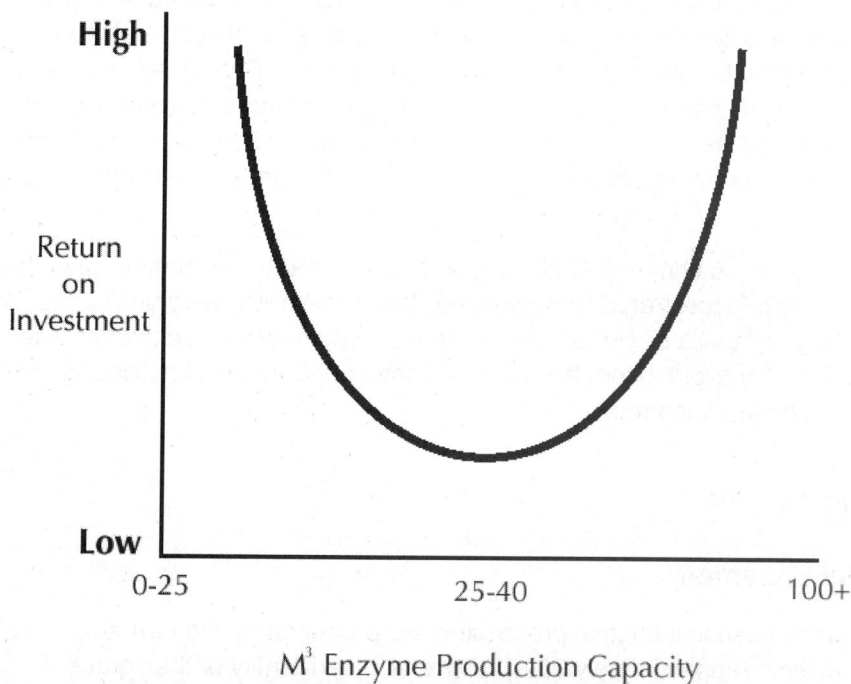

Figure 3.

The estimates show that nearly 60 per cent of the total world supply of enzymes is prepared in Europe, mainly within the European Community. Another 15 per cent is produced in North America, primarily 'in-house' for large scale application by large scale processors of natural materials, such as alcohol and sugar syrup. Numerous Japanese companies produce many, but not all, types of commercial enzyme, contributing another 12 to 15 per cent of the world production. The Russian and the Chinese markets probably use a wide variety of enzyme types for indigenous use, but are not yet active commercially. It is likely that their active entry into the market will expand the global market by a considerable degree.

BPP
PUBLISHING

Enzyme Types and Sources

Proteinases are a very important enzyme type because of their enormous use in the dairy (coagulants) and detergent industries, and collectively they account for approximately 40 per cent of all enzyme sales. Carbohydrases which are used in baking, brewing, distilling, starch and textiles, form the second largest group. The conventional approach to the division of world sales of enzymes is to assess them by their sectoral applications (detergent, dairy, textiles, starch, and 'other') as shown in Figure 1. It is useful to examine the 'other' section as it helps to determine the possible composition of the future markets. Currently the 12 main sectors under the 'other' market are alcohol, animal feed, baking, chemical biotransformations, diagnostics, fats and oils, flavour, fruit and wine, leather, protein (other than for milk coagulation, flavour and detergents), pulp and paper and water. These are the sectors that Biocatalysts Ltd. mainly operates in. Growth in these areas is expected to be very rapid and the division of sales in the year 2005 will be very different from that portrayed in Figure 1. This 'other' sector is likely collectively to be the largest section of the enzyme market, accounting for over 47% of the sales. This sector is expected to exceed $500 million worth of sales by 2005, accounting for approximately 70% of the growth of all industrial enzymes.

Out of the original 30 common enzyme types used in 1983, the number used has doubled, owing to accelerated Research and Development in both universities and biotechnology companies. The advent of Genetic Engineering Techniques, (see Appendix 3. for an explanation) has created many opportunities for specific enzymes to be manufactured.

Enzyme Types

Microbial Enzymes

Most enzymes used in industrial processing are produced by the fermentation of micro-organisms (approximately 90%). Currently, the identity of the source microbe is very important in the assessment of permitted use for food processing in most countries. The use of genetically modified organisms in the production of enzymes means that these have to be approved by food agencies, as 'novel' foods are supposedly created. These then have to be tested differently for approval. All information has to be open and transparent. In many cases too, a new enzyme preparation is likely to have a different compositional spectrum from the one produced in the traditional manner, with differing side activities. It could be that critical components of the customer's process were not identified when GMOs (Genetically Modified Organisms) were used. In some cases some side activities may well be absent, even if critical. Therefore in any new development, the customer has to be kept aware of the changes. For instance, previously all insulin (for diabetics) originated from pigs, with an enzyme used to convert the insulin to human insulin. A by-product from this process was sold cheaply for leather curing. As a result of the use of biotechnology, 50% of human insulin is now produced directly by fermentation and does not contain the by-product enzyme. This has meant that the by-product, used in the leather industry, has now become the *main product,* increasing the costs of leather curing. The advent of the new technology has created considerable problems in that industry sector. Nonetheless, producers are using sophisticated purification and recovery techniques to build up stocks of enzymes. These stock levels can pose problems, depending on supply/demand situations. Production changes usually take 6 weeks to implement and different applications may need differing purity standards. For many bulk produced enzymes, such as the ones used in detergents, dairy, starch and textiles, the systems produce enzymes continuously and the prices are effectively half those of about ten years ago.

Plant Enzymes

These include proteases such as papain, bromelain and ficin, enzymes of cereals and soya beans and the more specialised enzymes from citrus fruits. Increased supplies of plant enzyme are very dependent on growth cycles, climate, new long-term suppliers and world political and agricultural policies. This area is particularly ripe for the use of GMOs. The shortage of papain in recent years has been a good example of these particular issues affecting this market.

Animal Enzymes

These include pancreatic, lipases and proteinases, pepsins, pregastric esterases and rennets. These can be produced as ultra-refined entities or in bulk. The supply and demand of these enzymes depends on food and agricultural policies which control the numbers of livestock available for slaughter. Owing to viral and other problems such as BSE[1], there is a need for potential purchasers to take considerable safety measures. Consumers too are becoming more aware of the end products they consume. Owing to this, companies are increasingly purchasing enzymes that have been produced microbially or through genetic engineering processes. There is also an increasing demand for producing kosher certified enzymes for food production (see Appendix 4.).

---

1   BSE stands for Bovine Spongiform Encephalopathy, passed on to humans through ingestion of beef products which contain the disease. Humans suffer Creutzfeldt-Jakob Disease (CJD), leading to brain deterioration and death. Currently in the UK no-one is sure of the extent or prevalence of this disease in the general population. It is possible that the disease is prevalent in many other developed countries.

BPP PUBLISHING

Factors Customers Need to Consider when Purchasing Enzymes for Industrial Processes

For companies purchasing enzymes, it is important that they get a clear indication of how specific the chemical reactions are, the optimum level of acidity or alkalinity (pH) at which the enzymes perform, and the temperature range of performance. Activators and inhibitors are also of vital importance, as certain food processes need enzymes to be 'switched off' at the end of a particular process. Currently research is directed at producing molecules which can do this safely in food production, as it can be difficult to 'switch off' enzymes easily (enzymes often catalyse reactions, and continue to be effective until another chemical which stops the reactivity is introduced). Customers need to have similar analytical techniques to those used by the suppliers, so that the strength of an enzyme is clearly understood by both parties. The other key factors which purchasers take into consideration are availability with consistency in quality and activity in a particular enzyme type, together with a track record for safety. A supplier who is prepared to disseminate information actively on new and current developments is not only educating the customer (and potential customers), but possibly offering new and better processing methods. Finally price is always an issue and suppliers are required to establish enzyme purity and activity levels which are consistent with the price set.

Bulk enzymes are being produced more and more from GMOs (Genetically Modified Organisms) mainly by two European companies and one US company, Gist Brocades, Novo Nordisk and Genencor. Japan is weak in bulk enzyme production but strong in speciality enzymes, particularly for medical diagnostics. Its exports of bulk enzymes to Europe and the USA are consequently relatively low, but beginning to grow. In the UK, Biocatalysts Ltd., Rhone-Poulenc, Biozyme and Genzyme (the last two, diagnostics only) are the manufacturers of speciality enzymes. The research leading to this method of production has cost millions of dollars, with much of the development work taking place in the 1980s. The costs of developing GMO production for new enzymes range from tens to hundreds of thousands of dollars. Many, but not all speciality enzymes will be produced increasingly by GMOs, and will be cheaper and purer.

Non-GMO trade is expected to continue for some time. There are certain food manufacturers who will not use GMO produced enzymes, owing to the 'bad' publicity received in general by GMOs (see Appendices 3. and 4.). 'Other' processes justify the need for the 'side' (extra) activities of bulk enzymes, made traditionally for efficient performance. GMO produced enzymes do not contain side activities which are usually vital for the optimum performance of enzymes within the food industry. Companies like Biocatalysts Ltd. are in the market to purchase these enzymes, from which they can reprocess some of the enzymes they need.

Biocatalysts' Place in the Enzyme Industry

Biocatalysts Ltd. is rather special in that it offers a full technical service to present and potential customers, including giving clients access to a database of non-competing enzymes available commercially. As part of this service, Biocatalysts Ltd. offers valid cost comparisons between products whose performance is measured on different scales, as there is no internationally accepted scale. Enzymes, for instance, can be produced in different strengths, offering different levels of activity.

The pricing ranges reflect these differences; however, consumers may only be aware of prices and not strength and efficacy. In this sense, Biocatalysts Ltd. attempts to provide a high level of technical support to its customers. Biocatalysts Ltd. sells its products (see Appendix 9.) into the following markets:

Food

Many parts of the food industry use enzymes, mainly as processing aids. Examples include baking, brewing, protein modification, fruit processing and flavour production. Most bulk enzymes, as produced by the big manufacturers, are usable in many food processes but are not optimum for each particular process. Biocatalysts Ltd. specialises in producing optimum performing products for the food industry, which outperform (in function and price) the competing bulk enzymes. Examples of this are specific enzymes for apple and pear juice extraction, as opposed to using just one enzyme for both types of fruit.

Textiles

Most stone washed denim jeans are now enzyme washed. This is almost a commodity business, where a small percentage of a large market can be readily picked up by supplying special blends of enzymes and chemicals that produce specific types of styles of faded jeans. As faded jeans are going out of fashion, this is not seen as a long-term business, but this sector generates very useful short-term margins.

BPP PUBLISHING

Diagnostics

All babies born in developed countries are tested for a genetic disorder, PKU (phenylketonurea). A test involving the Biocatalysts enzyme Phenylalanine Dehydrogenase can be undertaken in minutes, replacing a slow labour-intensive method of detecting phenylalanine in the blood. Twenty-four million tests are done every year. Biocatalysts Ltd. is the only producer of this enzyme. Quanatase and ICN have received FDA (Food and Drug Administration) approval in the USA for this system. This means that the growth will now be very rapid over the next few years. The margins are good in this area. Customers are often tied into this market as, once a kit has been approved, they are very loath to change any of the components.

Market Breakdown of Sales for 1997 for Biocatalysts Ltd.

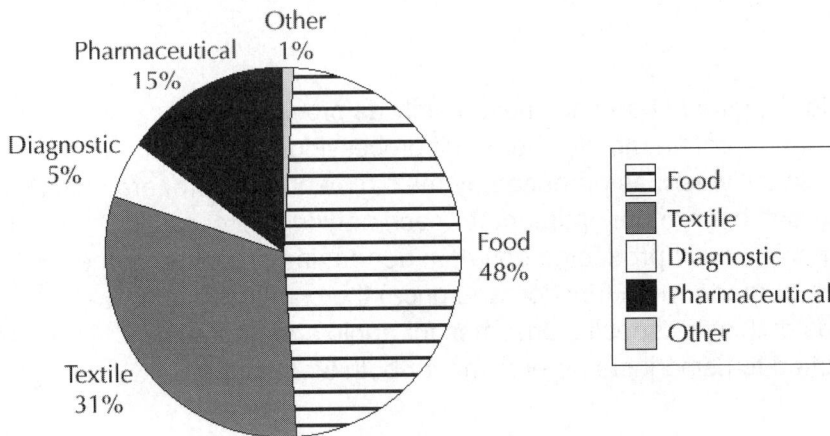

Other 1%
Pharmaceutical 15%
Diagnostic 5%
Food 48%
Textile 31%

Legend:
- Food
- Textile
- Diagnostic
- Pharmaceutical
- Other

Figure 4.

Biocatalysts Ltd. Geographical Sales for 1997

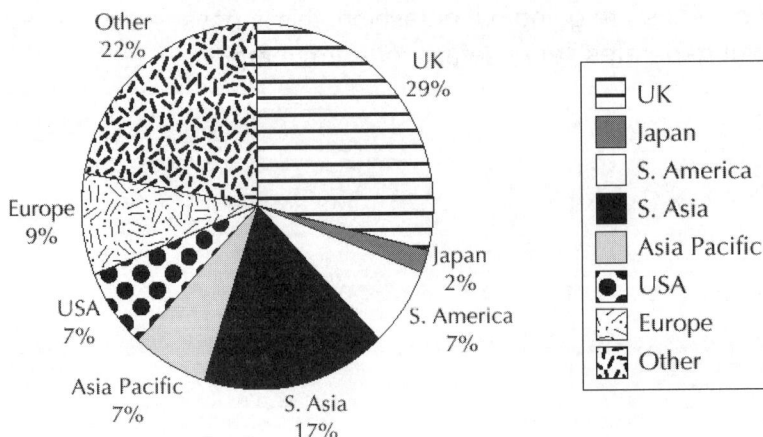

Other 22%
UK 29%
Europe 9%
Japan 2%
USA 7%
S. America 7%
Asia Pacific 7%
S. Asia 17%

Legend:
- UK
- Japan
- S. America
- S. Asia
- Asia Pacific
- USA
- Europe
- Other

Figure 5.

Figures 4. and 5. show the market and geographical breakdown of the main areas of sales for Biocatalysts Ltd.

Customer Focus

Biocatalysts Ltd. is unique amongst the world's enzyme companies. Its willingness to supply custom-tailored products for its clients means that the whole company focus is directed towards customers, attempting to provide total customer satisfaction. This customer focus has resulted in Biocatalysts Ltd. growing at more than twice the industry average over the past ten years. The company has many exclusive agreements with blue-chip companies around the world, who value the product and technical services that Biocatalysts Ltd. provides. Small- and medium-sized companies are also offered a competing range of services. Biocatalysts Ltd. does not make or sell high-volume commodity enzymes, such as those used in the detergent or starch processing industries. They operate in selected parts of the enzyme market where their technical support and willingness to work with customers on a one-to-one basis is highly valued. These enzyme sectors usually require, not single enzyme entities, but enzyme complexes, where the ratios of each of the components are crucial to the efficacy of the whole enzyme product and the customer's process. Biocatalysts Ltd. does not believe in the customers 'making do' with compromise enzyme products, just because that is the way they came off the fermenter. In order to be more customer focused, the fermentation for the manufacture of Biocatalysts is sub-contracted out. This allows for more flexibility and a focus on investment on enzyme technology, not in capital intensive massive stainless steel vats for large batches of production.

Research and Development

Much of the Research and Development programme is focused on the development of new enzymes and enzyme complexes, mainly identified by the customers. New application ideas and opportunities for the current range of blended enzymes are identified from contacts with clients. The development of these is mainly handled by technical sales staff (see Appendix 5.). Sales of current products (or variants of current products) for these new applications, accounts for much of the short-term growth in sales. Biocatalysts Ltd. has many allegiances with leading UK universities, where most of the basic research into new enzymes is carried out (see Figure 6.). This allows the company to focus its in-house scientists on the needs of its customers and keeping fully up-to-date with the latest developments in bio-research.

BPP PUBLISHING

R&D Cycle/Sales Cycle

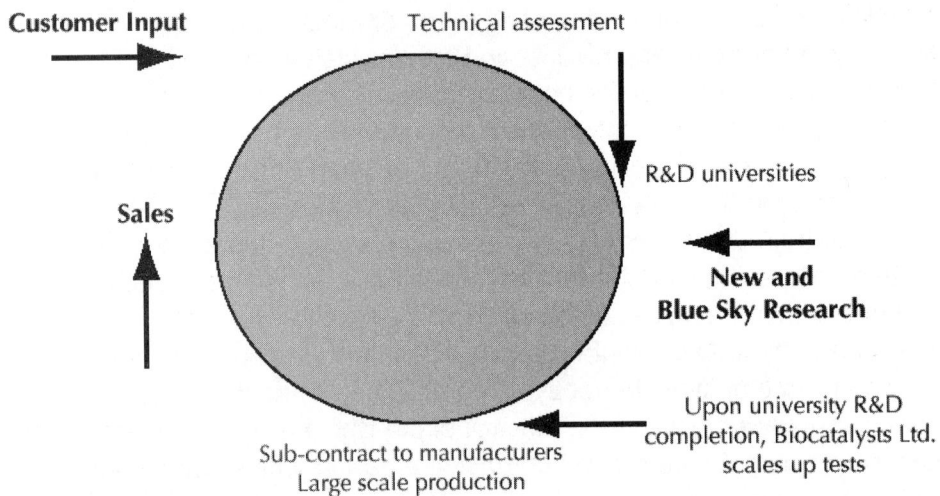

Customer Input

Technical assessment

R&D universities

New and Blue Sky Research

Sales

Upon university R&D completion, Biocatalysts Ltd. scales up tests

Sub-contract to manufacturers
Large scale production

Production

The production plant and laboratory take up around 8,000 square feet of a modern factory unit. The plant includes equipment for liquid and powder blending, fermentation (small scale) and filtration and pilot chromatographic purification and drying. Large scale fermentation is contracted out. The intention of the company is to continue sub-contracting fermentation as there is general over-capacity in the marketplace and to continue investing in downstream processing equipment. Additional investment of around £1 million would be needed to carry out all fermentation in-house, covering all the volume forecasts for the next five years.

The laboratory has all the necessary technical equipment, which is fully depreciated and can still function for at least a further five years. Quality control tests are carried out in-house on all incoming materials and finished products. The company has received the ISO 9000[2] accreditation. The factory is not fully utilised and it is estimated that sales could double with small additions to the existing plant and by employing one or two more production personnel. Batch sizes are flexible and most stock is kept as raw materials or work in progress to maximise flexibility.

---

2   ISO 9000 stands for Quality Accreditation of processes and products on a worldwide basis.

Marketing

The sales and marketing for the company is carried out by 5 people (see organisation chart in Appendix 5.), including the Managing Director. This team looks at the possibilities for new product development and sets out the long-term strategy for the company. The three active sales staff are either home or office based and they spend 80 per cent of their time on sales. The products are sold all around the world and 70 per cent of the products are exported. Most of the exports are generated by agents or distributors who often carry a range of imported products in their portfolio. Biocatalysts Ltd. has a presence in 35 countries. The sales team in the UK supports the agents in the other countries. Agents are used extensively by Biocatalysts Ltd. as their products can be classified as mainly being business to business. The use of agents is not without its problems, as in many cases the range of products offered by Biocatalysts Ltd. may form just a small amount of a particular agent's product portfolio. Unlike selling other products, the agents in the enzyme business need constant updating. The biggest issue facing the company therefore is the quality of the agents and the way they undertake sales. For example, Biocatalysts Ltd. has an enzyme for olive oil processing, so that yields can be increased. In Italy, there are numerous family farms with small olive oil processors. In this instance the agent needs to know something about that sector and also needs to 'educate' the farmers. In order to improve the sales focus, the company is now looking to recruit an agent who actually sells olive oil processing equipment to the farmers. Biocatalysts Ltd. produces a newsletter every six months. This is sent to all its distributors and customers and helps to update them on the current Research and Development activities of the company and any further developments in their current products.

As price is often an issue with many buyers, it is important to Biocatalysts Ltd. that it has the following factors in place:

a. The right agent, i.e. an agent who understands the different sectors well.

b. An agent who is working efficiently and effectively.

c. That the agent is selling the 'right' product.

BPP
PUBLISHING

The last issue of selling the 'right' product is very important, as enzymes come in differing strengths, and often customers may choose one brand over another simply on price, without realising the efficacy of the product(s). The agents are on a 5 per cent commission. Agents are a useful way of expanding the market, but Biocatalysts Ltd. is aware that there is no substitute for having its own sales marketing staff in the marketplace. However, the sales need to take off considerably before the company can justify recruiting another marketer. Most agents are difficult to control and the company relies a lot on their market research and knowledge of country specific issues. Agents mainly carry a range of products which they sell into different markets. Their motivation is often financial and they are therefore more willing to sell products which may offer greater returns. In many cases, they may not be adept at gauging incipient markets in enzymes. Currently therefore the quality of the agents is clearly an issue. Each year the company pays for all its agents to come for a few days' training sessions at the company headquarters. However, not all the agents attend these sessions. The training is particularly important as the markets have narrowed and niche markets require a greater degree of customer focus.

Marketing Issues

Targeting

It is important that Biocatalysts Ltd. develops a marketing strategy for the new products it introduces into the marketplace. One particular strategy could be the way in which innovators are targeted and then followed through with the early adopters. This strategy requires a sustained and expensive marketing effort. The other way in which markets could be opened up would be to bring in a big end-user from the outset, so that application trials could be carried out on an exclusive basis. This would probably mean lower margins, but guaranteed sales and income. More generally exhibitions and mailshots play an important part in the company's targeting strategy. The exhibitions also provide a forum for discussion for the agents. Targeting users is important if marketing effort is not to be dissipated. In order to target effectively, a considerable amount of market research needs to be undertaken for each country. This is costly and difficult, as the statistics and secondary information for many countries can be quite poor.

Web Site

Many biotechnology based companies offer excellent web sites which are both educational and interactive. Currently Biocatalysts Ltd. does not have a web site (but it does have an email address) and is looking to develop a fully interactive site, which can be used for both the agents as well as potential and existing customers. An added benefit would also be good links with its suppliers and the university R&D teams, providing them with updates on product availability, trialling results and scale-up problems or successes. However, the development of such a site will need resourcing and ongoing commitment with regular updating.

Pricing

Enzymes usually form a small part of most customers' product costs. The reliability of the product and service from the supplier is usually more important to customers than finding the cheapest source. In addition, alternative enzyme supplies cannot be identified from paper cost studies. The only way to find out whether an enzyme works and if it is cost-effective is to undertake a trial production run. If potential cost savings are small, many food manufacturers will be unwilling to do the test runs. Pricing therefore can be complex and needs to be customised according to the needs of the customers' product and process costs.

The Future

Food is arguably the most important product of consumption for the average person. Food is vital for sustaining life. At the same time it can be, certainly in well-developed economies and the wealthier sections of communities in most countries, a significant symbol of culture and refinement. The marketing of GMOs presents a new challenge in marketing communications. Currently many companies producing GMOs advertise discreetly. However, many companies, such as Monsanto, have created a very powerful web site devoted to the subject. There are many arguments about risks and benefits to the consumer and the need for open debate, whereas many pressure groups such as Friends of the Earth question the ethics of the production of GMOs in general. The whole debate is now out in the open and many newspaper articles are devoted to the subject. Given the sensitive nature of food and the adverse publicity generated by the BSE crisis, it is important to consider in a rational manner the main communication and advertising strategies that GMO producers could possibly adopt. In this respect Biocatalysts Ltd. has been open in its discussions on the subject (see Appendix 3.). In some instances, GMOs are likely to have positive benefits for the consumer, especially in the production of rennet or porcine based enzymes which would then be granted 'kosher' status as they are not animal derived (see Appendix 4.). This would then provide Biocatalysts Ltd. with a positive positioning strategy in niche markets. Most companies in this sector are likely to be considering effective ways of developing their communications strategies, so that the customers and downline consumers have a clear and rational picture of the issues involved.

BPP
PUBLISHING

Summary

Biocatalysts Ltd. has a range of different business markets with a 'near commodity' business in textiles, which needs little or no R&D. The 'New Technology' business is mainly in the food market and represents 50 per cent of the sales (see Figure 4.). The diagnostics (hi-tech) side of the business accounts for 10 per cent of the sales, but the margins are above average, as high development costs have to be met. The company is growing at 20 per cent per annum at a conservative estimate (see Appendix 6.). Biocatalysts Ltd. is generally quite well prepared for the advent of the Euro (see Appendix 7.). It is clear that there is considerable market potential within the enzyme industry; however, the advent of new genetic engineering techniques and the growth of new applications create their own marketing problems. Biocatalysts Ltd. has to consider how well it can grow into being an important, but respected, niche player in the marketplace.

Appendix 1.

Some Competitor Profiles

As described in the text, the enzyme business is quite complex and fragmented; nonetheless it is useful to consider some of the other companies in the business.

Some Suppliers of Enzymes for Biocatalysts Ltd.

Supplier	Country	Supplier	Country
Alko	Finland	Grinsted Products	Denmark
Amano Int.	Japan (UK)	Kyowa Hakko Europe	Germany
Biocatalysts Ltd.	UK	Larbus S. A.	Spain
Biopole	France	Meito Sangyo	Japan
Biocon (part of ICI Quest)	Ireland	Miles Laboratories	USA
Biozyme	UK	**Novo Nordisk**	**Denmark**
Boehringer	Germany	Oriental Yeast	Japan
Boll	France	Recordati	Italy
Calbiochem	USA	Rohm	Germany
Cultor	Finland	Rhone-Poulenc-ABM Brewing	France
Dafa S. A.	France	SAF-ISIS	France
E. Merck	Germany	Sigma Chemicals	USA
Fluka	Switzerland	Solvay Enzymes GmbH	Germany
Genencor International	**USA (Finland)**	Stern Enzymes GmbH	Germany
Genzyme	USA (UK)	Toyo Jozo	Japan
Girona S. A.	Spain	Viobin Corporation	USA
Gist Brocades	**The Netherlands**	Worthington	USA

Despite many companies producing enzymes, the market as a whole is dominated by three major suppliers: Novo Nordisk (50% of the world enzyme sales) with Gist Brocades and Genencor International having substantial market shares (together around 25%).

Japanese Companies

The Japanese companies tend to be complex with the enzyme business 'hidden' amongst the general shareholding. Also it is worth remembering that a lot of Japanese enzyme production is food related and is produced by 'surface' fermentation, giving poorer yields than their European counterparts.

BPP PUBLISHING

Nagase & Co. Ltd.

Figures for 1997	US Dollars
Net Sales (Total Trading Transactions)	4,608,766
Dyestuffs	414,301
Chemicals	1,714,671
Plastics	1,590,662
Electronic systems and materials	745,078
Healthcare and others	144,054
Net income	45,839
Net income per share	0.30
At Year End:	
Total assets	2,664,674
Shareholders' equity	958,217

Nagase has a subsidiary which is called Nagase Biochemical Sales Co. Ltd.

Amano Pharmaceuticals Co. Ltd.

With subsidiaries in Europe (Amano Enzymes Europe Ltd., Milton Keynes, UK) and the USA (Amano Enzyme USA Co. Ltd., Lombard, Illinois).

The company calls itself the 'World No. 1 Speciality Enzyme Producer Founded in 1899'. The company also produces Kosher certified enzymes.

Employees: 420, Products: 400, Patents: 50, Turnover: $92m.

Amano Sales Breakdown

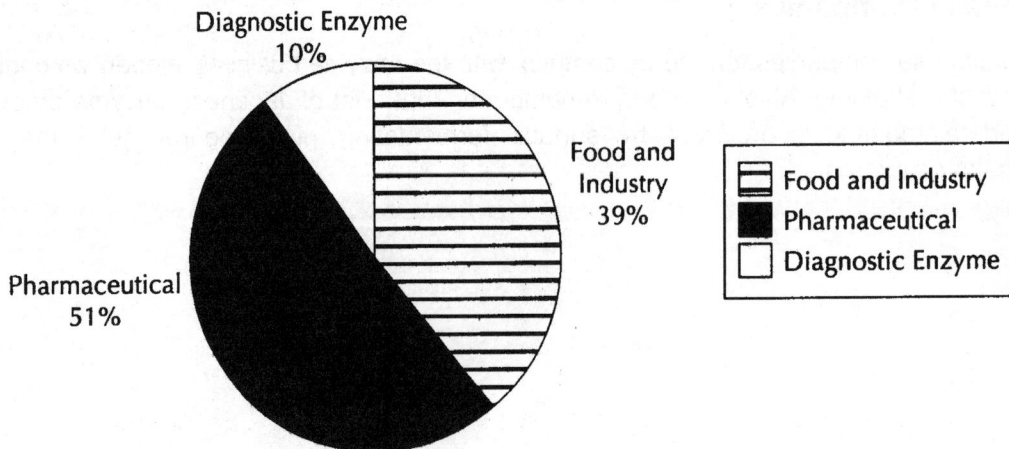

Diagnostic Enzyme 10%

Food and Industry 39%

Pharmaceutical 51%

Legend: Food and Industry, Pharmaceutical, Diagnostic Enzyme

Pharmaceutical Enzyme Area

Business Unit	Products
Digestive Enzymes	Regular type (Amylase, Protease, Lipase, Cellulase), Speciality type (Lactase, ∝-Galactosidase).
Anti-inflammation	Microbial protease (Crystalline protease).
Chiral Synthesis	Lipase, Esterase.
Others	OTC Medicines.

Food Industry Enzyme Area

Amano is focused on the production of speciality enzymes, with worldwide acceptance for food processing.

Business Unit	Application
Baking	Bread, Crackers.
Protein Hydrolysis	Flavour, Functionality, Dietary needs,
Fats/Oils	Hypo-allergenicity.
Starch Processing	Flavour, Functionality.
Brewing	Glucose, Maltose, Maltotriose, Isomaltose
	Oligosaccharides, Cyclodextrin.
	Japanese Sake Wine, Beer, Spirits.

The diagnostic area is growing and Amano are actively seeking new enzymes to improve the effective detection of diseases.

Tests	Items
Substrate determination	Glucose, Cholesterol, Triglyceride, Bilirubin, Free fatty acids, Others. (Used for health checks and individuals with cholesterol problems).

Key European and US Based Companies

Rohm

Produces high quality enzymes for baking and other food uses.

Danisco

Established since 1872. Food ingredients, sweeteners. Sales DKK 25 billion.

Novo Nordisk

Novo Nordisk's two core business areas are healthcare and enzymes. Novo Nordisk has about half of the world market for industrial enzymes. The enzyme business employs 3,000 people worldwide.

Key Strengths

A large company with a good R&D facility; internationally based with regional and local business development centres. The regional centres are based as follows:

Europe, Middle East and Africa	Paris, France
North America	Franklinton, NC, USA
Latin America	Curitiba, Brazil
Asia Pacific	Hong Kong, China

These RBDCs ensure that markets receive customer service matched to their own specific regional characteristics. They give Novo Nordisk the flexibility to adapt to local conditions and needs.

Financial Statement for the First Nine Months of 1998 (Unaudited)

	1998	1997	% Change
Net turnover	2,053	1,938	6
Operating income	422	346	22
Net financials	16	15	6
Income before tax	438	361	21
Tax	153	131	17
Net income	285	230	24
Employees at end of period	14,770	13,916	6
Earnings per share of DKK 10	3.82	3.09	24

Report on Enzyme Business (EB) Alone

EB sales rose by 1% in the first nine months of 1998. The modest sales increase is due in particular to a decrease in sales of technical enzymes. The market for industrial enzymes continues to be negatively affected by two factors. Firstly the situation in Asia has hit sales of industrial enzymes harder than previously expected and, as a result, sales in the region, including the textile area, are approximately 13% lower than in the same period last year. Around half of the decrease is due to weaker currency exchange rates in the region. Secondly, the value of the market for enzymes for the textile industry has decreased significantly as a result of a considerable decline in the number of blue jeans sales towards darker garments. Sales to the textile industry are thus 38% lower than last year. Exclusive of sales to Asia and to the textile industry, enzyme sales in the first nine months of 1998 increased 7% compared with the same period last year.

Against this background, the world market for industrial enzymes in 1998 is now expected to remain at the same level as in 1997. This also applies to Novo Nordisk's sales of industrial enzymes. It is anticipated that the financial impact of the reduced sales expectations will be countered by outgoing productivity improvements and cost-cutting measures in EB.

Biozyme

Established in 1971. The company is based in the UK and the USA.

Genzyme

This company is one of the oldest in biotechnology and was formed in 1981. The company is based in Cambridge, Massachusetts. It is mainly a healthcare company with much of the enzyme production developed for tissue repairs, therapeutics, surgical use and diagnostic tests. For the first nine months of 1998 its turnover was around $490 million. The revenues reflected higher sales of Ceredase and Cerezyme enzymes.

Gist Brocades

This company has worldwide operations, but the headquarters are in the Netherlands. The company is the world's largest antibiotics manufacturer within the pharmaceuticals sector. In the food market it offers baking, cheese and yoghurt making, brewing and fruit juice processing. Flavours and flavouring are another growth area. The company also produces enzymes for the animal feed industry, so that pigs and poultry can digest their foods better. Gist Brocades is very active in the growth markets of Asia and Latin America. The company is very active on the patent front. It employs 7,000 people in 70 locations, in more than 25 countries. Three quarters of all employees are based outside the Netherlands.

Genencor International

The company is based in the USA. It is the world's largest company dedicated exclusively to industrial biotechnology; through its new genetic engineering techniques, it develops and markets enzymes and biocatalysts. The company has hundreds of successful products, with more than 1,200 worldwide patents. The company has a $60 million facility in Stanford, California. Genencor International revolutionised industrial biotechnology with the world's first industrial-scale recombinant enzyme, and the world's first protein engineered industrial enzyme. These innovations introduced state-of-the-art genetic engineering techniques into the industry.

Appendix 2.

Major Industrial Enzyme Types and their Applications

Enzyme	Application
∝-Amylase	Corn syrup, baking, textile sizing, paper sizing, fuel alcohol, detergents, lens cleaners.
β-Amylase (Malt)	Beer, fuel alcohol, starch, production of maltose.
D-amino oxidase	Purification of L-amino acids.
Glucoamylase	Corn syrup, fuel alcohol.
Catalase	Egg desugaring, fruit and vegetable conservation.
Cellulase	Wine, beer, fruit juice.
Glucose isomerase	High-fructose corn syrup.
Glucose oxidase	Egg desugaring, oxygen scavenging, fruit conservation.
Invertase	Invert sugar.
Lactase	Dairy.
Lipase	Cheese.
Amyglycosidase	Starch, conversion of dextrin to glucose.
Proteinase	Protein (milk), production of peptone (soya bean), pre-treatment of soy sauce.
Papain, Proteases	Protein in beer, removal of turbidity, tenderising meat, cheese and flavour production.
Rennin (chymosin), Rennet	Casein, production of cheese.
Pectinase	Pectin, production of fruit juice, wine, beer, coffee.
Triacylglycerol lipase	Lipid, hydrolysis of lipid, flavour modification, cheese ripening, fat degradation.
Penicillin acylase	Semisynthetic Penicillin based antibiotics.
Pregrastric esterase	Cheese, butter flavour.
Protease	Detergents, lens cleaners.
Trypsin	Leather tanning.
β-Fructofuranosidase	Sucrose, production of inverted sugar.
β-Galactosidase	Lactose, decomposition of lactose.
α-Galactosidase	Raffinose, decomposition of raffinose.
Anthocyanase	Anthocyan, decolouration of anthocyan.
AMP deaminase	Adenylic acid, production of L-amino acid.
Aminoacylase	D, L-Acyl amino acid, production of L-amino acid.
Lysozyme	Egg white, against chlostridia in cheesemaking.
Lactase	Yeast, production of lactic acid, decomposition of whey.
Invertase	Sucrose, dethickening in chocolate.

Many industrial enzymes have multiple applications, as it makes good business sense to extend the utility of a product to as many applications as possible. This helps to increase sales and reduces the risk of having only a few customers. For example, alpha-amylase (α-amylase) is used in corn syrup manufacture, baking, textile sizing, fuel alcohol production, and an alkaline type, alpha-amylase, is used in detergents and lens cleaners.

Microbial Enzymes Legally used in Food Processing in the USA

Amyloglucosidase from *Rhizopuis juveus*	Degradation of gelatinised starch into constituent sugars, in the production of distilled spirits and vinegar.
Carbohydrase from *Aspergillus ginger*	a. Removal of visceral mass (bellies) in clam processing. b. Aid in the removal of shell in shrimp processing.
Carbohydrase from *Rhizopus, oryzae*	Production of dextrose from starch.
Catalase from *Micrococcus lysodeiktus*	Destruction and removal of hydrogen peroxides in the manufacture of cheese.
Esterase (lipase) from Mucor miehei	Flavour enhancer in cheeses, fats and oils and milk products.
α-Galactosidase from *Mortierella vinaceae* (free enzyme and mycelia) (var. raffinoseutilizer)	Production of sucrose from sugar beets, by addition as mycelia pellets to the molasses to increase the yield of sucrose, followed by the removal of the spent mycellial pellets by filtration.
Microbial Milk-clotting Enzymes from *Endothia parasitica bacillus cereus* *Mucor pusillus (var. Lindt)* *Mucor miehei (var. Cooney et emerson)*	Production of cheese if the enzyme was obtained from a pure culture fermentation.

BPP PUBLISHING

Appendix 3.

Genetically Modified Organisms

Genetically Modified Organisms (GMOs) are increasingly being used for production. There are many reasons for this, but some of them are:

- The production of purer enzyme products.

- Shorter development times for new enzymes.

- Reduced usage of energy and raw materials for production, giving reduced production costs.

In some countries, such as Germany, there has been a large negative reaction to GMOs. From a scientific point of view, there are no reasons for this negative response to GMOs for enzyme production.

The actual enzyme itself is identical whether it is produced by a wild-type organism or a GMO, although the end product will contain less impurities. In addition, enzyme end products do not contain any of the production organism, so the consumer is not exposed in any way to the GMO.

At the moment Biocatalysts Ltd. does not manufacture any of its enzyme products from GMOs, although it has several new enzymes under development which will be produced from GMOs. The first enzyme produced from a GMO is expected to be launched in 1999. These new enzymes will need special literature and a clear policy for communications.

The use of GMOs for enzyme production appears to offer many benefits; they are safe and efficient to use, and pose no threat to the environment or the end consumer. The end-user should be fully informed and promotional literature should clearly state if the production organism is a GMO.

Diagram to Show how GMOs are Made:

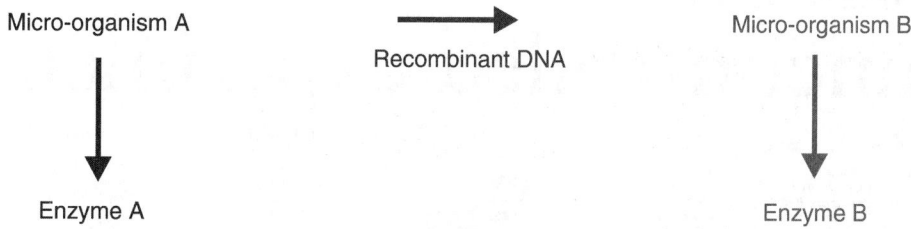

Micro-organism A

→ Recombinant DNA

Micro-organism B

Enzyme A

Enzyme B

A Typical Genetic Engineering Sequence

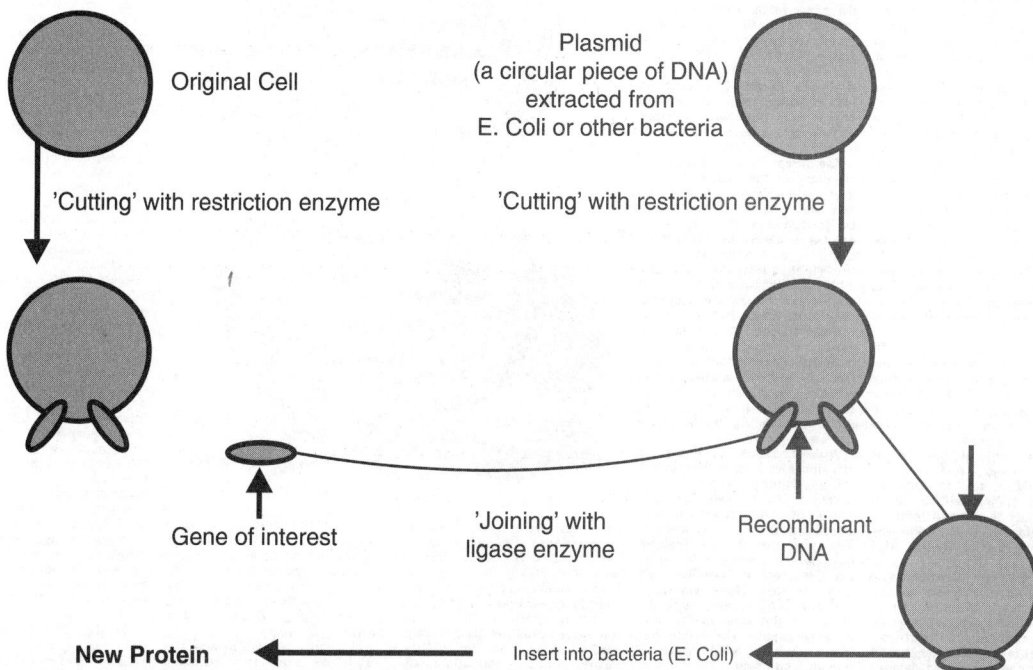

Original Cell

Plasmid
(a circular piece of DNA)
extracted from
E. Coli or other bacteria

'Cutting' with restriction enzyme

'Cutting' with restriction enzyme

Gene of interest

'Joining' with
ligase enzyme

Recombinant
DNA

New Protein ← Insert into bacteria (E. Coli) ←

One trait of living matter is the presence of genes which give a particular set of individual characteristics. Most genes are composed of DNA – deoxyribonucleic acid – which has a highly complex structure, consisting of the amino acids adenine, cytosine, guanine and thiamine, together with carbohydrate and phosphate groups, arranged in the pattern of a double helix. It is now possible to extract a fragment of DNA from one living micro-organism (e.g. plant cell or bacterial culture) to a second micro-organism, thus altering the genetic properties of the second micro-organism. Popularly this process is known as 'genetic engineering'; a technically more accurate term is 'recombinant DNA research'.

The new altered micro-organism would naturally possess different characteristics and, more importantly, different enzymatic properties. The way in which this is achieved is shown above.

BPP
PUBLISHING

FINANCIAL TIMES   WEEKEND FEBRUARY 13/FEBRUARY 14 1999

COMMENT & ANALYSIS

An uncontrolled experiment

Concern is growing over genetically modified food, write **Clive Cookson** and **Vanessa Houlder**

Might genetically modified foods become the next mad-cow crisis? Plants with altered genes are already pervasive in the food chain (see below). The view of mainstream scientists is clear: genetically modified foods that have been approved for human consumption are extremely unlikely to damage your health.

But the scientific wisdom was just as clear 10 years ago about mad-cow disease: the risk of BSE infecting people was negligible. The few maverick scientists who warned that the infection might cross the species barrier from cattle to people were attacked as irresponsible and received little attention. Unfortunately, they have turned out to be right.

The spectre of BSE haunts the current debate over genetic foods. Again, the vast majority of scientists pooh-pooh the view that eating genetically modified crops could pose any threat.

But this time consumer groups and politicians are listening to the minority who claim that added genes and the proteins they produce could pose a danger both to the environment and to human health.

"BSE has made people in Europe very sensitive to new technologies in the food supply industry, and very wary of scientists and government attempts to reassure them," says John Durant, professor of public understanding of science at Imperial College, London.

"It could be that the price of the BSE fiasco will be even greater outside the beef industry than inside it, if it makes the European public resist GM crops."

Public concern intensified yesterday after 20 international scientists signed a memorandum in support of controversial research that showed rats fed with an experimental kind of genetically modified potato suffered damage to their immune systems and changes to the size of their livers, hearts and brains.

Some of the findings were rapidly disowned by the Rowett Research Institute in Aberdeen, the institute where the work was carried out. It described the presentation of the work as "misleading" and asked Arpad Pusztai, the scientist involved, to retire.

The scientists who this week rallied round Dr Pusztai say his concerns are justified. Stanley Ewen, a pathologist at Aberdeen University medical school, says the work might even have disturbing implications for modified crops already in use, such as maize. Vivyan Howard, toxicopathologist at Liverpool University, says the growth retardation seen in young rats at the Rowett has serious implications, since underweight babies might show behavioural problems.

The researchers challenge the adequacy of the existing regulatory system in the UK and, by extension, the rest of the world. Dr Howard says: "The regulatory process needs to be more thorough, more objective and to ask the right questions." He and other scientists are calling for a moratorium on the use of genetically modified foods.

However, the fact is that such concerns remain those of a minority. Other scientists vigorously defend the existing system which, they say, involves detailed, case-by-case studies including feeding trials where necessary.

Professor Derek Burke, a biologist and former chairman of the UK government's advisory committee on novel foods, is "absolutely confident" about the safeguards in the existing system. The suggestion that the findings have any implications for existing GM crops is "absolute rubbish", he says. There was never any question that the particular genetic modification in the Rowett experiment – the potato contained a toxin – would enter the human food chain.

Lastly, he claims, the British regulatory system is more safety-conscious than that of the US.

"On medicine and drugs we are more relaxed. On food it is the other way round. It's a different attitude to risk."

One reason why the Europeans may be risk-averse is widespread ignorance both of how much genetically modified food there is and what has been done to the plants. While genetically modified plants are restricted in Europe to experimental field trials, commercial crops are marching across the fields of North and South America and east Asia, facing little consumer or political resistance. The total area planted worldwide has risen from 2.8m hectares in 1996 to 12.8m hectares in 1997 and an estimated 30m hectares last year.

Soya and maize are leading the way. The main modifications introduced so far enable plants either to kill insect pests or to resist a specific herbicide (so the farmer can spray the field with it to kill all the weeds without harming the crop.

Apart from the uncertainly over the facts, another barrier to public acceptance has arisen: all the benefits so far seem to have accrued to the farmers and the companies supplying them, while all the risks are born by consumers and the environment. More obvious public benefits – such as improved food qualities and gigantic improvements in productivity – remain promises.

Large-scale public surveys, such as those conducted by Prof Durant at Imperial College with George Gaskell at the London School of Economics, consistently show far more consumer opposition to genetically modified food in Europe than in North America. But the contrary is true of medical biotechnology; more Americans than Europeans express opposition to genetic testing. "We should avoid the stereotyped view that Americans are gung-ho about new technology and Europeans are not," Prof Durant says.

Besides BSE, which has not affected the US, he cites the very different views of agriculture on opposite sides of the Atlantic. "When Europeans think of wildlife and the rural environment, they think of farmland, and for them GM technology appears to be the next step in an unwelcome intensification of agriculture," he says. "Americans, in contrast, think of the wilderness areas in their national parks; they regard their farmland as part of the industrial system."

Whether the European concern or the American enthusiasm for crop engineering is more justified may not become clear for decades. Dr Howard says it will be extremely difficult to monitor the public for ill effects from GM food.

"Maybe, after 20 to 30 years, things might come to the fore," he says. "But you won't have any unexposed population against which to measure it. It is an uncontrolled experiment."

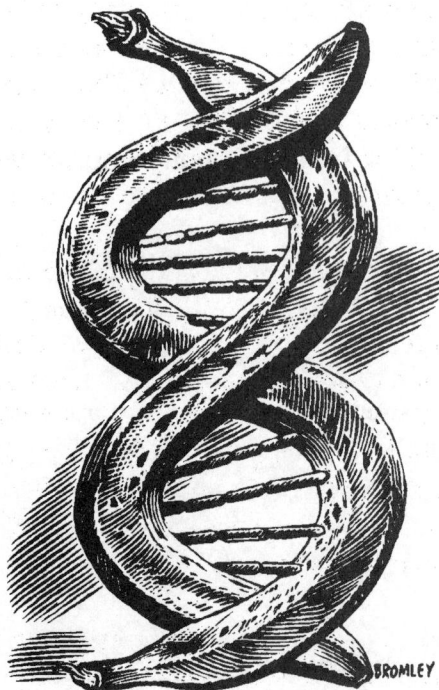

BROMLEY

A fridge full of modified genes

John Willman reports on what vegetables, fruits and foods life science groups have altered

A wide variety of genetically modified crops has been developed by the leading life sciences groups, ranging from potatoes and cauliflowers to lettuces and raspberries. They offer benefits such as better insect resistance, tolerance to chemical spray, better nutritional content and longer shelf lives after harvesting.

Only four are in use in the UK food industry and two of these have relatively restricted applications.

One is the genetically modified enzyme used to make vegetarian cheese, replacing rennet which is extracted from calves' stomachs. It is now increasingly used in making hard cheeses for general consumption.

The second is the genetically modified tomatoes used to make tomato paste. These tomatoes are less likely to rot on the plant and remain firmer after picking, producing a higher yield when turned into purée. As a result, the paste is cheaper and – according to Safeway, the supermarket chain – scores higher in consumer taste tests.

The other two are soyabeans and maize, both of which largely originate from the US. They are used much more widely – and in the case of soya increasingly hard to find in a non-modified form.

Soya is an ingredient in many products, including cakes and biscuits, chilled foods and vegetarian textured meat products as well as soya sauce and cooking oil. It is used in about 60 per cent of processed foods, though in some cases in very small quantities.

Most of the soya used in the UK comes from the US where genetically modified crops made up about a third of the harvest last year and the share is rising rapidly. Bulk shipments routinely mix modified and non-modified, and any food product that may contain modified ingredients must be labelled as such in Europe.

Maize is also used as a basic ingredient in many food and drink products, including breakfast cereals, crisps and snacks, petfood and processed foods. It is also a source of fructose used in soft drinks and confectionery. Europe is able to produce much of its maize needs so it is easier to keep genetically modified grain out of the UK food chain.

Under EU rules, a food using any genetically modified ingredient must be labelled accordingly. The only exception is derivatives of soya that contain none of the protein – such as oil.

The real question, however, is whether food manufacturers always know whether GM ingredients are in their products. One food company – which does not want to be identified – found traces of genetic modification in 14 out of 20 products it believed to be GM-free.

Genetically modified products

Ingredient	Used in
Enzyme to replace animal rennet	Vegetarian cheese and other cheeses
Tomatoes	Tomato paste
Soya	Chilled foods, cakes and biscuits, vegetarian textured meat products, processed foods
Maize	Crisps and snacks, cereals, pet food, processed foods

Appendix 4.

Vegetarian Enzyme Modified Cheese

Important changes in the dairy industry over the last ten years or so, have seen a significant move away from animal derived enzymes, such as calf stomach rennet, used in cheese manufacture, to microbially derived rennets. A similar, but more recent move has also occurred in the production of cheese derived flavour ingredients, such as Enzyme Modified Cheese (EMC) – an important and growing sector of the flavours market. The move away from animal derived products allows the cheeses and EMCs to be offered with both vegetarian, and kosher status – important and growing niche markets in the food industry.

Extra impetus has been given by recent concerns over possible BSE and swine fever transmissions. Many food and flavour suppliers are now starting to look for non-animal alternatives. However, much processed cheese is still made containing EMC, manufactured with animal derived enzymes. It is now generally agreed that there is a pronounced change occurring in the demand for EMC with vegetarian (and kosher) status, requiring the use of microbially derived enzymes in its manufacture. Of course, EMC is not only used in processed cheese but can be found as a flavour ingredient in a rapidly expanding selection of cheese flavoured snacks and convenience foods. It is even used in some pet foods!

Biocatalysts Ltd. is at the forefront of these changes, especially in EMC production. Whilst Biocatalysts Ltd. offers the conventional animal derived enzymes, it has always specialised in microbially derived enzyme products for vegetarian and kosher status EMC. Biocatalysts Ltd. offers a comprehensive range of well-developed formulations for a variety of cheese flavours, and has an active R&D programme for the introduction of new, microbially derived enzymes for new flavours. Biocatalysts Ltd. also offers a unique tailor-made formulation service if a customer has specific requirements that standard products do not fully satisfy.

BPP
PUBLISHING

Appendix 5.

Biocatalysts Ltd. Organisation Chart

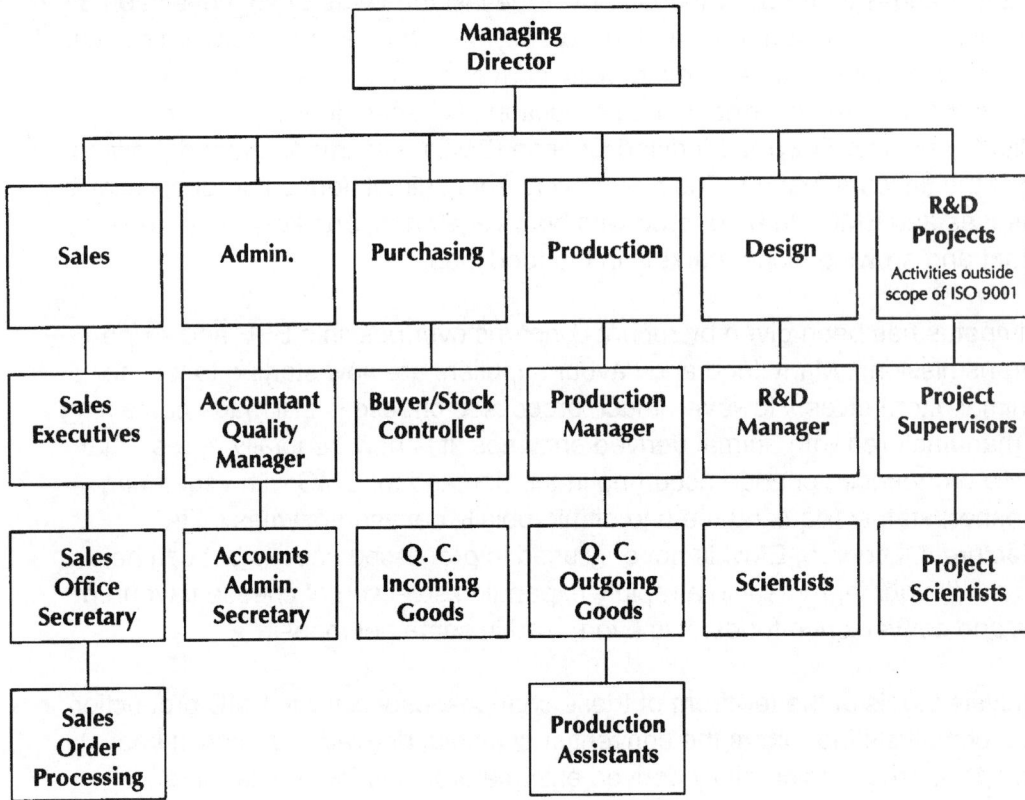

```
                          ┌─────────────────┐
                          │    Managing     │
                          │    Director     │
                          └─────────────────┘
```

Sales	Admin.	Purchasing	Production	Design	R&D Projects Activities outside scope of ISO 9001
Sales Executives	Accountant Quality Manager	Buyer/Stock Controller	Production Manager	R&D Manager	Project Supervisors
Sales Office Secretary	Accounts Admin. Secretary	Q. C. Incoming Goods	Q. C. Outgoing Goods	Scientists	Project Scientists
Sales Order Processing			Production Assistants		

Q. C. = Quality Control
R&D = Research and Development

Appendix 6.

Biocatalysts Ltd.
Abbreviated Balance Sheet

	1997		1996	
	£	£	£	£
Fixed assets				
Tangible assets		177,667		173,671
Investments		2		3
Current assets		177,669		173,674
Stocks	157,877		188,466	
Debtors	783,623		517,462	
Cash at bank and in hand	12,122		30,987	
	953,622		736,915	
Creditors: amounts falling due within one year	(508,073)		(399,078)	
Net current assets		445,549		337,837
Total assets less current liabilities		623,218		511,511
Deferred assets		10,138		10,138
Net assets		633,356		521,649
Capital and reserves				
Called up share capital		500,000		405,511
Capital reserve		–		7,089
Profit and loss account		133,356		109,049
Total shareholders funds		633,356		521,649
Attributable to:				
Equity shareholders		633,356		521,649

These financial statements are prepared in accordance with the special provisions of Part VII of the Companies Act, 1985, relating to small companies.

(Information supplied by Biocatalysts Ltd.)

Profitability 1994-1998 (1994 = 100)

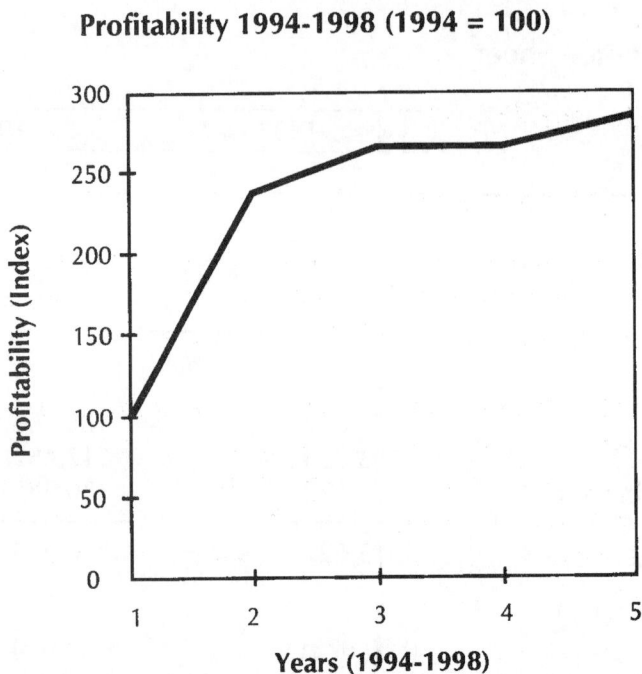

The company turnover is approximately £2.5 million.

Previous Years' Business Ratios

	1994	1995
Current Ratio	2.3	2.2
Acid Test	1.4	1.5
Stock Turn	4.9	4.8
Stock Holding (Days)	75	72
Payment Period	75	72
% Profit	4.9	8.2

The company is growing at 20-30% per annum. The sales profile follows the normal Pareto effect with 80% of the customers providing only 20% of the sales.

Appendix 7.

Biocatalysts Ltd. and Trading

Trading in the Euro (€), £s and $s

There is strong worldwide interest in how the new European money system based on the Euro €, is actually working (even if it is only how to get a computer keyboard with the new Euro symbol as part of the standard layout!).

More than two thirds of Biocatalysts' annual turnover is from export sales and it is used to working with different currencies. Biocatalysts Ltd. appears to be fully prepared for trading in the Euro. Biocatalysts Ltd. is able to offer quotations, take orders and, most importantly, accept payment in the Euro (€), American Dollars ($), and UK Pounds Sterling (£). All other currency transactions are usually 'translated' into one of the above three currencies.

Appendix 8.

Management Buyout History

1983 Biocatalysts Ltd. name registered.

1985 Work started on a new enzyme facility in South Wales.

1986 Biocatalysts Ltd. starts trading under the ultimate ownership of Grand Metropolitan.

1987 Management buyout financed by the Welsh Development Authority and Welsh Venture Capital Fund when Grand Metropolitan started to divest non-core businesses.

Collaboration with Universities

Biocatalysts Ltd. collaborates with around 8 different UK universities (Food and Biochemistry) and several European universities. In general, basic research is done at the universities (screening, gene cloning, new enzyme developments) before the laboratory processes are brought in for scale-up applications work. In addition, Biocatalysts Ltd. sponsors CASE awards at some universities on more speculative areas of enzyme research.

Appendix 9.

BIOCATALYSTS LIMITED
A manufacturer of speciality enzymes and formulator of enzyme complexes

BAKING

BREWING

FRUIT AND VEGETABLE PROCESSING

FLAVOUR

PROTEINS

DIETETICS

TEXTILES (GARMENT WASHING)

DIAGNOSTICS

PHARMACEUTICALS

ENVIRONMENTALS

Biocatalysts Ltd is unique amongst the world's enzyme companies. Our willingness to supply custom-tailored products for our clients means that the whole company focus is directed towards our customers and towards giving total customer satisfaction. This customer focus has resulted in Biocatalysts Ltd growing at more than twice the industry average over the past 10 years.

Biocatalysts Ltd is an independent company, located just outside Cardiff, the capital city of Wales. Biocatalysts, as our company name suggests, only makes and sells enzymes. We are not a division of a larger chemical, food ingredients or pharmaceutical company.

Biocatalysts Ltd has many exclusive agreements with blue chip companies around the world, who value the products and technical services we supply. But we are also happy to deal with both small and medium sized companies and our customer base has a full spectrum of company sizes.

Biocatalysts Ltd does not make or sell high volume commodity enzymes, such as those used in the detergent or starch processing industries. We operate in selected parts of the enzyme market where our technical support and willingness to work with customers on a one-to-one basis is highly valued. These enzyme sectors usually require not single enzyme entities but enzyme complexes where the ratios of each of the components are crucial to the efficacy of the whole enzyme product and our customer's process. We do not believe in our customers making do with compromise enzyme products just because that is the way they come off the fermenter! Our own fermentation for the manufacture of our enzyme products is sub-contracted out. This, we believe, allows us to be more flexible, our focus is on investing in enzyme technology – not stainless steel!

Our R&D programme is focused on the development of new enzymes and enzyme complexes mainly identified to us by our customers. We have many allegiances with leading British Universities where most of our basic research into new enzymes is carried out. This allows us to focus our in-house scientists onto the needs of our customers, whilst keeping fully up to date with the latest developments in bio-research.

If you are not sure that you are getting optimum performance from your current enzymes, or if you think your process could benefit by the use of enzymes, why not give Biocatalysts a try and find out what makes us unique amongst the world's enzyme companies.

BIOCATALYSTS

BPP PUBLISHING

E N Z Y M E S   F O R   T H E   F O O D   I N D U S T R Y

PRODUCT	CODE	PRINCIPAL ACTIVITIES	APPLICATION NOTES

BAKING

PRODUCT	CODE	PRINCIPAL ACTIVITIES	APPLICATION NOTES
AMYLASE	A011P	Amylase	Fungal alpha amylase, protease free, full range of activities to 100,000 SKB.
CATAMYL PLUS	C380P	Mixed amylases, Pentosanase	Anti-staling for bread.
COMBIZYME 261P	C261P	Alpha amylase, Proteinase, Pentosanase	For improving loaf volume, crumb texture & retarding staling in bread.
COMBIZYME 275P	C275P	Proteinase, Alpha amylase, Pentosanase	Protein modifier for biscuits & crackers.
COMBIZYME 359P	C359P	Pentosanase	Bromate replacer.
COMBIZYME 365P	C365P	Xylanase, Proteinase	Viscosity control in batters.
COMBIZYME 366P	C366P	Proteinase, Pentosanase	Metabisulphite replacer in biscuits & crackers.
➤ COMBIZYME 485P	C485P	Amylase, hemicellulase & protease	Metabisulphite replacer in biscuit manufacture.
DEPOL 112P	D112P	Glucanase, Xylanase	Viscosity control in batters.
DEPOL 222P	D222P	Pentosanase	Amylase free pentosanase.
DEPOL 267P	D267P	Alpha amylase, Pentosanase	Amylase/pentosanase formulated at working strength for direct incorporation into baking flour.
DEPOL 333P	D333P	Xylanase	High activity, amylase free hemicellulase.
DEPOL 364P	D364P	Xylanase, Cellulase	For viscosity control in batters & use in doughnut manufacture.
DEPOL 414P	D414P	Alpha amylases	Specialty amylase for French type bread.
➤ DEPOL 453P	D453P	Hemicellulase	Aspergillus hemicellulase without amylase for bread improvers.
➤ DEPOL 454P	D454P	Hemicellulase (xylanase)	Endo-xylanase for bread improvers.
PROMOD 223P	P223P	Proteinase	Bacterial protease for biscuits & crackers.
PROMOD 388P	P388P	Proteinase	Fungal proteinase for improving dough handling & bread texture.
PROMOD 451P	P451P	Proteinase	Fungal proteinase/peptidase for improving dough handling & crumb texture.

BREWING

PRODUCT	CODE	PRINCIPAL ACTIVITIES	APPLICATION NOTES
➤ AMG BC300	D339L	Glucoamylase	Production of lite beers.
➤ COMBIZYME 108L	C108L	Protease, Alpha amylase, Beta glucanase	High activity formulation for yield improvements in brewing.
➤ GLUCANASE 1XL	G011L	Beta glucanase	Improved mash & fermentation performance (run off & solubles) in brewing applications.
➤ GLUCANASE 5XL	G015L	Beta glucanase	Concentrated (5X) glucanase for improved mash & fermentation performance in brewing applications.
➤ PROMOD 144L	P144L	Papain	Beer clarification, removal of chill haze.

FRUIT AND VEGETABLE PROCESSING

PRODUCT	CODE	PRINCIPAL ACTIVITIES	APPLICATION NOTES
➤ CELLULASE 13L	C013L	Cellulase	Cellulose hydrolysis.
DEPOL 40L	D040L	Cellulase, Pectinases, Beta glucosidase	Versatile formulation for maceration, viscosity reduction & extraction of a wide range of fruits & vegetables including mangoes.
DEPOL 220L	D220L	Alpha amylase, Glucoamylase	Hydrolysis of starches during fruit processing.
➤ GLUCOSE OXIDASE	G168L	Glucose oxidase	Oxygen removal from fruit flavoured drinks.
MACER8 FJ	M263L	Pectinases	Improved performance in a wide range of fruit juice extraction applications (high pectin lyase, low pectin esterase).
MACER8 O	M265L	Pectinases	Significantly improved yield of olive oil & easier to handle waste.
MACER8 W	M264L	Pectinases	Improved extraction performance & flavour enhancement for white wine.
PECTINASE 62L	P062L	Pectinases	General depectinising applications & broad spectrum depolymerisation activity, particularly in fruit.
PECTINASE 444L	P444L	Pectinases	Highly active formulation for general depectinising applications.
CITRUS FRUIT PEELER			
PECTINASE 162L	P162L	Pectinases	Cost effective peeling of citrus fruits (automation aid).
➤ TANNASE	T510P	Tannase	Removal of tannins.

BIOCATALYSTS

New Products are Shown with ➤

ENZYMES FOR THE FOOD INDUSTRY

PRODUCT	CODE	PRINCIPAL ACTIVITIES	APPLICATION NOTES
FLAVOUR			
DEPOL 40L	D040L	Cellulase, Pectinase, Beta glucosidase	Versatile formulation for maceration & extraction in a wide range of vegetables including vanilla, carrots, tea etc.
DEPOL 112L	D112L	Glucanase, Xylanase, Beta glucosidase	Flavour extraction from fibrous botanicals.
FLAVORPRO 192P	F192P	Peptidases	Debittering of protein hydrolysates.
FLAVORPRO 373P	F373P	Glutaminase (Bacillus)	Conversion of glutamine into glutamate in protein hydrolysates.
LIPOMOD 187P	L187P	Esterase	Protease free microbial lipase for enzyme modified cheese (EMC) production. Cheddar type flavours. Kosher certification available.
LIPOMOD 224P	L224P	Esterase (protease)	Enzyme modified cheese (EMC) production. Cheddar type flavours.
LIPOMOD 299P	L299P	Esterase (protease)	Enzyme modified cheese (EMC) production. Cheddar type flavours.
LIPOMOD 29P	L029P	Esterase, Lipase (protease)	General fat hydrolysis & enzyme modified cheese (EMC) production.
LIPOMOD 338P	L338P	Esterase	Protease free microbial lipase for enzyme modified cheese (EMC) production. Blue cheese type flavours. Kosher certification available.
LIPOMOD 34P	L034P	Lipase, Esterase	Protease free, high activity lipase for hydrolysis of oils, tallow & fats including butter fat. Kosher certification available.
PEPTIDASE 436P	P436P	Aminopeptidase, Carboxypeptidase	Debittering of protein hydrolysates. Contains proline peptidase activity. Kosher certification available.
PEPTIDASE 433/4P	P433/4P	Aminopeptidase, Carboxypeptidase	Broad spectrum peptidases for debittering of protein hydrolysates.
PROMOD 215P	P215P	Endo-proteinase, Peptidase	For use with protease free lipases in enzyme modified cheese (EMC) production. Introduces protein notes. Kosher certification available.
PROMOD 446P	P446P	Endo-proteinase, Peptidase	For use with protease free lipases in enzyme modified cheese (EMC) production. Introduces protein notes. Kosher certification available.
PROTEINS			
BC PEPSIN 1:3000	P389P	Acid protease	Protein hydrolysis at acid pH values.
DEPOL 20L	D020L	Pectinase	For viscosity reduction of soya polysaccharides.
PROMOD 144L	P144L	Proteinase	Papain liquid 100 TU.
PROMOD 144P	P144P	Proteinase	Papain powder 100 TU.
PROMOD 184P	P184P	Proteinase	Bromelain powder.
PROMOD 192P	P192P	Endo-proteinase	Acid fungal protease with exo-peptidases.
PROMOD 194P	P194P	Proteinase	Neutral fungal protease with exo-peptidases.
PROMOD 24L	P024L	Proteinase	Neutral bacterial, general purpose liquid proteinase.
PROMOD 278P	P278P	Proteinase	Mixed fungal & bacterial proteinases for Stage 1 in the Biocatalysts eHVP (enzyme hydrolysed vegetable protein) Cascade: the bulk hydrolysis stage.
PROMOD 279P	P279P	Proteinase, Peptidase	Fungal proteases & peptidases for Stage 2 in the Biocatalysts eHVP Cascade: the debittering stage.
PROMOD 280P	P280P	Proteinase, Amylase	Mixed fungal & bacterial enzyme activities for Stage 3 in the Biocatalysts eHVP Cascade: the filtration aid stage.
PROMOD 298L	P298L	Proteinase	Broad spectrum bacterial proteinase, will rapidly reduce viscosity of soya protein pastes.
PROMOD 31L	P031L	Proteinase	Neutral bacterial, broad spectrum liquid proteinase.
DIETETICS			
AMYLASE	AD11P	Amylase	Aid for digestion of dietary starch. Ready for tableting.
BC PEPSIN 1:3000	P389P	Pepsin	Animal derived acid enzyme to aid protein digestion.
BROMELAIN 1200GDU	P523P	Bromelain	Broad spectrum plant protease to aid protein digestion.
CELLULASE CP	C013P	Cellulase	Aid for digestion of dietary cellulose. Ready for tableting.
DEPOL 333P	D333P	Xylanase	Aid for digestion of dietary hemicellulose. Ready for tableting.
HEMICELLULASE 334P	H334P	Glucanase, Cellulase, Xylanase	Aid for the digestion of dietary fibre. Ready for tableting.
LACTASE	L017P	Lactase	Aid for digestion of dietary lactose. Ready for tableting.
LIPASE, Rhizopus sp.	L036P	Lipase, Esterase	Aid for digestion of dietary fats & lipids. Ready for tableting.
PANCREATIN 4XNF	P211P	Amylase, Lipase, Protease	General aid for digestion. Ready for tableting.
PROMOD D24P	PD024P	Protease	Broad spectrum proteases for aiding the digestion of dietary proteins. Ready for tableting.

New Products are Shown with ➡

Page 36 of Biocatalysts

N O N - F O O D   G R A D E   E N Z Y M E S

PRODUCT	CODE	PRINCIPAL ACTIVITIES	APPLICATION NOTES
TEXTILES (GARMENT WASHING)			
→ CATALASE	C495L	Catalase	Inactivation and removal of hydrogen peroxide.
DESIZE 277L	D277L	Amylase	Very high activity bacterial amylase for cost effective garment & textile desizing applications. Can be diluted.
→ DESIZE 569P	D569P	Amylase	Very strong desizing amylase powder.
→ DESIZE (NON-ENZYMATIC)	D574L	Non-enzyme product	Desizing fabrics with difficult sizes or where minimal backstaining is required.
INDIFADE 7.5L	I07.5L	Cellulase	Range of liquid acid cellulase activities from medium to high activity. Ready to use,
INDIFADE 9L	I009L	Cellulase	cost effective formulations for bio-washing applications.
INDIFADE 11L	I011L	Cellulase	
INDIFADE 13L	I013L	Cellulase	
→ INDIFADE 9 LAS	I480L	Cellulase	Acid cellulase with anti-redeposition chemistry.
INDIFADE 426P	I426P	Cellulase	High activity, buffered mixed acid & neutral cellulase powder.
INDIFADE 501P	I501P	Cellulase	High activity, buffered acid cellulase powder with added anti-redeposition chemistry for an economical, near neutral type of stone wash effect.
→ INDIFADE 555P	I555P	Cellulase	Boosted cost effective neutral cellulase.
→ INDIFADE AGER	I478L	Non-enzyme product	Gives antique look to denims.
→ INDIFADE BRIGHT	I476P	Non-enzyme product	Optical brightener.
→ INDIFADE COLD	I539L	Cellulase	Cellulase for use in cool water (40 - 45°C).
INDIFADE LAS	I014L	Cellulase	High activity, liquid acid cellulase with added anti-redeposition chemistry for an economical, near neutral type of stone wash effect.
INDIFADE NC-1G	I001G	Cellulase	High activity, unbuffered neutral cellulase granules.
→ INDIFADE SOFT	I477L	Non-enzyme product	Specially formulated softener for denims.
INDIFADE SUPER	I474P	Cellulase	Highly cost effective, buffered neutral cellulase powder.
INDIFADE SUPER PLUS	I475P	Cellulase	Cost effective, buffered neutral cellulase powder with added anti-redeposition chemistry.
SOFTZYME	S425L	Cellulase	Bio-softening, anti-pilling formulation for cellulosic fibres (Tencel®).
DIAGNOSTICS			
ALKALINE PHOSPHATASE	A500L	Alkaline phosphatase	High stability reagent for immunodiagnostics.
GALACTOSE DEHYDROGENASE	G471P	Galactose dehydrogenase	For determination of galactose in blood of neonatals.
MANNITOL DEHYDROGENASE	M093P	Mannitol dehydrogenase	For determination of mannitol in sugar permeability test in human gastric disorders.
MYROSINASE	M044P	Myrosinase	Determination of glucosinolates in rape seed meal.
PHENYLALANINE DEHYDROGENASE	P098P	Phenylalanine dehydrogenase	For determination of phenylalanine in blood of neonatals.
→ GLUCOSE OXIDASE	TP 574P	Glucose oxidase - catalase free	Determination of glucose - available summer 1998.
→ GLUTAMINASE	G420P	Glutaminase	Determination of glutamine.
→ PEROXIDASE	P558P	Peroxidase	Immuno-diagnostics.
PHARMACEUTICALS			
LIPASE, Candida sp.	L034P	Lipase	Stereoselective hydrolysis of esters.
LIPASE, Pseudomonas sp.	L056P	Lipase	Stereoselective hydrolysis of esters.
LIPASE, Pancreatic	L115P	Lipase Esterase	Stereoselective hydrolysis of esters.
SEC ADH 300	S300P	Alcohol dehydrogenase	Synthesis of chiral alcohols.
TRYPSIN 250	T069P	Proteinase	Standard formulation for mammalian cell culture.
TRYPSIN IRRAD.	T070P	Proteinase	Irradiated formulation for mammalian cell culture.
TRYSIN SVF	T071P	Proteinase	Certified specific virus-free trypsin for cell culture.
ENVIRONMENTALS			
GREASE BIOSOLVE (COMBIZYME 209P)	C209P	Broad spectrum lipases & carbohydrases	High activity enzyme formulation for reduced fouling of grease traps & drain maintenance.
LATRINE DEODOURISER (COMBIZYME 253L)	C253L	Broad spectrum enzymes	High activity product for significant odour reduction in many waste treatment applications.
ODOURWAY 10X	O073L10	Mixed, broad spectrum	10X concentrated version. Available with a choice of perfumes.
ODOURWAY 20X	O073L20	Mixed, broad spectrum	20X concentrated version. Available with a choice of perfumes.

BIOCATALYSTS

New Products are Shown with →

CUSTOM TAILORED PRODUCTS:

This catalogue contains our standard products that are sold regularly to our customers. In addition we have many other products that have been developed exclusively for individual customers. If you do not think your current enzyme product is optimised for your process or would like an exclusive enzyme product (not available to your competitors) then contact the Sales department at Biocatalysts to find out how we can develop new enzyme products exclusively for your company.

If there are any enzyme activities that you are interested in that are not mentioned in our standard listing then please enquire; we have many new enzymes under development for release in the near future.

WORLD-WIDE SALES AGENTS:

Biocatalysts has an extensive network of agents and distributors in over 40 countries right around the world. Our most recent list is given in our company newsletter 'IN BRIEF'. This is sent out routinely to all clients on our database. If you would like to be added to our mailing list then please fill out a reader reply card included with this catalogue.

PACKAGING:

Biocatalysts products are packaged by weight (not volume) according to the following:

Powders (designated 'P' in product code)
Standard packaging   25 kg in fibre kegs or Lesac² lined square boxes.
Liquids (designated 'L' in product code)
Standard packaging   25, 215 and 1000 kg
Granules (designated 'G' in product code)
Standard packaging   25 kg
Other pack sizes are available including 1 and 5 kg on request.

DATA ACCURACY:

Whilst Biocatalysts makes all practicable efforts to ensure the accuracy of the information it gives, the data might be subject to change without notice. Biocatalysts cannot guarantee performance in any end application. Prior to carrying out any commercial application, clients should ensure that they are not infringing third party patent rights.

SAMPLES:

Product samples for trials are generally available on request. Please fill out and return an enquiry card included with this catalogue or contact the sales department at Biocatalysts.

PRODUCT DATA SHEETS:

Further information is available for each of the products listed in this catalogue. Please contact Biocatalysts for individual Product Data Sheets.

HEALTH AND SAFETY:

Always read and retain the Health and Safety data sheets supplied with each product, before use. If you are in any doubt about recommended product handling and safety, please contact Biocatalysts before use. Generally, when handling enzymes avoid contact with the skin and eyes and do not breathe dusts or aerosols containing them.

TECHNICAL SUPPORT:

Biocatalysts offers a Technical Support Service for all its products.

BPP
PUBLISHING

KOSHER STATUS:

Most Biocatalysts products are available with Kosher or Kosher Parve certification in accordance with current Orthodox Union requirements. Kosher certification requirements must be specified with order as retrospective certification cannot be issued.

TRADE MARKS:

COMBIZYME, DEPOL, INDIFADE, LIPOMOD, MACER8, PROMOD and the Biocatalysts logo including the cat symbol are trademarks of Biocatalysts Ltd.

ENZYMES FROM GENETICALLY MODIFIED ORGANISMS (GMOs):

Genetically modified organisms (commonly called GMOs) are being increasingly used by many companies for enzyme production. There are many reasons for this, but some of them include:

- the production of purer enzyme products
- shorter development times for new enzymes
- reduced usage of energy and raw materials for production giving reduced production costs

At the moment none of our products listed in this catalogue is derived from a GMO. We expect to launch our first enzyme produced from a GMO in 1999. All literature regarding these new enzymes will clearly state that they have been produced from GMOs. This is now the norm for the enzyme industry. It is our belief that the use of GMOs for enzyme production offers many benefits and that they are safe and efficient to use, and that they pose no threat to the environment or the end consumer.

ANIMAL DERIVED ENZYMES:

None of the enzymes listed in this catalogue is derived from a bovine (cow) source. One of our specialisations is to offer microbial derived alternatives to commonly available animal enzymes (e.g. our alkaline phosphatase). By not processing or dealing with bovine derived products we can ensure that there is no risk whatsoever of any of our products being contaminated with BSE.

The only animal derived enzymes included in this catalogue are from porcine (pig) sources. No primary processing of animal glands is carried out at Biocatalysts Ltd. All partially processed animal derived material comes from animal certified as healthy at the time of slaughter. Our premises are inspected annually by an Officer of the British Ministry of Agriculture, Fisheries and Food (MAFF) and an Approval certificate issued (copy available on request).

HACCP (HAZARD ANALYSIS AND CRITICAL CONTROL POINT SYSTEM):

As well as operating under ISO 9001 Biocatalysts Ltd also has additional operating procedures which conform to HACCP.

If you would like product datasheets, quotations or samples of any of the products in this catalogue or would like to be added to our database, please fill in the reply card and post or fax it back to Biocatalysts.

BIOCATALYSTS

4

Step 1: Overview of Biocatalysts

Introduction

Case step 1: the overview

This chapter will demonstrate how to get started on a case study and will show you how to establish the **context** of a case study. By the end of this stage in any case study, and at the end of this chapter in terms of Biocatalyst, you will be able to describe and explain the implications of:

- Your role and what you have been asked to do
- The company, its size, sector and key capabilities
- The main environmental challenges
- The customers
- The competitors

Skills and knowledge reminder: techniques and tools at overview

As we have already indicated, many of the analysis tools you have studied during Planning and Control will help you to organise and assimilate information quickly. You can identify those you will be able to use during the overview and will then analyse the information so they can be applied at the inview stages.

During this chapter you will see two techniques applied to this case study:

1. A mind map used to help sort out the information about enzymes (see 2.10)

2. A schematic to help pull together a picture of the various stakeholders and their needs and interests (see 5.5)

If you are unfamiliar with any of the basic tools and techniques we use in this section of the *Tutorial Text,* you will need to take time out to review your diploma notes.

1   WHAT ARE WE TRYING TO ACHIEVE AT THE OVERVIEW?

1.1   There are few people, students or tutors, who do not feel nervous at the prospect of tackling a major exam case. CIM cases do tend to fall with a thud on the doormat when they are delivered and, like Biocatalysts, they are typically 16-20 pages of narrative followed by a

BPP
PUBLISHING

similar volume of appendices. Clearly they represent a considerable piece of work: the challenge is where to start. It is the function of the overview to begin the process of bringing order and method to the case study.

1.2 The mistake at this stage is to keep reading the case without picking up a pen and actually doing something with the data it contains. Simply rereading the case will only give you a superficial picture: you need to really understand the business and the implications of what you are being told. You need to:

- First sort
- Then analyse

the clues and data provided, turning it in the process into relevant information which will eventually help you to make and justify a credible strategy.

So, what needs to be done?

1.3 You have already read Biocatalysts and thought about the business: now you are going to start work on it.

1.4 If you are not familiar with the sector (which of course most students won't be) the challenge of tackling issues generated by an unknown sector can itself be daunting. Remember we will bring order to the chaos of any business by applying our planning processes, objectively and rigorously.

1.5 What did you find out?

Action Programme 1

Even after one read of the narrative, you can probably answer these questions. Try and do this without referring back to the case.

(a) Is this a B2B or B2C case study and what are the implications of that?
(b) What is the product Biocatalysts are producing and why is it a challenging business?
(c) Who are you and what is your role in the case?
(d) What is the role of agents in Biocatalyst's market?

Turn to the end of this chapter to check your answers with ours.

1.6 Before you start getting down to any more detailed work on the overview, just take a few minutes to **familiarise yourself with the appendices**. What do they contain? Again do not try and do anything with this data, but simply assess what sort of information might be available to you once you analyse and cross analyse the various appendices. For example, Appendix 6 on page 29 gives you some headline financial information and, considered against some of the competitor information in Appendix 1 (from page 17), you can see how small the Biocatalyst operation is and that you will be able to assess its financial strength. Clearly Biocatalyst is a very small fish in a big and turbulent global pond.

2 BRINGING ORDER TO THE CASE MATERIAL

2.1 You won't understand the case study yet and shouldn't expect to but you are at least beginning to get a sense of the **scenario and scale**. There is no shortage of information but at this stage it is scattered throughout the narrative and appendices. In your overview you need to sort out:

- Information about the industry and its fortunes

- Information about Biocatalysts and its business

- Information about the products and markets (sorting out the general from the Biocatalysts specific)

2.2 Don't be surprised if the material seems muddled at first. As you work with it and sort it into relevant groups it will start to make more sense. Do avoid rushing into ad hoc analysis: it pays to work through the case thoroughly and logically, so that you can be sure that you have stripped out all the relevant data.

2.3 This next step in the overview process could take you two to six hours, depending on the complexity of the case. Take this task in two or three short bursts and don't worry at this stage about what you are going to do next.

2.4 **Note**

You must not do any research outside the Case Study as this will be penalised by the examiner. Additional information would only confuse the issues, so just use you own knowledge and the information given. In this instance, the Examiner has especially addressed the issues of anomalies which may be found in the case. There are likely to be some, so do not get bogged down in them, or in the detail of the case. You are working at the broader strategic level: flag up any assumptions you need to make and move on. However, the issue of websites is addressed in the case and it doesn't seem unreasonable for you, as a consultant, to visit Monsanto's website to get a 'feel' for the competitors and a flavour of the industry. **However,** do **not** get sidetracked by additional data; it is simply to help you understand more about the product. In reality, there is relatively little material that we spotted on our surfing of the web that would be of any obvious value, so don't worry if you don't have access or time. Certainly you must not bring 'facts' from any external search to bear on your answer in the exam. The world is as described by the examiner for the duration of the case.

2.5 **Reminder**

As you work through the case, keep an **information shopping list** so that you can use it later if we need to prepare for a research question.

2.6 **Head up pages** with key areas for analysis to help you sort through the case.

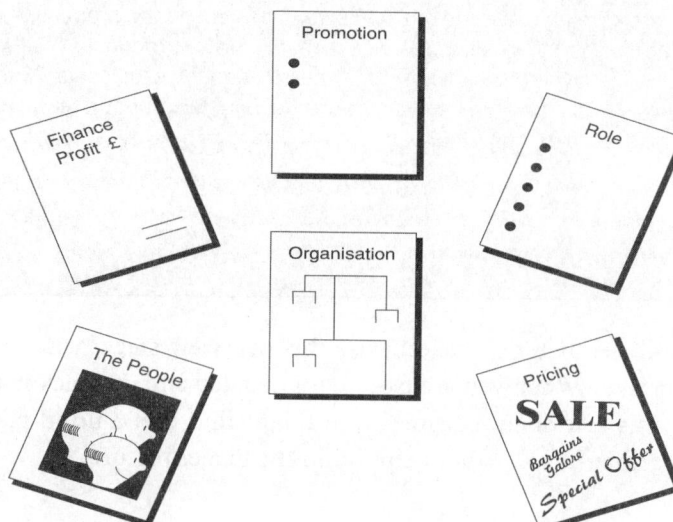

Examine every line and categorise all the significant information under a relevant heading.

(a) People
(b) Products
(c) Current performance, profitability etc
(d) Organisational structure
(e) Competitors
(f) Customers/audiences
(g) Potential environmental change, eg legislation or customer attitudes to GM products
(h) Brand and competitive position

The aim of the overview is to familiarise yourself thoroughly with Biocatalysts.

Take a further sheet of paper and use this to record information about the **consultancy role you have and make key notes about your client Stewart North**, his needs and interests and the expectation of the Board.

2.7 Note that with different cases you will need different headings. You will choose these based on what seem to be the key issues in the case. For example, if there was a lot of information on the brand or the sales force, you would pull that information together.

2.8 The idea is that at the end of this process you have, for example, all the financial information or macro environmental information together on one sheet.

Tutor Tip

- Do not be tempted at this stage to make decisions and/or jump to conclusions. Collect all the information and analyse it carefully before you start changing things.

- Try not to work in a mechanistic way as though this were an academic exercise; play your part. What questions do you think Stewart and the Board will want to ask? What extra information would you want if you were the consultant? **Remember to add these to your list of information needs – it may be invaluable later.**

- Take care with the appendices: currencies change - some are quoted in dollars, others in sterling, you may expect additional information in ECUs. We are apparently geared up to work in ECUs. Does that imply a strategy is needed for Europe?

- Do not just rely on what is written. Think about the business; try and picture it in your own mind.

- What do you know about the characteristics of marketing in an international business to business sector?

- Enzymes are raw material products, consumables used in the production process and they play a role in determining the quality of the customer's finished product. Their value is potentially high, and price is relatively insignificant as a percentage of total costs. Customers will tend to be relatively price insensitive (inelastic), but ensuring they understand the basis of comparison between different offerings is, it seems, a key issue.

- Channel management, promotion, particularly in relation to presenting GM products and pricing, all seem to be issues which could be on the Examiner's agenda: certainly the service element of the marketing mix is key to differentiating Biocatalysts's offering.

2.9 As you pull the materials together at this overview stage, you will find that the business becomes clearer. When you are faced with detailed and complex narrative in a case study, as we are in this case about enzymes, you might find that a mind map helps to bring various strands together in a way that helps build the bigger picture.

A Mind Map of Enzymes and their Market

Catalysts of the Living World

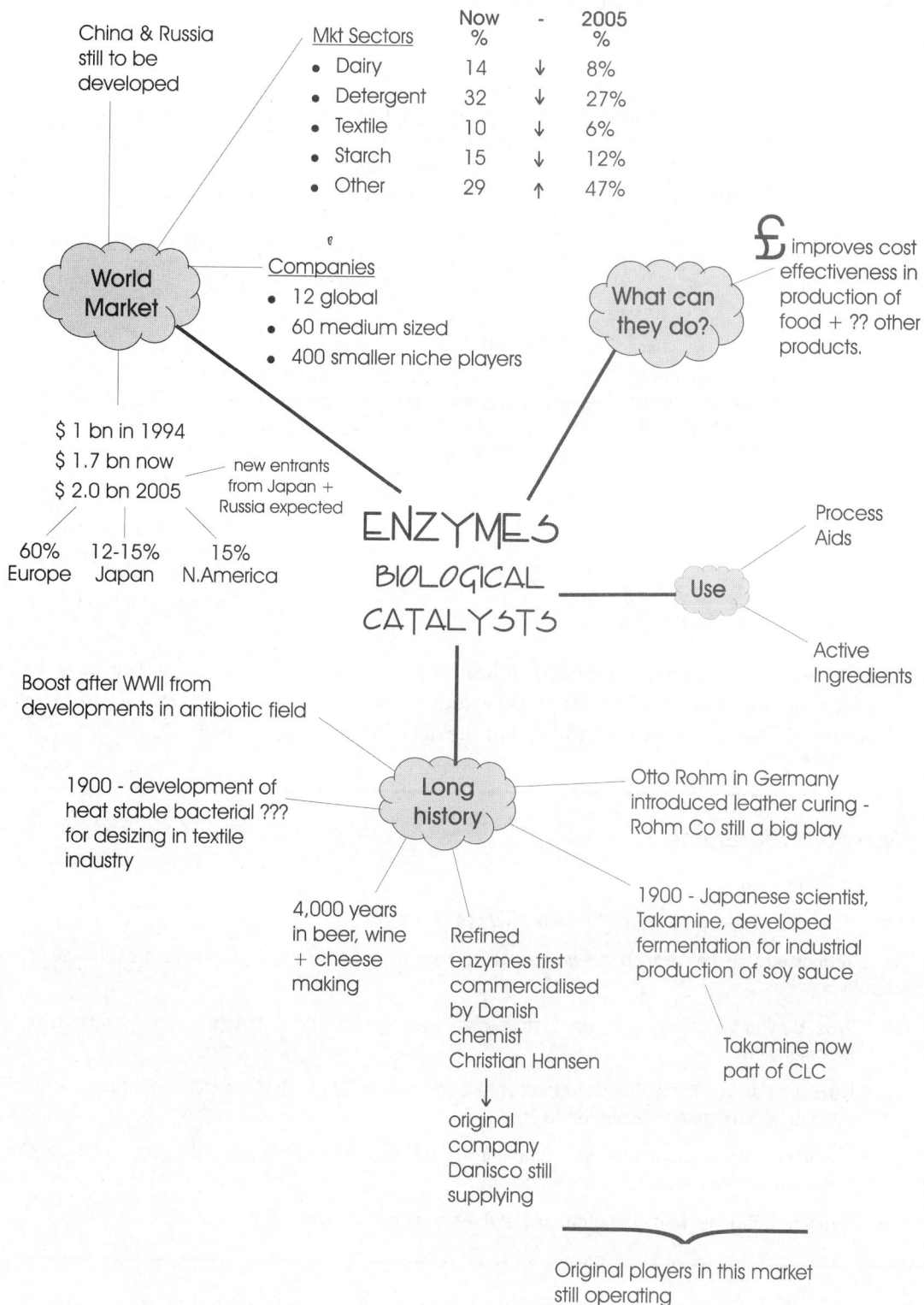

China & Russia still to be developed

Mkt Sectors	Now %	-	2005 %
• Dairy	14	↓	8%
• Detergent	32	↓	27%
• Textile	10	↓	6%
• Starch	15	↓	12%
• Other	29	↑	47%

World Market

Companies
• 12 global
• 60 medium sized
• 400 smaller niche players

What can they do?

£ improves cost effectiveness in production of food + ?? other products.

$ 1 bn in 1994
$ 1.7 bn now
$ 2.0 bn 2005

new entrants from Japan + Russia expected

60% Europe   12-15% Japan   15% N.America

ENZYMES
BIOLOGICAL
CATALYSTS

Process Aids

Use

Active Ingredients

Boost after WWII from developments in antibiotic field

1900 - development of heat stable bacterial ??? for desizing in textile industry

Long history

Otto Rohm in Germany introduced leather curing - Rohm Co still a big play

4,000 years in beer, wine + cheese making

Refined enzymes first commercialised by Danish chemist Christian Hansen
↓
original company Danisco still supplying

1900 - Japanese scientist, Takamine, developed fermentation for industrial production of soy sauce

Takamine now part of CLC

Original players in this market still operating

BPP PUBLISHING

3   ADDING CONTEXT TO TURN INFORMATION INTO INTELLIGENCE

3.1   Being a consultant or a case study student is a little like being a detective. You can't take the evidence at face value but need to read between the lines to really appreciate what is being said. Let's look at two extracts from the paragraph on page 14 under **targeting.**

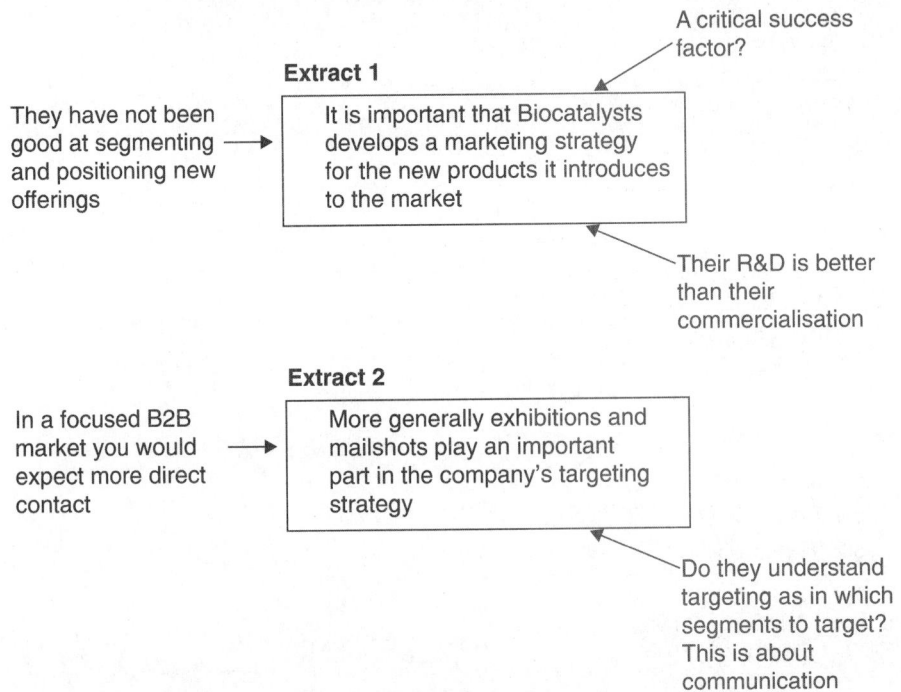

Extract 1

They have not been good at segmenting and positioning new offerings →

It is important that Biocatalysts develops a marketing strategy for the new products it introduces to the market

A critical success factor?

Their R&D is better than their commercialisation

Extract 2

In a focused B2B market you would expect more direct contact →

More generally exhibitions and mailshots play an important part in the company's targeting strategy

Do they understand targeting as in which segments to target? This is about communication

3.2   Data never becomes intelligence unless you consider it in terms of the case context, ensuring that contextual focus is very much the role of the overview. It provides firm contextual footings on which the rest of the detailed analysis can be built.

Activity Programme 2

Adding the context

Looking at this piece of data from the case study page 13:

The products are sold all around the world and 70% are exported. Biocatalysts has a presence in 35 countries.

(a)   What do you think about this, what impression does it create, what picture do you now have of Biocatalysts?

(b)   Now what do you think about it in the context of the case study. Biocatalysts had a turnover in 1998 of approximately £2.5m (page 30).

(c)   Would your assessment change if Biocatalysts was exporting low value/high weight products like bricks rather than enzymes and technology?

Compare your thoughts with our comments at the end of this chapter.

3.3   Remember that commercial credibility is key to your exam success and that credibility will be assessed by how relevant and appropriate your strategy is when judged in terms of the business context.

4 THE PITFALLS

Not too deep, not too shallow

4.1 One of the hardest things about case study is getting the analysis, both overview and inview, right. Analysis can be very reassuring, particularly when the alternative is to move on to the much more challenging and scary decision making!

4.2 You need to avoid analysis for its own sake. Ask yourself **why** am I analysing this – what kind of information will it generate and what will I do with it? Look for example at Appendix 9. You can use it to show a number of things:

- It provides some clues about the company's communication skills
- It shows how many new products they have as a proportion of the portfolio
- It identifies their key markets
- It provides clues about their potential differential advantages

Which of these pieces of information are important to you? In this case they probably all are, so you can analyse the information accordingly, but **be discerning.**

4.3 Typically, students fall into two camps:

(a) **Characterised by the superficial approach:** this person is likely to go into the exam with the headline picture of a **big** international player because they haven't identified from the analysis how **thinly Biocatalysts** are spread in terms of both products and markets. The additional information in the exam room is a real challenge to this candidate who often fails to see its relevance and is likely to jump to an obvious but wrong conclusion.

(b) **Characterised by 'too much analysis':** this candidate is likely to suffer from the dreaded Analysis Paralysis – never able to move on from the calculator and so goes into the exam room with little decision-making done before the exam. Their tendency is to repeat to the examiner or client what was told to them in the case, adding little of value. Before the exam, it is the case anomalies which really cause concerns for this candidate. The detail of numbers to three decimal places are scrutinised and considered, when all we really need is the big picture. In the exam room the killer for these over-prepared students is time – there is simply not enough of it to either:

- Work through their vast files of information and data , or
- Move on from the analysis to answering the questions set.

4.4 Which category are you most likely to fall into?

Superficial ☐

Bogged down in detail ☐

Take a few minutes to recognise your most likely pitfall and think about a strategy to overcome it.

(a) **For the superficial,** we advocate a timetable and clarity about the depth and breadth of analysis. Don't forget the value of cross referencing materials and if possible work with others to share ideas. Be sure to give time at least two weeks out of the four to your analysis.

(b) **For the potentially bogged down,** work to keep an holistic view; the bigger picture is critical in this strategic paper. Again a timetable helps – you **must** move on to decision making. Finally make yourself a promise **not** to get too concerned about anomalies. Make assumptions where necessary and move forward.

5 THE PRACTICE: COMPLETING THE OVERVIEW FOR BIOCATALYSTS

5.1   It is very difficult to undertake the case overview for you – it **must** be done by each individual if they are to have a meaningful view of the case – but below we have pulled some observations and comments together to help your overview analysis. You may like to have a go at this yourself before moving on.

5.2   **About the company**

(a)   **Biocatalysts** is well established in this industry, formed in 1986 and located in Wales. However, it has already had two transformations, starting life as a wholly owned subsidiary of Grand Metropolitan and, in 1991, becoming an independent company following a management buyout from Shell Ventures. (Page 2)

(b)   A leading developer and producer of specialist enzymes, the question seems to be **whether it has got the same ability to commercialise these innovative solutions**. We are told (page 2 paragraph 3) that the wide geographic sales and broad spread of sectors served gives a balanced portfolio with steady profitable, income streams. The question is do we believe this? With only £2.5 million turnover, this is a **small** company. You need to stay aware of this scale context as you work through the case, because the narrative reads as a much bigger global player operating in 35 countries and with pages of product offerings and a customising service for big and small companies.

(c)   It is certainly an interesting and topical sector; if you live in Europe, the ongoing controversy about genetically modified (GM) foods seems to roll on and on. There are some clear indications that, in your role as consultant to Biocatalysts, you may need to advise on how to handle the communication and PR challenges currently faced by biotechnology companies wanting to use GMOs in their production (Case Study page 24 paragraph 4). The organisation chart on page 28 shows a functionally organised business with no reflection of the international aspects of the business. R&D, design and production all seem to be involved in doing their own thing.

5.3   **Your role**

(a)   **Your role is clear.** You are an **independent consultant**, Joseph Mendes, apparently of some repute. (You must strive not to damage that hard earned reputation with your response to Biocatalysts' problems!)

(b)   You have been invited to develop a marketing report, to be presented to the Managing Director, Stewart North, prior to a piece of strategic work. Unfortunately, this brief (page 1) is not presented with as much clarity as we would like. It seems the Case Study itself represents this first stage in this process, the report, which has been sent in advance of the Board Meeting to Stewart North. It seems likely that in response to this you will get some additional information from Stewart and be asked your views on the strategic issues which will frame the next stages of presentation to the Board and preparation for the strategic exercise.

(c)   What you might be asked to report on is less clear than it has been in other CIM exams but you can assume the emphasis will be strategic not tactical. You **need to be able to discuss corporate positioning and competitive strategy as well as market segmentation,** short and longer term marketing plans, developing international markets, managing channels as well as the communication issues facing GM products.

5.4 Performance

(a) At first read of the case, Biocatalysts comes over as successful (20% growth, achieving double the industry average over the last 10 years: page 16) and seemingly very customer oriented. **However, for such a small business they seem very over-stretched.** Operating in 35 countries might mean they are trying to be all things to all people. They seem to be reactive to customers' needs, customising their offerings, but less successful at proactively developing a segment of the market as in the case of the olive farmers.

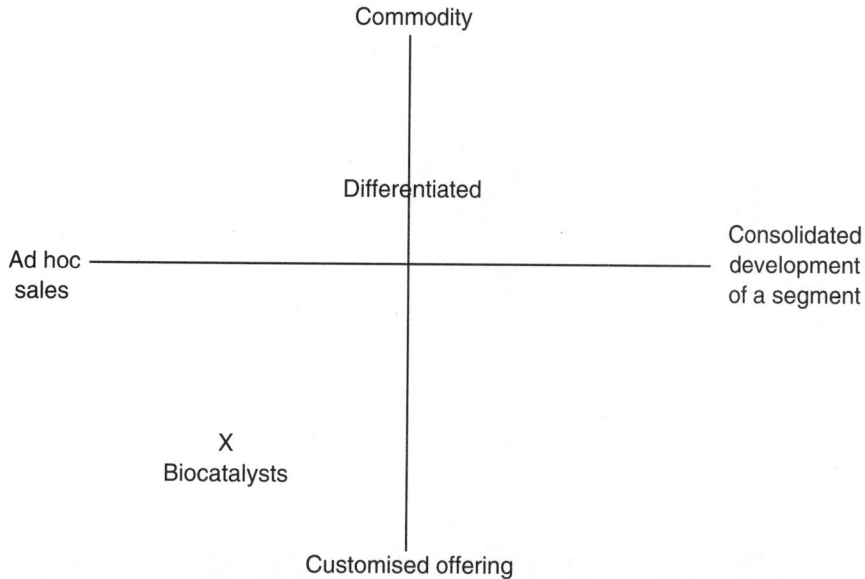

(b) It seems the company is mainly involved in a **niche of the market,** offering customised services, and it is said that this is a unique service, providing an important basis for sustainable competitive advantage. However, this is an **expensive process if additional demand is not generated.** In the last pages of the case you will see the listings of products offered by this company and there are a **large number of new products** in the list.

(c) The question of the product portfolio's balance is an obvious one to consider. Are there too many question marks/problem children and stars and not enough cash generated from the cows to fully exploit them? Certainly we know that 80% of sales come from 20% of customers (page 30), so an analysis of profitability by product and customer would I'm sure reveal some poor contributors. And the challenges of successfully commercialising innovations should be a framework for some of your planning.

5.5 Stakeholder concerns

The following schematic demonstrates how using models and diagrams can help you capture a lot of related data in a simple to review format.

Stakeholder concerns

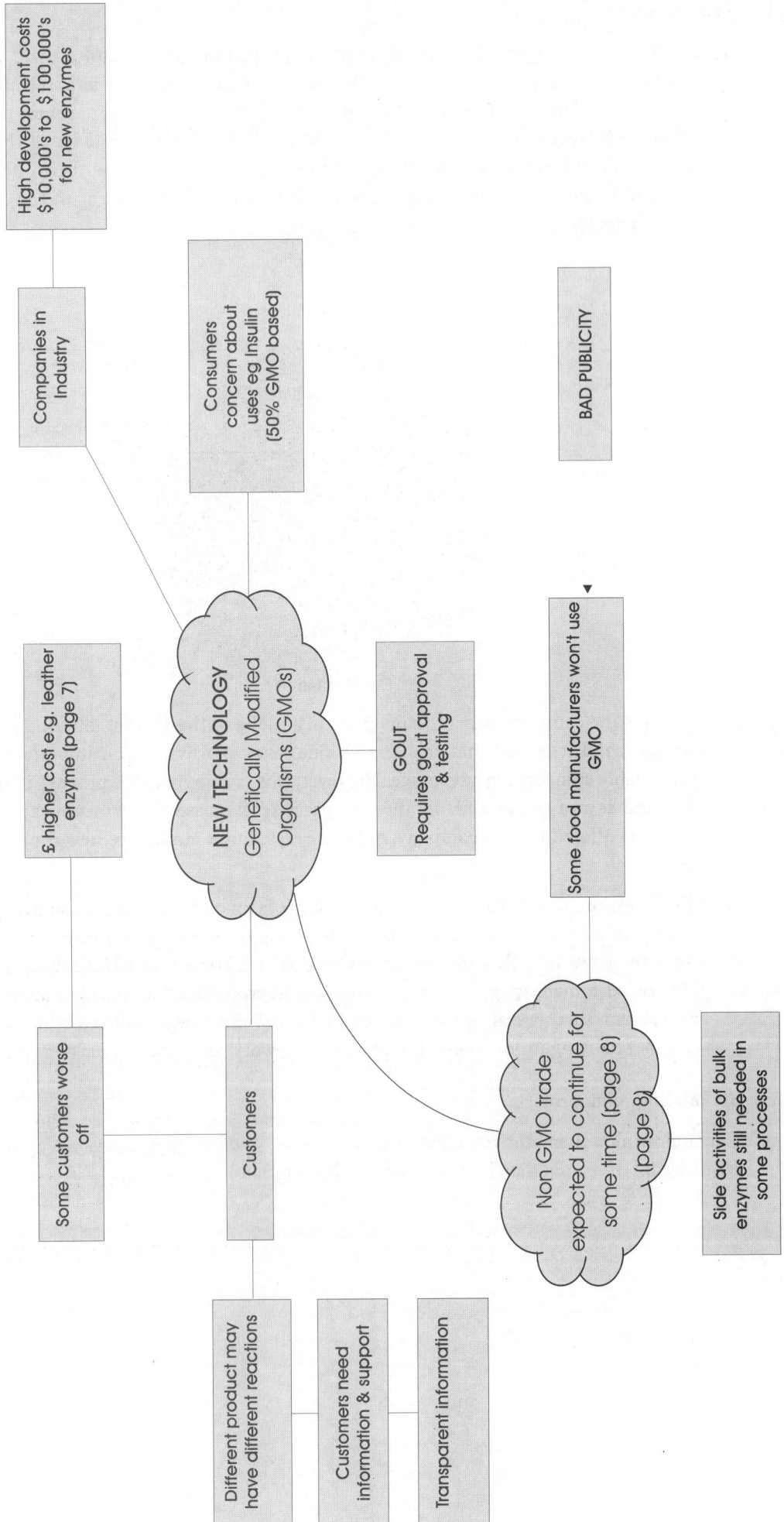

High development costs $10,000's to $100,000's for new enzymes

Companies in Industry

Consumers concern about uses eg Insulin (50% GMO based)

BAD PUBLICITY

£ higher cost e.g. leather enzyme (page 7)

NEW TECHNOLOGY Genetically Modified Organisms (GMOs)

GOUT Requires gout approval & testing

Some food manufacturers won't use GMO

Some customers worse off

Customers

Non GMO trade expected to continue for some time (page 8) (page 8)

Side activities of bulk enzymes still needed in some processes

Different product may have different reactions

Customers need information & support

Transparent information

5.6 Products and markets

The company launched 26 new products last year. 30% of sales are domestic and 70% are international.

The total product concept shows their perception of the product offering.

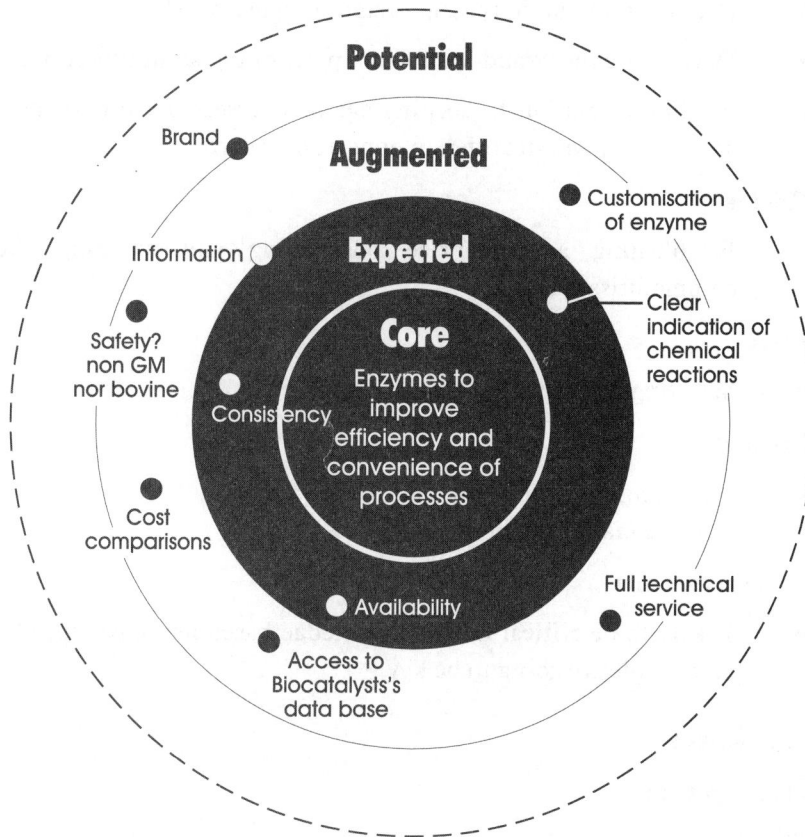

(a) The company is at the high value, low volume end of the market, offering catalysts which improve process performance across a range of sectors. They are a niche player, able to offer a customised solution to their clients and a full technical service, which should help them avoid price battles and commoditisation as the industry shakes down, with medium-sized players expanding or specialising.

(b) The niche sectors could get crowded, but it is a growing market. Potential is different in the various segments and you will need to sort this out. For example, the Diagnostics Market offers good margins and repeat business (as there are high switching costs) but Biocatalysts is one of three UK suppliers. Some segments like textiles are more price sensitive and protecting these customers from competitive action may be more challenging.

(c) This seems like a company well positioned for future success, with all the essential requirements:

- A unique service offering
- Excellent network of innovators and researchers
- A 'customer focused' culture
- Presence in markets across the world

5.7   **The Marketing Mix**

There are issues about all elements of the marketing mix which will need sorting out. Remember that, typically, the final case question is about one of the more tactical elements of the case.

(a)   **Promotion**

- Dealing with publicity issues relating to use of GMOs

- Developing the 'brand' values and positioning as an expert in the field

- Finding a solution to keeping agents overseas up to date, perhaps the internet and the new website offer an opportunity here

(b)   **Pricing**

- Establishing a value/price positioning and avoiding the slide towards commoditisation

(c)   **Place**

- Selecting and organising overseas sales

(d)   **Product**

- Managing the innovation and NPD process
- Commercialisation of new products

(e)   **The service mix**

- Likely to be critical in this knowledge based and customised market: processes and people are going to be key

5.8   **The Challenges**

The challenges are:

(a)   Turning stars into cash cows

(b)   Establishing a clear focus for activities, not trying to be all things to all people

(c)   A strategic plan: prioritising products and markets, and segmenting those markets is needed

(d)   International distribution needs reviewing and options evaluating

(e)   A clearer positioning is essential: whilst Biocatalysts have the opportunity to carve out a clear niche with customised services, their promotion comes across as an 'off the shelf' product catalogue.

Commodity enzymes

High price ——————————————————————————— Low price

X
Biocatalysts perceives
themselves to be here

Tailored enzyme
solutions

All sectors

X
Biocatalysts
seem to be here

Off the shelf
product

Added value
technical
consultancy

?
Should they be
here?

Selected sectors

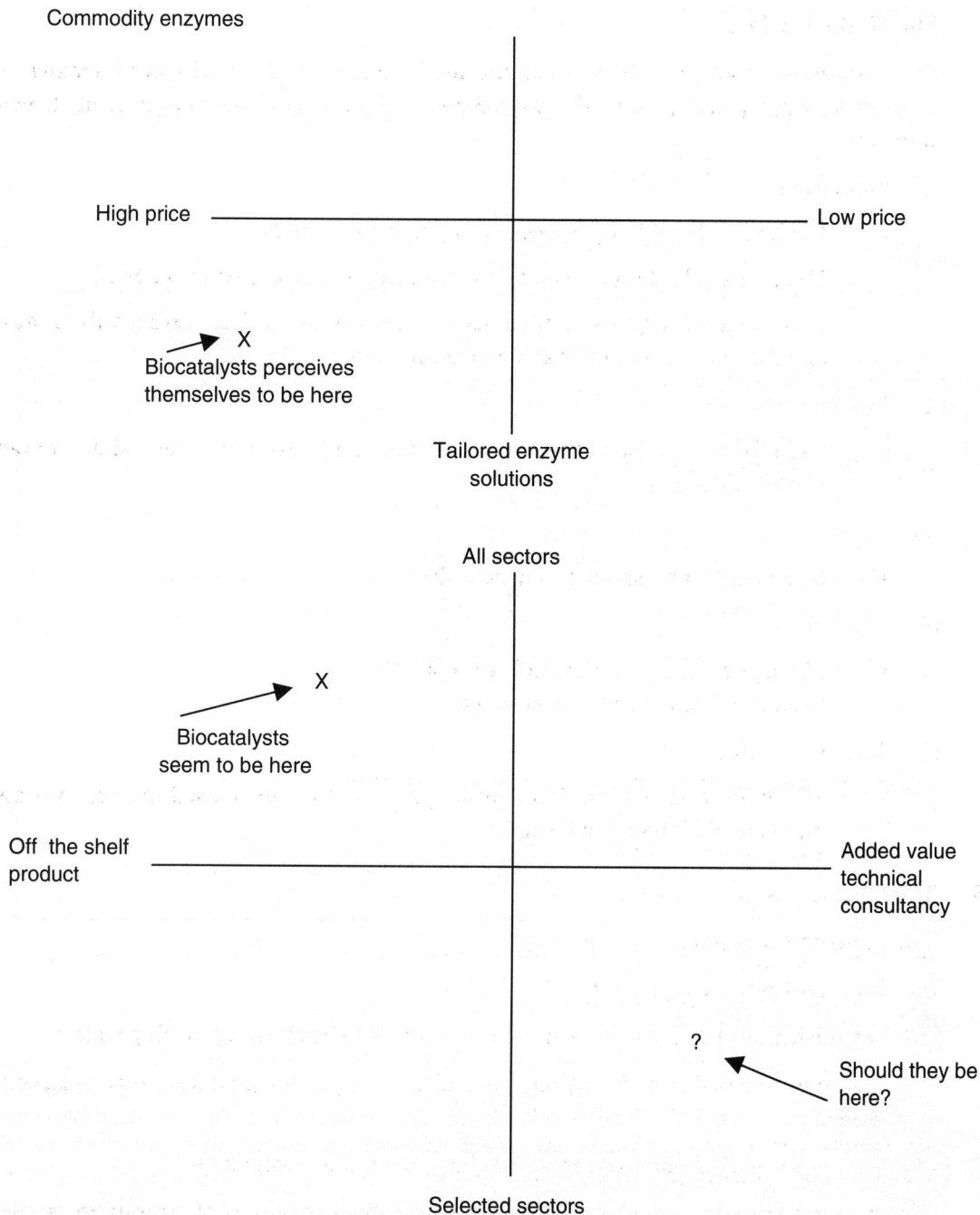

Where are you now?

5.9   By now you should have a much clearer picture of:

- Biocatalysts – the company and their business in terms of products and markets

- Current performance – financial, operational etc

- The company's competitive position and competitive advantage, actual and potential – focusing on the marketing mix

- The current organisation and the environment it is in

- The enzymes market, developments and challenges

- The market place for these products – now and in the future

- New product development at Biocatalysts

- Who the customers are and what matters to them

- The international markets

You should now feel much more ready to tackle the more detailed inview analysis but before you do, test your current understanding of the case.

Action Programme 3

SO YOU THINK YOU KNOW THE CASE..?

QUESTIONS

1   Who are you? What is your role?

2   How would you describe Biocatalysts Ltd?

3   What is the extent and current state of Biocatalysts's international business?

4   How is the product development work managed and paid for at Biocatalysts?

5   What is the value forecast for the structure of the world enzyme industry?

6   What sector of the market is Biocatalysts active in and what is happening to it?

7   What makes Biocatalysts unique?

8   What are the limitations to growth for Biocatalysts?

9   What is the customer's view of price in this market?

10   What is the PR dimension of communication which the company needs to face?

Action programme review

1   (a)   This is a business to business market (page 2); this means communication strategies are likely to be sales led and key account management and relationship marketing could be key aspects of Biocatalysts's approach to the market. As you might expect from a B2B firm Biocatalysts has a smaller number of higher value clients and corporate reputation rather than emotional brand values will be important.

(b)   Biocatalysts develops and produces speciality enzymes for industry. It is a challenging global business because it is growing and developing rapidly, but the advent of new genetic engineering techniques and new applications have created their own marketing problems (page 16).

(c)   You are Joseph Mendes, a marketing consultant who (like you) has no experience of this sector. This report is the output of Joseph's initial analysis into the firm and the market – you can expect to be asked to use this to help recommend future strategies.

(d)   Agents are largely involved in export markets.

2   *Adding the context*

(a)   It creates the picture of a large successful global player with a number of international markets. Its ethnocentric strategy could be explained by the high knowledge content of its services and the need to customise its services.

(b)   Instead of its global expansion being a strength, suddenly it seems more of a weakness. Here we have a business that has stretched itself too thin when it comes to its geographic markets at least. Only an average of 2% of its income, some £50,000, is generated from each country. Clearly there has been little market penetration strategy operating. You start to get a picture of a reactive and opportunist company more like the one we described in a) and the challenge would be to improve penetration and performance in their chosen markets.

(c)   An exporting strategy would probably be better replaced with local production, close to eventual markets, thus lowering distribution costs and either improving profitability or local price performance.

SO YOU THINK YOU KNOW THE CASE..?

ANSWERS

1   You are Joseph Mendes, you are a marketing consultant working with Biocatalysts Ltd.

2   A small Welsh-based independent company producing speciality enzymes for a range of industrial clients. They are in the low volume/high value end of the market.

3   70% of sales are exported currently to over 35 countries. Business is managed by agents, who are difficult to control and mainly motivated by finances. The agents earn a 5% commission.

4   Most of the basic research is handled by UK universities where they have many contacts. In-house scientists can focus on customer needs. Funding for higher margin products in diagnostics and pharmaceuticals comes from profits and from European and UK grants.

5   A rapidly growing market:

   1994 $1 billion
   1997 $1.3 billion
   1998 $1.7 billion
   2005 $2.0 billion

   A polarising market: 12 big global payers with clear positioning/distinct ranges; 60 medium-sized companies and 400 smaller players being forced out because of economies of scale. New competitors from Russia and China forecast.

6   The 'other sector' – likely to be worth over $500m by 2005 (representing 70% of the total market growth).

7   It provides custom-tailored products for its clients.

8   Current capacity would allow output to double. Further growth requires investment funds.

9   We are told price is always an issue, yet enzymes represent a small part of costs (so should be price inelastic) and liability and service is more important. Price comparisons are difficult and Biocatalysts offers a unique customisation service.

10   Genetically modified organisms are increasing by being used for enzyme products (page 24) and Biocatalysts has several under development. A clear communication plan and policy on communications is needed.

5

Step 2: The Interview – Internal analysis

Chapter Topic List

1	Introduction to planning route maps
2	Skills and knowledge reminder
3	Biocatalysts: product analysis
4	Biocatalysts: situation analysis
5	The pitfalls

Introduction

Case step 2: the overview

In this chapter we will:

- Review the knowledge and skills you will use in the internal analysis
- Identify the strengths and weaknesses of the Biocatalyst marketing audit
- Identify the strengths and weaknesses of the Biocatalyst business
- Consider the pitfalls at this stage of the process

1   INTRODUCTION TO PLANNING ROUTE MAPS

1.1   Throughout the file we will be guiding you through the process of analysis and decision with the use of the planning route maps. These maps enable you to quickly assess where you are now in the process and what the next stage is.

Purpose

1.2   At these second and third case steps we will be working on further but deeper case analysis. We need to really get to grips with the information available to us. Because our overview provided us with a real sense of the case context, we will be much better able to make sense of and appreciate the implications of our evaluations and assessments.

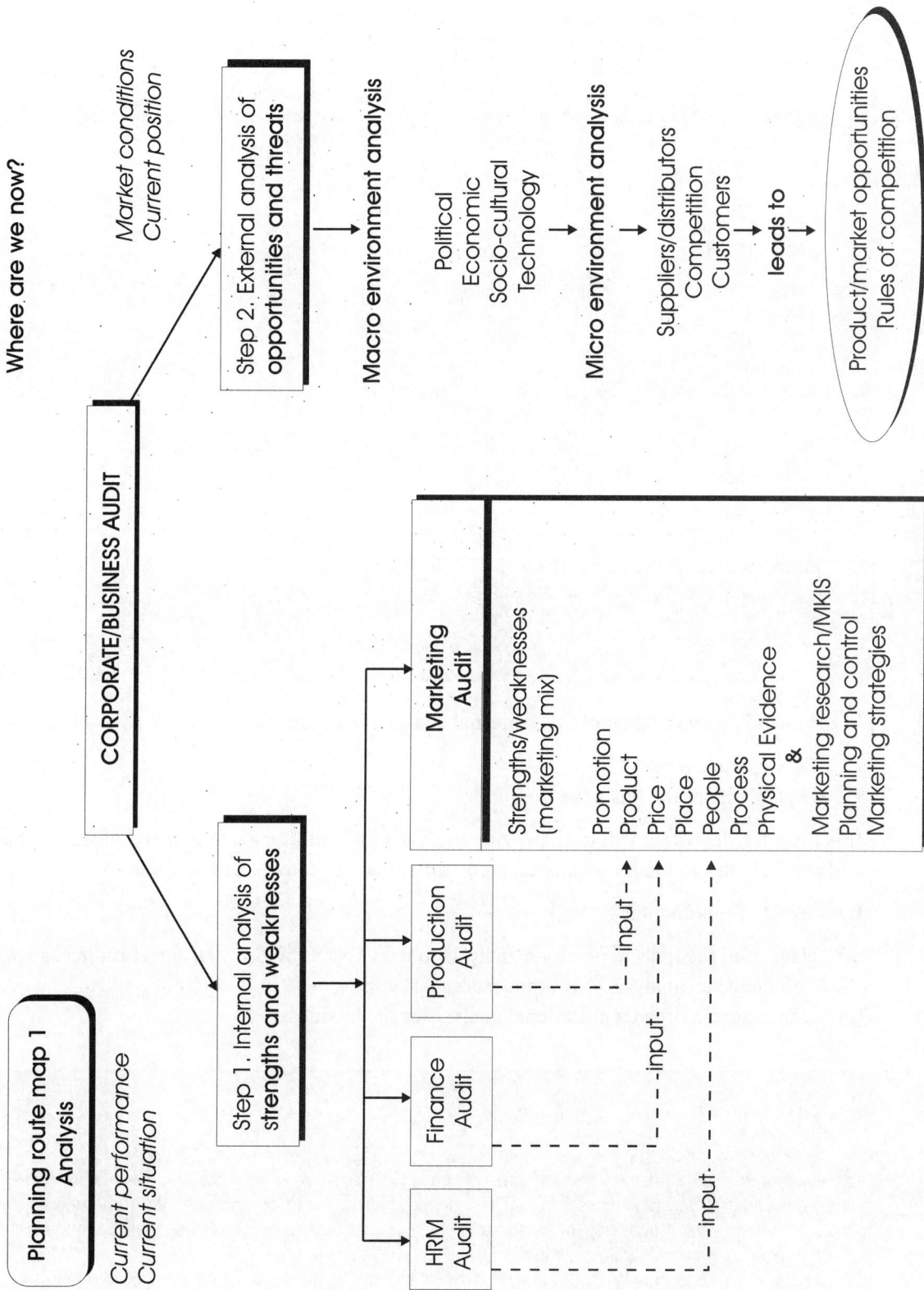

Where are we now?

Market conditions
Current position

Planning route map 1
Analysis

Current performance
Current situation

CORPORATE/BUSINESS AUDIT

Step 2. External analysis of **opportunities and threats**

Macro environment analysis

Political
Economic
Socio-cultural
Technology

Micro environment analysis

Suppliers/distributors
Competition
Customers

leads to

Product/market opportunities
Rules of competition

Step 1. Internal analysis of **strengths and weaknesses**

HRM Audit

Finance Audit

Production Audit

Marketing Audit

Strengths/weaknesses (marketing mix)

Promotion
Product
Price
Place
People
Process
Physical Evidence
&

Marketing research/MKIS
Planning and control
Marketing strategies

-- input --

-- input --

-- input --

© Juanita Cockton, 1997

Tutor Tip

As we said in Chapter 3, in practice, analysis steps are likely to be undertaken **simultaneously**. Amongst academics there is some debate as to whether it is most appropriate to undertake an internal analysis before or after the external one. Our overview alleviates that issue to some extent but in reality this audit stage can be sequenced however you like, as long as the internal position is then considered in the **context** of the external and *vice versa*. For example, at the end of our internal analysis, we would expect to be able to summarise our findings in a weighted and rated table of strengths and weaknesses. To do this, the external perspective must be taken into account because the assessment of strengths and weaknesses must be made against competitor's performance ie bench marked.

	Strengths	0	Weaknesses	
	+10			-10
HIGH				
MEDIUM				
LOW				

IMPACT ON BUSINESS PERFORMANCE

Point 0 indicates equal to the competitor(s). In this way we can review internal assessments in an external context. We will only be able to interpret our analysis in this way after both internal and external audits are complete, so we will do this in Chapter 7 as a stepping stone to establishing the critical success factors.

1.3 In case step 2, we will be taking the internal analysis first and our purpose is to assess the:

- Core competences
- Capabilities of the business

It is these factors which will both provide the basis for building a competitive advantage but will also help us establish that any recommendations are realistic and credible.

By the end of this chapter we will:

(a) Have used the tools of portfolio analysis to help assess the Biocatalysts's product range
(b) Completed an analysis of Biocatalysts's marketing
(c) Undertaken a broader situational analysis of the business

Tutor Tip

As we have already said, the case study is a very challenging paper for marketing students. Its completion requires you can demonstrate **not** just an understanding of your own discipline, but that you have a broader understanding of all business functions. In order to complete an internal analysis, you must therefore review financial, operational and HR issues facing the business and understand them and their strategic implications. As in the real world, you do not necessarily need to do this alone. You can work with others to break this analysis task down but, as we have indicated, you will need to think about managing that team and sharing the information you produce.

2 SKILLS AND KNOWLEDGE REMINDER

2.1 It is at the analysis stage where the tools of planning and control really come into their own. Different cases will lend themselves to different tools and you need to learn to be selective and not to worry if you have incomplete information:

(a) Use what you have

(b) Make assumptions if you need to, to fill gaps

(c) Remember to note the gaps on your information shopping list

2.2 Typically the tools and techniques you might need to use at this stage of a case study will include the following. (Again you will need to take time out to refresh your memory on how each of them is used if you have any doubts or knowledge gaps.)

- Ratio Analysis
- Benchmarking
- Product Life Cycle
- Boston Matrix
- GE Matrix
- Strength and Weaknesses Analysis

What needs to be done

2.3 What needs to be done and how much work is involved at this stage very much depends on the case study. You may have a lot or a little information on the products, marketing or resources of the business. You may have already done quite a bit of work at the overview stage which now needs incorporating or building upon. In this case study though, you can see the distinction between the **overview** and **inview** quite clearly.

(a) At **overview,** we looked at the generic enzyme products and tried to understand what they were and did

(b) We also had an **overview** of the Biocatalysts range – recognising its size, the proportion of new products and its sector focus

(c) At **inview** we need to get even more depth, looking for example at product profitability, if we have enough data

> **Tutor Tip**
>
> You may have already begun to appreciate how much paper can be generated when working on a case study and why file management is such a key skill for the successful student. To help keep your stress levels down by minimising lost pages and work, you should really take positive steps to organise your analysis now.
>
> Steps 2 and 3 are the most paper-intensive, particularly if you are working with a syndicate. You can start by organising your overview into internal and external factors and then working under specific headings like Product, Finance etc within these sections of your decision file.

2.4 By the end of this step we will be able to assess:

(a) Strengths and weaknesses of Biocatalysts's marketing activities

(b) Strengths and weaknesses of Biocatalysts's business situation

2.5 Remember internal analysis assesses the current situation, warts and all!. If staff morale is low, that is what needs to be identified. The fact a new incentive scheme is planned for next year or next month is not relevant. Our task is to evaluate the situation as it is **today**.

2.6 **The distinction between internal and external analysis is decided by controllability.** Low morale, profitability or brand perceptions are all internal controllable factors. Changing them may be difficult, take time and require investment but they can all be tackled. Factors like a declining birth rate, economic recession or introduction of a new technology are external and outside the control of the business.

3 BIOCATALYSTS: PRODUCT ANALYSIS

3.1 We will begin by looking in detail at the Biocatalysts's product portfolio.

Auditing the performance of products

This is undertaken by conducting product portfolio analysis. The intention is to determine which products are performing well and which are not in terms of their profitability, market share performance etc. A number of models can be used.

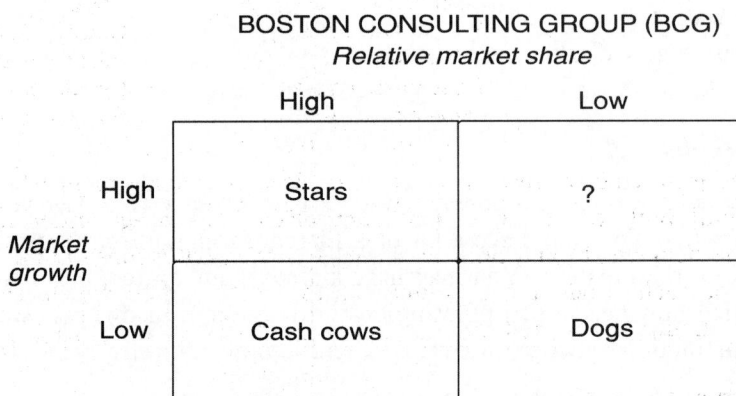

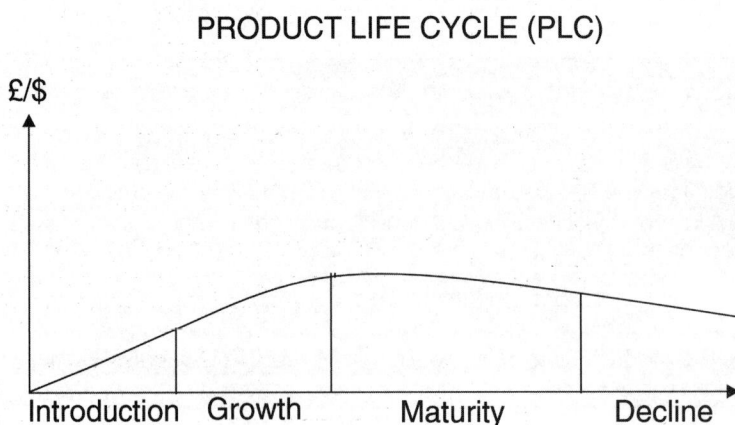

BOSTON CONSULTING GROUP (BCG)
Relative market share

	High	Low
High	Stars	?
Low	Cash cows	Dogs

Market growth

PRODUCT LIFE CYCLE (PLC)

£/$

Introduction Growth Maturity Decline

GENERAL ELECTRIC/MCKINSEY (GE MATRIX)

Product attractiveness

	High	Medium	Low
Strong			
Medium			
Low			

Competitive advantage

Criteria

Product attractiveness	*Competitive advantage*
eg	eg
Profitability of ...%	Value for money
Gain market share of %	Reliability
Fit with existing range	Quality (relative
Attract new customers	After sales service
Investment required	Reputation
Repeat purchase	Speed of delivery

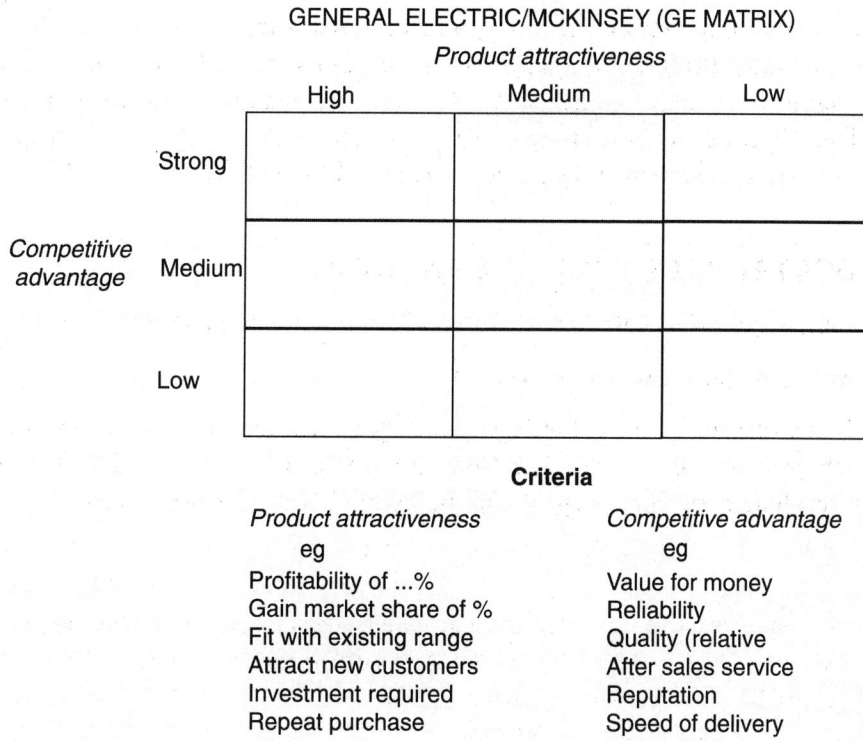

The **product attractiveness** criterion is decided by management who then prioritise and weight and rank the criteria. The **competitive advantage** criterion is determined by customers who weight and rank according to their perceptions of importance to them. The results for each product are plotted on the matrix. The results can determine which products should be invested in.

3.2 **The market context**

(a) We are working in a relatively new technology-driven and global market. We can use a Boston Matrix to help us assess the various Biocatalysts's products/markets within the whole sector.

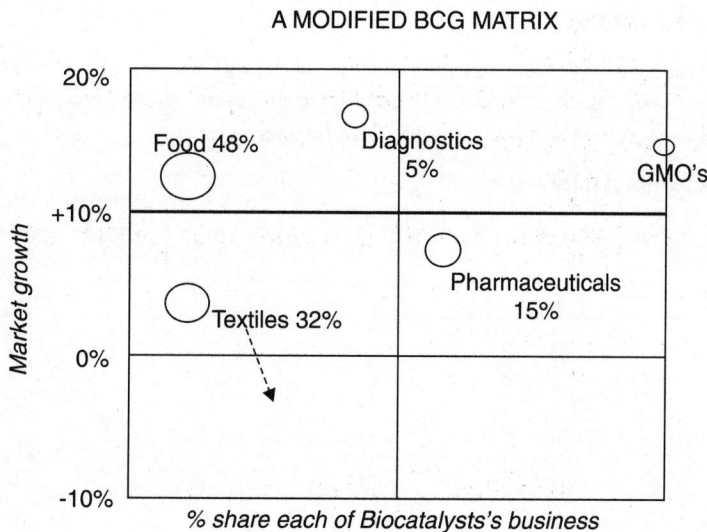

A MODIFIED BCG MATRIX

(b) You can see why these tools are so valuable, when you look at this grid and think about what it tells you.

Action Programme 1

Take five minutes to review this indicative BCG Matrix of Biocatalysts's portfolio and identify what this information is telling you.

-
-
-
-

Turn to the end of this chapter to compare your interpretation with ours. You may be wondering where we got the information to apply to our modified Boston Matrix.

Tutor Tip

It is quite acceptable to modify the various tools and models but do make it clear with your labelling. In this case we have used the extended grid which adds warhorses and dodoes to indicate products where the total market is in decline rather than growth. Because Biocatalysts is such a small player, we have used the relative share of their own market rather than relative market share.

Biocatalysts are too small to be market leader so all their products would turn up in right hand cells if assessed against market competitors.

    (c)   To build this matrix we needed information about:

- Biocatalysts's products
- The product/market sectors

Take a few minutes to look at where we found this and check it against the case study. You can see from this illustration how you need to cross relate data to turn it effectively into information, and then the intelligence we gleaned earlier.

Action Programme 2

You will remember we indicated that internal analysis could only be considered when viewed in an external context. The market information is just that in this example. We will also show how competitor information helps to give us some insight into Biocatalysts's position.

Biocatalysts's Product Information

Information on pages 34-36 in Appendix 9 is most helpful when you try to sort out the Biocatalysts's portfolio.

Biocatalysts product range

1	Baking Brewing Fruit and veg Flavour Proteins Dietetics	**Food industry** **48%**
2	Textiles (garment washing)	**Textile Industry** **32%**
3	Own specialist enzymes No npd	**Pharmaceutical industry** **15%**
4	Phen Dehyd Glactose Peroxidase etc	**Diagnostics industry** **5%**

Market information

3.3 **Food Industry** (from page 34)

(a) 12.5% of all new Biocatalyst's products/investments are in the food sector.

(b) In total, they have 71 old and 14 new products in this area.

(c) 48% of revenue means it represents the largest percentage of sales and Biocatalyst appear to get high margins in this sector.

(d) Their competitive advantage lies in:

- Niche production of specialist enzymes
- Kosher
- Tailored offering
- Safety

(e) This is where GMOs are currently causing concerns and in the UK and Europe the backlash of BSE etc is having a considerable impact.

(f) On average, each product in this part of Biocatalyst's portfolio represents 0.5% of total revenue.

(g) In the UK the closest competitor is Amano (Appendix 1).

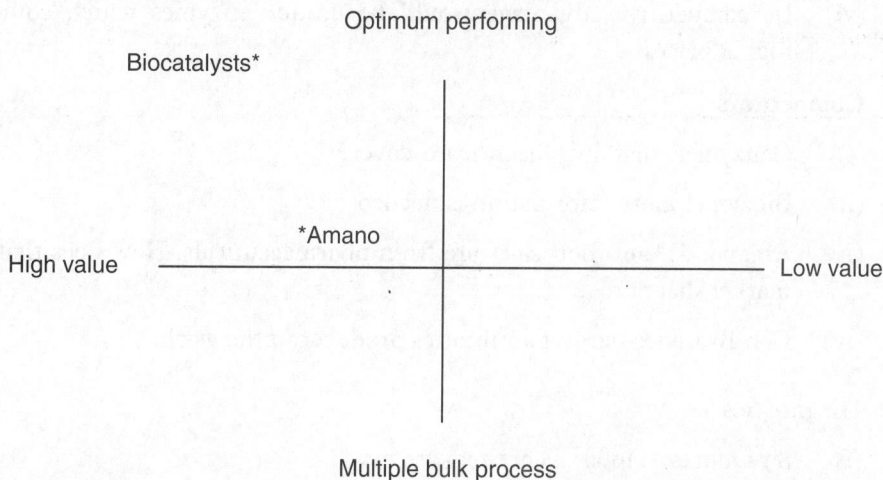

101

3.4 (a) **The Textile industry**

(i) 21 products in total and 9 are new ie 43%. It is clear that Biocatalyst's are investing heavily in this sector, with cost implications.

(ii) Yet this is a declining market.

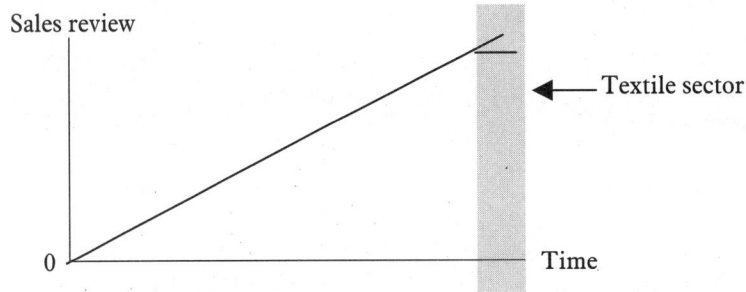

(iii) Gaining a share in a declining market is not an obviously strong strategy. The market, once mature, will commoditise and differentiation will be increasingly difficult and expensive. Biocatalyst will need to decide whether the level of investment needed to stay in this market is worthwhile.

(iv) Textiles represent almost one third (31%) of Biocatalyst's business

(b) **Competitors**

(i) Genzyme and Biozyme do not appear to offer many (if any) textile products.

(ii) What about Rhone-Poulenc: does it have textile products? More information is needed here.

(iii) There appears to be no major competitor in this sector, perhaps this is why Biocatalysts has commanded such a high share of sales from this market.

3.5 (a) **Pharmaceuticals**

(i) No new products out of a total of 7 offered – so no new investment. Why?

(ii) These represent 15% of total sales.

(iii) We have no real information on positioning or share in this sector.

(iv) Pharmaceuticals are not featured in the world market (page 4). Why not?

(v) Biocatalysts could be a niche player in a small market with high potential profitability.

(vi) Its competitive advantage would be unique enzymes which could command higher prices.

(b) **Competitors**

(i) Genzyme: what does 'healthcare' cover?

(ii) Biozyme: more information is needed

(iii) Amano: 51% of their sales are from pharmaceuticals. How does that translate to market share?

(iv) Gist Brocades: largest antibiotics producer in the world

3.6 (a) **Diagnostics**

(i) 8 products in total – 3 of them are new

(ii) They represent just 5% of revenue

(iii) Biocatalyst is a monopolist in PD enzyme (page 10)

(iv) In this sector customers become a captive audience with high switching costs that essentially tie them into a deal.

(v) This is another niche market which again does not feature in world figures.

(vi) There are new US customers which might lead to growth but also stimulate new competitors.

(vii) There are high margins to be made here and it is a profitable product range.

(viii) Biocatalyst is investing here and operates in several diagnostic areas and so can offer some depth of product range and experience.

(b) **Competitors**

   (i) Amano: 10% of their sales in Diagnostics which amounts to $9.2m a very large player in a small market

   (ii) Biozyme: more information needed

   (iii) Genzyme: more information needed

3.7 GMOs

Biocatalysts has two genetically modified organisms in development which they are due to launch next year.

Tutor Tip

As you pull your analysis together you will see how the picture builds and those information gaps close up.

3.8 Consolidating information

There are no short cuts to working through case information but you will find it easier if you find ways to summarise and consolidate it.

Product group	Sub Group	Number of products	Number of new products
Food	Baking	18	3
	Brewing	5	5
	Fruit & Veg Processing	11	3
	Flavour	14	0
	Protein	13	1
	Dietetics	9	2
Non Food	Textiles	21	9
	Diagnostics	8	3
	Pharmaceuticals	7	1
	Environmentals	4	0
		110	27

(a) A simple table shows the company's spread of activity – 110 products (plus 2 GMOs in development) offered to 10 sectors across food and non food based clients.

(b) Of the 110 products, 27 are new. Five of these are within brewing, a market the company has had no previous experience of. You do need to ask the question **why?**

(c) Has this come about because a researcher wants to work in this sector? If so, we would be worried about the product orientation this demonstrates.

or

Is this development in response to customer requests which shows the company as reactive? In this case we would want to look at the **screening process** for such requests. Does the company simply respond to the scientific challenge rather than assess the commercial feasibility of the new products being developed?

> **Tutor Tip**
>
> The analysis alone is not enough, you must think about what it is telling you. What are the implications?

(d)   Again mind maps and charts can help you to summarise and consolidate information.

Biocatalysts's product portfolio

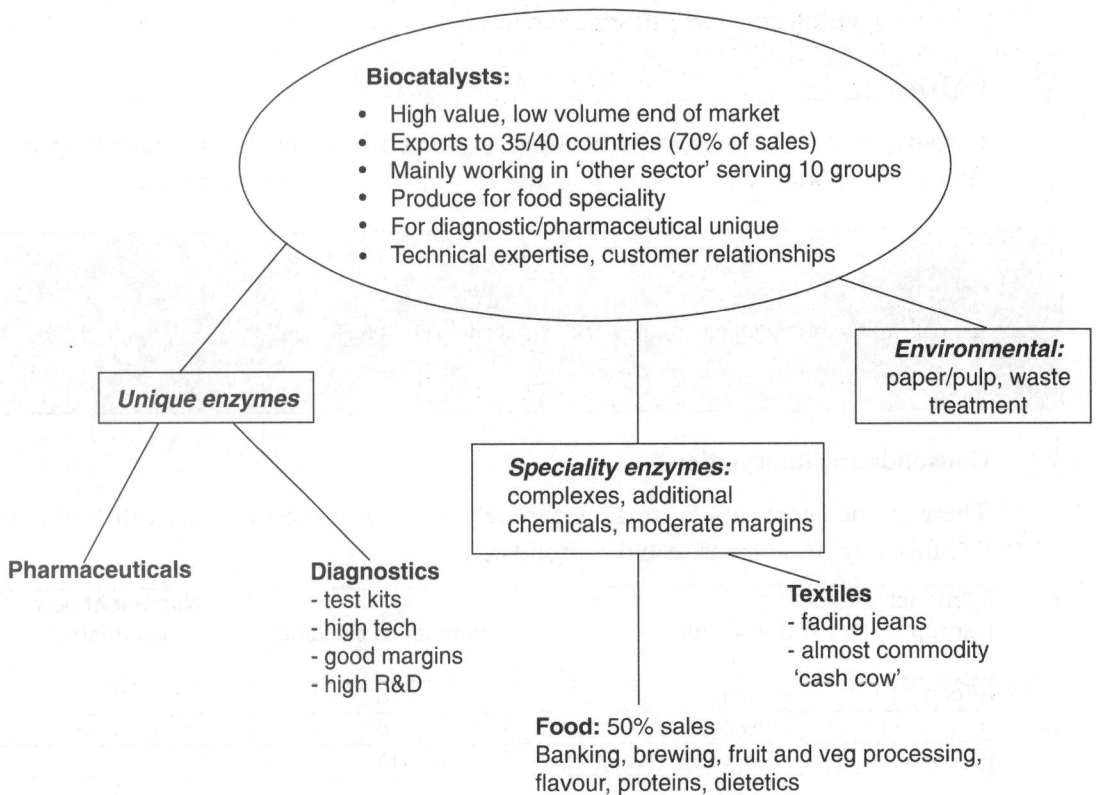

Biocatalysts:
- High value, low volume end of market
- Exports to 35/40 countries (70% of sales)
- Mainly working in 'other sector' serving 10 groups
- Produce for food speciality
- For diagnostic/pharmaceutical unique
- Technical expertise, customer relationships

Environmental: paper/pulp, waste treatment

Unique enzymes

Speciality enzymes: complexes, additional chemicals, moderate margins

Pharmaceuticals

Diagnostics
- test kits
- high tech
- good margins
- high R&D

Textiles
- fading jeans
- almost commodity 'cash cow'

Food: 50% sales
Banking, brewing, fruit and veg processing, flavour, proteins, dietetics

3.9   We often find positioning maps useful for clarifying information as well as communicating options and you can see in the one provided here how, in terms of its product, Biocatalyst appears to be uncertain about 'what business they are in' and how to position themselves.

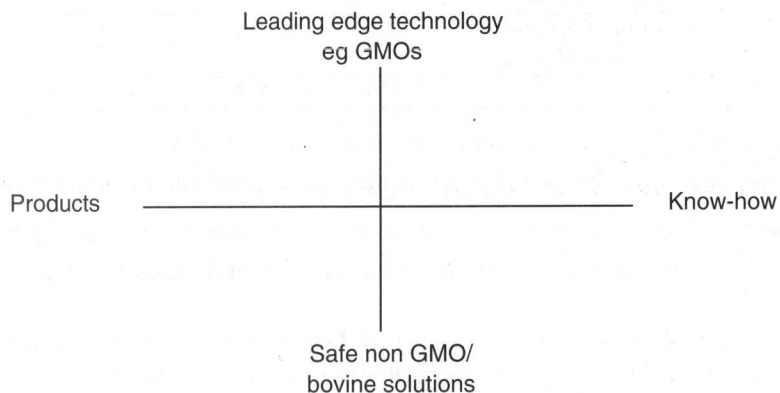

Leading edge technology
eg GMOs

Products ———————————————— Know-how

Safe non GMO/
bovine solutions

3.10 Any position could be tenable but for a very small business, such a big portfolio has them stuck in the middle of the road.

Action Programme 2

Auditing the rest of the marketing mix

Having looked in some detail at the 'product', take no more than 30 minutes to review your case materials and complete a summary strengths and weaknesses analysis for the remaining 6 'P's of the mix.

Tutor Tip

Remember: case studies are never complete, so do not be surprised to find gaps or limited information under certain headings.

Strengths	Weaknesses
Place	
Price	
Promotion	
People	
Physical evidence	
Processes	

Turn to the end of this chapter to compare your analysis with ours.

BPP PUBLISHING

4   BIOCATALYSTS: SITUATION ANALYSIS

4.1   To tackle a case study effectively, you need to address yourself to the whole business **not** simply the marketing activities. This requires that our internal audit is broadened to include:

(a)   Financial perspective

(b)   Operational overview

(c)   People overview

(d)   Pan-company issues, including culture, management skills, management information planning processes and new product development

4.2   When added to the marketing analysis, you then have a complete situational analysis which will enable us to:

(a)   Assess available resources

(b)   Consider issues of capacity

(c)   Identify any limiting factors

(d)   Establish corporate capabilities which could be used as a basis for establishing a competitive advantage

Tutor Tip

If you are working with a syndicate, you may rely on others to complete parts of your audit analysis for you. That is quite acceptable but you must take the responsibility of owning and understanding the output of that process.

In the exam room you could, for example, be faced with additional financial information and you need to know where it has come from and how to use it.

Optional activity

4.3   Before moving forward in this chapter, you might like to practise your analysis skills by pulling together an analysis of these other business areas.

Financial perspective

4.4   Biocatalyst's chosen market is one which requires **high investment** but **delivers high returns** as a result. New products are currently funded from profits and grants from the government and Europe. (The impact of losing grants is a pressing issue.)

4.5   The industry as a whole is growing steadily with sales raising from $1bn in 1994 to $1.3bn in 1997. This is expected to top $2bn in 2005.

4.6   With 70% of sales revenue coming from exports, the company is used to handling different currencies (although it usually only handles $s, £s, and Euros).

Creditors increased in 1997 over 1996 (up 27% or £109k); however debtors have increased by 51% (266k) in the same period.

4.7   Cash flow does not appear to be a problem at the present time. This is assisted by the company policy against stockpiling of finished goods: only raw materials and work in progress is generally held as stock.

- Current ratio > 2:1
- Acid test > 1:1

4.8 The business is growing by 20-30% pa but profitability (page 30) is not improving. There is a danger Biocatalysts is working harder rather than smarter.

Analysing financial information

During your studies of strategic marketing management, you will have covered financial ratios. There has been criticism of marketers' lack of financial skills and the Senior Examiner of Analysis and Decision has made it clear that this area will be tested. We have seen an increase in the financial data and need to be able to work the numbers and interpret financial information. There are many financial ratios but here is a reminder of the key ratios you are most likely to use.

Liquidity and working capital ratios

- Current ratio $$\frac{\text{Current assets}}{\text{Current liabilities}}$$

- Quick ratio (acid test ratio) $$\frac{\text{Current assets}}{\text{Current liabilities}}$$

Efficiency and turnover ratios

- Asset turnover ratio $$\frac{\text{Sales}}{\text{Average total sales}}$$

- Debtor days (average debt collection period) $$\frac{\text{Sales}}{\text{Debtors}}$$

- Average stock turnover period (days) $$\frac{\text{Sales}}{\text{Stock}}$$

Profitability ratios

- Return on capital employed (ROCE) $$\frac{\text{Earnings before interest and tax}}{\text{Capital employed}}$$

- Return on investment (ROI) $$\frac{\text{Net operating income}}{\text{Operating assets}}$$

- Return on sales (ROS) (net profit as a percentage of sales – net margin) $$\frac{\text{Earnings before interest and tax}}{\text{Sales revenue}}$$

- Gross profit as a percentage of sales (gross margin) $$\frac{\text{Gross profit}}{\text{Sales}}$$

- Return on net assets (RONA) $$\frac{\text{PBIT}}{\text{Sales revenue}} \times \frac{\text{Sales revenue}}{\text{Net assets}}$$

Debt and gearing ratios

- Debt ratio $$\frac{\text{Total debt}}{\text{Total assets}} \quad or \quad \frac{\text{Long term debt}}{\text{Shareholder equity}}$$

- Gearing ratio $$\frac{\text{Total debt}}{\text{Total assets}}$$

- Cash flow ratio $$\frac{\text{Earnings before interest and tax} + \text{depreciation}}{\text{Interest} + [\text{payment}/(1 - \text{tax rate})]}$$

Tutor Tip

Knowledge check: how many of these ratios are familiar to you? Skills check: can you use these ratios? You will need to be able to for the case study.

4.9 There are nearly always discrepancies in the numbers, for example, Biocatalysts's claim to have achieved growth of 20% to 30%. Is it 20%, 30% or somewhere in between? This is one of those occasions when we have to make an assumption before we can start working the figures. Anything from 20% to 30% is acceptable but once you decide what figure you are going to work with, you must remain consistent.

4.10 On page 30 there is reference to the company turnover being approximately £2.5 million. It does not tell us in what year. Again we must make an assumption and, at the time of working the case study, we assumed 1998. We can then work this figure backwards, using whichever figure we have assumed as growth, to give us a turnover figure for 5 years.

4.11 This page also has what is called a profitability index. It is not, in fact, a profitability index but a profit chart.

Action Programme 3

Using appropriate financial ratios, analyse Biocatalysts's financial data. Remember, information is scattered around the case study material, so make sure you collate all the information before you start.

Biocatalysts – working the numbers/key numbers sheet (pages 29/30)

4.12 Remember your figures might be different depending on what growth rate, and therefore turnover, you identified.

Liquidity/working capital

	1994	1995	1996	1997
Current ratio $\dfrac{\text{Current assets}}{\text{Current liabilities}}$			$\dfrac{736,915}{399,078}$	$\dfrac{953,622}{508,073}$
	2.3	2.2	1.8	1.8

(Good, 1.8 to 2.3 so fairly sound)

	1994	1995	1996	1997
Acid test $\dfrac{\text{Current assets, less inventory}}{\text{Current liabilities}}$			$\dfrac{548,449}{399,078}$	$\dfrac{795,745}{508,073}$
	1.4	1.5	1.4	1.6

(Good, greater than 1 so fairly sound)

Efficiency (productivity) and turnover

	1994	1995	1996	1997
Assets/T/O $\dfrac{\text{Sales}}{\text{Average total assets}}$			$\dfrac{1,601,562}{910,589}$	$\dfrac{2,002,952}{1,131,291}$
			1.8	1.8
Debtor days $\dfrac{\text{Sales}}{\text{Debtors}}$			$\dfrac{1,601,562}{517,462}$	$\dfrac{2,002,952}{783,623}$
(days)	75	72	118	143

(Poor risk bad debt/cash flow)

Stock turn $\frac{Sales}{Stock}$ =				$\frac{1,601,562}{188,466}$	$\frac{2,002,952}{157,877}$
	(days)	4.9	4.8	8.5	12.6
(Depends on 6 week lead time)					
Creditor days	(days)	75	75	91	93

4.13 This enables you to use very specific case material and therefore provides you with the opportunity to added value and offer insights into financial performance.

Tutor Tip

Have a look at the figures on page 30. This is a good example of how you need to take care with years and comparisons. The table makes you think profit margins are improving significantly: from 4.9% in 1994 to 8.2% in 1995.

There are two issues with this:

(a) Is 8.2% a reasonable return on investment in a high risk, high tech sector? Would the shareholders be better off putting their money in a bank?

(b) It isn't 1995, it is 1998. If you now look at the profitability index you can see the improved performances in 1994 – 1996, but profitability in 1997 and 1998 has levelled off or only increased marginally over the last twelve months.

The available financial analysis is weak. We have no profit analysis by:

- Country
- Product
- Sector
- Agents
- Sales people

We do know that 80% of business comes from 20% of the customers but we do not know whether this also represents 80% of the **profits**.

4.14 **Remember the marketer's impact on gross profit**

Marketing decisions impact directly on the gross profit margins of the business. Appreciating the implications of your decisions is critical to your ability to share responsibility for the financial health of the business.

(a) **Changing the customer mix**

Different market segments will have different gross profit potential. Large customers may be more or less profitable than small ones. There are no hard and fast rules, just the margins are likely to be different. Before deciding which segments to target, marketers must know which segments are most profitable.

(b) **Changing the product mix**

Different products will have different profit margins. Knowing which are your most profitable offerings is fundamental to decisions at a strategic and tactical level.

(c) **Changing the marketing mix**

Discounts or increased advertising might increase sales revenue and total profit but will depress gross profit margins. Decisions to change any element of the marketing mix will have financial consequences: marketers need to be aware of these and budget for them.

Tutor tip

Improving Profitability

Biocatalysts is unlikely to be the last case where we are faced with a need to improve profitability and it would be useful for you to ensure you are familiar not only with how marketing can impact on profitability, but on how it can be improved by actions across the business.

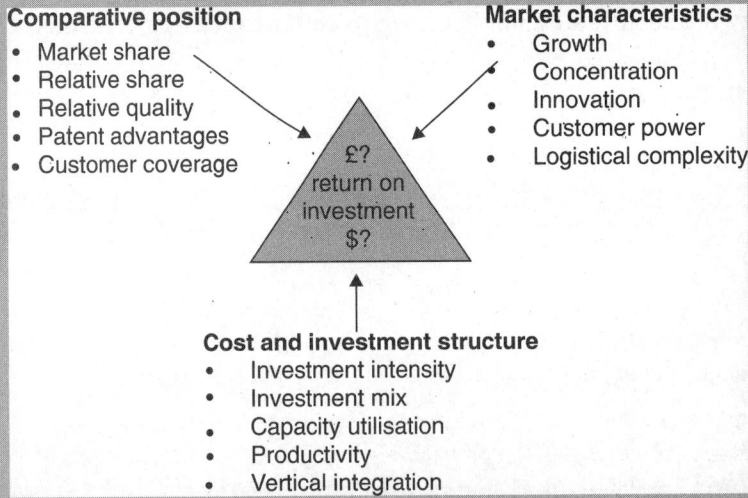

Comparative position
- Market share
- Relative share
- Relative quality
- Patent advantages
- Customer coverage

Market characteristics
- Growth
- Concentration
- Innovation
- Customer power
- Logistical complexity

£?
return on
investment
$?

Cost and investment structure
- Investment intensity
- Investment mix
- Capacity utilisation
- Productivity
- Vertical integration

Porter's value chain can be a useful model to help identify and communicate profit divers from across the business.

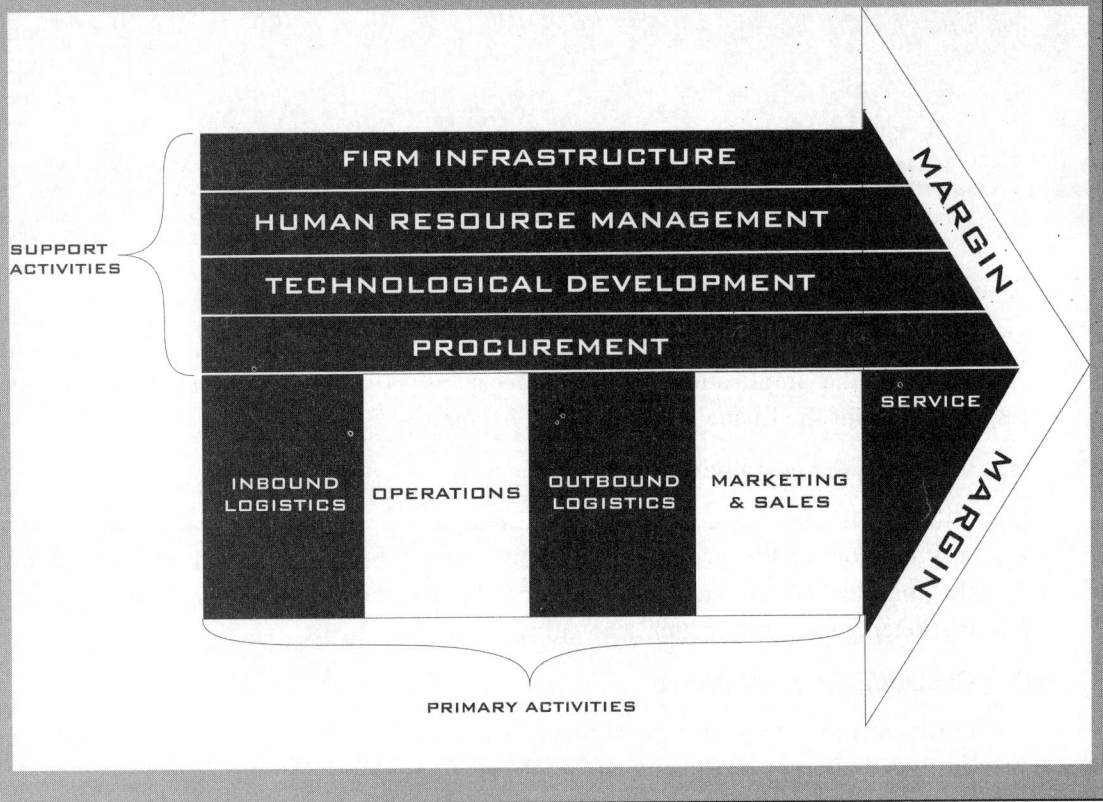

FIRM INFRASTRUCTURE

HUMAN RESOURCE MANAGEMENT

TECHNOLOGICAL DEVELOPMENT

PROCUREMENT

SUPPORT ACTIVITIES

MARGIN

SERVICE

MARGIN

INBOUND LOGISTICS | OPERATIONS | OUTBOUND LOGISTICS | MARKETING & SALES

PRIMARY ACTIVITIES

Operational overview

4.15   Biocatalysts Ltd have only one site: this is in Wales and is an 8,000 square feet modern factory unit.

Facilities include:

- Liquid and powder blending facilities

- Small scale fermentation/filtration equipment
- Pilot chromatographic purification and drying units

4.16 Batch sizes for all in-house production is flexible and the company is ISO 9000 compliant, enforcing the highest levels of quality control. All of the above machinery is fully depreciated but envisaged to be capable of another five years' output before replacement is necessary.

4.17 Customer requirements are established and the appropriate enzyme solution is researched by the Biocatalyst Ltd scientists (and researchers at various universities).

4.18 Large scale production/fermentation is contracted out. This has both good and bad aspects – good from the point of view of flexibility for the place/country of production and removal of the need for capital expenditure (for purchase and maintenance of facilities) but bad from the point of view of control. Quality control amongst other things can fall short of the required standards, facilities may not be available when needed and so on.

4.19 A £1m investment would enable all fermentation processing to take place in-house for the next five years (taking into account the sales growth we can expect). It should be noted that this could produce logistical problems in the transport of the finished product that would add to the costs of production and delivery of the final product.

4.20 Currently facilities already in place are not fully utilised. It has been calculated that in-house production could double with limited investment and only one or two more production staff.

4.21 Heavy investment after five years will be needed.

4.22 No fermentation takes place on site.

People overview

4.23 Currently there is a very simple structure in place with small teams for Sales, Administration, Purchasing, Production, Design and R&D projects. The structure is not marketing oriented at present which will need addressing.

4.24 Marketing/Sales is made up of five people including the MD (Stewart North). They look after new product development and long-term strategy. Of these five, there are three dedicated sales staff who spend 80% of their time directly involved with sales. This team of three is responsible for the relationship with the agents who conduct Biocatalyst's business to business sales.

4.25 Nearly all overseas sales are generated by agents and distributors. This has inherent problems such as that agents are not solely representing Biocatalyst Ltd and may sell competitor products in preference to Biocatalysts's; they need constant review, the quality of individuals varies. They are hard to monitor and they are not always motivated to educate the customers as they should.

4.26 Scientists are not full time employees and so their availability and commitment could be an issue.

4.27 There may be an element of 'pet project syndrome' when it comes to evaluating new opportunities.

4.28 High staff costs are minimised by using a project approach.

4.29 Contact with overseas sales teams is inadequate. A newsletter is sent out every six months to all distributors and customers. This details R&D advances and other changes in current products. Training sessions are held every year to bring agents up to speed with the current portfolio. Unfortunately many agents are absent from these meetings, drastically reducing their impact.

4.30 More and more, specialised/narrow niches are emerging and pressure is rising to provide dedicated sales teams who work only for Biocatalyst. Although it would be a challenge to replace all agents with dedicated staff in all countries, there are certain areas where potential volumes demand them, e.g. the Olive Oil sector and the PKU diagnostics enzyme recently approved for use in the USA.

5 THE PITFALLS

5.1 For the marketing student, the inview analysis can cause problems and there are a number of pitfalls you need to avoid:

(a) Focusing only on the **marketing aspects** and ignoring other **business issues and factors**

(b) **Ignoring the numbers:** yes we know it's tempting but the numbers will provide you with the keys to setting objectives and controls so work with them **not** around them.

(c) Failing to consolidate and summarise your analysis so that there are pages of information but you fail to use it as intelligence because it cannot be easily assimilated

Action Programme 4

Having worked through the internal analysis you should now be in a position to share your understanding of Biocatalyst with others.

Take no more than 20 minutes to prepare some brief notes in answer to a colleague's questions about Biocatalyst. Try and do this without referring back.

1   What are the key points you would make about the company's products?

Key Points

●

●

●

2   How would you summarise the strengths and weaknesses of Biocatalyst in relation to its current markets?

Strengths   *Weaknesses*

3   How would you summarise the company's overall weaknesses?

Check your answers with ours at the end of this chapter.

Action Programme Review _____

1   (a)   Over half of Biocatalysts's product/markets are high growth – net cash users not generators.

     (b)   The company is operating in four main sectors – so it begs the question, 'are they spread too thinly?

     (c)   The main cash cow, textiles, is a market going into decline.

     (d)   GMO's are a classic. They could be highly profitable or, if rejected by customers, immediately become a dog. I would be worried about future cash flow and funding the effective commercialisation of new products.

2   **Auditing the rest of the marketing mix**

     Strengths

     Place

     - Network of agents and direct sales covering 35 countries
     - Direct sales team, but it's very small

Implications
Little control over agents or access to the customer in international markets.

     Price

     - Euro may resolve our exchange problems for Europe in the future
     - Some new sectors and markets are attracting premium prices

Implications
A one-size fits all pricing strategy will not maximise returns for this business.

     Promotion

     - Key account handling exists in principle if not always in practice
     - They feel mailshots and exhibitions are important

Implications
There is more of a B2C feel to the communications thinking. Networking and relationship marketing need to be cornerstones for this sector.

     People

     - High calibre scientific staff
     - Flexibility in staffing should enable the right people for the right task and keep costs down
     - Links with University staff
     - 80% of five sales and marketing people's time dedicated to sales

     Physical evidence

Implications
In a service business physical evidence can add tangibility and value. It needs to be included in our thinking.

     Processes

Implications
Another black hole with no real insights but would be critical in ensuring customer satisfaction

Weaknesses

Place

- Inconsistent ability of agents to add value
- Problems of training and updating when Biocatalysts's business has limited total commission value to them
- Shipping costs
- Agents will be driven by commission
- No website

Price

- Pricing strategy is not delivering profits expected
- Some sectors are commoditising and prices are low
- Pricing strategy doesn't support the company's positioning
- How are exchange rates impacting on prices – who is taking the hit or benefits from fluctuations?

Promotion

- Personal sales coverage is weak due to limited resources
- Brand values are undefined and positioning is confused
- Communication with agents is patchy and unfocused
- No website for communication
- The literature is product led, offering few benefits and not focused on the various sectors with very different needs!
- Bad PR related to GM products

People

- No obvious marketing experiences
- There are question marks over the agents' motivation and capability
- Training not taken seriously
- High technical support promised but is it given?

> **Implications**
>
> Selling know-how is dependent on the people. There is a question as to the commitment and availability of this academic community

Physical Evidence

- No mention of any tangible aspects of the brand eg packaging, product literature, van livery, etc

4   1   **Key points about the Biocatalyst's products**

- Positioned at high value, low volume end of market, need to build strong positioning to counteract threats from changes in the market

- Have unique products: however need to protect them – intellectual property

- Diagnostics = good margins: however low percentage of current sales

- New product development led by customers – lack of focus

- Research part funded by grants – what if these were withdrawn

- Over represented in declining product sectors, many new products being produced in these

- GMO's could present both opportunity and threat: need to consider implications in terms of PR and marcomms

- Threats from competitors: they are producing products in a very attractive niche of the market

- Technical ability – but product led

2   **Biocatalysts's markets: strengths and weaknesses**

Strengths	Weaknesses
Experience in many markets	Overstretched serving too many sectors and countries
Diagnostic high margin	
Food sector expertise and high growth area	Never fully exploit sector/product potential
Pharma high margin	Textiles in decline
Seeks niches	Fragmented
Monopoly of PKU testing	Three players have 75% of market
	No market analysis
	No environmental screening
	Very competitive – many players
	Commoditisation of some markets
	8% profitability very low – some markets very unprofitable
	Little in-house overseas knowledge

3   **Overall Weaknesses**

- Reliance on other parties for sales and for R&D

- Resources spread thinly in over 35 countries

- Lack of production facilities leaving Biocatalysts at the mercy of other companies (time frames etc)

- Independent sales advisers are used who do not have it in their main interests to promote Biocatalysts's products all of the time(extended portfolios etc). These staff have no one to answer to.

- Lack of sales channels

- Communication channels to existing sales channels are unacceptably poor

BPP PUBLISHING

6

Step 3: External analysis

Introduction

In this chapter we will cover:

- The micro analysis for Biocatalysts:
  - market analysis
  - competitor audit
  - customer analysis

- The macro analysis for Biocatalysts

1   MAPPING THE CONTEXT: SKILLS AND KNOWLEDGE

1.1   The problem facing all organisations is that **they do not exist in a vacuum and so therefore they cannot plan in one.** It is the **changes** in their external macro and micro environments which create the **opportunities and threats** which drive their fortunes. Those who only look inwardly will be caught out by the environmental threats and will fail to respond to the opportunities. This has always been the case but in today's fast moving and dynamic markets, the environmental impact can be swift and significant. Only those really aware of their markets and environments can effectively capitalise on emerging opportunities or minimise the impact of the threats. The smaller the business, like Biocatalysts, the fewer resources they have to weather an environmental storm, and the enzyme market is one where change is a fact of life.

1.2   In this step of the case process, you need to look **outside** the business to establish the **external context** and conditions facing the case company.

1.3   In the situation analysis, you needed to assess the current position but in the **environmental audit you need to address the future.** Planning is about tomorrow not today, so we need to look forward and prepare the business for the markets of one, three, five or even ten years, time. **This planning horizon will often be clear from the case.** A business struggling to survive might expect to be concerned with short term strategy, whereas a capital intensive industry may be planning for a longer term future.

Tutor Tip

This immediately gives us a problem in case study. The CIM tells you **not** to look outside the case study and yet you are unlikely to have been furnished with environmental forecasts. You may be able to establish environmental trends from case information but you can also bring your common sense and personal and business experience to make reasonable assumptions about the future.

1.4 By the end of this chapter you will:

(a) Have created a market map for Biocatalysts

(b) Recognise the value of Porter's Five Forces and competitive strategies models in evaluating the micro environment

(c) Undertaken an environmental audit for this case

(d) Have considered the international aspects and the implications of different external environments on planning and strategy for a business like Biocatalyst

Skills and knowledge reminders

1.5 There are a number of tools and models which are helpful when completing the external audit. You may need to familiarise yourself with the following before approaching this chapter:

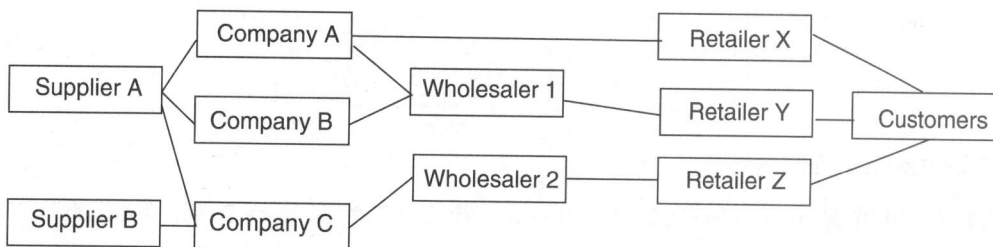

A market map

A market map is a useful visualisation of who's who in the market place and lets you look at who is working with whom and so on.

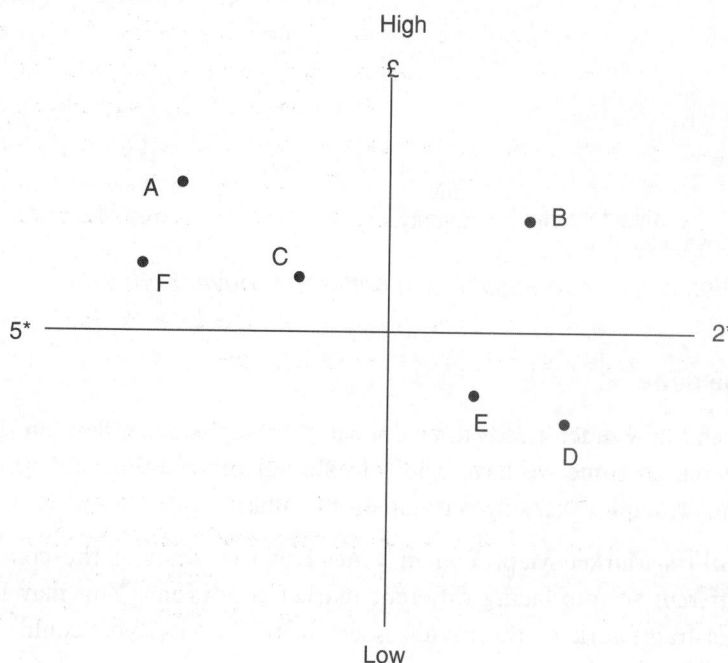

A positioning map. A positioning map is a very effective framework for identifying who the closest competitors are.

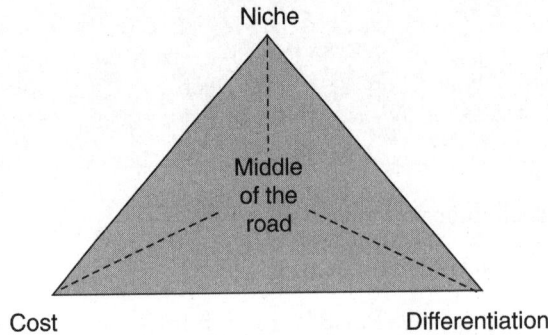

Porter's Generic Strategies

Porter's generic strategies encourages you to identify the strategy being adopted by the market players.

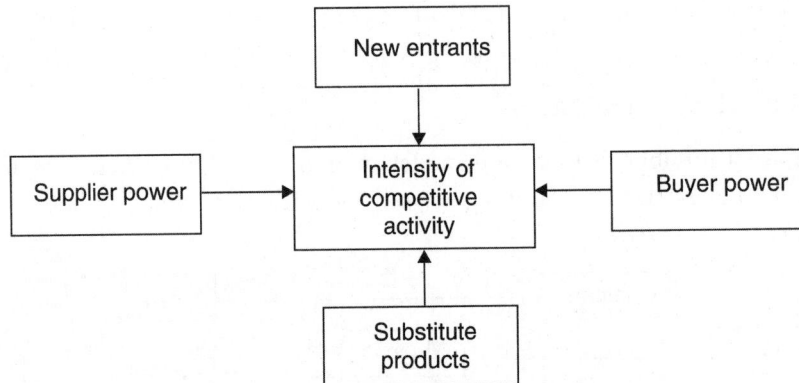

Porter's Five Forces

This will help you to assess the changes in market dynamics and forecast the likely direction of gross profit margins.

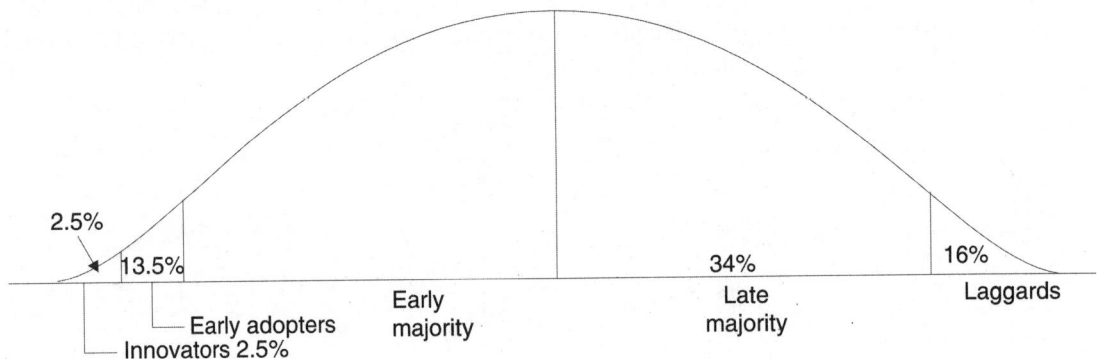

Diffusion of innovation curve: statistical patterns in buyer behaviour

What needs to be done

1.8 Again what and how much needs to be done at this step is dependent on the actual case you are working on. In some we have a lot of external information and in others very little. However, the principles will stay very much the same.

Step 1. Build a Market Map. You may need two or three if the company is active in different sectors facing different market conditions. You may have already used this framework at the inview stage in which case you could simply be adding detail now.

Step 2. Market dynamics are clearly important in understanding the business and we would try and extend the market map into a Porter's Five Forces Analysis and assess the implications of that.

Step 3. A competitor analysis is essential to any future strategy, so the next step is to sort out who is active in what markets and what strategies they are adopting. Again you will note that we began to collect some of that information when we were looking at the key Biocatalyst product markets in the last chapter.

Step 4. Customers are of course key, so we need to assess who they are, how the market is segmented and who is in the DMU. We will need to think of channels as customers in this process. We want to assess how customers are changing: what are the emerging needs or concerns.

Step 5. Finally we need to consider the external macro environment, PEST or SLEPT or PESTLE analysis. Your terminology is not important so long as you have considered all the key factors and influences facing the business:

- Political and legal
- Economic and demographic
- Social and cultural
- Technological and environmental

Step 6. **Market structure analysis – a check list**

Every market will differ in its characteristics so that it is difficult to be specific about structure. However, the following general analytical framework can be applied to most markets.

(a) What are the **market parameters?** In other words, what are its boundaries? The UK domestic market's parameters are the borders of the UK.

(b) How **big** is the market within these parameters?

(c) Is this market **growing,** stable or declining?

(d) How does the market **segment**?

(e) To what extent is **each segment** growing, stable or declining?

(f) Who are the **key players** in the market or segments? (Manufacturers, distributors, others.)

(g) What are the **key success factors** in this market or segment?

(h) What are the **buying behaviour characteristics** of this market or segment?

(i) Who are the **major market/segment competitors** and what are their distinctive competencies?

(j) What **future environmental factors** are likely to affect this market/segment?

(k) How easy or difficult is the market **and/or segment** to enter or exit?

2 BUILDING A MARKET MAP FOR BIOCATALYST

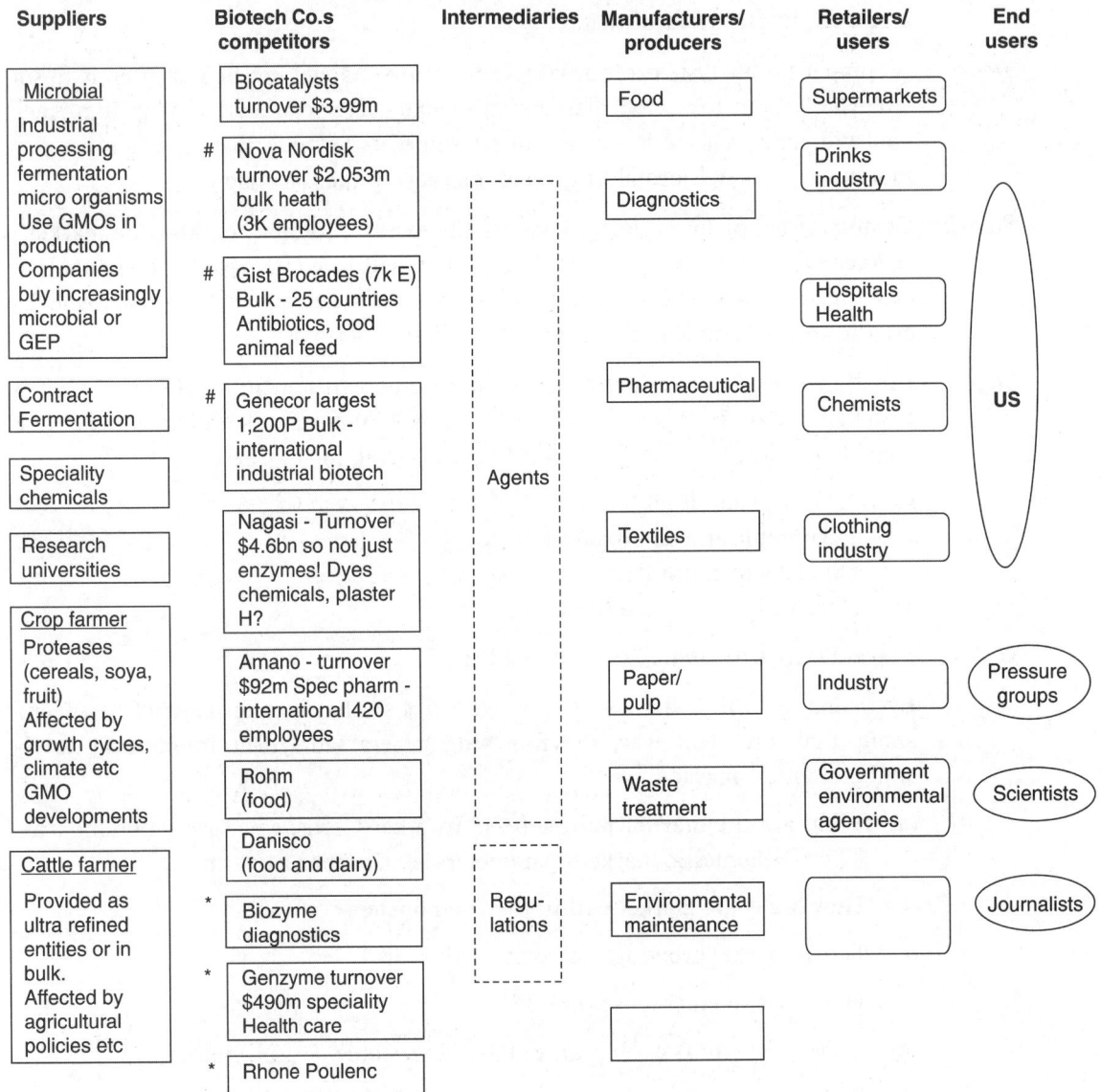

Suppliers	Biotech Co.s competitors	Intermediaries	Manufacturers/ producers	Retailers/ users	End users

Suppliers

Microbial

Industrial processing fermentation micro organisms Use GMOs in production Companies buy increasingly microbial or GEP

Contract Fermentation

Speciality chemicals

Research universities

Crop farmer

Proteases (cereals, soya, fruit) Affected by growth cycles, climate etc GMO developments

Cattle farmer

Provided as ultra refined entities or in bulk. Affected by agricultural policies etc

Biotech Co.s competitors

Biocatalysts turnover $3.99m

\# Nova Nordisk turnover $2.053m bulk heath (3K employees)

\# Gist Brocades (7k E) Bulk - 25 countries Antibiotics, food animal feed

\# Genecor largest 1,200P Bulk - international industrial biotech

Nagasi - Turnover $4.6bn so not just enzymes! Dyes chemicals, plaster H?

Amano - turnover $92m Spec pharm - international 420 employees

Rohm (food)

Danisco (food and dairy)

* Biozyme diagnostics

* Genzyme turnover $490m speciality Health care

* Rhone Poulenc

Intermediaries

Agents

Regu-lations

Manufacturers/ producers

Food

Diagnostics

Pharmaceutical

Textiles

Paper/ pulp

Waste treatment

Environmental maintenance

Retailers/ users

Supermarkets

Drinks industry

Hospitals Health

Chemists

Clothing industry

Industry

Government environmental agencies

End users

US

Pressure groups

Scientists

Journalists

2.1 In practice, you are unlikely to just sit down and complete a perfect market map for the case: you build it up and evolve it as you collect more information. This one is simple; it lists competitors but doesn't show how each of them is operating in terms of suppliers or access to customers. As we build our knowledge of competitors and customers through this step, you will be able to add more detail to the map.

Understanding market dynamics

2.2 Here is a table summarising the dynamics of the Biocatalyst market as produced by a student group working the case. It gives an idea of how you might synthesise this information, but compare it with the visual communication of the same material using the model. You can see how this gets information across quickly and can be a real asset in the exam room when time is at a premium.

Market analysis

Porter's model

Category	Remarks	Rating
Competitive activity	**General:** • Biocatalysts Ltd is a small company turnover just £2.5m – 70% export sales. • Biocatalysts Ltd provide full technical support, exclusive agreements and 1 to 1 relationship this high dependency relationship makes **switching** less likely • Biocatalysts Ltd operate in food 48%, textiles 31%, diagnostics 5%, pharmaceuticals 15% and other 1% • 12 major global producers all with relatively distinct offerings • 60 smaller range global producers • 400 very limited industrial quantity global producers • Geographically – 60% production in Europe, 15% in North America and 12-15% in Japan • Russian market large but undeveloped • Chinese market large (especially for food enzymes) but relatively 'closed' **Medical/diagnostic** (used for testing for abnormalities in humans) **sector:** • Japan weak in bulk enzymes but strong in speciality, especially medical diagnostics • Growth market • High margins **Textiles** (used for fading jeans) **sector:** • A near commodity business with little or no R&D required: this appears totally alien to Bio's offering • Moderate margins • Declining market **Food** (used to increase yields and quality) **sector:** • Moderate margins	Textiles: HIGH Other: MEDIUM
Buyers	**General:** • Price as a % of customers' production costs will be very low so price likely to be inelastic • A lot of product ignorance leading to some buyers focusing on price • Business to business market • Customers will often be very large and powerful • The needs of the deferred customer, the public, need to be considered ie fears in Europe leading to supermarkets not stocking • Agents selling many company products	Textiles: HIGH Other: MEDIUM
Suppliers	**General:** • Other enzyme producers (patents often in place) • University knowledge base • Fermenters (as this is outsourced)	MEDIUM

Category	Remarks	Rating
New entrants	**General:** • Growth market which is likely to attract others but high technical expertise may well act as a discouragement • Due to GMO option, R&D is lower, so ease of entry is higher • In-house option • Under-developed countries ie China and Russia	MEDIUM
Substitute products	**General:** • Traditional/natural production methods – but these are inefficient and of poor quality • Remember the GMO (lower R&D)/non-GO (higher R&D) option	LOW

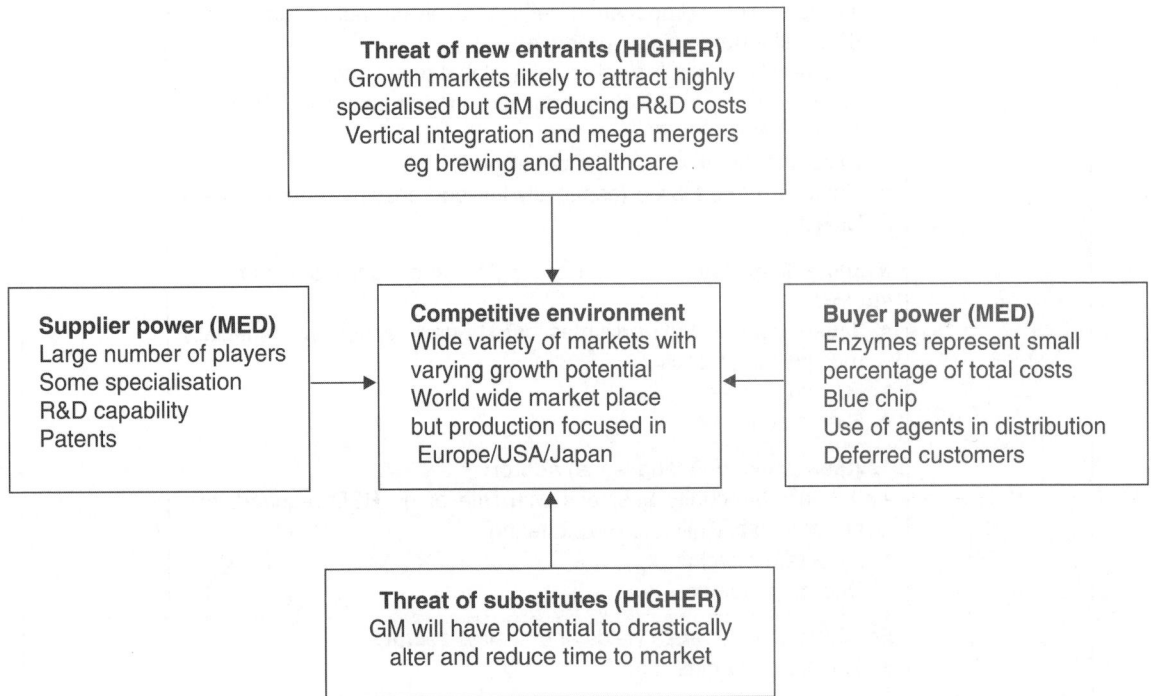

Threat of new entrants (HIGHER)
Growth markets likely to attract highly specialised but GM reducing R&D costs
Vertical integration and mega mergers eg brewing and healthcare

Supplier power (MED)
Large number of players
Some specialisation
R&D capability
Patents

Competitive environment
Wide variety of markets with varying growth potential
World wide market place
but production focused in Europe/USA/Japan

Buyer power (MED)
Enzymes represent small percentage of total costs
Blue chip
Use of agents in distribution
Deferred customers

Threat of substitutes (HIGHER)
GM will have potential to drastically alter and reduce time to market

A Five Forces Map of the Enzyme Market (version 1)

Tutor Tip

You should also be aware that in case study there is no single correct answer. The examiners are looking for rigorous process and justification which is credible but not some pre-determined standard approach. Sample answers and our approach should therefore be viewed as indicative rather than prescriptive. You can see this by looking at this alternative version of Porter's Five Forces developed by a different group – equally valid and accurate but perhaps you can see how you might choose the modified content in a model you were presenting if the questions or additional information were different.

If the focus was on international markets and developments, then the first version might be most useful but if the extra information was about a merger between key competitors, the second would have more impact.

```
                        ┌─────────────────┐
                        │  New entrants   │
                        │  Japanese and   │
                        │  Russian firms  │
                        │    expected     │
                        └────────┬────────┘
                                 │
                                 ▼
┌──────────────────────┐  ┌─────────────────┐  ┌──────────────────────┐
│   Supplier power     │  │     Rivalry     │  │     Buyer power      │
│                      │  │ 12 global players│  │                      │
│ • Purchase enzymes   │  │ 60 medium sized │  │ • End users increasingly│
│   from other         │─▶│ under pressure  │◀─│   concerned with safety │
│   users for          │  │ 400 smaller     │  │   eg BSE, GMOs       │
│   reprocessing       │  │ intensifying    │  │ • Some parts of market│
│ • Relationships with │  │ competition and │  │   commoditising eg   │
│   university staff   │  │ market          │  │   textiles, customers │
│ • Sub-contractors    │  │ consolidation   │  │   have lots of choice │
└──────────────────────┘  └────────▲────────┘  │ • Some customers weak,│
                                   │            │   with high switching │
                                   │            │   costs eg diagnostics │
                          ┌────────┴────────┐  └──────────────────────┘
                          │   Substitutes   │
                          │ DIY - purification│
                          │     and recovery │
                          │     to re-use    │
                          │     products     │
                          │ GMO - options with│
                          │     new technology│
                          └─────────────────┘
```

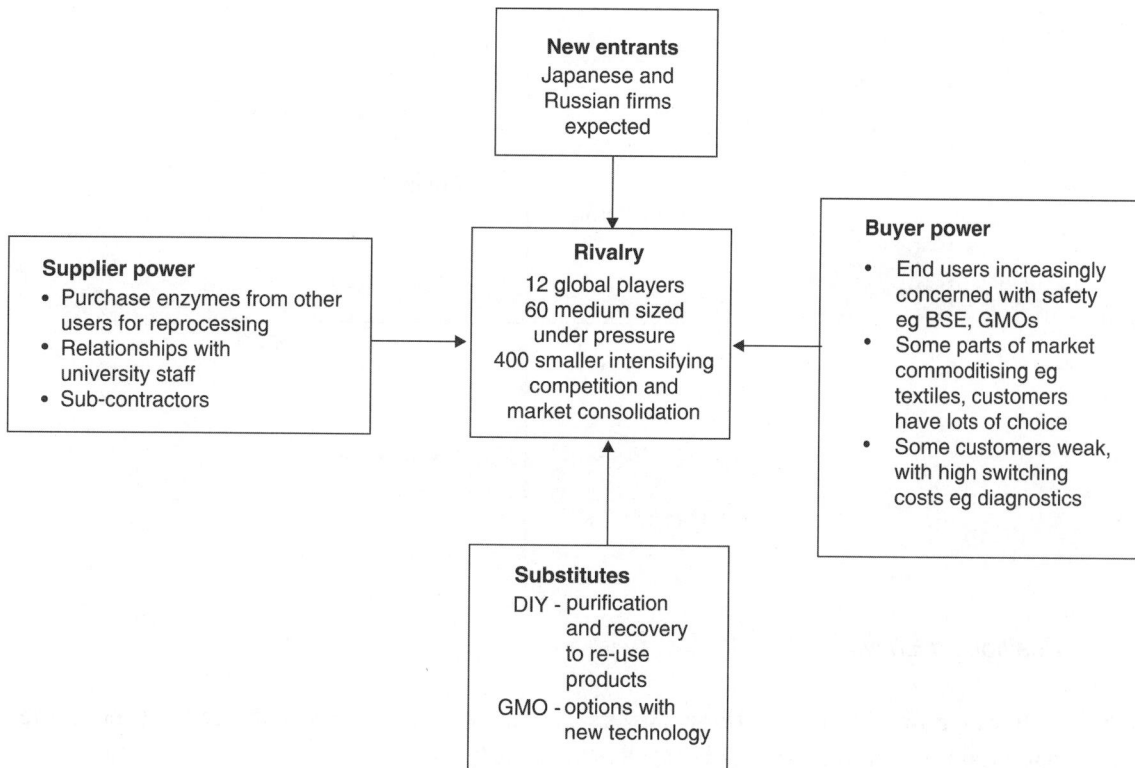

Porter's Five Forces (Version 2)

Add the competitor dimension

2.3 Business would be a lot easier without competitors.

Action Programme 1

Assessing Competitor Responses

Take a few minutes to think about what you already know about competitors and how this knowledge could help you get a more detailed insight into how competitors in a case context might behave.

1 Who are likely to be the most aggressive competitors - those operating in a growing or mature market place and why?

2 If a new entrant, moving into a market which was itself in late growth or early maturity, wanted to avoid head to head competition with the existing players in that market, what strategy should they adopt?

3 Who would you expect to be the most aggressive competitor in an established market place: the market leader, market challenger or one of the other players?

4 Are there any circumstances when a smaller firm might respond more aggressively to a competitive threat?

5 In the Biocatalyst case, how do you expect competitors like Amano and Rhom to respond to changes in Biocatalysts's strategies?

Check your answers with ours at the end of the chapter.

Who are the real competitors?

2.4 In a large marketplace the existence of a player in the market does not necessarily make them a major threat (although it will probably mean they could be a potential one). In cases, as in business, you need to identify the closest competitors. Positioning maps are an easy framework to use for this.

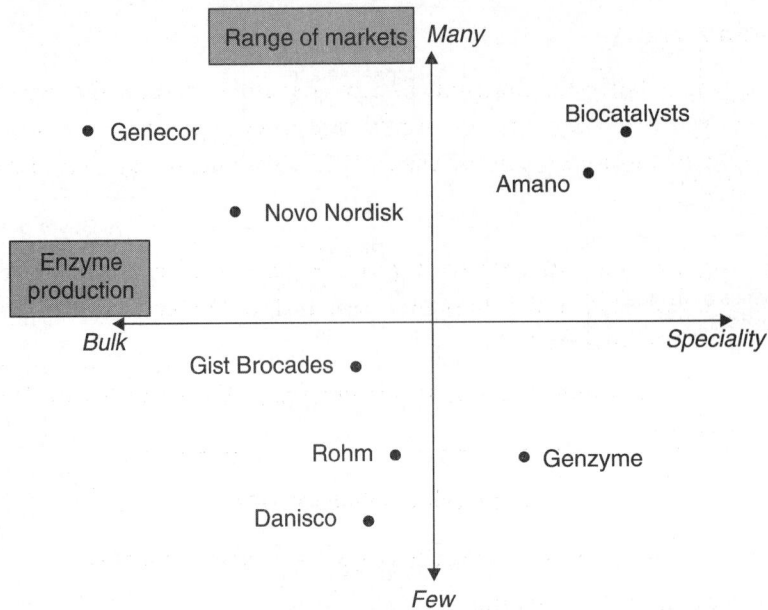

Positioning Enzymes

2.5 You can now see that of these players Amano are the closest competitor (hence their potential interest in acquiring Biocatalysts's expertise).

Companies like Genencor and Novo Nordisk are really in a quite different part of the market with expertise in volume production.

Understanding competitor strategy

2.6 Once you know who the competitors are you want to understand the competitive strategies they are adopting. Porter's Generic Strategies model will provide a simple framework for recording and communicating this information. Remember – those in the middle of the road are most vulnerable so could be targets if you needed to win market share.

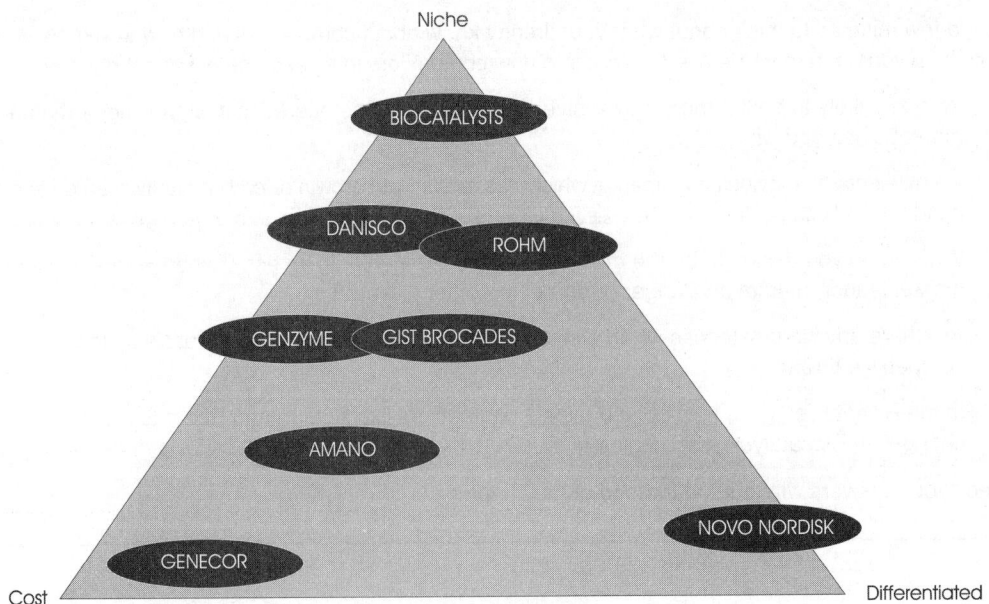

Porter's generic competitive strategies for enzymes

This analysis is perhaps a little kind to Biocatalysts. Whilst they are clearly niche players, their lack of product or market focus has left them much more 'middle of the road' and also, therefore, in a vulnerable position.

Adding the customers

2.7 As marketers, it is fairly fundamental that we remember to add the customer dimension. Changes in buyer behaviour can have significant impact on business success and we need to bring our understanding and knowledge of the customer to any strategic assessment or decision-making.

2.8 This is the work which will eventually provide the basis for effective segmentation. At a macro level, we will need to define the markets and understand their needs and, at a micro level the decision making unit.

You can see here how a student group tackled this part of the analysis for Biocatalysts.

Understanding the Markets

The world market for enzymes is growing, doubling in the 10 years from 1994.

World market for industrial enzymes:

1994	$1 billion
1997	$1.3 billion
1998	$1.7 billion
2005	$2 billion

The Biocatalysts customers come from a number of industries.

Distribution of enzyme sales by product sector:

Year	Other	Detergents	Diary	Textiles	Starch
1994	29%	32%	14%	10%	15%
2005	47%	27%	8%	6%	12%

'Other' market = growth

The rest in decline

Breakdown of 'other' market:

- Alcohol
- Animal feed
- Baking
- Chemical biotransformations
- Diagnostics
- Fats and oils
- Flavour
- Fruit and wine
- Leather
- Protein (for milk coagulation, flavour and detergents)
- Pulp and water
- Water

It is clear that this 'other' sector is becoming increasingly significant to Biocatalysts so this is worth some further review and analysis

---

Action Programme 2

Mind mapping 'other'

Take 20 minutes and produce a mind map or schematic which consolidates the information and analysis we have available about 'other' customers.

Compare your analysis with ours at the end of this chapter.

2.9 **Analysis of customers by industry.**

(a) Biocatalyst's customers are in 35 countries including:

•	UK	29%
•	Spain	17%
•	South America	7%
•	Asia Pacific	7%
•	Japan	2%
•	Europe	9%
•	USA	7%
•	Other	22% (28 countries)
		100%

•	Sales in Food	48%
•	Textiles	31%
•	Diagnostics	5% (now 10%)
•	Pharmaceuticals	15% (all figures from 1997)

These customers include blue chip, medium and small accounts, buying products and services. The **pareto** rule applies with 80% of the sales going to 20% of the customers.

(b) **Food**. Biocatalysts' products are used as a processing aid. Competitive advantage is function, security and cost in use. This includes baking (bread, biscuits, crackers, batters), brewing, protein modification, fruit and flavouring.

   (i) **Decision Making Unit (DMU):** mainly industrial businesses involved in food and beverage processing of ingredients to produce branded consumer goods. Examples are Hovis, Premier biscuits, Ryvita, Tetley, Robinson's. Also flavourings for snack food and cheese manufacture with Enzyme Modified Cheese (EMC).

   People involved are food technologists, industrial buyers, process production and quality staff.

   (ii) **Critical issues**

   • Consistent quality for customers' production efficiency
   • Cost in use is competitive
   • Complies with legislation and consumer trends (GM and bovine safety)
   • Communication between technical service, agents and customers

(c) **Textile**. Products are used as washing agent that causes the stone-washed effect on jeans. The competitive advantage is low with a declining fashion based market buying on price as a commodity.

   (i) DMU: industrial buyers and production staff

   (ii) Critical issues • Correct product specification as set
                        • Competitive pricing at time of purchase

---

Action Programme 3

Analysing diagnostics

Take 15 minutes to complete the same analysis of the diagnostic sector. Compare your answer with ours at the end of this chapter.

(d) **Pharmaceuticals.** Cell cultures and hydrolysis of esters. Competitive advantage unknown.

    (i)   Critical issues • Technical service support

                                 • Consistency and quality of product

    (ii)   DMU: similar to diagnostics market with less due diligence

(e) **Environmental.** Waste water treatment for odour reduction and lower drain maintenance. Competitive advantage unknown

    (i)   DMU: the customer, the local drainage and sewerage authorities (these civil servants include maintenance managers and procurement officers). The workers will feed back the performance and ease of use of the product and packaging.

(f) **Other markets**

Alcohol	World wide demand; near-commodity business
Animal feed	BSE and safety issues, high volume low margins
Chemical	Green issues for industry, opportunity for environmentally friendly products
Biotransformers Fats and Oils Leather Protein	} information gaps
Paper and Pulp	Environmental issues and packaging waste regulations.

Combining product/market information

2.10 From this next chart, you can see how a student has linked product information with end use to give us a further perspective on the variety of customers the company is trying to satisfy.

BPP PUBLISHING

Biocatalyst's current products by sector

Sector	No. of Products	New Product	End use.
Baking	19	3	Bread, biscuits, crackers, batters
Brewing	5	5	Beer
Fruit and Veg	12	3	Fruit juice, wine, citrus fruits
Flavourings	14	0	Vegetables, fibrous botanicals, ECM
Proteins	13	1	Bacterial proteinase Soya
Dietetics	10	2	Aid for digestion ready for tableting
Textile	21	9	Stone-wash, cost effective development
Diagnostics	8	3	Immuno-diagnostics, food testing
Pharmaceuticals	7	0	Cell cultures, hydrolysis of esters
Environment	4	0	Waste odour reduction, drain maintenance

COMPETITOR SUMMARY

Competitor	Geographic focus	Target markets/ product range	Market share (of $1.7bn	Supplier to Biocatalysts	GMO	Summary
Novo Nordisk	Worldwide (RBCDs)	Industrial and technical enzymes including textiles	[50%]	✓	?	RBDCs allow flexibility to adapt to local conditions Also in healthcare Cost cutting and productivity improvements
Genencor	Worldwide	1,200 patents	[12.5%]	✓	✓	Largest company devoted exclusively to industrial biotechnology State of the art production capability
Genzyme		Medical-diagnostics, therapeutics and surgical			?	Mainly healthcare $490m turnover
Amano	Production in Japan/ USA/UK	Pharmaceutical/food/ diagnostic 50 patents	[7%]	✓	?	'World No 1 speciality enzyme producer' Surface fermentation?
Gist Brocades	Worldwide especially in growth areas of Asia and South America – 70 sites	Food and agriculture Very active with patents	[12.5%]	✓	?	
Nagase					?	Part of $4.6bn turnover company
Biozome		Baking/food		✓	?	
Rohm		Food/sweeteners		✓	?	
Danisco					?	
					?	FDA approval for PKU test in USA

Table 2

Adding the macro dimensions

2.11 Finally, to complete your external audit, you will need to build up the picture of the changing external environment for the enzyme market. Here you can see such an environmental audit completed and prioritised helping you to summarise and consolidate the many clues provided within the case study.

Political/legal	Economic	Social/demographic	Technological
• Food sector – politicians increasingly responding to public's **concerns** • Food and medical sectors – tight legislation controlling release of new products • Food sector – packaging disclosure laws • All sectors – employment laws • All sectors – worldwide trade agreements/ barriers/ embargoes	• Food sector – higher yields could lead to an over-capacity and an agricultural recession in the medium term • All sectors – large parts of Wales classed as Economic Development Areas inc grant assistance • All sectors – strong pressure on industry from analysts/city to improve productivity ⇒performance enhancing technology (ie enzymes) will be in demand. • All sectors – worldwide trade so UK's involvement in EMU could be important • Exchange rate risk from trading across 3 currencies - $, £ and the euro • Worldwide recessions eg instability in Asia • Merging of large Blue Chip companies • China and Russia	• Food sector – expected population growth will require higher food yields. • Food sector – widespread anti-GM feeling in European society building on BSE scare. This includes well organised pressure groups. Far less the case in other continents. • All sectors – increasingly 'green' sensitive society in developed countries • Food sector – developing countries however want reliable food sources and are not 'green' • Textile sector – some linkage to fad and fashion through involvement in textile industry ie faded jeans • Medical sector – people becoming more health conscious so medical and diagnostic trade will become more important • Increasing demand for global brand foods]• Global warming ⇒ medicines required and reliable crops	• All sectors – high new product R&D costs but reducing where GMOs are used. • Food sector – strong growth area ⇒ an agricultural revolution is taking place as important as that in electronics • Food sector – GM food is actually already widespread • All sectors – reliance on universities for research • All sectors – Internet makes them more accessible, including deferred customers' products

Table 3

Moving on

2.12 You have now completed the detailed inview and overview analysis essential to providing the detailed understanding of the case context. In the next chapter we will look in more detail at how you take the next steps to action by sorting and refining the internal and external analysis and identifying the critical success factors.

Before moving on, take a few minutes to reflect on what you have learnt about the process of analysis and how it can best be completed. Look at the pitfalls we have identified and take the time to tackle this end of chapter activity.

Pitfalls

2.13 **The most common pitfalls when completing the external audit**

(a) Focus on PEST analysis and forget to really work on the micro analysis of competitors and customers

(b) Try to do **two steps** at once during the macro analysis so instead of

- threat of recession

the student says

- falling sales because of recession

This is going from the **external factor** to the **product/market implication**. This is a mistake because an environmental change could generate **both** product market opportunities and threats.

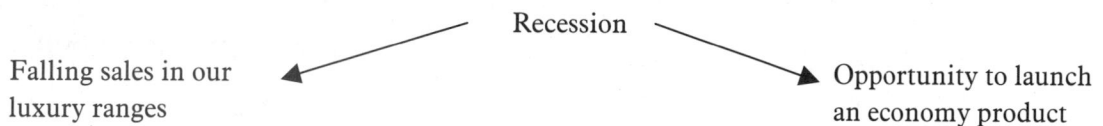

Recession → Falling sales in our luxury ranges

Recession → Opportunity to launch an economy product

Make sure at this step you stick to the uncontrollable and external PEST factors, and leave the translation into product/market implications until Step 5.

2.14 **Failure to think ahead**. The external analysis requires that we try to think ahead even though forecasting is **not** a very precise art. Keep it reasonable and realistic but use your own knowledge and look ahead.

Action Programme 4

We have handled a lot of data and information in this step of the case process. Are you using this to build a clearer picture of Biocatalyst and its challenges?

Take a few minutes to work through the following questions which might help you consolidate your thoughts.

1 Why would a change in Government policy regarding the funding and support of biotechnology be significant to Biocatalyst?

2 Competitor Amano has 400 products and an income of £92m. How might this information help us set an objective for Biocatalyst?

3 Is a differentiated strategy an option for Biocatalyst?

4 Why are GMOs an important issue for Biocatalyst and what impact might decisions about them have on strategy?

5 Why is the 'other' sector of the enzyme market potentially attractive to Biocatalyst?

6 Take 10 minutes to produce a checklist of questions to pose about competitors which you could use in future cases.

Compare your answers with ours before moving on.

Action Programme review_____

1   *Assessing Competitor Responses*

    1   Those working in a mature market because winning new business means taking customers away from someone else.

    2   They should target the 'laggards' who will be the only new customers still entering the market place. In this way they can win market share without taking customers from someone else.

    3   The market challenger normally who will be focused on winning market share and can often best do this by taking on smaller players rather than the market leader.

    4   Yes, if this was its core market and more important to it or if the challenge being made was a direct head to head one.

    5   Probably hardly at all. They are significantly bigger and Biocatalyst is a small niche player. Amano may, however, be interested in acquiring them for their expertise and patents but that would probably be the extent of things.

2   *Mind mapping 'other'*

The 'other' sector of the Enzyme Business

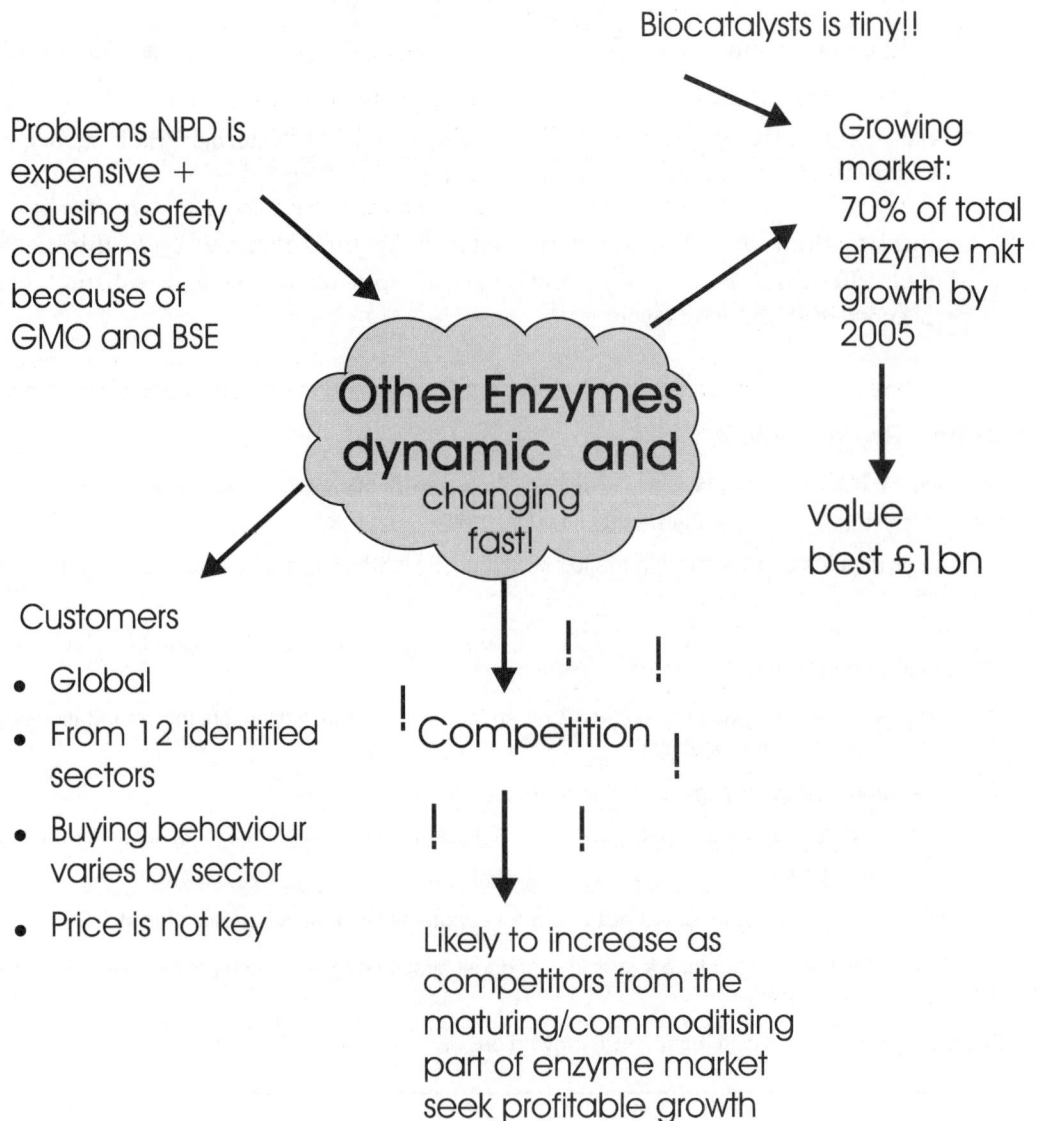

Biocatalysts is tiny!!

Problems NPD is expensive + causing safety concerns because of GMO and BSE

Growing market: 70% of total enzyme mkt growth by 2005

value best £1bn

Other Enzymes dynamic and changing fast!

Customers

- Global
- From 12 identified sectors
- Buying behaviour varies by sector
- Price is not key

Competition

Likely to increase as competitors from the maturing/commoditising part of enzyme market seek profitable growth

3   *Analysing Diagnostics*

Diagnostics. Medical applications for determination of presence and immuno-diagnostics. The competitive advantage is technology-based with partnership agreements.

Testing for genetic disorder, blood tests, gastric disorders, determination of glocosinates in rape seed meal.

DMU. This is a highly scientific environment with leading edge technology transformed into commercial reality. The DM is protracted with extensive independent testing and field trials before approval; these include medical bodies, associations and FDA approval. This work would be championed by the drug companies looking to supply the diagnostic kits via the medical profession. Dealing with scientists, doctors, professional supply chain managers, process engineers and marketing.

Critical Issues
- Unique formulation and confidentiality agreements
- Quality and consistency of product and process performance
- Medical approval for targeted markets
- Technical support and partnership approach

4   1   Much of Biocatalysts's work attracts grants which could be reduced or stopped. The Government could also influence the extent of support provided by university research if their priorities changed.

2   This means Amano (based in the same sector of the market place) earns some £230k per product compared with approx. £22k per Biocatalyst product. This is a useful benchmark indicating how product rationlisation and improved marketing of say 30 instead of 112 products could increase revenues to say £7m.

3   Not really - it is too small a player, a niche or multi-niche approach feels more credible.

4   GMOs are the cause of much concern amongst the general public, particularly in Europe. The decision to include or reject them from the portfolio will strongly influence both the corporate positioning and which customers will be attracted to the company.

5   Because this sector is growing and profitable, whereas others like textiles are increasingly mature and commoditised. Biocatalyst has the skills, competence and experience to focus very effectively on this £1bn part of the market.

6   A competitors checklist

A great deal can be accomplished in understanding competitors by relatively simple numerical analysis and financial and market review. Here is a checklist of questions about competitors you should find answers to.

Question	Answer
(a) How many?	
(b) Size	
(c) Growing or declining	
(d) Market shares and/or rank orders	
(e) Likely objectives and strategies	
(f) Changes in management personnel	
(g) Past reaction to:	
(i) price changes	
(ii) promotional campaigns	
(iii) new product launches	
(iv) distribution drives	
(h) Analysis of marketing mix strengths and weaknesses	
(i) Leaders or followers?	
(j) National or international	
(k) Analysis of published accounts	

BPP PUBLISHING

7

Step 4: Prioritisation and critical success factors

Chapter Topic List
1 Prioritising analysis
2 Prioritising strengths and weaknesses
3 Prioritising opportunities and threats
4 Critical success factors (CFCs)

1 PRIORITISING ANALYSIS

1.1 Professional marketers have a duty to present analysis in a way that is of value to senior management and the organisation. This requires going further than just establishing SWOT; it requires making connections and inferences, drawing conclusions and, ultimately, providing insights that ensure decision making is based on valued information.

1.2 During analysis, the SWOT and other auditing techniques help to determine the current situation. For the results of the audit to be of any value, SWOTs etc must be **prioritised to ensure the organisation is focused on those issues that matter most,** for example the weaknesses and threats that will impact on organisational success.

1.3 A long list of SWOT terms might provide an improved understanding of the current situation but it can be a daunting step to move from this list to decisions. There are also always constraints on resources, money, time, processes and people, and so priorities must be established to determine what is important and must be invested in, and what can wait.

1.4 There are some helpful techniques for prioritising analysis. We will now describe others.

2 PRIORITISING STRENGTHS AND WEAKNESSES

2.1 It is of course helpful for employees to comment on the organisation's strengths and weaknesses. However, much more important are the **external** perceptions and opinions on the organisation's performance.

2.2 Customers, suppliers, distribution channels and other stakeholders should be canvassed for their opinions. For example, a technique that can help identify what is important to customers and prioritise its importance is the **semantic differential**.

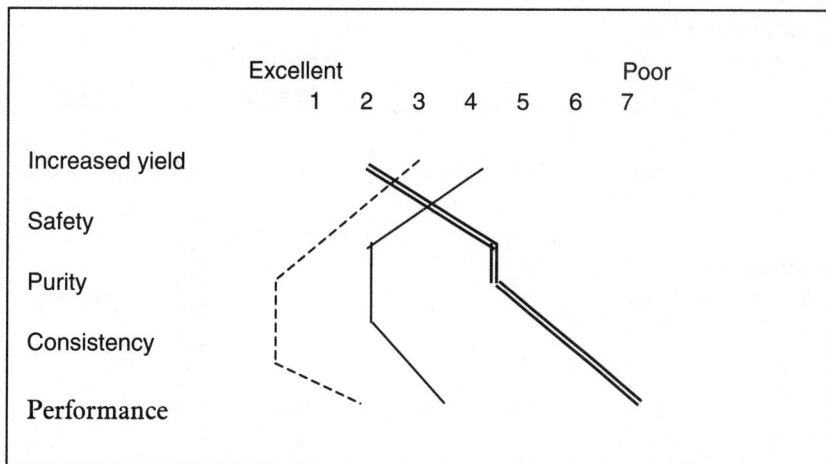

```
                    Excellent                    Poor
                    1   2   3   4   5   6   7

Increased yield

Safety

Purity

Consistency

Performance
```

Biocatalysts   ————
Competitor A   ═══════
Competitor B   - - - - - -

2.3   Please note, this is not meant to suggest that this is how Biocatalysts's results would look. We do not have the information to enable us to do this. It is an example of how we might be able to identify performance if we did have the information.

2.4   Management can then use this information to rank activities as strengths and weaknesses and to establish some understanding of the importance of each activity to customers. There is no point in an organisation identifying a weakness and allocating resources to improving performance if it is of no importance to the customer. Resources must be used where they will do the most good, or where there is an opportunity to maintain or develop competitive advantage.

| Activities | Prioritising strengths and weaknesses | | | | | | | | |
| | Strength | | | Weakness | | | Importance | | |
	Major	Medium	Low	Minor	Medium	Serious	High	Medium	Low
Promotions reach									
People									
technical skills									
service skills									
Process									
simple									

BPP PUBLISHING

2.5 Activities can be weighted and rated to enable marketers to determine whether eg a strength is major, medium or low.

		Performance		
		Excellent	Average	Poor
Importance (to customer)	High	Maintain	Improve	Urgent attention
	Average			Improve
	Low	Over investing	Monitor	Monitor

2.6 Another factor to take into account when prioritising weaknesses is the effort involved in dealing with the weakness. Is it simple a matter of investing more money, for example a computer could solve the problem? Or will a major change be required in processes, people skills, organisation structure and so on?

2.7 Speed may also be a factor. How quickly can the organisation solve the problem? Can it be solved within the planning period and in time to make a positive difference to the organisation?

3 PRIORITISING OPPORTUNITIES AND THREATS

3.1 Prioritising **threats** forces us to consider the **likelihood** of something happening and how **serious** the threat is. Constraints on resources prevent us from developing contingency plans for every likely threat: it would be impractical. To avoid or at least reduced a 'crisis management' syndrome, we do need to establish threats which are most likely to occur, during the planning period.

(a) **Threats matrix**

		Likelihood of occurrence		
		High	Likely	Unlikely
Seriousness	Very			
	Average			
	Low			

(b) The aim is to make sure we are focused on threats that could damage our prospects and jeopardise business performance. This technique forces us to consider the likelihood of something occurring and how serious it is. We can then decide whether resources should be allocated to develop contingency plans or whether we simply monitor the situation.

3.2 In the same way, we cannot pursue every opportunity that presents itself, and often it is not appropriate for us to do so if it does not fit with our strategic objectives and goals.

Opportunities matrix

<table>
<tr><td rowspan="2"></td><td colspan="3" style="text-align:center">Probability of success</td></tr>
<tr><td>High</td><td>Medium</td><td>Low</td></tr>
<tr><td>High</td><td></td><td></td><td></td></tr>
<tr><td>**Attractiveness** Medium</td><td></td><td></td><td></td></tr>
<tr><td>Low</td><td></td><td></td><td></td></tr>
</table>

Action Programme 1

Try and complete both threats and opportunities matrix for Biocatalysts.

Compare your answer with ours at the end of the chapter.

3.3 **Realities of the case study analysis**

(a) Usually we do not have the right, or enough, information to enable us to prioritise analysis, and in the case study we cannot go out and obtain the information we want. Therefore we must make some **intelligent and reasonable assumptions**. If we have done a professional job on analysis, there will be enough information to make reasonable assumptions and the results of analysis can be used to provide the evidence to support these assumptions.

(b) Remember that one of your objectives is to pass the examination. **If we can get the Critical Success Factors right, we will have identified, broadly, the question areas.**

4 CRITICAL SUCCESS FACTORS (CSFs)

4.1 The terminology varies from company to company for example Significant Performance Indicators (SPIs), Key Results Areas (KRAs), but Critical Success Factors is one of the most common terms used.

4.2 The stepping stone from analysis to decision is agreeing critical success factors which can only be determined from the results of analysis. These are the factors that will impact on the organisation's ability to pursue the opportunities it has identified and intends to implement.

4.3 Critical success factors are any factors essential to the success of organisation and strategy and can include:

- Profitability and cash flow
- Market development and market position
- Productivity
- Identifying/developing competitive advantage and new product development
- Marketing orientation, employee attitudes and public responsibility
- Marketing management skills and personnel leadership
- Competitive positioning and product leadership

Each CSF will have key issues associated with it issues that influence/affect the CSFs. Examples are given below.

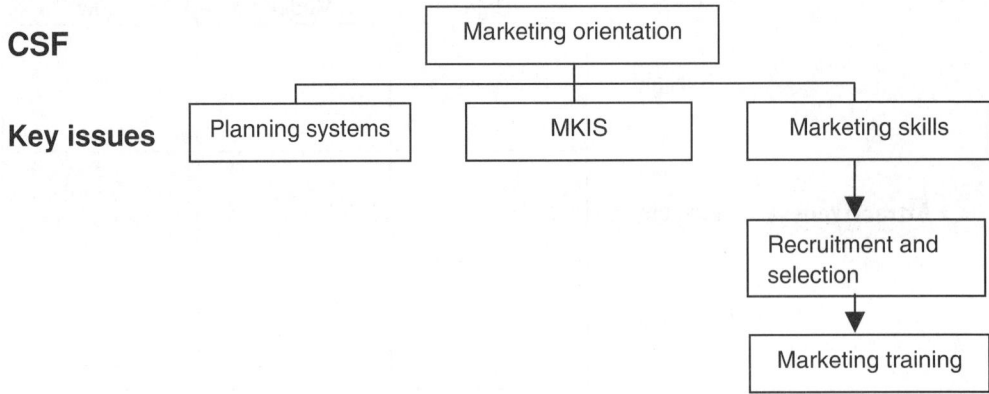

CSF

```
                    ┌─────────────────────────┐
                    │  Marketing orientation  │
                    └─────────────────────────┘
```

Key issues

Planning systems	MKIS	Marketing skills

```
                                      ↓
                              ┌──────────────────┐
                              │  Recruitment and │
                              │  selection       │
                              └──────────────────┘
                                      ↓
                              ┌──────────────────┐
                              │ Marketing training│
                              └──────────────────┘
```

4.4 Identifying and agreeing CSFs ensures corporate decisions are focused on the issues that will produce the desired results. Major problems/obstacles to success must be dealt with; for example delivering products that customers want may require re-structuring the organisation. Resources must be allocated to support critical success factor outcomes.

Action programme 2

From your analysis, identify the Critical Success Factors you believe Biocatalysts face, and compare them with ours at the end of the chapter.

Action Programme review

1 **Threats matrix**

Likelihood of occurrence

		High	Likely	Unlikely
Seriousness	Very	Growing anti GMOs	Government withdraw funding	
	Average	Competitors merge Legislation	Russia or China enter market	
	Low			

Remember some of the issues that emerge can be both opportunities and threats depending on the organisation's ability to identify and address the opportunity or threat.

Opportunities matrix

Probability of success

	High	Medium	Low
High	Diagnostics Food		
Medium		Environmental products	
Low		Changing fashions eg faded jeans	

Attractiveness labels rows: High, Medium, Low

2   Biocatalysts's CSF's

CSFs	*and*	**Key issues**
• Competitive positioning		Competitive strategy Brand/values Marketing skills
• Distribution		Agency skills/expertise/knowledge New channels/Web
• New Product development		Processes Marketing information Marketing skills
• Communications		Strategic and integrated Marketing skills Brand Changing perceptions
• Marketing information		International problems
• Relationship marketing		Stakeholders/nurture relationships
• International market entry		Level of involvement
• Funding/cash flow		Cost efficiency, profitability, growth

BPP PUBLISHING

8

Step 5: Establishing strategic direction. Corporate/business decisions

Introduction

In this chapter we will:

- Turn our environmental analysis into a forecast and quantified objective to establish a planning gap for Biocatalysts

- Assess the role of vision and mission, and developing them for Biocatalysts

- Use the Ansoff matrix to identify strategic options for the business

- Develop and use criteria for evaluating and selecting strategies to fill the planning gap

- Consider the potential pitfalls for students working at this critical case stage

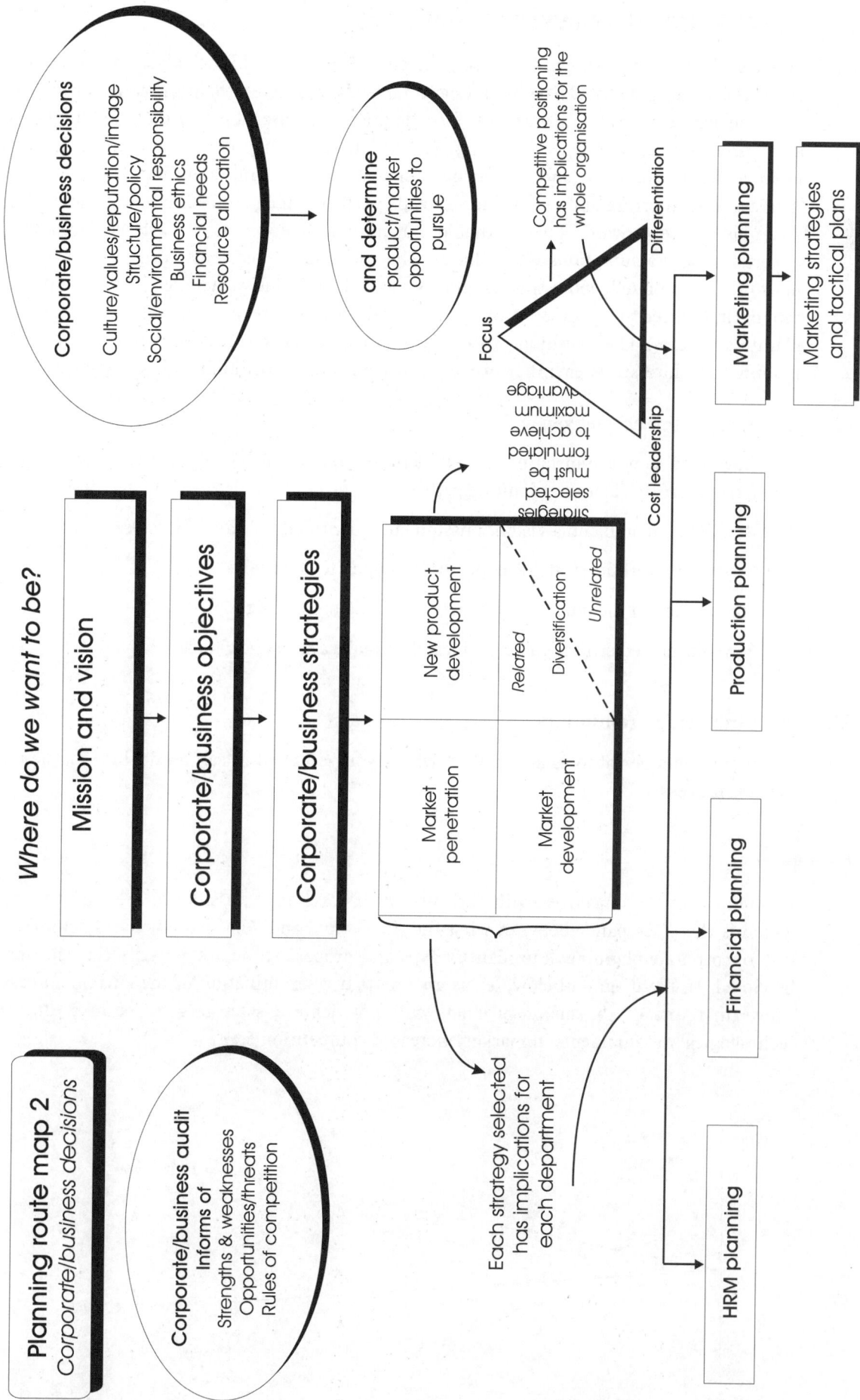

Corporate/business decisions

Culture/values/reputation/image
Structure/policy
Social/environmental responsibility
Business ethics
Financial needs
Resource allocation

and determine product/market opportunities to pursue

Competitive positioning has implications for the whole organisation

Differentiation

Focus

Cost leadership

strategies selected must be formulated to achieve maximum advantage

Marketing planning

Marketing strategies and tactical plans

Where do we want to be?

Mission and vision

Corporate/business objectives

Corporate/business strategies

Market penetration

Market development

New product development

Related Diversification *Unrelated*

Production planning

Financial planning

HRM planning

Each strategy selected has implications for each department

Planning route map 2
Corporate/business decisions

Corporate/business audit
Informs of
Strengths & weaknesses
Opportunities/threats
Rules of competition

© Juanita Cockton, 1997

1 ESTABLISHING STRATEGIC DIRECTION

1.1 So far we have been working to establish the current position of Biocatalyst's business. You have seen a number of tools, techniques and models employed to help us really get to grips with the 'where are we now' question for this business. Case step 5 is the one which will allow us to answer 'where are we going'. It is the first real step down the path of decision making. Many students (and, in fairness, managers) find this a difficult step to take. Analysis is comforting and reassuring. It keeps you busy and productive but at some point you must move forward. This is that point, and from now on you will be faced with uncertainty and assumptions which have to be addressed if decisions are to be made. Try not to worry too much about this; it reflects the real world but remember that assumptions can be monitored by your control systems and that we are only working through the planning process. The planning process is iterative, and decisions made now can still be modified or addressed later if they prove unworkable at the operational planning level.

1.2 By the end of this chapter you will:

(a) Have seen how a translation of your environmental audit can provide a bottom line forecast for Biocatalyst's planning gap

(b) Be able to recommend a vision, mission and quantified objective for Biocatalyst

(c) Have identified the strategic opportunities open to Biocatalyst

(d) Have reviewed the multifactor matrix as a decision making tool

(e) Have developed criteria to help Biocatalyst make a strategic choice

Skills and knowledge reminders

1.3 There are a number of tools and models which you will need to call on during this step of the case process.

Gap analysis

1.4 By comparing the objectives with the current forecast, it is possible to measure the gap which is the discrepancy between what the firm wants and what it is likely to achieve. A task of corporate planning is to identify gaps and propose strategies whereby the gaps may be closed. In the diagram below, let us assume that re-examination of the current forecast shows that one of the major products will not achieve sales targets (perhaps due to technological developments in market, increased competition etc).

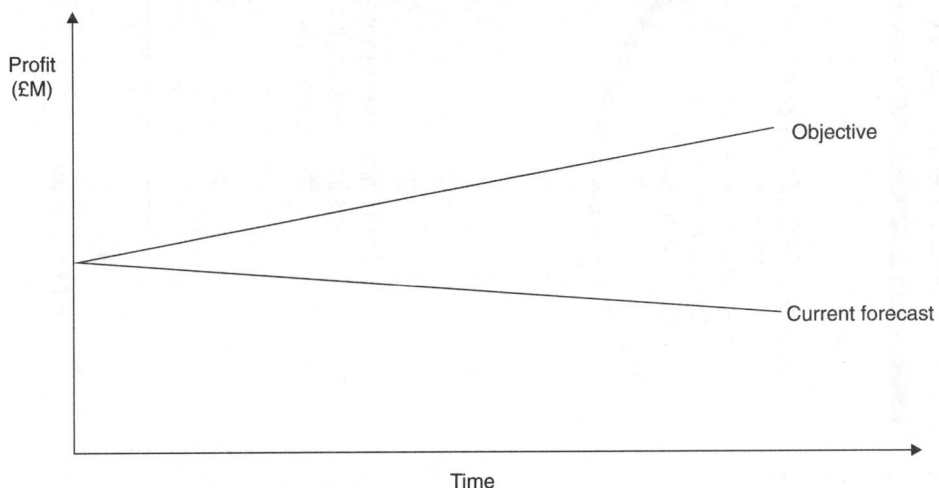

1.5   **Ansoff matrix**

	Existing products	**New Products**
Existing markets	Market penetration strategy 1. More purchasing and usage from existing customers 2. Gain customers from competitors 3. Convert non-users into users (where both are in same market segment)	Product development strategy 1. Product modification via new features 2. Different quality levels 3. New product.
New markets	Market development strategy 1. New market segments 2. New distribution channels 3. New geographic areas eg exports	Diversification strategy 1. Related 2. Unrelated

The Ansoff matrix is an excellent framework for helping you to identify and communicate the strategic options facing an organisation. It can usefully be modified to create a nine box grid which logs existing, **modified** and new products (and markets).

1.6   Trade-offs inevitably occur between levels of risk and levels of return. When considering entering new markets or new market segments for example, (Ansoff's market development strategy) the following trade-offs are likely.

	Low exit barrier	**High exit barrier**
Low entry barrier	Low stable returns	Low risk returns
High entry barrier	High stable returns	High risk returns

1.7   A variety of matrix analyses can be used. You can invent your own according to your particular product and market situation or, better still, the one in the case study. However, here are some established matrices which have a degree of universality as well as a history of success.

1.8   **The multi-factor decision matrix**

To be customer focused, organisations must make all decisions based not just on what they want but also on what makes sense from the customer's view.

There may be a very attractive opportunity in the market but whether it is right for your business to exploit it is determined essentially by the customer's perception.

This model helps the company assess:

(a)   The quality of the opportunity
(b)   The potential competitive advantage they would gain by exploiting it

Strategy attractiveness

	High	Medium	Low
High	▓	▓	
Medium	▓		
Low			

Competitive advantage (Business strengths)

In this exam, the examiners are interested in process and so want to see the criteria you develop from the case study to drive this model.

1.9 Other models can help you assess what approach to adopt once a strategy has been selected. Of these:

(a) The directional policy matrix considers the amount of competition against the attractiveness of the opportunity (but does not take account of customers and so is less useful we feel)

(b) The Arthur D Little model looks at the stage of the industry life cycle against competitive advantage and so does take account of the customer but not the objectives and needs of the firm

1.10 As always, no one tool will do everything for you: each can add to the picture, so be prepared to call on any if it helps a particular case.

(a) **The directional policy matrix (George Day)**

Market attractiveness / **Degree of competition**

Market attractiveness	Strong	Medium	Weak
High	PROTECT POSITION • Invest to grow at maximum digestible rate • Concentrate effort on maintaining strength	INVEST TO BUILD • Challenge for leadership • Build selectively on strengths • Reinforce vulnerable areas	BUILDS SELECTIVELY • Specialize around limited strengths • Seeks ways to overcome weaknesses • Withdraw if indications
Medium	BUILD SELECTIVELY • Invest heavily in most attractive segments • Build up ability to counter competition • Emphasise profitability by raising productivity	SELECTIVITY/MANAGE FOR EARNINGS • Protect existing program • Concentrate investments in segments where profitability is good and risk is relatively low	LIMITED EXPANSION OR HARVEST • Look for ways to expand without high risk otherwise, minimise investment and rationalise operations
Low	PROTECT AND REFOCUS • Manage for current earnings • Concentrate on attractive segments • Defend strengths	MANAGE FOR EARNINGS • Protect position in most profitable segments • Upgrade product line • minimise investment	DIVEST • Sell at time that will maximise cash value • Cut fixed costs and avoid investment meanwhile

(b) **Arthur D Little matrix**

Stage of industry maturity

	Embryonic	Growth	Mature	Ageing
Dominant	Grow fast Build barriers Act offensively	Grow fast Aim for cost leadership Defend position Act offensively	Defend position Increase the importance of cost Act offensively	Defend position Focus Consider withdrawal
Strong	Grow fast Differentiate	Lower cost Differentiate Attack small firms	Lower costs Differentiate Focus	Harvest
Favourable	Grow fast Differentiate	Focus Differentiate Defend	Focus Differentiate Hit smaller firms	Harvest
Tenable	Grow with the industry Focus	Hold-on or withdraw Niche Aim for growth	Hold-on or withdraw Niche	Withdraw
Weak	Search for a niche Attempt to catch others	Niche or withdraw	Withdraw	Withdraw

Competitive position (row axis label)

Establish a vision and mission

1.11 These are important starting points for any planning process and both need to be developed to provide the parameters of our planning.

(a) **Visions** are aspirational: to be No. 1 or the recognised expert in a particular field. They will help inform our objective setting.

(b) **Mission statements** answer the question 'what business are we in?' and will help us in the selection of appropriate products and markets.

Tutor Tip

You have already given some consideration to visions and missions in order to do your analysis. You cannot identify competitors or draw market maps if you haven't defined the business. What you are addressing now is:

WHAT BUSINESS **SHOULD** THEY BE IN?

Take care with cases which supply you with visions and missions: they can be product focused or just red herrings. We would advise you to carefully review and if necessary challenge any 'statements' which might have been made earlier.

Revisit our analysis to help us quantify our planning gap

1.12   **Auditing the present and forecasting the future**

(a)   It is only when we have a clear picture of where we are now (and how we've come to arrive here) that we can decide realistically where we want to be in the future. This relationship between auditing and forecasting can be seen in the following figure.

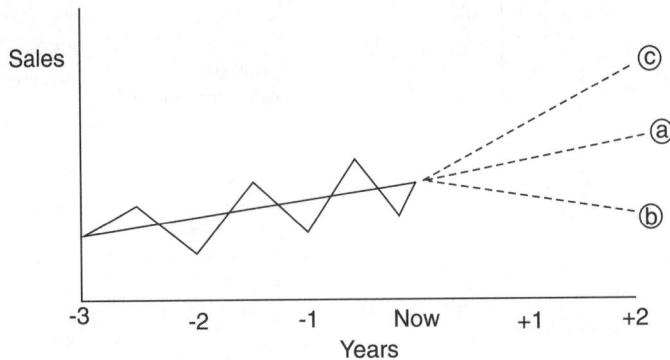

Auditing and forecasting

(b)   Here you can see how sales for the last three years have been plotted and a line of 'best fit' added. One approach is to simply extend this line indicating where (all things being equal) the business could expect to be in two years (a).

However all things are not equal. Some people might argue that the more recent past is a more reliable indicator of the future than the more distant past and so weight the last year accordingly. Furthermore one or more of the external environmental factors may be on the verge of radical change.

   (a)   The collapse of Amano or a sudden surge in consumer support for enzyme based products could boost Biocatalyst sales to (c).

   (b)   A backlash of opinion about GMOs or a sudden economic recession could make (b) a more likely scenario.

(c)   Your external analysis completed at Step 3 and reviewed in the opportunities and threats matrices in the last chapter will inform this bottom line forecast of your planning gap. In essence you are trying to add the forecast of how profitable the business would be if we stuck with the current products in the current markets.

Having established the bottom line, we now need to add the top line, created once you have set a realistic objective.

(d)   Again this decision should not be made until the external analysis is complete. You may want to double your profits this year but is that realistic given the market and environmental conditions?

In the diagram below, the economy may be booming (leading to a 'high' objective for sales) but competitive activity may be intense, leading to poorer forecast results.

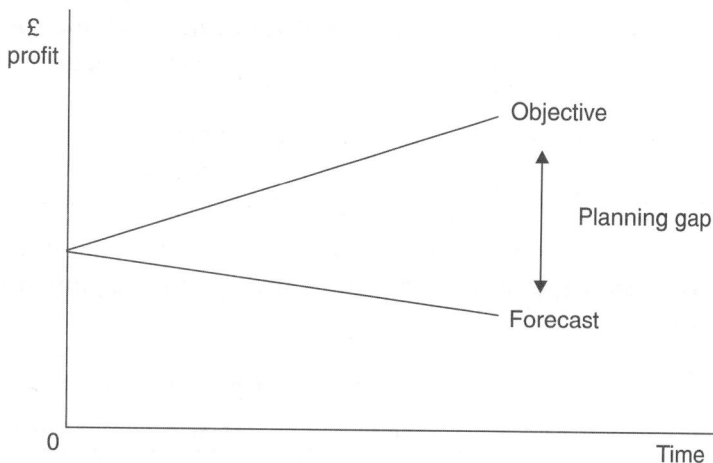

(e) We will now have established a planning gap which is realistic and credible because it was informed from analysis rather than wishful thinking.

Tutor Tip

In practice, the objective will often be a trade off between what the stakeholders aspire to achieve and the assessment of what is realistic or reasonable. There are two things you should bear in mind when writing up a case answer:

(a) Acknowledge the stakeholder's expectation

(b) Justify your objective

.... it is conservative because

.... it is bullish because

Complete your Ansoff matrix

1.13 The opportunities identified in your environmental audit should now provide us with the context for identifying product market opportunity:

(a) Technology breakthrough creates the opportunity for new diagnostic products
(b) Political change provides funding for new development of GMO products
(c) Business growth increases demand for textile and food based products

Completing the Ansoff matrix requires you to look at your environmental analysis and say 'so what'? If this changes, what are the product market implications?

Selecting strategies

1.14 This is the heart of decision making and examiners will be looking hard at how you do this. Decisions made need to be:

- Objective
- Customer focused
- Justified

The multifactor matrix criteria will be scrutinised and it **must** be case specific:

Not	But
Increase revenue	The potential to generate at least £220k per opportunity; this is 10 times more than currently achieved but reflects the 'best of breed' competitor Amano

Notice in this example the criterion is not only **quantified** and **case specific** but **justified**. You leave the examiner in no doubt that you understand what you need to do and how to do it.

Filling the planning gaps

1.15 Once the criterion is determined, the various strategic options can be applied to it. You will **not** need to show the calculation of **weighting** and **rating** but simply acknowledge it has been done.

Strategy attractiveness

1.16 Those strategic options in the high and high/med boxes are those you will implement in order to fill the planning gap.

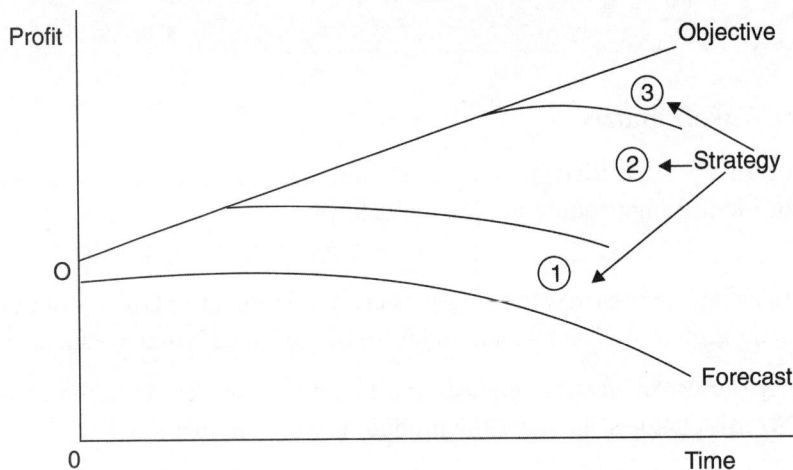

1.17 All the business has to do now is:

(a) **Assess the business implications** of selecting these strategies which we will consider in Step 6

(b) Develop the **operational plans** needed to implement these selected strategies which we will work on in Step 7

Action Programme 1

A knowledge review

Before we complete this step for Biocatalysts take a few minutes to check that you are completely happy with the process and tools which underpin this stage.

1   How will you decide on a reasonable objective for the case company?

2   Where will the criteria for assessing the strength of competitive advantage come from?

3   What do you do if the potential contribution of the strategies in the high/med cells of the matrix are insufficient to fill the planning gap?

4   What characteristics would you expect the examiner to be looking for in a 'good' mission statement?

2   BIOCATALYSTS: WHAT NEEDS TO BE DONE

Tutor Tip

You are now ready to start making decisions and you will need to own these in the exam room. If you are working in a syndicate group, it has been quite appropriate for you to share your work up to now but take care from here on in. If the examiner gets twenty scripts from the same centre with a word perfect mission statement, he or she is likely to assume a group answer, which will result in an automatic fail. Discuss and review together by all means but the words need to be yours.

A vision

2.1   Remember the vision is an aspiration. It needs to be realistic and something which will inspire the organisation to strive for its achievement. A good vision can act as something of a 'crie de coeur' for the business.

Action Programme 2

Establishing a Vision

Take a few minutes to look at the following possible visions for Biocatalyst. Which would you reject and why? Which would you choose?

1   It is our vision to be the global leader in the development and production of enzyme solutions for industry.

2   We are in the business of providing enzyme solutions to our clients.

3   We want to be the first choice provider for organisations who have 'other sector' clients who have enzyme problems or opportunities.

4   We want to be the biggest producer of bulk enzymes in the food and textile industries of Europe.

5   We want to be the acknowledged technical leader in UK based enzyme research.

Turn to the end of the chapter for our comments.

2.2   Take another 10 minutes to craft your own vision for Biocatalysts.

> A Vision
>
>
>
>
>
>
>
>

Check it for:

- Relevance
- Realism

What business is Biocatalysts in?

2.3   We must now tackle the mission statement. What do you think of this for Biocatalysts?

> We are in the business of helping our globally-based customers improve the efficiency and effectiveness of their processes through the provision of tailor made enzyme solutions, employing leading edge technology, combined with over 13 years of experience and expertise.

Comments

....

....

....

It is a little long winded but it incorporates the **customer benefits** of 'efficiency and effectiveness'; it has focus; it is for processes and there is a hint of differentiation built around the technology in safe hands.

An alternative mission

2.4

> We will be the leading global supplier of specialised enzymes to diagnostic, food processing and GMO sectors within five years.

2.5   Again take 10 minutes to craft your own mission

> A Mission for Biocatalysts
>
>
>
>
>
>
>

Check it for:

- Distinctiveness
- Focus on customer benefits

Tutor Tip

When using a vision or mission in the exam, do first check it makes sense against the additional information and questions set. For example, if you set out to be No. 1 in Europe and the extra information is about opportunities in Japan, you will need to review your vision.

Action Programme 3

Establishing the Planning Gap

Establishing a planning gap

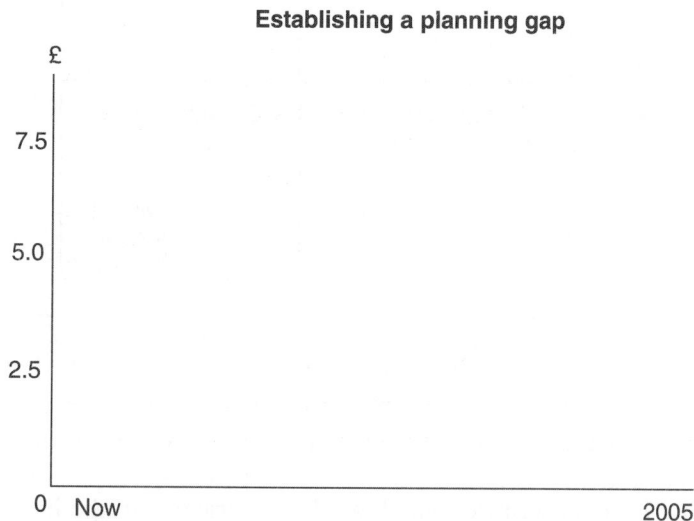

Before you turn to the end of this chapter to look at our thoughts on a possible planning gap, have a go at producing one for yourself:

1   Check out current revenue and profit

2   What do you think will happen to both if Biocatalyst continues to operate as it has with the same products and markets?

3   Next, think about the future environment and what the shareholders might expect, and try and set a realistic objective

4   Can you justify your decisions?

Do not agonise about these decisions: be brave and a little bold. Remember you are in essence quantifying the added value marketing might give to this business.

Now turn to the end of the chapter to see our planning gap but remember there will be many variations equally acceptable. Ours is only a sample developed to show you the process.

The strategic options

2.6   The only problem now we have established the planning gap, is to decide how to fill it.

2.7   The first step is to identify the options. The company can only expand its business with combinations of products and markets. Its strategic options are based around four strategies:

- Market penetration
- Market development
- Product development
- Diversification

151

BPP PUBLISHING

Action Programme 4

Ansoff options

We have begun to populate the Ansoff Matrix for Biocatalyst – what can you add?

Products

	Existing	New
Markets — Existing	• Increased penetration of olive oil growers	• GMOs
Markets — New	• Asia markets for current products	• Consultancy services / • Bulk enzyme production

2.8 Having identified the strategic alternatives **open to a business**, the next step is to decide which are **most attractive** for the business. Remember there may be an excellent opportunity in the market, but your firm may **not** be suited to exploiting it.

2.9 You are looking for opportunities which are both attractive to the business and where the business has the propensity to deliver a competitive advantage.

Making strategic decisions

2.10 The **multifactor matrix** is an excellent framework to ensure you have taken account of both the attractiveness of the opportunity and the potential competitive advantage.

2.11 Examiners will be looking for evidence that you can adapt the theory to meet the specific context of the case. That means case specific criteria are needed. What you do **not** need to do is add the weighting and rating to calculate each strategic option. It is highly unlikely you would have the data to do this in a meaningful way anyway.

2.12 What you **do** need to do is explain that you would, or indeed have, weighted and rated the alternatives and then demonstrate the assumed or potential outcome on a multifactor framework.

Action Programme 5

Biocatalyst Decision Criteria

Take ten minutes to think about the criteria you could use for assessing Biocatalysts' options.

You only need 5-6 in each list, but make them as case specific as possible.

Strategy market attractiveness

1...

2...

3...

4...

5...

6...

Competitive position

1...

2...

3...

4...

5...

6...

Our example is provided for you at the end of this chapter.

Biocatalysts's strategy attractiveness

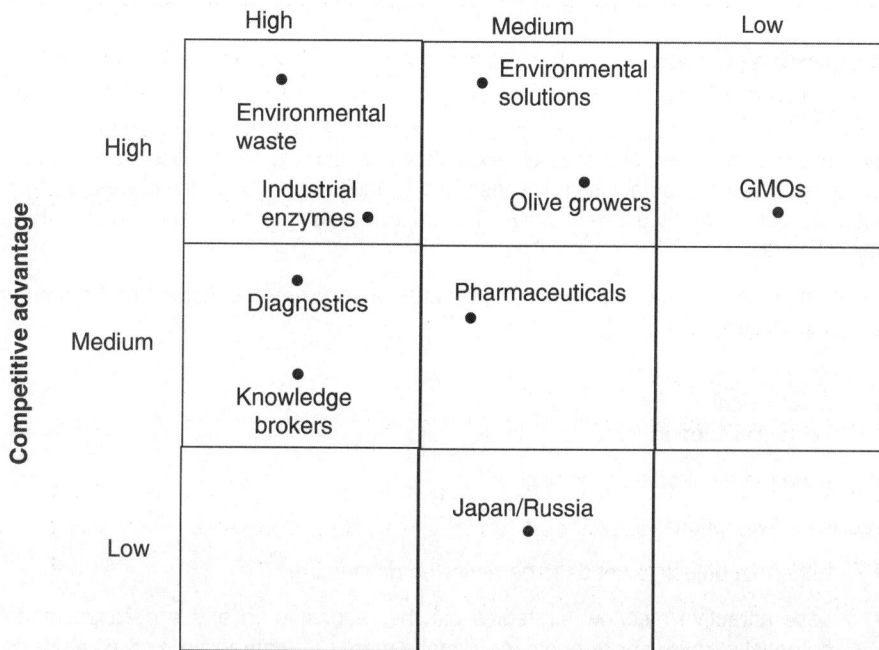

2.13 Note that there is **no single right or wrong answer as to where to log opportunities on this matrix**. The examiners will be looking for your thought process and in the exam you would want to highlight the selected strategies and comment on their justification. You may like to conclude your strategy section with a completed planning gap, showing how your selected strategies will fill it.

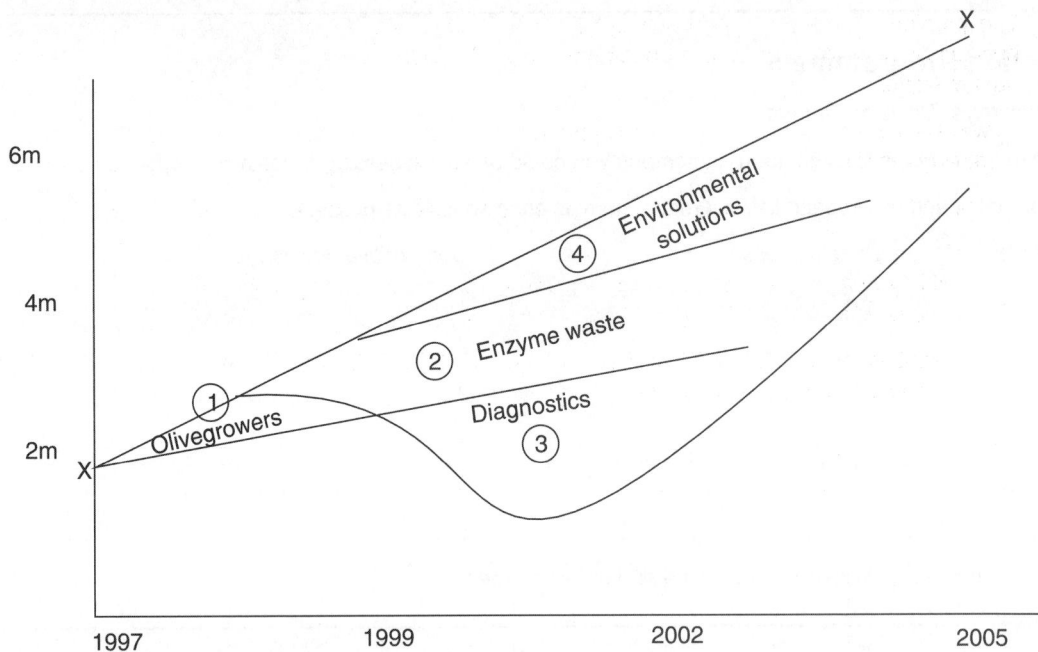

Filling Biocatalysts's planning gap

Action Programme review

1   *A knowledge review*

   1   By considering likely stakeholder expectations, current and past performance and what competitors seem to be achieving. These to be considered against the general state of the market but there can be many different views. The important thing is to be specific and able to justify the objective set.

   2   It should come from the customers buying criteria so always an aspect of the marketing mix. So for Biocatalysts:

   •   Safety
   •   Customisation
   •   Technical support

   may all be more important than price

   3   There are two options:

   •   Either the objective needs to be reviewed downwards

   •   Less attractive med/low strategies can be reconsidered and a decision made about their potential to review or re-engineer to make them more attractive. For example, if this strategy was unattractive to the firm because of the high levels of investment needed, perhaps a partner could be found.

   4   Simple, distinctive and based on customer benefits **not** product features

2   *Establishing vision*

   1   Simply unrealistic – Biocatalyst is a tiny global player.

   2   No, this is a mission statement, not a good one as it has no source of differentiation incorporated in it.

   3   This is quite good – it provides a niche focus 'other sector' and would need the company to build a reputation for problem solving. It is a vision which might appeal to the scientists who make up the Biocatalyst community.

   4   This is not the business Biocatalysts are in; bulk production is a different sector and is not one in which they operate with core competence.

   5   This could be appealing to the staff but is too narrow a focus to provide commercial returns in this global market.

The problem, as we saw in our analysis, is that profits are not growing although revenue is. The business is currently spread too thin in terms of products and markets and new products are developed but not exploited.

However they are positioned to increase revenues if the global distribution is sorted and some pro-active marketing is added – so a slightly bullish objective of £6m or even £8m revenue could be justified.

Notice that, at approximately £250k per new enzyme, this would need 14 launches over 1998 – 2005: less than last year!

The real key though is the profit. If you assume a 15% gross profit margin this needs to be increased from its current low level to £1.5m by 2005.

Rationalisation of products and markets will be needed to get rid of unprofitable activity. Such a strategy would make the planning gap look like this:

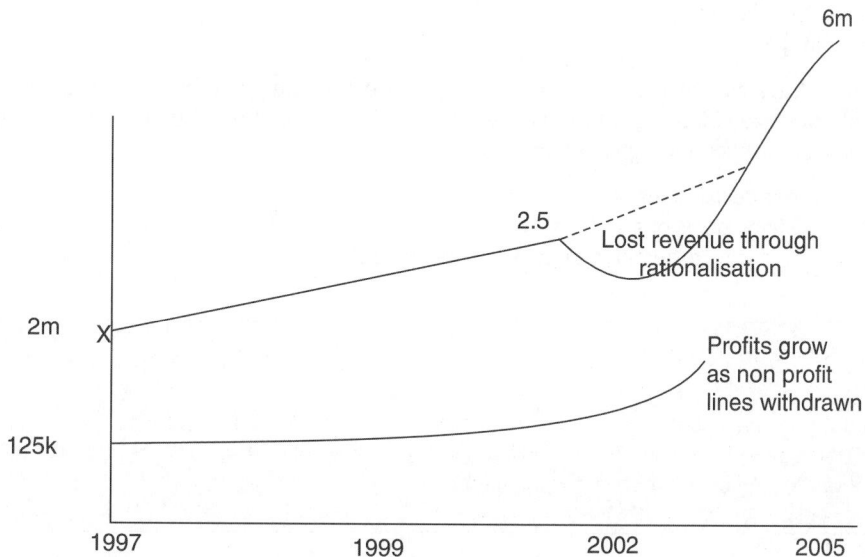

Tutor Tip

Look at how adding legends to your diagrams helps with the process of justification and explanation

---

3   **Establishing the Planning Gap**

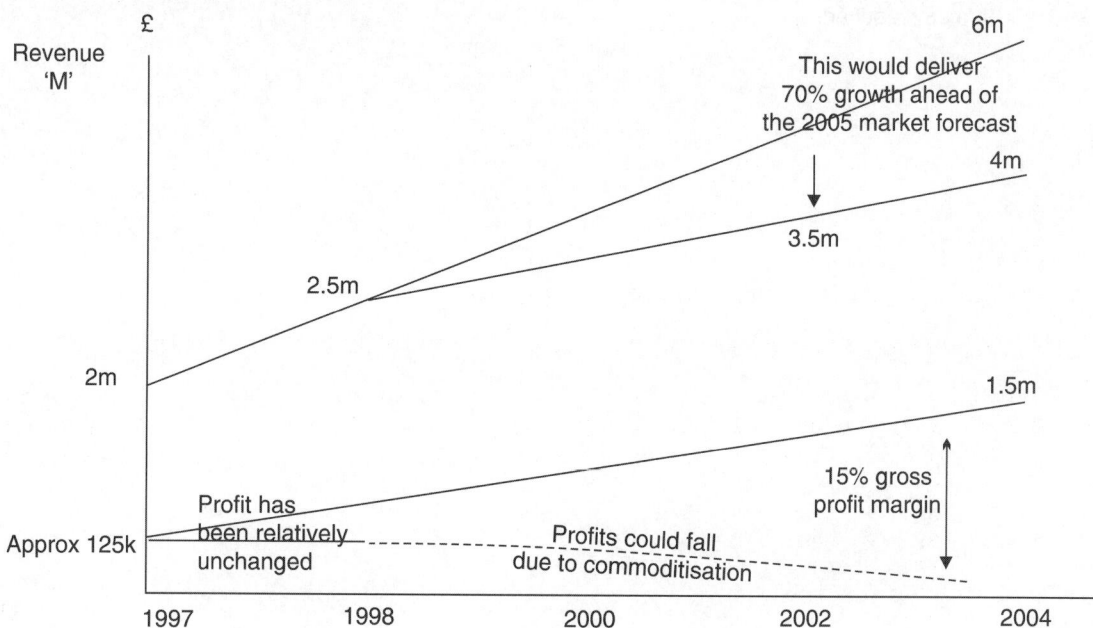

BPP PUBLISHING

You can see we have included both the profit and revenue picture on one graph. You may prefer to do it on two.

The pitfalls

This is the Case step which perhaps causes students the biggest problems and not surprisingly there are a number of potential pitfalls which need to be avoided.

1   **Not making decisions is perhaps the most obvious pitfall.** Students are often unwilling to decide on an object or preferred strategies because they are worried their decisions will not be in line with the examiner's opinions. Instead they try and sit on the fence. You can spot scripts of these candidates by the 'weasel' words they employ:

- Perhaps
- On the one hand
- On balance
- Maybe

As we have said before, there are no single correct answers to a case study, so the examiner will not have fixed ideas about the right strategy. What he or she will be looking for is evidence that you have worked through a logical process resulting in :

- Clear decision making
- Justified decisions
- Convincing arguments in favour of those decisions

Tutor Tip

If you are not confident about the recommendations you are making, it is unlikely you would convince the case organisation or the examiner. The successful selling of strategy in business is being directly tested in how you present your case proposals.

2   **Failing to add the numbers.** We appreciate most marketers hate the thought of numbers, but trust us, it is essential. Objectives and decisions criteria need quantification and those numbers must be drawn from the case study. You must understand them and be able to work with them.

3   **Failing to use the analysis to inform decision making**. Too many candidates fall into the trap of treating each case step in isolation and the result is commercial nonsense.

There is no point in recommending a strategy of expansion through acquisition if a business has no cash.

Neither is a long-term product development strategy sensible if there is a short-term survival strategy required.

4   *Ansoff options*

A number of options emerged during analysis.

Products

	Existing	New
Existing	Environmental maintenance Waste treatment Textiles Health care Unique speciality foods Alcohol, baking, fats/oils Fruit/wine, flavour, protein Animal foods, leather Paper/pulp Chemical biotransformation	More testing kits GMOs By-products High tech diagnostic New Tech foods Full consultancy service Technical backup service
New	Geographic - eg Russia China USA Japan New industries/sectors Oil spillage Pharmaceutical Licensing	Knowledge brokers Backward Forward integration

(Markets on vertical axis: Existing / New)

5   *Biocatalysts's decision criteria*

Evaluation of strategic options

Each strategy must be evaluated for its attractiveness to the business and the competitive advantage/position it offers. The best evaluation tool for this purpose is the GE matrix. Management will agree and prioritise the criteria for strategy attractiveness and research on customers can determine the competitive position. We already have some information on why customers buy which would form this criteria, for example:

Strategy/market attractiveness

1   Profitability of net less than X%
2   Marketing growth potential
3   Levels of competition
4   Investment required of not more than X%
5   Synergy with existing operations
6   New skills required
7   Speed to implement
8   Degree of risk

Competitive position

1.   Improving efficiency
2   Cost effectiveness
3   Convenience
4   Safety
5   Availability
6   Consistency and quality
7   Value for money
8   Technical support

Weighting and rating the criteria enables us to plot the strategies on the matrix to reveal which strategies are worth pursuing and should be rejected.

Biocatalysts need to plan for the short- and medium-term. In this fast changing, dynamic market longer term strategies can be difficult to identify. Strategy selection will need to provide immediate profits given our financial position, followed by medium-term strategies that will grow the business and establish a competitive position.

9

Step 6: Business implications: developing and implementing strategic marketing plans

1 BUSINESS IMPLICATIONS OF MARKETING PLANS

1.1 Marketers developing marketing strategies and plans to meet the challenges and demands of the business environment must think of the **implications to the business of developing and implementing their plans.** These implications will usually be to the business as a whole as well as to marketing. Marketers who fail to consider these issues are not thinking or acting strategically and jeopardise the chances of success. **Business implications include:**

- Culture of the organisation and whether or not it has a marketing orientation
- Structure
- Financial and funding
- Processes
- People
- Communications and information systems

1.2 **Marketing implications** are inevitably interlinked with business implications and are those strategic issues associated with marketing activities which include:

(a) **Customer focus** (implicit in a marketing orientation and dependent on good marketing intelligence, marketing information systems and the ability to segment markets)

(b) **Product/services** offered and the quality, benefits and value they represent to the customer (including e.g. accessibility – place, value for money – price)

(c) **Customer service** (implicit in the people, processes and physical evidence policies)

(d) Communications, positioning and the brand

Tutor Tip

With some case studies more time would be spent on this than with others, depending on how obvious or serious the business implications are. With Biocatalysts, for example, clearly there were business implications, and a few notes need to be made on what these are. Some might come up as a question eg establishing a marketing information system, or might need to be referred to briefly, if relevant, within a strategic marketing plan question.

---

2 MARKETING ORIENTATION

2.1 A marketing orientation ensures that management's key tasks are to determine the needs and wants of selected target markets, and to adopt appropriate structures and design activities to meet those needs. Marketing research is a key activity and marketing intelligence forms the basis of decision making. Marketing programmes are tailored to meet the needs of specific, selected groups of people with similar needs and characteristics.

Clues to marketing orientation

People

2.2 **Board level/senior management**

Marketing is represented at board level by qualified marketing professionals. The Chief Executive, from whatever background, has a marketing qualification or training.

2.3 **Staff**

People are valued and trusted by the organisation and this is reflected in internal policies and procedures, and in management attitudes to employees.

Culture and structure

2.4 The values of the organisation are reflected in the way staff are treated, how responsive the organisation is to the local community and the responsibility assumed for social and environmental issues.

Customers are not considered the sole responsibility of marketing and sales, but the responsibility of everyone in the organisation. All employees understand their role and contribution in delivering benefits to customers; they know who their customers are and what is important to them.

2.5 Organisational structure is designed to meet the challenges of external demands rather than internal convenience. Continuous improvement is a corporate goal that is assimilated into departmental, team and individual objectives.

Tasks and processes

2.6 **Strategies**

Senior management are concerned with the long-term future and direction of the organisation and developing strategies that reflect the reality of the market place. Marketing plays a pivotal role in determining what product market opportunities the organisation pursues. Financial resources for marketing are determined by objectives to be achieved, not spare cash left over.

2.7 Marketing information

(a) There is a **formalised** Marketing Information System (MKIS) feeding into a Management Information System (MIS) and **primary marketing research is regarded as an essential activity**. Management decisions are based on the results of marketing research activities and reflect business strengths and competitive positioning.

(b) The business understands its business environment, the likelihood and nature of opportunities and threats and how well it is performing compared with competitors. It understands customer behaviour and the values customers attribute to the organisation's brand(s).

2.8 Co-ordination and integration

(a) Planning and control is recognised as the most efficient and effective way to use limited resources and organise activities. Activities across the organisation are co-ordinated and integrated by senior management to ensure consistency of delivery and take advantage of maximising value-added opportunities.

(b) Departments understand each others' problems and needs, and work in partnership to solve problems and accomplish overall departmental and corporate objectives.

(c) This partnership philosophy extends to suppliers, distribution channels and other stakeholders who are included in the planning process and whose activities are assimilated into the organisation's plans.

2.9 Communications

Communications, internal and external, with employees, customers and all stakeholders, incorporate values and positioning, and reflect the needs of different target groups. Two-way communications are encouraged, with mechanisms for listening as well as talking.

2.10 New product/service development

New product development involves the customer either directly or through marketing intelligence and customer contribution to this process is considered fundamental. Customer service is designed in at the start, developed with the product or service and is seen as key to competitive advantage and customer retention. Different customer needs are reflected in different products, and services are designed to meet those needs.

2.11 Measuring effectiveness

Setting targets and standards is regarded as pivotal to successful outcomes and measuring effectiveness as an integral part of planning. Employees have customer satisfaction performance targets as well as the usual easily quantified targets. Evaluation of successes and failures determines the nature of future plans.

2.12 Training and development

Training and development of employees is recognised as key to ensuring business success, and marketing and customer service training is **not confined to marketing personnel**. Appraisals form part of continual improvement, and the development and motivation of employees is seen as a significant management task. Training and development is also seen as the most effective way of ensuring employees are prepared and able to accept and implement change in response to market conditions.

Innovation and organisation culture

2.13 An important aspect of marketing orientation is innovation. This is the only way businesses can stay ahead. Central to innovation is an **environment that allows creativity**. Control therefore, must be flexible and is able to adapt when circumstances demand a different approach.

2.14 A key driver of innovation is **attitude**.

(a) People in the organisation are not interested in following but in leading, wanting to be first. This attitude will also affect the type of innovation.

(b) Incremental innovation is less risky, costly and more likely to succeed due to its nature. The business learns as it evolves and, because the innovation is usually built on something the customers already know and understand, they are likely to appreciate the 'new' benefits.

(c) Innovation can be revolutionary and involve 'megaprojects' or 'do everything'. This requires heavy investment, the 'unknowns' are greater including the market's response and the learning curves are far steeper. It is only usually an option if it is a matter of business survival (due to falling so far behind the competition) or the innovation is known to meet a significant identified need and has guaranteed commercial viability.

Continuous improvement

2.15 An attitude of, and systems for, continuous improvement is also essential in developing an innovative culture and environment. Change can be very disruptive and threatening, leaving people concerned with issues that are not productive and lead to low morale.

2.16 Change can be gentle and continuous, a part of everyday life, so people are used to it and work with it. This requires flexibility in structures, systems and processes so that events can evolve gradually, but continuously, where appropriate. An attitude of wanting to improve on what is done now is encouraged through rewards and recognition. Continuous improvement is included in personal and team targets.

3   STRUCTURE

Key factors affecting organisation design/structure

3.1   **Internal influences**

- **Mission**: corporate objectives and strategies
- **Culture**: management style/attitudes to control will be reflected in design
- **People**: skills requirements and levels
- **Task**: the product made and the way work is organised
- **Processes**: technology

3.2   **External influences**

(a) **Location**: some industries are affected by their necessity to be in a certain geographic location eg mining industry and this will affect structure

BPP PUBLISHING

(b) **Customers**: organising around customers can be driven by necessity or a desire to differentiate

(c) **Legal/political**: eg organisations producing dangerous or toxic products.

Centralised versus decentralised operations

3.3 The extent of centralisation and decentralisation depends on a number of factors including size of organisation, number of markets it operates in, industry type, products and processes. Usually the more complex and competitive the environment the greater the need for decentralisation.

(a) **Advantages of centralisation**

    (i)   Facilitates the co-ordination of marketing

    (ii)   Can dilute low management expertise in some areas

    (iii) Should result in better control

    (iv) Ensures transfer of ideas across teams

    (v)   Avoids duplication of effort and therefore reduces costs

(b) **Advantages of decentralisation**

    (i)   Allows local responses

    (ii)   Improves effective local performance

    (iii) Improves management development

3.4 **Structural options**

- Functional eg finance, marketing, product
- Territory eg north, home countries
- Product
- Market
- Process/technology
- Knowledge/skills eg paediatrics, radiology
- Matrix

4 STRATEGIC ROLE OF THE BRAND

4.1 The brand plays a more significant role than ever before. Its value to the organisation as a source of competitive advantage and means of securing customer loyalty has been recognised and the nature of brand management has changed as a result.

Brands and their strategic role

4.2 Managing brands at a **tactical** level has always been easier than at strategic level. It did not require co-ordination across the organisation or consideration of integrating business activities.

4.3 The role of the brand has become much more 'strategic' in the last decade. This has been driven by brands appearing on balance sheets as assets. Suddenly organisations realised the financial value of brands. To build and maintain financial value requires a strategic approach, which in turn requires long-term commitment to the brand, investment and innovation.

4.4 It also requires effort to co-ordinate and integrate all business activities to represent the desired meaning and values of the brand.

Objectives and benefits

4.5 There are a number of objectives, and benefits, of brand management including:

- Building demand and building/holding margins
- Protection (eg reputation and quality)
- Added value
- Competitive advantage
- Customer loyalty and repeat purchase

What is a brand?

4.6 A brand is more than just a physical product or service; it can help build relationships with customers. This is particularly important in markets where the organisation has no face to face contact with customers eg fmcg. A brand is also more than just the component parts that make up a product, it has **additional values attributed** to it by customers.

4.7 A brand adds value to the product. Added value often has more potential to differentiate one product from another than core and expected functional benefits.

Where is value added?

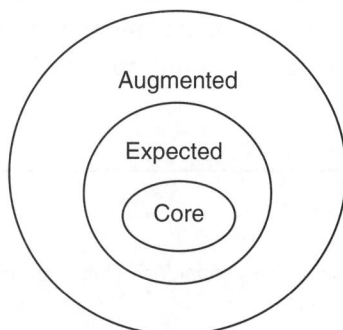

Augmented

Expected

Core

The brand (and its values) represents the total benefits received from offering both tangible/functional benefits and intangible/emotional benefits

Brands and corporate image/reputation

4.8 Image and reputation come from a number of sources. How the business performs in its markets can help build a positive image and reputation (or not). Customers' views and perceptions, and competitor actions, will also affect image and reputation.

4.9 A key factor in building a positive image and reputation will be the **effectiveness** of the organisation's **communication activities**. Fundamental to this will be the brand and what it has come to represent. The brand can be (and increasingly is) the company name or product names.

4.10 The communications effort, amongst other things, should be concerned with promoting **positive associations** with the brand that are meaningful and valued by customers. Sony is a good example of a brand that is perceived as trustworthy and reliable, with high quality performance. This reduces the customer's need to take time deciding between brands: the Sony brand is trusted and so the **perceived risk** is lessened.

Brands, corporate culture and customer service

4.11 Corporate culture can affect perceptions of the brand either positively or negatively. An organisation that receives bad publicity for the way it treats its staff is likely to damage its image in the eyes of its publics. An organisation that values its staff and is perceived as a good place to work will add value to the brand. This also extends to its role in the local community, society and environmental responsibility.

4.12 Customer service, increasingly a source of competitive advantage, is one of the most difficult elements of the marketing mix to manage. Variability in service affects customers' perceptions of the value of the brand.

4.13 To ensure consistent and desired customer service levels, the right people need to be recruited, employees need to feel valued and receive the appropriate customer service training if the desired levels of service are to be achieved and maintained.

Brands, positioning and the marketing mix

4.14 The marketing department does not have **control** over all of the marketing mix: the whole organisation is involved. The marketing department should, however, have **significant influence** over the marketing mix, particularly if the brand is to perform effectively and provide a source of competitive advantage.

4.15 The entire marketing mix must represent and reflect the brand values. Any inconsistencies confuse customers and damages the brand's reputation and performance. The marketing task is to ensure that, in the first place, it understands the brand values as perceived by customers and, secondly, manages the mix to build positive brand values and effectively position the mix in the market.

Action Programme 1

What brand values would you recommend Biocatalysts consider? Think about what they do well and how they need to build a niche position in the future.

There is no feedback for this Action Programme.

---

5 STRATEGIC AND INTEGRATED MARKETING COMMUNICATIONS (IMC)

5.1 Key to achieving a unique position in the market place, and managing the strategic role of the brand, is ensuring that all the ways in which the organisation communicates with its publics, both directly and indirectly, are consistent. Everything the organisation does and the way it does it reinforces the positioning values. There should be no confusing or conflicting messages.

5.2 This requires a strategic approach and planning and the rewards include:

- Improved effectiveness of communications with selected targets
- Improved efficiency in use of resources
- Improved profits as a result of above two
- Improved competitiveness

5.3 The organisation does not simply communicate through its marketing mix promotional activities. There are four main levels at which the organisation communicates, spanning strategic and tactical levels.

5.4   **Strategic communication levels** are the industry (or institutional) and company levels and include:

- Corporate actions (eg social responsibilities, influencing industry and government)
- Corporate identity – brand values
- Management style and behaviour
- Corporate strategies
- Positioning

5.5   Integrated communications require vertical and horizontal co-ordination of activities.

Corporate vision, mission and communications

5.6   **The company's mission statement defines the purpose of the business.** The role of strategic marketing communications is to **signal that purpose** to the market and reinforce the message through regular, planned promotional activities. The company's aspirations are defined in the vision and this also is communicated to the market. The messages signal future intentions and aspirations to the market.

5.7   Fundamental to the success of these messages is that the **market believes** what is communicated. Developing credibility is core to messages of business purpose and vision: therefore the organisation's know how and capabilities are given prominence.

Corporate culture and communications

5.8   The **culture of the organisation** is expressed through the **behaviour of the people** within the organisation, both management and staff. The culture is the personality of the business and increasingly culture is playing an important role in adding value to the corporate brand. The organisation's reputation may be built through quality, reliability, innovation and so on, and these become part of what the company is known and respected for. Positive attributes become core communication messages.

5.9   The values and attitudes held by people in the organisation are reflected in the way people are treated, both internally and externally. They also reflect attitudes to risk, and influence strategic choices. These values and attitudes communicate the sort of 'personality' the organisation has, and will have a positive or negative impact.

Management style and communications

5.10   **The culture of the organisation significantly affects the style of management.** The extent to which management trusts and respects employees is demonstrated in the extent of supervision and control. Rules, regulations and procedures all reflect attitudes towards employees perceived capabilities and how they are valued (or not). This trust and respect is passed on to customers through employee attitudes to service. Customers will either feel they have been processed or that they have been served. The result of this communication with the customer is either an impersonal experience that resulted in the customer feeling uncomfortable, unhappy and/or unsatisfied or a personal experience where the customer felt valued and expectations were at the very least met or exceeded.

BPP PUBLISHING

Corporate image/identity and communications

5.11 Corporate image is achieved through the combination of:

(a) Culture: its personality, values and attitudes

(b) Visual cues: the physical evidence e.g. buildings, logos, colours

(c) Behaviour: performance (eg competitive and reliable) and integrity (conducting business, eg with awareness of, social and environmental responsibilities, ethics)

All these organisational issues are interwoven.

Corporate strategy, positioning and communications

5.12 **Competitive positioning** and growth strategies depend on effective marketing communications to achieve the overall goal. Customers may position a company in their minds but it is up to the organisation to influence that position positively and in line with their strategic goals. This position follows on from the mission and vision, and is reinforced through the company's performance in the market.

5.13 Growth strategies depend on identification of specific market segments to target with specific products. The success of these strategies depends on the effectiveness of the marketing mix including communication messages targeted at those existing and new segments. Different strategies will require different messages; for example, market penetration messages are targeted at existing customers with whom a relationship has already been built. This will differ from market development where messages are targeted at new customers who will not be so familiar with the organisation.

6 INTERNATIONAL MARKETING STRATEGY

6.1 The same processes and frameworks are used in international marketing. The difference is the complexity and increased need for co-ordination and integration of strategies, particularly if global strategies are to be pursued.

6.2 As well as vertical planning systems, there is a need for horizontal planning systems, a framework for senior management to co-ordinate and harmonise Strategic Business Unit plans. The goal is to maximise competitive advantage through sharing best practice and skills and develop coherent global strategies.

International business operations

6.3 Structure and control present problems for international companies, and structuring and re-structuring has become part of normal life for the multi-national in a bid to find the 'best' structure for managing international activities. Organisations have centralised control and decentralised control and back again.

6.4 There are no easy answers or perfect solutions. The international market place is changing rapidly, not least because of the impact of technology. Organisations must therefore remain flexible and ensure that continuous improvement and adaptation is part of day to day operations.

Managing across borders

6.5   Organisation culture and the influences of national culture affect both management style and communications. Marketing is responsible for responding to the needs of external customers and stakeholders. Marketing management must therefore respond to the needs of internal employees to ensure those external customers and stakeholders receive what they want.

(a) **Staffing policy**. Decisions include whether to recruit locally, post home country staff to overseas appointments or a combination of both. There are advantages and disadvantages to recruiting local people (see your international notes). Staff should receive support and training for overseas assignments and communications systems should ensure employee/s feel as in touch as they did before moving abroad. This requires extra effort from the organisation, not the same effort. Motivation must take account of differences for example, while Maslow's hierarchy of needs is still valid, the order of the needs changes depending on the culture.

(b) **Training programmes**. Factors to consider include and learning styles and expectations, training methods available, training skills available and attitudes to training. If training is not common practice in a culture, it may be seen as threatening, a criticism of performance. It is important to communicate the purpose and benefits of training and ensure people perceive training positively.

(c) **Communication programmes**. Factors to consider include language and interpretation, style and tone, expected forms of communications, technology availability, symbolism and cultural influences e.g. meaning of colour and use of humour. In high power distance cultures employees will expect to be 'told' what to do and communications are one-way. If the manager wishes to encourage two-way communications and involve employees, plans will be needed to change employee expectations and perceptions of their role in decision making. In low power distance cultures, two-way communications will be the norm. Employees expect to be allowed to clarify instructions and challenge actions.

Action Programme 2

Consider the implications of Biocatalysts' business and strategic marketing. What might affect their ability to implement strategic marketing plans and what changes may they have to make?

6.6   All of these issues impact directly or indirectly on marketing planning. Marketers need to ensure they have taken account of the impact and incorporated, where appropriate, actions to address the business and marketing implications of the mission, vision, corporate objectives and strategies selected.

6.7   In this chapter we have discussed the business implications that may arise as a result of developing strategic marketing plans. In fact, for Biocatalysts, all of these issues are relevant. For example they need to adopt a marketing orientation if they are going to achieve their goal of being a respected 'niche player'. This cannot be achieved with their current business and marketing planning skills.

6.8   Strategic and integrated marketing communications will also be essential to success. Particularly as Biocatalysts do not have much cash to fund communications activities and so must ensure that everything they do will maximise results.

6.9 Their international development has been unmanaged and appears to be ad hoc. There is no clear strategy and, given their financial performance, they cannot afford to operate in this way any longer. Again, to produced successful results they need to develop coherent international plans and this may require re-structuring the business.

7 PITFALLS

7.1 Sometimes the exam questions do not ask specifically for you to identify implications for the business of the recommendations you have made. The danger is of failing to incorporate these vital issues within your answers even if they have not been specifically asked for. We do not suggest that you spend much time discussing them but, for example, if adopting a marketing orientation or customer focus is essential to the success of building a brand or integrated communications strategy, you should briefly refer to the need to change the culture to a marketing orientation.

Action Programme review

2 There are many factors you might include here:

- The lack of customer orientation
- Shortage of funding and uncertainty of funding
- Lack of marketing skills
- The product focus of technology staff
- The product focused business structure
- Lack of information

Changes which would be needed:

- To restructure around customer groups
- To establish an effective marketing information system
- To establish internal marketing skills

10

Step 7: Marketing strategy

Chapter Topic List

1	Marketing planning
2	Marketing objectives
3	Marketing strategy: segmentation
4	Marketing strategy: positioning
5	Marketing strategy: targeting
6	International marketing strategy
7	Separating processes from plan
8	Customer service and relationship marketing

---

1 MARKETING PLANNING

1.1 Marketing objectives and marketing plans cannot be developed until the organisation has made decisions on which broad product market opportunities it intends to pursue. You will see from the planning route map that marketing plans need to be developed for each business strategy selected and, for each segment identified, tactical plans will be developed and implemented.

2 MARKETING OBJECTIVES

2.1 When senior management have communicated their decisions, marketing can set marketing objectives for each business strategy selected by the business.

2.2 The marketing objective is translated from the business objective. So for example a business objective of £1.2 million profit and forecast gross profit margin of 10% can be translated into a marketing objective of £12 million revenue. If we are able to value customers and/or markets in financial terms then marketing objectives can also be interpreted in these terms.

How are we going to get there?

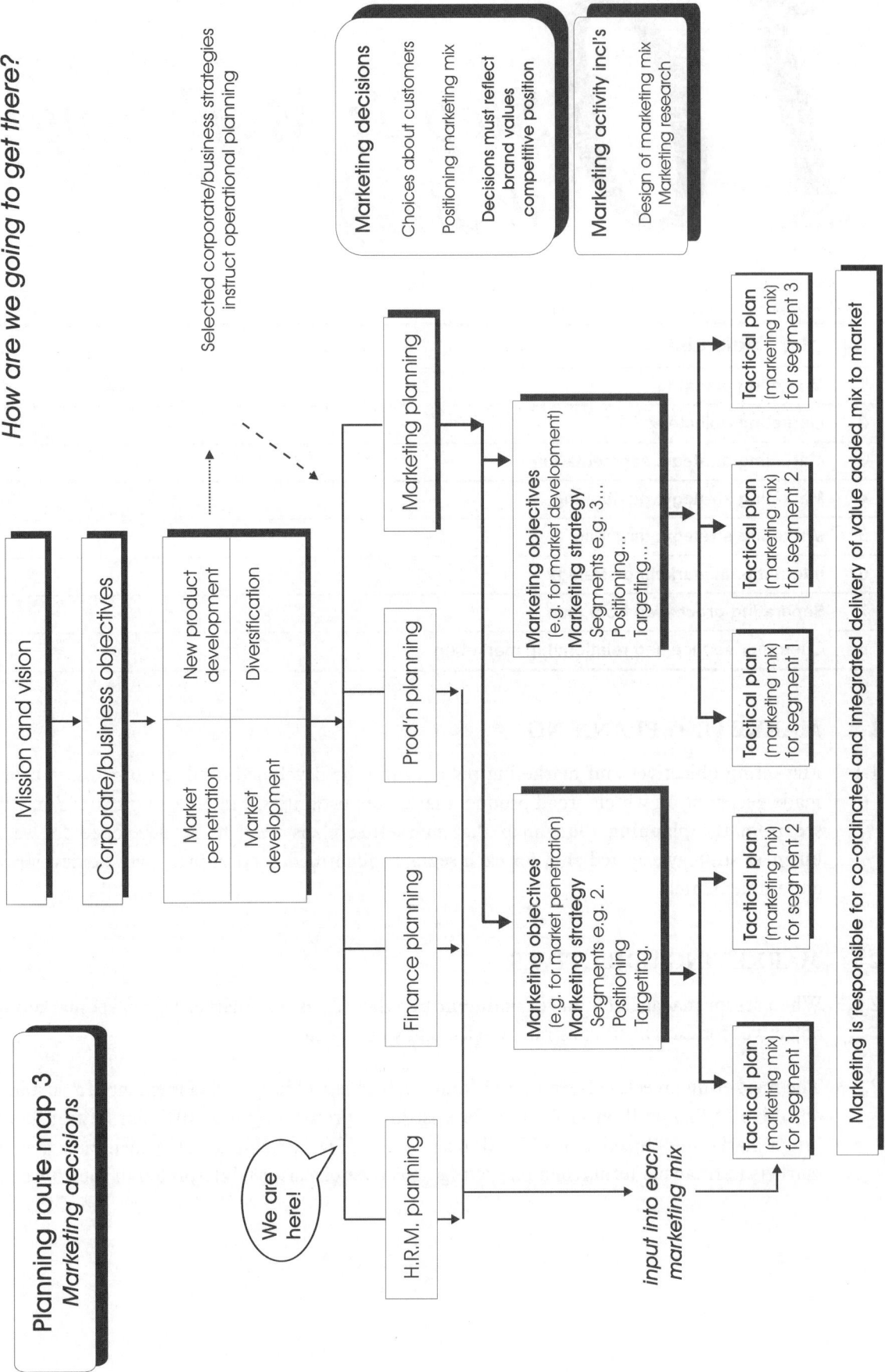

Planning route map 3
Marketing decisions

Mission and vision

Corporate/business objectives

| Market penetration | New product development |
| Market development | Diversification |

Selected corporate/business strategies instruct operational planning

H.R.M. planning

Finance planning

Prod'n planning

Marketing planning

We are here!

Marketing objectives
(e.g. for market penetration)
Marketing strategy
Segments e.g. 2.
Positioning.
Targeting.

Marketing objectives
(e.g. for market development)
Marketing strategy
Segments e.g. 3....
Positioning...
Targeting...

Marketing decisions
Choices about customers
Positioning marketing mix
Decisions must reflect brand values competitive position

Marketing activity incl's
Design of marketing mix
Marketing research

input into each marketing mix

Tactical plan (marketing mix) for segment 1

Tactical plan (marketing mix) for segment 2

Tactical plan (marketing mix) for segment 1

Tactical plan (marketing mix) for segment 2

Tactical plan (marketing mix) for segment 3

Marketing is responsible for co-ordinated and integrated delivery of value added mix to market

© Juanita Cockton, 1997

This will be cascaded further when we get to tactical plans as for example:

- Products sold
- Brand awareness
- Customer numbers

can all be calculated from your revenue objective.

Action Programme 1

Using your analysis and business objectives, set a marketing objective for each strategy you have selected.

Check that the figures work and that it is an interpretation of the business objective. Also is it realistic given Biocatalysts's strengths and market conditions?

---

3 MARKETING STRATEGY: SEGMENTATION

3.1 As markets become more competitive, there are increasing constraints on **budgets**. This coincides with consumers having more choice. How can resources be used more efficiently, and effectively to ensure consumers choose their products? Segmentation achieves this by identifying target groups for marketing purposes.

Key Concept

Segmentation is the process of splitting customers into different groups, or segments, within which customers with similar characteristics have similar needs. By doing this, each one can be targeted and reached with a distinct marketing mix.

3.2 Successful segmentation can be a key source of competitive advantage. Unfortunately, of those businesses that do bother to segment their markets, few consciously adopt an approach that maximises their competitive advantage, opting instead for traditional methods of segmentation.

Knowledge brought forward

Here is a brief reminder of segmentation techniques

Traditional methods of segmentation

Geographic

- Postcode, city, town, village, rural, coastal, county, region, country, climate

Demographic

- Age, sex, family life cycle, family size, religion, income, occupation, ethnic origin, socio-economic group

Psychographic

- (AIO) Personality traits, attitude, family life cycle, lifestyle, VALS, product specific

Behavioural

- Benefits sought, purchase behaviour, purchase occasion, usage

Geodemographic

- Combines geographic and demographic **plus** overlay of psychographic **and** patterns of purchasing behaviour; most well known are ACORN and MOSAIC

Business to business

- SIC codes, process or product, geographic, size of company, operating variables, circumstances, purchase methods

Increasingly organisations are developing segmentation models combining the above, the DMU and personality characteristics (eg loyalty, attitudes to risk, beliefs and values).

3.3 Decision Making Unit – (DMU)

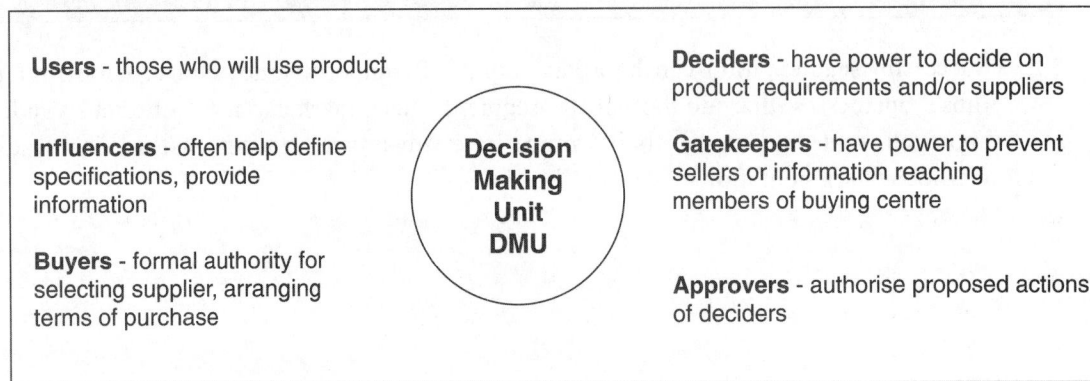

Users - those who will use product

Influencers - often help define specifications, provide information

Buyers - formal authority for selecting supplier, arranging terms of purchase

Decision Making Unit DMU

Deciders - have power to decide on product requirements and/or suppliers

Gatekeepers - have power to prevent sellers or information reaching members of buying centre

Approvers - authorise proposed actions of deciders

Action Programme 2

Who is the customer?

How many of the roles in the DMU above can you identify for Biocatalysts?

Decision making units are also valid in consumer markets.

Company's own segmentation techniques

3.4   As well as using some of the more traditional methods of classifying the information, organisations should be gathering more precise information about their customers tailored to the exact needs of the organisation. This information should provide answers to needs and motives. It can then inform product and promotion development and insights into achieving competitive advantage. It requires systematic gathering of information on their motives/needs from customers over time.

Action Programme 3

Segmental analysis

Choose one or two Biocatalyst markets and think about:

- Who buys
- What is bought
- Where
- When/how
- Why

You may have gaps or have to make assumptions but complete what you can and turn to the end of the unit for a Biocatalysts Segmental Analysis.

Tutor Tip

We often do not have as much information as we would like effectively to segment markets. We will have broad industry sectors and sometimes we will have some information about business to business customers or consumers. We can make realistic assumptions about segments and identify any information gaps that would help us improve segmentation.

We should be able to make recommendations on **how** we can improve segmentation. This is when the segmental analysis process and the identification of information gaps can help us.

---

4   MARKETING STRATEGY: POSITIONING

4.1   **Positioning takes place in the minds of customers**. They evaluate and compare companies, products and services, and position them according to the values they attribute to them based on their experience. Companies have influence over positioning, most significantly through communications, product quality and customer service. Positioning is critical to competitive advantage. The more value customers perceive, the greater the competitive advantage.

4.2   **Positioning is based on rational and emotional evaluations**. The functional benefits of a product are easily copied by competitors and provide little opportunity to differentiate. Emotional evaluation, often intangible values attributed to the product such as status, can offer much more opportunity to differentiate the product offering to appeal to customers.

4.3   **Successful positioning requires a realistic approach**. To aim for a 'world leader' position when there is no chance of this happening, particularly if resources and marketing skills are lacking, is unproductive. However realism should be balanced with vision. It is realistic to aim for a 'lead' position, for example, a leader in a segment/s, in industry or a particular process or technology.

BPP PUBLISHING

4.4 Successful positioning requires commitment, investment and sustained effort. Leave it up to the customers and they may not bother. Worse, the competition may decide to position you, for example, Qualcast very successfully re-positioned Hover mowers.

Positioning and the competition

4.5 Know your position. Are you a market **leader, follower, challenger or a nicher?** These positions will affect the strategies adopted. Decisions influence the position and resources will be allocated and strategies designed to build and maintain actual position. Know where you are going. There may be a need or desire to change position. This will require a change in strategy.

Firms A, C, F

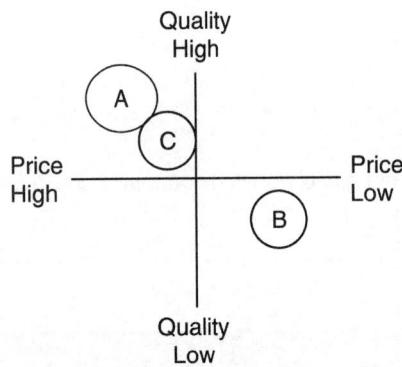

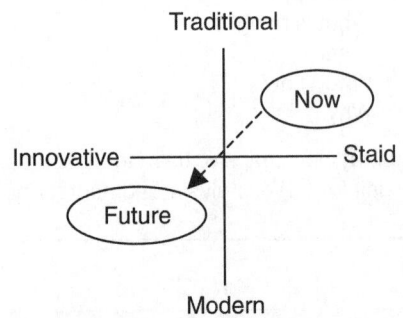

Action Programme 4

Decide how you would position Biocatalysts for the Diagnostic sector. Remember the buying criteria identified during analysis: what matters to customers, on what basis do they make decisions on which product/services to buy?

Compare your answer with ours at the end of the chapter.

Blank positioning maps for you to use

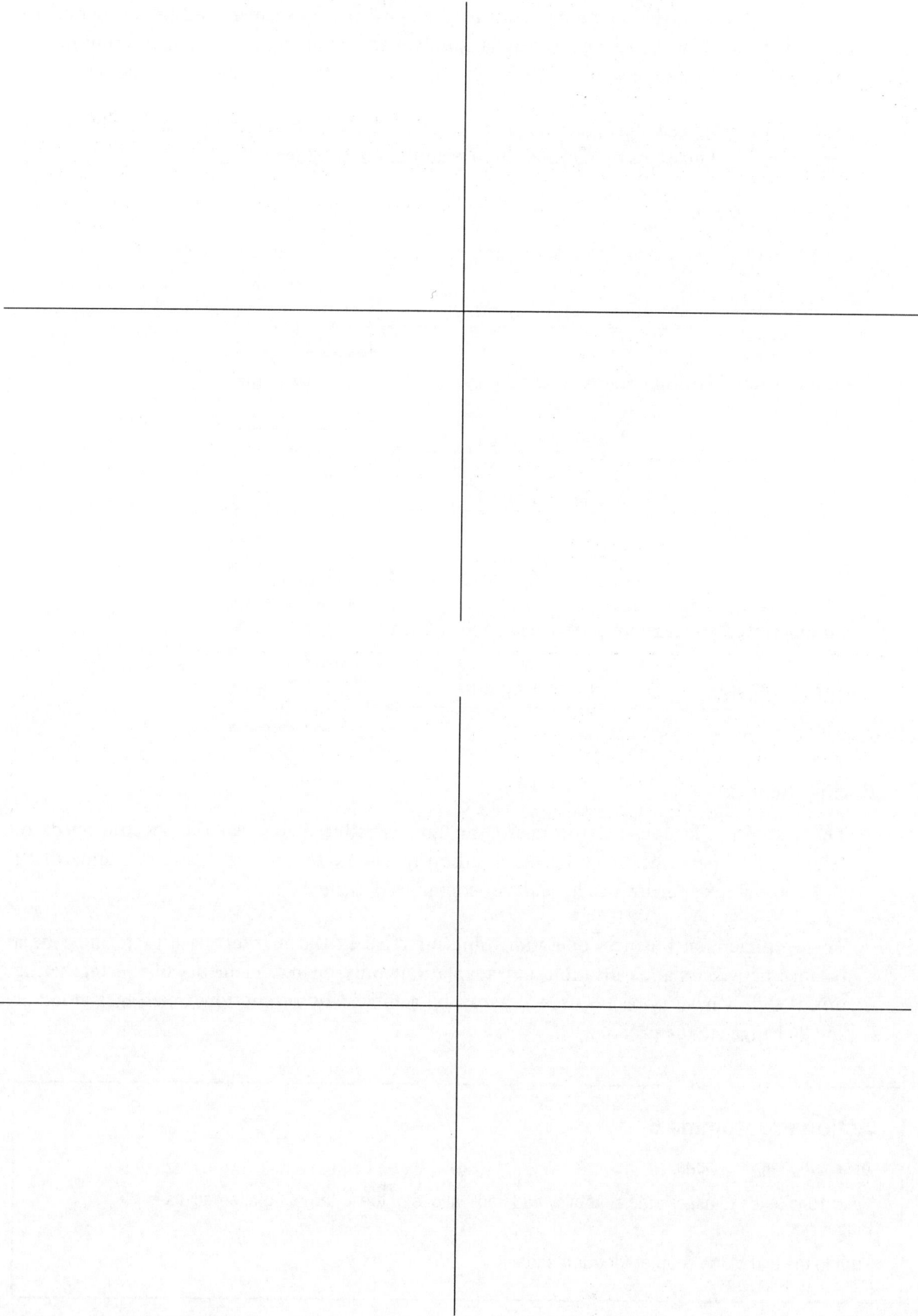

5 MARKETING STRATEGY: TARGETING

5.1 The word 'targeting' is too often confused with 'targets' (segments). Targeting makes the connection between the segments identified, the positioning strategy and the design of the marketing mix. The targeting strategy is simply a statement on how the marketing mix is used eg undifferentiated to the whole market or differentiated to identified segments.

5.2 Information acquired during analysis will determine which targeting options are viable both in terms of business operations and marketing effectiveness.

5.3 The choices are these.

Undifferentiated strategy (one marketing mix unchanged for entire market)

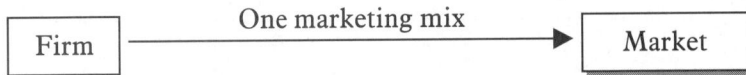

| Firm | → One marketing mix → | Market |

Differentiated strategy (tailored to meet needs of selected segments)

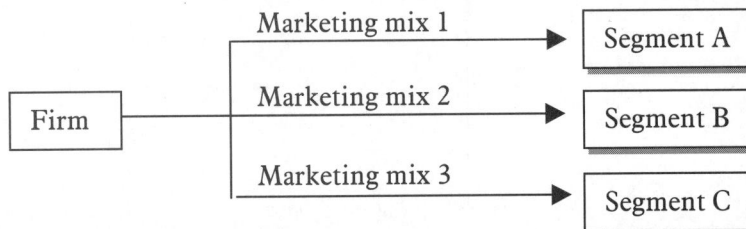

Firm	→ Marketing mix 1 →	Segment A
	→ Marketing mix 2 →	Segment B
	→ Marketing mix 3 →	Segment C

Concentrated strategy (undifferentiated for a niche)

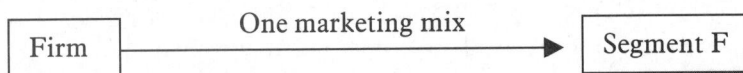

| Firm | → One marketing mix → | Segment F |

Tailoring the mix

5.4 To maximise effectiveness, the marketing mix is tailored to meet the specific needs of selected customers. Ideally, to maximise efficiency, marketing mixes should be standardised and so provide opportunities to achieve economies of scale.

5.5 To be efficient in business operations **and** effective in the market place there must be a balance between standardisation and adaptation: only change elements of the marketing mix that will have impact. Often this can be achieved by promotional messages alone or small changes to the product.

Action Programme 5

Assessing target options

Take 10 minutes to assess the suitability and implications of these targeting alternatives for Biocatalysts.

Turn to the end of the chapter for our feedback.

---

6 INTERNATIONAL MARKETING STRATEGY

Marketing planning: planning for differences

6.1 In some instances, differences will have to be accepted and planned for: in fact these differences, from a marketing perspective, may be essential to success.

(a) Customer service is significantly influenced by culture. What is expected in one culture is not necessarily expected in another. For example, self-service has become part of Western life. In other parts of the world, customers do not expect to serve themselves in any exchange with a business.

(b) When selling, in some cultures the price is publicised and that is the price people expect to pay. In other cultures the expectations is that you will always bargain over price. In some parts of the world fast and direct negotiations are the norm; in others, time is taken over building a relationship before any negotiations can begin.

6.2 The same frameworks and tools can be used to develop marketing plans. There are, however, some extra considerations.

(a) **Country selection** should be an objective process (Harrell and Kiefer matrix).

(b) **Methods of entry** must also be evaluated for their suitability in terms of levels of involvement as well as managing control. An increasingly important trend is SAs, JVs, M&As as a means of developing international markets. It is also significantly affecting the nature of competition.

(c) **Segmentation**: standard techniques can be used in many markets such as identifying strategically equivalent segments (SES) and acknowledging similarities and differences across rather than within markets. Segmentation can be based on consumers not countries. In some markets, however, it cannot be assumed that the same customer characteristics apply. Geodemographic Euromosaic, VALS 2 (Europe) and Euro-styles, RISC Euro type.

(d) **Positioning**: changing markets can mean having to change position. For example product use might change (Japanese using strimmers to cut lawns) and benefits may be sought for different reasons (eg four wheel drive in most European countries and part of the USA is often about adventure; in other parts of the world durability and reliability really do matter if you are driving through difficult terrain. Decisions on global, regional, country, market or segment positioning.

7 SEPARATING PROCESS FROM PLAN

7.1 All the activities described in this chapter so far are part of the process we go through to reach effective marketing decisions. The outcomes of these decisions are then recorded in the marketing plan. Plans are communication documents. They inform people of decisions made, actions to be taken, by whom, when and where.

Tutor Tip

Reference has been, and will be made to the need for communications in the examination to be persuasive. When developing outline plans for the exam, as with the real world, we must **explain** and **justify** our decisions and recommendations. Recommendations usually require senior management to allocate resources, people, time and money and they will only be prepared to do this if we can justify that what we proposed will result in successful outcomes. The examiner will be looking for justification.

7.2   The outcomes of the marketing planning process are decisions recorded in the plan; your activities in this chapter have been reaching those decisions. So you will now have:

- Marketing objectives
- Segments identified to target
- Positioning of the marketing mix
- Targeting strategy adopted

The marketing plan must reflect the competitive position of the business strategy.

Marketing strategy: statements (decisions) for marketing plan document

Segmentation
Statement on:

Segmentation type used

or

Segment construction based on needs/solutions combined with traditional approaches where appropriate

Segments selected

Descriptions/characteristics of segments

eg

Segment 1 profile >
            age ...
            occupation ...
            interests ...
            needs ...
            etc

or

Segment 1 >
            Acorn Category D
            group 9
            (with brief
            description)

+ needs/motives where known

Positioning
Statement on:

Positioning of the marketing mix (customer perceptions of value)

Link to competitive position

Sub brand position (if relevant)

Where position now and where re-positioning to (if relevant)

eg

Targeting
Statement on:

How the marketing mix will be constructed for the marketplace

eg

Concentrated targeting strategy

Marketing mix will be undifferientiated and focus on selected niche being targeted

or

Differentiated targeting strategy adapting marketing mix for each selected segment

Segment 1 Product V8 Promotional message emphasis on ease of use

Segment 2 Product Tb1 Promotional message emphasis on multi-purpose use

(Only require very brief example of major differences)

8 CUSTOMER SERVICE AND RELATIONSHIP MARKETING

8.1 Before we move on to tactical implementation, there are some other important issues to consider when developing marketing strategies and plans. These are strategic issues and they are influenced by people and policies vertically and horizontally across the organisation.

Customer service and relationship marketing (CRM)

8.2 Organisations are turning to customer service as a way of achieving and sustaining competitive advantage. Customer service, for companies faced with increasing competition and more demanding customers, is no longer a choice but a necessity if they are to survive. Consumer protection is increasing and tolerance of poor service has never been lower.

8.3 The launch of customer service initiatives was beset with superficiality and exemplified by slogans paying lip service rather than being representative of service values. Organisations are now coming to terms with the full implications of what delivering good customer service means.

What is service?

8.4 Service involves two key elements.

(a) **The actual product or service** the customer receives, and benefits and solutions to problems. Businesses have steadily improved in this area through efficiency and quality drives.

(b) **The personal service:** way in which the product or service is delivered and the interaction between companies and customers. This is probably the most visible aspect and often the one on which the company is judged. This has been neglected through lack of training the right people with the right skills.

Developing customer service

8.5 Culture has been referred to throughout the file but note in particular that if management distrust employees and believe in high levels of supervision and control, are poor at communicating, giving little understanding to staff of the purpose of the business or of the customers served, then employees will feel de-motivated and undervalued. In these circumstances, establishing a customer care culture will be difficult.

8.6 There may be an atmosphere of trust and respect between management and employees, where the company believes in its social and environmental responsibilities, and staff understand the purpose of the business and customers served, are motivated and feel valued. In these circumstances the company is in a strong position to develop a customer care culture.

8.7 Until the appropriate culture and values have been established, efforts to implement customer care programmes are futile and will result in limited short-term success. They may even do more damage than good if customer and staff expectations are raised only to be disappointed.

Customer's chain of experience (moments of truth)

8.8 Customers come into contact with a company in a number of different ways, at different points and with a number of different people during any transaction. These pre-transaction, transaction and post-transaction activities are the customer's chain of experience, and whether or not this experience is good or bad depends on the organisation's efforts to understand the customer and manage the experience.

8.9 The customer will come in contact with both **processes** and **people** and both have the potential to **add value** to what the customer receives, thereby providing opportunities for competitive advantage.

8.10 A review should be undertaken to determine:

- The customer's chain of experience
- The customer's expectations and buying criteria
- Opportunities to improve the experience

8.11 The design of future processes and training of staff should reflect the goal of at least matching experience with expectations or, better, exceeding expectations if any competitive advantage is to be secured.

Customer relationships

8.12 Customer relationships are about the long-term value of a customer and the building of long-term relationships. In many business to business industries, ensuring continued business has always required investing considerable time, over the long term, in building relationships with customers. Reasons varied but include the following.

(a) **Need for trust** and **reduce risk**. This is particularly vital if:

   (i) The product or service has to do with saving, maintaining or improving life, for example in the caring professions

   (ii) Large sums of money are involved, meaning that the investment has to be seen to be of benefit and to solve problems, for example in aerospace companies

(b) **Need for security.** If secrecy, privacy or sensitivity are issues the customer has to believe their interests will be protected, for example in financial services.

(c) **Need for time.** If projects have long time scales (eg 5, 10 even 15 years) businesses have to be patient and think and act in the time scales typical of the industry, for example, in the military.

(d) **Need for co-operation.** Working partnerships with customers are a feature of business operations especially where input from customers is required in product development.

8.13 Many businesses do not operate, or previously have not operated, in this way. While demand exceeded supply there was no incentive to do so. As markets become increasingly competitive, companies are looking for ways to improve customer retention and 'relationship marketing' hold the answers.

What is relationship marketing?

8.14 Relationship marketing involves the bringing together of quality, customer service and continuous improvement, managed through marketing activities.

8.15 Clues to an organisation's ability to adopt a relationship marketing philosophy and develop relationship marketing strategies have been covered in other areas of the file, in particular marketing orientation.

The loyalty ladder

8.16 Relationship marketing requires organisations to change the emphasis of their activities from focusing on acquiring new customers to building mutually beneficial long-term relationships with existing customers. This does not mean that there is no strategy for acquiring new customers, just a change in emphasis.

Through customer service, the aim is to move customers up the loyalty ladder.

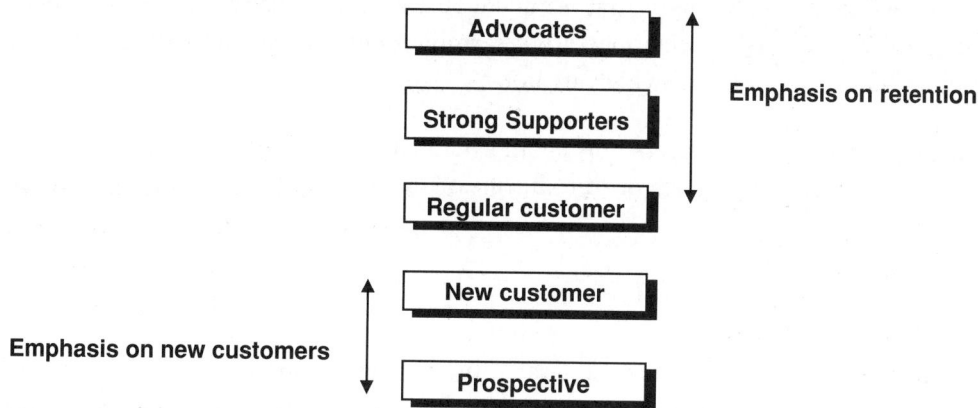

Adapted from Christopher, Payne, Ballentyne

Holistic market approach: seven markets

8.17 Relationship marketing does not assume that customers are the only market (or stakeholder) that exists and strategies are developed to build relationships with all its markets.

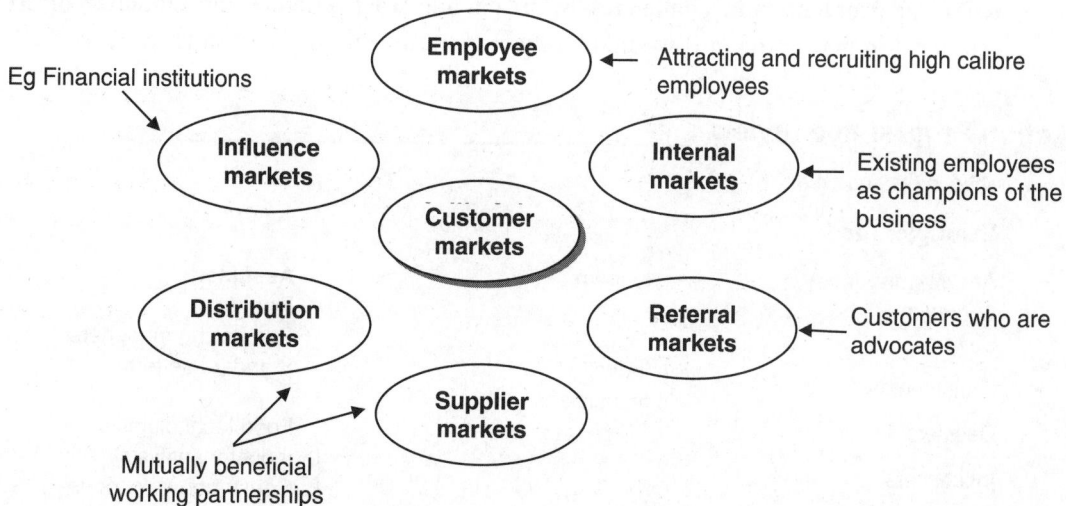

Adapted from Christopher, Payne, Ballentyne

8.18 Integrated marketing and communication strategies designed to build long-term relationships with all markets are essential to success.

Relationship transitions

8.19 Relationship strategies must take account of the customer's life cycle and transitions in the relationship. Transitions and stages are points where there is a high risk of losing the customer due to the changes taking place and the different needs that are emerging. The changing needs and relationship need to be understood and strategies designed appropriate to the needs of that stage or transition to help ensure that customers remain loyal and highly satisfied. The emphasis is on working partnerships and two way communications.

Managing expectations

8.20 Managing expectations is one of the marketing manager's key tasks but it is too often disregarded, and promotional activities make claims and promises that little resemble the experience. Customers' expectations are determined both by factors within the control of the organisation and by some which are not.

8.21 Strategies for managing expectations should be incorporated into the marketing plan with marketing influencing areas of the business that impact on both expectations and experience.

The Biocatalysts customer

8.22 You can see in the Biocatalysts Case Study how important customer relationship management is, and how inadequately it is currently being dealt with. Biocatalysts could be developing relationships with:

- Their agents
- Directly with their customers

8.23 If they position themselves in the specialist end of the market, the creation of **advocates** would be essential to establishing preferred supplier status to niche users. It is easy in this case to see Biocatalysts as customer focused but actually they respond to customers' technical problems and challenges in an ad hoc way. There is no evidence of strategic relationship marketing or it would be reflected in their financial performance.

Action Programme review_____

2   *Who is the customer?*

Example: food

At company level	Known	Assumed
Approvers		Finance
Buyers		Purchasing managers
	{ Industry	Standard setters
Gatekeepers	{ technicians	
Deciders		Food technologists
		{ Industry analysts
Influencers		{ Consumer watchdogs
Users		Production staff

Note. Beyond this industry DMU, there would be the end-consumer and the people influencing their decision to buy GM products or not.

Biocatalysts – segmental analysis

Who buys	What is bought	Where	When? How	Why
Food and drink industries	Enzymes	Direct	Seasonality foods/drugs Initially sample trials	**Buyers have common needs:** Increase yield, improve efficiency, cost effectiveness, safety (track record), expertise, consistent quality and activity, to be kept informed (Openness, transparency), guidance on developments, availability, reliability, strength, purity, value for money reflects quality
Mass and niche markets Diagnostics*		or through	Small batches	**Food:** information on animal derived enzymes, safety, guidelines allergenic potential, kosher certified enzymes, reassurance additional chemicals are safe for human consumption, improve/alter texture, extend life of food products, improve processing eg faster fermentation, flavour enhancement, depectinising, peeling, easier to handle waste products
Textiles		agents	Bulk	**Diagnostic:** high specificity, high sensitivity, stable products, ideally product that can be versatile, stable in small scale and bulk production (for R&D trailing then commercial production). Information on financial stability of firm as one kit been approved Diag Co loath to change a component therefore purchase is quite a large commitment to the supplier
Pharmaceutical Pulp/paper Water Animal feed Environment			Currency issues	**Textile:** product that will maintain its stability in bulk production, wide ranging heat stability

Other stakeholder needs and objectives

FDA. Needs: ensure product produced safe for consumer, health and safety procedures met, clearly documented procedures
Objectives: protect consumers and promote public health, alert of potential danger, work with government to promote uniform activity in food/drug related matters, assist manufacturer in understanding how to comply with good practice standards, remove unsafe/ unlawful products, work with international harmonisation committees to develop accepted standards, monitor companies with regulations

Investigators and industry analysts: open and transparent information and procedures reputation

Trade bodies/associations/professional societies: access to company documentation, is endorsement sought?, encourage ethical practices, conduct research, represent industry effectively, keep up to date

Many have characteristics in common including buying criteria. Some reasonable assumptions can be made on specific criteria.

BPP PUBLISHING

4   Positioning Biocatalysts

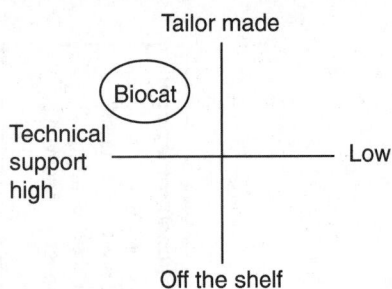

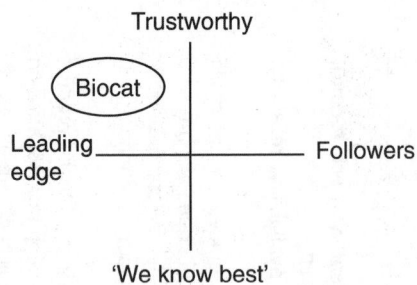

```
              Tailor made                              Trustworthy
                   |                                        |
              ⟨ Biocat ⟩                              ⟨ Biocat ⟩
Technical          |                      Leading          |
support   —————————+————————— Low         edge  ———————————+——————— Followers
high               |                                        |
                   |                                        |
              Off the shelf                          'We know best'
```

5   *Assessing targeting options*

Undifferentiated

Biocatalysts already offer customised solutions: their strength is their expertise and ability to customise so undifferentiated not a realistic option. Also offers no competitive advantage opportunities.

Differentiated

This requires ability to deliver a broad range to variety of customers. Medium to large size players have strength and resource to do this. Biocatalysts do not.

Niche

Requires expertise and customisation and to work effectively on a global scale can also adopt multi-niche strategies. Works well in highly specialised or narrow markets. This fits well with Biocatalysts's position.

11

Step 8: Tactical plans for the marketing mix

1   IMPLEMENTING MARKETING STRATEGY

1.1   Implementation is an area that is too often undertaken as an unrelated activity to the business and marketing strategies. The marketing mix tactical plans implement the marketing and business strategies.

1.2   It is assumed you are knowledgeable about developing tactical plans. There are also strategic issues associated with each element of the marketing mix, for example new product development requires a strategic and integrated approach, the type of product or service will affect communications plan at a strategic level, and these will be discussed briefly.

Tutor Tip

You are not expected to spend much time on this part of the plan. The paper is strategic and tactical plans used to demonstrate to the examiners that you know how to implement strategy. They will be looking for consistency and integration of your plans, assuming you have been asked for one.

What is important is any strategic issues associated with the marketing mix. You might cover these under 'Business Implications' or, depending on the question asked, it might be more appropriate in the tactical plan.

BPP
PUBLISHING

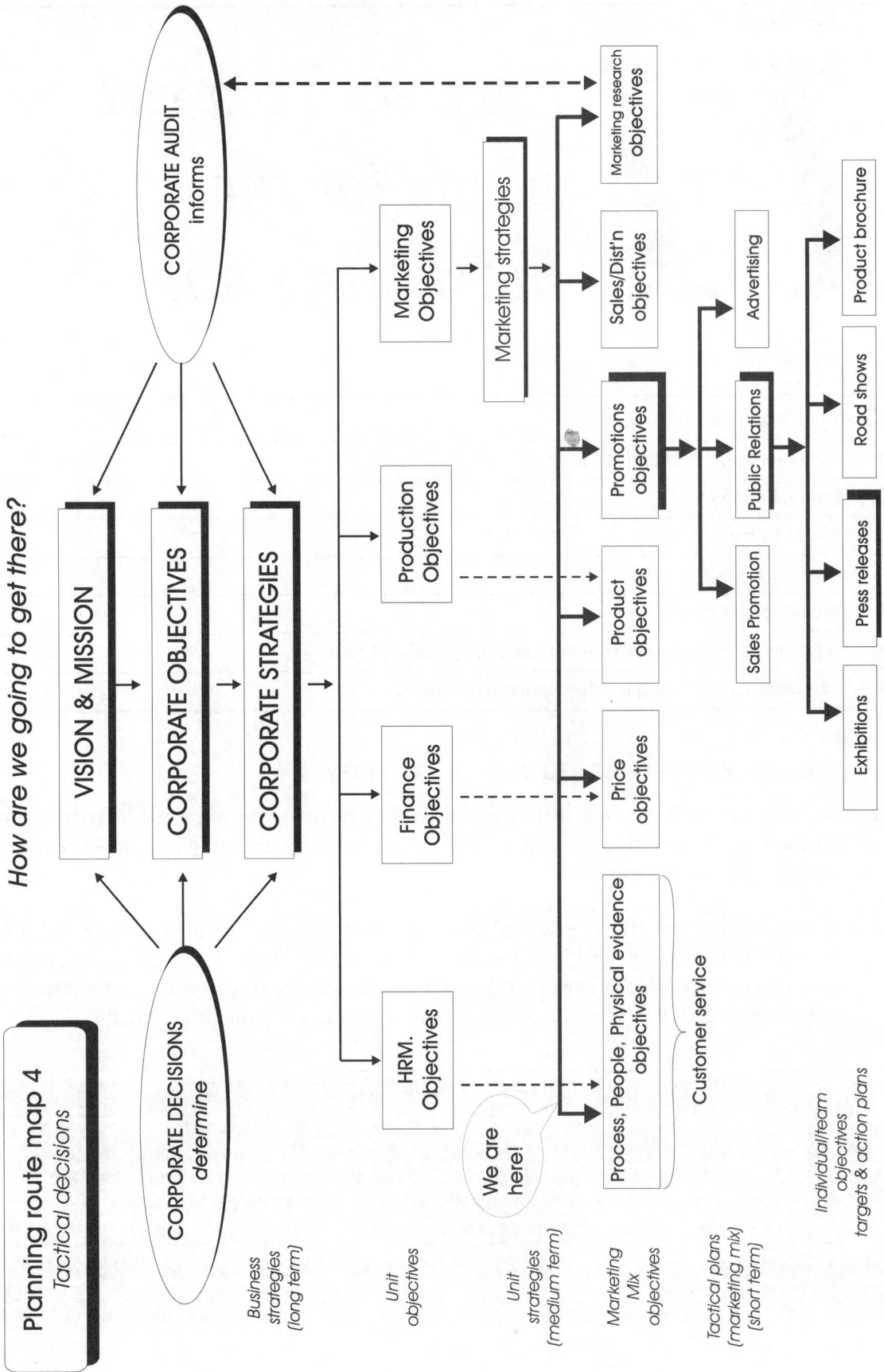

How are we going to get there?

Planning route map 4
Tactical decisions

© Juanita Cockton, 1997

2 PRODUCT STRATEGY

2.1 Central to the purpose of the business is the product/service provided that meets customers needs. Marketing is not concerned with product features but with the benefits perceived by the customers.

2.2 Meeting customer needs in a competitive business environment is not the only challenge facing marketers, they must do so in a way that either is:

(a) **Unique, innovative**, truly new

or

(b) **Differentiated** in some way from the rest

2.3 **Factors affecting product strategy**

(a) **Quality policy**. This is concerned with, for example, the level of quality (implications for position), physical components (life span, replacements), technology and social preferences (patterns, trends and timescales)

(b) **Product category. Search product**: here the purchase decision is made by evaluation (eg size, colour) and comparison (eg performance against competitors). **Experience product**: the purchase decision cannot be based on sensory perceptions or comparison it must be experienced. **Credence product**: the purchase decision cannot be by comparisons or experience as the product/service will be different each time.

(c) **Product life cycle**. The plc can be very difficult to determine in many industries. The stage the product is at in its life cycle does have implications for the marketing effort, so some endeavour must be made to establish its life cycle stage.

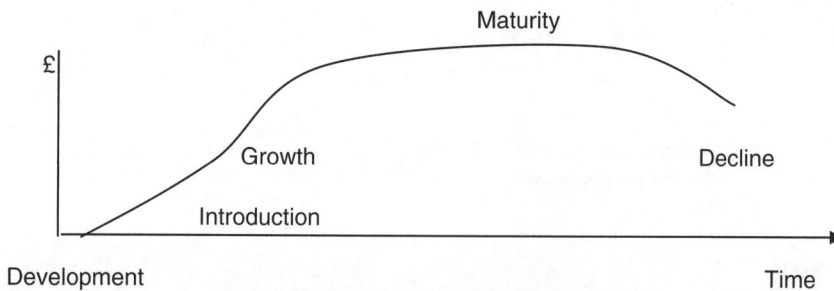

Each stage of the product life cycle requires different strategies to ensure maximum profits are achieved. Different industries/products have different life cycles, s can be seen from the following.

The product life cycle and impact on the business

Introduction	Growth	Maturity	Decline
Competition limited	Competition growing	Competition intense	Competition declining
Sales low	Sales rapid	Sales peak	Sales falling
Profits nil	Profits rising	Profits stable	Profits falling

The product life cycle and marketing planning

Introduction	Growth	Maturity	Decline
Product basic	Product extensions	Product modifications	Product rationalise
Price cost-plus	Price penetration	Price competitive	Price cut
Promotions heavy	Promotions heavy	Promotions uniqueness	Promotions minimal
Place selective	Place extend	Place extend	Place rationalise

BPP PUBLISHING

Total product concept

2.4 If products do not offer some competitive advantage their time in the marketplace will be a short one. Trying to develop competitive advantage is becoming increasingly difficult and the basic product rarely provides opportunities in this area unless it is unique.

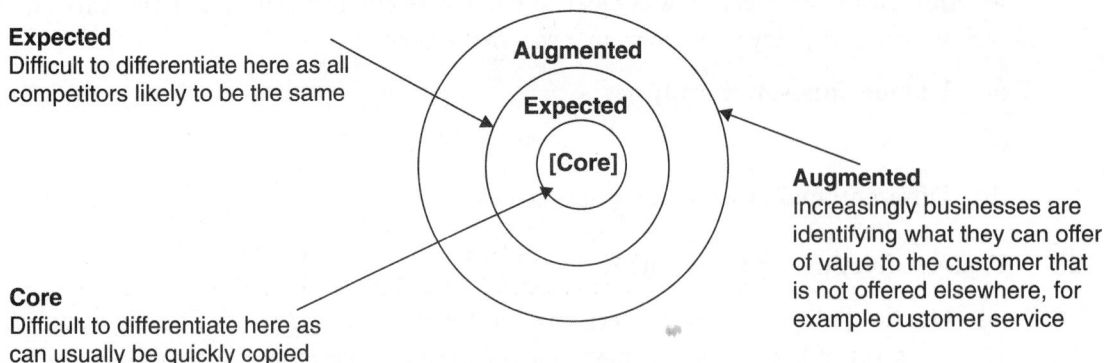

Expected
Difficult to differentiate here as all competitors likely to be the same

Augmented

Expected

[Core]

Augmented
Increasingly businesses are identifying what they can offer of value to the customer that is not offered elsewhere, for example customer service

Core
Difficult to differentiate here as can usually be quickly copied

'Product' for Biocatalysts

2.5 For example, with Biocatalysts we know that important issues in product development include to increase yield, to improve efficiency, cost effectiveness, safety (track record), expertise, consistent quality and activity, to be kept informed (openness, transparency), guidance on developments, availability, reliability, strength, purity, value for money reflects quality and similar analytical techniques.

Other issues that also need to be planned for include, for example, where Biocatalysts's products are in the product life cycle.

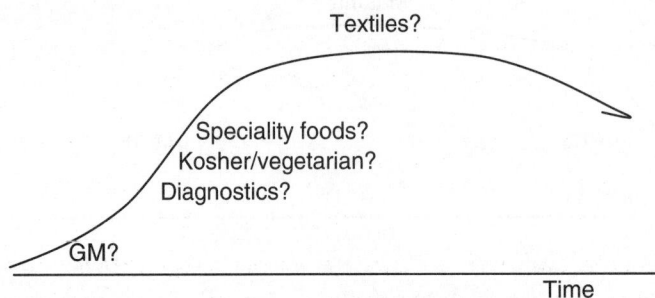

Textiles?

Speciality foods?
Kosher/vegetarian?
Diagnostics?

GM?

Time

2.6 **NPD.** Another issue for Biocatalysts was that of developing new products **reactively in response to any customer** instead of **proactively in response to selected customers** in the context of **business goals and market conditions**.

2.7 Products must also be appropriate to the markets they are developed for including international markets.

New products and market growth

2.8 During the screening process of new product development, one of the tasks for marketing will be to determine the speed of market development. A number of factors will affect new product sales.

Diffusion of innovation process

2.9 Determining how quickly a new product is likely to be accepted by the market requires an understanding of the people most likely to buy and of who in the market will be most likely to purchase the product on its launch. The diffusion of innovation curve or adoption process provides some insight.

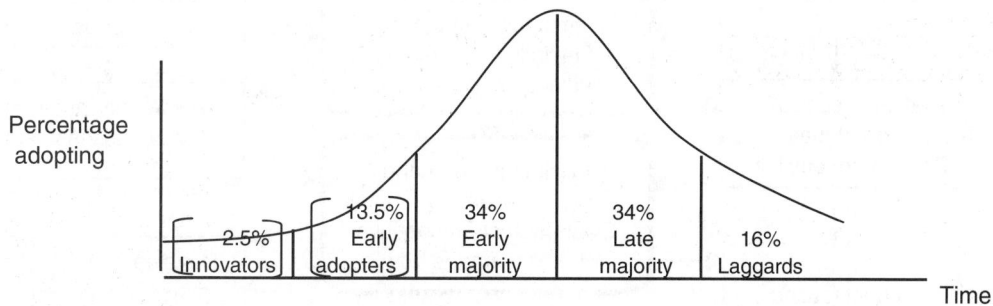

2.10 The number of people initially interested in buying innovative products may be small, therefore targeting these people is critical. The marketer's task is to identify the innovators and early adopters and ensure marketing activities are targeted specifically at these people.

2.11 Factors affecting speed of diffusion

- Complexity of the new product (the more complex/different the longer the take-up period)

- Relative advantage (the greater the advantage the faster the take-up)

- Compatibility (with existing lifestyles etc compatibility speeds take-up)

- Ability to try (if it can be used and benefits are experienced the faster the take-up)

- Communications (how easy/difficult is it to promote the benefits: if it is very new and different, it might be difficult to get the message across initially, slowing down diffusion)

New product development

2.12 Staying ahead of the competition requires a company to continually update its product and service range to meet the changing needs of its markets. Customers are more demanding, sophisticated and less inclined to stay loyal to a company that does not provide the benefits sought and service expected.

2.13 New product launches have suffered notoriously high failure rates in some industries usually because new product development was internally driven by 'good ideas people' rather than externally focused on identifying customer needs. The process of new product development should be a combination of both and, to ensure the process meets the challenge of speedy 'time to market' demands, the process should ensure several NPD activities are undertaken, at the same time in parallel to reduce the development period.

New Product Development process

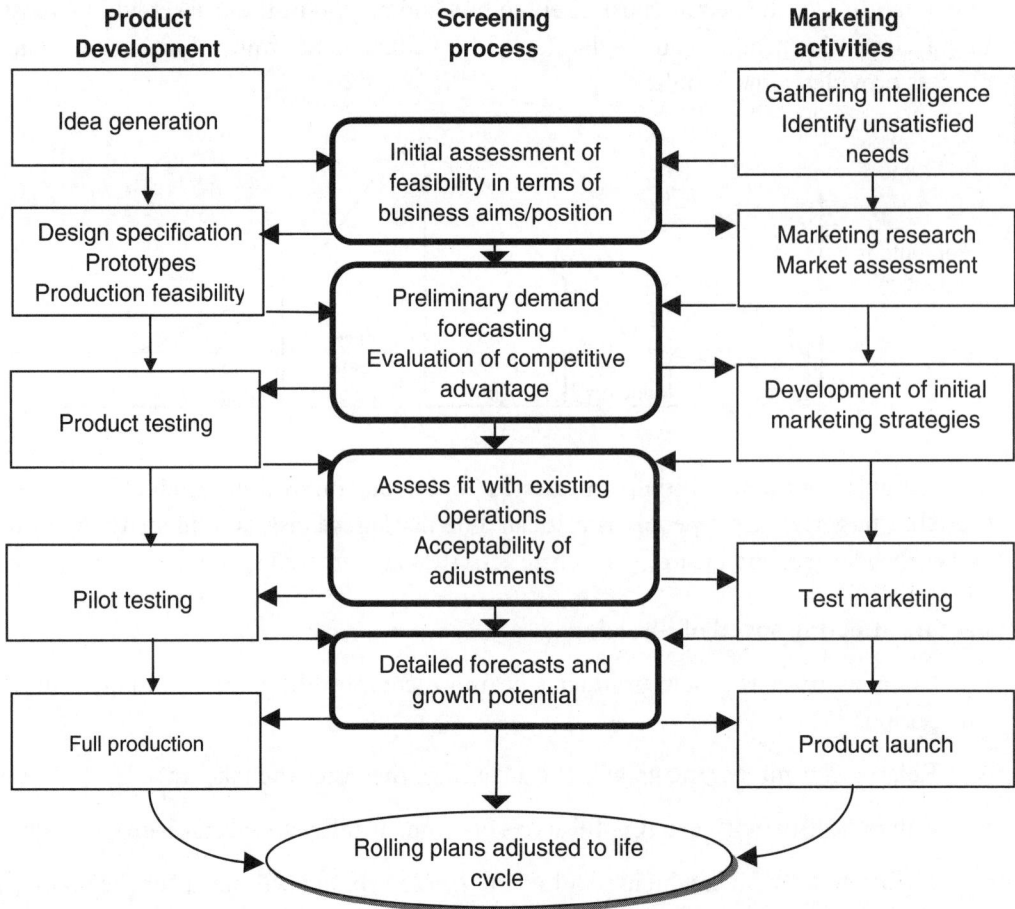

Product Development	Screening process	Marketing activities

- Idea generation
- Initial assessment of feasibility in terms of business aims/position
- Gathering intelligence Identify unsatisfied needs
- Design specification Prototypes Production feasibility
- Marketing research Market assessment
- Preliminary demand forecasting Evaluation of competitive advantage
- Product testing
- Development of initial marketing strategies
- Assess fit with existing operations Acceptability of adiustments
- Pilot testing
- Test marketing
- Detailed forecasts and growth potential
- Full production
- Product launch
- Rolling plans adjusted to life cvcle

3 PRICE STRATEGY

3.1 At a strategic level, decisions on price will include the range and movement of price during the planning period. Price should not be set as a cost plus exercise. This does not take account of market conditions or of the company's vision and positioning.

3.2 **Critical factors that define range of strategic pricing options**

- Real costs and profits
- Product or service value to customer relative to value offered by the competition
- Market segment differences and positioning
- Likely competitive reactions
- Marketing objectives

3.3 Positioning: product quality/price

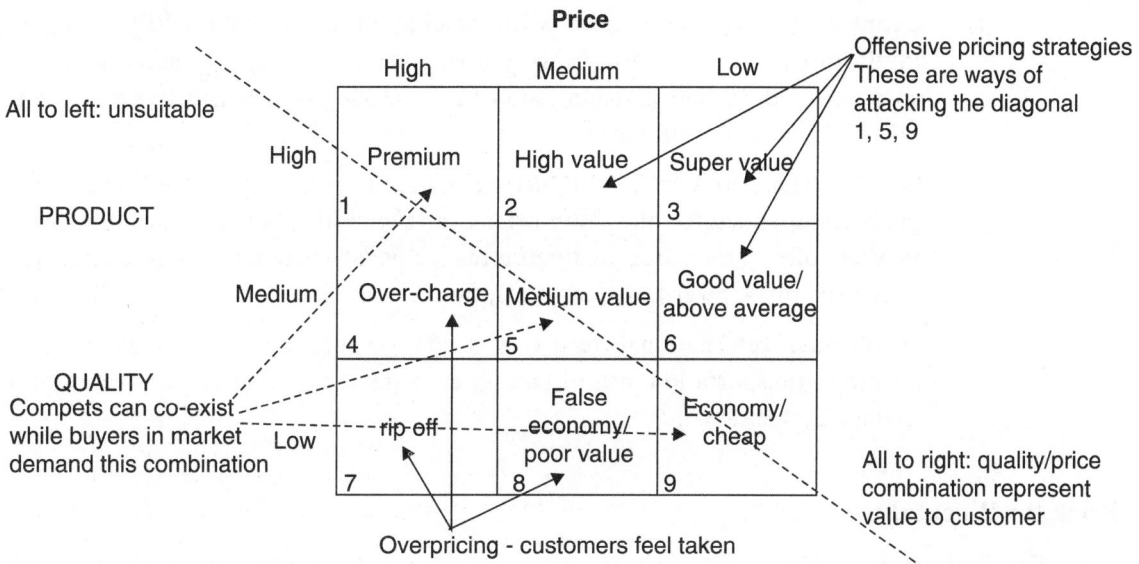

Strategic pricing

3.4 Here are some **examples** of what strategic pricing can achieve.

(a) Gain customer trust by reducing price when costs decline substantially and when the drop is easily noticed

(b) Weaken competitors by choosing key market segments in which to launch price promotions

(c) Win customers from competitors by offering multiple items at low total price (perhaps including products or services not offered by rivals)

3.5 There are two main ways to **implement strategic pricing**.

(a) **Skimming** (gaining high profits)

(i) **Rapid skimming:** high price, high promotion/gain high returns, high awareness

(ii) **Slow skimming:** high price, low promotion/gain high returns, promotion unnecessary, word of mouth more appropriate eg cult

(b) **Penetration** (market entry or increasing share)

(i) **Rapid penetration:** Low price, high promotion/gain market share rapidly

(ii) **Slow penetration:** Low price, low promotion/gain market share, low promotion spend typical with own label brands

3.6 **International pricing strategies and issues**

(a) **Forms**

- **Ethnocentric**: uniform around the world

- **Polycentric**: subsidiaries set whatever price they want

- **Geocentric**: does not fix worldwide price/ignore subsidiary price decisions balance between the two

(b) **Techniques**

    (i) **Transfer pricing.** Concerned with pricing of goods sold within company: implications on value for cross border taxation purposes; should optimise corporate rather than divisional objectives (cause problems if division is profit centre impacts of profit performance)

    (ii) **Gray markets or parallel importing.** Unauthorised importing and selling of products intended for one (high priced) market and sold in another (low priced) market: often arises due to fluctuating value of currencies between countries (other reasons - lower transport costs, fiercer competition, higher product taxes)

    (iii) **Incoterms.** International terms of trade (export license, currency permit, packing, transportation, bill of lading, customs export papers, wharfage/storage, invoicing, insurance)

Price for Biocatalysts

3.7 For Biocatalysts, a significant strategic issue is that they have been customising products using their expertise and high technical skills but their **financial performance suggests they are not charging premium prices for premium products**. Decisions will need to be made on pricing in relation to their desired position.

4 PLACE STRATEGY

Distribution audit

4.1 Reasons for a distribution audit include a need to improve control, improve productivity/performance, improve market effectiveness or establish resource requirements. This audit takes place at the strategic and tactical level.

4.2 A **strategic distribution audit** should take place every two to four years and include a review of **market profile** (structure, existing markets, potential markets PEST factors), **competitor profile** (number, location, strengths and weaknesses, distribution standards, potential competitors), **customer profile** (location, behaviour needs) and **channel profile** (buyer/supplier strengths and power, differential costs and technology use).

4.3 A **tactical distribution audit** should be ongoing and include a review of **product profile** (mix, range, seasonality, patterns, handling, innovation), **process/system** (ordering, delivery, technology, customer experience, logistics, service levels), **cost/efficiency** (order processing, data processing, materials handling, inventory control) and **sales/promotion** (sales force performance, standards and targets, and promotional effectiveness)

4.4 **Evaluation criteria: current distribution channels (efficiency and effectiveness)**

Financial criteria	Non financial criteria
Order quantities/value/cycles	Delivery times/reliability/condition/materials handling
Profitability	Customer service satisfaction/problem handling
Margins	Inventory management
	Marketing capability/performance
	Competitive performance
	Value added

Distribution channel selection

4.5 Developing strategies will require consideration of channel length and breadth.

(a) **Channel length:** will vary from industry to industry/country to country depending on requirements (market and legal). Consider extent of added value through chain:

- Vertical integration (ownership of distribution outlets) improves ability to differentiate, improves access

- Contractual eg franchising

- Conventional eg agents, distributors

- Direct marketing

(b) **Channel breadth:** meets market coverage needs.

Intensive Distribution	Selective Distribution	Exclusive Distribution
Mass market coverage Low priced products Convenience Impulse buy Sought by mfr. of high volume/low value goods	Balanced coverage Knowledgeable dealers Specialty goods Search characteristic Industrial markets Shopping around in consumer markets	Restricted coverage High priced luxury goods No competing products May require expert advice

(c) **Evaluation criteria: potential distribution channels**

Financial criteria	Non financial criteria
Sales turnover of outlets	No. of outlets/geographical location/accessibility
Pricing policies	Promotional co-operation
Profitability	Competitive products Reputation/quality/size sales force Terms of business/stocking policies Product characteristics. Buyer behaviour Degree of control

4.6 It may be worth considering the Internet.

(a) **Internet distribution strategy dependent on a number of factors**

- Customer groups served – their needs, preferences

- The role and power of current intermediaries

- Size of business and ability to adopt/embrace company-wide technology (structure, operations)

- Culture of the business – innovative, low risk avoidance

- Products/services provided (digital, non digital, value per unit, volumes, level of incorporated technology)

(b) **Internet as a direct distribution channel**

The Internet provides an ideal channel for digital product categories (software, text, image, sound). Examples of industries/businesses that can benefit include publishing,

BPP PUBLISHING

information, services, technology companies (computers, software, entertainment games), multi media (films, music etc) and financial services.

The increasing ease of the Internet as a search tool is likely to change buyer behaviour from a tendency to be reactive to promotion/sales to being proactive and searching for information and engaging with sellers who can provide what is wanted.

(c) **Internet as an indirect distribution channel: intermediaries**

Many products and services cannot be distributed down the line and therefore intermediaries are still needed. The role of the internet in these circumstances can be:

- Communications and information channel
- Transactions
- Extranet link with intermediaries who distribute goods
- Co-ordinating/monitoring physical logistics

As with any intermediary strategy, a business must have clear objectives of what it expects from its intermediaries. Internet distribution strategies may require the role of the intermediary to be redefined. Is the Internet just extending the chain or adding value? Traditional intermediaries may eventually disappear if they do not redefine the value they add and the role they can play in e-commerce.

4.7 **Distribution channel management**

Channel management is another area that is too often neglected. Once appointed, there tends to be an attitude of 'get on with it'. Distribution channels are key to success and should provide a source of competitive advantage, but they can only do so if managed properly. Some of the issues include:

(a) Service and support: identifying dimensions of service that customers value and prioritise, and determine costs of providing that service against expected revenues

(b) Agree and set performance standards and targets and monitoring of performance standards and day to day operations

(c) Communications and relationships: partnership approach

(d) Availability, reliability, convenience, speed of delivery, order sizes and product variety

Place for Biocatalysts

4.8 **Biocatalysts have not been managing their channels**. There is clearly evidence in the analysis, of poor revenue generation in some markets, particularly overseas markets. Evaluation of existing channels and of new channels is critical, as will be their need to manage channels more effectively in future. Channel management must also improve international development.

4.9 Given Biocatalysts's weak financial position, they should consider utilising the Internet to their advantage.

5 PROMOTIONS STRATEGY

5.1 Promotional activities are the company's key means of communicating with its publics, customers, suppliers, distributors, and so on. Communications are, or should be, mostly under the control of the business and used to best advantage by developing an integrated communications strategy.

5.2 During marketing research, the identification of target markets will have included assessment of the means of reaching the targets through appropriate channels with the appropriate promotional mix.

Key factors affecting promotional mix selection

- Business to business or consumer market
- Mass market, numerous segments or niche
- Product or service
- Technology (both in terms of product/service and media channel)

5.3 The selection of promotional tools will also be determined by the objectives set. A number of response hierarchy models have been developed which attempt to understand the process of buyer behaviour and therefore what we are trying to achieve with our communications.

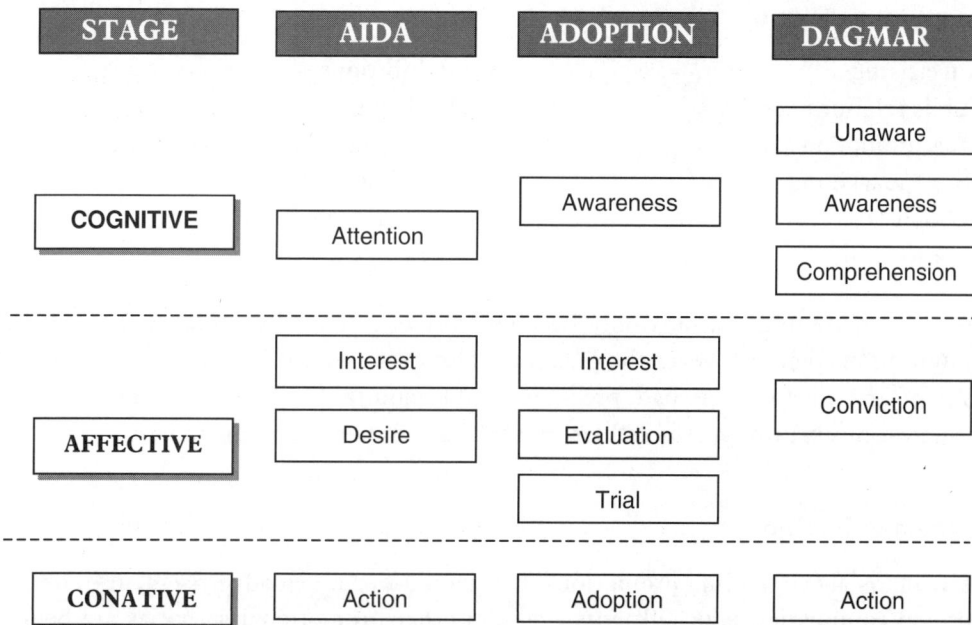

STAGE	AIDA	ADOPTION	DAGMAR
			Unaware
COGNITIVE		Awareness	Awareness
	Attention		Comprehension
	Interest	Interest	
AFFECTIVE	Desire	Evaluation	Conviction
		Trial	
CONATIVE	Action	Adoption	Action

5.4 Using AIDA for example, if we have achieved **attention,** then the task is to generate **interest** and move potential buyers through the stages of **desire** and **action.** Interest might be achieved through public relations activities, while desire might be created through sales promotion and action through sales. When the task is understood, it is usually easier to estimate the time it may take to achieve the task.

5.5 It is important that promotional design takes account of the targets. At whom are the messages being targeted and therefore what is likely to be the most effective promotional tool and channel to reach them.

5.6 The DMU (Decision making unit) is another useful model for understanding better the people being targeted: identify needs and target messages to their specific problems or benefits sought.

5.7 Another useful model is the well known Maslow's hierarchy of needs. This model identifies needs that motivate individuals. Promotions linked to the target market's needs become much more effective than those that are not related to the target's needs.

BPP
PUBLISHING

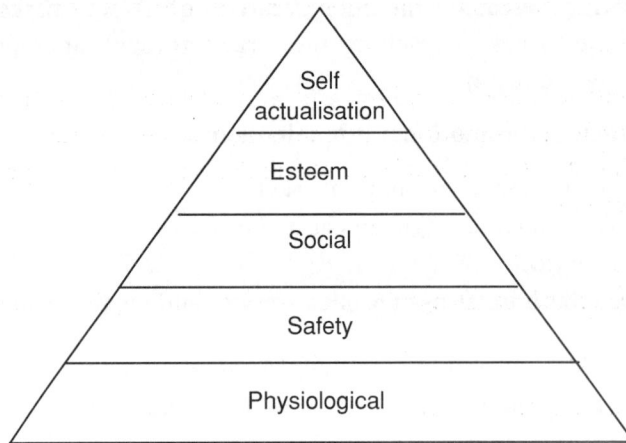

Maslow's hierarchy of needs

Promotional techniques

- Advertising
- Public relations
- Sales promotion
- Direct marketing
- Publicity
- Sponsorship

- Exhibitions
- Packaging
- Point of sale and merchandising
- Word of mouth
- Corporate identity
- Personal selling

5.8 These tools of communications only become truly effective when integrated through the communications plan. However the plan must also take account of publicity not within the control of the business eg bad press, word of mouth. Crisis management is part of communications planning, as is influencing the less obvious communications.

Above and below the line

5.9 Advertising is above the line promotions. It is paid for space eg advertisement in a journal, poster and commission is usually involved. All other promotional activities are below the line with the exception of direct marketing. This has recently repositioned itself as through the line promotions.

Profile, push and pull strategies

5.10 **Profile strategies** are typically concerned with strategic communications and can be targeted at a broad range of stakeholders, both internal and external. Profile strategies will focus on building reputation and status, image and brand values and so on.

5.11 Communications are designed to either **push** the product/service out or **pull** people in. Typically push strategies are used to push products into distribution channels and a sales force is critical to the success of push strategies. Pull strategies are used to pull customers into the outlets to buy and typically advertising is successful for pull strategies. A combination of both is usually required.

Media decisions

5.12 There are two types of decisions facing the marketer:

(a) **Inter media** decisions: which media category to use eg TV or press

(b) **Intra media** decisions: which medium within the category to use eg Daily Telegraph or Times

Media channel/s selection should provide the best access to the target audience the company is trying to reach. The objective is to reach as many of the target audience as possible cost effectively. The development of new channels is opening up opportunities for businesses not before possible.

Internet communication strategy

5.13 (a) Many of same processes and rules apply.

- Need for objectives
- Strategy: push, pull and profile
- Positioning and messages: consistent with brand values and targets
- Targets: identifying who talking to
- Promotional techniques: can use on-line brochures
- Controls: measuring effectiveness

(b) **Differences**

(i) Targets are still limited and often poorly defined: assumptions made about who is on line

(ii) On line communications is interactive and can engage target audiences in a way traditional communications cannot

(iii) Dynamic, instantly updating, moving, changing in direct response to customer demands

(iv) Different measures for on line activities

(v) Role of the database management

(vi) Information overload

(c) **Factors to consider**

(i) How are (or can) brand values interpreted? Will the internet affect perceptions in anyway and if so how?

(ii) Ensuring it is a two way process: capturing customer information

(iii) Matching experience with expectations: ensuring communications are clear, unambiguous, helpful, avoid 'click help' syndrome (ie no help at all)

(iv) Because it is dynamic, must engage, interact

(v) Do not use as an alternative to all other forms of communication, in particular if a telephone call will do the job better make the call.

Promotion for Biocatalysts

5.14 Biocatalysts's promotional activities need to become more strategic and focused. Their major problem is cash so any recommendations must be realistic in terms of budgets and the context of the industry they are in. Business to business promotions need not be expensive activities and most certainly should not be extravagant campaigns.

5.15 Building and maintaining a strong brand over time will be important. Maintaining and building their reputation for quality and expertise are potentially powerful brand values and any promotional activities should be designed to build the brand. Remember that in different countries there are different attitudes to GMOs, for example, and this needs to be considered when building brand values.

5.16 Biocatalysts promotional activities require a strategic and integrated approach to marketing communications including international ones.

6 CUSTOMER SERVICE AND CUSTOMER RELATIONSHIP MANAGEMENT

People

6.1 People impact on customers both directly and indirectly. The marketing manager has to consider the influences and impact on the marketing mix and how it affects overall customer service, impressions, experience and company/product positioning.

Contact

6.2 Firstly the marketing manager needs to determine who directly and indirectly influences the customer's experience. Once the nature of contact is identified, decisions can be made on service, training, operations, policies and procedures appropriate to desired contact outcomes. Too often, outcomes of contact are not considered or prepared for resulting in mixed experiences for customers. It cannot be left to chance as its influence on customer perceptions are significant.

Process

6.3 The role of processes in customer service and product delivery has often been underestimated and usually attention to efficiency has been concerned with cost reductions and internal operations rather than added value and customer satisfaction. People within the organisation who are responsible for delivery, either directly or indirectly, usually rely on processes to support that activity. The processes are often key to the product or service being delivered and take many forms and have a variety of functions.

Design must consider the degree of contact a customer will have directly and indirectly with processes. The higher the contact, the greater the opportunity for problems and inconsistencies and the more difficult it can be to manage and control. Processes should be kept to a minimum and be simple and easy to use.

Physical evidence

6.4 Customers are influenced by many factors when making decisions to purchase a product or service. An important factor, particularly to the service industry, is the role of physical evidence. Often intangible, for example atmosphere, its influence is no less important. It can play a key role in forming impressions and perceptions of a company and the position it holds within the competitive environment.

6.5 Factors such as buildings, furnishings, layout, colour schemes and associated goods such as carrier bags, tickets labels etc. should be considered in positioning and the overall design of the marketing mix. There are two kinds of evidence that customers experience.

(a) **Peripheral evidence**: possessed as part of the purchase but has little or no independent value eg bank cheque book, admission ticket. Peripheral evidence 'adds to' value of essential evidence only as far as the customer values these **symbols** of service. They provide tangible evidence of an exchange.

(b) **Essential evidence**: cannot be possessed by the customer but an important influence. The appearance of a hotel, the 'feel' of the branch of a bank, or of the aircraft are all essential evidence that provide **clues** to quality and standards and are often intangible in nature.

6.6 It is therefore important to pay attention to **external factors** (physical size, shape, frontage of buildings, materials used, outside lighting, entrances, signs and logos, vehicles, parking areas) and **internal factors** (layout, colour schemes, equipment, materials and support materials eg stationery, lighting, space and its use, heating and ventilation).

7 INTERNATIONAL MARKETING MIX ISSUES: SOME REMINDERS

7.1 The **international marketing mix** must be designed appropriate to market conditions, particularly cultural. Decisions on the extent of standardisation v adaptation should be balanced with the need for economies of scale, profitability and consistency, and meeting the diverse needs of different markets.

Personal selling in international markets

7.2 Personal selling in international markets is often more important because of the restrictions on promotional techniques, for example bans on advertising or sales promotion and restricted use of media channels.

7.3 Within a country there can be a mix of languages and literacy and a range of cultural diversity, for example in countries where tribes exist. This puts demands on the sales team and requires a high level of diverse skills from individuals and across the team.

7.4 Selling in international markets requires an understanding of the cultural differences in communications and negotiations. In some cultures, people are more willing to trust each other than in others. This needs to be understood because if the willingness to trust is low and people are suspicious, the task of selling becomes much more difficult and potentially complex. Attitudes to change, already discussed, also affects negotiations. In cultures where people tend to resist change, the sales task can become difficult if it requires people to accept something new and/or different.

7.5 **Key factors affecting the success of negotiations**

(a) **Gender**. In some cultures, women are not expected to negotiate contracts or sell goods and services. It can be difficult for women from cultures where this is normal practice to accept they cannot operate in some markets. For example, women from cultures where there is equality between the sexes, such as Scandinavia would be likely to find this difficult.

(b) **Age**. In Western economies, it is typical for young people to be in responsible managerial jobs, negotiating high value contacts. In other cultures, for example South East Asian, this is not typical or expected. It can cause offence if a young manager is sent to negotiate a contract in, say, China.

(c) **Status and rank**. The status of those you are negotiating with must be matched with people of equally high rank and authority or again you can cause offence and jeopardise the negotiations.

(d) **Authority**. In some cultures the person negotiating is the person with the authority to make the decisions, eg Western cultures. In other cultures, the person with authority might not be involved in the negotiations and has to be referred to for decisions and approval, as is typical in China.

7.6 Recruitment, selection and training of personnel selling in overseas markets is key to success. Depending on the complexity of the culture, eg high context, it may be more appropriate to recruit locally or, depending on the complexity of the technology eg highly technical/innovative, it may be appropriate to recruit internally. Either way, recruitment, selection and training will be designed to equip personnel with the skills needed to operate successfully in overseas markets.

Customer service (3Ps) for Biocatalysts

7.7 Customer service in this case study is pivotal in transforming their technical capability into an offer that adds value. Biocatalysts's expertise and ability to advise and guide customers in a way that enhances the customer's performance is central to business success.

Customer service in international markets

7.8 Customer service has become the battleground for attracting customers and building customer loyalty. Most other elements of the marketing mix can be copied and offer little opportunity to differentiate the business from the competition. Customer service in many markets is poor and any organisation that can deliver excellent customer service will have a distinct competitive advantage.

7.9 The problems of customer service are the intangibility and variation of service received. Even within a company, the quality of service can vary from person to person. In an attempt to build brands and reputation and improve performance, many businesses have set service standard goals and implemented customer service training.

7.10 It becomes even more difficult to standardise service when businesses start to operate in international markets. The organisation has to establish whether it is appropriate to standardise customer service. People have different attitudes to customer service in different cultures. For example, attitudes to waiting for service include these issues.

(a) **Time**. Is waiting for service viewed as wasting time or is it seen positively as an opportunity to socialise? In Europe, time spent in a restaurant is not only for eating but also for conversation and relaxing over a meal. Japanese people waiting for service in a restaurant would view this as poor service.

(b) **Rules**. It is traditional in some countries to 'wait your turn'; in other words queuing for service is typical and this can range from expectations of short queues and time to long queues and time. In other cultures, queuing is not a cultural norm and people expect to fight for what they want.

(c) **Power**. In cultures where power distance is strong, it is seen as acceptable for 'superiors' to bypass the queue. Less powerful people expect to wait longer.

Automation and service

7.11 In Western societies, automation of service has become the norm. We serve ourselves in restaurants, petrol stations, supermarkets etc. In other cultures people expect personal service, time taken to get to know the person providing the service and to understand their requirements; the relationship is important.

7.12 A company's customer service policy must reflect the different cultural expectations and staff development and training should reflect these cultural differences. This can become a problem if the goal is standardisation of customer service to improve quality. However, some aspects of service can be standardised to represent the corporate image and brand values while other aspects specific to culture can be adapted to meet the needs of the local market.

Action Programme 1

You now need to develop tactical plans for each of the marketing strategies you have developed. A tactical plan is needed for each segment. The differences between each plan might be very small, for example the promotional mix messages might be different or service provided, and they will reflect the valued added for that segment.

BPP PUBLISHING

12

Step 9: Control

Chapter Topic List

1 CONTROL: INTRODUCTION

1.1 Controlling business performance and planning activities is as important as the planning process and is, indeed, an integral part of that process, but control will require different skills. Control is about making sure we do what was intended. It is important to start by distinguishing levels of control. Control issues are too often dealt with as a tactical activity. As the focus of planning moves to a strategic focus, so must control.

1.2 There are broadly three levels of control:

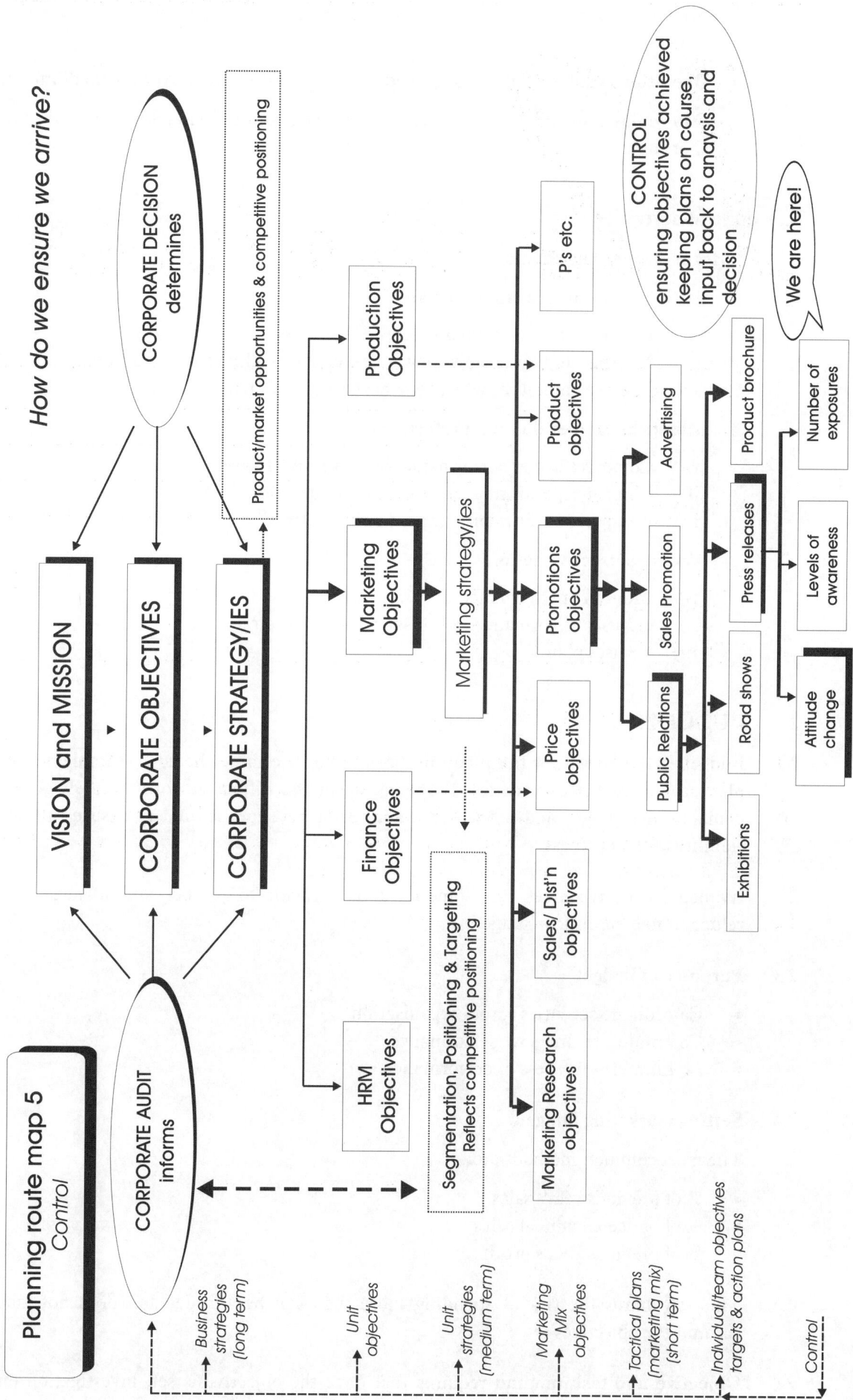

Planning route map 5
Control

How do we ensure we arrive?

CORPORATE DECISION
determines

Product/market opportunities & competitive positioning

VISION and MISSION

CORPORATE OBJECTIVES

CORPORATE STRATEGY/IES

CORPORATE AUDIT
informs

CONTROL
ensuring objectives achieved
keeping plans on course,
input back to anaysis and
decision

We are here!

HRM Objectives

Finance Objectives

Marketing Objectives

Production Objectives

Product objectives

P's etc.

Marketing strategy/ies

Segmentation, Positioning & Targeting
Reflects competitive positioning

Marketing Research objectives

Sales/ Dist'n objectives

Price objectives

Promotions objectives

Advertising

Sales Promotion

Public Relations

Press releases

Product brochure

Road shows

Exhibitions

Number of exposures

Levels of awareness

Attitude change

Business strategies (long term)

Unit objectives

Unit strategies (medium term)

Marketing Mix objectives

Tactical plans (marketing mix) (short term)

Individual/team objectives targets & action plans

Control

© Juanita Cockton, 1997

BPP PUBLISHING

(a) **Strategic control** will be concerned with overall business performance over the long term

(b) **Operations control** will be concerned with unit performance over the medium term

(c) **Day to day tactical** will be concerned with team and individual performance over the short term

Key control activities

1.3 **Performance measurement**

(a) **Setting performance standards and targets**

    (i) Informs employees what is required of them
    (ii) Informs employees how they are excepted to achieve it (conditions)
    (iii) Informs employees when they have to achieve targets

(b) **Measuring and evaluating performance**

    (i) Compares actual performance against standards set
    (ii) Compares performance against the competition
    (iii) Compares performance against best practice

(c) **Taking corrective action**

    (i) Monitors performance
    (ii) Adjusts performance in line with standards/targets, or
    (iii) Revises plan

2 BUDGETS

2.1 Budgets are required for the planning horizon to determine the cost of implementing the plan against expected revenues. Problems lie in the difficulties of accurately forecasting demand for products and services, so monitoring revenues is vital to ensure the financial stability of the business.

2.2 Availability of resources can sometimes be difficult to predict and managers can be reluctant to commit to a budget.

2.3 **Purposes of budget**

- Co-ordinate activities across organisation
- Communicate financial performance
- Monitor effectiveness of performance

2.4 **Setting marketing budgets**

The most common methods are:

- % of previous year's sales
- % of budgeted annual sales
- % of previous year's profit

2.5 This safeguards the risk of spending more than can be afforded but does not take into account the objectives set.

2.6 **Objective and task method** requires that once the objective is set, investigation on how much it will cost to achieve the objective is undertaken. This then has to be balanced against what can be afforded but if achieving the objective in the long term is vital to business survival and success, profits may have to suffer in the short term.

3 FINANCIAL AND HUMAN RESOURCE IMPLICATIONS

3.1 Any recommendations and plans will have both financial and people implications. Marketers have, in the past, been criticised for ignoring these critical issues when developing plans.

3.2 A review of each recommendation made for its implications on business operations is required. In practice the **justification** for each course of action would play an important role in persuading senior management to accept the proposals made and the same applies to the exam case. Any proposal will cost money and require other resources and senior management have to be convinced the expenditure will see worthwhile returns.

3.3 Financial implications (example)

- Capital investment
- Risk
- Revenue
- Profit, profitability
- Working capital
- ROI/ROCE   Also consider major or new projects
- Creditors/debtors   eg re-organisation/structuring
- Stock   new markets (exporting)
- Liquidity   new product development
- Depreciation   additional costs (patents, legal etc)
- Budgets
- Financial control

3.4 Human resource implications (example)

- Known/expected staff losses due to normal wastage
- Transfers in/out
- New appointments
- Promotion plans
- Current staffing requirements
- Future staffing requirements
- Surplus/shortfall in staffing requirements
- Current skills needs
- Future skills needs
- Training requirements (costs/timing)
- Changes (eg conditions of employment, health and safety)

3.5 A good marketer will make the link between the resource implications and benefits of using these resources and consequences of not using them. The task is to use these benefits and consequences to persuade management of the value of the strategies and plans you have developed.

3.6 In the case study, you are using the same process to persuade the examiner that, based on your analysis, you have developed credible plans to ensure the organisation achieves its goals.

4   SCHEDULING

4.1   All plans have a planning horizon, a time within which the plan must be executed and objectives achieved. Activities are also often dependent on each other: one activity must be completed before another can commence, so scheduling activities to make the best use of time is necessary.

4.2   Gantt charts, and for planning that involves hundreds of activities, critical path analysis, are useful techniques for ensuring activities have deadlines and are scheduled according to sequence.

Simple Gantt Chart

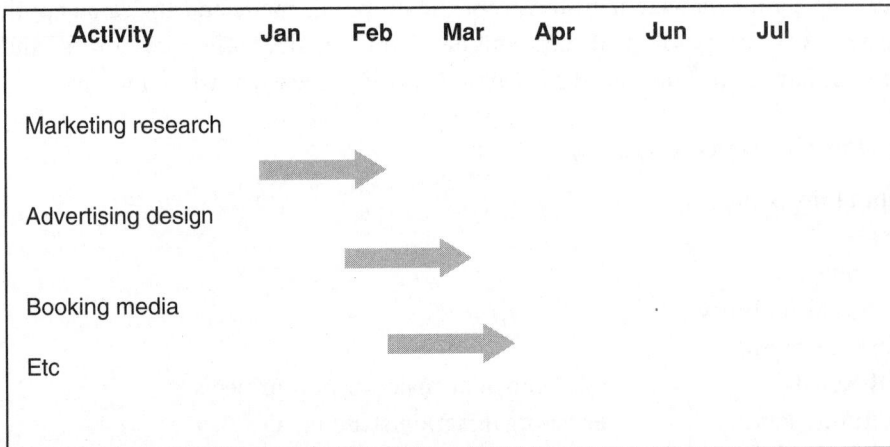

Activity	Jan	Feb	Mar	Apr	Jun	Jul
Marketing research						
Advertising design						
Booking media						
Etc						

Simple Critical Path Analysis

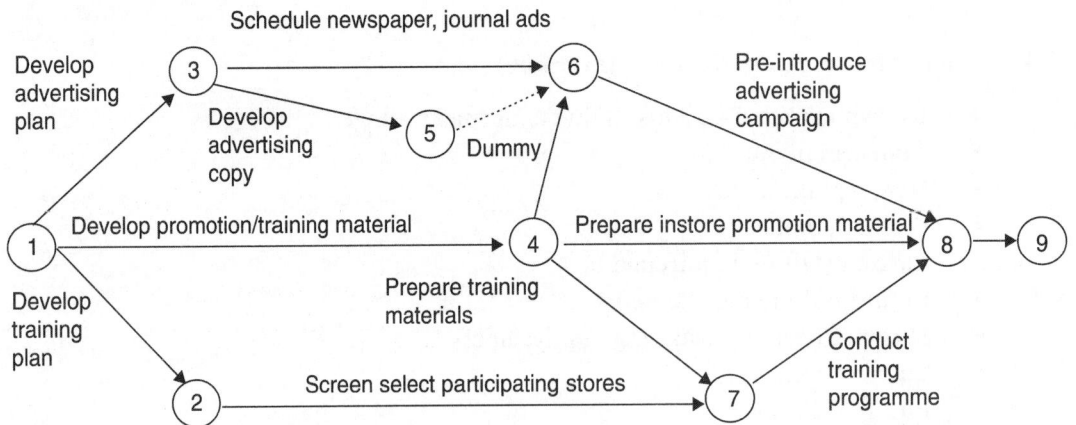

5   BENCHMARKING

5.1   Increasingly, businesses are looking at the competition to determine how well their own performance compares. Competitive benchmarking requires that a business identifies key performance indicators to benchmark against the competition and against best practice which may be a company outside the company's own industry. This benchmarking forces an external focus on performance and provides opportunities for the company to establish a base with the intention of out-performing the competition in the eyes of its customers.

5.2 How easy it is to benchmark the competition will depend on the industry. If it is intense, competitive information will not be easily accessed: in other industries where technology is 'newsworthy', information flows freely. If there are few competitors and they are concentrated in one area it is usually easier to acquire information. Benchmarking partners can be established which requires trust, open communications and mutual exchange of information.

5.3 It may be unrealistic to attempt to be 'the best' but improvement targets are important.

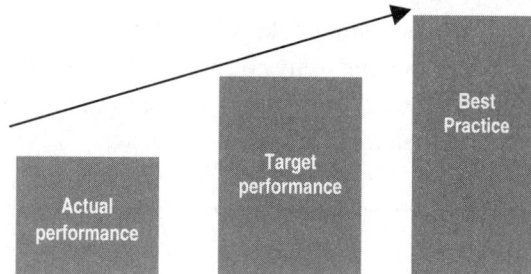

Warning: competitive benchmarking is not about copying the competition, it is about out-performing them, doing things well but differently.

6 MEASURING MARKETING EFFECTIVENESS

6.1 Quantitative and qualitative measures must be used to establish the effectiveness of marketing.

	Comment
Product	Contribution to sales revenues and volumes, contribution to profit, increasing market share, accessibility to new markets, reliability and durability, adaptability
Price	Impact on profits, impact on sales volumes, perception of value for money, attraction of new sales, customer loyalty
Place	Support and service to us and customer, reliability and consistency, added value (specify), accessibility, claims procedures, condition of goods
Personal selling	Sales by customer and by product, customer call frequency, average sales value per call, average cost per call, number of new customers obtained, customer retention
Promotions	Advertising (queries generated and conversion rates, attitude change – pre, during and post testing), PR (column inches), sales promotion (sales volume and sustainability)
People	Attainment of targets set, productivity, efficiency measures eg order turnaround, problem solving, delivery of training (content, presentation, visuals etc)
Processes	Reliability, speed, simplicity
Physical evidence	Perception of material evidence e.g. atmosphere/impressions created by offices, reception, training support materials, exhibition stands, impact on awareness, recall

	Comment
Customer service	Measure customer complaints (numbers, types), analyse levels of repeat business, analysis of chain of experience (customer contact points)
Marketing research	Methodologies used, accuracy of information, utilisation of information, accuracy in determining future information needs, analysis of usefulness in decision making

6.2 Measuring marketing effectiveness cannot take place without information. Measurement should be in the context of the business environment and should include indications of competitive performance. This requires the design, implementation and management of an effective marketing information systems.

Action Programme 1

Complete your plans by establishing the controls you require. Consider a realistic budget, establish a timetable and confirm what you are going to measure and how. This does not need to be a lengthy activity, keep it brief.

Compare your answers with ours at the end of this chapter.

---

7 MARKETING INFORMATION AND KNOWLEDGE MANAGEMENT

7.1 At the heart of knowledge management is the culture of the organisation. Culture will affect the way and extent to which knowledge can be managed. Beliefs, attitudes and values, management style and communications all influence culture. The culture should also reflect an enthusiasm for learning.

7.2 Potential conflicts include knowledge ownership and management must acknowledge joint ownership, where appropriate, and recognise individual contribution, their intellectual capital, encourage the sharing of knowledge (informed employees are more likely to reciprocate with information), and give rewards and recognition (performance measurement should take account of the value of knowledge).

Three key elements to knowledge management

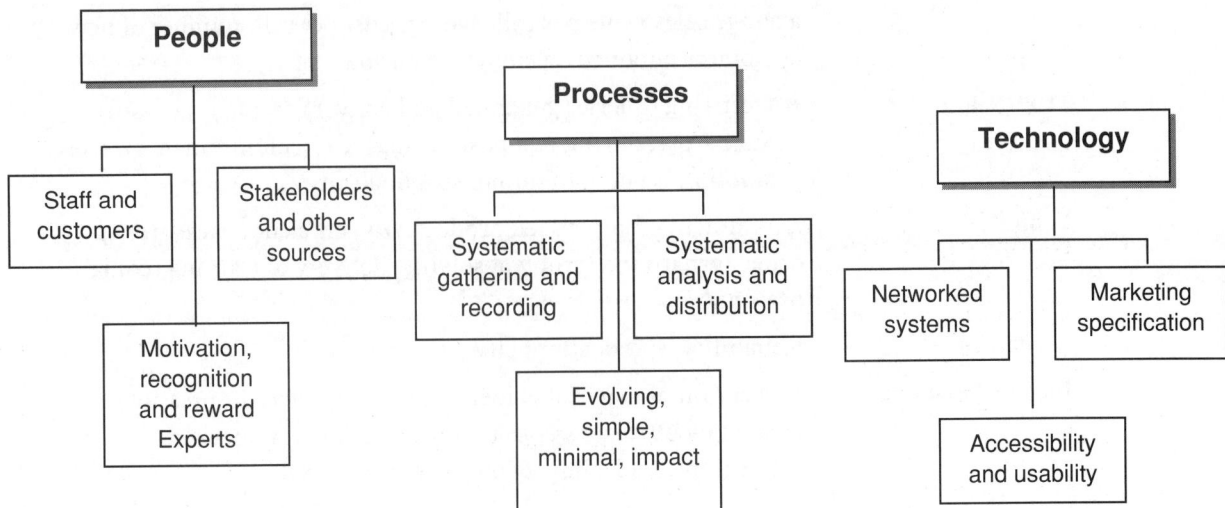

J. Cockton © 2000

Marketing information and database management

7.3 Research and gathering information as part of the customer relationship building and maintenance process leads to the need for database management. The strategic goal of database management is quality marketing intelligence that helps to build good long-term relationships that, in turn, lead to 'highly satisfied' and 'loyal' customers and results in profits.

7.4 Database management is not about the technology. It is about the outcomes – customer knowledge. Good database management often means changing the information you gather, moving from product knowledge management to **customer knowledge management.** It requires changing the 'mind set' from concentrating on the products you sell to concentrating on the different kinds of customers who buy. Moving from product expertise to **customer expertise.**

Management and Marketing information systems

7.5 Pivotal to control is the establishment of information systems. The monitoring, gathering, analysis and reporting of information allow the business to control its internal operations and be prepared for external opportunities and threats. Most businesses are gathering in information in various forms all the time but the difference between a successful business and the less successful will often be the formality of that information gathering process. Making connections between pieces of information makes the difference.

The role of a marketing information systems in control

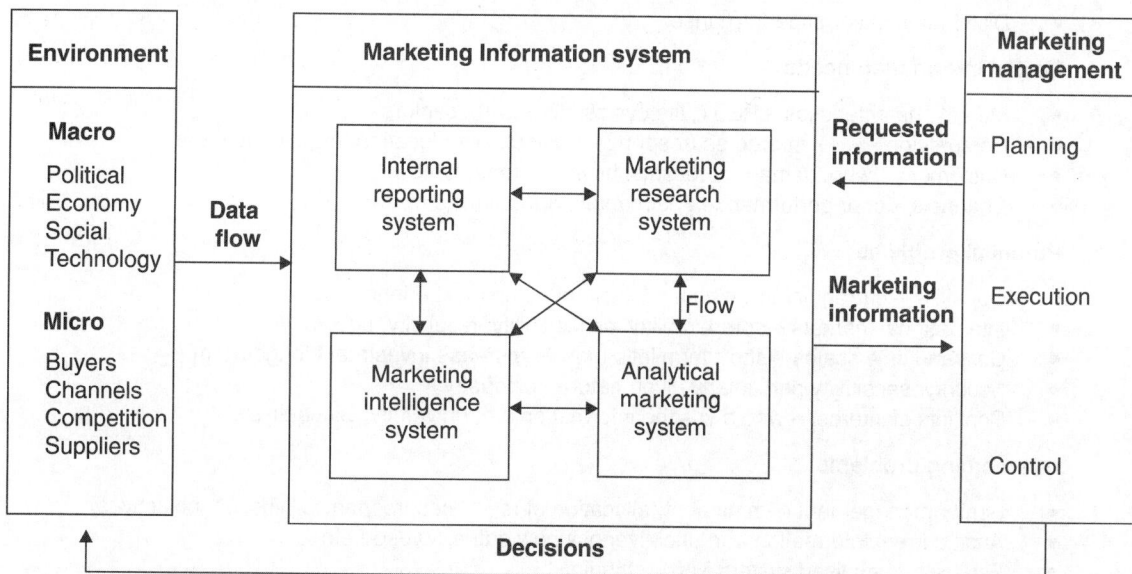

7.6 An MKIS ensures an ongoing information flow that enables the business to be prepared for events as they unfold. It accesses information from numerous sources in a variety of ways to build a complete picture of external opportunities and threats, market characteristics and dynamics.

Action Programme 2

A more strategic control issue is that of management and marketing information systems. Briefly consider the information system needs and how you would tackle them.

Compare your answer with ours at the end of the chapter.

Action programme review

1   Budget - Obviously Biocatalysts's financial constraints are a real problem. You need to think creatively, for example marketing research costs can be significantly reduced by working with customers who will be willing to share information and through participating where appropriate in omnibus research and of course partnerships with universities.

They are already spending some money on marketing – we could use this to far greater effect with more focused strategies and, as Biocatalysts's financial situation improves, increase marketing spend.

Schedule - remember Biocatalysts has some short-term survival needs as well as the longer-term vision.

Measurement - key issues include financial performance and critical cash flow, market position and share, product performance and communication.

2   **Introduction**

- Importance of marketing information (and fast developments in biotechnology)

- Consequences of not knowing/understanding market dynamics (eg changing nature of competition with competitors adopting more strategic positions)

- Biocatalysts current situation re marketing information

Internal information needs

Biocatalysts performance S/W
- Financial performance
- Marketing skills levels
- Management skills levels
- Planning and control systems and processes (product/market selection etc)
- Competitive position and strategy
- Market share and performance by country, industry, segment (value customers)
- Distribution channel performance

Market information needs

- Market characteristics – PEST, life cycles etc growth, sectors
- Competition – who, strategies (response profiles), size, location/market coverage
- Customers – who, demand forecasts, buying criteria, DMUs
- Channels – poor performance and market implications

Potential problems

- Our skills – current information held, lack resources, experience
- International markets – comparability, accessibility, reliability, accuracy
- Cost and time scales – short term little money, increase investment longer term
- Security, sensitivity particularly given nature of industry
- Conflicts of interest – who owns the information e.g. university, Biocatalysts?

Overcoming problems

- Senior management commitment (allocation of resources, responsibilities, set objectives)
- Audit current information and effectiveness how gathered/used etc
- Establish formalised system MKIS - funding
- Role/selection of agents/distributors
- Sources of information – governments, embassies, trade associations etc
- Contacts – formalise network of stakeholders (global) e.g. universities
- Role of interactive website
- Planning process for

Formalised gathering and analysis of information for planning and control purposes

Marketing Information System MKIS

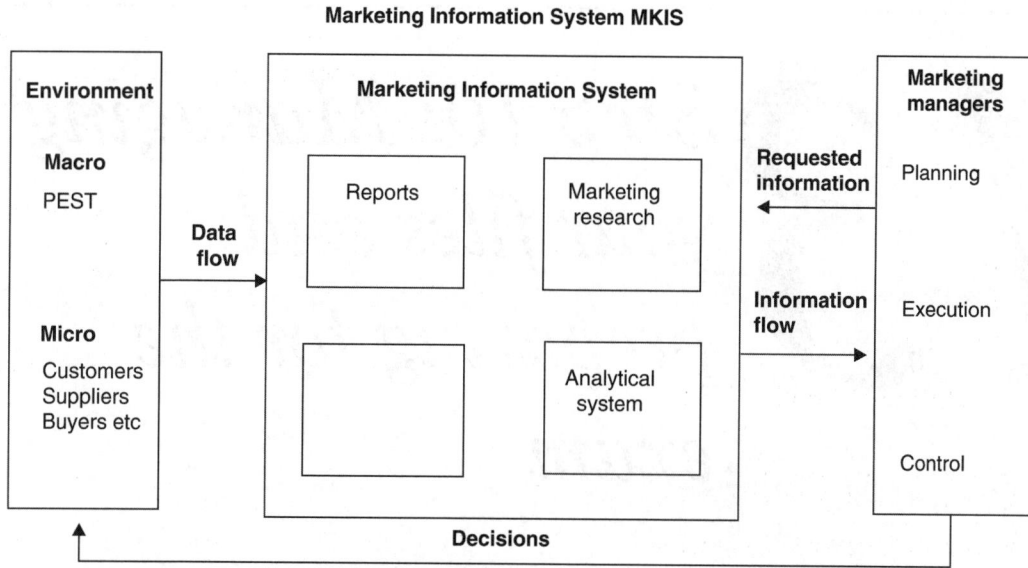

Step 1. Design

- Evaluate current information, flows, sources etc. S/W and processes
- Review requirements e.g. use in decision making, identifying, collecting, recording, analysing, reporting, storing, retrieval, removing outdated, use for control
- Involve staff in design – project teams

Step 2. Technology

- Evaluate systems – meet needs of everyone, flexibility, networking

Step 3. Implementation

- Project teams develop implementation plan
- Staff training
- Test run
- Monitoring and evaluating

13

Step 10: Managing your files and preparing for the exam

	Chapter Topic List
1	Open book: file management
2	Preparing for the modified open book exam

1 OPEN BOOK: FILE MANAGEMENT

1.1 Depending on which style of examination you are preparing for, your final preparation will differ. If you are in the modified open book programme you will still need to organise your materials and thinking as well as:

   (a) Preparing a six side A4 appendix
   (b) Annotating your exam case study which can be taken into the exam room

1.2 If you are taking the open book exam, one of the greatest obstacles to you passing will be the paper and books you take in with you. An open book exam is often seen as an opportunity to take a supermarket trolley full of 'helpful' material into the exam. For some students, this is a sort of insurance against anything unexpected happening on the day; for others it is because they have not done the work and they think they can get through by plagiarising the work of others. It will not work.

1.3 We recommend one good book for reference, possibly one you have been working with or you feel is most suitable.

1.4 The pre-prepared material you take in can be the worst obstacle. The well prepared student, and particularly the over prepared student, can find themselves sorting through paper for three hours with increasing anxiety and chaos. For this reason, we strongly recommend you take in outline notes only, designed as reminders of possible structures and key points and to act as prompts. By the time you have finished working the case study; you will need little reminding, you will know the case better than your own company.

1.5 We recommend **two files:**

   (a) One containing all your analysis, which you should not need to refer to but take just in case you do

   (b) The other file is your working file which will contain a summary of the **analysis** and outline plans and frameworks

1.6   To ensure you work effectively in the examination, you must organise your file to help you access the correct information quickly. Ensure you have dividers clearly marked of different plans, structures etc. The following is a general recommendation of possible headings.

Tutor Tip

Please be very disciplined and keep your paper down to a minimum. A key numbers sheet (or two) is important. You are aiming for 2 or 3 pages per section. Remember, if you are writing out fully prepared plans you are planning to fail.

File management: a file contents checklist

WHERE ARE WE NOW?

SUMMARY OF ANALYSIS (Background/current situation)

1a.   Internal audit: strengths and weaknesses

Statements on:

- Purpose
- Profitability
- Structure
- Culture   **Corporate**
- Processes/task
- People

(or Men/women, money, machines, materials and markets)

- Integration
- Image/influence
- Planning and control   **Marketing**
- Current strategy
- MKIS
- Marketing research

- Product
- Price
- Place
- Promotion   **Marketing mix**
- People
- Processes
- Physical evidence

Examples of models you can use at this stage:

- Financial ratios
- Portfolio analysis (Boston, GE, Shell etc.)
- Product life cycle
- Strengths/weaknesses performance/importance matrix
- Positioning maps

Remember you are summarising, adding value and providing insights. You will not be able to make statements on every area; there will be gaps.

BPP PUBLISHING

1b.   External audit: opportunities and threats

Statements on:

- Political/legal
- Economic
- Social/cultural   **Environment**
- Technology
- Industry
- Market/s

- Who buys
- Intermediaries
- What is bought
- Where is it bought   **Customer profiles**
- When is it bought
- How is it bought
- Why is it bought

- Main competitors
- Strengths/weaknesses
- Strategies
- Market share   **Competitor profiles**
- Product range
- Competitive advantage

Remember to include channels and other key stakeholders where appropriate.

Examples of models you can use at this stage:

- Porter's five forces
- Threat matrix
- Opportunity matrix
- Positioning maps
- Multifactor matrices

RESULTS AT END OF 'ANALYSIS'

You will be able to describe:

- Company performance
- Market conditions
- Current position
- Customer behaviour and issues
- Competitive situation

Summary of analysis should focus on:

- Critical success factors
- Key issues
- Major problems

WHERE DO WE WANT TO BE?

CORPORATE DECISIONS

2. Vision and mission statements (if appropriate)

Statements on:

- Future direction/what the business aspires to be
- What business we are in/purpose
- Reflect actual or desired position

3. Corporate objectives

- Quantified objectives
- Meet financial needs of business
- Growth needs of business

Example of models that can be used: gap analysis and forecasting techniques

4. Business/competitive Strategy

Statement on:

- Strategic options open to business
- Justification of those selected/rejected
- Selected strategies to be pursued

(Note: each strategy will require a marketing plan)

Example of models that can be used: Ansoff matrix (to develop strategic options)
GE matrix (to evaluate strategic options)

Statement on:

- Competitive nature of strategies to be pursued
- Implications for business

Example of models that can be used:

- Porter's generic competitive strategies
- Do any international and/or strategic brand issues need to be included?

HOW ARE WE GOING TO GET THERE?

MARKETING DECISIONS

---

5. Marketing objectives and 6. Marketing strategy

- Corporate objectives interpreted as marketing's task
- Segmentation, positioning and targeting

---

7. Tactical Plans

Statements on:

- 7.1 Product
- 7.2 Price
- 7.3 Place
- 7.4 Promotion **(UNLESS separate communications plan)**
- 7.5 People
- 7.6 Processes
- 7.7 Physical evidence

Each individual plan includes:

- Objective/s or aim: what is to be achieved
- Details on actions: how it is to be achieved

Each plan should take account of:

- Constraints: internal and external
- Implications: financial and human resources

File should include, where appropriate plans for:

- Marketing orientation
- Managing change
- Internal marketing
- Relationship marketing and customer service
- Implementing and maintaining MKIS
- Outline marketing research plan/list of information needs

Briefs on:

- Appointing/briefing marketing agencies
- Commissioning marketing research
- Managing outside resources

RESULTS AT END OF 'DECISION'

You should have marketing plans for each selected business strategy and have:

- Explained and justified recommended courses of action
- Plans for organisational issues arising from case specific issues

HOW DO WE ENSURE WE ARRIVE?

CONTROL

---
8. Control

8.1 Budgets

A financial plan for the planning period showing:

- Expected revenue generation for period of plan
- Expected expenditure for period of plan
- Expected profit for period of plan

8.2 Timetable

Short, medium and long term planning horizons.
Detailed actions: what will happen when and in what sequence (Gantt)

8.3 Measuring performance

Setting targets (often expressed as objectives)

Financial

- Profitability
- Short and long term solvency
- Working capital
- Shareholders investment

Marketing

- Communications
- Sales
- Product and price
- Distribution

People

- Setting performance standards
- Monitoring performance

Note: whatever you recommend in your plans should have some element of control

---
9. Contingency plans

Plans developed to deal with unlikely events/changes during planning horizon

---

RESULTS AT END OF 'CONTROL'

- Identification and allocation of responsibilities

- Systems and procedures for evaluating performance

- Checks for ensuring plan proceeds on course/time, mechanisms to trigger corrective action

Do you need to set up a MKIS or develop a marketing research plan?

BPP PUBLISHING

Tutor Tip

It is very important to remember this contents checklist is not exhaustive and does not cover every point. Every case study is different and has its own unique circumstances. What else do you need to include?

Action Programme 1

For the practice case study, you do not really have to do this activity. However this is often the area students find most difficult, reducing all the hard work into notes and checklists and organising into a file in a way that will help rather than hinder.

It is a good discipline to practise file management and check whether or not this is a personal strength or weakness.

2 PREPARING FOR THE MODIFIED OPEN BOOK EXAM

Developing a Case Study appendix

2.1 The modified open book examination means you:

(a) Cannot take a case file into the exam room

(b) Can develop a six page appendix to attach to your exam answer

(c) Can take your annotated copy of the case study into the exam

CIM has given relatively little guidance on how best to use this new opportunity.

2.2 You will see in our sample answers to the case one or two examples of these pre prepared appendices and you will be able to draw some conclusions of your own.

What you should NOT do

2.3 You should not:

(a) Try to incorporate all your analysis squashed into six sides

(b) Try to produce a strategic marketing plan in advance of the question and additional information

(c) Try to second guess the questions; if you are wrong your appendices will be less useful

(d) Present analysis without added value

What you should do

2.4 You should:

(a) Think about how best to use your A4 sheets in the context of the case

(b) Ensure you add the commentary, business implications or links which the examiner understand 'why' this analysis is valuable or relevant and how it might inform strategy

(c) Use models and frameworks: it will save you time in the exam

(d) label them and number them for easy reference in your answer script

(e) Make your figures and illustrations big enough to be read by an ageing and tired examiner!

(f) Remember the value of colour and white space

(g) Go for quality rather than quantity

(h) Be clear whether your sheets are supporting analysis or decision

The headings and framework given earlier in this chapter for file management will help you organise content logically.

14 *Biocatalysts Ltd: the examination*

BIOCATALYSTS LTD

DO NOT LOOK UNTIL YOU ARE READY TO SPEND

THREE HOURS DOING THESE AS A MOCK EXAM

---

1 EXAM HINTS

1.1

This table shows how many minutes to allocate to each question in a three hour exam based on the number of marks per question. The time allocated includes planning and checking time. You will not be spending all this time writing.

Marks	Minutes
5	9
10	18
15	27
20	36
25	45
30	54
35	63
40	72
45	81
50	90
55	99
60	108
65	117
70	126
75	135
80	144
85	153
90	162
95	171

1.2 **Equipment, aids and exam centre**

(a) Good quality pens – **not** highlighter or felt tips: use colour for models, underlining etc but **not red**: use a ruler where appropriate when drawing models

(b) Calculator (in the past has not been needed but take one just in case)

(c) Tipp-Ex fluid or similar (in good condition)

(d) Stencils for drawing charts, boxes, models etc: pre-prepared models (to scale where appropriate) are useful: use black felt tip for pre-prepared examples so you can trace on exam paper

(e) Watch/clock

1.3 Make sure you know where the exam centre is and where you can park (do you need permission, change etc). If travelling by public transport, where is the nearest station etc and how long does it take to walk from the station to the centre, train/bus times and so on.

1.4 Allow plenty of time on the day: you will not be allowed into the exam room 15 minutes after the start. Check with the exam centre when they intend to start the examination and be prepared for there to be other people in the room taking other exams. Their exams may be shorter and they may leave earlier.

1.5 **Examination and presentation techniques**

(a) **Always** plan your answers. Even if you have prepared well and anticipated questions successfully, you will still need to plan your answers, particularly to take on board the additional information. You will **not** be able to use your pre-prepared material as you have developed it, (except the analysis work for closed book exams). You must be selective in the material you draw on and it will require modification to meet the specifics, emphasis and slant of the question. This is where well prepared students often fail.

(b) Another area where the well prepared student fails is **poor time management**. Time and again this comes back as a problem. Manage your time and be disciplined about moving on to the next question. If you have run out of time on a question, leave space to go back to it later, if you have time.

(c) Structure your answer to keep you focused on the question **and** make it easier for the examiner to mark your script. Where appropriate, use headings from the question to help keep you focused. Always use report format, unless otherwise stated.

(d) **Use good communication skills**. Get your points across succinctly: explain and justify where appropriate (never make a recommendation without some explanation and justification). Be persuasive: you would have to use this skill if you were trying to convince senior management of the validity of your recommendations and the same is true for the examiner. Do not allow the examiner to get lost (or worse bored!) in a wall of words that wanders around the point.

(e) **Demonstrate both knowledge and experience**. Do not leave the examiner to fill in gaps and guess whether or not you know the theory or how to apply it: they will not do that, it is not their job. Make the connection and links: the point of the case study examination, in particular, is for you to demonstrate your skills as a marketing professional.

(f) **Do not deliver what you want to as opposed to what the question has asked for**. Unless the question specifically asks for analysis, you are expected to deliver decisions. The quality of your analysis is tested through the quality of your decisions. If a 'current situation' type question is asked for, do not deliver SWOTs. You are expected to give an overview of the current situation that adds value, an interpretation of the current situation that provides insights. A SWOT cannot do this.

(g) Use plenty of white space – aim for 25%. A wall of words is hard on the eyes (and the brain!) and immediately signals to the examiner that report format is not understood.

(h) **Always** check your answer: particularly important when you have had to adjust your prepared work to take on board additional information. Check for integration and consistency.

2   THE EXAMINATION PAPER

Additional information to be taken into account when answering the questions set.

Owing to the problems in the South Asian and South American economies, Biocatalysts is likely to face an erosion of margins within its textiles business. Clients are demanding cheaper enzymes for jeans and other textiles production. The agents in the key offices in Hong Kong and Singapore are also finding that they need more time and support from the Head Office in Wales. They are, however, finding that some of the specialist food enzyme demand is growing, although many of the potential customers require high levels of technical support.

Examination questions

Based on your analysis of Biocatalysts' competitive position, and after further discussion with the Managing Director, as the appointed marketing consultant to the Managing Director, you are to prepare a report which should address the following.

Question 1

Produce a strategic marketing plan for Biocatalysts Ltd for the next five years, justifying your recommendations.   **(50 marks)**

Question 2

Biocatalysts Ltd sells a diverse range of products into many geographical areas. Critically assess the best possible international marketing strategy that the company should follow, taking into account the generally poor performance of its agents and distributors.

(25 marks)

Question 3

Given the long-term prospects of the development of genetically modified organisms (GMOs) for the production of enzymes, develop a marketing communications strategy for Biocatalysts Ltd.   **(25 marks)**

(100 marks in total)

3   READING THE EXAM PAPER

Tutor comments on examination paper

3.1   Remember exam technique is vital to your success and the first action you need to take is to note the marks for each question and allocate the appropriate time to each question.

The additional information

3.2   Next you need to read the entire paper, additional information and all questions. Then you need to look for clues on what is being asked for.

Additional information

> 'Owing to the **problems** in the **South Asian** and **South American** economies, Biocatalysts is likely to face an **erosion of margins** within its **textiles** business'

Already you have clues on how you should develop your answer.

We now know there are problems with some economies which will affect Biocatalysts's margins and that textiles is not an attractive option.

> '**Clients are demanding cheaper enzymes** for jeans and other **textiles** production.'

How does this fit with your analysis and decisions, particularly on Biocatalysts' position? Were you intending to stay in textiles? Does staying in textiles fit with Biocatalysts' potential position? How does it fit with their strengths?

> 'The **agents** in the **key offices** in **Hong Kong** and **Singapore** are also finding that they **need more time and support from the Head Office** in Wales. They are however finding that some of the **specialist food enzyme demand is growing** although many of the **potential customers require high levels of technical support**.'

So specialty food enzymes are looking attractive and Biocatalysts's expertise and technical skills can be used to help position them as a premium priced service.

The questions

Question 1 is asking for the strategic marketing plan, question 2 for an international strategy (with specific reference to agents) and question 3 for a communications plan (with specific reference to GMOs).

Question 2 and 3 mean we do not have to spend much time on international issues, 'Place' or 'Promotions' in question 1. We can refer the examiner to questions 2 and 3. It does mean that in question 1 our strategic marketing plan must refer to and reflect an international focus.

4   A SAMPLE ANSWER

> **Planning your answer**
>
> Now you have examined the examination paper to determine precisely what you have been asked for, you can start to plan your answer.
>
> **Tutor comments on example answers**
>
> Please note this is an example only. You may have tackled the question differently. Providing you answered the specifics of the questions and within a marketing framework, there is no reason why your answer is not as good or better.
>
> The most important lesson to learn from this is, how much could you write in three hours (broken down into 90 minutes and 45 minutes × 2)? This is what you need to know before you go into the exam.

Contents

Leave the first page blank, go back when you have finished and complete this page. Normally you would include subheadings but this may be too time consuming in the exam

1   Five year strategic marketing plan

1.1   Current situation
1.2   Mission, vision and business objective
1.3   Business strategy and competitive position
1.4   Marketing objectives
1.5   Marketing strategy (segmentation, positioning, targeting)
1.6   Marketing mix plans (product, price, technical support)
1.7   Control (budget, scheduling, measurement)

2   International marketing strategy

2.1   Country/market selection
2.2   Agents and distributors
2.3   Methods of entry and levels of involvement
2.4   Marketing objectives
2.5   Marketing strategy
2.6   Tactical plans
2.7   Control

3   Marketing communications strategy

3.1   Communications objectives
3.2   Communications strategy
3.3   Targets
3.4   Promotional activities
3.5   Control

4.1 **Question 1**

1. **Five year strategic marketing plan**

1.1 **Current situation**

1.1.1 **Market conditions**

The biotechnology industry is young and very dynamic and technology is a key driver of developments and change, both of which occur with increasing frequency. Governments in many countries have supported developments in biotechnology through funding and a reluctance to over-regulate the market. Pressure from consumers may change this.

Economic conditions have been relatively stable in Europe and North America, but as highlighted in the additional information, this stability is not reflected across the globe, with South Asia and South America suffering from economic downturn.

Predicted future market growth in enzymes is from $1.7 billion to $2 billion by 2005. The greatest opportunity is the growth in 'other' eg animal feed, baking, fruit and wine, speciality applications and is predicted to be very rapid and collectively likely to be the largest section of the enzyme market exceeding £500 million sales by 2005. Bulk enzymes will increasingly be produced from GMOs. Some of Biocatalysts' markets are predicted to decline, for example textiles, while value will increase with total growth. Markets need to be examined for future viability.

Market/industry life cycle

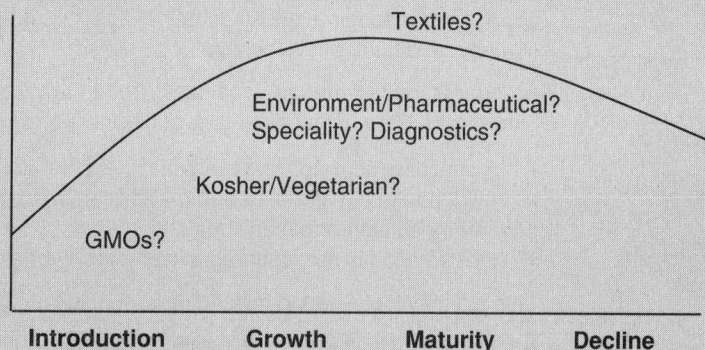

1.1.2 **Competition**

The nature of competition is changing. In this young industry, competitive 'positions' have not been an issue until now. Competitors are now clearly thinking about future positions. This would indicate a move to a more strategic marketing approach and you can expect clear competitive positions to emerge.

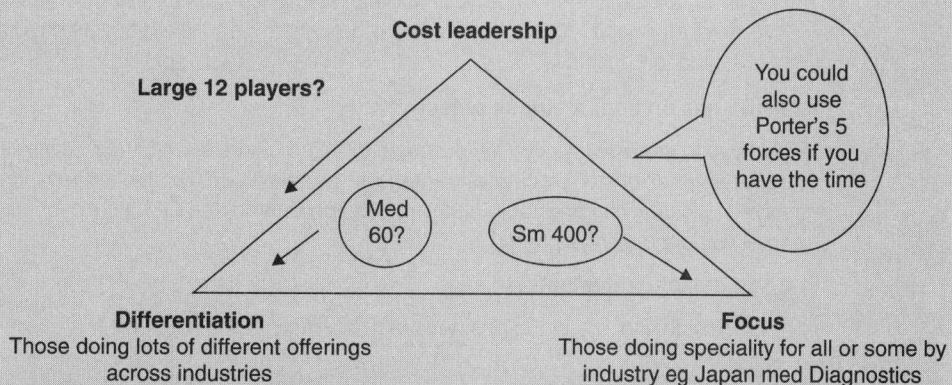

With the competitive information we have, it is difficult to be precise about competitors as we are not always comparing like with like but some assumptions can be made. Novo is a major player with 50% of the market. Gist and Genecor share 25% of the market. These players are most likely to have the potential to develop cost leadership positions. The remaining 25% of the market is shared by the rest of the biotechnology companies so the competition amongst these players is likely to become increasingly intense.

The 60 medium-sized companies are most likely to have enough market share to enable them to segment their markets and adopt differentiated positions. The remaining 400 small players will not have the strength to take on the medium and large players and are likely to look for opportunities to develop niche markets.

1.1.3 Customers

The end consumer significantly influences your customers who are typically manufacturers, producers and retailers and their future decisions will be based on what is acceptable to the consumer.

The industry has a complex network of many stakeholders that influence, directly and indirectly, what the industry does. For example MAFF, universities, industry analysts, FDA, HACCP etc.

1.1.4 Biocatalyst's current position

The business has highly qualified experts providing strong technical competence. With high levels of technical support becoming an expectation, this will be a key strength. Biocatalysts are innovative and have a track record of developing customised products and are good at customer relationships. However the customer focus is tactical not strategic or marketing orientated and new product development has not included business screening or marketing input suggesting a product orientation. This is evident from their poor financial performance. No segmentation seems to take place resulting in Biocatalysts tending to do anything for anyone.

A concern is that three sales people appear to be looking after 35 countries. The poor performance in some of the overseas markets, for example as little as £40,000 from Japan in 1997 and £140,000 from the USA, suggests this is not working. There does not appear to be an international strategy. There does not appear to have been a rigorous process for appointing, managing and evaluating agents and distributors. There is a lack of clear strategy, and competitive position.

Broader issues of market conditions, trends and competitive activities do not seem to be considered. Overall there is a lack of planning and control, evident in:

- Lack of up to date marketing intelligence. (lack of analysis)
- No monitoring of the market (performance, developments)
- Competitor information is patchy
- information is not gathered systematically or analysed methodically

This will inevitably lead to missed opportunities and threats.

An analysis of financial performance indicates a lack of control and is of immediate concern. The business has grown faster than the industry average but profits are low, running at around 6%. At the moment they are fairly liquid and able to cover liabilities. However increased debtors days (75 in 1994 to 143 in 1997), together with paying creditors faster than receiving debts suggests availability of funds and cash flow could become critical. The cash balance has come down to £12,000, down 61% ('96 on '97).

In conclusion the market is changing rapidly, competitors are becoming more strategic in their approach, customers are more demanding and Biocatalysts have some critical issues facing the business.

1.2 Mission, vision and business objective

Biocatalysts need to clarify the purpose of the business and their aspirations. Decisions will include whether or not Biocatalysts intend to pursue GMO production and, if so, the time scales involved. Biocatalysts are not in a strong position to launch a GMO product into the current hostile market without a clear strategy.

1.2.1 Mission statement

Biocatalysts are in the business of providing...

> Add your mission and vision here

1.2.2 Vision

To be...

1.2.3 Business objective

A profit objective is recommended to keep the business focused on what it must achieve and to provide a measure.

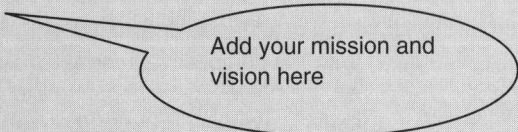

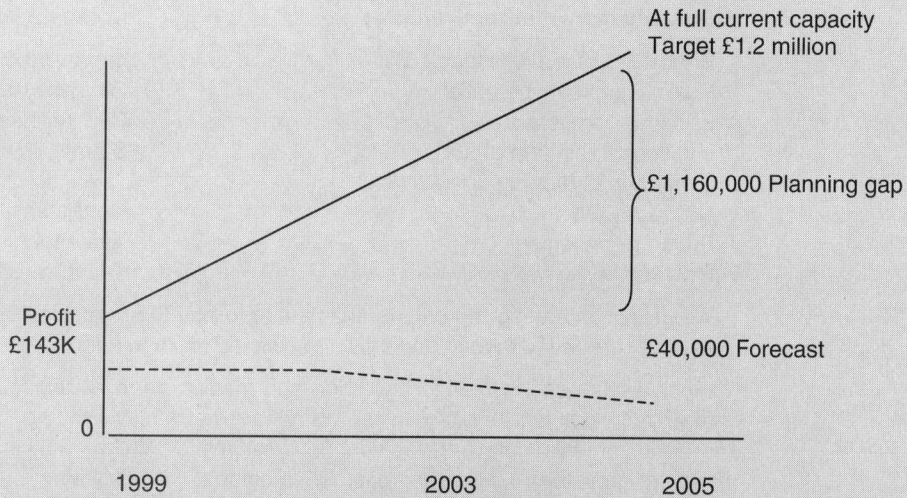

This profit objective requires an increased margin to 10%.

A company can grow when a market is growing substantially. However, given the rapidly changing nature of the market and increasing competition, to carry on as Biocatalyst is now, the forecast is likely to be a decline. With such low profits, unless a clear strategy and direction is implemented, there is a danger Biocatalysts will not be around in 2005.

Strategies now need to be identified to fill the planning gap.

1.3 Business strategy and competitive positioning

A number of options emerged during analysis.

PRODUCTS

		Existing	New
MARKETS	Existing	Environmental Waste treatment Textiles Health care Unique speciality foods Alcohol, baking, fats/oils Fruit/wine, flavour, protein Animal foods, leather Paper/pulp Chemical biotransformation	More testing kits GMOs By products High tech foods Full consultancy service Technical backup service
	New	Geographic - eg Russia China USA Japan New industries Oil spillage Pharmaceutical Licensing	Knowledge brokers Backward forward integration

1.3.1 Evaluation of strategic options

Each strategy must be evaluated for its attractiveness to the business and the competitive advantage/position it offers. The best evaluation tool for this purpose is the GE matrix. Management agree and prioritise the criteria for strategy attractiveness and research on customers to determine the competitive position. We have some information on why customers buy. This would form one of the criteria.

BPP
PUBLISHING

Strategy/market attractiveness	**Competitive position**
Profitability of not less than 10%	Improving efficiency
Marketing growth potential	Cost effectiveness
Levels of competition	Convenience
Investment required of not more than X%	Safety
Synergy with existing operations	Availability
New skills required	Consistency and quality
Speed to implement	Value for money
Degree of risk	Technical support

Weighting and rating the criteria enables us to plot the strategies on the matrix to reveal which strategies are worth pursuing and which should be rejected.

Biocatalysts need to plan for the short and medium term. In this fast, changing, dynamic market, longer term strategies can be difficult to identify. Strategy selection will need to provide immediate profits given your financial position, followed by medium term strategies that will grow the business and establish a competitive position.

The information we do have suggests the most attractive strategies are:

> Use additional information. You could plot these (and rejected) on the GE matrix.

- Short term market penetration strategy diagnostics

- Short to medium term market development strategy – Speciality foods

- Medium term new product development strategy – Technical support with selected products and as stand alone service

> You could indicate how much each strategy will contribute.

More accurate and up to date marketing research will confirm validity of this selection and profitability.

1.3.2 Competitive position

Strategy selection must be more focused than has been the case to date. The mission and vision will guide strategy selection and formulation. Biocatalysts cannot be all things to all people so product rationalisation and customer segmentation is going to be important. When formulating strategy, a clear competitive position should emerge and this can only be established through a co-ordinated effort by the business.

Analysis shows there are 12 major players in this market. Their size makes a cost leadership position possible. This is not an option for Biocatalysts given their size. The investment is too great. Increasingly even large companies are moving towards a differentiation strategy to improve their competitive position. 12 major players and 60 medium sized companies will be vying for positions using a differentiation strategy.

This leaves some 400 small companies, including Biocatalysts, to decide how they are going to compete. Analysis of the market and trends and Biocatalysts's strengths would indicate that a niche strategy would be the best option.

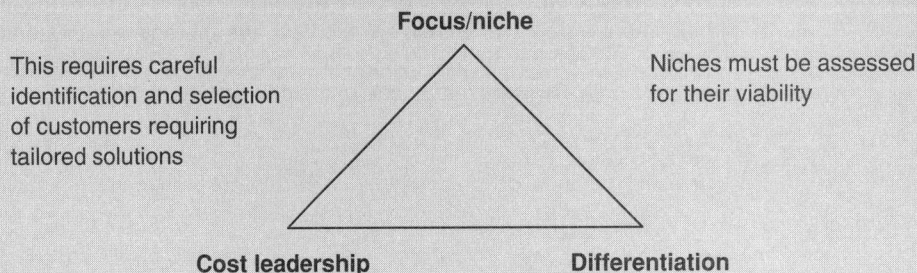

Focus/niche

This requires careful identification and selection of customers requiring tailored solutions

Niches must be assessed for their viability

Cost leadership   **Differentiation**

1.4 Marketing objectives

An overall marketing objective is recommended to generate £12 million revenue by 2005 to deliver a £1.2 million profit.

Marketing objectives must then be further broken down by industry/market and for each strategy eg:

Diagnostics 35%   £4.2m (from £100K 1997) at 12% = £504K
Pharmaceuticals 35%   £4.2m (from £300K 1997) at 12% = £504K
Food 30%   £3.6m (from £960K 1997) at 5.3% = £192K

1.5 Marketing strategy

A marketing strategy will need to be developed for each business strategy selected. The following plan is for speciality foods.

1.5.1 Segmentation

More information is required to segment the market effectively. However we do have some information, which will enable us to make a start.

Options for segmentation include initial segment bases determined by industry sectors, so for speciality foods, Kosher and vegetarian producers. Product, process and size of company may provide some opportunities for segmentation but none for competitive advantage. We must identify decision making units and needs and motives for buying. Many of these emerged during analysis. For example:

NEEDS	Users	Influencers	Deciders	Buyers	Approvers	Gatekeepers
Purity	X					
Cost efficiency				X		
Increase yield			X			

Research will improve information on precise needs and motives for Kosher and vegetarian foods. The technical support required may also affect segmentation. You may find customers from different sectors have commonalities by which we can segment. The advantage of this type of segmentation is that it can be used again, with small modifications and improvements, across national and industry boundaries.

1.5.2 Positioning

The positioning of the marketing mix should reflect the desired competitive position and customer needs. For example:

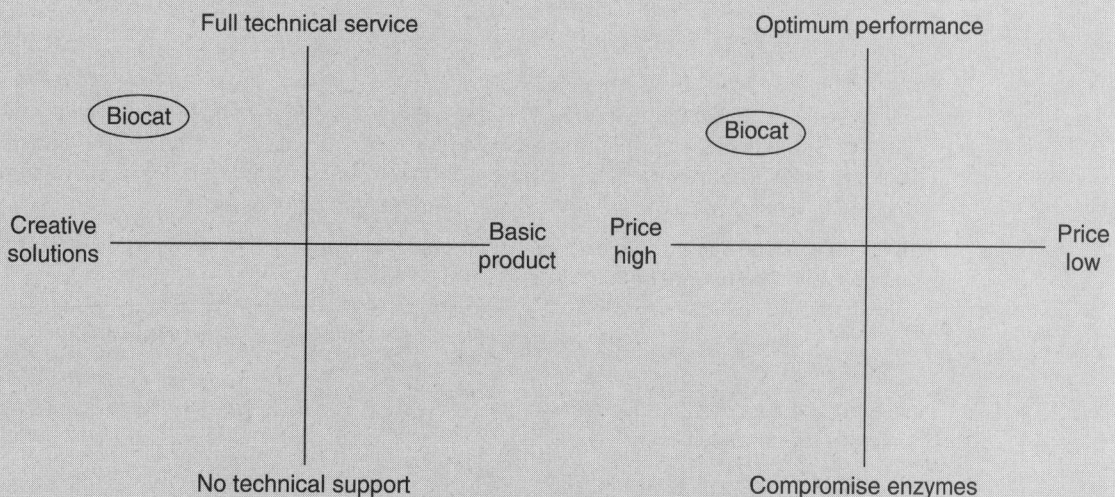

Full technical service — Biocat — Creative solutions / Basic product — No technical support

Optimum performance — Biocat — Price high / Price low — Compromise enzymes

It is important to establish current competitor positions and to monitor this activity and ensure Biocatalysts maintain a position that differentiates itself from the rest.

The role of the brand will be crucial in communicating and establishing desired position.

BPP PUBLISHING

1.5.3 Targeting

It is recommended that Biocatalyst pursue a multi-niche strategy. It would be risky to pursue only one niche for two reasons. The speed of change might result in a new entrant taking an interest in the niche and a single niche might not support the desired growth objectives.

The targeting strategy will therefore be differentiation. Specific needs of niches will be identified and marketing mixes designed to meet those needs.

1.6 Marketing mix plans

A distinct marketing mix plan will need to be developed for each niche targeted. By way of illustration, this plan is for speciality vegetarian foods.

1.6.1 Product

Objectives: to be determined: number of products sales by sector/market should be established

Actions: To rationalise the product range and ensure focus on profitable niches
To identify precise needs and possible future needs of vegetarian enzymes

1.6.2 Price

Aims: To reflect value for money and added value technical service: to achieve profit objective through premium price that reflects technical service

Actions: Research on price in the market and clarify price sensitive areas, complexities
Review sources of supply
Review impact of currency and exchange rate

1.6.3 Place

See answer 2

Additional information used here

1.6.4 Promotion

See answer 3

1.6.5 Customer service and technical support (service 3Ps)

Aims: To provide full technical support that will add value and differentiate the company to establish clear competitive position

Actions: Research customers, existing and potential, to establish nature of technical support needed

Evaluate current skills levels, both technical and customer care, and identify training needs

Design training programmes and review recruitment policy to meet above

1.7 Control

1.7.1 Budget

Cash flow is a problem and the reality is this will affect the marketing budget. However with a more strategic, efficient and focused plan, the current budget can be used much more effectively. Biocatalysts should consider alliances with customers on some activities e.g. research to help finance plans. Omnibus research might be of use.

If Biocatalysts are to survive and succeed, money will need to be spent on marketing and a recommended budget of X%.

You would need to specify

1.7.2 Scheduling

It is not the intention to detail every activity, these will be included in each plan, but rather to cover broadly key tasks.

Activity	Jul-Sep 99	Oct-Dec 99	2000	2001	2002	2003	2004	2005

Marketing research

Segment market

Review and implement formal planning and control systems (incl. NPD)

Rationalise product range. Re-design marketing mixes

Staff training

Implement market penetration

Implement market development   and on going

Implement N.P. development

Market monitoring

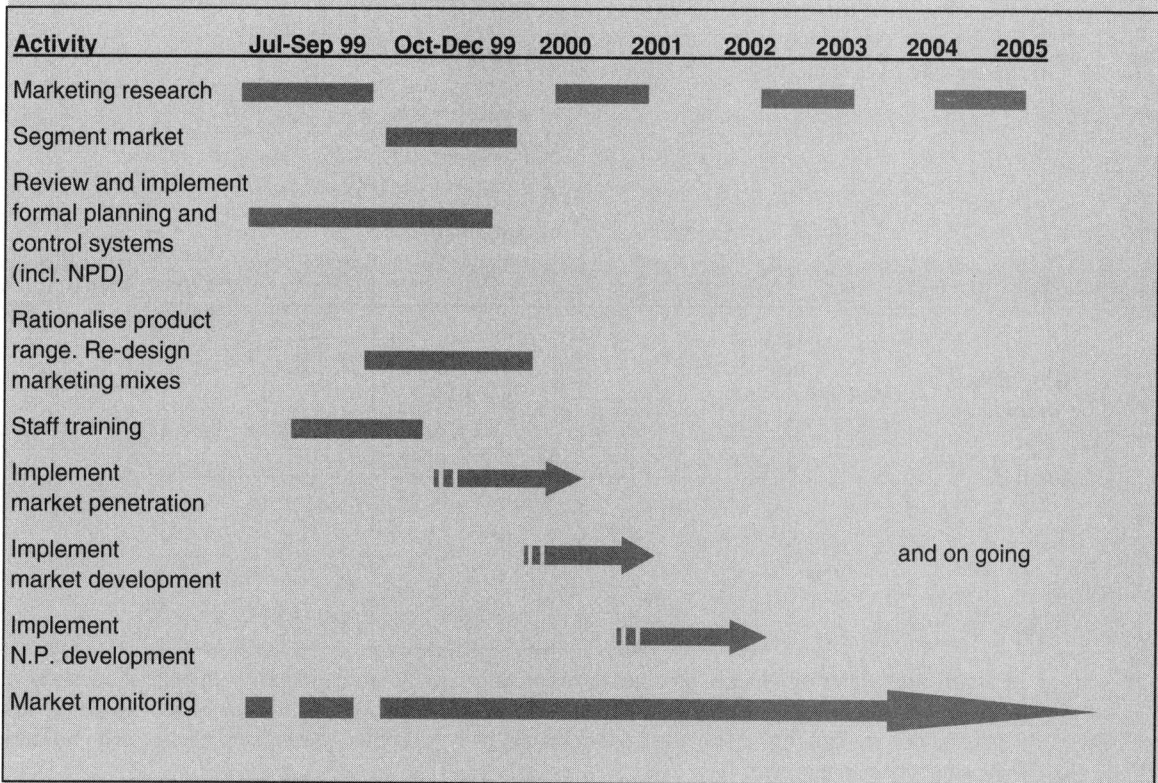

1.7.3 Measurement

Biocatalysts must track performance and ensure they are on course. Performance measures will include:

- Profits and profitability

- Product sales by sector

- Effectiveness of competitive positioning (customer, supplier, distributor surveys to track attitudes and perceptions)

- Customer satisfaction and loyalty

- Technical support performance

4.2 Question 2

2. International marketing strategy

The strategic marketing plan developed above has outlined vision, mission, business objectives, competitive position and issues on product and some market selection.

The intention in this plan is to recommend how Biocatalysts's international efforts can be very much more effective than they currently are.

2.1 Country/market selection

Not all markets are performing well and decisions need to be made on which markets to develop, particularly in view of Biocatalysts's limited resources.

A useful model for evaluating which countries or regions to operate in is the Harrell and Kiefer model. It works on the same principles as the GE matrix but the dimensions and criteria are different.

Criteria to enable the business to evaluate the attractiveness of the market eg:

Country attractiveness	Biocatalyst's capabilities
Political stability, risks and legal requirements	Experience of market
Economic conditions/growth	Investment required
Infrastructure	Management skills
Local technical skills and knowledge	Existing channel performance
Levels of competition	Control issues

BPP PUBLISHING

We know from the additional information that the South Asian and South American economies have problems. Added to this, these markets have been significant textile markets, a market that appears to be commoditising, possibly in decline.

	High	Medium	Low
High	Europe	North American	
Medium		S E Asia	
Low			

Biocatalyst's capabilities (vertical axis: High, Medium, Low)

> Use information from the case. Better than we have!

Europe and North American are stable markets where food, particularly specialist food, is a rapidly growing market. North America is very competitive and would be difficult, initially, for Biocatalysts to manage, given their financial situation. Europe, however, is closer to home and showing significant growth.

2.2 Agents and distributors

We must evaluate and rationalise the current network. The results of the analysis suggest performance is mixed. In some markets, Biocatalysts are hardly making enough money to make it worthwhile. The additional information suggests that agents in Hong Kong and Singapore are performing well as they are described as '**key offices**' so both these markets and agents are likely to be part of Biocatalysts's future developments in the medium-term when the economic situation improves. What we must establish for the short- and medium-term is the strength of distribution channels in Europe.

2.2.1 Evaluating current

As mentioned in the additional information, market conditions vary and will also need to be taken into account.

The GE matrix is again a very useful tool for evaluating distribution channels. The criteria will be different for evaluating distributors. Criteria will include for example:

Distribution attractiveness/performance

Order quantities/value
Profitability
Delivery performance
Technical know-how, experience, knowledge
Customer technical support capabilities (including problem handling)
Marketing performance (activities)
Market performance (penetration, development)

The customers' view of the effectiveness of distribution channels is important. They should be surveyed and their criteria will be similar to that discussed in part 1.

The evaluation process is two way. Biocatalysts need to establish their performance from the channels' point of view. Their criteria will include:

Reliability
Support – both technical and marketing
Profitability
Consistency
Compatibility
Motivation and communications

This exercise will result in identification of those agents and distributors that Biocatalysts will want to continue working with.

Development of an international strategy for Biocatalysts includes decisions on levels of involvement in different markets as this will determine methods of entry selected.

2.3 Methods of entry and levels of involvement

Other viable options for Biocatalyst to consider include:

2.3.1 Joint ventures

2.3.2 Strategic alliances

Under each of these headings you would discuss the advantages and disadvantages of each, **not** as a theoretical exercise but drawing on case material and in view of Biocatalysts's aspirations. In particular what is appropriate given your strategy selection?

2.3.3 Licensing

2.3.4 Wholly owned subsidiary

2.4 Marketing

Once countries/regions have been selected and methods of entry identified, marketing objectives by market can be established. Marketing research will clarify market value and therefore what Biocatalysts can realistically aim for. However there will be a minimum acceptable level for the market to be viable.

Illustrate your quantified marketing objectives by market. Make sure they link back to the business objective

2.5 Marketing strategy

The marketing strategy will be developed along the lines illustrated in the five year plan. Specifically, segmentation will identify similar niches across Europe initially, other regions later, that can be targeted. Positioning should have a broad theme for all niches and each niche will have specific needs and values. Research will identify any market-specific issues.

2.6 Tactical plans

Marketing mix design must reflect the constraints of the country including laws, standards and cultural issues.

You could expand briefly on the marketing mix but time would be against you

2.7 Control

Span of control increases with market development. Control issues include the extent of centralisation and decentralisation, and managing and motivating channels of distribution.

An important strategic issue will be the structure of the organisation as this impacts on control.

Budgets need to be set by market and measures of control would be similar to those outlined in the five year plan with performance measures for market and channel performance.

4.3 Question 3

3. Marketing communications strategy

Our communications strategy should focus on our customers and key stakeholders. However, as mentioned, in the current situation, there is increasing hostility in the market about GMOs in particular and, more generally, the biotechnology industry is beginning to suffer from some of the backlash. We therefore cannot ignore what is happening in our customers' markets. The responsibility for this hostility lies partly with governments and particularly with biotechnology companies, so we must be part of the solution.

BPP PUBLISHING

Consumers in developed countries are usually better educated and informed and are more sophisticated and demanding. Governments and large companies have, in the past, presumed they know best and made decisions about goods and services with little, if any, consultation with consumers. Consumers want to be informed and will make decisions about purchases based on that information.

Biocatalysts has the opportunity to build a brand that represents quality, safety and ethical practice so is of value to our customers who in turn have to address the needs of their consumers.

3.1 Communications objectives

Broad aims can include the intention to inform, reassure and if necessary persuade and change attitudes towards biotechnology and GMOs. However it is important to be clear about what is to be achieved. Aims can include the need to raise awareness or attention, generate interest, create a desire and encourage action.

It is difficult to quantify objectives until we have some indication of number of customers and stakeholders we need to influence. Once this has been established we can set quantified objectives. For example:

To raise awareness from X% to X% within three years of the benefits of GMOs

To change attitudes towards GMOs from a negative view of X% to a positive view of X% within five years

3.2 Communications strategy

Because of Biocatalysts' limited financial and marketing resources, some realistic decisions will have to be made about the development of communications strategy.

Biocatalysts should have a push and profile strategy. It is essential to ensure effective use of all resources and maximum impact on the marketplace.

A pull strategy is unrealistic and must be left to your customers. Biocatalyst's role could be to provide evidence and information to help customers communicate more effectively with consumers. This support might encourage customers to return the support and help with the funding of some communication activities.

Biocatalysts customers' pull strategies will play a significant role in dealing with negative perceptions and cannot be ignored.

3.2.1 Push

This strategy will be designed to encourage and persuade existing and new distribution channels and business to business customers to purchase Biocatalysts's enzymes and services.

3.2.2 Profile

This strategy is intended to promote broader issues to a wider audience, the complex and very influential stakeholders involved in this industry.

The communications strategy will build the brand and competitive position over time.

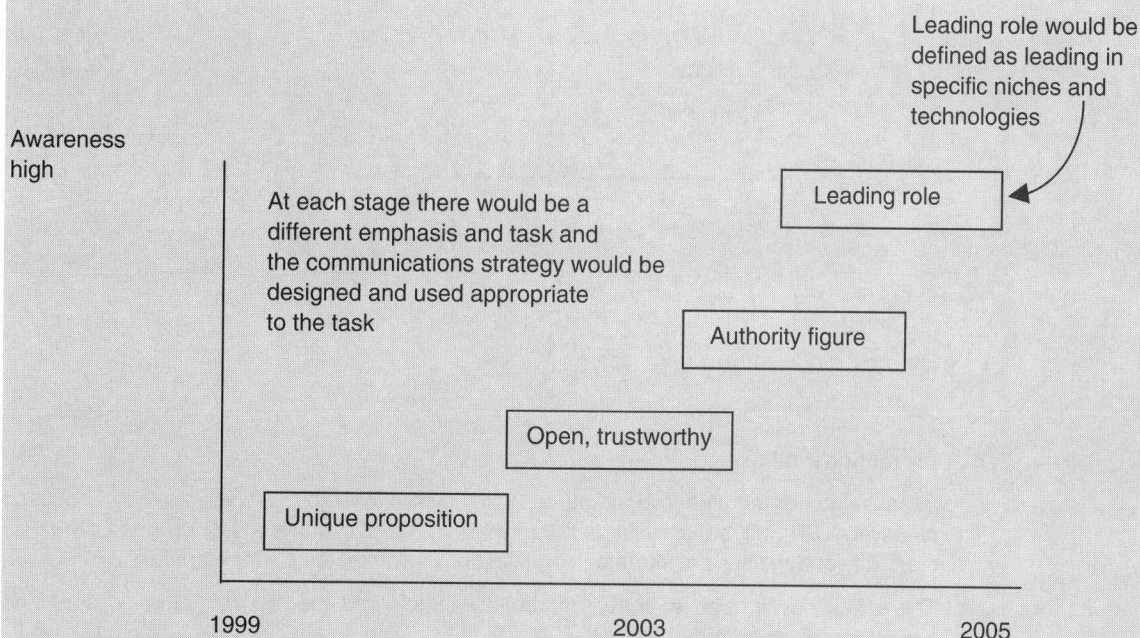

Awareness
high

At each stage there would be a
different emphasis and task and
the communications strategy would be
designed and used appropriate
to the task

Leading role would be
defined as leading in
specific niches and
technologies

| Leading role |

| Authority figure |

| Open, trustworthy |

| Unique proposition |

1999   2003   2005

3.3 Targets

The targets for communications will be broader than the marketing strategy. The reason for this is the need to influence the significant number of stakeholders involved that in turn influence, directly or indirectly, developments in the biotechnology industry. These stakeholders include:

Performance network - stakeholders directly influencing include:

- Suppliers, MAFF, FDA, universities, agents/distributors, industry producers, consumers, competitors, employees

Support network - Stakeholders that indirectly influence include

- Pressure groups, industry analysts, investigators, scientists, journalists, trade bodies, religious groups, slaughterhouses, environment agencies, food and drug agencies, governments

All stakeholders need to be targeted with clear, tailored messages and promotional mixes to ensure effective communications.

3.4 Actions

3.4.1 Positioning and messages

The key issue to address in this business is that of trust. Consumers have lost faith with businesses and governments and no longer trust them to make decisions that are in the best interests of consumers.

This is an opportunity for Biocatalysts to position themselves as trustworthy and as the biotechnology company that puts safety first. Testing procedures would take account of consumer concerns, not just the profit motive. Creativity is going to be vital and Biocatalysts, while able to provide the information, do not have the creative communications skills. An agency will need to be considered.

BPP PUBLISHING

Reputation for trust and safety

Biocat

Rigorous testing
procedures

Minimal testing
procedures

Disregard for public concern

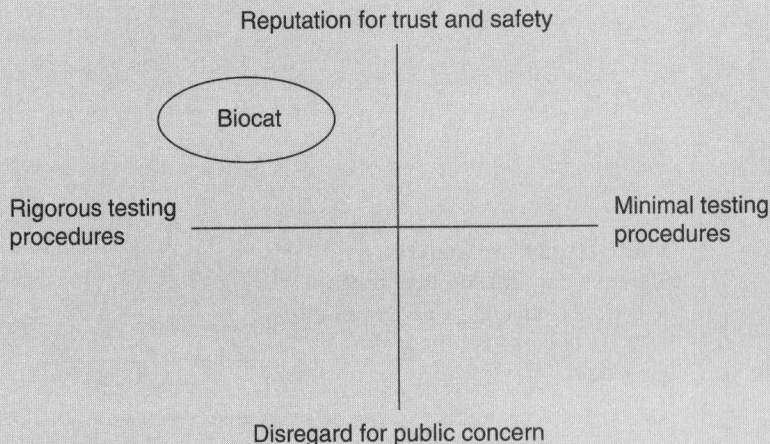

3.4.2 Promotional mix

Because of limited financial resources, the promotional budget will have to be used creatively. PR will be a main feature, which is in Biocatalysts favour because of its credibility and the current interest. Identifying newsworthy items will be crucial.

There has never been a better opportunity to tap into the 'human interest' story and encourage media to print.

Push strategy – sales force, technical support team, brochures, exhibitions, trade press

Profile strategy – PR, papers at seminars and conferences, explore opportunities for sponsorship

3.5 Control

You would need to specify

3.5.1 Budget

Biocatalysts's cash flow problems means that, until improved market penetration leads to improved profits, the communications strategy, though crucial, will have a slow start. However until research is completed the design of the campaign cannot start in earnest.

Other sources of funds should be reviewed and allocation of existing marketing budgets examined for more effective use. This can be used in the short term with more funds allocated as profits improve.

A budget of £X is recommended for the first year, increasing to £X for years 2 – 4. By year 5 the success of the campaign should lead a lower volume of funds being required. However the communications effort will remain vital and should be sustained.

3.5.2 Schedule

Activity	Jul-Sep 99	Oct-Dec 99	2000	2001	2002	2003	2004	2005
Marketing research	▬			▬	▬		▬	
Design of campaign		▬						
Launch of campaign 'Confronting the issues'			▬					
The brand build 'USP'				▬▬▬▬▬▬▬▬▬				

3.5.3 Measurement

Measurements will include tracking attitudes to GMOs, biotechnology companies generally and Biocatalysts in particular, awareness levels and so on.

Part C
Practice cases

15

Tackling a Practice Case: City of Daugavpils

Chapter Topic List

1	Introduction
2	City of Daugavpils: text and appendices
3	Step 1: Initial overview

---

1   INTRODUCTION

Tackling a Practice Case: City of Daugavpils

1.1   You may have already been practising your case study skills by working the Biocatalysts case study, as we demonstrated the approach in section B. This second case is one you really should work through yourself, using the materials we have provided as samples against which you can monitor and benchmark your own output. Simply reading the material is really not good enough. Case study analysis, as you have seen, is made up of a series of techniques which you need to develop and practices for yourself so that by the time the exam case is issued, you are confident about tackling it, whatever the business or sector.

1.2   In the second half of this manual, you will find two more cases. We have included the next, City of Daugavpils, with analysis and decision material developed by student groups actually working the case study. The final case study, World Class International, is to give you a final rehearsal case and is supported only with general guidance and some tutor comment.

BPP PUBLISHING

1.3   For City of Daugavpils, we will remind you at each stage of the case of the steps you should be following and then present you with our material and any necessary tutor comments. We will not be reminding you of 'how' to tackle each step, so if you are in doubt, you will need to refer back to section B.

By the end of this chapter, you will have:

(a)   Read the City of Daugavpils case
(b)   Completed your overview analysis
(c)   Compared your analysis with our tutor comments and feedback
(d)   Tested your understanding of the case

Case Step 1

Complete the overview

1.4   Consult Chapter 4 for detailed 'how to' guidance.

(a)   Read the case study

(b)   Stop and think about the case context

(c)   Sort out the case narrative into topic areas eg finance, marketing environment etc

(d)   Identify what is included in the Appendices and what information their analysis might generate

(e)   Remember to start your information shopping list

The Chartered
Institute of Marketing

Case Study
December 2001

Strategic Marketing Management: Analysis & Decision

City of Daugavpils

© The Chartered Institute of Marketing

BPP
PUBLISHING

Case Study – December 2001

Strategic Marketing Management: Analysis & Decision

Important Notes

The examiners will be marking your scripts on the basis of questions put to you in the examination room. Candidates are advised to pay particular attention to the *mark allocation on the examination paper and budget their time accordingly*.

Your role is outlined in the candidates' brief and you will be required to recommend clear courses of action.

You WILL NOT be awarded marks merely for analysis. This should have been undertaken before the examination day in preparation for meeting the tasks which will be specified in the examination paper.

Candidates are advised not to waste valuable time collecting unnecessary data. The cases are based upon real world situations. No useful purpose will therefore be served by contacting companies in this industry and candidates are *strictly instructed not to do so* as it would simply cause unnecessary confusion.

As in real life, anomalies will be found in this Case situation. Please simply state your assumptions where necessary when answering questions. The CIM is not in a position to answer queries on Case data. Candidates are tested on their overall understanding of the Case and its key issues, not on minor details. There are no catch questions or hidden agendas.

Additional information will be introduced in the examination paper itself which candidates must take into account when answering the questions set.

Acquaint yourself thoroughly with the Case Study and be prepared to follow closely the instructions given to you on the examination day. To answer examination questions effectively, candidates must adopt a report format.

The copying of pre-prepared "group" answers written by consultants/tutors is strictly forbidden and will be penalised by failure. The questions will demand analysis in the examination itself and individually composed answers are required to pass.

Candidate's Brief

Daugavpils is Latvia's second city and, in Soviet times, was an industrial powerhouse. Now after ten years of Latvian independence, it is a shadow of its former self.

In March 2001, a new Mayor, Richard Eigims was elected together with a new administration. He is a businessman and self-made millionaire. After a thorough review of the city finances and organisation, he created a new department to advise him on business and marketing. Ilya Podkolzins has been appointed to head this new department.

You are a Marketing Consultant funded by the European Union pre-accession funds and have been assigned to Daugavpils to help address the above challenges. At a meeting you will present your findings to Ilya Podkolzins, who will share them with the municipality.

N.B. The municipalities in Latvia are similar to the American model where the Mayor, as the leader of an elected majority, runs the town. Most of the facilities are controlled by the municipality.

Important Notice

Additional information will be provided at the time of the examination. Further copies may be obtained from The Chartered Institute of Marketing, Moor Hall, Cookham, Maidenhead, Berkshire, SL6 9QH, UK.

BPP PUBLISHING

City of Daugavpils

Introduction

This case is set in the city of Daugavpils in the Latgale region of Latvia. Daugavpils has had a turbulent past and an interesting history. As the result of the momentous changes in Russia and Soviet withdrawal from the city in 1991, it has become a city which is trying to stabilise itself and find a new meaning for its existence. It has a mayoral system which is based on the American model where the Mayor carries a lot of influence and power, and is not just a figurehead for the citizens. The country itself is polarised as Riga has the base of power and wealth with cities such as Daugavpils being regarded as backward and poor. There is little understanding of the region and its potential in Riga, the capital of Latvia. The new Mayor Richard Eigims is determined to create a new future for the city. Part of creating this future lies in marketing the city within and outside Latvia. Riga is the centre of power and prosperity in Latvia.

The Country, Latvia

Latvia has a long and somewhat chequered history, being controlled at various times by Sweden, Russia, Poland and Germany over the last 800 years. The national identity was established during a brief period of independence between the World Wars. The Nazi holocaust and the Soviet Pogroms resulted in a large percentage of the nation being displaced, killed, or replaced by ethnic Russians and other Soviet peoples. The last phase of Russian control ended in 1991, marking the opening of the 'Iron Curtain'. Latvia's leaders are anxious to seal their country's independence from Soviet rule by forging stronger links with the Western economies.

Latvia is in the centre of the three Baltic States. To the south, Lithuania has strong geographical and historical links with Poland. Together they once formed an empire that reached the doors of Moscow and threatened Russia. Estonia has strong cultural and geographic links with Finland. They share a common language and culture and have many business links. This leaves Latvia with nominal friends across the Baltic Sea, namely Sweden and Denmark, and greatly dependent on Russia.

Latvia now has strong economic links with the west and nearly two-thirds of its exports go to the European Union (EU). The country is preparing for EU entry and is beginning to fulfil many of the requirements for full status. However, in spite of the growing links and business with the EU, the country is still highly dependent on the flow of Russian oil through the country. A large proportion of its income is derived from transit services as up to 15% of Russian oil is exported from the port town of Ventspils. Russia therefore has a great interest in what happens to the country. Another reason is that 30% of the population is Russian. The current government's somewhat contentious policy of only granting citizenship to Latvian speaking individuals has left some of the Russian speaking population stateless. Many of the ethnic Russians are uneasy about Latvian being the main language. The country, as a result of historical events, has been left with a mixed demography and a Soviet economic legacy. As a result, Daugavpils is essentially Russian speaking and presents the country with the challenge of dealing with

2

ethnic and economic variations. Unemployment in the area has been rising steadily, ever since the collapse of the Russian empire, with its large and inefficient factories. Latgale is one of the poorest regions in Europe with a high concentration of small farms and an ageing population. These factors pose a specific challenge for the country, especially as most of its resources are located in Riga. In the long term it will also pose a challenge for the EU, when it extends so far east. Latvia as a country only has a few attractions from an economic point of view, if Porter's competitive advantage of nations is taken into account. Porter considers that the key factors in determining a country's competitive advantage are as shown below (*Figure 1.*). Latvia has been pushed towards the west, largely as a result of the economic crisis in Russia in the late 1980s and early 1990s (*for economic details see Appendix 1.*).

Figure 1. – Porter, 1998

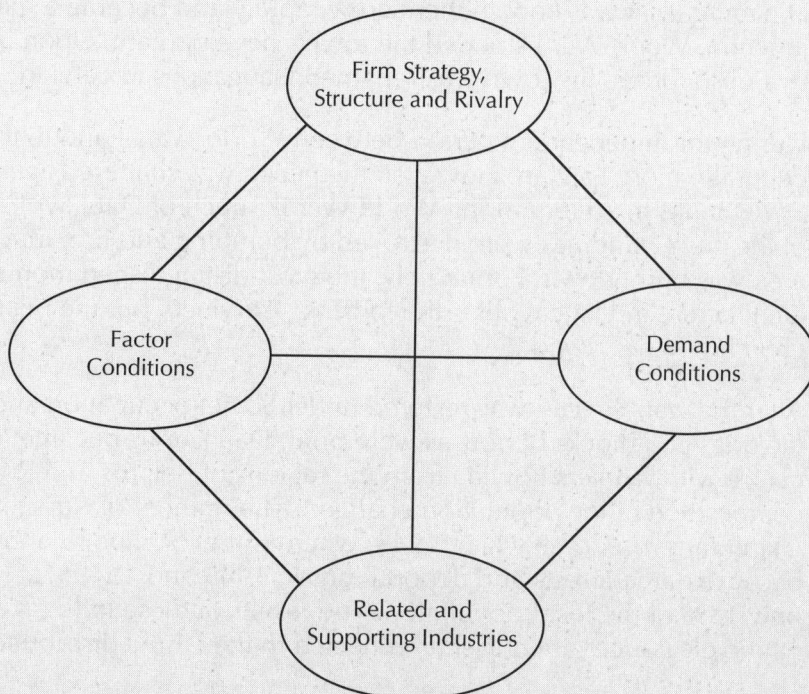

A major problem that is holding Latvia back, in common with the other Former Soviet Union (FSU) countries, is the Soviet management system. This has given rise to very hierarchical, authoritarian, military style organisational structures. In the fast moving commercial sector, these structures are extremely inefficient and inflexible. They are not competitive, but they are the current role models. This makes it even more important to attract back former Latvians with knowledge of western methods and culture. Currently there are large numbers of successful Latvians living in the USA and Canada. Without their knowledge of western practices, it will take one or two generations to move from the Soviet model to the western model. The key element in changing the culture of the individuals who were used to a centrally planned and largely inefficient economy is instilling the importance of developing and implementing a market oriented view of business, (*see Appendix 2. for country statistics*).

City of Daugavpils

History

The city was formed in 1275 by Ernest von Raceburg, Master of the Livonian Order. The new town was sacked by Lithuanians twice within the next 100 years. Soon there were occupations by the Poles and the Russian Czars. Instead of rebuilding the old castle, Ivan the Terrible built a new fort. It was later controlled by Poland and became a major trading centre. Jesuit monks settled there in 1620 and peace and prosperity returned. However, this was shattered by a war between Poland and Russia. Following this, the Swedes ruled the area for a short period. The next period saw the city being exchanged several times between the Russians and the Poles. Eventually it was ruled by the Russians. In 1810, a remarkable fortress was being built along the Daugava to keep out the French, under Napoleon's command. However, the French managed to occupy the structure while it was still being built. After the Napoleonic wars construction was resumed with the help of 10,000 Russian soldiers and 30,000 workers. In the 1860s, Dinaburg (as it was known then) grew rapidly and became a major railway junction. World War I stopped the town's development. Upon liberation in 1920 by Polish forces, the town was renamed Daugavpils in Latvian.

During this independent period between World Wars I and II, the town became culturally more Latvian. However, the peace was shattered again by the arrival of Soviet tanks in 1940. During World War II, much of Daugavpils was ruined: 72% of the city's buildings were destroyed by bombing and fire; much of the downtown area was burnt down. Fortunately, the most distinguished monument of history and architecture in Daugavpils – the fortress – survived, but the beautiful baroque style church was destroyed.

After the war, the city was restored under Soviet occupation and several new factories and blocks of houses were built. Daugavpils became a large industrial centre with workers flowing from the regions of Belarus and Russia. The ethnic composition of the population changed. The number of Russians, Belarussians and Ukrainians rose to 69.4% in 1949, whereas the local population decreased because of the arrests and deportations in 1945 and 1949. Latvians constituted only 13% of the local population. The results of these influxes of individuals and ethnic clearances are currently reflected in the ethnic distribution of the town.

Table 1. – Demographics – Ethnic Distribution

Ethnic Origin	Daugavpils City
Latvians	14.36%
Russians	58.61%
Poles	13.25%
Belarussians	8.27%
Ukrainians	2.83%
Lithuanians	0.84%
Romanians	0.34%
Estonians	0.03%
Other	1.48%

Geography

Daugavpils is the second largest city in the Republic of Latvia, located 232km from the capital, Riga. Its closest neighbours are the Republic of Lithuania (25km to the border), Belarus (33km to the border) and Russia (120km to the border). This juxtaposition of three countries has been of great benefit to the city over the centuries, enabling it to become an important hub of transport and trade in eastern Latvia. Railroads connect Daugavpils with Riga, St. Petersburg, Moscow, Vilnius, Panavezius and Saulai, (*see map of Daugavpils in Appendix 1.*).

Daugavpils is located in southeastern Latvia on either side of the Daugava River. This river is 1,020km long with 367km lying within Latvia. The river ends its run in Riga and enters the Baltic Sea. The city is located in the southeastern part of Eastern Latvia's low-land, on the Jersika plain, (*see Appendix 1.*). It is surrounded by the Latgale heights in the north-east, and by the Augzeme heights in the south and south-east. In the east, it borders on the protected Augsdaugava region. The city lies on unusual geological formations, with abundant sandstone slate and clay available within its environs. These deposits have been used for buildings for many centuries. Daugavpils has a continental climate, being about 200km inland from the sea. The highest temperatures are around 34°C and the lowest around -25°C. Precipitation is around 650mm per annum and the sunlight hours are around 1,809 per annum. The land around the city is well endowed with water, having 15 large lakes (with approximately 350 small ones), 8 rivers, numerous brooks and economically significant water reserves. The area has outstanding natural beauty and is well forested with approximately 10,400 hectares of trees. The forests and lakes support a wide range of mammals and fish.

BPP
PUBLISHING

Politics

The Mayor of Daugavpils effectively runs the town and is responsible for schools, hospitals, local police, street cleaning, rubbish collection and disposal, sewage, water treatment, heating, etc. and a wide range of property and local businesses.

The local elections in March produced a new Mayor, Richard Eigims. He is the leader of the Latgales Light Party and has 7 of the 15 seats. His party has formed a coalition with the Social Democrats (1 seat) and the Human Rights Party (2 seats) for a total of 10 seats.

The previous Mayor and leader of the Daugavpils City Party, Alexei Vidavskis, had 13 of the 15 seats. This was reduced to 5 seats at the March elections. He now leads the opposition. This is a new development as Daugavpils was effectively a "one-party state" from independence to March 2001. The City Party has its roots in the former Communist Party.

The Latvian State Government changes about every 12 months and appears to be based on the Italian model. As a result, most local politicians form their own parties. They avoid affiliation with national political parties as this can lead to unpopularity when that particular government goes out of favour. This creates problems for creating a consistent brand image for the city.

Religion

There are churches for the following religions in Daugavpils: Catholic, Lutheran, Jewish, Baptist, Old Orthodox and Orthodox. This broad range of religions is a demonstration of the multi-cultural society that is Daugavpils. The two with the largest following are the Catholic and Orthodox churches. The former is actively supported by the Polish community. The churches are full most Sundays and during religious festivals, but, with the exception of the Catholic church, the congregations largely comprise older women.

Regional Development

To date, regional development has been fragmented and unco-ordinated. In order to address this, the Latgale Regional Development Agency (LRDA) was formed. The LRDA has produced the first regional development plan in Latvia. They have pioneered co-operation amongst the region's municipalities and are raising the region's profile in Riga. EU Project Partners are based in the LRDA Daugavpils office, together with two other projects.

Education

Daugavpils has a University of around 3,000 students. Originally it was dedicated to teacher training, but latterly the demand for teachers has gone down significantly owing to low birth rates. This institution is in the process of changing its mission to support local business and transforming itself into a full University. Now there are 500 students taking business related courses. There is an affiliation with both Salford University in the UK and a Riga based business school.

There are many good schools in Daugavpils. Unfortunately, they have generally become polarised as "Russian" or "Latvian". English is emerging as a required language, in addition to Latvian and Russian. School number 9 has an excellent academic record and has won many English Speaking contests.

Health

There is a large local hospital which is being partially modernised with a loan from the World Bank. With a staff of 900, it is the largest single local employer. There is also a small Nurses Training College of about 150 pupils. In Soviet times there were several large, attractive "sanatoria" in and around Daugavpils. They were very popular with Russians, especially from St. Petersburg. They were somewhere between a convalescent home and a health farm, and served as both. After independence, they all fell into disuse and have been closed. A good example of this is a very grand 19th century building on the banks of the Daugava. There are excellent views and beautiful grounds, but the building has been abandoned and has fallen into disrepair. Interestingly enough, Lithuania has kept some of these sanatoriums going and they are proving to be popular amongst the Latvians! Doctors' salaries are low and vary between 10-150 lats a month. Most are state employed. Many are also very dedicated and return to Latvia after spells abroad. (*For details on healthcare, see Appendix 2.*). Currently the city has no plans for developing 'health tourism'. Health tourism is a growing market in countries such as India, where many westerners feel that they can get better care at cheaper costs with excellent doctors.

Multi-cultural Society

The Daugavpils District is ethnically diverse with over 20 nationalities living in peace and harmony. This is a major achievement that goes largely unrecognised outside the area. The inevitable growth of Latvian nationalism after independence, e.g. through the language laws, has increased local tension and provoked an equal and opposite nationalist backlash amongst the other communities. However, there is still a high rate of inter-marrying and social and cultural activities across ethnic boundaries. There are many flourishing societies that promote social cohesion, e.g. Latvian-Belarus, Latvian-Lithuanian, Latvian-Polish societies. There is also a small Roma community that co-exists with the other ethnic groups. Latvia has a Roma representative in the parliament (Saeima).

The city's Culture Hall was opened in 1937. It includes a theatre and an acting company with an average age of 30. There have been productions of works by Russian writers, Faulkner and Lorca. Plans are being started for the refurbishment of this theatre so it can again take its place as the cultural heart of the city.

Agriculture

There is a lot of subsistence farming around Daugavpils that will go through the painful transition to medium sized, multi-function farms as part of the EU accession, e.g. the SAPARD programme. There is little local preparation for this. However, the Naujenes Pagast in the Daugavpils District is a good example of Rural Development. The community is based around a disused Soviet airfield, which they are redeveloping as a local business and social centre.

The Elderly

Approximately 29% of the Daugavpils population are pensioners on very low incomes and with few assets. Families generally care for their elderly, but there are those who have no support and end up in Homes.

The Unemployed

Unemployment is high in this area – how high is difficult to judge because after 6 months, claimants drop out of the system. It is estimated at 28% or double the "official" figure. The State Employment Services is legally obliged to document details of training, job vacancies, etc. only in Latvian. This is clearly a disadvantage for those whose native language is not Latvian.

Education

Education in Latvia begins at seven, with compulsory basic education lasting 9 years.

The number of pupils at basic school level in the year 1998-1999 was 293,385. Education is generally free and accessible. The country places a great importance on education and the literacy rates are higher than many developed countries at around 95%, (*for further details on Daugavpils see Appendix 2.*).

Marketing Issues

As a result of the problems that the city faces and the opportunities that exist, the Mayor has created a new structure to help to promote Daugavpils, (*see Appendix 3.*).

The marketing needs of the city are complex and touch on different sectors in different ways. Initially, the biggest challenge facing the city council is understanding and counteracting the poor perception of Daugavpils in Riga. As Riga is the powerhouse of the Latvian economy, little thought is given to the far off city lying to the east of the country.

Marketing for Business Growth

The city, as explained before, lies at the crossroads of many different countries. In many ways it looks both to the east and the west. However, it is likely that investment for growth will come more readily from the west and the EU. The Daugavpils District Enterprise Support Centre is a business focal point in the Daugavpils District. They are currently running two US sponsored projects. US Peace Corps volunteers have assisted in the development of this NGO. This is a multi-lingual centre and all training material is available in both Latvian and Russian.

Foreign investment is vital to the regeneration of this industrial area. So far the following foreign companies have taken the plunge: Zieglera, Rhodia, Axon Cable and Swedtex; one German, two French and one Swedish. Rhodia has bought a very large site containing many serviceable buildings. The largest covers 10 hectares! This is the local equivalent to a business park and represents an excellent opportunity for any foreign companies wishing to invest here. Axon Cable has bought two buildings and employs 80 people making cables for computers. Swedtex is a Swedish textile company making ladies' stockings. It employs 70 people and plans to double its workforce. In addition to this, Le Bois Massif of France is starting to build wooden houses for export to the west. It expects to employ 120 people by next year. Others attracted to the site include Falck, a Danish security company which has its local headquarters in an office block, Aga the German-Swedish industrial gases company and Magistr, a local company which buys and recycles waste from Rhodia's operation. Magistr also employs 220 people and supplies high quality ropes and fishing nets to companies around the world. The company was founded and is run by individuals who were cybernetics experts in the former Soviet army.

Then there are the "dinosaur" companies left over from the Soviet era. Generally they supplied one item for the whole of the Soviet Union. At independence, their main market disappeared overnight. For the few that survived, employment is 10% of the previous number. For example, the Driving Chain Company made bicycle chains for the whole of the Soviet Union. It continues to survive through creative schemes such as supplying a Belarus factory with bicycle chains with payment in finished bicycles which it then sells locally. Much progress has been made and the factory recently gained ISO9000 certification. The city is a key railroad juncture for the former Soviet empire and as a result of this, railway coaches were built and engineered in the city. This has left a legacy of good engineers and craftsmen. Zieglera, a German company manufacturing heavy-duty grass cutters has taken advantage of this fact.

The city council needs to develop a marketing strategy that will attract new businesses from international sources to the region. Currently, there is a lack of a coherent marketing plan to attract business to the area.

The city has:

a. A plentiful supply of cheap labour with average wages running at $60 a month.

b. A good, skilled labour force left over from the Soviet era.

c. Huge factories which are currently lying empty.

d. An old decaying industrial infrastructure.

e. An educated population.

Figure 2. – Multiple Audiences for Daugavpils

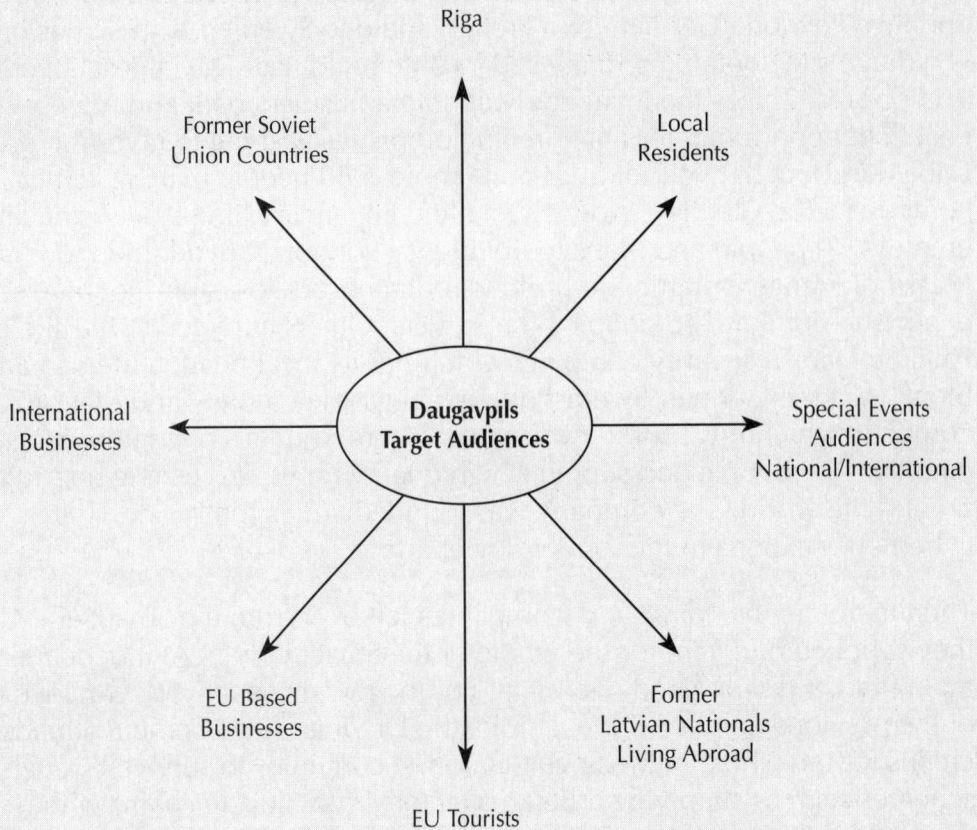

Riga

Former Soviet Union Countries

Local Residents

International Businesses

Daugavpils Target Audiences

Special Events Audiences National/International

EU Based Businesses

Former Latvian Nationals Living Abroad

EU Tourists

One of the first studies into assessing cities, took place in the Netherlands. The cities were assessed on the basis of a scale developed by Ashworth and Voogd. They considered the following issues:

- Qualities of the site.
- Transport infrastructure.
- Land cost.
- Possibilities of subsidies.
- Attitude of authority.
- Commercial contacts.
- Residential amenity.
- Labour markets.

These particular areas were then assessed and a general 'potency' score was developed. This allowed a competitive analysis of different cities. Based on this, differential marketing strategies can be developed. In another study the key elements in the promotional image of 16 medium sized Dutch towns were studied.

Table 2. – Information Produced by Towns in the Netherlands

Types of Information	% of Towns
Tourism marketing	81%
Tourist overview	69%
Description of monuments	56%
Historical	56%
Description of museums	50%
Town guide	50%
Town map	50%
Historical account	44%
Water recreation facilities	31%
Description of coat of arms	31%
Sport facilities	31%
Parking facilities	31%
Other public services	31%
Lists of monuments	25%
Lists of cafes/restaurants	25%
Calendar of events	19%
List of commercial firms	19%
Description of public parks	6%
Description of housing	6%
Description of schools	6%

Tourism marketing is now becoming an important part of most cities' strategies. However, tourism marketing is probably one of the most difficult areas to develop successfully. Daugavpils generally has a very negative image. For instance, a recent poll of residents showed that 75% would wish to live elsewhere. Most individuals in Riga have a poor image of the city and generally feel that it is backward and too close to the Russian border. The ethnic mix of the population also deters local Latvians from visiting the town. Yet the town has many positive assets. It has:

- Beautiful churches.
- An excellent pedestrianised centre with beautiful architecture.
- Pleasant parks.
- An old historical fort.
- Tree lined avenues.
- A good but old tram service.
- Beautiful unspoilt countryside dotted with lakes.
- Friendly and generally helpful people.
- Safety.
- An excellent ice hockey stadium.

BPP
PUBLISHING

Figure 3. – Positioning of Cities

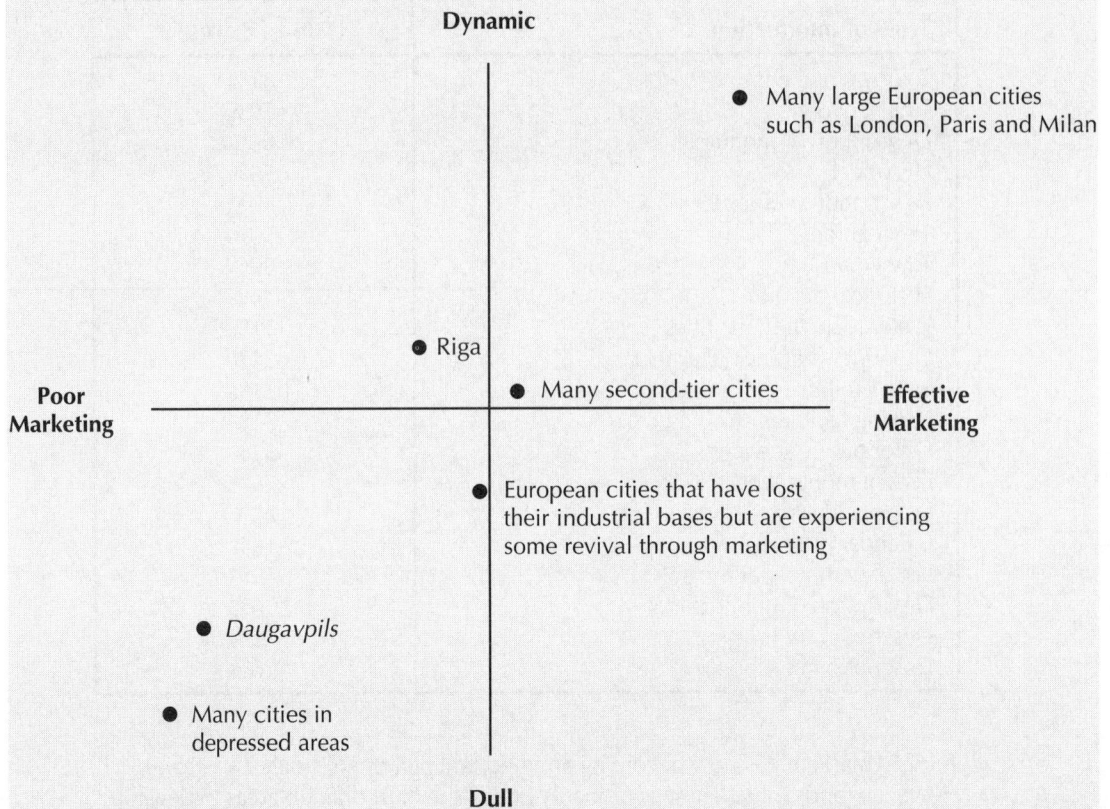

Dynamic

● Many large European cities
such as London, Paris and Milan

● Riga

Poor Marketing

● Many second-tier cities

Effective Marketing

● European cities that have lost
their industrial bases but are experiencing
some revival through marketing

● *Daugavpils*

● Many cities in
depressed areas

Dull

Source: Ranchhod, 2001

The figure above shows some of the key ways in which cities are perceived both by locals and the general public.

In many ways the city has to create a positive image out of a negative. Although the history is somewhat chequered, there are many ways in which it could be sold to potential tourists. For instance, the great Soviet writer Pushkin was actually imprisoned in the great fort.

An example of a city that has created a positive image is Bradford in England. For many decades it suffered a poor image coupled with an industrial base which was declining inexorably. The city council recognised this problem and allocated £100,000 to expand and search for tourist markets. They undertook an audit and promoted some of the key sites used for television programmes such as *Wuthering Heights*, *Emmerdale Farm* and *Last of the Summer Wine*. They also took into consideration its industrial heritage, based on the National Museum of Photography, Film and Television. The city also cleverly promoted its ethnic mix by promoting the city as the 'Curry Capital of the North'. The city was promoted for short breaks in order to entice people from local cities. Package holidays were offered to travel agents. As tourists began to flood into the city a degree of confidence returned to the residents and local businesses.

The surrounding area of Daugavpils offers a different kind of experience for individuals interested in hunting and fishing. The immense history also offers scope for development. The region has plenty of attractive natural landscapes. Several lakes and two significant highland areas – Augszeme and Latgale highlands – are located in the Daugavpils region. A number of historical monuments and religious buildings provide good background for the development of tourism. However, the tourist industry still has a lot of room for development, (*see Figure 4. and Appendix 2.*), as the popularity of the region is significantly below average in Latvia and cannot be compared with the most prosperous regions in the Baltic States. Some of the most popular spots in the region are the Daugavpils Fortress from the 17th century, Peter-Paul Cathedral, a fortress built in the beginning of the 19th century, the Boris-Gleb Church, Vaclaiciena Palace and other churches built over the centuries. One of the most dramatic edifices is the Duke Jacob's Channel in Asare (500km long), built in 1667-1668 to link the two rivers, Vilkupe and Eglaine, to connect the Daugava and the Lielupe water routes so that traders could reach the sea without going through customs in Riga.

Figure 4. – Tourism Figures, Daugavpils Region

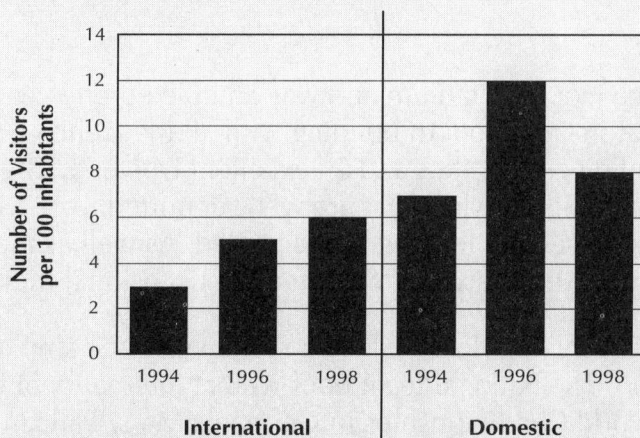

The Airport

Although Daugavpils is the second largest city in Latvia and although some very big companies are located there, it is still regarded as a development area. Owing to the lack of flight connections, the business environment has difficulties in exploiting new markets as well as attracting investors and tourists. The current Daugavpils airport is a former Soviet military airport with a runway of 2,500m. When the Russian army left, all technical installations and equipment were dismantled, including the landing lights. The airport needs updating. During the Soviet period, Daugavpils was a busy airport serving more than 60,000 passengers per year. There were 7 daily flights to Riga, one daily flight to Moscow and one to Minsk. The big factories also used air transportation for cargo in connection with sales and supply. The airport is owned by the municipality and a number of business people. The Daugavpils region and the Daugavpils City Government as the major stakeholders have a great interest in opening the airport for commercial and tourist traffic as it is such an important pivot for developing a marketing strategy for the region. Within a 100km radius of Daugavpils, there are 800,000 people. It is by far the biggest city after Riga in Latvia. A survey carried out by a group of Danish consultants showed the key export markets and the key destinations for passengers, (*see Appendix 1., Table 5.*)

13

255 BPP
PUBLISHING

Sport in Daugavpils

There are three major sports facilities in Daugavpils:

- Lokomotiv Stadium.
- Ledus Halle.
- Football Stadium.

Lokomotiv Stadium

This is the only speedway (motorcycle racing) stadium in the Baltic States and hosted the European Championships on the 14th to 15th September 2001. There has been a very basic facility here for some years, but last spring a new stadium was built and the facilities greatly enhanced for the European Championship. This stadium holds 4,000 spectators. Latvia has a very good speedway team which participated in these championships.

Ledus Halle

This is the Ice Hockey Stadium and was completed one year ago. It holds 3,000 spectators in a modern building with all the facilities expected in a new arena, including good toilets and an excellent cafeteria. There is a local league of about 8 teams (still growing) that are well supported. Last winter, they had their first "sell out" when the leading teams played. As well as the local league, there are matches between Latvian towns and the occasional friendly international.

Ice hockey is very popular in Latvia and the World Championships will be held there in 2006. The national team does well at international level and beat the USA at the last World Championships in Germany. Many Latvian fans travelled to Germany to support the national team.

Football Stadium

The local team is called Dinaburg, the old name for the town. They do very well in the Latvian national league, finishing 2nd or 3rd. They have qualified for the UEFA Cup tournament this season. There is a local league of teams within the town.

Other Sports

In addition to the above, there are 3 large swimming pools, tennis courts and volleyball courts. Daugavpils is home to an Olympic Gold medallist, a biathlete (skiing and shooting) and Miss Universe (body building).

Internet Marketing Communications

Internet marketing is set to play an increasingly important part in the marketing of locations. Currently Daugavpils has a site but it is basic and slow and has few hyperlinks to anything of real interest. Fishing for instance is an increasingly important international sport, yet it is difficult to get into the fishing site in Latvia.

The importance of the new technologies is being increasingly recognised by the tourism industry, with the World Tourism Organisation Business Council (WTOBC, 1999) describing the Internet as... "having a greater impact on the marketing of travel and tourism... since the invention of television". They are also being recognised, in particular, by public sector organisations such as local authorities, which commission a range of tourism marketing programmes/services. Increasingly, Government Tourist Offices (GTOs) are playing an important role in the promotion, marketing and management of tourism destinations. This type of service benefits both the industry and tourists. The service can be improved and its efficiency can be increased by the utilisation of information technology. In the future it is quite possible that good IT systems will enable individuals to undertake a 'virtual tour' before embarking on a trip. The Internet is driving the changes within the tourist industry with travel and tourism pages taking up a large proportion of the World Wide Web. Hence, for local authority tourism providers, the Internet and WWW are of critical importance. This can be further confirmed by the rapid changes taking place in the tourism market environment today, including:

- Consumers are increasingly demanding greater, instantaneous access to higher quality, timely visitor information.

- Effective marketing is becoming increasingly important as markets become increasingly competitive, vying for the 'cash rich-time poor' visitor pound.

- Resource pressures within local authorities to provide 'global' tourism marketing/marketing communications on shoestring budgets, are increasing. Electronic forms of communication can navigate traditional barriers to awareness and can help to reduce value chain costs (of intermediaries and agents, distribution and logistics, etc.).

- The greater usage, acceptance and abundance of new technologies within society generally and specifically within the tourism marketplace today – particularly by consumers in lucrative long haul international markets such as the United States of America. Technologies are impacting upon consumers and travel trade tourism providers in a huge way.

The WTOBC argues... "the destinations that will win (in the Information Age) will be those that can satisfy this thirst for information, that can convince the tourist online that their destination and the products that can be experienced there are worth the time and expense of visiting", and... "If you are not online you are not on-sale" (1999).

Internet Strategy Model Guidance

The WTO argues that the **web-objective setting process** is very important for DMOs such as public sector local authorities. They must clearly define a role for their web sites that the commercial sector does not already fill, setting objectives in the context of wider public/private sector partnerships. Decisions therefore must be taken on the web construct and how it will affect (strategically and practically) value chains and intermediaries, particularly concerning e-commerce development. In addition to setting clear web objectives, the WTOBC argues that best practice **Internet marketing strategy** must also **specify web site functionality**, resourcing the project via appropriate **internal and external (agency) human resources**, **testing and piloting the site**, **monitoring and evaluation**, and finally, **promoting** the web site.

The WTO model approach is detailed below, (*see Table 3.*).

Table 3. – Model 'Functionality' Criteria

Home Page	Virtual, multi-media tours, live cams	**Virtual Brochures**
Logo/brand	Visitor comments	Registering compulsory for first time users
Text description	Customer forms (to request information)	Information from the site included
Photograph/graphic of destination	Online registration form	Can the brochure be edited?
Moving/changing text		
List of internal links	**Search Facility**	**Accommodation Information (Non-interactive)**
Click on graphic to enter site	Key word search available?	One list of accommodation options
Language/translation option	Use of directories to search?	Listed on the basis of location
List of awards given to site		Listed on basis of style (i.e. hotel)
Number of visitors to site	**Online Shop**	Listed on the basis of price
Email address	Clothes/souvenirs/books/maps?	
Local time	Minimum order value?	**Accommodation (Interactive)**
Gateways	Do you have to register to shop?	*(Can search the database to find…)*
		Style of accommodation (hotel, hostel)
General Information about the Site	**Interactive Trip Planner** *(can search database to find…)*	Location of accommodation
Photographs of destination	How to get to the destination	Price
Climate, geography, topography	What to do	Facilities of accommodation providers
Clothing	Attractions/events	*Information provided on…*
Money	Where to stay	Address/phone/fax details
Shopping hours	Transport	Photograph of accommodation
How to get to destination	Tours	Text description of accommodation
Public transport	Hire	Room rates
Telecommunications	Where to look for further information	Check in/check out times
Culture and customs		Child facilities
Suggested itineraries	**What is included in the results?**	Quality accreditation rating
Events and attractions	Name, address, phone of service provider	Link to email and URL of provider
Destination specific activities	Fax number	Online booking through the web site
Maps	Photograph of service provider	
	Pricing information	
Features of the Site	Textual description of service offered	
Language options	Link to email and URL of provider	
List of site contents on every page		
Link back to home on every page		
Site map		
Information on site design		
Statistics on site usage		

Adapted from WTOBC, 1999: Pages 156-157

In many ways Daugavpils has to consider these and branding strategies for the area. The current logo is shown below. The entrances to the city also have the monuments as depicted in the photos shown.

The Current Logo

The Entrances to the City

Summary

The city of Daugavpils is in many ways symptomatic of the plight of many cities in Europe. The situation in Daugavpils is particularly interesting because it finds itself in a situation where it has to market itself both to Russia and the east, and also to the EU. However, one of the biggest challenges facing the Mayor and the council is the perception of the city both in Riga and amongst the residents themselves, (*see Appendix 3. for a profile of new Mayor and the organisation chart*). The city has an interesting past and some beautiful locations; however, the brand image is poor. The marketing communications are carried out by a Personal Assistant to the Mayor who handles the PR for the city. In fact, the case presented the city with a PR opportunity and this was exploited for the purposes of local television and national TV. The budget spend on marketing is rather fragmented. A high quality book on the region has been produced as well as some leaflets. There is little co-ordination between the departments and little in the way of a comprehensive marketing exercise. Part of the problem lies in the centralist Soviet approach where marketing had little or no meaning. The Mayor has a formidable task ahead of him. He realises that the city has many strengths and there are many opportunities to further its cause. The general feeling is that marketing is likely to play a major role in rejuvenating the city.

17

Appendix 1.

Article 1. – Latvia Facts and Figures

FT file

- **Area:** 64,589 sq km
- **Languages:** Latvian and Russian
- **Currency:** Lat
- **Exchange rate:** 2000 av $1=0.60614 lats
  June 8 2001 $1=0.6356 lats
- **Time:** Two hours ahead of GMT
  (GMT during summer time)

Constitution

- **Population:** 2.37m (January 2001)
- **Main towns and population**
  (January 2000)

Riga (capital)	788,000
Daugavpils	115,000
Liepaja	95,000
Jelgava	71,000
Ventspils	46,000

Constitution

◦ **Official name**
Republic of Latvia
◦ **Legal system**
After the failed coup in
Moscow the Latvian government declared
on August 21 1991 that the transition
period leading up to the restoration of
independence had ended and in effect
established legal continuity between the
1918-40 republic and the present state
• **National legislature**
The 100-seat Saeima (parliament) is
identical to the pre-second world war
legislature. Only Latvian citizens and
those resident in Latvia before June 27
1940 are eligible to vote. The Saeima's
term is four years

• **Electoral system**
Proportional representation with a five
per cent threshold for parties to enter
the Saeima
• **National elections**
October 1998 (legislative); June 1999
(presidential); next elections due in June
2002 (presidential) and October 2002
(legislative)
• **Head of state**
President, elected by the Saeima;
currently Vaira Vike-Freiberga
• **National government**
A coalition government headed by Andris
Berzins was sworn in on May 5 2000; it
currently consists of the People's party,
Latvia's Way and the FFF-LNIM

Economic summary

	2001	forecasts 2002
Total GDP ($bn)	7.4	8.0
Real GDP growth (annual % change)	4.5	4.0
GDP per head ($)	3,110	3,390
Inflation (annual % change in CPI, end period)	3.4	2.9
Agricultural output (annual % change)	2.0	1.0
Industrial production (annual % change)	5.3	4.0
Recorded unemployment rate (% of labour force)	7.6	7.5
Money supply, M2 (annual % change)	6.8	7.4
Foreign exchange reserves ($m)	900	950
Budget balance (% of GDP)	-2.0	-1.0
External debt (% of GDP)	36.5	35.7
Current account balance ($m)	-485.7	-522.0
Merchandise exports ($m)	2,271.7	2,542.2
Merchandise imports ($m)	-3,346.5	-3,639.0
Trade balance ($m)	-1,074.8	-1,096.8

Main trading partners (share of total trade to world 2000)

EXPORTS

Russia	Sweden	Finland	Germany	UK	EU
4.2%	10.8%	n/a	17.2%	17.4%	64.6%
11.6%	6.7%	8.6%	15.7%	n/a	52.4%

IMPORTS

Sovereign credit rating

Moody's **Baa2**   Standard and Poor's **BBB**   Fitch IBCA **BBB**

Sources: Economist Intelligence Unit; Thomson Financial Datastream

Source: Financial Times, Friday, 15th June 2001

Political Structure

Official name	Republic of Latvia.
Legal system	After the failed coup in Moscow the Latvian Government declared on 21st August, 1991 that the transition period leading up to the restoration of independence had ended and in effect established legal continuity between the 1918-1940 republic and the present state.
National legislature	The 100-seat Saeima (parliament) is identical to the pre-Second World War legislature. Only Latvian citizens and those resident in Latvia before 27th June, 1940 are eligible to vote. The Saeima's term is four years.
Electoral system	Proportional representation with 5% threshold for parties to enter the Saeima.
National elections	3rd October, 1998; next elections due June 2002 (presidential) and October 2002 (legislative).
Head of state	President, Vaira Vike-Freiberga, elected by the Saeima on 17th June, 1999.
National government	A new government, headed by Andris Berzins, was sworn in on 5th May, 2000; it consists of three parties from the previous coalition – People's Party, Latvia's Way and the FFF-LNIM – as well as the small New Party.
Main political parties	Ruling coalition: People's Party (24 seats); Latvia's Way (21 seats); For Fatherland and Freedom-Latvian National Independence Movement (FFF-LNIM, 16 seats); New Party (8 seats); Opposition: For Human Rights in a United Latvia (FHR, 16 seats); Social Democratic Workers' Party (SDWP, formerly Social Democratic Alliance, 14 seats); Independent (1 seat).

Council of Ministers	**Prime minister**	Andris Berzins (Latvia's Way)
	Special tasks minister for co-operation with international financial institutions	Roberts Zile (FFF-LNIM)
	Special tasks minister for state administration and municipal reform	Janis Krumins (New Party)
Key ministers	**Agriculture**	Atis Slakteris (People's Party)
	Culture	Karina Petersone (Latvia's Way)
	Defence	Girts Valdis Kristovskis (Latvia's Way)
	Economy	Aigars Kalvitis (FFF-LNIM)
	Education and science	Karlis Greiskalns (People's Party)
	Environmental protection and regional development	Vladimirs Makarovs (FFF-LNIM)
	Finance	Gundars Berzins (People's Party)
	Foreign affairs	Indulis Berzins (Latvia's Way)
	Interior	Mareks Seglins (People's Party)
	Justice	Ingrida Labucka (New Party)
	Transport and telecommunications	Anatolijs Gorbunovs (Latvia's Way)
	Welfare	Andrejs Pozarnovs (FFF-LNIM)
Central bank governor	Einars Repse	

Source: EIU Country Report, October 2000

BPP PUBLISHING

Economic Structure

Annual Indicators

	1996	1997	1998	1999	2000[a]
GDP at market prices (LVL bn)	2.8	3.3	3.6	3.7	3.9
GDP (US$ bn)	5.1	5.6	6.1	6.3	6.4
Real GDP growth (%)	3.3	8.6	3.9	0.1	4.0
Consumer price inflation (av; %)	17.6	8.5	4.7	2.4	2.8
Population (m)	2.5	2.5	2.5	2.4	2.4
Exports of goods fob (US$ m)	1,488.0	1,838.0	2,011.0	1,889.0	2,059.0
Imports of goods fob (US$ m)	2,286.0	2,686.0	3,141.0	2,916.0	3,289.4
Current account balance (US$ m)	-280.0	-345.0	-651.0	-642.0	-570.9
Foreign exchange reserves excl. gold (US$ m)	654.1	704.0	728.2	840.2	940.0
Total external debt (US$ bn)	0.5	0.5	0.8	0.9	1.0
Debt-service ratio, paid (%)	2.4	4.3	2.5	4.8	8.3
Exchange rate (av; LVL: US$)	0.551	0.581	0.590	0.585	0.615

29th September, 2000 LVL0.615:US$1; LVL0.542: €1

Origins of Gross Domestic Product 1999	% of Total	Components of Gross Domestic Product 1999	% of Total
Agriculture, hunting and forestry	4.0	Private consumption	65.5
Manufacturing	14.9	Public consumption	19.0
Electricity, gas and water supply	5.0	Gross fixed investment	25.0
Construction	7.6	Increase in stocks	1.4
Services	68.4	Exports of goods and services	46.7
Total incl. others	**100.0**	Imports of goods and services	-57.6
		Total	**100.0**

Principal Exports 1999	% of Total	Principal Imports 1999	% of Total
Wood and wood products	37.3	Machinery and equipment	22.0
Textiles	15.4	Chemicals	12.0
Metals	11.5	Mineral products	11.4
Machinery and equipment	4.9	Transport equipment	8.3
Foodstuffs	3.8	Metal products	7.0

Main Destinations of Exports 1999	% of Total	Main Origins of Imports 1999	% of Total
Germany	16.4	Russia	15.2
UK	10.7	Germany	10.5
Sweden	10.7	Finland	9.1
Russia	6.6	Sweden	7.2
EU	62.5	EU	54.5

[a]EIU estimates

Source: EIU Country Report, October 2000

Quarterly Indicators

	1998 3 Qtr	1998 4 Qtr	1999 1 Qtr	1999 2 Qtr	1999 3 Qtr	1999 4 Qtr	2000 1 Qtr	2000 2 Qtr
General Government Consolidated Budget (LVL m)								
Revenue	414	403	370	393	397	430	394	420
Expenditure	406	459	375	446	425	488	395	458
Balance	7	-56	-4	-53	-28	-58	-1	-38
Output								
GDP at 1995 prices (LVL m)	699	669	657	697	700	687	693	730
% change, year on year	2.4	-1.7	-1.5	-1.1	0.2	2.8	5.5	4.8
Industrial production index[a]	99.3	88.6	86.8	84.5	94.4	99.8	104.5	105.2
% change, year on year	-0.7	-11.4	-13.2	-15.5	-5.6	-0.2	4.5	5.2
Employment, Wages and Prices								
Employment ('000)	1,047	1,033	1,028	1,035	1,046	1,041	1,037	1,039
% change, year on year	-0.1	-1.0	-1.9	-2.1	-1.1	-0.7	-0.3	0.4
Unemployment rate (% of the labour force)	7.4	8.5	9.8	10.1	9.7	9.2	9.1	8.7
Average monthly wages (LVL)	136.5	140.8	132.6	141.0	142.6	147.7	141.4	149.3
% change, year on year	11.7	8.7	7.8	6.1	4.5	4.9	6.6	5.9
Consumer price index (1995 = 100)	133.4	133.9	135.9	136.5	136.1	138.0	140.4	140.7
% change, year on year	3.9	2.8	2.5	1.8	2.1	3.1	3.2	3.1
Producer price index	115.7	113.3	110.5	110.0	110.4	110.6	111.4	111.2
% change, year on year	2.3	-0.5	-4.0	-4.9	-4.6	-2.3	0.8	1.1
Financial Indicators								
Exchange rate								
LVL: US$ (av)	0.597	0.572	0.579	0.593	0.589	0.580	0.591	0.603
LVL: US$ (end-period)	0.583	0.569	0.590	0.598	0.579	0.583	0.596	0.600
LVL: Ecu/€[b] (av)	0.666	0.671	0.648	0.625	0.617	0.602	0.582	0.562
LVL: Ecu/€[b] (end-period)	0.683	0.666	0.634	0.618	0.618	0.586	0.569	0.573
Interest rates (av; %)								
Deposit	4.7	6.0	5.5	4.9	4.9	4.9	4.0	4.8
Lending	14.9	16.2	16.9	15.7	12.1	12.1	10.1	10.9
Money market	2.9	7.1	5.2	4.4	4.5	4.7	2.5	2.6
M1 (end-period; LVL m)	619	601	613	652	624	639	670	707
% change, year on year	19.7	6.0	6.5	0.8	0.8	6.3	9.4	8.5
M2 (end-period; LVL m)	980	959	955	1,012	1,006	1,038	1,109	1,186
% change, year on year	16.7	6.7	3.3	-1.7	2.6	8.3	16.1	17.3
Dow Jones RSE index[c] (2nd Apr 1996 = 100)	113.5	98.0	81.9	83.9	70.9	87.8	116.6	108.7
Sectoral Trends								
Cargo turnover by rail (m t/km)	3,243	3,266	2,744	3,237	3,104	3,125	3,480	3,127
% change, year on year	-1.8	-13.2	-15.0	0.3	-4.3	-4.3	26.8	-3.4
Cargo handled in ports ('000 tonnes)	13,027	13,498	12,438	14,014	11,905	10,676	13,327	13,199
% change, year on year	5.9	4.5	-5.6	11.3	-8.6	-20.9	7.1	-5.8
Foreign Trade (LVL m)								
Exports fob	262	247	245	254	255	254	275	291
Imports cif	-476	-487	-375	-422	-440	-487	-416	-485
Trade balance	-214	-240	-130	-168	-185	-233	-141	-194
Foreign Payments (US$ m)								
Merchandise trade balance	-299	-372	-179	-236	-264	-348	-189	-262
Services balance	53	45	80	91	89	81	125	124
Income balance	22	8	-29	3	-5	-17	-24	-11
Current account balance	-195	-278	-102	-127	-149	-264	-64	-130
Reserves excl. gold (end-period)	739	728	746	887	768	840	847	832

[a]Corresponding period of previous year = 100. [b]Ecu before 1999. [c]End-period.

Sources: Central Statistical Bureau of Latvia, *Monthly Bulletin of Latvian Statistics*; IMF, *International Financial Statistics*; Bank of Latvia, *Quarterly Bulletin*; Standard & Poor's, *Emerging Stock Markets Review*.

Source: EIU Country Report, October 2000

21

Inflation

The lat's peg to the IMF's SDR has shielded Latvia from most of the international inflationary pressures caused by oil price rises. The most recent spike in oil prices, the future strength of the euro and growing domestic demand will accelerate inflation slightly in the coming months, but annual average inflation for 2000 will not exceed 3%. Inflationary pressures from producer prices will remain almost non-existent in the short term, but are likely to build up as economic growth increasingly allows producers to pass costs on to consumers.

Exchange Rates

The lat is pegged to the IMF's currency basket SDR and at the moment its stability is secure. At the end of August the Bank of Latvia's currency and gold reserves were US$920m, which provides more than 4 months of import cover. The lat is expected to remain constant against the SDR during the forecast period, and given the low level of inflation in Latvia, the real appreciation of the lat will be small.

External Sector

The current account deficit widened in the second quarter of 2000 on the back of a deteriorating balance of trade and we expect this trend to continue as economic recovery boosts domestic demand for imports. High oil prices bring higher revenue for the Latvian transit sector, and the economic recovery in Russia will boost transit to Russia as well.

Forecast Summary
(% Unless Otherwise Indicated)

	1999[a]	2000[b]	2001[c]	2002[c]
Real GDP growth	0.1	4.0	5.0	3.0
Industrial production growth	-4.7	4.6	6.0	6.0
Gross agricultural growth	-7.3	1.0	2.0	1.0
Unemployment rate (av)	9.1	7.4	7.0	6.8
Consumer price inflation				
Average	2.4	2.8	3.4	4.8
Year end	3.2	1.8	5.0	4.4
Short term interbank rate	14.2	15.0	13.0	13.0
Government balance (% of GDP)	-4.2	-2.5	-1.5	-1.0
Exports of goods fob (US$ bn)	1.9	2.1	2.3	2.6
Imports of goods fob (US$ bn)	2.9	3.3	3.6	4.0
Current-account balance (US$ bn)	-0.6	-0.6	-0.6	-0.7
% of GDP	-10.3	-9.0	-8.8	-9.6
External debt (year end; US$ bn)	0.9	1.0	1.2	1.4
Exchange rates				
LVL: US$ (av)	0.585	0.615	0.620	0.591
LVL: ¥100 (av)	0.514	0.576	0.597	0.597
LVL: € (year end)	0.586	0.569	0.607	0.607

[a]Actual. [b]EIU estimates. [c]EIU forecasts.

Source: EIU Country Report, October 2000

Fast Recovery Fuels Trade Deficit as Investment Grows

As a result of the fast growth in imports, the trade deficit has started to increase again. In January-July 2000 the trade deficit was LVL407m (US$610m), up by 13.9% from the same period in 1999. Latvia – like other emerging markets – has traditionally run large merchandise trade deficits in order to finance its substantial investment needs. Now that the Latvian economy is growing rapidly, the attendant growth in investment is once again exerting pressure on the country's external balances.

The reason behind this dynamic is that Latvia's main exports are relatively low in value added. Timber exports and textiles constitute around 50% of exports – sawn wood alone accounts for some 35% of Latvia's exports to the EU – and Latvia has so far not been able to upgrade its productive capacity in a way that would allow it to compete in EU markets with more advanced products. Conversely, on the import side the most important single category is machinery and mechanical appliances, which make up some 20% of imports, showing Latvia's need to import technology in order to upgrade its productive capacity – a process necessary if the country is to move towards the production of goods with higher value added.

Trends in Foreign Trade
(LVL m Unless Otherwise Indicated)

	1999 1 Qtr	1999 2 Qtr	1999 3 Qtr	1999 4 Qtr	2000 1 Qtr	2000 2 Qtr
Exports fob	**246**	**254**	**255**	**254**	**275**	**291**
of which:						
to the EU (%)	65	63	60	62	68	64
to the CIS (%)	10	12	14	12	8	8
Imports cif	**-375**	**-422**	**-440**	**-487**	**-416**	**-485**
of which:						
from the EU (%)	56	57	54	52	53	54
from the CIS (%)	14	13	16	17	15	17
Trade balance	**-129**	**-168**	**-185**	**-233**	**-141**	**-194**
% of GDP	15	17	19	23	15	18
Export unit values (% change, year on year)	-1.5	-0.5	-5.5	-4.1	-1.8	-2.0
Import unit values (% change, year on year)	-7.1	-7.5	-4.7	-1.8	-5.9	-6.3

Source: Central Statistical Bureau of Latvia, *Monthly Bulletin of Latvian Statistics.*

Import Bill Drives Current-account Deficit

After a substantial quarter-on-quarter fall in January-March 2000, the current-account deficit widened again in the second quarter of the year, reflecting a pick-up in import demand that increased the merchandise trade deficit by 35%. Whereas, according to revised data, the current-account deficit in the first quarter of 2000 amounted to LVL33m (US$56m), in the second quarter of the year it more than doubled, reaching LVL78m. Year-on-year comparisons show that, although in US dollar terms the current-account deficit remained stable, in lat terms the second-quarter deficit also widened in comparison with the same period of 1999. However, in the context of the recovering economy the current-account balance has improved, falling from a deficit of 8.1% of GDP in the second quarter of 1999 to one of 7.4% of GDP.

Source: EIU Country Report, October 2000

Article 2. – Map of Daugavpils

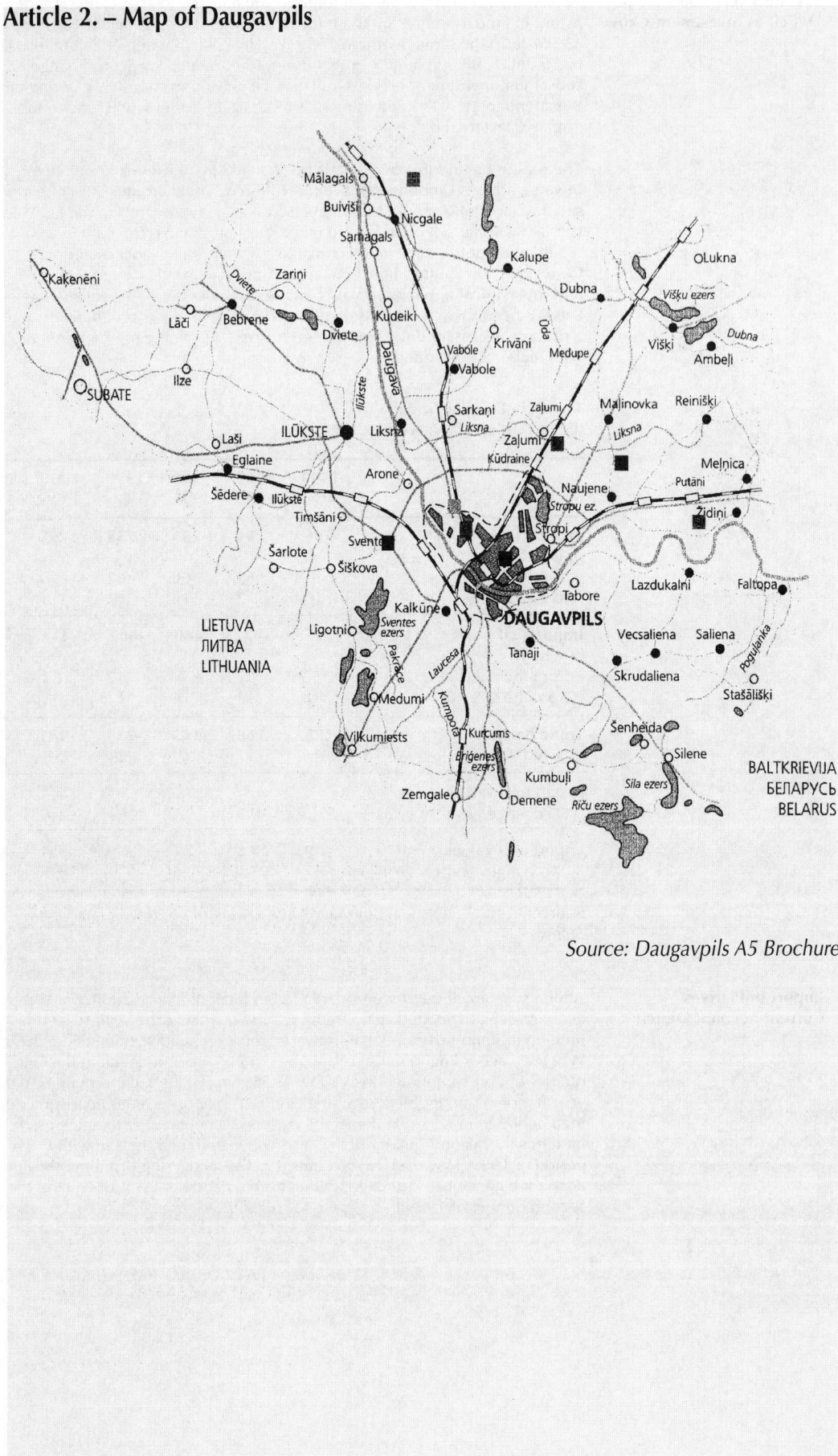

Source: Daugavpils A5 Brochure

Article 3. – Daugavpils' Links with other European Cities

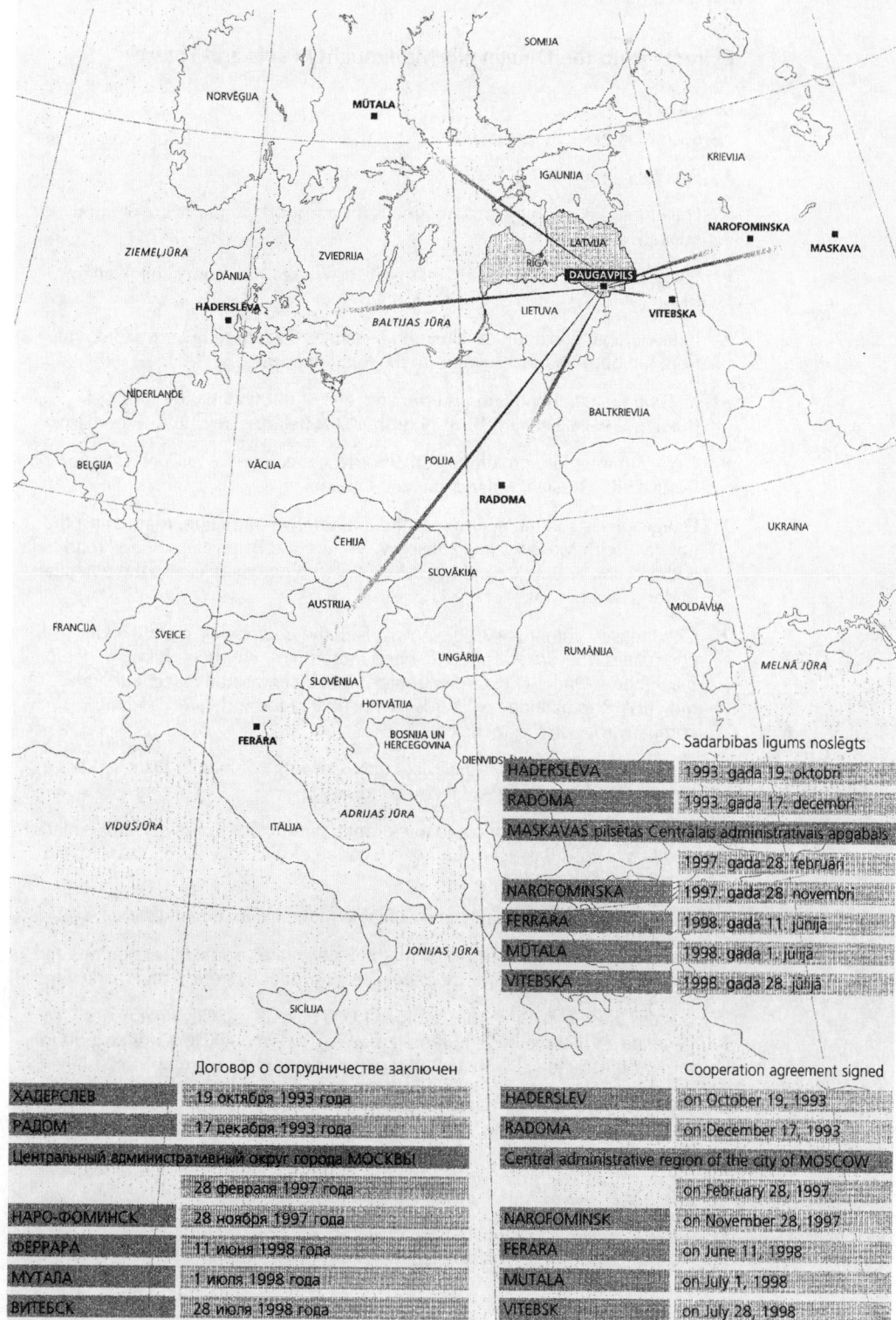

Sadarbibas ligums noslēgts	
HADERSLĒVA	1993. gada 19. oktobri
RADOMA	1993. gada 17. decembri
MASKAVAS pilsētas Centrālais administratīvais apgabals	
	1997. gada 28. februāri
NAROFOMINSKA	1997. gada 28. novembri
FERRARA	1998. gada 11. jūnijā
MŪTALA	1998. gada 1. jūlijā
VITEBSKA	1998. gada 28. jūlijā

Договор о сотрудничестве заключен		Cooperation agreement signed	
ХАДЕРСЛЕВ	19 октября 1993 года	HADERSLEV	on October 19, 1993
РАДОМ	17 декабря 1993 года	RADOMA	on December 17, 1993
Центральный административный округ города МОСКВЫ		Central administrative region of the city of MOSCOW	
	28 февраля 1997 года		on February 28, 1997
НАРО-ФОМИНСК	28 ноября 1997 года	NAROFOMINSK	on November 28, 1997
ФЕРРАРА	11 июня 1998 года	FERARA	on June 11, 1998
МУТАЛА	1 июля 1998 года	MUTALA	on July 1, 1998
ВИТЕБСК	28 июля 1998 года	VITEBSK	on July 28, 1998

Source: Daugavpils A5 Brochure

BPP
PUBLISHING

Appendix 2.

Extracts from the Daugavpils Municipality Facts and Figures

Daugavpils

- Second largest city of Latvia.

- First mentioned 1275.

- Developing economy – big crossroads for transport, centre of culture and education.

- Located in SE of country on banks of Daugava, 230km from capital city of Riga.

- In favourable geographical situation because adjacent to Belarus (33-35km from the border) and 120km from the Russian border.

- In 2000 the city population is estimated at 114,000 inhabitants (58.59% Russian, 14.4% Latvian, 13.3% Polish, 8.3% Belarussian, 2.8% Ukrainian).

- Owing to the close proximity of the borders, there are three Consulates in Daugavpils, Russian, Belarussian and Lithuanian.

- Daugavpils is a manufacturing centre and transport junction. Main transport links are with Moscow, St. Petersburg, Vilnius and Panavezius. Good road links with Lithuania, Belarus and Russia are developing. There is also the potential to develop a new airport.

- City industry comprises 30 big enterprises and companies, metalworking companies, Pievadkedes PLC (car and motorbikes, children's bikes, agricultural machinery), Dauer-D PLC (electronics), Zieglera Masinbuve (agricultural mowers), Rhodia Industrial Yards (synthetic threads and yards) and the company Magistr (synthetic cables).

- Light industry companies include: clothes sewing companies Daugavpils suveja, Dinaburg apgerbs, Linko-D and Triad.

- Also general production companies – milk production Kraslava Dairy, Antaris and Daugavpils Bakers; Pallada produces alcoholic beverages; Annas-V and Aviz'D are fish producers.

- Products are of high quality and compete in the external market.

- Dinaz has active co-operation with the Baltic States, some FSU countries and the West, and trades in transit of petroleum products, storage and marketing.

- Besides these companies are another 2,000 businesses. City enterprises generate an income of 52 million lats a year, of which 30% is from export to the West, 40% to FSU. Some 9,000 people work in these companies.

- The city has a bus and tram system. There are more than 1,100 other businesses (shops, kiosks, cafes). Major companies amongst them are Antaris, Gurons and Ditton BC.

26

- In Daugavpils almost all the major Latvian banks are represented. Investment projects are also being realised related to water supply and sewage purification; they are being funded by the World Bank, Phare, NEFCO and others (US$22.3m).

- Daugavpils is an important cultural centre in the East of Latvia. There are 27 schools for general education, 4 extra-curricular establishments, 29 kindergartens and 9 technical institutions, 'Sun School' Art College and a Music College.

- Each year 1,000 teaching and engineering students graduate from the Daugavpils Pedagogical University and Riga Technical University.

- The city has revived the theatre, working with national and cultural institutions, has a cinema, cultural centre and other cultural organisations. The Daugavpils Ice Hall has also been built.

- The city is also actively working towards an Exhibition Centre.

- Daugavpils has many architectural, historical and cultural monuments. The largest and most important of them is the Daugavpils fort, built in the 18th century.

- The city has an environment of many beautiful lakes. Daugavpils has the potential for development of foreign tourist trade.

Daugavpils History

Daugavpils has a long history. This began in 1275 when the Livonians built the first stone castle – Dinaburg. During the Livonian war (1558-1583) Daugavpils moved to a new location 19km down the Daugava. The city has had many different names: Dinaburg (1275-1893), Borisoglebsk (1656-1667), Dvinsk (1893-1920) and Daugavpils (since 1920).

Twinnings

Daugavpils is twinned with:

- **Hadersleva (Denmark)**
  Legal contract 19.10.93
  District matters
  Cultural exchange programme
  Municipality specialist experience exchange programme
  Lions Club collaboration
  Charity work with orphanages and old peoples' homes

- **Radom (Poland)**
  Legal contract 17.12.93
  Cultural exchange programme
  Teachers and students exchange programme
  Promotion of business contacts

27

- **Russian Federation Moscow City Central District Administration**
  Legal contract: 28.02.97
  Business, cultural, educational contacts

- **Narofomiks (Russian Federation)**
  Legal contract: 28.11.97
  Students' development programme
  Cultural development programme
  Municipality co-operative programme
  Promotion of business contacts

- **Ferrara (Italy)**
  Legal contract: 11.06.98
  EU integration matters

- **Mutala (Sweden)**
  Legal contract: 01.07.98
  Municipal co-operation programme

- **Vietbsk (Belarus)**
  Legal contract: 28.7.98
  Promotion of business contacts
  Cultural exchange programme
  Municipality specialist experience exchange programme
  Teachers and students exchange programme

- **Tampere (Finland)**
  Co-operation agreement signed between Daugavpils Municipal Enterprise, Daugavpils Udens and Tampere city water supply and sewage company, signed in 1996 and extended in 1999.

City Development Priorities

Agreed priorities for the city.

Most important objectives of city development:

- To improve economic development.
- To improve employment.
- To improve streets and roads.
- To ensure all have the right to culture and education.
- To improve security in town.
- To give all citizens healthcare.
- To give all citizens safe, healthy, pleasant and motivating environment.
- To save the city centre as an important part of European cultural and historical heritage.
- To create modern architecture and to preserve architectural heritage as an important quality of the city's scenery.

Projects in Daugavpils

General development of city.

– Project for Daugavpils water supplies and sewage
  Financed by: Bank of International Reconstruction and Development, NEFCO, Sida (Sweden), DEPA (Denmark) EU Phare, Finnish Ministry of Environmental Protection, Latvian Government, Daugavpils Municipality and Municipal PLC, Daugavpils Water
  General costs of project: $22.3m
  Daugavpils Municipality input :   L1.8m
  Project co-ordinator: Daugavpils Executive Director Richard Draba
  Term of project: 1996-2001

– Research on how dangerous industrial waste is created in a region and management of such waste
  Financed by: VARAM, Finnish Ministry of Environmental Protection and Daugavpils Municipality
  General costs of project: L94,900
  Daugavpils Municipality contribution: L5,000
  Project co-ordinator: (Environmental Projects VARAM) Vlads Pjankovskis
  Term of project: 1999-2001

– South Latgale Household Waste Project, implemented in terms of investment programme – '500'
  Project foresees creation of a joint system of waste management for Daugavpils, Kraslava, Preili regions and the creation of one waste tip.
  Financed by: Finnish Ministry of Environmental Protection, B\ip, BSG
  General costs of project: L7.2m
  Daugavpils Municipality contribution: L364,000
  Project co-ordinator: (Environmental Projects VARAM) Vlads Pjankovskis
  Term of project: 1999-2003

– 'Daugavpils and Mutala – 2010' – ways to develop Daugavpils city and analysis of the surrounding environment

– Emergency Management
  Financed by: SWEBALTCOP, Mutala Municipality and Daugavpils Municipality
  General costs of project: SKr2,092,000
  Project co-ordinator: Inga Melnikova, Daugavpils Municipality
  Term of project: 1999-2001

29

– General management point for crisis situations
Project finance given by: Swedish Nuclear Safety Institute and Daugavpils Municipality
General costs of project: L45,500
Daugavpils Municipality contribution: L17,800
Project co-ordinator: Daugavpils Municipality, G. Zvirbulis and others from the Municipality State Emergency Services – professionals for crisis management and City Health Department – R. Margevics and A. Faibusevics
Term of project: 2000
(Further details of improvements to be made and deadlines)
Improvement and development of the management centre:
Swedish Safety Institute plans to finance until 2003 the purchase of different equipment and logistics, for the sum of approximately L2,000
Latvian State Emergency Services, Ministry of Internal Affairs provided equipment for modem connections and information/communication systems

– Latgale Region Development Plan
Project financed by: EU Phare
General costs of project: L500,000
Project co-ordinator: Inara Stalidzane, Latgale Region Development Agency (LRDA)
Term of project: 1999-2000

– SPP Pilot Project 'Urban Development'
Financed by: EU Phare
General costs of project: (L371,000) €700,000
Project co-ordinator: Maija Muceniece, LRDA
Term of project: 2000-2001

– LRDA Capacity Improvement for Working with Pre-structural (EU) Funds
Financed by: Danish Government
General costs of project: (L111,392) DKr1,547,100
Project co-ordinator: Iveta Puzo
Term of project: 2000-2001

Daugavpils Education Department

– State Programme for Latvian Language LAT 2
Financed by: LWAP Latvian State Language Acquisition Programme
Co-ordinator: Silva Kucina (Latgale Bureau) and Vitalis Cirss
Term of project: Ongoing in all teaching institutions

– Nord Prison Project – teaching prisoners in Griva jail

– Reconstruction of heating system in educational institutions and control systems for heat consumption
Financed by: Daugavpils Municipality and Department of Education

30

– Improving effectiveness of use of revenue and improvement of quality of education in educational institutions (phases 2 and 3)
Financed by: World Bank

– Latgale Programme
Financed by: Ministry of Education and Science

– Establishment of examination centre for professional education in South Latgale
Financed by: Ministry of Education and Science and EU Phare

– LEIS (Latvian Educational Information System)
Financed by: Ministry of Education and Science

– Socrates Project in city schools, EU Educational Programme
Financed by: EU
Co-ordinators: City Educational Institutions and Department of Education, IZM

– State Investment Programme Full Reconstruction of the 1st Gymnasium's Boarding School
Financed by: Latvian Government and Municipality
Co-ordinators: Daugavpils Municipality and Department of Education

– Project for rehabilitation of abused children
Financed by: Ministry of Welfare and Department of Education
Co-ordinators: Department of Education and Centre of Psychological Support

– Renovation of Polish Secondary School Sports and Culture Complex
Financed by: Latvian Government and Polish Government
Co-ordinators: Daugavpils Municipality and Department of Education

Health and Social Care

State Health Reform pilot project: Optimisation of infrastructure system of healthcare in Daugavpils and Kraslava regions.

Daugavpils sub-project should be realised:

- Daugavpils PVA (healthcare system) improvement and transfer of children's hospital.

Objectives:

- To empower the network of healthcare activities.
- To improve PVA services, quality and intensity.

31

BPP PUBLISHING

Tasks:

- Former children's hospital wards/rooms – 5 healthcare practice places to be installed which are placed according to traditional microareas of the town.

- Transfer the Daugavpils children's hospital to the available empty space in City Central Hospital.

- Create regional centre for Oral Health in the former children's hospital.

- Create regional rehabilitation centre in facilities of former children's hospital.

Financed by: Latvian Government and World Bank
General costs of project: US$1,035,700
Project co-ordinator: Dr A. Faibvusevics, Director of Daugavpils Municipality Health Department
Term of project: 1999-2001

Culture and Recreation

Diary for the year 2000, anniversary of 725 years of establishment of the city, with different events throughout the year.

January:
- Sacred Music Festival with Choral Competition.

March:
- Festival for Latvian Minority Children's Folk Festival.
- Charity concerts in Kalupe, Kalkune, Auseklitis and Priecite Orphanages.
- Two big concerts in Latvian Cultural Centre and Culture and Sports Centre.

April:
- Traditional art days 'Moving with Time'.
- Jazz Festival, 6th International Traditional Jazz Festival (France, Sweden, Belarus and Latvia).

May:
- Children's competition 'Sunbeams' – singing, dancing and arts.
- Week of Slavic Culture, concerts, Polish, Russian, Belarussian culture. Also, Scientific Conference 'Dinaburg – Dvinsk – Daugavpils' – scientists from 6 countries.
- Daugavpils 725 celebrations 31st May to 4th June; visit of the President of Latvia; exhibition of candelabra; concerts; first stage of Baltic Water Motorcycle Championships.

32

September:
- Annual Poetry Days.
- 7th Festival of Chamber Music.

October:
- Swedish Days in Daugavpils. Mutala's Music School string quartet, Jazz Group, wall hangings and seminars on EU affairs, water protection, medicine.

December:
- Traditional Christmas Tree – switching on of lights by Latvian Prime Minister.
- Second day of Christmas activities.
- New Year Celebrations – fireworks.

City Sports

Table 4. – Children's and Youth's Sports Schools

Number	Name of School	Number of Pupils	Type of Sport
1	School Board	613	Football, weight lifting, fencing, shooting, canoeing
2	School Sports Committee	574	Field and track, basketball, swimming, boxing, Greco-Roman wrestling, free wrestling
3	Specialised Volleyball	926	Volleyball, tennis, hockey
	School Total	2,113	15 sports categories

Sports Clubs

Includes:

- 23 social sports clubs (darts, stiga, football club, basketball, boxing clubs, Lokomotiv, VK, tennis clubs, etc.).

- Two education establishment clubs (DP University, Railway Technical School).

- Six different companies' clubs (SC Daugava, Police SK, Dinaburg Football Club, Speedway Centre, etc.).

33

BPP PUBLISHING

Sport Groups

Includes:

- 26 educational based groups.
- Eight company based groups.

Personnel Working with Sports

Number of employees in sports work – 189.

Including 46 coaches, 100 in schools and educational establishments, and 43 in clubs and sports centres.

Sports Centres

- Stadia – 3 (Celtnieks, Lokomotiv and football stadium Esplanade).

- Sports grounds – 40 (volleyball, basketball, football, multi-sports, tennis courts).

- Swimming pools – 10 (25m indoor pools, 6; non-standard, 3; 50m outdoor pools 1).

- Shooting galleries – 3.

- Sports halls – 45.

- Track and field centre – 1.

- Rowing centres – 2.

- Karting and moto tracks – 2.

- Sports hotels – 2.

- Ice hall – 1.

Popular sports in the city – speedway, volleyball, football, weight lifting, track and field, basketball, freestyle wrestling and hockey.

34

Airport Survey Results:

Table 5. – Airport Survey Results

Russia	21%
CIS	14%
Belarus	11%
Lithuania	5%
Germany	16%
Others	33%
	100%

Table 6. – Top 5 Destinations

Moscow	22%
St. Petersburg	20%
Minsk	16%
Berlin	8%
Warsaw	6%
Others	28%
	100%

Table 7. – Impact on Business if there are Flight Connections

Significant	59%
Some	24%
None	17%
	100%

Table 8. – Number of Travellers

Persons	Year	Month	Week	Day
International	4,162	347	83	14
To Riga	6,051	504	121	27
	10,213	851	204	41

Current Train Passengers	Daugavpils-Riga 1996
Fast Train	63,767
Slow Train	27,540
	91,307

Figure 5. – Daugavpils: Breakdown of Area

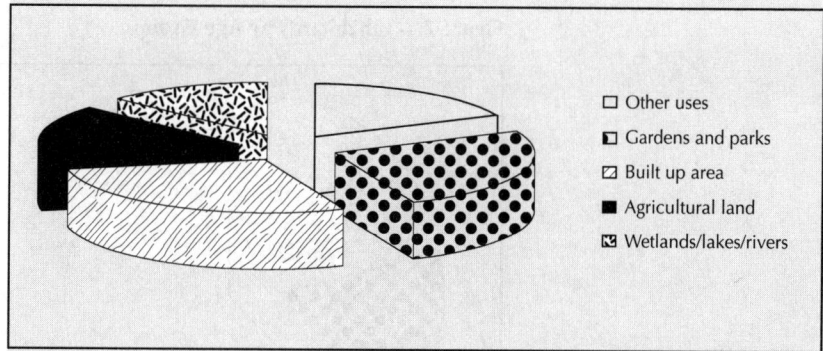

- ☐ Other uses
- ▨ Gardens and parks
- ▨ Built up area
- ■ Agricultural land
- ▨ Wetlands/lakes/rivers

Figure 6. – Population Changes

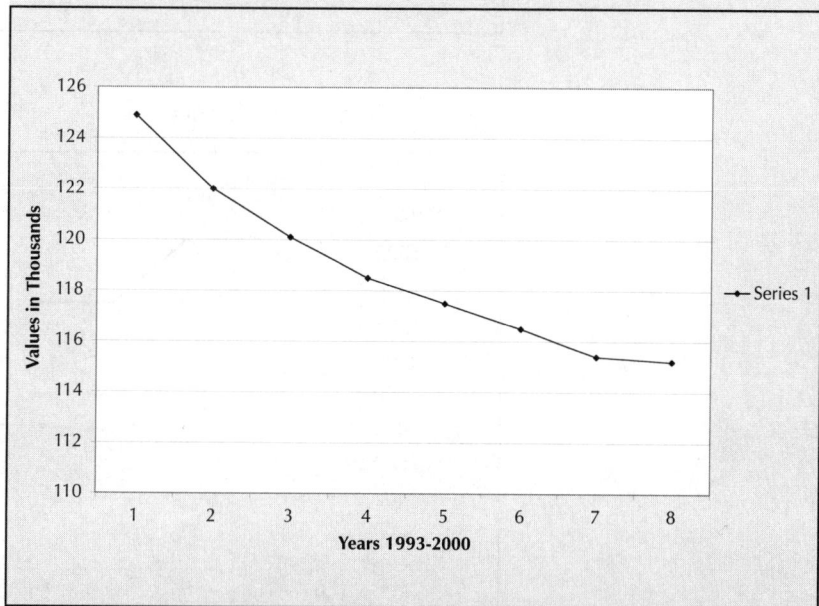

Figure 7. – Inhabitants by Age Group

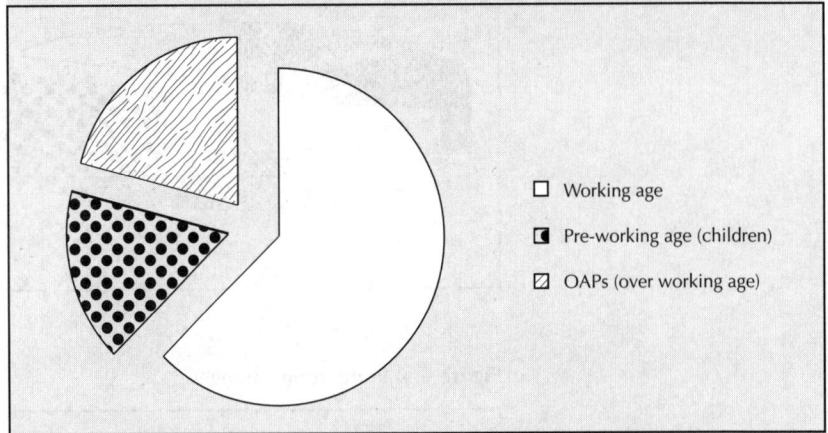

☐ Working age

◖ Pre-working age (children)

▨ OAPs (over working age)

Figure 8. – Death and Birth Rates

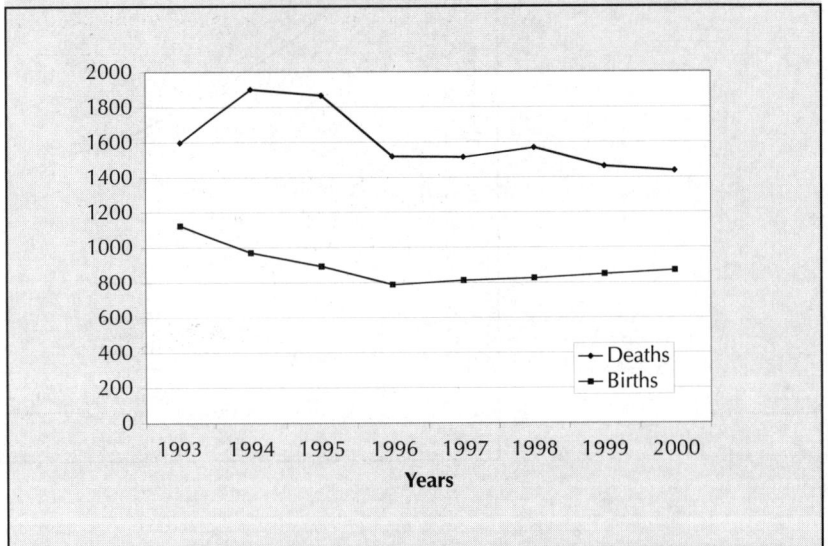

Figure 9. – City Income Sources

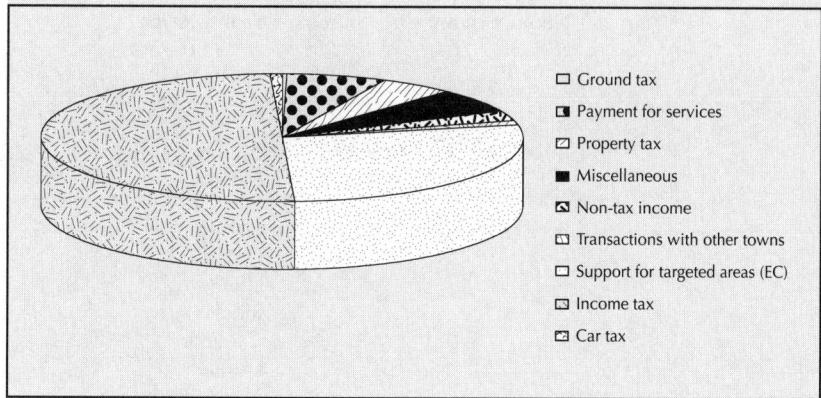

- ☐ Ground tax
- ◨ Payment for services
- ▨ Property tax
- ■ Miscellaneous
- ◪ Non-tax income
- ▨ Transactions with other towns
- ☐ Support for targeted areas (EC)
- ▨ Income tax
- ▨ Car tax

Figure 10. – Daugavpils' Budget Expenditure for 2000

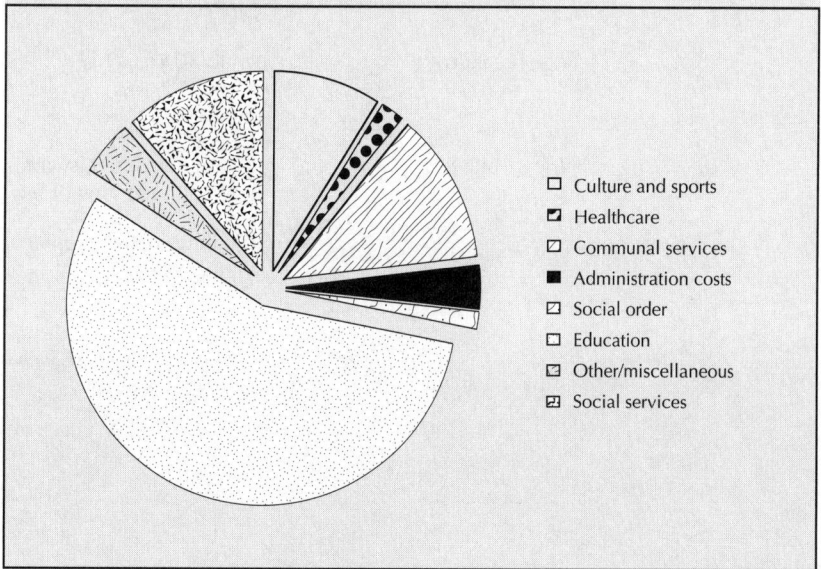

- ☐ Culture and sports
- ▨ Healthcare
- ▨ Communal services
- ■ Administration costs
- ▨ Social order
- ☐ Education
- ▨ Other/miscellaneous
- ▨ Social services

Analysis of Demands in Rural Tourism

Latvia

Number of tourists	Year	1996	2,468
		1997	3,630
		1998	6,200
		1999	6,621 (for 10 months)

Breakdown into countries	Latvian tourists	89%
	Foreign	11%

Foreign tourists	Germany	15%
	Finland	14%
	USA	10%
	India	10%
	Canada	6%
	France	6%
	Netherlands	5%
	Denmark	4%
	UK	4%
	Russia	3.5%
	South Africa	3.5%
	Other	20%

Age breakdown	Up to 30 years old	45%
	30-40	28%
	Over 40	27% (locals)

Trip's objectives	In summer: water, swimming, bath, eating, horses, host-guide, renting of bicycles and sport games.
	In winter: baths, fireplace, celebrations, eating and winter sports.

Source: Compiled by Irina Gorkina,
Daugavpils Enterprise Support Centre, Latvia, 31st July 2001

40

Health Statistics

From the Yearbook of Healthcare Statistics in Latvia, 2000
Published by the Ministry of Welfare

Overall trends in Latvia:

- Reform of the health system is decreasing the total number of hospitals and increasing the number of outpatient institutions.

- Lack of money is decreasing the number of outpatient visits and increasing mortality after urgent surgical operations.

- Deaths still exceed births but the gap has narrowed to 12,019 in 2000.

- Population density has declined from 37.8 (1999) to 37.5 (2000) people per sq km compared with a European average of 116.

- Decrease in population in rural areas has been more marked, making provision of healthcare in rural areas even more expensive per capita.

- Females make up 53.7% of the population and this has been constant since 1989.

- 61% of the inhabitants are of working age (15-59).

- 21% are 60 or over; there is a considerable increase in the population over working age in Ventspils, Daugavpils and Rezekne.

- The large gap in life expectancy between males and females (11.1 years) identifies Latvia as a developing country (gap is 5-7 years in developed countries).

- Life expectancy at birth (1999): male 64.7 years, female 75.4 years compared to the UK at 74.9 and 79.9 respectively.

- Poverty increases use of psychoactive substances (alcohol, tobacco, drugs), depression, suicide, deviant social behaviour and criminality, risk of unsafe food.

- Diptheria in Latvia is the highest in Europe; it peaked in 1997 and there were 264 cases in 2000, i.e. 10.9 per 1000 inhabitants; only 54.3% of population are immunised.

- Polio has been eliminated through immunisation.

- In 2000 sexually transmitted diseases increased markedly.

- HIV cases rose from 247 to 467 and deaths from AIDS from 17 to 24 (1999 to 2000) for all of Latvia.

41

BPP PUBLISHING

Table 9. – Main Causes of Death by Age in Latvia (2000)

	0-14 Years	15-59 Years	60 Years +
Total	361	7,458	24,383
Infectious/parasitic diseases	10	229	144
of which tuberculosis	0	196	92
Neoplasms	28	1,293	4,312
Circulatory system diseases	5	2,143	15,717
Respiratory system diseases	5	285	567
Digestive system diseases	3	327	668
External causes of which:	96	2,561	1,118
Transport accidents	22	543	43
Alcohol poisoning	0	181	55
Drowning	35	175	69
Suicide	5	540	223
Homicide	9	409	125

Table 10. – Daugavpils

	Total	0-14 Years	15-17 Years	18 and Over
Latvia	2,424,150	432,215	103,791	1,888,144
Daugavpils	114,510	18,513	4,994	91,003
	4.72%	4.28%	4.81%	4.82%

	Live Births		Deaths		Change	
	Total	Per 1,000	Total	Per 1,000	Total	Per 1,000
Latvia	19,396	8.0	32,844	13.5	-13,448	-5.5
Daugavpils	833	7.2	1,462	12.7	-629	-5.5
France		12.6		9.2		3.4
Germany		9.6		10.4		-0.8

	Lyme Disease		Tick borne Encephalitis	
Per 1,000	1999	2000	1999	2000
Latvia	11.5	19.5	14.4	22.4
Daugavpils	12.1	24.5	0.0	6.1

Page 43 of City of Daugavpils

Per 1,000	Syphilis		Gonorrhea	
	1999	2000	1999	2000
Latvia	63.2	42.1	45.1	30.7
Daugavpils	133.9	81.2	71.9	74.2

Total	Registered Mental Patients		of Which New Patients	
	1999	2000	1999	2000
Latvia	63,323	62,108	7,629	6,577
Daugavpils	4,740	3,577	532	332

Per 1,000	Latvia		Daugavpils	
	1999	2000	1999	2000
Physicians	33.0	33.6	34.0	36.7
Medical personnel	62.9	61.6	94.5	92.2
Hospital beds	90.5	85.2	142.8	141.1
Outpatient visits		4,700		5,000
Laboratory tests	905	877	980	458
Physiotherapy	102	105	95	78
Diagnostic tests	52	51	41	34
Radiology	82	87	70	69
Emergencies	208.8	206.1	33.0	33.0

Table 11. – Ministry of Welfare: Hospital Bed Utilisation

	Average Bed-days Per Patient		Bed Turnover		Bed Occupancy %	
	1999	2000	1999	2000	1999	2000
Latvia	12.1	11.6	24.4	25.1	81.1	79.5
Daugavpils	11.3	11.4	23.6	21.6	73.2	67.5

Table 12. – Local Authority: Hospital Bed Utilisation

	Average Bed-days Per Patient		Bed Turnover		Bed Occupancy %	
	1999	2000	1999	2000	1999	2000
Latvia	8.6	8.3	32.6	34.0	76.8	77.3
Daugavpils	8.2	7.9	37.2	38.7	83.3	83.2

43

Appendix 3.

Article 4. – The Mayor of Daugavpils

Source: Magazine: National Geographic, 24th May 2001, Author: Andrew Petrov

Daugavpils (Continued)

4
№ 21 (407)
24 мая 2001 г.

NATIONAL GEOGRAPHIC

Вести

«Здесь будет город-сад!»

ЛАТГАЛЬЦЫ

Латгальцы (лат. latgalieši), население историко-культурной области Латвии — Латгалии, говорящее на верхнелатышском диалекте латышского языка. Латгальцы — потомки латгалов. Термин «латгальцы» в литературе употребляется с начала XX века. С древнейших времён латгальцы особенно тесно связаны со славянскими народами, что находит отражение во всех сферах быта и культуры. В результате особых исторических условий (оторванность от других территорий, населенных латышами, более медленное социально-экономическое развитие и др.) в материально-духовной культуре латгальцев сохранились своеобразные архаичные элементы. Большинство верующих — католики. Локальные особенности в культуре латгальцев быстро исчезают.

Большая Советская Энциклопедия

Автозаправка «высокой культуры».

(Окончание. Начало — на 3-й стр.)

— Можно ли в Латгалии где-нибудь отдохнуть, ведь до Вены или до Швейцарских Альп не каждый доберется?

— Таких мест в Латгалии много — это же озерный край! Под Даугавпилсом есть озера Свента, Стропы, под Краславой замечательные места, в Аглоне — Цириши (там мои родители живут). Куда поехать — у нас есть. У нас на планы по созданию новых зон отдыха с самыми комфортными условиями и благоустройству старых.

— Вы позволяете себе расслабиться с помощью алкоголя или табака?

— Я расслабляюсь с помощью спорта и русской бани. Зимой после бани плаваю в проруби. И этого достаточно.

Голосуй — а то...

— Выборы не показали вам, что политика — грязное дело?

— Я не считаю, что политика — грязное дело. Просто некоторые люди делают ее грязными руками.

— Вы сделали для себя какое-нибудь неожиданное открытие в должности мэра?

— Сделал. Большое открытие. Пройдя испытание предвыборной кампанией, я понял, что людей нельзя обмануть. Они хотят иметь свое мнение и верят делам, а не словам. Они умеют отделить правду от красиво упакованной лжи. Нам поверили, и мы обязаны оправдать доверие людей.

— Существует ли конфликт между Эйгимом-мэром и Эйгимом-бизнесменом?

— Он есть. Хотя бизнес и руководство городом в чем-то похожи, как бы меня ни убеждали в обратном. Но как мэр Даугавпилса я гораздо сильнее ощущаю моральную ответственность — за людей в первую очередь. В каких-то ситуациях предприниматель Эйгим поступал бы гораздо жестче, чем мэр. Или, наоборот, мягче. Поэтому сейчас во мне происходит внутренняя «перестройка».

— Вас никогда не тянуло в Ригу?

— Трудно ли увольнять людей с работы? Совесть потом не мучает?

— Когда увольняешь руководителя, который нарушал трудовую и финансовую дисциплину, всегда помнишь, что у него есть семья, дети. Но есть семьи и у тех, кто страдает от такого «руководства», и их гораздо больше. Поэтому приходится принимать довольно жесткие решения, но всегда — в рамках закона. Я никогда не руководствуюсь эмоциями в таких вопросах. И членов «чуждых партий» не собираюсь преследовать. Для меня выборы закончились 11 марта.

О душе

— Что значит для вас благотворительность? Порыв души? Или трезвый расчет, как считают некоторые?

— Это помощь самому себе. Когда помогаешь — освобождаешь душу от тяжелого груза. Ты же видишь, как тяжело живут люди, видишь глаза детей-сирот. Как можно не делиться, если у тебя, грубо говоря, карман распирает от прибыли? Те, кто имеет деньги, просто обязаны, я не побоюсь этого слова, помогать ближнему. Тем более что люди с доходом в 10 латов отдают на богоугодные дела 50 сантимов. Это — весомее моей помощи...

Так — победим!

— Какая проблема номер один для Даугавпилса?

— Это проблема для всей Латгалии. Безработица. Ее сразу не

— Я бы мог уехать в любую часть мира и не иметь тех проблем, которые имею здесь. Но я родился в Латгалии, здесь живут мои родители, здесь могли мои бабушки и дедушки. И я хочу быть полезным своему краю.

— Вы не заметили, что среди вашего «электората» много женщин?

— Мне многие об этом говорят. Да и в думском аппарате у нас много женщин. По-моему, это говорит лишь о том, что пришло время прекрасного пола. Не зря же у нас президент — женщина. Много подобных примеров и в других странах. А мужчины начинают утрачивать позиции по чисто профессиональным критериям, и для меня половая принадлежность сотрудника не имеет никакого значения. Профессионализм и порядочность — вот что должно быть на первом месте.

— Вы ощущаете себя в своем возрасте?

— Тяжело обмануть свой организм. Нет—нет да и напомнит он о том, что тебе не 18. Если он не подскажет это в утренние часы, то сделает это в дневные.

— Или в ночные...

— Или в ночные. Другое дело, что надо стараться, чтобы не износиться раньше времени. 40-летний человек не должен иметь организм 60-летнего.

решить. У нас нет волшебной палочки. Ее можно решить только постепенно и совместно с другими районами. Латгалия — это не только Даугавпилс, но и Резекне, Лудза, Ливаны... Только объединенными усилиями можно победить безработицу.

— В Даугавпилсе осталось хоть одно предприятие, работающее на полную мощность?

— Есть у нас предприятие, которое работает почти на полную мощность. Это «Локомотив» — один из старейших заводов Латвии.

— А можно ли без восстановления производства решить проблему безработицы?

— Вряд ли. Один бизнес этот воз не потянет. Производство нужно налаживать, и мы начинаем это делать. Начало с конвейерного завода... Но, я думаю, два месяца — это не тот срок, за который можно восстановить заводы и фабрики.

— Чего, по-вашему, не видно из Риги? Какие там мифы о Латгалии особенно живучи?

— Мифы о Латгалии рождались не в Риге. Мы, латгальцы, сами способствовали их созданию. Все зависит от нас самих. Нас будут уважать, если мы будем дело делать, а меньше говорить.

— Что такое латгальский характер? И есть ли вообще у латгальцев какой-то особый менталитет?

— Есть. У латгальцев имеются свои отличительные черты. Это целеустремленность, напористость и работоспособность. Эти качества и помогут нам добиться успеха.

— Спасибо за беседу. И — до свидания...

Ложка дёгтя

Предвыборные баталии попортили Рихарду Эйгиму немало крови. Журналисты обозвали его популистом, а конкуренты уличили будущего мэра во многих грехах — от контрабанды нефтепродуктами до... незнания латышского языка.

И если обвинения в контрабанде оказались несостоятельными, то за второй пункт конкурентам удалось зацепиться. Комиссия по государственному языку выявила, что кандидат в мэры Даугавпилса Рихард Эйгим слабо знает латышский. Стать городским головой ему тем не менее удалось. И сейчас мэр с нетерпением дожидается июня, чтобы на повторном экзамене продемонстрировать свои лингвистические способности.

ЛИЧНОЕ ВПЕЧАТЛЕНИЕ

Мэр Даугавпилса Рихард Эйгим, безусловно, представляет собой тип руководителя новой формации. Не красноословя ради, а, глядя в календарь, можно даже сказать — руководителя XXI века.

Он не похож ни на советского председателя горкома, ни на «нового латгальца». Он не любит произносить длинных речей и кормить народ обещаниями. Умеет организовать нормальную работу без авралов и трудовых подвигов. Нравится женщинам и вызывает уважение у представителей сильного пола. Является личностью, как сейчас модно говорить, харизматической — за ним хочется идти с песнями, но не строевым шагом. И кажется, что все у него получится. Очень бы этого хотелось...

№ 21 (407) 24 мая 2001

4-звёздочный мотель Stalkers.

Source: Magazine: National Geographic, 24th May 2001, Author: Andrew Petrov

Translation of Magazine Article for CIM Case Study

Article 4. – Main Text

Latgale has a special position in Latvia. The mixture of races and cultures makes this region multi-faceted. But self-satisfied Rigans have always had a lordly, condescending attitude towards Latgale: what can you get from those "Changals"? (Riga nickname for Latgalians; Latgalians call Riga people "Chuily" meaning interpreter). They drink, they do nothing. If they are lucky they become hired helps or farm labourers. They speak a terrible dialect of Latvian. There are even Russian and Polish speakers. But the region's backwardness is understood by many people as an historic inevitability.

However, the "National Geographic" editorial staff do not believe in such myths. That is why they have decided to organise the first Latgalian expedition to get an answer to the question, Quo vadis Latgale? The first place on our journey is Daugavpils – the unofficial capital of the "Land of the Blue Lakes". And here is our first interview – with its Mayor, Richard Eigims.

Richard Eigims – "There will be a Garden-City!"

The new Mayor dreams of turning Daugavpils into a little Vienna.

Richards Eigims has managed the city's economy for only two months. It is too early to draw any conclusions, but the appearance of flower beds near the municipality creates an optimistic mood.

The first thing that impresses is that Eigims, from being a "simple" businessman, has built the only 4-star hotel in Latgale, 20 kilometres north of Daugavpils. Wedding parties now drive to his "Stalkers" petrol station for photographs. Daugavpils newlyweds have a new tradition. The thing is, such a picturesque petrol station does not exist in Riga, let alone the whole of eastern Europe! Everything around is green with plants, the fountains work, and there are fish splashing in the pond.

But from 11th March, 2001 there was a new beginning for Richard Eigims – he became the new City Mayor. So life is not only about fountains...

So onto our first interview with the new Mayor in his office – the coffee invigorating, the sweets sweet and the conversation open.

"Please tell me what journalists' questions annoy you the most and I will ask something different."

RE: "There are no such questions. All questions are good (smiles). Journalists ask journalistic questions – it is your work. We, those who are asked, cannot choose: I like this question, but don't like that so I am not going to answer it. It simply does not happen like that."

"Has getting onto the list of millionaires in "Klubs" magazine made you feel happy?"

46

RE: "My attitude to this is very calm. That is to say, it was not invented by me. This magazine got their numbers from somewhere, different numbers, and introduced them to their readers. That's how it happened."

"But isn't it some kind of recognition of your business success?"

RE: "I already felt successful enough before my name appeared in this magazine."

"Could you tell our readers about your car and your home? What do you drive? Where do you live?"

RE: "I am constantly asked what do I have and how much did it cost. I don't hide anything. In one of the newspapers, I read a funny thing about myself. They were telling how millionaire Eigims differs from other millionaires. It turned out it was because I owned an MT3 tractor!"

"And how much was this tractor?"

RE: "It was purchased in 1992 for approximately L3,000. Now, of course, it is worth much more."

"And how many foreign cars have you got?"

RE: "One. It is a Renault Safrane. I have had this car since 1993. It is good for our roads, it's got a powerful engine and it satisfies me. And it cost – I am anticipating your next question – L25,000."

"And where is your house?"

RE: "I have a three room flat in Daugavpils. I don't have villas on islands, although I could have them. But I believe there should be someone living in a house. What is the point of having a villa that you visit once a year?"

"Everybody knows you are a car racer and ice hockey player. But which do you prefer?"

RE: "Both are interesting. I don't think I need to tell you about enjoying the risk and the excitement. Besides it helps me in my work. It helps me to work efficiently. During the winter, I play ice hockey from October until May. But the racing is good, because it starts in May and finishes in October. The same cycle as in work. I call it 'well planned sport'."

"That sounds very active. But how do you really relax? When did you have your last holiday?"

RE: "I have my holidays every year. Those who "skip" holidays act, to my mind, extremely thoughtlessly. All the people who have worked with me went somewhere for their holidays. I will introduce this approach in the municipality. People who don't plan rest for themselves, will be instructed to take a break. I am also against work at the weekends. What can you expect from morally and physically exhausted workers?"

"By the way, where do you like to spend your holidays?"

RE: "Usually, I separate my holidays into two parts. For two weeks in the winter, I am dedicated to downhill skiing. In the summer, I like the seaside."

"The Red Sea, the Mediterranean?"

RE: "At any... any ocean... summer drives me to the ocean."

"Where do you ski?"

RE: "In Switzerland."

"Probably in Davros?"

RE: "No. Although I've been there a couple of times. It's too busy and noisy in Davros. Many world famous people and those who follow them. But I want to relax... I've found a quiet place, but I don't want to name it!"

"Are you afraid that all our readers will rush there? But where else do you feel at home, where else could you live?"

RE: "I like Vienna very much – it's one of the most beautiful cities! What parks there are! I would like to create something similar in Daugavpils..."

Is it possible to relax in Latgale? Not everyone can go to Vienna or the Swiss Alps.

RE: "There are many nice places in Latgale – it is the Land of the Blue Lakes! Near Daugavpils we have the lakes of Sventa and Stropi, near Kraslava there are remarkable places, in Aglona, in Cirishi (where my parents live). There are many places to go. And we have plans for creating new relaxation areas with very comfortable facilities and plans to upgrade the old places."

"Do you use the help of alcohol or smoking to relax?"

RE: "I relax with the help of sport and Russian Baths (sauna). In winter, after the Russian Bath, I swim through a hole in the ice. And that is enough!"

"Didn't the elections show that politics is a dirty business?"

RE: "I don't think politics is a dirty business. Only some people do it with dirty hands."

"Did you make any unexpected discoveries yourself in your new position of Mayor?"

RE: "I did... a big discovery. Having gone through a very demanding pre-election campaign, I have recognised it is impossible to cheat people. They have their own opinion and believe in deeds not words. They know how to sort out the truth from the nicely packaged lie. They have placed their trust in us and we must justify that trust."

"Is there any conflict between Eigims the Mayor and Eigims the Businessman?"

48

RE: "There is, although business and city management are similar in many ways. But, as Daugavpils Mayor I feel a moral responsibility, the need to put people first. In some situations, Eigims the Businessman would act much tougher than Eigims the Mayor! Or, to put it another way, I am a softer touch as Mayor. That's why now, inside myself, there is a kind of "rebuilding" going on."

"Is it difficult to fire people? Aren't you conscience stricken afterwards?"

RE: "When you fire a manager for work or financial indiscipline, you always remember they have a family and children. But those who suffer from such mismanagement also have families and they are much more numerous. That's why we have to take tough decisions, but always within the limits of the law. I never base such decisions on emotions. And I'm not going to hunt down members of the "strange" parties. For me the elections finished on the 11th March."

About the soul...

"What does charity mean for you? An impulse of the soul? Or is it a sober decision as some people think?"

RE: "It is about self-help. When you help, you make your soul free from a heavy weight. You see how hard life is for most people, you look into the eyes of the orphans. How can you not share if, in a manner of speaking, your pockets bulge with money. Those who have money are obliged (and I'm not afraid of that word) to help their neighbours. Even more, people with only 10 lats will give 50 santimes to charity. This is far more significant than my help."

"Haven't you ever been drawn to Riga?"

RE: "I would leave for any part of the world not to have the problems that I have here. But I was born in Latgale, my parents live here, the graves of my grandmothers and grandfathers are here. And I want to help my native land."

"Didn't you notice that many of those that voted for you were women?"

RE: "So people tell me. Also in our city administration there are many women. To my mind it only indicates that the time for the fair sex has arrived. It is not a coincidence that our President is also a woman. There are many similar examples in other countries as well. Now men can lose their positions when judged on purely professional criteria. For me the gender of a staff member has no importance. Professionalism and integrity – that's what counts."

"Do you feel your age?"

RE: "It's difficult to cheat your own body. Now and again it reminds you that you are not 18 any more. If it doesn't remind you in the morning, it will during the day."

"Or at night..."

BPP PUBLISHING

RE: "Or at night. The other thing is that you should live so that you don't wear yourself out prematurely. A 40-year person shouldn't have the body of a 60-year old."

"What is the number one problem for Daugavpils?"

RE: "It's a problem for the whole of Latgale. Unemployment. It can't be solved at once. There is no magic wand. It can only be solved gradually and together with the other regions of Latgale – it's not only Daugavpils, but Rezekne, Ludza, Livani… only with our joint efforts will we overcome unemployment."

"Is there at least one enterprise left in Daugavpils that works to full capacity?"

RE: "We have an enterprise that works nearly to full capacity. It is "Lokomotiv" (makes/repairs trains) – one of the oldest factories in Latvia."

"Can the problem of unemployment be solved without restoring production capacity?"

RE: "Hardly. One business can't take up this load. Production needs to be increased and we have made a start. We've started with the canning factory. But two months is too little time in which to restore the many factories and businesses."

"From your point of view, how does Riga see this area? What are their myths about Latgale?"

RE: "Myths about Latgale were not born in Riga. We, the Latgalians, allowed them to develop. Everything depends on us. We will be respected if we work more and talk less."

"What is the Latgalian character? Is there a different Latgalian mentality?"

RE: "There is. Latgalians have their own distinct features. These are – purposefulness, energy and a capacity for work. These qualities will help us achieve success."

"Thank you for the interview – goodbye."

50

Boxed Articles

A Spoon of Tar – Pre-election fights raised the blood pressure of Richard Eigims. Journalists called him a populist and rivals accused him of many things from smuggling oil products to poor knowledge of the Latvian language. And even if the smuggling accusations had no ground, the second point was successfully used by rivals. The Commission of the State Language found that, as a candidate for Mayor, Richard Eigims did have a weak knowledge of Latvian. Despite this he has managed to become leader of the city. And now the Mayor waits impatiently for June and the chance to demonstrate his linguistic skills in the next examination.

Personal Impression – The Daugavpils Mayor is undoubtedly a new type of manager. A manager for the 21st century.

He's not like a Soviet style leader, nor like a "new Latgalian" as he doesn't like to give long speeches or feed people with promises. He knows how to organise work with crises. Women like him and men respect him. He is a charismatic leader and as the popular expression goes, people follow him with songs, not out of duty. And it seems everything will be successful – we hope so.

"Latgale – an ancient, historical area in the east of Latvia inhabited by Latgalians. During the 10th to 13th centuries there were three principalities, Jersika, Koknes and Talava. In the 13th century it was conquered by German knights.

From the beginning of the 17th century, the south-eastern part of this territory, south of the River Aivieksne, became part of the Zadvina Dukedom. In 1629, it became part of Pzech Posplita. From 1772-1917, it was within the borders of Imperial Russia (Dvina Province) and then the western part of Vitebesk Province. Since 1918, it has been part of Latvia."

From the History of the Motherland – Great Russian Encyclopaedia

51

BPP
PUBLISHING

About Richard Eigims

Richard Eigims was born on the first of May 1962 in a small village, Vishki (Daugavpils District). After local school he went to the legal faculty of Latvia University. Since 1993 he has been president of Stalkers, a joint stock company, trading in oil products. Under him, Stalkers has been included in Latvia's list of top company tax payers. In 1999, Eigims was acknowledged as Daugavpils Person of the Year. This March he became Mayor of Daugavpils, beating the former Mayor, Alexei Vidavskis. But in May he appeared in the Latvian list of millionaires published by the magazine "Klubs" (and not for the first time). A great sportsman – a champion of Latvia in car speedway and a champion of Daugavpils in ice hockey. Actively works for charity: helps asylums, schools, poor people and the church. Divorced with two children, 17 year old Christina and 16 year old Alexander, who study in the Russian Gymnasium.

When last year, Richard Eigims got into the list of the 100 millionaires of Latvia, he was laughing about it with his friends. Obviously, such a possibility had not occurred to him. In addition, just the day before the article was published, the newly discovered millionaire had bought a pair of shoes in the local market for only L14. The shoes turned out to be very comfortable, he later reported.

A year later "Klubs" again included Mr Eigims in their list of millionaires that now comprised 150 names. And journalists resurrected the story about the shoes to show that millionaires were just people.

And they are not without charity. Mr Eigims has for several years made Christmas gifts to children throughout Latgale, and provides equipment to the school's first form. He is also a sponsor of local ice hockey.

In January, this magazine reported that Mr Eigims had installed electricity in Daugavpils Lutheran Church, where there had been no light at all for several years. We also can recall a story about the reconstruction of a church in Dagda.

52

Article 5. – Daugavpils the City

Source: Magazine: National Geographic, 24th May 2001, Author: Andrew Petrov

Translation of Magazine Article for CIM Case Study

Article 5. – Main Text

Travel without a map – I have seen the city.

There are very beautiful women and a ticket for the tram costs 10 santimes, but the people are generally poor and rely on unemployment benefit.

The weather welcomed our arrival. On this warm May evening from the Riga bus station a bus has cast off towards Daugavpils exactly on time. There were no adventures on the journey and many traditional scenes of forests, fields, farms and meadows passed rapidly by. But the Latgalian scenery was nicely typified by the many storks' nests on the tops of telegraph poles. After a ride of three and a half hours, we arrived in Daugavpils.

I was loafing about the city… by Andrew Petrov.

My acquaintance with the Latgalian capital began the following morning. A normal working day was beginning. What was striking? An absence of crowds of people hurrying about with anxious and gloomy faces – a normal attribute of big cities. The unhurried rhythm of the city life, the calmness and cordiality of its people lifted my heart. True, this feeling only lasted two days – the length of my stay in Daugavpils. Perhaps after a week or two, I would have missed the hustle and bustle of Riga. But certainly not in two days.

It is clear that the inhabitants of Daugavpils have more problems than Riga. Just think of the impact of high unemployment. But it does not reflect in their stoicism and benevolence. The abundance and beauty of the local women and girls cannot help but bring tears to a man's eyes. Already at the bus station, it was possible to see Aphrodite selling ice cream. Unfortunately, at the offer to take her photograph, the goddess responds rather unexpectedly. She makes off with her handcart to get away from the strange tempters. Such modesty, but we are not from Playboy!

In the city park, we had the opportunity to talk with three charming pupils from the 11th grade of the Polish school, Oksana, Lena and Natasha. These girls love the town of their birth very much, but their future plans include studies in Riga or abroad. Unfortunately, in the local Pedagogical Institute studying is quite costly. Thus, "flow away the brains" …well you know what I mean.

It's nonsense to come to another town and not visit the local market. And there we hear the all too familiar ventriloquism, "Cigarettes, cigarettes!". But unlike Riga, spirits were not offered at all. On the contrary, live chicken and ducklings can easily be bought. Although around this miniature zoo, there are more spectators than buyers. The city market in Daugavpils is a bit smaller than Riga's "Matveichiks". I did try to compare prices, but soon got bored. (I hope housewives will forgive me). Some goods were 10-15 santimes cheaper than Riga, some did not differ in price. But these differences are only really important for the city dwellers, whose incomes are much more modest than those in the Latvian capital.

54

After getting acquainted with the centre of the city, I made my way to an unusual attraction of Daugavpils – a jail with a poetic, national name of "The White Swan Hotel". When the photographer starts clicking away standing on a bridge, we suddenly hear a disembodied voice from a loudspeaker saying it is forbidden to photograph this prison! We shout in reply, assuming the voice to be from security, that we do not photograph you but the railway. (It really does run nearby). "They say they photograph the railway" – negotiations continue via the loudspeaker. But we never knew how this conversation ended as by then we had completed our filming and left.

55

BPP
PUBLISHING

Figure 11. – City Organisation Chart

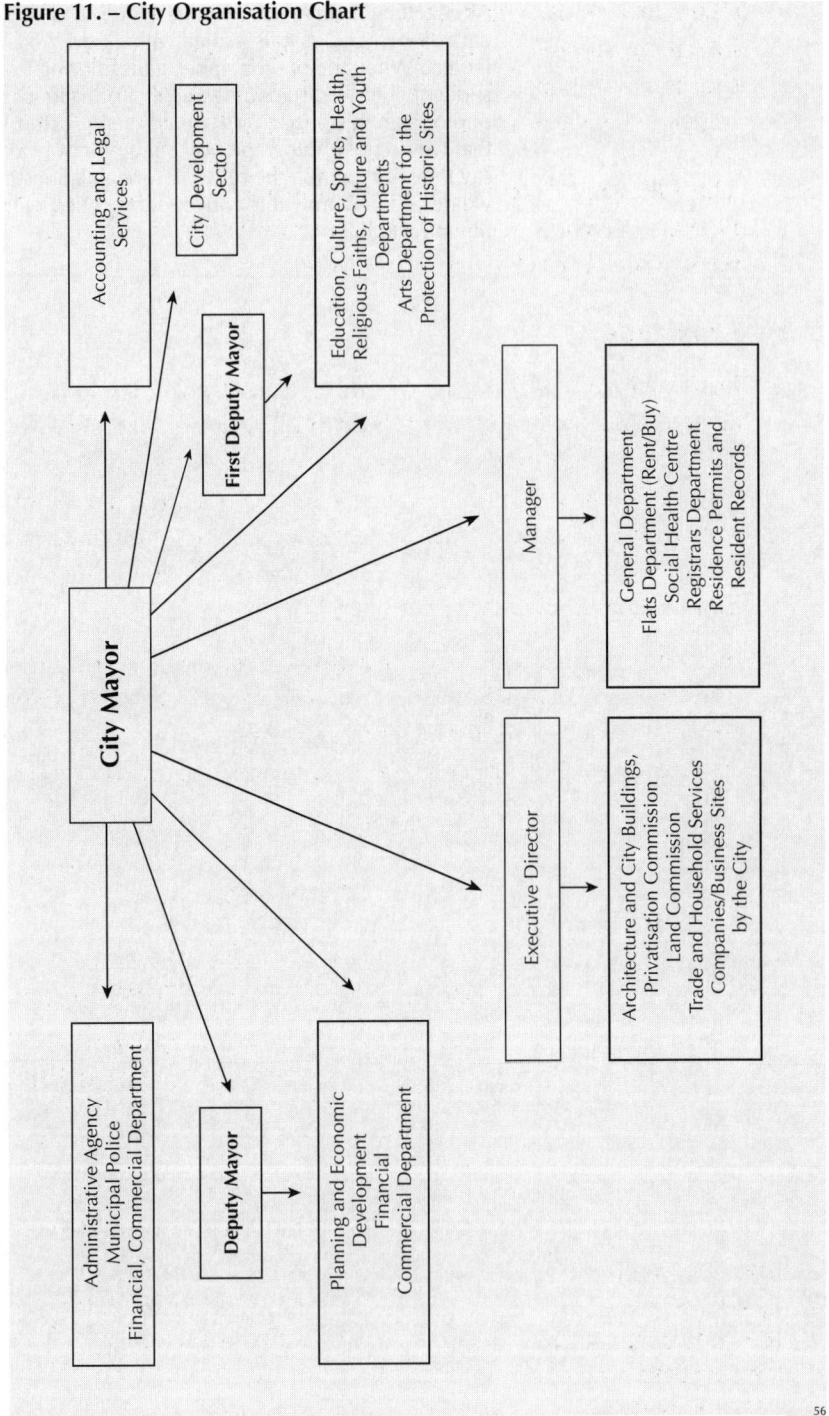

3 STEP 1: INITIAL OVERVIEW

3.1 This is an example of a very different case study from what you are used to. It is a not for profit organisation and tackles a contemporary issue: 'place marketing'. It contains a great deal of environmental information and data, which could be off-putting. Do *not* let the sector or lack of your knowledge of it scare you. In this case, you are also operating in an international context, but the case process remains unchanged. Remember that whatever the case is about, it is the same for **everyone** and simply serves to re-enforce how transferable our marketing and planning skills are.

3.2 The following notes are tutor comments, which will help you to assess your overview. Before reviewing them, complete your overview. Please note that the page references below refer to the page references of the case.

3.3 **About the City**

Daugavpils (C of D) is the second City in Latvia, but run down from its industrial glory days during Soviet times. Politically, Latvia prefers links with the West and Europe to building closer ties with Russia. Today, almost two thirds of Latvian exports go to the EU (page 2, paragraph 4). The country is preparing for EU membership and an economically stronger second City would be advantageous to this political and economic ambition. This is the sort of benefit which may help in winning any business case for investment in C of D from Riga politicians.

Its troubled past has led to a situation where Latvian citizenship is only offered to Latvian speakers. As the inhabitants of Daugavpils are mainly Russian speaking, this must clearly position them as somewhat 'second class', struggling to manage a mix of people and interests (page 2, paragraph 4) and perceived by Riga as 'remote'.

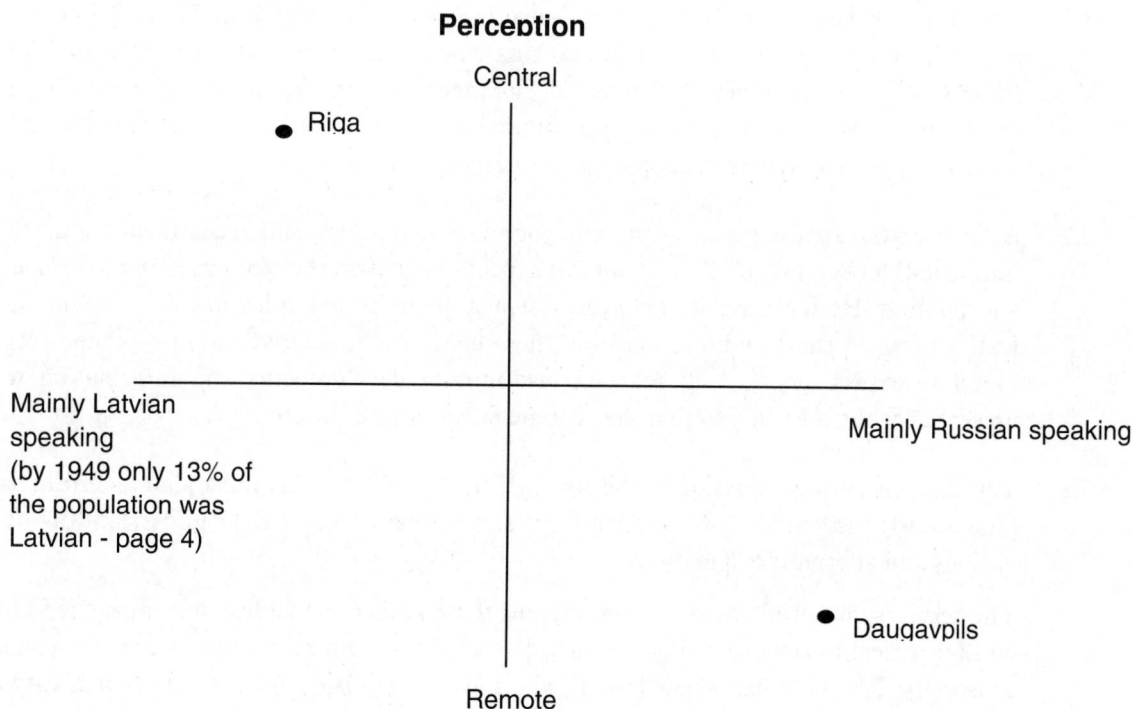

Perception

Central

● Riga

Mainly Latvian
speaking
(by 1949 only 13% of
the population was
Latvian - page 4)

Mainly Russian speaking

● Daugavpils

Remote

3.4   In common with other former ex-Soviet countries the old structures and decision making centralist systems do not deliver the fast moving flexible responses to market conditions needed to be the commercially successful today (page 3).

Its geographic location is, in fact, a positive, with good rail links and close to the borders of three neighbours:

- Republic of Lithuania (25 km)
- Belarus (33km)
- Russia (120 km)

The description of the climate and geography on page 5 are worth reviewing. Try to get a picture in your mind of the area and the sort of visitors or industry it could attract.

3.5   To date regional development has been fragmented and un-coordinated (page 6, paragraph 6) but there is the Latgale Regional Development Agency (LRDA) with EU partners based in their offices in Daugavpils.

However, on page 8, paragraph 5, we have a clear indication of the key issue which is stated as being 'raising the City's profile in Riga'. What is less clear, is why? The political influence and authority (or ability) to divert funds etc from Riga are not immediately clear. We are not sure who the key influences are in Riga. Certainly if you are seeking to change popular stereotypes, this would be a difficult and long term task. Think about the images we have of Londoners, Brummies or Mancunians – true to type or false, they are hard to change and the short term economic benefits of doing so would not be clear.

Actions rather than words are more likely to challenge and change the status quo.

That perception of a declining City, an ageing population made up of 20 nationalities, geographically in the centre of things and places but percieved politically as remote and not Latvian, is the sense I have as I consider what the case asks us to do.

3.6   Your role is clear. You are a marketing consultant funded by European Union pre-accession funds. You are reporting to Ilya Podkolzins who has been appointed by Mayor Richard Eigims to head up a new business development and marketing department. It seems reasonable to assume that if the EU has funded your consultancy project they will also fund some marketing activities in support of your recommendations.

3.7   As Ilya Podkolzins is going to present your views, findings and recommendations to the municipality (Candidate's Brief), you can expect his questions at your meeting to be specific and pointed. He will need to be clear, not just about your arguments, but also about the justification for them and will insist on these being well prepared and up-to-date. You can therefore expect any and all relevant last minute developments and information to be presented at the meeting, so that they can be factored into the strategy.

3.8   You can expect the discussions to be strategic in nature. The City must plan its future based on a realistic assessment of its capabilities and resources and a clear understanding of the options and alternatives open to it.

The services and products it focuses on, and the markets and audience it must then target, will be critical to re-positioning the City of Daugavpils and rebuilding the area's economic prosperity. The City has a new leader, who has a clear vision to create a Garden City and this is key to providing a focus for initiatives and local effort. It would be easy to be sceptical, but a review of how a marketing approach has helped turn around the fortunes and change the image of a number of towns and cities in the UK, does give an insight into what can be achieved. Bradford is mentioned, but Glasgow now has an international reputation for its Arts and Dockland areas. With vision and strategy, a lot is possible.

3.9 This case will, however, have many facets to it. There are a number of complex stakeholder groups whose support will be needed and a communications plan to win their support. Cash will be needed, as well as recommendations for achieving the desired re-positioning of the City's image. The challenge in this case is to win support and investors, not the customers who may eventually use the City's facilities and amenities. This is a Business to Business model of marketing not a B2C one.

The key issues and possible exam questions will always become more obvious as you work through the analysis. It is certain that you will need to be prepared with short term as well as long term recommendations. Remember, the Mayor is elected and will want some 'quick wins'. A plan which only delivers benefits to the City over 10 years is unlikely to win many voters.

You can however be confident that the focus will be strategic <u>not</u> tactical - your exam success depends on just three things:

- Thorough analysis
- Used to support clear and realistic recommendations
- Presented convincingly with stakeholder benefits highlighted

The challenges

3.10 The summary on page 17 of the case is most useful. We have a picture of a City currently in a poor situation but with potential. Resources are limited, so strategies are needed both to **boost** the available resources and to **apply them** to the opportunities will deliver tangible benefits to the area and where there is a potential for competitive advantage.

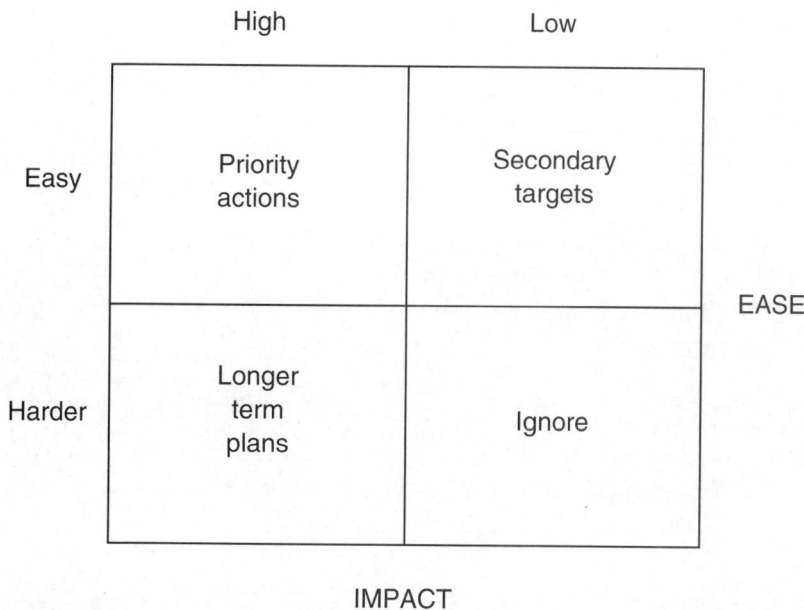

	High	Low	
Easy	Priority actions	Secondary targets	
Harder	Longer term plans	Ignore	EASE

IMPACT

An impact/ease grid shows that the goal is to identify options which will deliver high impact benefits in terms of inward investments, employment creation and 'the local income multiplier'. The easier these are to deliver, the more attractive the opportunity will be. Some factors are listed below:

- Ease of winning political support
- Synergy with stakeholder objectives (on page 28 the City's development priorities are clearly spelt out)
- Levels of investment needed

- Independence of the project vis a vis other infrastructure developments and support
- Speed of implementation

3.11 Of course, although the opportunity is attractive to the City this does not mean that the City is positioned to exploit that opportunity.

Its potential competitive advantage must also be considered. For example, in an extreme scenario, the City may like to be host to the next allocated Olympic Games, but its potential to win such a bid would be unlikely.

The **multifactor matrix** is likely to be very useful in this case in helping to decide which opportunities the City of Daugavpils should focus on. Your criteria for such evaluation will be the foundation stones of the justification for your recommendations.

Michael Porter's model in the Case (page 3) provides a framework for assessing potential competitive advantage in this context. The diagram on the next page is taken from 'The Competitive Advantage of Nations'.

Porter describes this model as a diamond representing the determinants of National advantage.

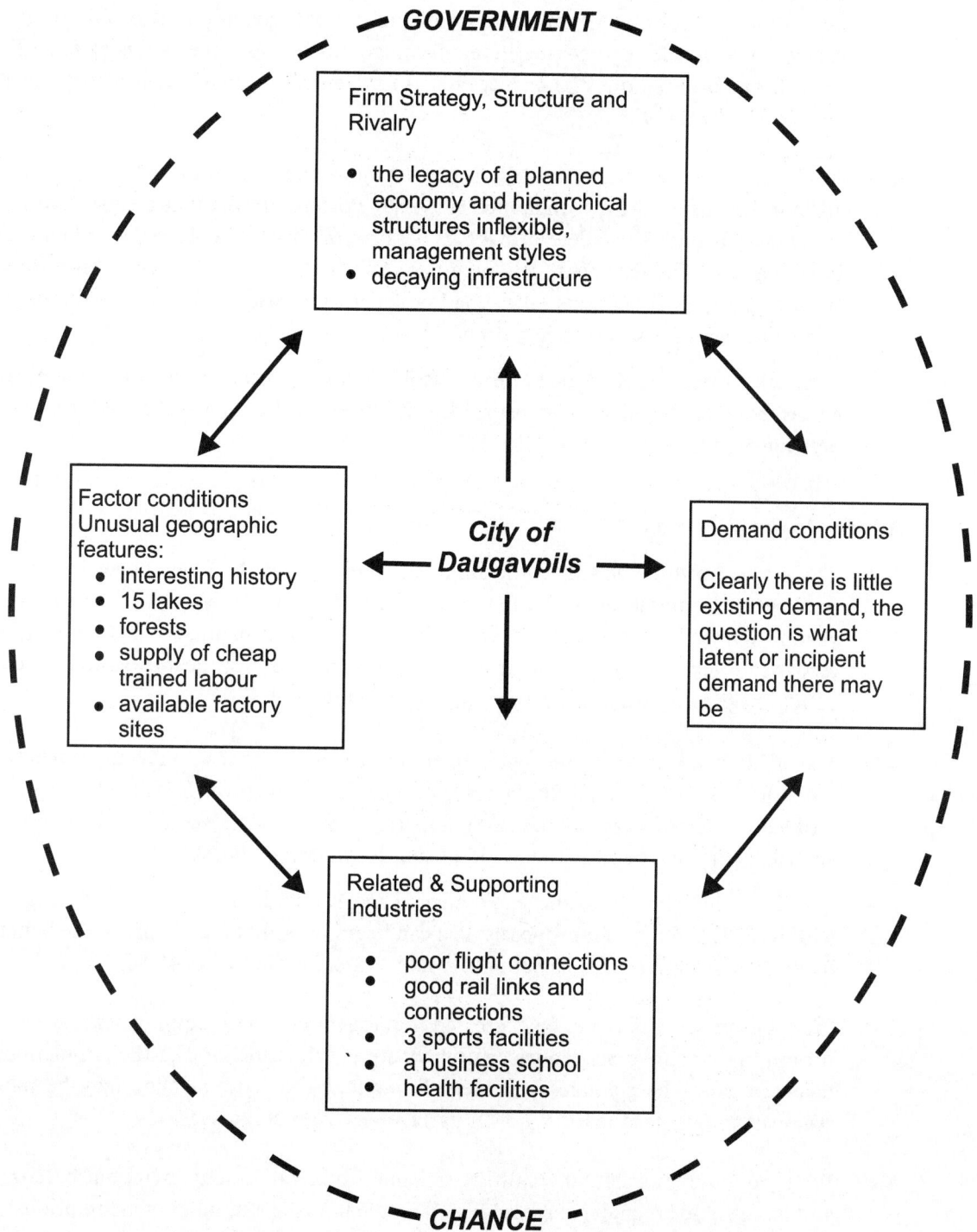

Porter's Diamond model diagram for the City of Daugavpils showing:

GOVERNMENT (outer dashed circle, top)

Firm Strategy, Structure and Rivalry
- the legacy of a planned economy and hierarchical structures inflexible, management styles
- decaying infrastrucure

City of Daugavpils (centre)

Factor conditions
Unusual geographic features:
- interesting history
- 15 lakes
- forests
- supply of cheap trained labour
- available factory sites

Demand conditions
Clearly there is little existing demand, the question is what latent or incipient demand there may be

Related & Supporting Industries
- poor flight connections
- good rail links and connections
- 3 sports facilities
- a business school
- health facilities

CHANCE (outer dashed circle, bottom)

3.12 Porter says the more favourable the four determinants are, the more likely the industry or country will be to succeed, though good conditions are no guarantee of competitive advantage.

In fact, the more dynamic the natural environment, the more likely some firms will fail, as resources will not be allocated equally. However Porter's view is that those who do survive are likely to also fare well in an international arena.

Tutor Tip

3.13 We have started to add the case materials to this Porter model for you. This is not intended to be definitive but to give you an example of applying theory to practice. Work on this, modify, develop and complete it as you feel necessary.

3.14 Porter goes on to say 'the diamond is a mutually re-enforcing system, the effect of one determinant is contingent on the state of the others. Favourable demand conditions for example will not lead to competitive advantage unless the state of rivalry is sufficient to cause firms to respond to them. Advantages in one determinant can also create or upgrade advantages in others.'

3.15 Applying this model to the C of D, it clearly shows that the conditions are not positive in all four dimensions of the diamond. However, Porter believes that competitive advantage based on only one or two determinants is possible in natural resource dependent industries, involving little sophisticated technology or skills – although this may be an unsustainable advantage as global copycats enter the market. In the case of Daugavpils the opportunity offered by fishing reserves may fit in here.

You will notice two factors to this model are also central to the theory – chance and government. Both generate opportunities and threats, which have changed the competitive position of nations.

Adding to the summary

3.16 There is more to be added to the summary provided in the case. There is a new Mayor (perhaps an example of political impact). This Mayor is a successful person and has a vision. Within two months of office, flowerbeds were planted. This sort of **physical evidence** of change will be important to motivating the local people, as well as creating a better image for visiting influencers and potential investors.

3.17 Mayor Eigims, it is worth noting, is likely to have a propensity to favour **tourism,** having built the first 4 star hotel 20kms outside the City (page 46). Locally, he seems to have created a new concept, a 'destination petrol station' with such an attractive physical environment it has become the local hot spot for wedding photos!

He tells us he enjoys risk and excitement (page 47). If the Mayor is a key decision-maker within the DMU for your proposals, you can begin to build up a picture of the benefits he is likely to be swayed by. Do pay attention to his interview on pages 46-80.

3.18 City objectives are likely to be expressed in terms of increased employment targets or other inward investment goals. Tourist numbers are provided per 100 of the population, but do take care with the statistics provided throughout the Case, as they may be national or regional, not just for the City and similarly, check your currencies.

3.19 We have some information about the stakeholders' requirements here, but because the EU and its agencies are major stakeholders, it is safe to make a number of assumptions:

- The current poor economic situation needs to be addressed before EU membership can be attained by Latvia

- Political interests in Riga would therefore be supportive of development in their second city

However, competition for development and marketing resources will be intense at EU and national level, which means that you will need to make a persuasive and strong case for any additional resources. This is not a cash rich nation and remember the examiners will be looking for evidence of your commercial credibility i.e. do you recognise the constraints of the context you are working in?

3.20 The communications and stakeholder management are issues which could be on the examiner's agenda and the brand development is important for long term market presence. Is there any real differential advantage in what the City can offer? Why should an enterprise choose to locate here rather than the Capital or indeed another country?

Who are the competitors and what external environmental factors are changing the market for inward investment?

3.21 Demand is influenced by many factors. What influences the choice of an industrial location? Remember for example, the impact of external economies of scale which explains why similar firms locate in the same area, attracted by a trained workforce or appropriate infrastructure etc.

Remember to think about all the key stakeholder groups, including the local residents – these are the Mayor's constituents and their ongoing support will be important.

3.22 Recognising the Stakeholders

In this case the stakeholders are critical. Who are they and what do they need? How can they be segmented? What do you need from them and what 'business case' and techniques could be used to win their support?

> **Tutor Tip**
>
> * As you work through the Case detail, use the tools and models to give structure and help sort the material so that the data provided becomes marketing information. For example, use your market maps to build up the picture.

3.23 This approach helps you clarify who is who.

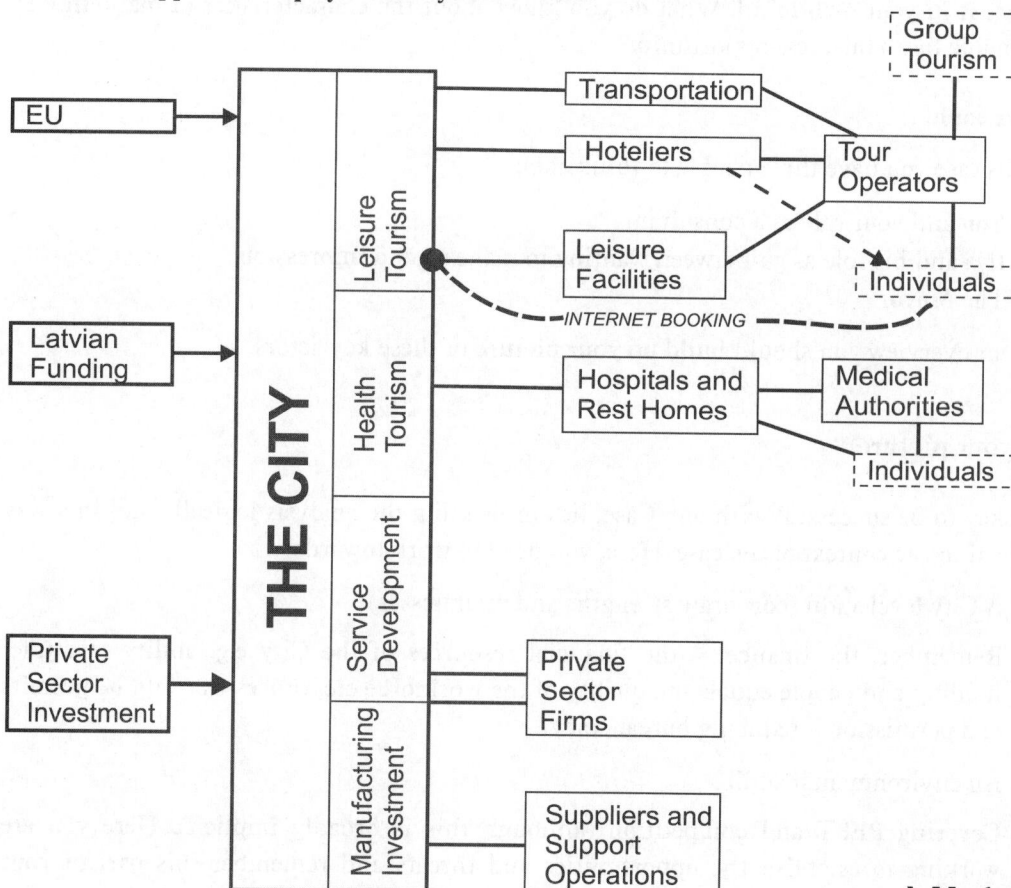

A Market Map for the City

Remember, this is essential to a B2B case. We need to help the City:

- Win funding
- Attract companies

In tourism this means a push and pull strategy.

3.24 You can also use mindmaps to help you sort through and make sense of your analysis at this preliminary stage.

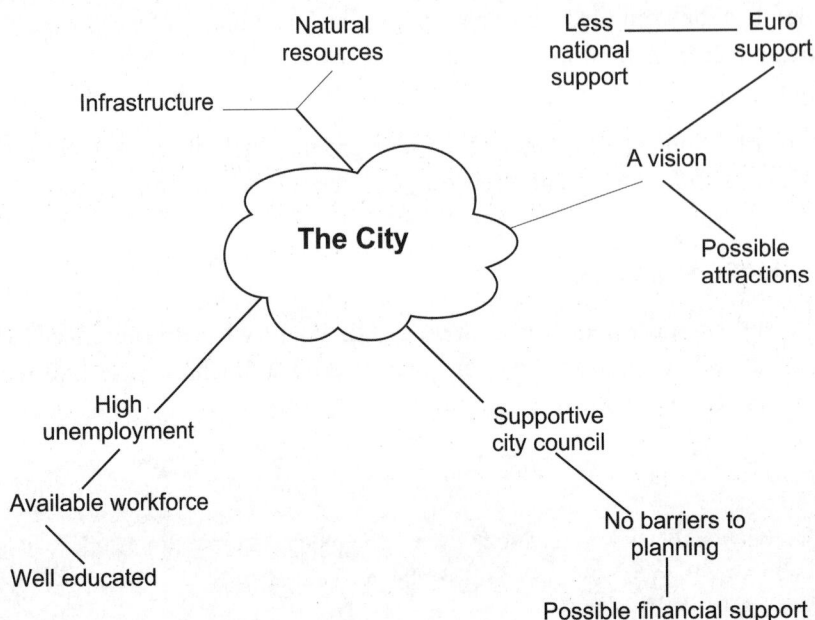

3.25 Do not just rely on what has been written. Think about the City of Daugavpils. Try to picture it in your own mind. What do you know about the characteristics of marketing an intangible like a business opportunity?

3.26 **The People**

In this case you have three people to think about.

- You and your role as a consultant
- Ilya and his role as go-between wanting to make a good impression
- The Mayor

In your overview you should **build up your picture** of these key actors.

Build up your picture

3.27 The key to be successful with any Case, lies in tackling the analysis logically and in a way relevant to the context of the case. Here, you need to work towards:

(a) A City level audit (corporate strengths and weaknesses)

Remember, the finance = the financial resources of the City e.g. ability to attract funding and people equals the quality of the workforce etc, processes could be permits and permission – reducing bureaucracy.

(b) An environmental audit

Covering PEST and competition (although this is broadly implicit). Here you are working to establish the opportunities and threats and remember this part of your analysis should be forward looking. EU support, website opportunities and membership of the EU are all aspects of this audit.

(c)   At market/customer level

The offer, or potential offer the City has, needs to be looked at in a slightly different way and you will find this easier if you do this for 3 targets.

Tourism, Ventures and Initiatives	New Business Investment	Local Population

You will see for example that:

- The scenery and geography is part of the 'product' for a tourism venture

- The available factory space and easy planning processes could be part of the offer for a new business, whilst low labour costs reduces the price tag

3.28   Work through the strengths and weaknesses for each market and then consider the specific product/markets this might let the City target eg fishing and shooting tourism.

Stakeholder issues

3.29   Managing stakeholders is a high profile element of this Case, so you need to analyse who the stakeholders are, what their needs are and their current perceptions or concerns. The stakeholder map provided by the examiner needs considerable work.

3.29   In this case, we think you will find it easiest if you start by sorting all the information about the City of Daugavpils and then looking at:

- What business is the City in, particularly the Mayor and his administration
- Who might want to locate or invest in the City and why?
- Who are the competitors?
- What has to be done to attain a competitive advantage?
- What does the City have to offer?
- What are the possible bases for adding value?

3.30   With the information available, complete what you can. You have limited information to let you know about buyers priorities or buying behaviour, but sort out what you can.

(a)   Identify what information you can from the data and check if anything can be gleaned by relating information from one part of the material to another. See what can be done with what information you have.

(b)   You may find having pieces of paper with key headings on each will help, giving you a structure for sorting the material out. Remember to think about your role, your objectives and those of your client and paymaster.

> **Tutor Tip.** Information gaps abound. From the beginning of your analysis keep a shopping list of information needs, it will be helpful later. Organise your work carefully in an indexed analysis file.

3.31   If you have not yet completed your own overview analysis, do take the time to do that now. You need to be aware of the case detail before you move on.

Action Programme 1

You should now be feeling more comfortable with the case study, both the context and the nature of the issues faced by C of D. Use the following questions to test your understanding and check your answers with ours at the end of the chapter.

Questions

1. Who are you and what is your role?

2. As this Marketing Consultant, who are your main 'customers'?

3. Name the three Baltic States.

4. Why does Latvia lack a National Identity?

5. Describe the geographic location of C of D

6. Name two potential tourist attractions and two business attractions of C of D

7. What is the currently held perception of C of D?

8. What is a City in the business of?

9. Whilst there is little information in the Case on competition, who might their competitors be?

10. What are you competing for?

11. Name three challenges facing C of D

12. Which framework, referred to in the Case, helps determine Competitive Advantage in this context?

13. Why would political interests in Riga be supportive of development in their City?

14. The newly elected Mayor has a vision of C of D being similar to which European City?

15. What qualities do you see the Mayor bringing to the City?

16. Whilst many of the recommendations may take five to ten years to realise, why will the Mayor also want to see some quick wins?

Tutor Tip

- Getting to grips with a Case study quickly depends very much on your approach to it. If you treat a case like a puzzle waiting to be solved, you will find yourself reading and re-reading the case, but never really getting into it. The solutions will **not** simply jump out at you, even if you learn the narrative by heart. Instead, you must try and role play a Case study. Imagine this is a work project - once you had been introduced to the key players, you would know who they were. Think about what it might be like to work at C of D, what is morale like at the culture? Put yourself in the case and the case process will become much easier.

Action Programme Review

1 Who are you and what is your role?

- Marketing Consultant funded by EU pre-accession funds, assigned to C of D to help advise on business and marketing.

2 As this Marketing Consultant, who are your main 'customers'?

- New Mayor, Richard Eigims, as the key decision maker and influential in DMU, Ilya Podkolzins who heads up the new Dept. who I am reporting back to with recommendations, and EU, for whom I work and will advise on my findings and allocation of marketing funds.

3   Name the three Baltic States.

- Latvia, Lithuania and Estonia

4   Why does Latvia lack a National Identity?

- Independence only last 10 years. Formerly ruled by Poles, Swedes, Germans and Russians

5   Describe the geographic location of C of D

- Proximity to Russia, Belarus and Lithuania. 232 km from Riga. Daugava River on either side of the City leading to Baltic Sea. Latgale region. 30% forest, lots of lakes, low lands, good rail links, beautiful scenery. Continental climate.

6   Name 2 potential tourist attractions and 2 business attractions of C of D

- Snow Ski-ing, Water ski-ing, boating, camping, climbing, historical sites, rail links to St Petersburg. Former 'health farms'. Sports Facilities. Water and rail links for business. Skilled and cheap labour force. Existing un-used factories. Current businesses that have set up which might provide economies of scale or related services for new businesses. Fishing reserves

7   What is the currently held perception of C of D?

- Backward, multi-cultured but mainly Russian, depressed, has nothing to offer, ageing population, located in the heart of things but remote politically

8   What is a City in the business of?

- Providing conditions which attract enough 'business opportunities' to provide an appropriate standard of living for its people.

9   Whilst there is little information in the Case on competition, who might their competitors be?

- Other European Cities, at home and abroad.

10   What are you competing for?

- EU project Funds
- Inwards business investment
- Tourists
- Tourism investment

- National Funding
- Business skills
- Skilled workforce

11   Name 3 challenges facing C of D

- Change the image amongst key audiences with a repositioning programme
- To position the City to attract tourists and businesses
- To win the support of the local people for the re-development programme
- To tackle unemployment

12   Which framework, referred to in the Case, helps determine Competitive Advantage in this context?

- Michael Porter's Determinants of National Advantage. See page 13 of Case Guidance Notes

13   Why would political interests in Riga be supportive of development in their City?

- The current poor economic situation of Latvia needs to be addressed before EU membership can be attained. Riga alone cannot address this. Development of their 2nd City will help.

14   The newly elected Mayor has a vision of C of D being similar to which European City?

- Vienna – a garden City.

15   What qualities do you see the Mayor bringing to the City?

- Thrives on risk and excitement
- Locally born and bred
- Successful businessmen
- Modest and charitable

- Charming to the women, respected by men
- Leads by example
- Wealthy

16   Whilst many of the recommendations we make may take 5 or 10 years to realise, why will the Mayor also want to see some 'quick wins'?

To win votes in the short term.

16

City of Daugavpils: Steps 2 – 4

Chapter Topic List

Introduction

In this long chapter you will:

- Work through the internal and external analysis for City of Daugavpils

- Compare your approach with that of the other students to help you assess and improve your own technique

- Prioritise activities and establish City of Daugavpils critical success factors

1   COMPLETING THE ANALYSIS FOR CITY OF DAUGAVPILS

1.1   Once you have a broad understanding of the Case Study, you are much better placed to tackle the more detailed audits and analysis. This is the time consuming part of your case work and remember, if working with others, you can share the work load.

1.2   For each step in the process, we have provided you with some sample material and tutorial comments. We suggest you take this practice case a step at a time; complete one part of the analysis and review our feedback before moving on to the next step. Utilise the tools and models because they will help not only to pull material together for you but also to communicate your assessment to others.

1.3   By the end of this chapter you will have:

(a)   Undertaken and reviewed the internal analysis of City of Daugavpils
(b)   Undertaken a micro and macro external audit
(c)   Consolidated your analysis into a SWOT framework
(d)   Identified the critical success factors and key issues facing City of Daugavpils

2   STEP 2: INTERNAL AUDIT, STRENGTHS AND WEAKNESSES

The internal audit: Strengths and Weaknesses of marketing

The first part of your in-view analysis requires you to assess the strengths and weaknesses of the City's current marketing. Work with the marketing mix headings and think about the current offer for:

1.   Residents and employees

2.   Business

3.   Tourists

When you have completed this, compare it with the notes and samples below.

Strengths and weaknesses of the current marketing activity

Tutor Tip

The marketing mix for a place needs to be evaluated from a number of perspectives. At the very least, there will be a marketing mix for residents and employees, for local businesses and for tourists and visitors.

We will therefore review the mix from each of these perspectives.

2.1   Marketing mix – The residents and employees

(a)   **Strengths – Product**

Town administration

- Current projects funded by municipality include:
- City developments, educational developments, health and social care

Developments

- Culture and recreation developments and City sports
- Daugavpils budget expenditure indicates the main priorities of municipality: (1) education, (2) communal service and (3) services

University education

- The one University in Daugavpils, which can accommodate 3,000, is re-focusing on business.
- University is linked to Salford University in UK and business school in Riga.
- Education is so good, so the young get jobs abroad.

Schools education

- 27 schools for general education, 4 extra-curricular establishments, 29 kindergartens and 9 technical institutions, 'Sun School Art College' and a music college. (Kindergarten could support working mothers?).

Entertainment

- Refurbishment plans aim to make the theatre the 'cultural heart of the City'
- Theatre company is young
- Cinema available (don't know if it is used for conferences)

BPP PUBLISHING

Unemployment support

- State unemployment service posts training and job ops

City development

- An excellent pedestrian centre with beautiful architecture/flowers/pleasant parks/tree lined avenues

Sports facilities

- Lokomotive stadium refurbishment – European championship host (motor cycle and racing)

- New Lede Halle – hosts national and international hockey

- Football stadium

- Various other sports centres/groups/clubs

Property

- Providing housing for the elderly with no family

Residents and employees
(Place to live, work and belong)

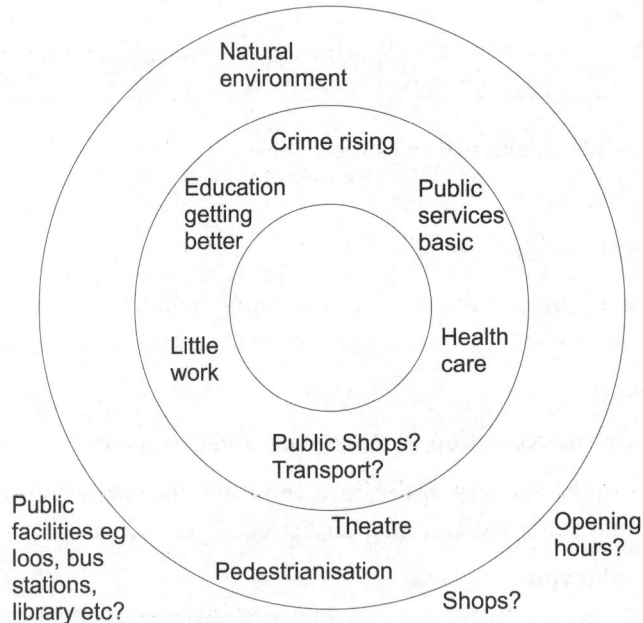

Natural environment

Crime rising

Education getting better

Public services basic

Little work

Health care

Public Shops? Transport?

Public facilities eg loos, bus stations, library etc?

Theatre

Pedestrianisation

Opening hours?

Shops?

Tutor Tip

Models like the **total product concept** can help communicate as well as help with the analysis.

(b) **Weaknesses – Product**

Town Administration

- Development projects appear un-coordinated. Questionable use of funding on most projects due to lack of research evidence

Education

- Schools are polarised as 'Russian' or 'Latvian' – encourages cultural divide

- Education at local University is expensive and some candidates go elsewhere because of cost

Security

- Health – hospital is undergoing refurbishment
- Street cleaning, rubbish collection and disposal
- Sewage – projects
- Water treatment – projects

Action Programme 16.1

Improving the analysis

Look at this work on the product and spend 5 minutes considering how this could be modified or improved.

Check your answer with the feedback at the end of the chapter.

(c) You can see from the next 3 grids how it is possible to build the picture up, based on interpretation and implications drawn from the data you have.

Daugavpils analysis – marketing mix audit: residents/employees

STRENGTHS	WEAKNESSES
Product (defined as housing, employment, services, shopping facilities etc)	
We don't really know! Assume housing passed its best/fairly run down? Probably outdated shopping facilities?	
• Good education • Sports facilities good • P27 Cinema, theatre, cultural centre, ice hall	• Poor work prospects
Price (defined as cost of living, rates, actual and potential earnings)	
• Probably cheap	• Earnings low, unemployment high
Place (defined as location in relation to living, working and transportation)	
• Infrastructure needs investment	• Working generation are leaving
Promotion (defined as information, promotion/image building on City)	
• Getting better – image new mayor, some PR articles • Football team not exploited in promotions	• Image is dull • Probably been poor • Daugavpils is a multilingual/multicultural society. This means standardised communications are not appropriate
People (defined as people who deliver services, demographics)	
• Skilled labour force • Mayor is local and offers a vision of the future	• Cannot attract people who want a high quality life style

STRENGTHS	WEAKNESSES
Processes (defined as those that facilitate living/working eg paying taxes)	
	• Bureaucratic
Physical evidence (defined as nature environment, ambience, design and architecture)	
• Natural environment good? Lakes, forests etc	• A **petrol station** is the best place to take a picture?

2.2 **Strengths and weaknesses of the offer for businesses and inward investment**

(a) These can be summarised in the diagram below.

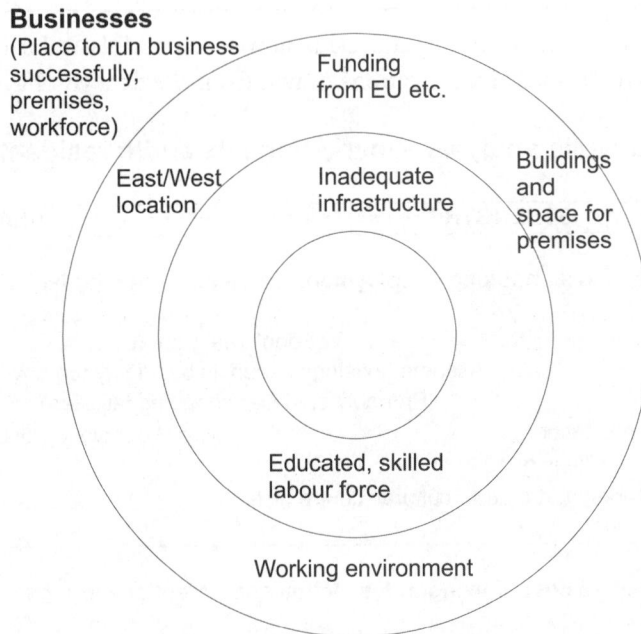

Businesses
(Place to run business successfully, premises, workforce)

Funding from EU etc.

East/West location

Inadequate infrastructure

Buildings and space for premises

Educated, skilled labour force

Working environment

(b) **Daugavpils analysis – marketing mix audit: businesses and inward investment**

STRENGTHS	WEAKNESSES
Product (defined as buildings/factories, natural/associated resources, vibrate)	
	• Old disused buildings/empty factories
Price (defined as cost of rates, rent, grants, wages)	
• Probably cheap land etc	
• Cheaper labour	
• Economic regeneration	
• Low rates	
Place (defined as location to customer, infrastructure)	
• Strategic hub between east and west	• Infrastructure poor
• Rail links	• Poor flight connections

STRENGTHS	WEAKNESSES
Promotion (defined as information, promotion/image building on City)	
	• Poor image
People (defined as labour force, unskilled, skilled, professional, educated, availability etc)	
• 500 business graduate pa available • Well educated, multi-lingual • Engineering skills • Purposeful people	• Net immigration from area
Processes (defined as services that facilitate business operations)	
• Planning permissions could be helped through at local level	
Physical evidence (defined as nature environment, ambience, design and architecture)	
• Improving environment	

Tutor Tip

There is something of a 'catch 22' in the City. To attract tourists, the town needs infrastructure, to build the infrastructure, they need employment and inward investment.

Understanding what they could potentially offer to attract 'jobs' to the area will be key.

2.3 **Strengths and weaknesses of the offer for visitors**

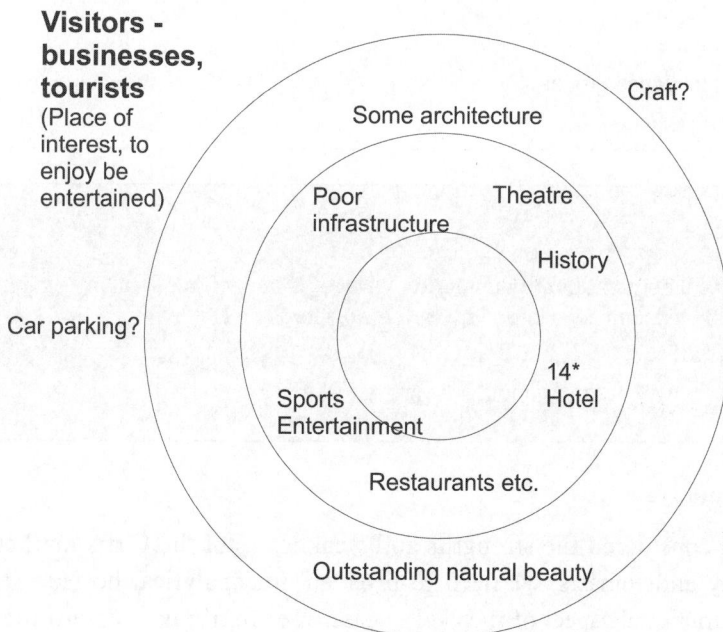

Visitors - businesses, tourists
(Place of interest, to enjoy be entertained)

Craft?

Some architecture

Poor infrastructure

Theatre

History

Car parking?

14* Hotel

Sports Entertainment

Restaurants etc.

Outstanding natural beauty

BPP
PUBLISHING

(b) Daugavpils ANALYSIS – MARKETING MIX AUDIT Tourist Visitors

STRENGTHS	WEAKNESSES
Product (defined as attractions) • Lakes, forest, some architecture • 4* hotel • Sports facilities • Places of historic interest	• No tourism strategy
Price (defined as value for money) • Probably cheap but little value for money	• Dual pricing for locals and tourists
Place (defined as location) • Meeting of cultures? • Infrastructure to and within the City	• Poor regularity, variety of flights
Promotion (defined as public relations) • Twinning of towns • EU lobbying • National Geographic articles • Mayor's interviews	• Latvia brand awareness low, Daugavpils has no real brand image • No PR for European Championship Racing
People (Defined as attitude/personality) • Friendly community • Considerate people	• Uncertain political position of ethnic Russians may cause unrest
Processes (Defined as Information Technology) • Basic internet site	
Physical Evidence (Defined as nature environment, ambience, design and architecture) • Natural resources, mountains, lakes, wildlife, people • Sports centres • Cultural influence groups • Improving City centre	

Tutor Tip

• Do not be concerned about gaps you have due to lack of information – they will exist. If you have to make assumptions later, you will be able to do so

• You may also need to prioritise your strengths and weaknesses analysis, if you have the information on what's important to customers

2.4 Functional analysis

(a) Having considered the strengths and weaknesses of the City's marketing for residents, industry and tourists, we need to broaden our analytical horizons to incorporate the other functional aspect of the C of D case. We are trying to determine the competencies and capabilities.

(b) You need to be clear about the available resources and constraints eg: do C of D have money for investment or the potential to attract grants and so on? If you do not do this case step well, it is likely you will recommend strategies which cannot be delivered eg doubling the number of jobs within two years or attracting one million Lats in world investment.

Tutor Tip

The exchange rates at the time of the case were as follows. You need to put numbers into context so you get a sense of the costs, but in this case it is necessary to ensure you are working in one currency.

Exchange rates at November 2001

1 US Dollar	=	0.63 Latvian Lats
1 Latvian Lat	=	1.59 US Dollars
1 Latvian Lat	=	1.80 EURO
1 EURO	=	0.55 Latvian Lats
1 Euro	=	0.88 US Dollar
1 US Dollar	=	1.13 EURO

(c) **Task:** Take the time now to undertake your own analysis of the 'corporate' position the town is in currently.

(d) **Daugavpils Analysis – Corporate (City organisation) Audit**

STRENGTHS	Page	WEAKNESSES	Page
Purpose (Vision, mission, direction)			
New mayor with successful business background	2		
Richard Eigim's Visions and Values	47		
• Improve economic development and employment	28		
• Improve streets, roads and security			
• Ensure all have education, healthcare and culture			
• Improve environment			
• Save City centre European cultural, historical heritage			
• Create modern architecture, preserve architectural heritage for projects			
Structure			
• New department for business and marketing	1	• Still has soviet management system	3
• Mayor's party (7 seats) formed coalition with Social Democrats (1) and Human Rights Party (2) for seats	6	• Bureaucratic, authorisation, military (inefficient/inflexible)	
Culture			
• New business style approach		• Still bureaucratic, central control, red tape	
Financial performance and economy			
• EU and other funding		• Heavily reliant on Russia	
• Income transit services?	3	• Ageing population 29% elderly (33k)	
• City population 114,000 60% Russian, 14% Latvian, 13% Polish, 8% Belarus and 3% Ukrainian	26	• Unemployment rising 28%+ (32k min)	

STRENGTHS		Page	WEAKNESSES		Page
• 900 employed in hospital		7	• Birth rate falling (17%), Population falling (8%)		3, 8
• Region population 800,000		18			8
• Pupils 300,000: Students 3k (500 are business related)		8			
• 2/3rds exports go to EU		2			
• Fulfilling accession criteria		2			
• Deaths falling (8%),					
Projects		29, 30			
	L'000	32			
Water/sewage ($33.3m)	1,800.0				
Industrial waste	94.9				
Household waste	7,200.0				
Crisis management	45.5				
Latgale development plan	500.0				
SRP urban development	371.0				
LRDA pre-structural EU	111.4				
Total	L10,122.8				
Health/social care	$1,035.700				

2.5 Summarising the strengths and weaknesses analysis

Potential impact on the town's prosperity	Strengths	Weaknesses
High	• New mayor, vision and style • Skilled people • Natural resources, lakes etc • Central location • Availability of stadium and facilities • Low costs of doing business	• Limited financial resources • Run down image • Lack of hotels • Bureaucracy and red tape • Lack of sophisticated marketing strategy
Low	• Attractive town centre • Successful sports teams • Cultural heritage and mix of people	• Not being a member of the EU • The poor image amongst other nationals outside the City

Tutor Tip

This strengths and weaknesses summary is much more useful than the simple lists because it demonstrates your ability to consider your analysis in terms of its business implications.

For those developing pre-prepared analysis appendices for the exam, you should always employ this more sophisticated development of presentation.

Action Programme 16.2

Making a comparison

The work you have just looked at is fine: it covers many of the key points, and the summary strengths and weaknesses table really helped to bring it all together. But now take 10 minutes to review this second example of a student analysis of the situational audit for C of D.

Make notes on what the differences are, which is better and why, and turn to our comments at the end of the chapter.

A second version of the corporate audit

2.6 **Corporate audit**

    (a) **Mission, vision, purpose**

        (i)   Many City priorities are given (p28 case study) **(Strength)**, but not apparently prioritised, co-ordinated or demonstrating buy in from the residents of the City **(Weakness)**

        (ii)   Richard Eigims has a Vision to turn the City into another 'Vienna' 'A Garden City'**(Strength of vision)** although it is not clear that this is what the residents want**(Weakness)**

        Overall there is a lack of succinct Vision and Mission.

    (b) **People/Culture**

        (i)   **Strength**

- Diverse history resulting in a stable, multi-cultural/lingual platform:

- 'Friendly' and skilled local population. Appear to live in relative harmony with each other and offer a warm welcome to visitors.

- The Mayor is a role model, based on his personal success in business. He speaks highly of the potential of Daugavpils and knows how to handle the media.

- Latvian nationals overseas could potentially add a beneficial Western cultural element.

Key challenge

To address poverty from unemployment and harness the local diversity in a positive co-ordinated manner. 'To help the people help themselves as a cohesive unit'.

        (ii)   **Weaknesses**

- **History/multi-culture.** Latvian and Russian subculture are currently divisive and unco-ordinated. This does not create a good corporate image, nor has it been exploited to promote diversity.

- But the **friendly and skilled population** is elderly and probably need to adapt their skills for the new challenges ahead.

- The Mayor shows few signs of being able to inspire his people as a united group to success. (He does not speak good Latvian) '75% of the people would like to leave Daugavpils'.

- **Latvian nationals overseas** maybe unwilling to return to Daugavpils.

(c) **Structure**

    (i) **Strengths**

- New department for business and marketing.

- Mayor's party (7 seats) formed from coalition with Social Democrats etc.

- **Geographical structure.** 'A Crossroads of four Countries' presents obvious transit trade advantages and strengthens the local Train Build/Repair Business.

- **Rail and trams** are examples of infrastructure strengths.

- **Factory Infrastructure** well disposed toward some 'Single item mass production' eg Yarn for Rhodia, Bike chains for Belarus.

- **Areas of outstanding natural beauty** provide good outdoor activities eg sailing, hunting, fishing, hiking.

- **Educational structure** is well funded.

- **Alliances** with EU/FSU/USA.

Key challenge

To understand what Business or Businesses the City is 'in' and develop assets accordingly. It does not matter if City's business is Airports, roads, hotels.

    (ii) **Weaknesses**

Still has a Soviet style management system, which is bureaucratic, and authoritarian.

- The **Geographical Structure** has not been exploited as a 'Gateway to the East' for EU and other non FSU Countries.

- **Airport, Roads and Hotels** represent Infrastructure weaknesses.

- **Factory infrastructures** are deemed inefficient for many types of production, eg sawn timber trade

- **Areas of outstanding natural beauty** appear not to have been developed to expand the leisure opportunity

- But the **educational structure** may not assist with multi-cultural integration.

- Are **alliances** coordinated and fully exploited?

(d) **Process/Technology**

    (i) **Strengths**

- **Education** is high priority and there is a 95% literacy rate.

- **Health provision** can be provided by committed doctors who work hard despite low rates of pay.

- **FSU management style** is effective when trading with FSU.

- **Coalition local government** should give a broad platform of political support.

- **Strong regional development** funding and some evidence of Municipality coordination.

- Some evidence of **rural development** eg Naujenes Pagst.

Key challenge

To define objectives and prioritise and coordinate process development in line with overall objectives.

(ii) **Weaknesses**

- Little evidence of vocational **Educational** or **Education** targeted at the Business Needs. 'Brain Drain' potential.

- **Health provision** is poor and getting poorer. With an elderly/poor population this could be a growing problem (Figures suggest that on average Daugavpils is above the national average).

- **FSU management style** does not promote flexible, adaptable, market orientation.

- **The coalition local government** may have problems agreeing consensus direction. Also has no association with National Politics which may present problems in obtaining funding and building Corporate brand.

- Lack of coordination and prioritising **NGO** and **GO Regional Development** and in line with Business Priorities.

- Much subsistence **rural activity** which will require transformation on EU accession.

(e) **Financial and economic performance**

Latvia is a relatively stable and growing former Soviet Union economy trading on the borders between Russia and the EU. It is well placed to capitalise on its under-utilised production capabilities and market itself as a place in which business can be transacted.

(i) **National strengths**

- Sustained Economic (GDP) growth is forecast to continue.

- GDP per head of $3,400 makes this comparable to South Africa, indicating that Latvia's more than a developing country.

- Exchange rate stability owing to IMF SDR pegged LAT gives confidence to investors/helps exporters maintain prices.

- Inflation appears to be well managed centrally (EU entry criteria).

- The National debt is serviceable and at a relatively low level.

- There is a good spread of export destinations – largest concentration 16% Germany.

- Latvia retains strong Russian trading links – can promote itself as a 'beach-head' into Russia.

- Producer prices demonstrate productivity gains being achieved.

- The Latvian banking industry includes foreign-owned institutions and appears 'trusted' by community.

BPP PUBLISHING

(ii)   **National weaknesses**

- Overall size of economy is small GDP $6.4bn, total population 2.4m and so offers little domestic market to foreign investors.

- Oil transit income is sensitive to world oil price fluctuations.

- Export concentration (62%) to EU. Latvia is increasingly tied to EU trading cycle, now heading for recession.

- 38% wood products – low value add so total export income flat.

- Rising trade deficit as a result of import growth. However, there is evidence that technology is being imported and translated into production efficiency and increasing competitiveness.

- Agricultural growth is poor as a result of small farms. Acceptance of EU Common Agricultural Policy will be difficult.

- Internal lending rates at c.8% over base appear high and constraining to development finance. Evidence of scarce deposits – probably offshore

- Dependence upon the IMF for currency stability

- Government deficit likely to rise as a result of forthcoming elections

(iii)   **Financial and economic Performance:** the city

Daugavpils

- Extremely high unemployment is a drain upon fiscal resources.

- The ageing population and associated health care cost implications (21% 60+).

- Unable to fund own infrastructure developments, reliant on third party support in excess of $22m.

- Falling population due to health/migration issues.

- Spends huge amount of own resources on education for others benefit.

- Daugavpils area represents 33% of Latvian population but lacks weight at administrative centre – Riga.

(iv)   **Financial and economic performance:** information gaps

- There is a lack of information to benchmark Latvia's performance and size with international comparatives.

- The lack of government income/spending budget information does not allow for an assessment of local financial resources. Is Daugavpils allocated a fair share relative to its importance in population terms? It may not be getting enough for education.

- The regional economy is not being measured by the Bank of Latvia.

- Incentives for FDI? Does Latvia have trade treaties/special access to Russia?

- No marketing budget information at national or local level.

- Tourism figures appear confused and not centrally collated/analysed.

(f) **Influence/image of marketing in the city**

   (i) **Strengths**

   - The Mayor is passionate about change and improvement.

   (ii) **Weaknesses**

   - He has had **minimal impact** to date. He has not **countered the negative perception** of Daugavpils in Riga and with own citizens. The image of Daugavpils is that it is too close to Russia, old, decaying and backward.

   - The website presentation embodies this perception.

   - The Mayor's PA manages communications.

   (iii) **Brand values of the City (attributes)**

   - **Potential to exploit** multi-lingual skills
   - Area of natural beauty (geology) and history (fort, fortress)
   - Natural resources (sandstone slate, clay, forests, water, animals, birds)
   - **Logistics infrastructure** (railway junction) and transport hub
   - **Negative perception** – regarded as backward and poor by Rigians
   - Little understanding of the region generally
   - Lack of understanding of region's potential
   - Multi-ethnic mix is perceived as negative by Latvians
   - More ethnic discriminatory laws – language
   - **No hooks** for attracting businesses
   - Letting past **successes wither** – sanatoria
   - **Not exploiting potential** in history, landscape, monuments, waterways

Competitive advantage/Differentiation

2.7 The purpose of this part of the analysis is to help you establish both the current position and potential competitive advantage for the City.

Look at both the summary below, and then the model in paragraph 2.8, which though complex really helps to communicate some key issues quickly. This is so much more useful for an exam context – a real snapshot that demonstrates analysis and insight.

Summary List
- Beautiful churches, old historic fort
- Excellent pedestrianised centre, beautiful architecture
- Pleasant (!) parks, tree lined avenues
- Beautiful unspoilt countryside dotted with lakes
- Good old tram service
- Friendly, generally helpful people!
- Safety
- Excellent ice hockey stadium
- Lakes, forest, mountains, wildlife
- Multi-lingual staff
- Available space and workers
- Enthusiastic Mayor

Are these really sources of competitive advantage or just what people expect – especially visitors?

If you were the examiner, or the Mayor, which presentation of competitive advantage would mean most to you? Which would demonstrate the presenter's strategic competence most effectively?

2.8 Positioning the City

(a) Models such as the product life cycle are highly adaptable and could be put to good use here, again to help you analyse the position and later to use to communicate this understanding to the examiner.

(b) **City organisation development stage**

City organisation development stage

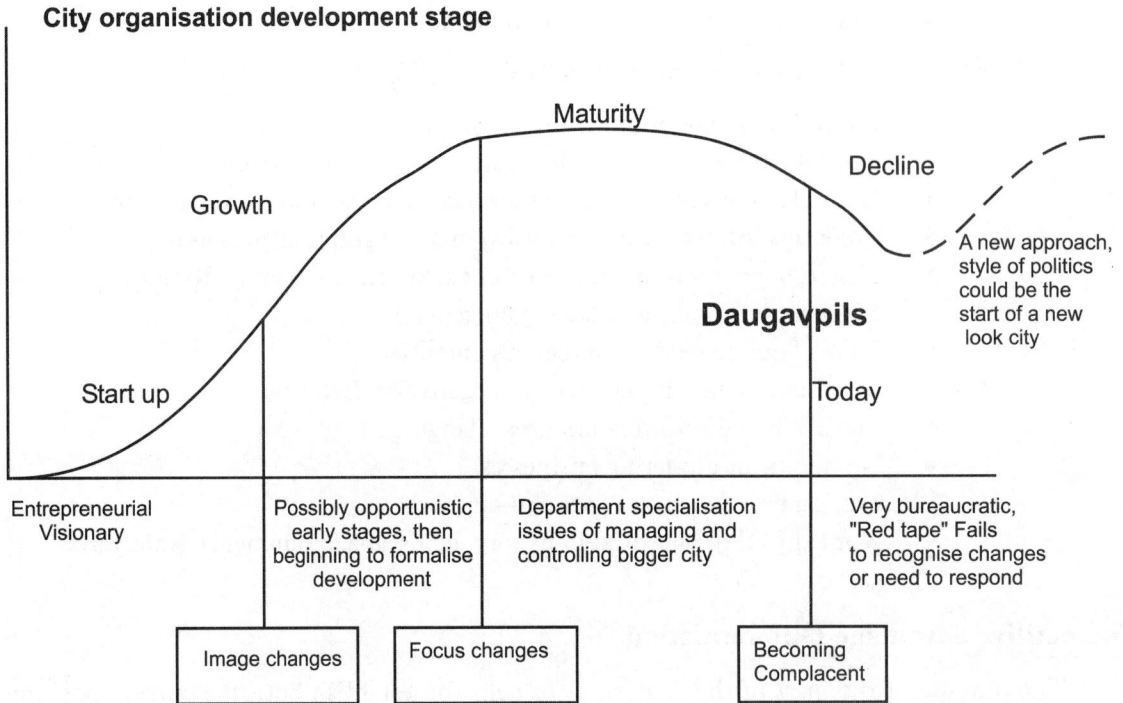

Entrepreneurial Visionary	Possibly opportunistic early stages, then beginning to formalise development	Department specialisation issues of managing and controlling bigger city	Very bureaucratic, "Red tape" Fails to recognise changes or need to respond
	Image changes	Focus changes	Becoming Complacent

(c) **City business/earnings stage**

City business/earnings stage

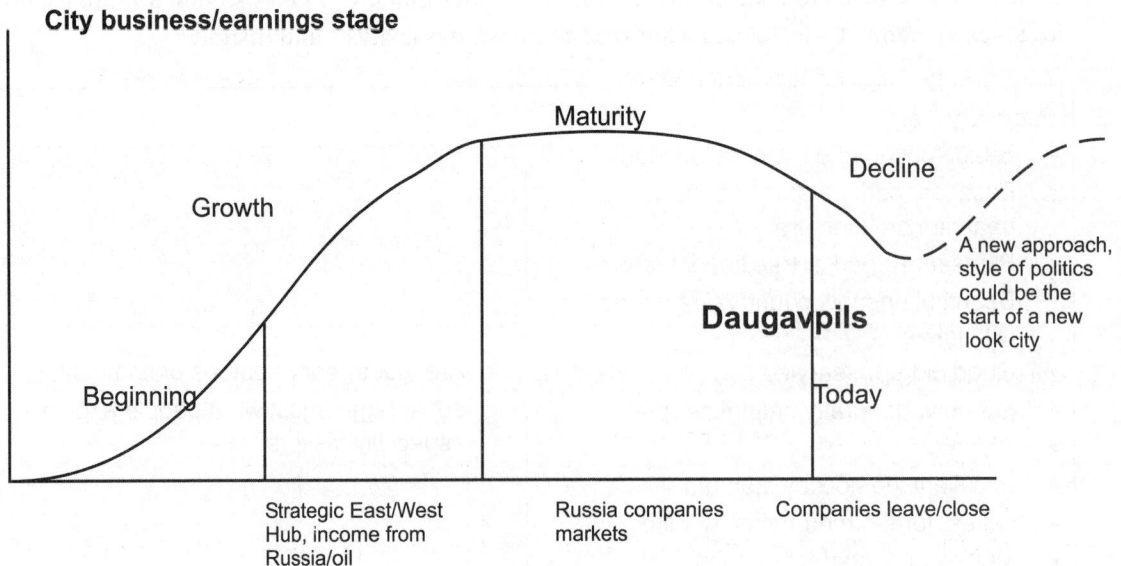

	Strategic East/West Hub, income from Russia/oil	Russia companies markets	Companies leave/close

Perceptual or positioning maps serve a similar purpose in this case. You can use them, as this group has, to show the **current** positioning and add arrows to show the **desired** re-positioning.

Perceptions

(a) Situation

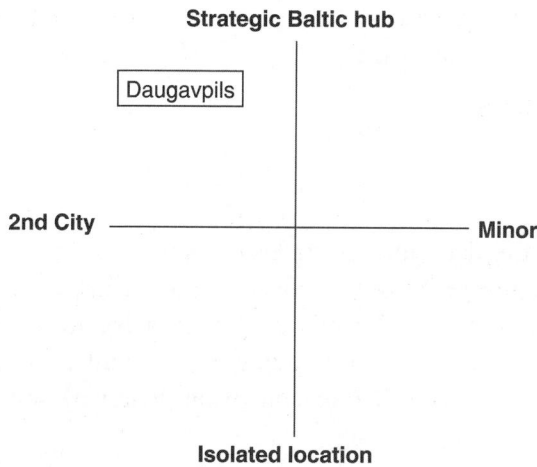

(c) Workforce

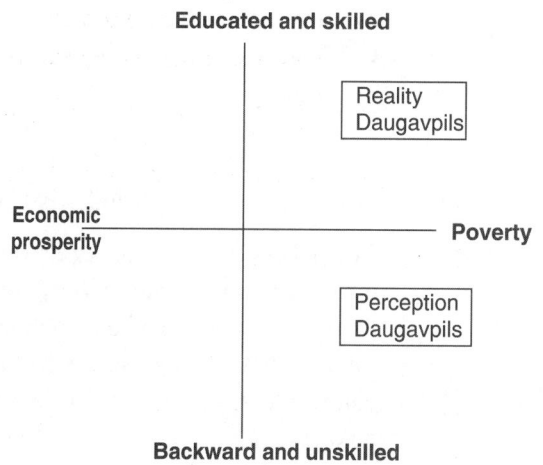

(b) Attractiveness

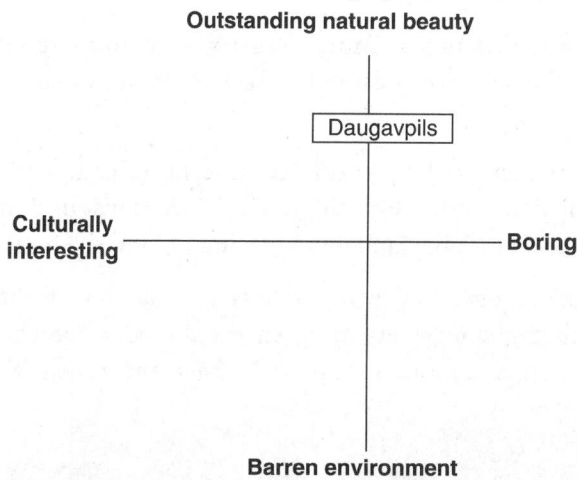

(d) Society

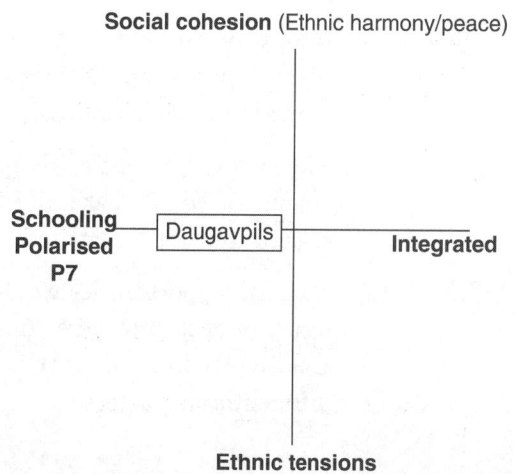

Tutor Tip

Did you remember your information shopping list? Well done if you did. It is important for the Case exam to keep one in case you get a research or MKIS question.

2.9 **Information gaps**

- What are their measures of success?
- Alignment between development projects and marketing strategy.
- Who is co-ordinating IT?
- Who advises the mayor on policy. What is their knowledge, skills and capabilities?
- How frequently is data collected and how, by whom?
- Income from Higher Education; how many graduates remain in Daugavpils?
- Segmentation research: who are the customers?
- What do the customers want from the government?

BPP PUBLISHING

- What services should they be providing?
- What is the most effective value proposition, short and long term?
- What roles should the region/City play?
- What is the best operating model?
- With whom should the region/City partner?
- Success of current development projects
- How does Daugavpils score on the diagnostic scale?
- How is the data compiled who does it, how timely?
- Internet take up data?
- TV ownership data (for possible digital penetration)

2.10 Summary of the internal position

To make sure you are interpreting the data you are gathering and making sense of the information available to you, you need to get into the habit of summarising what you have found out. Imagine you are describing the reality of the City to a friend, but not one interested in taking the exams. Take a minute or two to pull out a few bullet points of how you would sum up Daugvapils and its prospects, before comparing them with our thoughts below.

(a) Daugvapils is a city with a chequered past and a potentially promising future.

(b) Currently, it is run down economically with an ageing population and high unemployment. Stopping the skills drain is a priority.

(c) Inward investment is the key to re-generation. More industry leads to more jobs and higher tax income. This enables better facilities and attractive environment thereby attracting more investment.

(d) The area has potential, its position and skilled workforce in terms of engineering and languages could make it ideal as a centre for call centre operations in European organisations. Low labour costs and available land and buildings add to the potential.

(e) Tourism opportunities would take longer to develop on a large scale, but in the short term, budget travellers looking for somewhere different could be a target. Again Daugavpils location, hotels and the natural resources do have the potential to be differentiating factors.

3   STEP 3: ADDING THE EXTERNAL ANALYSIS

3.1   Your next step is to add the external analysis, at micro level. Take the time now to work through this next part of your analysis again, before reviewing the examples of student work and our commentary. You need to look in detail at:

- Stakeholders
- Customers
- Competitors

You have probably realised that you may need to focus on these issues for inward investment and tourism separately as the factors may be different.

Building the Picture

3.2   In the overview in the last chapter, you saw a market map developed for this Case and this is a highly useful starting point, particularly with a complex case.

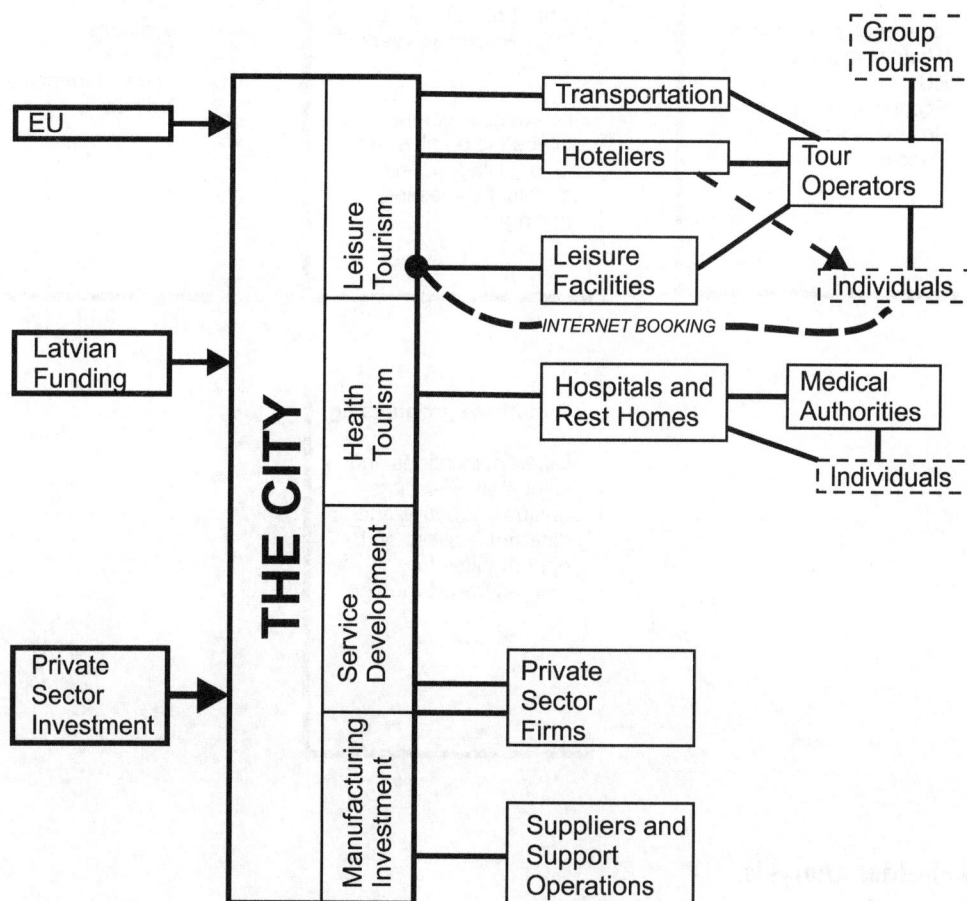

Competitive position

3.3   Porter's five force analysis, on the next page, is also an excellent model for giving you an overall view of the market but also for demonstrating the changing dynamics within the market place. In this case, few, if any, students actually chose to use Porter's Five Forces. We have included an example of how Porter could have been used to help evaluate the market for C of D.

Competitive structure of the industry

New entrants eg

Other less developed/
developing Eastern
European countries

FSUs

Other emerging countries
with "special" interests,
advantages

Supplers eg

Natiobnal government
World Institutions
EU
Economic Trading blocs
Businesses
People

Industry rivalry

Other Latvian towns
Other Baltic towns and
cities

Increasingly competitive
competing on all levels
eg for skilled workers,
tourists, businesses,
funding

Buyers eg

Business
Tourists
Agents (Tourism)
Airlines

Substitute products eg

Different locations and
cities that offer more
unique, attractive and/or
different facilities and
opportunities for
competitive advantage

Stakeholder analysis

Tutor Tip

In this Case and other Cases dealing with not for profit organisations, you are likely to find the
stakeholders particularly complex and you will need to pay particular attention to them. The following
represents a particularly useful analysis from one group. Notice the added value that comes from
ranking and categorising each stakeholder group's expectations.

3.4 The relationship map which follows is complex, but if you take time to consider it, it is quite useful.

*O = Objective, N = Need, M = Motive
** H= High, M = Medium, L = Low

Stakeholder	Interest*	Expectations	Ranking**
• Local inhabitants	N	• employment, growth, prosperity, security, pride	H
	-	• none	H
• Riga inhabitants	N	• employment, growth, prosperity, security, pride	H
• Local Latvians	-	• employment, growth, prosperity, security, pride	M
• Ex-Latvians	O	• increased goods & cultural people exchange	M
• Twin cities	M	• employment & reasonable wage, relationships,	L
• University	O	• recognition, reputation	
• Religions	O	• keep churches going, health & happy population	L
• Travel agents	O	• more hotels, more higher standard sport	M
• Event organisers		• facilities, ROI, growth	H
• EU	O	• ROI, relationships, Latvia to meet entry criteria,	H
		• Latvia to have good brand image and PR	
• World bank	O	• increase health care & education standard loan re-payment	H
• International Gov	O	• ROI, relationships, improve infrastructure	H
• Russia	M/O	• Latvia's security	H
• Latvian Gov	M/O	• EU entry, national economy, re-election, employment, relationships, infrastructure	H
• Local parties	M/O	• local economy, re-election, employment, relationships, infrastructure	H
• LRDA	O	• regional development	H
• Mayor, Richard Eigims	M/O	• local economy, re-election, employment,	H
		• influence, power, relationships	
• Marketing dept, Ilya Podkolzins	N/O	• number of tourists, businesses attracted perception change of population	H
• Business	O	• growth, ROI, relationships, cheap labour, subsidies, not polluted ground	H

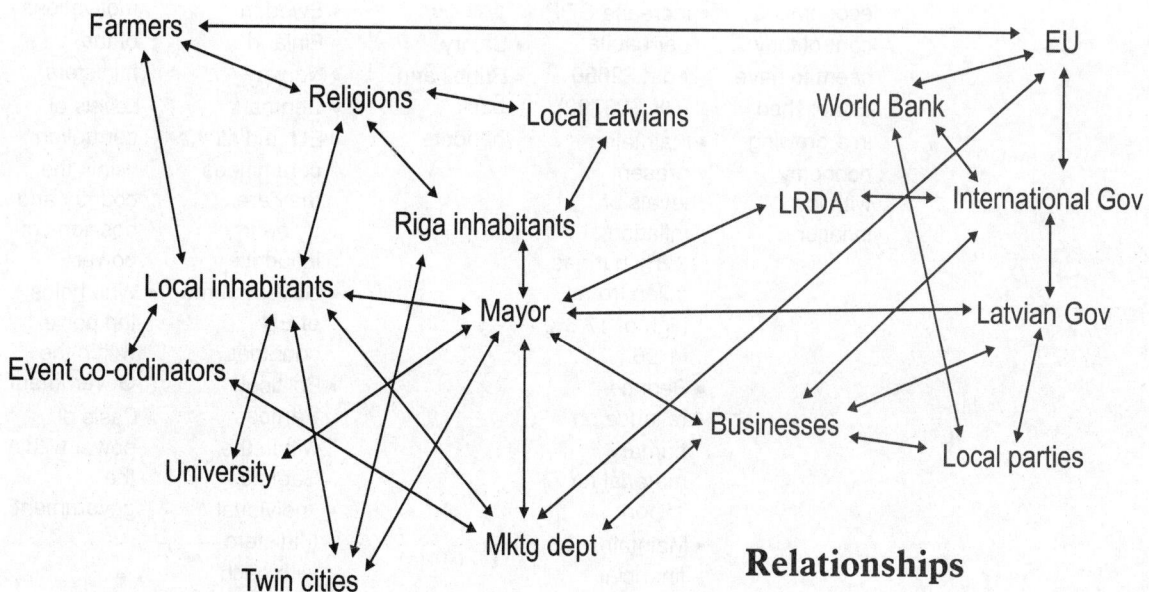

Relationships

A different approach to stakeholder analysis

3.5   The analysis below contains the same detail for each key stakeholder group. Here, you get a feel for both the depth and quality of analysis which is both possible and expected.

Universities/schools

Critical issues: funding, academic recognition, student number, jobs for graduation students.

Stakeholder	Objective	Needs	Motives	Relationships	Info Gaps
Universities/ schools	• Help the community rejuvenate - support local business • Rise profile overseas – Salford uni • Attract non-local people into the area	• Funding • Students (low birth rates at moment) • Teachers • Teaching materials and resources • Twintown support – exchange support	• Support community • Improve employment with graduate • University encourages outsiders to come to the area	• Riga and Salford university • Municipality, • State Govt (finding 30.7 • Dept of Education, World Bank	

Latvian State Government

Critical issues: entry into EU, economically productive 2nd city, income and investment, economic growth, lowering unemployment, developing positive relationships with other national governments.

Stakeholder	Objective	Needs	Motives	Relationships	Info Gaps
Latvian State Government	• Obtain EU membership • Increase the prosperity of the country • Maintain economic control they seem to have established in a growing economy with low inflation	• A 2nd city to meet EU qualification criteria • Reduce the external debt • Increase GDP per capita from $2666 (UK $23792) • Maintain present levels of inflation, 2.8% but has fallen from high of 17.6% in '96 • Reduce reliance on primary material for export • Maintain financial support from EU	• Get re-elected at the elections due in Oct 2002 (representative) • Personal ambition • Salary • Bribes and back handers	• Other regional Governments • Russian • Belarus • Lithuania • Sweden • Finland • Norway • Denmark • EU and all the committees they are trying to influence • Governments of EU countries • Political Parties within the Saeima • Individual Ministers with each other	• Whether we know all the members of the govern-ment • Personal motivations of the ministers • Levels of corruption within the country and positions of power • Who holds the power within the Government • Basis of power within the government

3.6 Another stakeholder model

In the final example of how you might handle stakeholder data, we include this creative example of a stakeholder map produced by one student. Here, you will notice that the closer to the centre of the circle, the more important the stakeholder.

STAKEHOLDERS

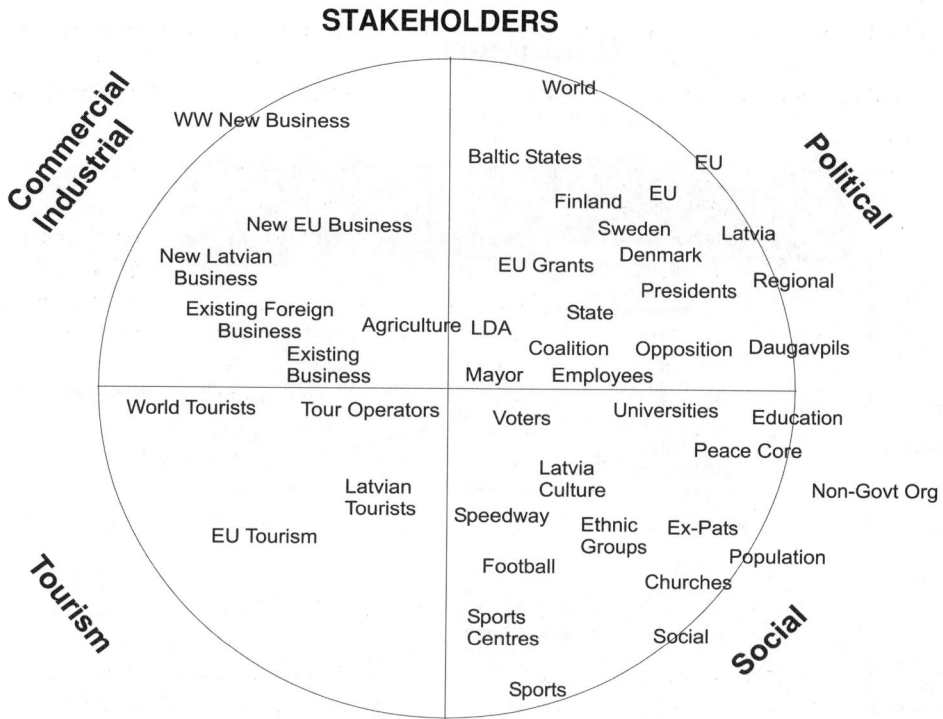

3.7 **Customer analysis**

The customer analysis had to be completed for the business and tourist customers. Again, notice how the pictorial approach helps handle large amounts of complex data effectively. It is followed by an equally thorough narrative analysis but, again, the template style used is highly effective.

(a)

Customers

Market Map - Business

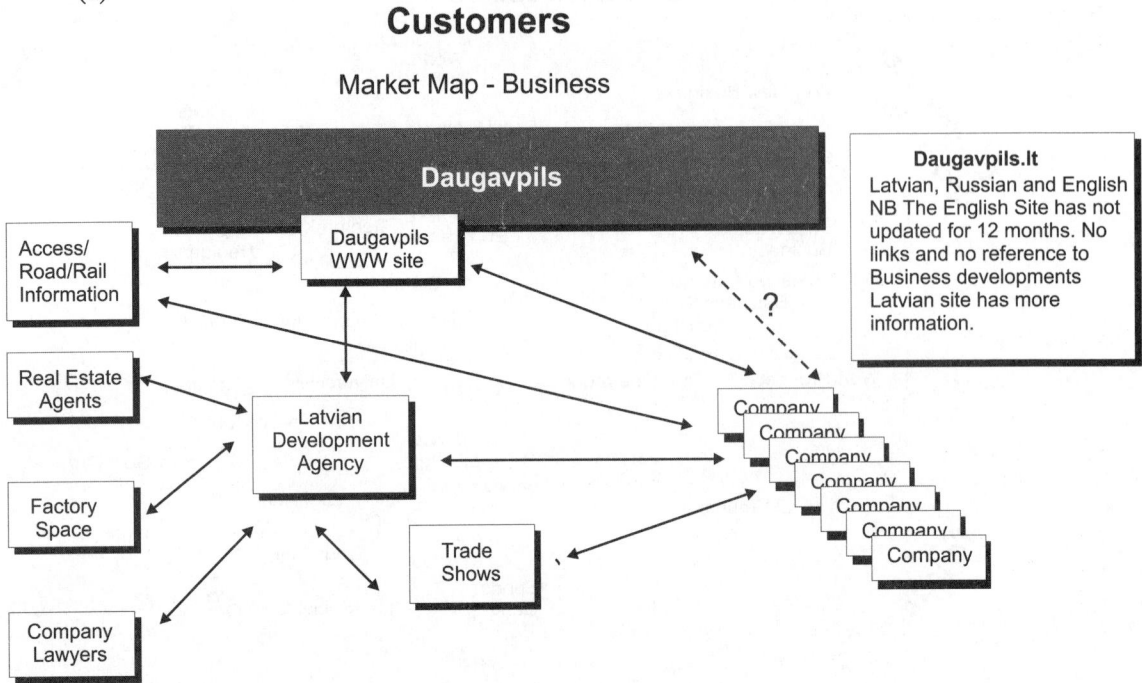

(b)

Customers

Market Map - Tourist

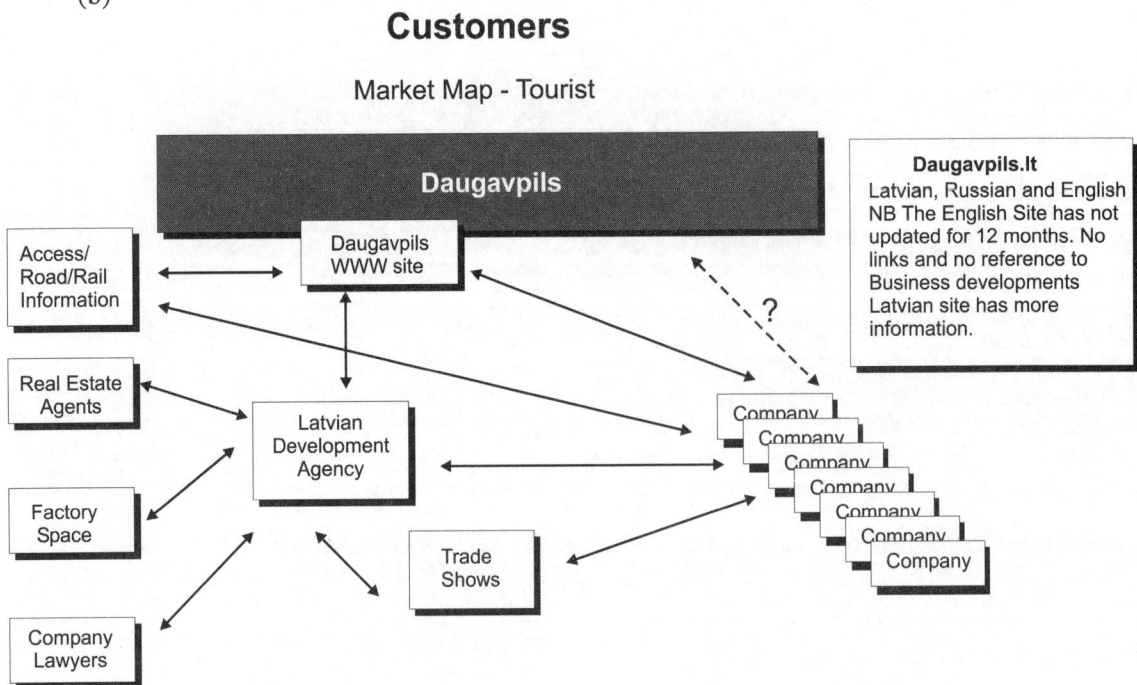

(c)

Who buys? (business, consumers or both?)	What is bought? (our and competitors products)	Where is it bought? (channels, outlets and intermediaries	When?	How? (payment and buying process	Why? (needs and benefits sought)
• Nationals, Former Soviet Union countries • Riga • Local residents • Former Latvian Nationals living abroad • EU tourists (very low 6,200 in 1998) • EU based businesses • International businesses	**Recreation** • Holidays – very low numbers in 1998 (6,200 in total for rural Latvia • Sports events • Speedway (Euro champs In September 2001) • Football (local and UEFA) • Fishing – very low numbers • ICE Hockey – world champions in 2006 **Business goods: foreign companies** • Timber products (ie Boss Masiff – export) • Ropes and net (Magistr – world exports) • Grass cutters (Zielera – export) • Stockings (Swedtex – export) • Computer cables (Axon export) **Latvian companies** • Car, bikes, machinery (Pievadkedes) • Bicycle chains (DCC – Belarus) • Oil products and storage (Dinaz transit arrangements.	• Assuming the products are moved by road and rail Good links to FSU and Baltic states. • Airport does not appear to be used to the maximum • capacity as conduit for • businesses, products or tourists. • 30% export to West • 40% to FSU	• No information available but assume that tourists would come during the summer for warm weather and countryside activities.	• £52m Lats pa in exports some which is bartered for other goods – DCC export chains for bicycles.	• Attitudes to town by local is not good – 75% wish they live else-where. • Goods tend to be high quality for export but basic pro–ducts like ropes net and timber products. • Expectations are not high because the FSI sys-tems and processes still exist. • Tourists expect choice and lots of information on potential destinations for holidays. • This is expected via the web, brochures tourists offices etc... D has no significant presence in any of these places/ media

3.8 Further segmental analysis

Again, we hope the work from these students shows you both the depth of analysis possible and gives you further ideas on how best to organise your own work. We want to emphasise that simply analysing material without context and insight, generates data (and often lots of it), but little useful information. Take time to think about what you are doing and what you need to know. The segmental analysis of the customers for this Case is not quite over.

Remember, this information will help you to determine the most effective way of segmenting the various markets, so if C of D goes for tourists, which ones, backpackers or business travellers?

See how the following pieces of analysis and sensible assumptions start to make the picture much clearer.

Segments

(a) **Businesses**

Local	Buying criteria – business
• Heavy duty manufacturing (cat, bikes, ropes and nets – magistr) • Farming (subsidence moving to medium) • SMEs (2,000 small businesses) • Engineering (DCC) – basic • sports (various) • Government employment old FSU style (hospitals, schools, environmental, buses, trams) **International** • Basic engineering – grass cutters • Basic production lines (timber buildings, stockings, cables for PCs etc) • Storage for oil products	• political (ie stability, inflation, exchange rate, EU entry criteria, government marketing skills • Labour (ie cheap, qualified, educated) • Ground (ie cost, not polluted) • Law (ie employment, authorities attitude) • Infrastructure (ie airport, rail, road, transport services, good housing) • Services (ie good water supply ,sewage purification) • social behaviour (ie crime, disease (Aids rate high), state of mind (suicide rate high)) • Cultural offer (ie museums, churches, fort, event calendar) • Subsidies • Commercial contacts and supporting industries • Competition

(b) **Visitors/tourists (in 1999, 6,621 for 10 months**

Local (89%)	Buying criteria – tourism
• Sports fans • Sports teams • Latvian tourists (low numbers) but 89% of total for area **International (only 11% of total in 1999)** • German (15%) • Finish (14%) • American (10%) • Indian (10%) • Canada (6%) • France (6%) • Others (39%) **Age** • Up to 30 , 45% • 30 – 40, 28% • Over 40, 27% (all locals) **Activities** • Swimming, baths, eating, horse riding, bikes, sports, winter sports, celebrations etc	• Holiday packages • Political (ie stability, inflation, exchange rate) • Hotel (ie rating, capacity, value for money) • Quality (ie food, service, accommodation, hospitality) • cultural offer (ie museums, churches, fort, events calendar) • Infrastructure (ie airport, rail, road, transport services (tram)) • Facilities (ie children friendly) • External environment (ie not polluted, lakes, forests) • Information access (ie website) • Sports facilities (ie pools) • Languages spoken • Safety • Climate

Of course, the buying criteria list will be helpful in any multifactor matrix work we do – it is the basis for C of D to assess their possible competitive advantage with each segment or market.

(d) You will also note the **information gaps** sheet. How does it compare with yours?

Missing information

Who buys? Business, consumers or both?	What is bought? Our and competitors products	Where is it bought? Channels, outlets and intermediaries	When?	How? Payment and buying process	Why? Needs and benefits sought
• No information on the buying habits of the locals. • Is there a marketing organisation other than Podkolzins Mayor, his PA and me?	• No accurate number for tourists in Latgale and Daugavpils region.	• What are the distribution channels for business products? • Are there tourist bodies in existence? Where does Ilya Podkolzins fit in the Mayors organisation? • No hotels mentioned in the town or immediate surrounding area (only Mayors hotel 4* to north of town).	• When is the best time to visit Latvia/Dp? Is the surrounding hill area potentially suitable for winter sports? • Is the airport usable in winter and what is its capacity for passengers and freight?	• Is there a budget for tourism? • Is there a marketing budget? Is there a budget for business development?	• There is no indication of what the towns people want

Competitor analysis

3.9 This is an interesting Case Study where we have relatively little about competitors, but based on our assumptions and our international knowledge, it is possible to pull together a picture of the competitors.

(a) If you find a similar gap in your Case exam, check you have not missed anything, but then make the assumptions you need to be able to move on.

(b) This reminds us how important it is to have studied the syllabus for International Marketing Strategy before moving on to Case. It is indispensable when faced with a Case like this.

(c) You should note how important it is for a City to understand the competitive forces of its **customers'** markets in order to position itself successfully.

BPP PUBLISHING

3.10 Competitors

(a) Riga

- Centre of prosperity in Latvia
- Most of the resources are based in Riga
- Appears less culturally diverse than Daugavpils
- Distance 232km
- Daugavpils population does not seem inclined to go to Riga (5%)
- Better websites

(b) **Ventspils** appear to have money from oil transportation –

(c) Most of the other towns of note seem to be based in north and closer to Riga and therefore an airport.

(d) **Estonia** has cultural and geographical links with Finland, assisted by the similarity of the Finnish and Estonian language.

(e) **Lithuania:** Vilnius is the same distance away as Riga but Lithuania has fewer similar-sized towns.

- Competition for investment and also cheap labour, etc.
- Also facing similar problems

(f) **Competitor – other former Soviet Union**

- Not in EU and therefore no access to EU funding for development
- Huge logistical problems
- More well known tourist attractions (particularly in North)
- More political clout owing to size and history

(g) Less developed countries will have similar cheap labour etc

(h) UK commonwealth countries probably have better English language skills. This language advantage also applies to ex-French colonies, South America (Portugal and Spain)

(i) **Competitors – tourism**

Where would you rather go? Florence, Los Angeles, Lima or Daugavpils?

Holiday destinations

- Summer holiday destinations
- Winter holiday destinations
- Historic/beauty destinations
- Sports facilities destinations (including fishing)
- Health 'tourism'

Other information

- Steeped in history
- Over 1,100 shops, cafes and kiosks
- Diverse culture offerings – theatre, cinema, cultural centres
- Considerable beauty (countryside, lakes, parks)
- Diverse sports facilities
- Opportunity to develop the airport
- Wants to develop links with west

Tutor comment

3.11 Once again, the models show their value, providing snapshots of the situation and demonstrating clearly how you have interpreted things. These tools are invaluable in the exam and in your day-to-day work as a marketing planner. The range used by these students is as shown.

- Porter's generic strategies approach for both tourism and inward investment.

- Positioning maps – notice how general international marketing knowledge is integrated in them.

- The diffusion of innovation model. This is a very impressive and creative application of a tool more commonly associated with New Product Development

(a) **Porter's Generic Strategies: Tourism**

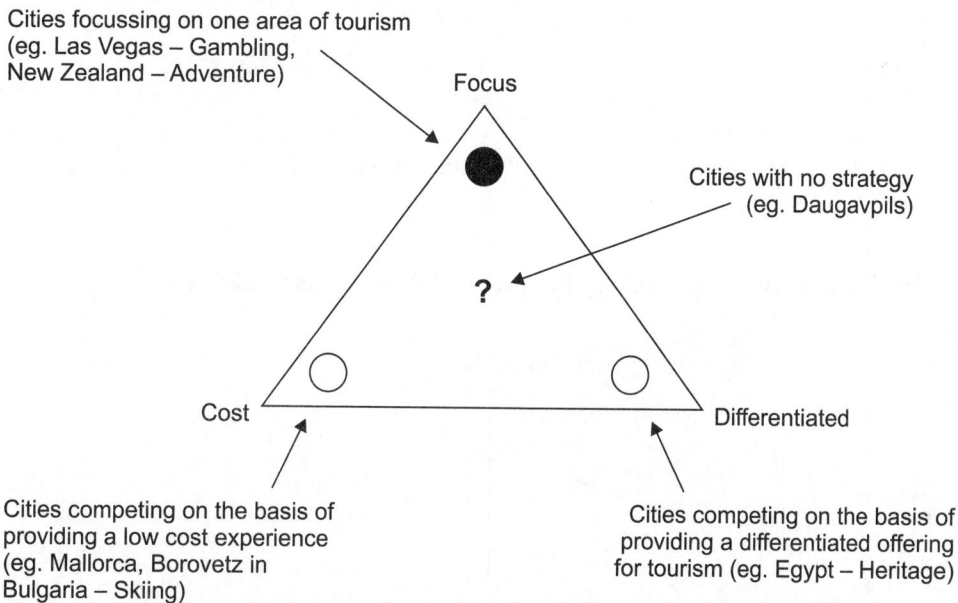

Cities focussing on one area of tourism
(eg. Las Vegas – Gambling,
New Zealand – Adventure)

Focus

Cities with no strategy
(eg. Daugavpils)

?

Cost

Differentiated

Cities competing on the basis of
providing a low cost experience
(eg. Mallorca, Borovetz in
Bulgaria – Skiing)

Cities competing on the basis of
providing a differentiated offering
for tourism (eg. Egypt – Heritage)

(b) **Porter's Generic Strategies: Business**

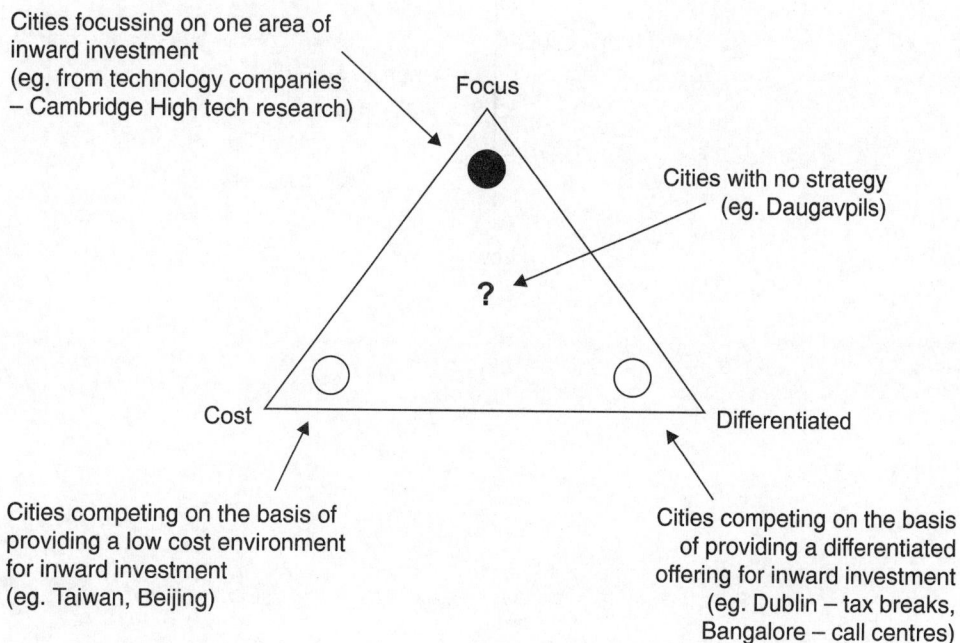

Cities focussing on one area of
inward investment
(eg. from technology companies
– Cambridge High tech research)

Focus

Cities with no strategy
(eg. Daugavpils)

?

Cost

Differentiated

Cities competing on the basis of
providing a low cost environment
for inward investment
(eg. Taiwan, Beijing)

Cities competing on the basis
of providing a differentiated
offering for inward investment
(eg. Dublin – tax breaks,
Bangalore – call centres)

(c)   **Competitive Positioning: Tourism – holiday type vs costs**

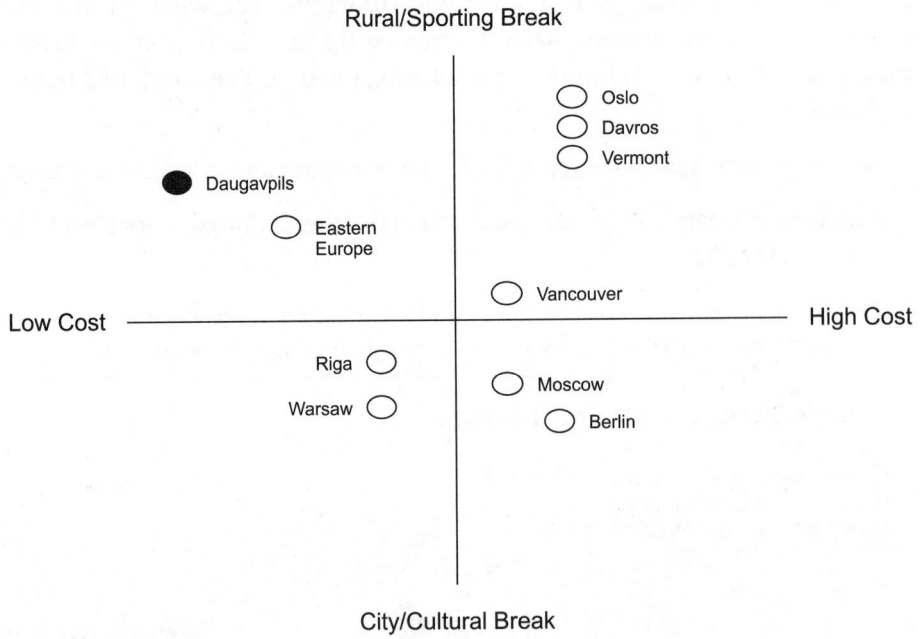

Rural/Sporting Break

○ Oslo
○ Davros
○ Vermont

● Daugavpils
○ Eastern Europe

○ Vancouver

Low Cost ———————————————— High Cost

Riga ○
Warsaw ○

○ Moscow
○ Berlin

City/Cultural Break

(d)   **Competitive Positioning: Business – labour costs vs skill level**

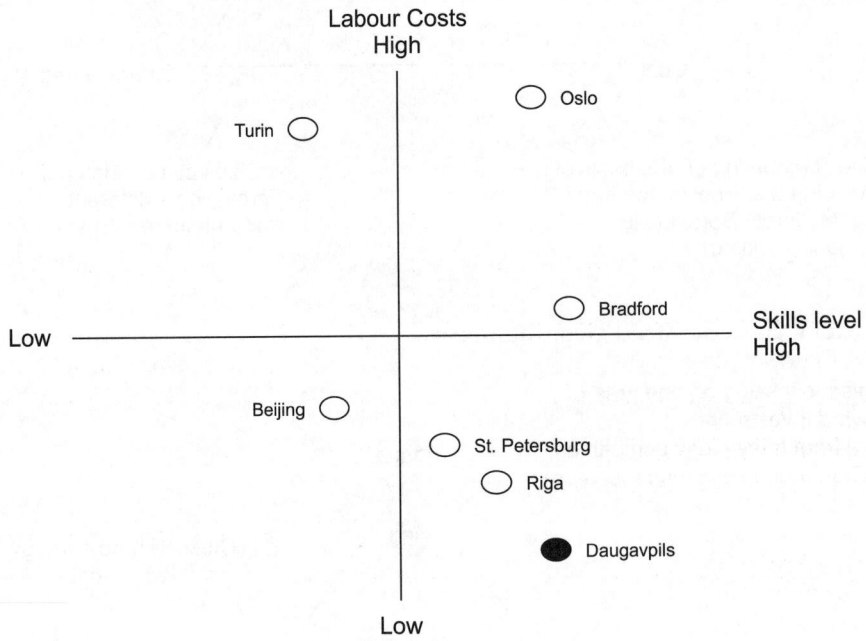

Labour Costs
High

Turin ○

○ Oslo

Low ———————————————— Skills level
High

○ Bradford

Beijing ○

○ St. Petersburg
○ Riga

● Daugavpils

Low

(e) **Diffusion of Innovation: Maturity of tourism**

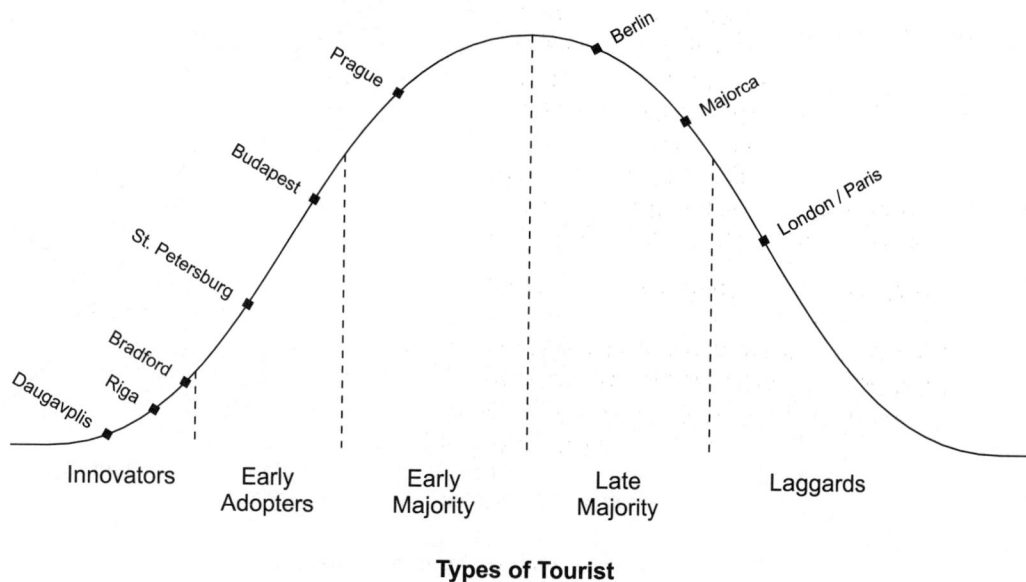

Types of Tourist

(f) **Diffusion of Innovation: Tourism – accessibility vs sophistication**

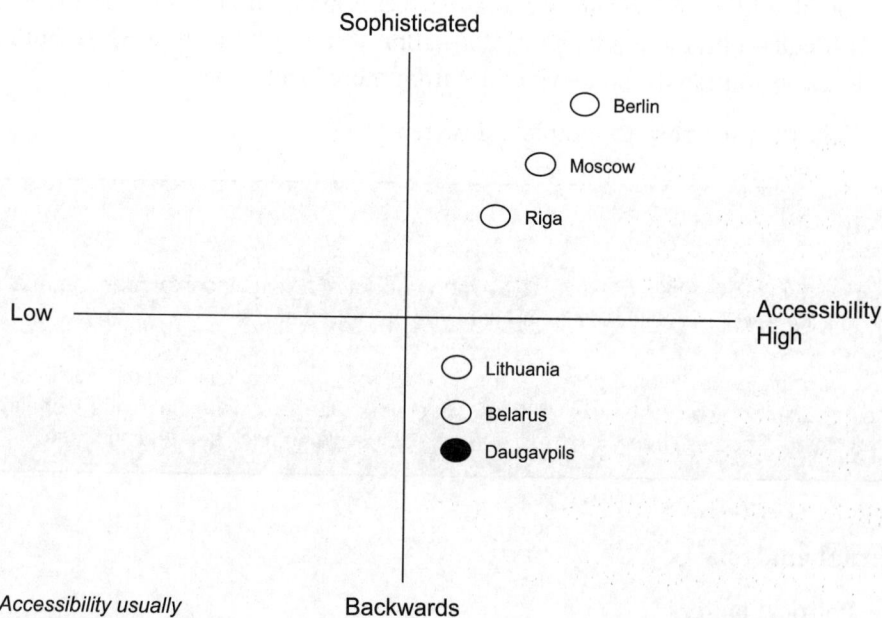

Note.   Accessibility usually depends on the airport.

(g) **Diffusion of Innovation: Levels of inward investment**

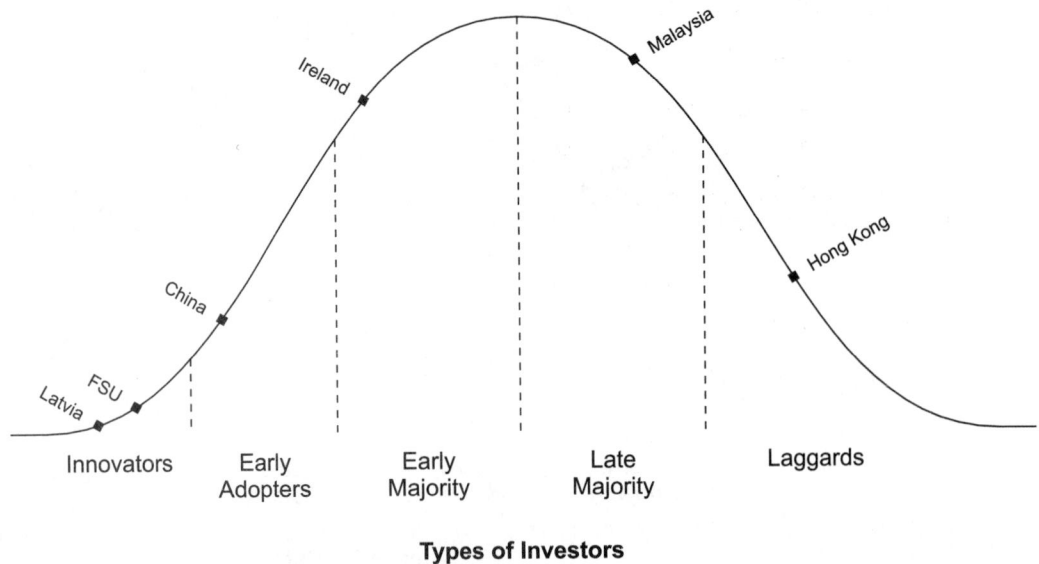

Types of Investors

4 PEST ANALYSIS

4.1 Finally, to complete your audit, you need to complete the macro or PEST analysis. By now, you should have a strong sense of the Case material and this last piece should not be too difficult – but, there is a lot of information you might like to work at, both regional and City level, so you can differentiate wider from more local issues.

Take the time now, to complete this step.

> **Tutor Tip**
>
> You will by now be getting used to both the depth of analysis students generate and the value added by considering the 'implications' of the data you pull together.
>
> You won't have this level of detail yet (the impetus of the actual case exam adds quite a bit of rigour to most student's analytical skills) but we hope your analysis does have the benefit of 'implications' highlighted. If so, well done, if not, do make a point of going back and adding these.

External analysis

4.2 **Political factors**

    (a) **Political – Rest of world**

        (i) **Opportunities**
- Different types and styles of governments

        (ii) **Threats**
- Political terrorism
- Economic crisis in Russia may lead to political instability

    (b) **Political – Latvia**

        (i) **Opportunities**

- Preparing to enter EU
- Reducing trade barriers

- Inward investment
- Ethnic Russians in government 30% – common culture with Daugavpils
- Independence from CIS

(ii) **Threats**

- Elections in 2002
- Government changes frequently

(iii) **Facts about Latvia**

- Gained independence in 1991
- State government changes every 12 months
- Only Latvian citizens and those resident before June 27 1940 can vote
- Citizenship only granted to Latvian speaking individuals.
- Elections:
  - June 2002 (presidential)
  - October 2002 (legislative)

(iv) **Foreign trade agreements**

- Attempting to forge strong links with West
- Preparing for EU entry
- Indulis Berzins (Latvia's Way), Foreign affairs
- Painful transition to multi-function farms for EU accession

(c) **Political – City of Daugavpils**

(i) **Opportunities**

- Coalition government – representation for all population
- Mayor – figurehead and overall control
- Three consulates – Russia, Belorussian, Lithuanian
- established contacts with east
- Foreign trade agreements – town twinning – east and west promotes foreign trade

(ii) **Threats**

- Coalition government –
  - too many opinions
  - political uncertainty
- No political contacts with West

(iii) **Facts Daugavpils**

- Twinned with:
  - Haderslev, Denmark (EU)
  - Mutala, Sweden (EU)
  - Ferara Italy (EU)
  - Radoma, Poland (pre-EU accession)
  - Moscow, Russia
  - Naro-fominsk, Russia (suburb of Moscow)
  - Vitebska, Belarus
- Municipal governments similar to the American model. The Mayor runs town and facilities.

- Eigim is leader of Latgales Light Party – not represented in the national parliament. Party holds 7 of 15 council seats. Formed coalition with Social Democrats and Human Rights Party (both government opposition parties). Previous Mayor, Alexei Vidavskis lost 6 of 13 seats – change from an effective one party state. The City party has no government representation.

- SAPARD programme is helping farming environment.

(iv) **Implications**

- Can exploit business links for foreign trade
- Grants can be obtained for cultural exchanges with other EU (and pre-accession) countries
- Will off financial support of meets economic and other criteria
- Managed by Latvians and not EU – which is not usual
- Regional development
- Interested in re-opening airport
- LRDA – Latgale Regional Development Agency
- Produced first regional development plan in Latvia
- LRDA pioneered co-operation amongst region's municipalities

4.3 Economic factors

(a) Economics – Rest of World

(i) **Opportunities**

- Currency fluctuations – linked to stable currency market

(ii) **Threats**

- Oil price fluctuations
- Potential US and EU recessions

(b) Economics – Latvia

(i) **Opportunities**

- Major exports to the EU
- 68% GDP comes from services

(ii) **Threats**

- Unemployment rising
- Poverty increasing
- Most imports from the EU (may be able to buy cheaper)
- Main exports – low added value

(iii) **Exports – Latvia**

- Main exports are low value added
- Sawn wood accounts for 35% of exports to EU. Unable to upgrade and compete with EU markets

(iv) **Imports – Latvia**

- Fast growth in imports has increased trade deficit
- Runs large trade deficit to finance substantial growth
- Mechanical appliances show Latvia's need to import technology in order to upgrade its productive capacity

(c) **Economics – Daugavpils**

  (i) **Opportunities**

- EU funding
- High spend on education (over 50%)
- Plentiful supply of cheap and skilled labour (cheaper than Riga)
- SAPARD investment
- Better trade

  (ii) **Threats**

- Low spend on healthcare
- Low paid doctors
- No official record of unemployment
- High employment
- Agricultural reforms will lead to increased rural unemployment

  (iii) **Facts**

External

- Economic crisis in Russia

Daugavpils

- Hospital being modernised with loan from World Bank
- Business generate 5.2m lats pa ($81.3m)
- Details of jobs only in Latvian
- Claimants drop out of system after 6 months
- Employment companies left over from Soviet era 10% of pre-soviet times
- Plentiful supply of cheap labour. Wages $60 per month
- Wages much more modest than Riga
- 2000 businesses in Daugavpils

  (iv) **Implications**

- Loans will need repaying. IBRD loans are often accompanied by stringent fiscal measures
  - Inflation and GDP
  - Origins of GDP
- Huge service element – tourism in Riga
  - External funding (via projects)

  (v) **Employment**

- Unemployment rising since independence
- Demand for teachers gone
- 2,000 businesses in Daugavpils
- Doctors dedicated by low paid 10-150 lats per month ($16-$236)
- Painful transition to multi-function farms for EU accession
  - SAPARD programme helping farming environment
- In Eastern bloc – mid-wives and community nurses are often referred to as 'doctors' may explain difference in salary
- Likely to lead to migration to cities of unskilled workers and further unemployment

(vi) **May help prevent rural exodus**

- Not particularly helpful to 58% of the population
- No official record of number of unemployed – estimated 28%
- Legacy of good engineers and craftsmen

4.4 Society and culture

(a) **Social/cultural – Rest of World**

(i) **Opportunities**

- Social and cultural diversity

(ii) **Threats**

- Different business operating styles
- Communist style business structures – historical

(b) **Social/cultural – Latvia**

(i) **Opportunities**

- More deaths than births
- Families generally take care for their elderly – life expectancy gap

(ii) **Threats**

- 53% rural economy
- Citizenship only granted to Latvian speakers
- Falling birth rate
- Increased crime, suicides, depression, use of drugs and alcohol, and sexually transmitted diseases

(c) **Social/cultural – Daugavpils**

(i) **Opportunities**

- Friendly, helpful hard workers
- Education is key (95% literacy, schooling is free, universities and affiliations to Riga and Salford)
- High proportion to go on to higher education
- English language is being promoted
- Death rate is higher than birth rate

(ii) **Threats**

- Little cultural cohesion between Russians and Latvians
- Latvian language forced over Russian
- Population falling
- Birth rate falling
- Russian and Latvian schooling split

(iii) **Facts**

- 53% rural
- Daugavpils has similar number to other towns
- Many more Latvians outside Riga than in
- Population is falling (8%)
- Birth rate is falling (17%)
- Deaths are falling (8%)
- People leaving area is falling (90%)

(v)   **Implications**

- Likely to be poor – not potential customers
- Likely competition
- Other towns not included – Jakabkils and Rezekne equal size to Ventspils and may be culturally closer
- Fewer people to support
- Fewer in school
- Labour force decreasing
- Ageing population
- Have all the 'brains' already left?
- Perception may be misguided
- Difficult culture to change – less innovation
- Potential for urban population to spend money in countryside
- Potential source of lobbying for funds for leisure activities to make citizens feel good about town

(vi)   **Demographic – Daugavpils**

- Figures broadly similar to rest of Latvia
- 28% of working population is unemployed (31,920)

Changes in lifestyle

- 75% of population want to live elsewhere: however only 5% have ever been to Riga.

Work behaviour

- Soviet management system is hierarchical and authoritarian
- There is need to change culture – used to central planning
- Painful transition to multi-function farms for EU accession (53% of Latvian population live outside major cities) .

Leisure activities

- Situated on lowland plains – Jeriska plain. Also surrounded by Latgale and Augzeme heights
- 15 lakes (350 small ones), 8 rivers, 10,400 hectares (4,200 acres) of forests/trees. Supports wide range of wildlife and fish
- Karina Petersone (Latvia's Way) is Culture Minister

Implications

Distribution of income

- Likely that it has followed those in power under 'Soviet' administration – nomenklatura.
- Eigims would have needed connections to become a millionaire in ten years – did he use old connections?

4.5   **Culture**

(a)   **Religion**

- Catholic
- Lutheran
- Jewish
- Baptist

- Old Orthodox
- Orthodox
- Mostly Polish
- Most Latvians are (were) Lutheran – brought in by Germans – plain, non-emotional

(b) Values and beliefs

- Multi-cultural
- Used to centrally planned economy
- 75% wish to live elsewhere
- Rigans see Daugavpils as backward
- Keen on sport
- Education valued
- Invasions/history had effect

Implications

- May be difficult to position city effectively
- Don't take responsibility for actions
- Don't take pride in city probably agree with Rigans
- Competitive
- Keen to learn

(c) Cultural Education

Schools

- Education 7-16
- Falling birth rate = reduced demand for teachers
- English emerging as required language
- ~13k pupils in 29 schools (~500 per school)
- Over 50% of budget spent on education
- Russian/Latvian split on education

Implications

- Appears that a majority go on to higher education
- Russians have to learn a 3rd language – or ignore Latvian
- Shows commitment but is it too much – efficiency
- Which schools do Poles and other ethnic groups favour
- Perpetuates cultural divide

(d) Higher education

- 1,000 students graduate from two Universities (teacher training and Riga Technical)
- Approximately 70% go onto higher education
- Nine technical institutions
- Art college
- Music school
- 150 pupils at Nursing School
- Teachers less in demand what replace it? Redundant lecturers
- Students of Riga Technical University may stay in Riga – Daugavpils loses know-how
- Potential to convert to University to prevent students going to Riga
- What sort of jobs do these end up in?
- Karlis Greiskalns (People's Party), Education and science minister

- 5 projects underway to improve infrastructure and develop education system
- High level of investment in education. Other political pressures may lead to this budget being cut
- May be interested in and lend support to outside sources of income – foreign students
- Better education facilities for an y foreign students

(e) **Cultural: Language**

(i) **External**

- Estonia has common language with Finland

Latvia

- 30% of population is (speak) Russian
- Citizenship only granted to Latvian speaking individuals leaving some Russian speaking people stateless

Implications

- Finland may show preference to doing business with Estonians
- May be more inclined to visit Daugavpils – less negative
- Source of potential conflict
- Large proportion of population may not be able to understand political communication – feel alienated

(ii) **Daugavpils**

- Essentially Russian speaking
- Town signs not in Cryllic script
- Schools polarised into Russian and Latvian
- English emerging as required language in schools
- Job details only in Latvian
- Daugavpils District Enterprise Support Centre – multi-lingual – all info in Latvian and Russian

Implications

- May not be able to 'read' western script easily or intuitively
- Doesn't reflect multi-cultural society
- Presumably taught in own language – citizenship, perception by Rigans
- More able to do business with N Americans and Europeans
- As much as 85% of population may have difficulty understanding
- Positive sign – shows it can be done if there is a political will

(iii) **Cultural/Social orientation**

- Families generally care for their elderly
- Project for rehabilitation for abused children

Implications

- Still sizeable ethnic group
- Russian population forced migration – negative perception of city ended up in
- No indication of societies to promote integration of Russians with others

4.6   **Technology**

(a)   **Technology: Latvia**

(i)   **Latvia**

- Imports 20% of Machinery and mechanical appliances. this shows the need to import technology to upgrade productive capacity

- Anatolijs Gorbonuvs (Latvia's Way), Transport and telecommunications

- Karlis Greiskalns (People's Party), Education and science minister

(ii)   **Opportunities**

- Good rail and air links; adequate road links
- Good websites

(iii)   **Threats**

- Need to import technology to upgrade capacity

(b)   **Technology: – Daugavpils**

(i)   Daugavpils

- Poor website, slow and few links
- Infrastructure

(ii)   **Opportunities**

- Bus and tram systems
- Good rail network links
- Proposed development of road networks
- US$22.3m investment in sanitation (foreign)

(iii)   **Threats**

- No operational airport
- No apparent existing investment in technology or infrastructure
- Poor website

(iv)   **Facts**

- Distance from other cities
  - Riga – 232km
  - Lithuania – 25km
  - Belorussia border – 33km
  - Russia border – 120km
- Good tram system but old.
- Current **airport** not functioning (Russians took all equipment with them).
- Developing good **road** links with Lithuania, Belorussia and Russia
- Key **railroad** juncture for USSR.
- Anatolijs Gorbonuvs (Latvia's Way), transport and telecoms

US$ 22.3m invested in infrastucture

Daugavpils water and sewage project – financed by many including Phare, IBRD: US$22.3m.

4.7 **Market conditions**

(a) **Market conditions – Latvia**

- Soviet structure holding back Latvia – hierarchical, authoritarian
- Need to attract back ex-Latvians to help change business culture
- English emerging as required language in schools

Implications

- May find transfer to tourist industry difficult but 64% of GDP is gained by 'Services'
- Why does it have to be ex-Latvians – may all decide to go to Riga – more sophisticated
- Easier for North Americans and Europeans to undertake business

(b) **Market conditions: Daugavpils**

- Regional development uncoordinated
- Pedagogical University to support local business – 500 students taking business related courses
- Details of jobs only in Latvian
- Rhodia (industrial Yarns) – bought a large site = business park
- Good engineers and craftsmen in city (from Soviet area when it manufactured trains)
- Plentiful supply of cheap labour ($60 per month)
- Huge factories lying empty
- Rigans see Daugavpils as backwards
- Current airport is not functioning (Russians took all equipment with them)
- Prior to closure of airport, the Russians had used it for cargo and it served 60,000 passengers per day.
- 2,000 businesses in Daugavpils
- Investment being made in infrastructure.

Implications

- May take longer than planned to improve
- May create more businesslike employees
- Russians may miss out on jobs
- Space for inward investors
- Transferable skills
- Cheaper than Riga
- Potential. Planning regulations could help or hinder businesses
- Need to change perception
- May deter inward investors and tourists
- Presumably large enough when/if re-developed

(c) **Environment**

(i) **Raw materials**

- Most of the resources based in Riga
- High concentration of small, subsistence farms – SAPARD helping

349 BPP
PUBLISHING

- Support wide range of wildlife and fish
- Abundant sand stone slate and clay region
- Lies on Daugava River 15 lakes (350 small ones), 8 rivers
- 10,400 hectares (4,200 acres) forests/trees
- Foreign money likely to follow resources
- Food production
- Food production – appears to be exploited already by local businesses
- No mention of quarrying – potential
- Some industries need a lot of water
- Source of wood – already being exploited

(ii) **Pollution**

- Daugavpils water and sewage project – financed by many including Phare, IBRD; US$22.3m)

- Research on management of industrial waste – financed by Finland and Daugavpils; L94,000 (US$0.15m)

- Household waste management project – financed by VARAM, Finland and Daugavpils; L7.2m (US$11.3m)

- Decaying industrial environment

- Implies there is a problem – has waste polluted rivers being promoted for leisure activities

(iii) **Environment – Role of government**

- Atis Slakteris (People's Party) – Agriculture Minister

- Vladimirs Makarovs (FFF-LNIM), Environmental protection and regional development

- Investment (Phare, IBRD) seems to concentrate on sewage clean up

- Need to 'lobby' to ensure correct allocation of investment

- Need to 'lobby' to ensure correct allocation of investment

- Implies it must have been pretty awful

(iv) **Environment – Appeal**

- Lies on Daugava River. Says its 1,020km long – but does not look like it on map. Ends run in Riga and Baltic sea

- Situated on lowland plains – Jeriska plain. Also surrounded by Latgale and Augzeme heights

- 15 lakes (350 small ones), 8 rivers, 10,400 hectares (4,200 acres) forests/trees. Support wide range of wildlife and fish

- Temperatures 34C (84-90 F) to –25 C. Rainfall 650mm per year. Sunlight hours 1,809 per annum

- Possible cruise from Riga

- Pleasant surroundings for locals, tourists and inward investors

- Leisure

- Tourism may be seasonal owing to weather

- 72% destroyed in WW2

- Post WW2 – Soviets built factories and blocks of houses

- Lies on Daugava River. Says its 1,020km long – but doesn't look like it on map. Ends run in Riga and Baltic sea.

- 15 lakes (350 small ones), 8 rivers, 10,400 hectares (4,200 acres) forests/trees. Support wide range of wildlife and fish

- No mention of ex-Latvians financing rebuild – how connected do they still feel?

- Unlikely to be attractive or well built

Tutor Tip

You can see from this analysis that the students have added a heading 'implications'. Under this heading they have provided insight to the analysis. Reaching some conclusions about what the analysis is telling them.

This analysis has been well structured and lots of information has been extracted from the case. In places it is a little skimpy, for example no comment on technology for the rest of the world.

---

5 A REVIEW OF THE SITUATION AND OPTIONS

5.1 This must be one of the more unusual and challenging Case studies that has been set, although the exam covered did tackle the marketing of the UK town of Gravesend. This summary should help you lock the final pieces of your analysis and review of other people's work together.

An emerging market economy with little experience of marketing and market place economics, Daugavpils has to compete for investment opportunities on a global basis:

- For EU funding from development towns and cities across Europe
- For industry with low cost locations from Asia Pacific as well as other parts of Europe

5.2 The City is in a bit of a mess at the moment. Employment levels are just over 30% of the 114,000 population and 75% of residents would rather live somewhere else: hardly a great ad for the place. There is run down local industry and a lot of small local enterprises with 2,000 operations employing just 9,000 people. We know that there us a lack of western business experience and marketing skills, so we are sure you will have considered how support from the council could help these local entrepreneurs increase their sales and output. This is the equivalent of a market penetration strategy for the City, it may generate relatively small increases in employment but would be relatively quick and would generate considerable awareness of the Mayor's initiatives.

5.3 Here are a few thoughts:

- Business students could 'mentor' local companies
- The website could include information on local goods and services
- Trade visits to/from other parts of Latvia or overseas could be organised
- Help in funding external investment partners, 'business angels' could be given

5.4 As far as attracting new investment, the City has to offer any incoming business a commercial opportunity – ie locating in Daugavpils has to provide the inward investor with a potential business benefit – lower costs or added potential revenue. A review of Porter's basis for competitive advantage of a nation has shown the City's **infrastructure** and **demand conditions** to be broadly unfavourable but there are things which could drive a strong competitive advantage for certain organisations.

(a) The natural resources in the area – the blue lakes, scenery and fishing stocks have the potential to attract tourists. You might think about whether the diffusion of innovation model would give you some insight into those travellers prepared to be innovators and early adopters of 'new' destinations. It will be some time before the City has the infrastructure and facilities to compete for 'mass tourism'.

(b) The local heritage and literary connections are of course also unique and might allow some targeted development of special interest groups and for a second City stopover on tours to Riga or even neighbouring countries.

(c) The problem with tourism is that while it does generate some relatively low paid jobs, the market for the tourist market is global and intense. However, the growing sector of this market could be the medical market. The local environment and experience of this sector could be a basis for a strategy which would generate jobs for medical staff as well as hospitality services. This market could be segmented by the level of medical intervention needed, from providing acute services to a health farm with convalescence and rehabilitation segments between these extremes. This could be a B2B or B2C opportunity with targets for health contracts with various authorities or marketing direct to individuals.

(d) Industry is a different issue. There is an available workforce which is a low cost option to other European cities but these cost differentials will fade if and when Latvia converges with the rest of the EU. Investment needs to be sustainable and it seems positioning the City in a more positive way would be preferable.

(e) The multicultural nature of the City means language skills are high and English is a common language. This would make Daugavpils an excellent centre for call centre operations and may build on the strong telecoms links of Denmark and Sweden.

5.5 We know you will be going on to consider these options and alternatives and will be aware of the time any of these developments is likely to take realistically. Whatever strategy you propose, the City must cope with managing the expectations of a wide range of stakeholders – not least the local population. As you prepare to move forward from analysis to decision-making, think about what might help. Updates on progress, Mayoral briefings and involvement of the local population on improvement initiatives would all help in the processes of regeneration. The Mayor's vision of the Garden City is a bit 'me too'. The Blue Lakes idea seems more original but the concept of improved physical evidence is a good idea. Think how others have done it. The most attractive village competitions could become the prettiest street and re-development or adoption of local parks and common areas could be encouraged.

5.6 We think you will need to be prepared to help the City make the business case for public funding, national or international in nature. A clear vision and strategy and view on the economic benefits resulting from such investments is key but so to is the political benefits in terms of helping Latvia meet EU entry criteria. These are also topics you will need to tackle.

About the current position

5.7 The current position is very much a focus for your brief, but do take care not simply to present analysis as lists of strengths and weaknesses or PEST factors. The Mayor will not be impressed if he is expected to do all the thinking! Take time to think through how best to structure an answer to such a question.

5.8 In any answer, you will need to highlight your understanding of the importance of maintaining the support of the various stakeholders and your recognition of the need for a strategys, which provides **short-term improvements** as well as **long-term sustainable development.**

5.9 Improving employment does seem to be an objective which will deliver many subsidiary benefits and goals, and so generally seems safe to work with. Remember to present your analysis positively and try and show how apparent negatives could be turned to advantages e.g. the multi ethnic mix of the population gives excellent language skills.

5.10 Now you have completed the analysis and compared your work with the student samples provided. The important thing at this stage, is to turn this information into 'Case intelligence', which requires you to pull the threads together, in a meaningful way, in light of the 'context' of the Case. Spend no more that twenty minutes – one side of A4, to summarise the competitive advantage (ie internal strengths and weaknesses) of the City. Besides the strengths and weaknesses, consider the conclusions this leads you to, ie what is the potential for exploiting the strengths or tackling the weaknesses.

5.11 Try using a model to structure your answer in a way you could use in the examination. Remember simple lists of the factors will **not** impress the examiners. Strengths need to focus on areas of opportunity.

Strength	Opportunity
• Outstanding natural beauty ⟶	• Potential for outdoor tourism
• Skills in heath care + local and natural environment ⟶	• Potential for health tourism

BPP PUBLISHING

Strengths – New business orientated leader, visionary, EU and others funding and support.

Weaknesses – Soviet style management systems, lack of business/marketing skills, lack of domestic rivalry.

However – Some industries have re-invented themselves, so some signs of innovation.

Strengths – Nordic demand, increasing EU interest.

Weaknesses – Limited demand (heavily dependent on Russia who have many problems).

However – Country is a channel for some products on route to other countries (could add value?).

Chance

City strategy, structure & rivaly

Factor conditions

Demand conditions

Related & supporting industries

Government

Strengths – Engineering skills, area of outstanding beauty (eg. lakes, wildlife).

Weaknesses – Infrastructure, lack knowledge/skills for hi-tech industries.

However – Educated so can retrain. Potential to upgrade infrastucture.

Strengths – In its infancy?

Weaknesses – Little/no internationally competitive industries. Contact and coordination with suppliers appears poor; little obvious relationship between, or in direct support of other industries. Value chains **not** structured, so linkages with suppliers are optimised.

However – Do they optimise business school links?
Exchanges and projects with many of the twinned cities.

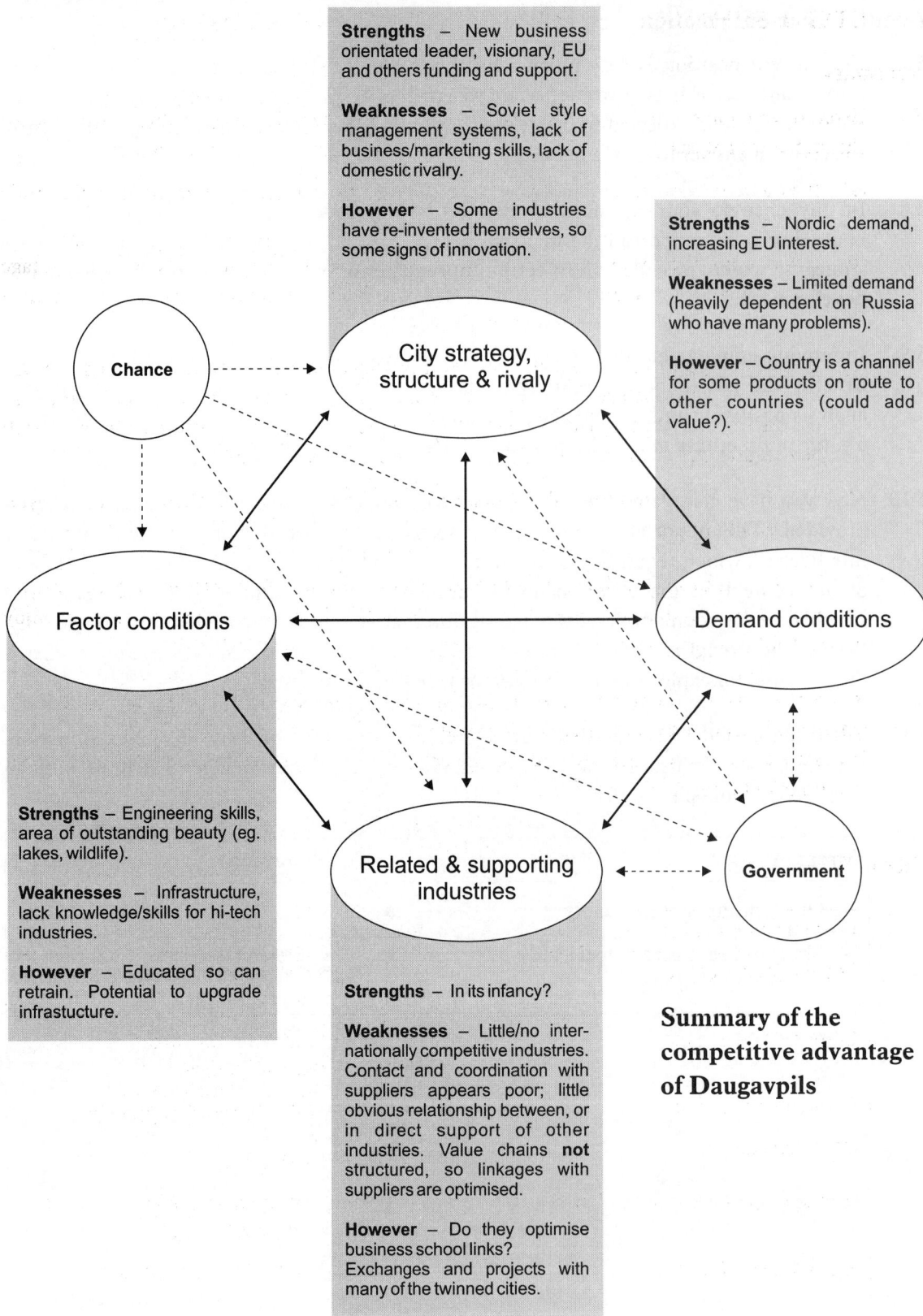

Summary of the competitive advantage of Daugavpils

6   STEP 4: SUMMARY AND CRITICAL SUCCESS FACTORS

Summary

6.1   Even if you have not completed the analysis of Daugvapils yourself, but have worked through our analysis, you should be able to analyse the City's is current situation

(a)   It is at a crossroads and needs a clear strategy to provide the impetus for economic recovery.

(b)   It has a number of assets, which can be utilised as a basis of competitive advantage These include its natural beauty on the blue lakes, its central location, its resource availability and the leadership of the Mayor.

(c)   There are opportunities but the core and expected elements of the infrastructure will need to be right, before mainstream tourists can be attracted. There are push and pull factors in marketing a place – a lack of the 'hygiene' factors will push people away. Pull factors are sites of interest, facilities or the natural environment.

(d)   The City cannot exploit all its opportunities at once so will need to be selective. Resources are limited.

6.2   So, the City has problems, but is not without hope. Your next task is to identify the critical success factors and key issues which are essential if the City is to re-position itself and enjoy the fruits of economic growth.

6.3   Remember, critical success factors can be defined as those internal changes or challengers, which are literally critical to success, for example establishing a market orientation. The key issues are those actions need to address the critical success factors for example, re-structure around clients and improve the MKIS.

City of Daugavpils

Critical Success Factors	Key Issues
Economic prosperity	Attracting/retaining businesses, people tourists
Competitive positioning	Natural environmental advantages Manufactured advantages
Branding and image	Current internal/external perceptions
Communications	Brand values Internal marketing
Managing stakeholder relationships	Segmentation, communications Mutual benefits, influence
E-strategy and web	Link to communications and raising awareness
Changing culture to a marketing orientation	Marketing planning and control systems Marketing information systems

6.4   **Other key issues to consider in planning**

(a)   Raising money could be the main problem – businesses should see problem as theirs also and they collaborate to resolve eg US town improvements paid for by a special tax (proved very successful).

(b) This stage is very important as it can lead us to identifying the possible question areas. Look at how these CSF's are reflected in the case clues pulled out for City of Daugvapils.

Identifying possible question areas

6.5 Your analysis and CSF's leads you to the strategies and plans your organisation needs to pursue to achieve its goals. In the Case study this of course means the potential questions that could be asked in the exam.

6.6 We need to ensure our efforts, before the exam, are both focused and productive. It is useful to go through the **Case study and highlight specific clues to possible questions.** For example

Page	Comment
3	'key element in changing culture ... is instilling the importance of developing and implementing a marketing orientated view of business'
6	'problems for creating a consistent brand image for the City'
8	'biggest challenge understanding a counteracting the poor perception of Daugavpils in Riga.'
17	'biggest challenge facing mayor perception of City in Riga and amongst residents.'
9	'City council needs to develop a marketing strategy that will attract new businesses from international sources to the region'
11	'tourism marketing us becoming important part of most cities' strategies...'
15	'internet marketing is set to play an increasingly important part in the marketing of locations'
16	'internet marketing strategy'
17	'logo... brand image is poor... marketing communications carried out by assistant..'
27	'Daugavpils has the potential for development of foreign tourist trade...'

6.7 These clues do not identify guaranteed questions that could be asked on the day. They provide ideas on the issues the organisation needs to address. As we do not know the questions, our pre-exam preparation can only therefore guide us and must be in outline only. For the Daugavpils Case study we prepared students for the following questions.

City of Daugavpils

Preparation planning exercise – Assume a time scale of 5 years:

1. Develop a strategic marketing plan to attract industries (of your choice) to the City of Daugavpils. Agree how you will competitively position the City to attract this business.

2. Develop a marketing strategy for attracting tourists to the City of Daugavpils. Agree what product/services you will offer and how the City will develop to appeal to the tourists you are targeting.

3. Develop a communications strategy to change the image of the City of Daugavpils (to three key targets of your choice). Explain the key brand values and image you will be developing.

4. Develop an internet strategy for the City of Daugavpils. What key factors do you need to take into account in developing you strategy and what are the implications?

6.8 The task now is to work through the process of developing strategic marketing plans and other plans eg communications, in outline only, to act as prompts to help you on the day.

Once this step is complete, you have crossed the bridge from analysis to decision making. We tend to think that we have broken the back of a Case study by this point in the process. Once you know where you are, deciding where you are going and how to get there seems fairly straightforward.

But before you leave this analysis stage, we would like you to take some time out to think about what you have learned, which will help you be more effective through these analysis steps in your Case.

Take your time to consider the following questions and turn to the end of the chapter for our feedback.

Action programme 16.3

Improving your Effectiveness

1. Imagine you were briefing a newcomer to Case study analysis. What tips would you give them to ensure they managed themselves and the process effectively?

2. How do you decide which models or frameworks to use during analysis stage?

3. What do you do if you are missing data which would allow you to use a model properly, for example, there was no information on supplier power when you were completing a Porter's Five Forces Analysis?

4. You will be faced with lots of data, tables and information in a Case study. What do you need to be aware of, alert to, before using these to generate information?

5. You have seen a number of different examples of analysis and models used during this chapter. What conclusions have you drawn about a 'best practice' approach?

---

7 AN EXAMINATION FOOTNOTE

7.1 The quality of your analysis will be judged by the quality of your decision making and your ability to justify your work.

7.2 However, it is sometimes assessed more directly by a first 'situation analysis' question.

7.3 You need to be prepared to answer an exam question which asks for your critical assessment of the company/City and its current position. Do not be tempted to reproduce SWOT or lists of analysis. You need to interpret your assessment, spelling out to the board the implications of your analysis and the critical success factors.

The 'where are we now' question may be asked in different way.

- As a full question, in which case some depth will be required,

- As an introduction or contextual background to another question, for example, what are the strategic options facing the business?

You should be prepared to do this for The City of Daugavpils.

In either case, make sure to factor in and highlight the implications of any additional information given in the exam room.

Action Programme Review

1   This listing of the key facts drawn from the Case can be used as the stepping stone you need to complete an in-depth analysis, but next, you must ask yourself what this means. What are the implications?

There are no page references, and not enough quantitative or qualitative comment. Is this a big City? How many graduates are there elsewhere?

2   **Feedback**

These differences in approach are included to show you there is more than one way to tackle your analysis and you need to develop the approach that is most effective for you.

I personally like the strengths and weaknesses grid, which shows at a glance, the balance of strengths versus weaknesses and can have page numbers added. You can set these up as templates and easily fill them in as you work through the material. The summary of the strengths and weaknesses 'sorted' in terms of impact or importance really helps. However, in this case, the second example of analysis – the more 'narrative' approach, has more depth and in particular the development of a key challenge at each point is really useful.

3   **Feedback**

1.   To get organised from the beginning:

- Set up an analysis file with sections
- Keep analysis filed and organised
- Pull different strands or analysis together in one-page summaries
- Plan your time, using several short burst to work through the analysis

2.   Any models which help can be used at any stage of the process. There are no right and wrongs, use those which work best with the available data.

3.   You can still use or modify the model to take account of the gaps. You can either:

- Note the gap, or
- make a reasonable assumption

4.   Ensure it is:

- Relevant
- Up to date
- Reliable (where has it come from?)
- Uses the same definition

Like using a secondary data you need to be careful. Case data can still be unreliable or out of date. A customer satisfaction survey, completed three years ago and before the launch of a significant new competitor, would be of limited value. Check dates/weights and currencies for comparability and consistency.

Make sure you:

- Add depth – include information which allows you to show both the business position and its market context.

- Commentary or indications that you understand the business implications are particularly appreciated.

17

City of Daugavpils: Decision Making: Steps 5-10

Introduction

In this chapter of the City of Daugavpils practice case, you will work from the completed analysis to the end of the decision-making processes. This prepares you for tackling the exam paper.

1 STEP 5: THE CORPORATE AND BUSINESS DECISIONS FOR THE CITY

1.1 This is what you have established.

- The City is currently in economic decline. It faces rising unemployment, younger people are leaving the city and there is a deteriorating infrastructure.

- It has the leadership and potential to re-position itself for economic regeneration. If you look at the example of Bradford given in the case (and other British cities which lost their manufacturing bases) you can see this is not an impossible objective.

1.2 If you are working the Case with us, you should now take the time to think about the following.

(a) **A vision for the City**. The Mayor has a vision of Daugavpils being a 'Garden City' – this may not be enough to create a unique European positioning. You can make your own judgement.

Your vision should be aspirational and establishes how your clients want the City to be recognised in the future. It will link directly to how the 'City' brand will need to be built if the vision is to be realised across all stakeholder groups.

Do not spend too long agonising about the precise form of words: simply get a sense of direction for the business.

> A Vision for the City of Daugavpils..
> ....
> ....
> ....

(b) A **mission statement** is then required to provide the planning framework or parameters for the management team. Remember the characteristics:

- Short and memorable
- Benefits focused
- Geographically bounded where appropriate

> A Mission for the City of Daugavpils...
> ....
> ....
> ....

(c) **Adding the numbers**: finally, you will need to establish the **planning gap**. What is happening today and what **objective** is realistic?

(i) In this Case, you need to determine a meaningful measure which would make sense to and be supported by the Mayor, Council and local residents, all of whom may have different priorities.

(ii) In private sector companies, profit is the integrating target. For this case, you could be tempted to use the amount of inward investment, number of tourists attracted, but perhaps the most useful measure would be **jobs created**.

(iii) There are no specific rights and wrongs here, the only key thing is to have a qualified and realistic target. Ask yourself, what are the City objectives and priorities likely to be. These are important as they are your client's agenda.

1.3   What are the City objectives likely to be?

- Increased taxes from increased revenues people/ industry increased number of businesses

- Reduced unemployment (or increased employment)

- Visitor revenue – Tourists and travellers, sports fans, business people

- Funding (attracting/winning) – for various projects

1.4   P28 City development priorities (City income sources P39)

- Improve economic development and employment

- Improve streets, roads and security, create modern care

- Improve environment, save City centre – cultural, historical, heritage (protecting architecture)

Now choose your measure and complete your planning gap. Remember to add labels to your axis and a title.

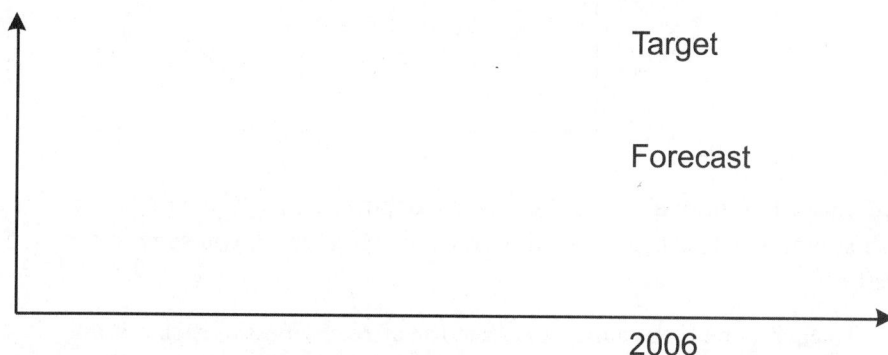

Target

Forecast

2006

1.5   Vision, mission and planning gap (Example 1)

(a)   **Vision.** To rejuvenate the City of Daugavpils as a vibrant and exciting place where people aspire to live, work and visit.

(b)   **Mission.** To cultivate economic prosperity, a healthy environment and cultural, leisure and sports activities and interests that enhance the quality of life. We will do this through the provision of work, housing and economic development that meets the needs of the people and business in a fast changing global environment.

(c)   **City/corporate objectives**

(i)   **Short term:** to reduce unemployment by 5% within 2 years
(ii)   **Medium term:** to reduce unemployment to 14% by 2006
(iii) **Long term:** to reduce unemployment to 3% by 2010

Action Programme 2

Making Strategic Direction Matter

- If you were the examiner how would you respond to this answer?

- What is good and bad about it, and what could be improved?

- What lessons can you learn about how to approach this part of the planning process for the exam Case?

Check your thoughts with the feedback at the end of the chapter.

---

2 FILLING THE PLANNING GAP

2.1 Once you have established the planning gap, you can turn your attention to how the City of Daugavpils could fill it. Where are the new jobs going to come from?

Your analysis should have equipped you to complete an Ansoff matrix, identifying the strategic alternatives. Use the matrix here to model the opportunities you have identified: which products and which markets?

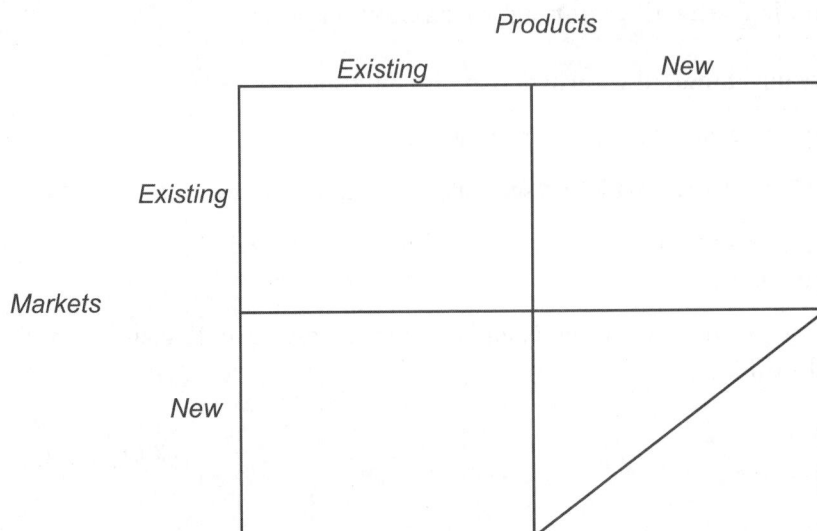

Products

	Existing	*New*
Existing		
New		

Markets

2.2 City of Daugavpils

You must then think about evaluating the opportunities. You will need to use a framework, such as a multifactor matrix for this. What criteria would you suggest for the following two cases.

- To enable the City council to assess the attractiveness of each option.

- To model customer behaviour: what would 'customers', whether tourists or inward investors, use to assess the attractiveness of Daugavpils as opposed to alternative destinations or locations?

> **Tutor Tip**
>
> This is a very important and telling part of the Case process. You need to ensure your criteria are more case specific and if possible quantified and even justified. Knowing how to make objective decisions is a key management skill.

2.3 Evaluating and selecting strategies

List the criteria you would recommend for evaluating the product/market options open to the City.

Evaluation criteria for the City council to use	Evaluation of customer criteria customers might use
1. _____	_____
2. _____	_____
3. _____	_____
4. _____	_____
5. _____	_____
6. _____	_____
7. _____	_____

Tutor Tip

Let us just re-enforce that point about the importance of the criteria. The examiners will be interested in your choice – so make them as Case specific as possible and as specific as possible.

No. 'Increase employment': This is not quantified.

Yes. 'Generate at least 500 extra jobs': This is quantified and can be assessed for realism.

Action Programme 3

Take a few minutes to compare this student example below with your own work.

- What is your opinion of it?
- How could it be improved?
- What lessons does it teach you about this part of the planning process?

Our comments are included at the end of the chapter.

Products

	Current	New
Current	Expand local business	Two-centre holidays Sports centres Conference hotels
New	Attract European tourists	

Markets

Ansoff's Growth Vector Matrix

BPP PUBLISHING

2.4 You could flesh out the matrix by noting how strategies could be delivered. But remember, there is a danger in moving from the strategic to the tactical.

Products

	Existing	*New*
	Tourists • More from Germany, Finland, USA, India, Canada, France, Netherlands, Denmark, UK, Russia, South Africa • Health farm, hunting and fishing Sports events (ice hockey, football, motor cycle racing) *Business* • More oil • Encouraging Latvian business to relocate to Daugavpils • Improve local business processes	*Tourists* • Cultural events • Entertainment (theme park type) • Sports events 'World Championships' • Recreation - hiking, camping *Business* • High tech industrial park • Attracting local chains • Water Park • Bottled water • Call centres
New	*Tourists* • New geographic areas eg. Eastern Europe, Norway, Sweden, Western Europe (med) *Business* • Satellite industries	*Tourists* Sports education *Business* Gambling Hydro power

Markets labels: *Existing* (top row), *New* (bottom row)

2.5 Evaluating the options – A student example

Your criteria may be different from these, but check yours for relevance and numbers.

City's criteria	Customers' criteria
1 Prosperity to generate over 500 jobs	1 Location
2 Local income/employment multiplier greater than 2 (ie every €100 inward investment or spending generates €200k + plus increase in local income).	2 Availability of pull factors - for tourist attractions and hotels etc - for industry workers and space
3 Impact on local environment (ie no pollution)	3 Friendliness/flexibility of local people
4 Synergy with the values and positioning of the City	4 Environment: - Safety - Attractiveness
5 Prosperity to build skills or attract other activities	5 Cost

This is fine. If you have been able to add even more numbers that is great. The customer criteria are credible but are not very specific. Do be sure in cases where you get more customer data that you use it.

> ## Tutor Tip
>
> If you get Case questions with additional information that can be incorporated with your criteria, make sure you use the new data. For example: the Mayor believes he has only two years to make an impact...., so, you would add, positive return within 24 months as a criterion and highlight it.

Corporate plan evaluation of strategic options

Using the multifactor mix

2.6 This model is an excellent tool for demonstrating and communicating quickly and clearly the options and relative attractiveness. You should make sure of several things if you want to maximise your marks.

- Make it clear that the criteria represents the justification for why specific strategies have been chosen.

- Emphasise that the weighting and rating has been done.

- Pull out your selected strategies (making sure any proposed by the **examiner** via the questions are in the high/high zone) and say a few words about each.

Strategy attractiveness

		High	Medium	Low
Competitive position	High	• Increase local processes • Engineering Centre • Health tourism • Develop airport		
	Medium	• Develop call centre Furniture centre • Develop two centre holidays • Develop sports tourism • Increase national tourism	• Distribution centre • Fish farming • Develop niche holidays	
	Low			

There is a planning gap of over 18,000 jobs. You can use the planning gap again this time to communicate your selected strategies, showing how, over time, you expect them to build towards the City objectives.

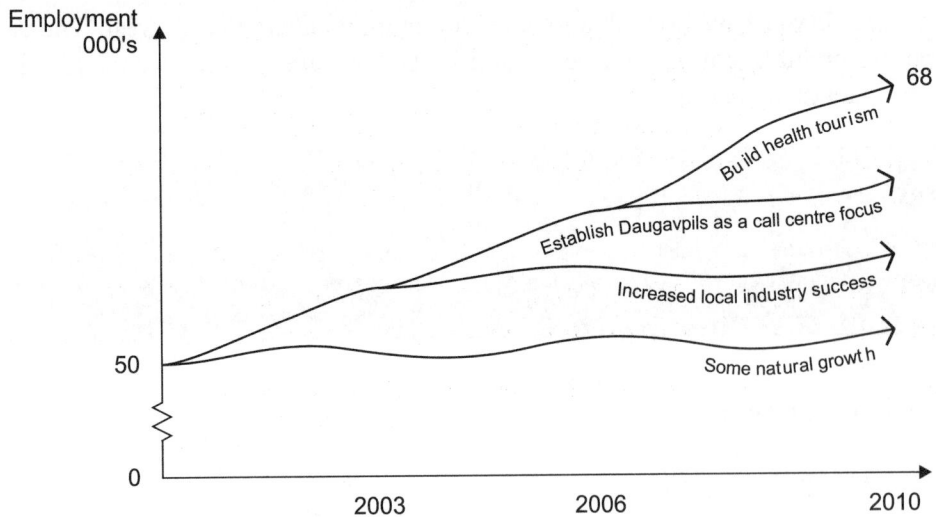

Do not worry if these selected strategies don't match yours. **As long as your strategies are credible and can be justified, the examiner will be happy**. Do, however, think about the time scales involved. Helping local firms improve their marketing would be a lot quicker and easier than building the infrastructure for sanatoria and rest homes.

3   STEP 6: BUSINESS IMPLICATIONS

3.1   It is one thing to establish a new vision, a bold objective and define a new mission statement. It is quite another to bring these changes about. Deciding strategy is obviously important because it provides a focus, and ensures resources and efforts are integrated. But, we must now return to those critical success factors we identified at Step 4.

3.2   These were the **implementation** factors which had to be addressed if any future strategy was to be **achieved**. We will take a couple of these as examples and review how students actually set about tackling these issues.

Tutor Tip

In the exam, you may simply need to highlight the business implications and comment upon them, in order to support your strategy. On the other hand you could be faced with a whole question on a critical success factor or a key issue. For example in Biocatalysts:

- Organisation/structure
- Changing to a customer orientation
- Improving the process of new product development
- Using e-strategy to reduce costs and improve effectiveness
- Implementing a CRM strategy
- Building the brand

3.3   At this step of the process, we would encourage you to re-visit your critical success factors and outline thoughts and strategies for tackling them. The CSF's can come up as exam questions and often include things that must be in place before your marketing plan can be effectively implemented.

In this Case for example, you might look at:

- Building a re-positioned City brand

- Maintaining stakeholder relationships

- Building an effective e-strategy to support the strategies selected for tourism/investment and local business

Keep these notes short, a maximum of one page, although the following example of a communication strategy is rather fuller to give you an idea of the structure. See what you think of this student answer.

4 STRATEGIES FOR COMMUNICATIONS ADDRESSED TO RIGA, TOURISTS AND INTERNATIONAL BUSINESSES

4.1 Changing the image of Daugavpils in eyes of the Riga authorities

(a) **Situation**

   (i) *Internal performance*

- Strategic geographical location
- Regional plan will help attract external investment as a recognised document to international businesses
- Municipality restructured with view to bring marketing orientation
- Physical evidence of things starting to change (flower beds)
- Increase in optimism of population
- Educated diverse skilled population
- Mayor is dynamic and has vision of the future
- Cultural tension

   (ii) *External issues*

- For EU accession Latvia will benefit from a politically stable and economically productive second city
- Agricultural unemployment may rise due to measures to attain EU membership
- Political instability, due frequent to elections at local and national level
- Increase in cultural tensions between Latvian and Russian speakers

(b) **Towards a brand vision**

   (i) *Developing a competitive advantage*

- Strengths
- Skilled workforce
- Centre for education
- Centre for Culture
- Land of the Blue Lakes
- Cross roads between East and West – strategic location
- Transport infrastructure
- Industrial sites
- New Mayor

   (ii) A sustainable competitive advantage is Daugavpils' physical location

   (iii) **Vision: To provide an environment for physical prosperity and to be a recognised centre of culture within a breathtaking physical environment**

(c) **Objectives**

   (i)   To change the perceived image of Daugavpils in the eyes of Riga from a negative perspective to a positive one within the next 2 years.

   (ii)   To develop positioning as Latvia's second city and change from **awareness** of Daugavpils to **interest** within 5 years.

(d) **Targets**

   (i)   Who is within the DMU what are their key concerns?

- Latvian State Government
- Entry into EU
- Economically productive second city
- Income and investment
- Economic growth
- Lowering employment

People of Riga currently think of Daugavpils as a backward place, with lazy people and heavy drinkers, not a place they would like to visit or reside in.

Businesses in Riga

- Profit
- Skilled workforce
- Infrastructure to support them
- Incentives, location and need for low investment costs
- Ability to distribute products efficiently

(e) **Strategies**

   (i)   Profile influencing stakeholders to change perceptions and build reputation and status, moving their mental image of Daugavpils towards our brand vision

   (ii)   Pull: demonstration of change (flowers) will create interest in the area

   (iii)   Push: promoting business experience in the Daugavpils area through non-governmental organisations and support groups and existing businesses

(f) **Positioning and messages:** to follow

4.2 **Communications strategy for attracting tourists**

(a) **Situation**

   (i)   *Internal performance*

- 4,800 international tourists visited the region in 1998. English is becoming a more prominent language.

- Little infrastructure to support tourists (poor air connections and only one hotel mentioned)

- City moving to a marketing orientation, so greater focus on audiences

- Area of outstanding and natural beauty with attraction of historical importance and cultural diversity

- High profile sports events attracting tourists to the area

- Good network of sports clubs and associations

- Lack experience in tourism

(ii) *External issues*

- Access to the Latvia and Baltic region is difficult

- Country not promoted heavily as a tourist destination shown by limited number of visitors at present

- Hours of daylight in certain seasons, temperature extremes

(b) **Towards a brand vision**

(i) Developing a competitive advantage

- Skilled workforce
- Centre for education
- Centre for culture
- Land of the Blue Lakes
- Cross roads between East and West – strategic location
- Transport infrastructure
- New Mayor
- Sustainable Competitive Advantage is: Daugavpils physical location

Vision. To provide an environment for economic prosperity and to be a recognised centre of culture within a breathtaking physical environment

(c) **Objectives**

To raise awareness of Daugavpils as an international tourists destination to 20% of tourists in the market for Eastern European Holidays in 2 years and to build this up to 40% within five years.

(d) **Targets**

Who is within the DMU and what are their key concerns?

(i) **Latvian Government tourist office**

- Funding
- Attracting tourists
- Investment in tourist infrastructure
- Relations with foreign tourist offices

(ii) **Foreign Government tourist offices**

- Clear communications from destinations
- Guarantees of safety for travellers
- Economic and political stability

(iii) **Tour operators**

- Clear communications from destinations
- Guarantees of safety for travellers
- Investment in tourist infrastructure
- Economic and political stability

(iv) **Latvian tourists**

- Easy access
- Tourist attractions
- Contrast to where they live Independent International Tourists
- Somewhere different to go, a bit of the beaten track so unspoiled

(e) **Strategies**

- Profile: influencing stakeholder to change perceptions and build reputation and status, moving their mental image of Daugavpils towards our brand vision

- Pull: Use of internet to attract independent travellers, investment in tourist infrastructure

- Push: promoting Daugavpils to tour operators and Government Tourist Organisations

(f) **Positioning and messages:** to follow

4.3 **Communications strategy for international business**

(a) **Situation**

(i) Internal performance

- Number of existing foreign companies already bringing investment and expertise to the City

- Rhodia business park providing infrastructure to foreign companies

- Plentiful skilled, cheap labour force in particular engineering and craftsmen

- Good transportation infrastructure and strategic geographic location - links to Lithuania, Russia, Belarus

(ii) External Issues

- End of Soviet era and independence since 1991 has forced industry to change - need for re-structured organisations who can operate competitively

- EU accession briefing change of focus to west / western approaches

(b) **Towards a brand vision**

Developing a competitive advantage

- Skilled workforce
- Centre for education
- Centre for culture
- Land of the Blue Lakes
- Cross roads between East and West strategic location
- Transport infrastructure
- Industrial sites
- New mayor
- Sustainable competitive advantage

Vision: To provide an environment for economic prosperity and to be a recognised centre of culture within a breathtaking physical environment

(c) **Objectives**

(i) To increase awareness of City amongst foreign businesses looking to expand internationally to 5%.

(ii) Generate 100 enquiries to City from foreign businesses (assuming 10% conversion rate) in the next 5 years.

(iii) Attract ten new foreign businesses to the City over the next five years

(iv) Ensure perception of City from existing foreign businesses remains positive over the next five years

(d) Targets

Who is within our DMU and what are their key concerns?

(i) Existing foreign businesses in City

- Plentiful skilled cheap labour
- Cheap land
- Good infrastructure and transportation
- Tax incentives
- Co-operation and attitude from City

(ii) Existing foreign businesses in Latvia

- Location/land,
- Infrastructure workforce,
- Incentives cooperation and attitude of City

(iii) Foreign businesses looking to expand internationally

- Economic and political stability,
- Exchange rate stability,
- Location/land, Workforce,
- Infrastructure,
- Distribution

(e) Strategies

(i) Profile: influencing stakeholder to change perceptions and build reputation and status, moving their mental image of Daugavpils towards our brand vision

(ii) Pull: use of Internet to attract business investment

(iii) Push: use of sources on info for foreign investors, use of intermediaries with influence

Tutor comments

4.4 The notes above provide some very helpful pointers for developing different communication strategies and, importantly, identifying sources of competitive advantage which will feature heavily in messages.

4.5 What would have been useful (with objectives), would have been a **quantified objective** for some reference to raising awareness. We have population numbers and know key stakeholders, so you could set 100% for awareness level for key stakeholders (and a lower percentage of the population as a whole) over a defined timescale.

4.6 Quantified objectives were set in the business and tourist markets but **not sensibly**. A 20% awareness of all tourists in two years (even though this is Eastern European holiday makers) seems ambitious given:

- The timescale
- The difficulty of identifying global travellers considering an Eastern European holiday
- Latvia is not established as a holiday destination

4.7 There are similar reservations about the objectives and strategy for businesses. You will not have time on the day to think this through.

4.8 **Targets for Riga.** The comment, positioning and messages was mentioned in all three headings, but there were no **notes** under these. This in fact would be central to any communication strategy.

BPP
PUBLISHING

5 STEPS 7, 8 AND 9: OTHER OPERATIONAL MARKETING PLANS

5.1 For every business strategy selected at Step 5, to fill the planning gap, you need to be prepared to present detailed operational marketing plans (objectives, strategy and control) which would implement them.

> **Tutor Tip**
>
> Again, there is no intention here to prepare full answers, but to work through the progress of segmentation positioning and tactical planning, so you can convince the examiner of your ability to implement a strategy.

A student example: strategy to attract new businesses to the City

5.2 These are outline notes only as provided by a student group. We have presented this outline with tutor comments on the right, so that you can see them in context. This is a genuinely strategic marketing plan, because the students presented the business context and options first.

Student example	Tutor comments
Attracting industries to Daugavpils **A strategic marketing plan**	
1 Current Situation • Recognition of need to move from Soviet style economic activity to Western model. Evidence of this being the appointment of visionary mayor - businessman who can relate to the needs of industry and associated benefits for the City. Business and marketing department set up. • High quality products • Skilled and educated workforce which is competitive internationally on cost and willing/able to retrain if necessary • Transport hub and it's geographical location means east/west link could be exploited. • Foreign investment - businesses and agency thus attracting other new and satellite companies • Interested stakeholders - looking to move D forward	The advice on current situation was to ensure that the summary provided insight. The danger is that the more obvious comments are made, often strengths, weaknesses, opportunities and threats but no value is added by making the connections and links between different pieces of information that allow you to make inferences and, reach conclusions from the analysis.
2 Current situation - internal (City) **Daugavpils is a City in decline. This is typified by:** • 28% unemployment • Failure to move away from hierarchical soviet management structures • Closure of the Soviet 'dinosaur' companies leading to huge and empty factories • Decaying industrial infrastructure due to assumed lack of investment. • Reliance on subsistence farming	This comment is a good example of providing insight. The comment is that Daugavpils is a City in decline. It then goes on to provide evidence that supports this statement.

Student example	Tutor comments

3   Current situation - external (Latvia)
• **Political**
  Latvia wants EU membership but has an unstable government
• **Economic**
  Developing country which has seen considerable economic growth
  Stable economy linked to IMF currency basket
• **Social**
  Highly literate
• **Technological**
  Investment will be required to compete internationally
	These comments have now slipped back into a summary that does not add value.

4 Critical success factors • Improving economic prosperity by attracting new business • Repositioning the perception of Daugavpils to be recognised as high quality and low cost • Develop a marketing orientation • Managing stakeholders relationships	The 'repositioning the perception ... as high quality and low cost' is a little misleading. Is this for businesses, residents or tourists? Is it possible to be both 'high quality' and 'low cost'? Given that our CSFs should focus our exam preparation, reference to brand building and communications might have been better.
5 Mission To improve the lives of our citizens (economic, cultural and social) by attracting new business, redeveloping the City as a commercial hub and increasing employment.	This mission is rather narrow for a City, in terms of the stakeholders covered and rather vague in terms of its purpose.
6 Vision To be recognised as the commercial capital of Latvia with a highly skilled and sought after workforce by international companies	This vision is much more focused.
7 Daugavpils objectives Currently have 70,000 working age, 20,000 unemployed (=28%) (Latvian unemployment 7 %) Therefore objective is to get 15,000 employees back to work. This will give: • 6.5 million Lats in income to employees • 2 million Lats extra income tax • 75% reduction in social service benefit	Please note we have not checked these numbers as we can all work from a different set of assumptions in this case. However the process they have gone through has been well thought through and these are credible objectives for a City.

Business Strategy for Daugavpils
8   Existing products and markets
    Wood & textiles
8.1   Existing products, new markets
    Selling bikes within Latvia and internationally
    Selling fishing nets internationally
8.2   New products, existing markets
    Sport/leisure tourism products
8.3   New products & markets
    Health facilities
    Hydroelectric power
    Clay, sandstone etc
    Using economically significant water reserves	

Student example	Tutor comments
Evaluating strategic options	The students missed out criteria for evaluating their strategic options. This results in students delivering a strategy that does not appear to have been evaluated, so the rationale for selecting strategies are not explained and pursuing this strategy is not justified.
	The use of a planning gap at this point, would have enabled the students to establish which selected strategies would fill the gap in the short, medium and long term.
Competitive strategy **12 Strategy:** **Create a thriving, synergistic business community by capitalising on:** • Location and communications links – gateway between East and West • Human capital – potential workforce - skills, costs, adaptability, Russian speaking • Natural resources - water, wood, sandstone, factory space • Alliances and relationships - EU, twinning, partners • Economic stability • Porter's diamond?	The competitive nature of their strategy has started well with an explanation and justification Interestingly the students knew they should have used Porter's diamond model, but were unsure how to. You have already undertaken this exercise and have an example.
13 Marketing objectives **To achieve City objective of 15,000 new jobs** • Currently 30 major companies/supporting network = 1,600 employees per company • Assume 10% fixed number of employees, therefore an additional 10 major companies should gain the 15,000 employment opportunities • Marketing objective is to have 10 new major companies and the supporting network in place by 2006	Again the rationale behind the setting of the marketing objectives is sound. We have not checked the numbers and we must remember that we have to make assumptions in the absence of information to guide us.

Student example	Tutor comments
14 Segmentation **141 Two main targets:** • Companies • Workforce **142 Identified by** • Conduct competency/skills audit of existing/potential labour force • Identify target industries with synergy to the City strengths eg manufacturing industries (high value add), use natural resources - wood to end product, and people strengths - craftsmanship/engineering • Identify training gaps • Implement retraining programme to support recruitment of the target companies	Given the strategy the students were concentrating on, they have the right idea here and have identified some factors that would help in segmentation eg manufacturing industries, use natural resources. However they have slipped into 'issues around' attracting businesses rather than discussing either what the **characteristics** of their segments are or, in the absence of this information, how they might segment. Business needs in particular would be a helpful way for a City to segment its markets. It could then evaluate to what extent City strengths match business needs.
Positioning Highly skilled Reality Low cost labour — High c[ ] Perception Unskilled We need to change the perception to match the reality.	This positioning map correctly identifies issues that would be of interest to a business. More positioning maps could be used or reference to other issues such as natural resources, strategic location. The use of the model is also powerful in revealing the task, the reality and the perception and therefore what needs to be done to change the perception.
16 Targeting	Another heading was missing, that of targeting. This simply requires a statement on whether or not the City would differentiate its offering to businesses or keep it undifferentiated. In other words, do they recognise differences in the businesses they want to attract and if so how are they to differentiate their marketing mix?

BPP PUBLISHING

Student example	Tutor comment
17 Marketing Mix **17.1 Product** • Thriving commercial capital with great access to East and West **17.2 Price** • Competitively priced (lowest cost but moving towards sustainable competitive pricing) **17.3 Place** • Distribution network/agents throughout EU and FSU **17.4 Promotion** • Consistently, dynamically branded, growing City promoted across Europe. Jobs marketed in appropriate languages. **17.5 People** • Highly valued, motivated, adaptable, skilful, loyal community **17.6 Process** • Fully integrated, coherent, planning and control systems **17.7 Physical Evidence** • Busy modern, industrial estate and City, retaining architectural heritage. Urban renewal	The students were working under time constraints so their marketing mix was very brief. You would need a little more detail and remember what the examiner is looking for is consistency and credibility. Would this marketing mix implement business strategy and achieve corporate objectives? There was no comment about which segment this marketing mix was for. If the students' targeting strategy was 'undifferentiated' then they would only need one marketing mix for all businesses they want to attract. If however, their targeting strategy was 'differentiated' they would need to identify the segment and develop a marketing mix for that segment.
18 Control **18.1 100,000 Lats budget required, over 5 years, for profile strategy to attract the 10 major businesses** **18.2 Timetable** • 1st 6 months research and groundwork. Tactical planning. Produce materials • 2nd 6 months exhibition/event follow-up. Travel and profile. Target recruitment of 1st business • Year 2 - 1 more business • Year 3 - 2 more • Year 4 - 2 more • Year 5 - 4 more	The controls were very tactical and failed to track performance eg businesses attracted, income generated. There was also a lack of explanation on what they were spending money. Either in 'control' or earlier on in the plan there should have been some reference to 'business implications' eg the need to change the culture of the City council to achieve a more marketing orientated approach to business planning.

Overall comment

This was a good example of the process you need to go through for each strategy selected. However, you will note that we have identified some weaknesses which could usefully be addressed.

6 ADDITIONAL MARKETING PLANNING TIPS

6.1 **Marketing objectives** are translated from the corporate objectives and might include:

Objectives for:

- Businesses
- Tourist numbers
- Business travellers
- Sports events

There is insufficient enough information to be specific about marketing objectives, but enough to provide some guide.

6.2 **Segmentation**

We are segmenting several very different markets. The following is a guide to groups you need to consider.

(a) **Business community**

Travel trade

- Tour operators focus themes
- Travel agents and retailers
- Airlines

Other industry

- Hi tech
- Manufacturing
- Oil related
- Satellite

Education

- Universities
- Business Schools

(b) Tourists

- Experienced 'independent' traveller
- 'Package tour' traveller
- Action holidays (activities laid on)
- Explorers and Adventurers
- Exotic resorts, elitist
- Special interest – sport, culture, ecotourism
- Relaxation
- Visiting friends and relatives
- Hunting, shooting, fishing
- Walkers, ramblers, forna and flora
- Sports fans - winter, summer, water

(c) Business visitors

- National/international seminars, conferences and exhibitions
- Company visits and forums

(d) Segmentation - stakeholder groups

- Residents and employees

(e) Local and National governments

- Trade
- Health
- Education
- Law enforcement

(f) Institutes (World, financial and trade partners): EU, WTO, NEFCO, VARUM

BPP PUBLISHING

6.3 **Positioning**

As we are dealing with different groups, needs and motives, we need to think about positioning in terms of these different groups. Positioning in the business market will be quite different to positioning in the tourist market.

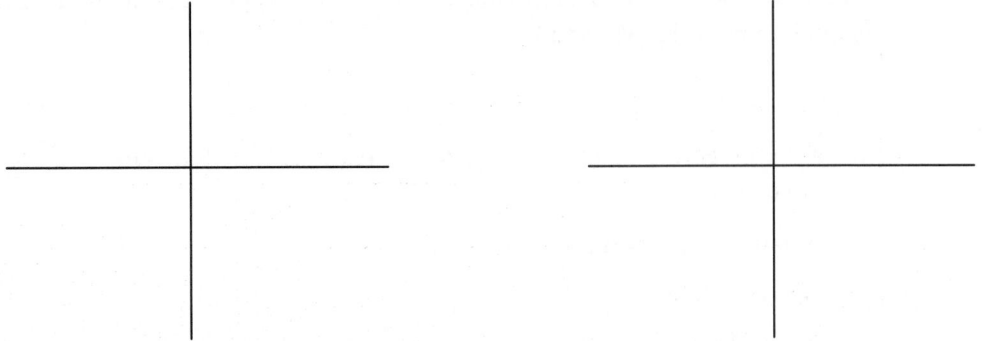

Business   **Tourists**

The issues to consider when identifying values for positioning includes

Time sensitive	vs	Insensitive
Reputation for...	vs	Unknown
Many facilities	vs	Few facilities
High quality	vs	Low quality
Cosmopolitan	vs	Insular
Purpose of visit	vs	Primary, secondary

6.4 **Possible city life cycles at present**

A city provides a wide range of facilities and services to a wide range of people and businesses and needs to ensure investment meets future, as well as current needs. The following are examples of the sort of **phases** cities have experienced.

(a) Shopping

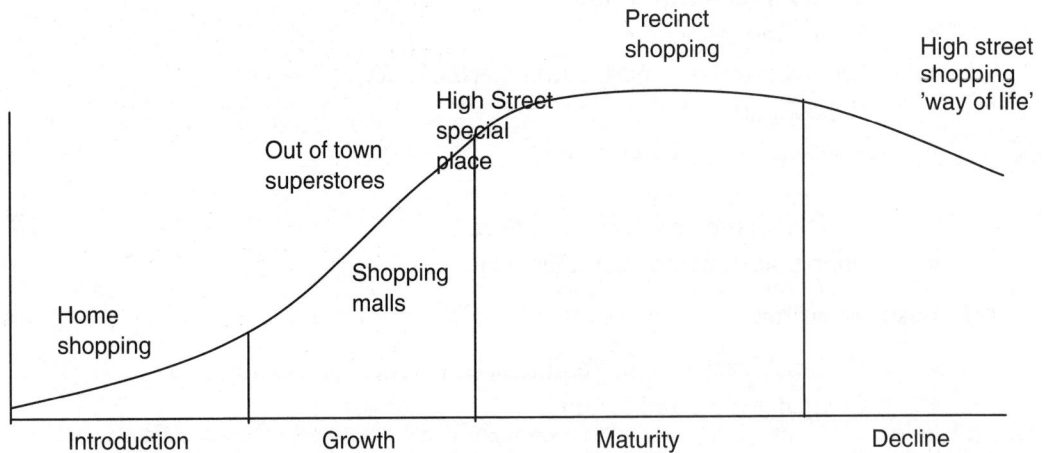

(b) **Leisure/entertainment**

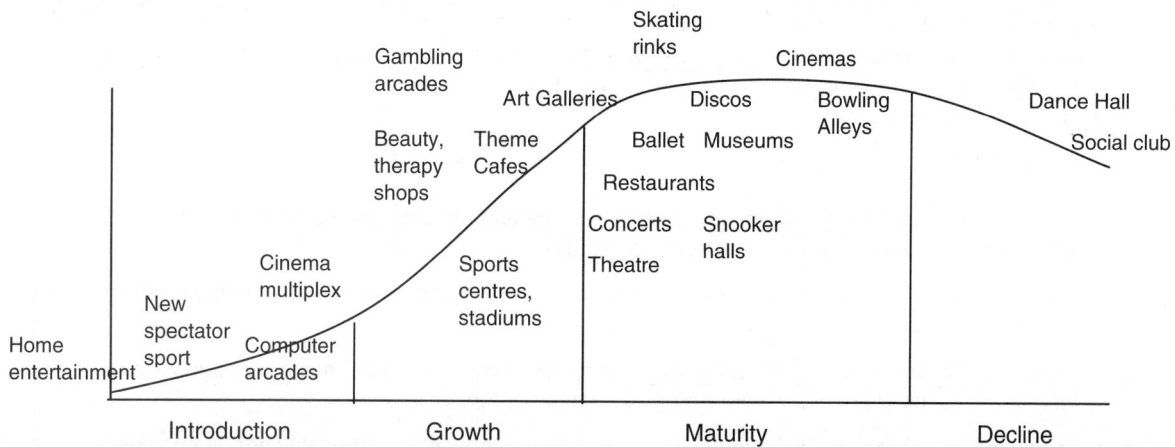

Tutor Tip

The process outlined in paragraphs 6.1 to 6.4 shows what you need to go through for each strategy selected. You cannot rely on just one outline in case the examiner focuses on another strategy for example, tourism.

It is however, a strong and easy to follow framework which will ensure you have all the key information at your fingertips. This structure is in no way intended to limit your creativity, you can and should use different models and frameworks as appropriate to the Case study.

Having considered this student example and tutor comments, take a moment to look at these tutor guidance notes which make some specific points about segmentation and positioning.

Pitfalls

6.5 There is one big potential pitfall to avoid. You prepare notes but write up a plan. In the exam, you would need to flesh this out with more comment and justification. It is not enough to simply copy out the notes.

7 STEP 10: FINAL PREPARATION AND FILE MANAGEMENT

Final preparation

7.1 The following notes represent a last minute briefing which will help you as you consolidate your notes and thoughts before moving on to tackle the exam paper as a practice.

7.2 **Remember, when tackling the questions**. Keep your work clear, strategic and justified, add budgets, timetables and comments about control and feedback

Task

7.3 Now take the time to pull your notes and materials together and plan a time when you can sit down and tackle these questions. Ideally, work in exam conditions - in the three hours. Time management is always a problem in exams, but it is particularly difficult in the Case study - one of the main reasons why well prepared students fail.

As you try out this practice paper, think again about how well organised your materials are. How could you prepare better?

Remember, it is an open book exam, so you can refer to notes and textbooks if you need to.

7.4   You are now ready to move onto the exam paper itself, but before you move on, take a few minutes to look at these final questions to help you consolidate your Case preparation skills.

Action Programme 4

Checking case preparation skills

1   It is unlikely you will have enough information to be certain about decisions: how then can you justify setting a quantified objective in a Case study?

2   Examiners are interested in what strategy you recommend, not how you decide on the strategy. True or False?

3   Visions and missions are mainly a PR exercise for the business, but the best way of generating them is to brainstorm one with your college syndicate group. True or False?

4   Evaluation criteria need to be Case specific - examiners are looking for quality not quantity of factors. True or False?

5   The best way to be prepared for the exams is to write your plans out in full. Then, all you have to do is copy them out in the exam room. True or False?

Check your answers with ours at the end of this chapter.

Action Programme review_____

1   *Reviewing the decision steps*

Step	Process
5	Corporate/business decisions

- Vision and mission
- Corporate objectives
- Strategic options
- Strategic choices

6   Business implications
     What must the business do or change if these selected strategies are to be implemented?

7   Marketing strategy

     For every selected business strategy, you need to develop:
- Marketing objectives
- Segmentation
- Positioning
- Targeting

8   Tactical planning
     Implementing the strategies needs tactical marketing plans covering the 7P's

9   Controls
     Who does what, what budget is needed and how will progress be monitored?

10   File management/appendix development
     Organising your materials in preparation for the exam

2   *Making strategic direction matter*

The problem with so many visions and missions created in exam contexts is that they end up being very bland. The student is worried about being too radical, suggesting anything which might 'offend' the examiner and so a 'one size fits all' alternative is created.

The example shown here is workmanlike, no one could disagree with it, but it is not inspirational.

'To position Daugvapils as the City of the Blue Lakes'

or

'To establish Daugvapils as the first choice for Europeans seeking recuperation and health tourism'

There is an opportunity for some creativity and uniqueness here, but remember your strategy will need to deliver or start to deliver the vision.

The mission is also fine, but perhaps a little long winded - consider this:

'We are in the business of building economic prosperity for our residents by exploiting our competitive advantage as a location for European call centre activities'.

The objectives are fine, quantified over time, but the lack of visual presentation means the examiner must think about them. They also show a reduction target in the short term, but an unemployment target thereafter - do keep your numbers consistent.

BPP PUBLISHING

Re-working the Planning Gap

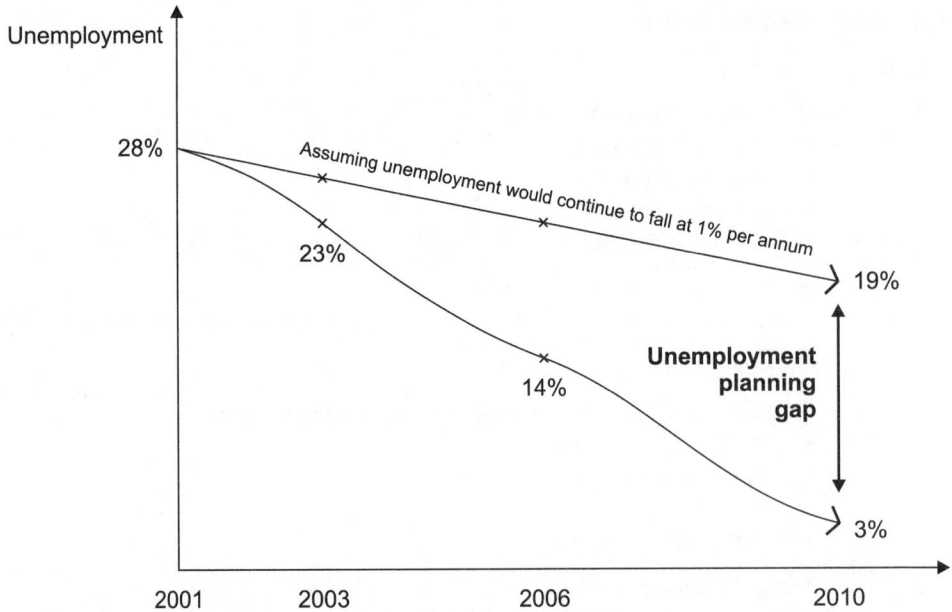

See what a difference the visual presentation makes, but working on unemployment numbers shows how you need to adapt the models.

Unusually, the target line is below the forecast, because you want to make unemployment fall faster than it is doing naturally.

If you feel uncomfortable with this, you could simply go for employment growth

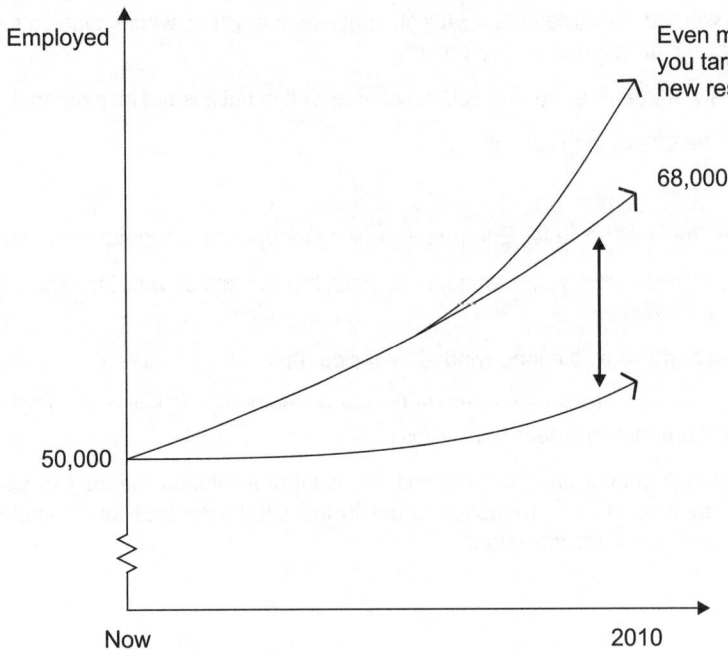

A review of the analysis

In case you aren't sure where the numbers have come from, you can calculate the following from the Case:

Population: 114,000

Working age 6% 70,000

Unemployment 28% 20,000 (28% of 70,000)

Employed 50,000 (70,000 minus 20,000)

Planning gap can be based on 20,000 unemployed or 50,000 unemployed

You can see how you could generate 'more than full employment' (usually defined as 3% unemployed) if you also attract inward migration.

A final note on objective setting for this Case.

Because the balanced scorecard was one option as a framework, you could, as this student group did, use that as a framework for setting the aligned objectives.

Using the balanced scorecard approach to develop marketing objectives

Citizen

Short term	Medium term	Long term
To create 600 new jobs by	To create 9,000 jobs by	To create 13,000 jobs by

Financial

Short term	Medium term	Long term
To increase the efficiency of local businesses by 1% by 2003 (currently, the GDP per capita for city enterprises is 1% – based on 2,000 city	To attract 20 large international enterprises to the city by 2006	To attract 25 large international enterprises to the city by 2010

Learning and growth

Short term	Medium term	Long term
To encourage international enterprises to sponsor 25 business course places		To create jobs for 4,000 engineering graduates by 2010

Internal

Short term	Medium term	Long term
To share city improvement plans with our residents	To implement a fully functioning MkIs by 2006	To improve our residents' quality of life by 2010

Tutor Note

This shows your ability to use current thinking and models, but do make sure your objectives are consistent and aligned. However, using the framework of the model shown on the next page would help communication.

The balanced scorecard provides a framework whereby you can translate strategy into operations.

BPP PUBLISHING

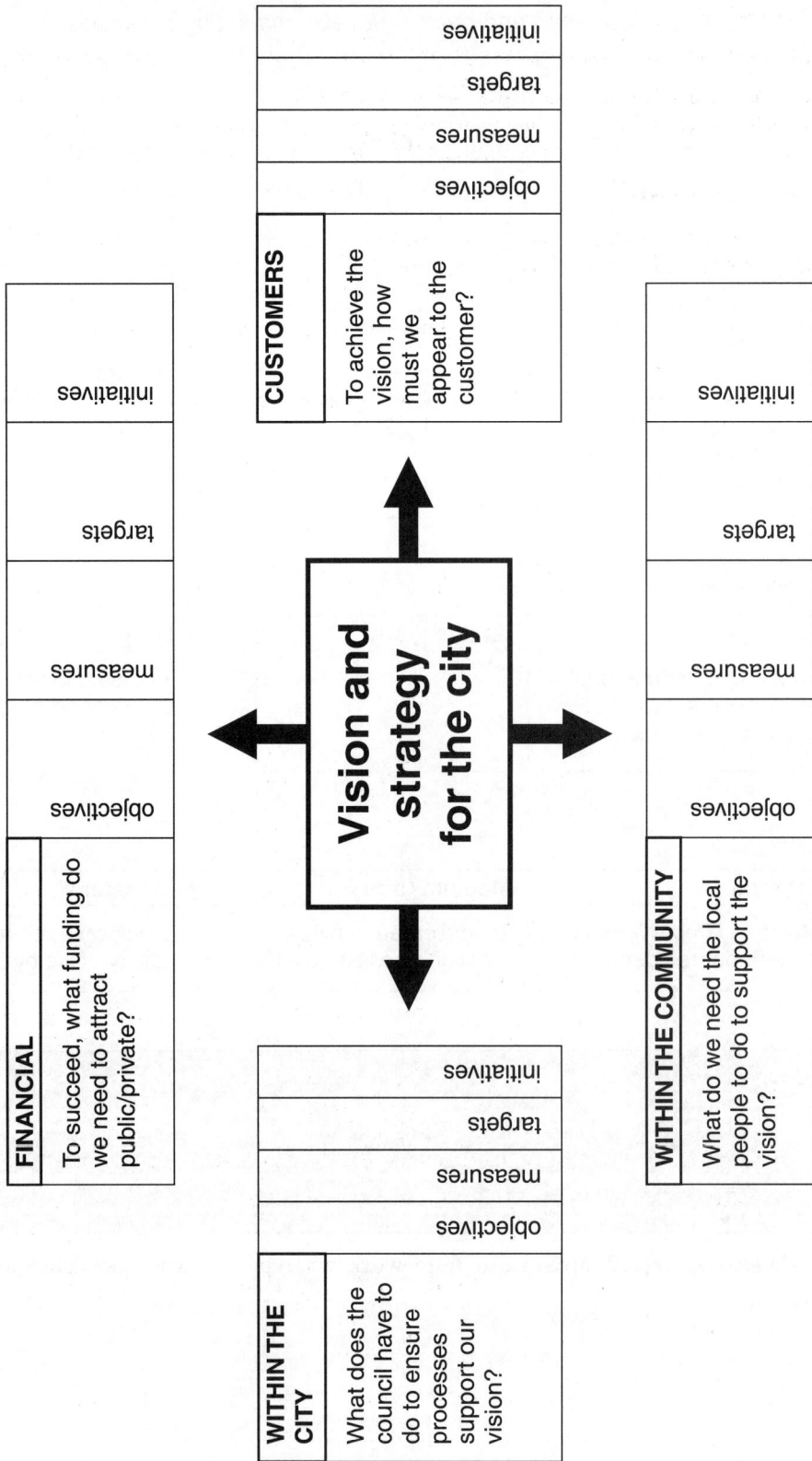

	objectives	measures	targets	initiatives
CUSTOMERS To achieve the vision, how must we appear to the customer?				

Vision and strategy for the city

	objectives	measures	targets	initiatives
FINANCIAL To succeed, what funding do we need to attract public/private?				

	objectives	measures	targets	initiatives
WITHIN THE COMMUNITY What do we need the local people to do to support the vision?				

	objectives	measures	targets	initiatives
WITHIN THE CITY What does the council have to do to ensure processes support our vision?				

3   *Action Programme*

Although this would probably be a 'pass' from the examiners, we do not find this particularly convincing.

Strategic options are limited. It is presented in a theoretical way, ie. labelled as Ansoff rather than strategic options facing the City. The examiner will accept this theoretical approach, but our view is to be commercially credible, you behave and work as you would expect a consultant to work.

An Alternative Example

Now look at this second student sample, it looks more rounded, is presented as you might to a client and shows some creativity and the holistic approach.

18

The City of Daugavpils Exam

Introduction

In this chapter you will:

- Work the City of Daugavpils case under exam conditions (allow 3 hours)

- Consider tutor comments and examiner feedback for Daugavpils

Tutor Tip

Daugavpils exam paper

In this chapter, you will have the opportunity to tackle the actual exam paper under exam conditions, no matter how much or little of the analysis you have completed. We would strongly advise you to take the time out to tackle an actual paper.

To be of value, you really need to do this under exam conditions.

- Take some time to organise your notes and files, even if it is made up of the sample material we have provided. Part of the real art of an open book case exam is managing your material in the room and only if you have actually tried this, will you be able to decide how best to organise yourself in future.

Once you have prepared yourself, make the time to tackle the paper, ideally in:

- An undisturbed environment
- A single three hour sitting

If that is **not** possible, tackle it in two or three timed sessions. Do not cheat and give yourself any longer. Managing time is one of the biggest obstacles to Case success and the more prepared you are, the harder it is to fit everything in.

By the end of this chapter, you will have:

- Seen the Daugavpils question paper and considered the additional information
- Undertaken Daugavpils as a practice exam paper
- Reviewed your own exam technique and approach
- Reviewed the examiner's comments

BPP PUBLISHING

The Chartered
Institute of Marketing

Postgraduate Diploma in Marketing

Strategic Marketing Management: Analysis & Decision

9.54:   **Strategic Marketing Management: Analysis & Decision**

Time: **14.00-17.00**

Date: **7th December, 2001**

3 Hours Duration

This paper requires you to make a practical and reasoned evaluation of the problems and opportunities you have identified from the previously circulated case material. From your analysis you are required to prepare a report in accordance with the situation below. Graphing sheets and ledger analysis paper are available from the invigilators, together with continuation sheets if required. These must be identified by your candidate number and fastened in the prescribed fashion within the back cover of your answer book for collection at the end of the examination.

Read the questions carefully and answer the actual questions as specified. Check the mark allocation to questions and allocate your time accordingly. Candidates must attempt ALL parts. Candidates should adopt a report format; those who do not will be penalised.

© The Chartered Institute of Marketing

City of Daugavpils

Examination Paper

Additional Information

The new Mayor Richard Eigims has recently been on visits to major cities in Europe. He has been on a fact-finding mission to help to improve the city's image in Europe and in Latvia. As part of this exercise, the case study writer was invited onto a prime time television broadcast in the country. Also working with the Mayor's office is Nigel Seymour-Dale, an experienced Consultant with the Voluntary Service Organisation of the United Kingdom. Nigel has worked with many multinationals in the past. He is currently helping the council with an impending visit from His Royal Highness the Prince of Wales from the UK. This visit is of vital importance to the city in its quest for greater international recognition. The United Kingdom Embassy in Latvia is arranging this visit from Prince Charles.

BPP PUBLISHING

Examination Questions

As a Marketing Consultant appointed by the Mayor of Daugavpils you have been asked to address the following:

Question 1.

Assess the current situation in Daugavpils and outline a marketing strategy for three years.

(40 marks)

Question 2.

Critically analyse the key issues involved in creating a distinctive brand image for Daugavpils. *(Note: This question does not ask for a marketing communications plan).*

(30 marks)

Question 3.

Discuss how the Internet could be used as part of a strategy to attract international investment and tourism to the region of Daugavpils.

(30 marks)
(100 marks in total)

3

2 EXAMINER'S COMMENTS

General comments

2.1 This case study was rather unusual as it was based on the marketing of a city in a country which was part of a centrally planned economy during Soviet rule. After several years of freedom, Latvia and the city itself are getting to grips with fundamental issues in marketing. The city of Daugavpils administration is beginning to understand the extent of the problems facing the city and is now working on ways of increasing income through marketing. There are various avenues available for improving the status of the city. These are discussed at length in the case. Students have to be imaginative in terms of the marketing strategies they could develop. The city faces a real problem of identity and of growth. The perception of the city in Latvia itself is poor. This was the first CIM case to be set in an Eastern European country.

The case has no personalised comments, is factual and contains no 'red herrings'. Nonetheless, as usual , there is the problem of an extensive range of detailed information. There is a need to develop clear and concise insights into the key issues involved in developing a strategy.

2.2 Given this scenario, it was good to see candidates demonstrating a good understanding of the international dimensions and the e-commerce issues. Most examiners were pleasantly pleased with the level of answers given. In general, the pass rates were good, but the poorer centres still performed badly.

2.3 Key points on student performance

(a) There was less of a tendency to produce 'group' answers, apart from three scripts from Singapore, which contained identical answers.

(b) Question 1 was reasonably well answered. However, some students still fail to justify their strategies. Porter's diamond and other models were used appropriately. Some candidates still have a problem with time and sometimes tend to use this question for 'dumping' all their ideas.

(c) Question 2 seemed to create problems. Many candidates are still 'locked' into the 'planning' mode. The question asked for issues in branding, allowing students to consider branding theory and settings. However, many students presented superficial and fragmented answers. Communication issues in marketing are still poorly taught at some centres.

(d) Question 3 was generally well handled and many students seem to have grasped the relevance of the Internet. In spite of this, it was surprising that many candidates are still unaware of its possibilities. It was even more surprising that the World Travel Organisation model described in the case was not used sensibly.

Summary on students' performance

2.4 This year's pass rate is higher than usual. It appears that the gulf between international centres and UK centres is closing. The gulf is now between good centres and bad centres. As marketing becomes complex and undergoes many changes, it is important that centres are given the right guidance. At the same time it is important that prospective candidates are urged to attend teaching sessions at the right establishment. Currently the gulf between the poor students and the good ones is getting greater, yet at the same time, the number of better (middle range) students is increasing. The new style of cases and the tutor sessions are helping with standards. Perhaps more candidates are sitting the case as the final

Diploma examination. We need to understand these changes so that momentum is not lost. The key to better success is the ability to apply marketing knowledge to the questions set. It is interesting to note that the pilot centres are still doing well. Finally, Prince Charles was sent a copy of the case and a very favourable letter was received in response.

Key issues

2.5   Looking at the case in length, the examiner identified the key issues below.

(a)   Developing marketing within a population, which does not understand this.

(b)   Improving the perception of the city.

(c)   Competitively positioning the city within Latvia and Europe/USA.

(d)   The city does not have a marketing budget.

(e)   Using its position as a transition point between East and the West.

(f0   An airport with the potential to become hub.

(g)   Developing a coherent brand image.

(h)   Selling the city/s tourism and leisure facilities.

(i)   Developing aspects of the Internet.

(j)   Exploring the possibilities of exploiting the city alliances.

(k)   Developing focused and targeted marketing for local/national/international clientele.

(l)   Current recessionary climate.

(m)   Latvia is regarded as stable and the currency is stable.

(n)   No key staff dedicated to marketing.

(o)   PR focused on the Mayor Richard Eigims.

(p)   The potential for developing medical tourism.

(q)   The potential for raising money through the EC for marketing development.

(r)   Further marketing of the sporting facilities and fishing as a sport.

(s)   Developing the balance in marketing to Latvian and Russian speaking individuals.

(t)   Allocating a reasonable (£100,000 approx) budget to marketing

(u)   There is a possibility of developing the brand through sports sponsoring.

2.6   **The answers**

According to the examiner, this case is reasonably straightforward and does not contain many surprises. It was important, therefore that the following issues were considered.

1   The application of theory.

2   The amount of international marketing theory/application that the students could apply to the case. The amount of communication theory that they could also apply.

3   The candidates needed to think strategically and not tactically.

4   The answers given had to be realistic and practical.

5   A degree of innovation and lateral thinking was rewarded.

6   It was important that the questions were answered within the given context.

7   The additional information is quite important and shows the possible impact of HRH Prince Charles's visit to Latvia, and Daugavpils itself.

Question 1: Assess the current situation in Daugavpils and outline a marketing strategy for three years.

2.7   This question requires students to use many of the strategic planning models used by marketers. Candidates will then need to consider the following.

(a)   Consider the objectives that they wish to set for the city for thee years.

(b)   Take into account a reasonable but small budget to start with.

(c)   Consider segmentation of the various areas that need marketing, such as tourism, business, sports and health.

(d)   In the longer term consider how the budget could be increased through EC grants.

(e)   A strategic vision and mission needs to be developed.

(f)   In the short term consideration needs to be given to increasing growth in tourism from national areas such as Riga.

(g)   The administration needs to consider how it can entice European nationals from the EC and also Latvians living in America.

(h)   The city offers interesting sites an tranquility at a very low cost. This needs exploiting.

(i)   How should the airport be developed?

(j)   For PR purposes, hw can Price Charles's visit be build on?

(k)   In the very short term PR and communications are going to be very important.

(l)   The city's brand image is diffuse and each entrance to the city has different symbols., This needs to be unified.

(m)   Models such as Porter, Ansoff, BCG, GEC, Shell directional and GAP could be used it the analysis of the case, modified for use in the public sector.

(n)   What are the constraints to the given strategy? How can the administration follow a market led strategy? What would be a realistic marketing budget?

(o)   How should the organisation chart be redeveloped to create and maintain an emphasis on marketing?

(p)   Developing the role for the Internet.

2.8   Points in a strategic plan.

1	Set corporate objectives
2	Identify target markets
3	Set marketing objectives
4	Develop marketing strategy and tactics
5	Organise control systems

2.9   Given the points above, the best answers showed a clear grasp of the following.

> 1   A good analysis of the current position
>
> 2   The development of a strategic plan with fully developed implementation strategies.
>
> 3   A good justification of the strategies to be adopted.

Question 2. Critically analyse the key issues involved in creating a distinctive brand image for Daugavpils.

2.10   Some key factors that should be analysed and assessed are as follows.

(a)   The city has a logo, but does not have a distinctive brand image.

(b)   The entrances to the city do not have a single identity. The statues are all disparate.

(c)   The city image has to be gradually built up with a distinctive offering and strap line.

(d)   Developing the need for branding within the city administrators and the city itself.

(e)   The importance of credible communications with the press and having a sustained public relations exercise with the national press.

(f)   Making effective utilisation of the Internet.

(g)   Developing a major poster campaign to push the brand in Riga.

(h)   Working closely with locally based companies to understand the key selling points of the city and using these in the brand offering to outside investors.

(i)   Developing the band within the context of marketing the country as a whole.

(j)   Consideration of repositioning the brand: psychological repositioning. **The people's beliefs about the city need to be changed and discussed.**

(k)   Reweighing values and understanding the key values of the city...offering history, tourism and business possibilities.

(l)   Considering budgets and constraints for communications.

These and any other relevant points should be taken into consideration.

Finally the students should consider how these factors could be seamlessly linked up with the strategies that the company has developed.

2.11   **A good answer will take into the following.**

> - Critical analyses of the key issues.
> - Links with the overall strategy.

Question 3. Discuss how the Internet could be used a part of a strategy to attract international investment and tourism to the region of Daugavpils.

2.12   This question offers a range of interesting options to students. The key issues to consider are actual Internet possibilities and the links with an international audience.

2.13   In essence, the Web will be used for publishing and database marketing. Such a site only offers information and promotional material. The site can be made interesting by having site, sound, video and pictures. It is essential that the administration has a well-developed map of Daugavpils, with an illustration of its tourist features and also its business potential.

2.14 Candidates should be able to use ideas developed in the case.

    (a) The logo for the site should be better developed.

    (b) Photographs of the key sites need to be shown.

    (c) The site should have key language options.

    (d) The site should have good hyperlinks to sister sites of the twinned cities.

    (e) There should be interactive trip planners.

    (f) The city's brochure should be put online.

    (g) The key accommodation outlets both in the city and the outskirts need to be shown.

    (h) Key routes to the city need to be shown.

    (i) For potential investors, there should be a section showing the key benefits for investing in the city.

    (j) the site should be linked to potential investors, such as banks etc.

    (k) Develop hyperlinks to key busies sites, especially where companies are looking for investment possibilities.

    (l) Hyperlinks with business sections of the Financial Times.

2.15 These and other ideas for internet development should be considered. At the same time, the team should be ensuring that international development continues through the normal diplomatic channels in each of the countries where Latvia is represented. Key to success are links within the EC sites.

2.16 As usual, coherence, strategic thinking, justification and detail featured in the answers were duly rewarded. The case is quite long and there is considerable amounts of data so that candidates had the chance to fashion a range of interesting answers. Creativity and innovation were rewarded.

19

A Final Practice Case: World Class International

Introduction

In this chapter:

- You will be able to work through a final practice case, further developing your own skills and case technique in advance of the exam.

1 INTRODUCTION: THE CASE

1.1 In this chapter you will find our third and final case study, included to provide you with the opportunity to work through the process independently and fine tune your skills and techniques.

1.2 You need to treat this very much as a dry run for the final exam, so take the time to review and reflect on the processes, how long each stage takes you and where you still have knowledge or process gaps.

Tutor Tip

You might find it helpful to create templates of tools, checklists for each stage in the process which will provide you with your own customised DIY guide to help you when the final case arrives.

1.3 You will find in this section:

- The World Class International Case
- Some guidance notes to get you started

In the next chapter, you will find examiner's comments and detailed student answers.

Action Programme 1

Start by reading the World Class International case as far as the end of the narrative and turn the pages to see what is included in the Appendix. You will see this is quite a different sector – service based and essentially a consumer market.

BPP PUBLISHING

The Chartered
Institute of Marketing

Case Study
June 2002

Strategic Marketing Management: Analysis & Decision

World Class International (WCI)

© The Chartered Institute of Marketing

Case Study – June 2002

Strategic Marketing Management: Analysis & Decision

Important Notes

The examiners will be marking your scripts on the basis of questions put to you in the examination room. Candidates are advised to pay particular attention to the *mark allocation on the examination paper and budget their time accordingly.*

Your role is outlined in the candidate's brief and you will be required to recommend clear courses of action.

You WILL NOT be awarded marks merely for analysis. This should have been undertaken before the examination day in preparation for meeting the tasks which will be specified in the examination paper.

Candidates are advised not to waste valuable time collecting unnecessary data. The cases are based upon real world situations. No useful purpose will therefore be served by contacting companies in this industry and candidates are *strictly instructed not to do so* as it would simply cause unnecessary confusion.

As in real life, anomalies will be found in this Case situation. Please simply state your assumptions where necessary when answering questions. The CIM is not in a position to answer queries on Case data. Candidates are tested on their overall understanding of the Case and its key issues, not on minor details. There are no catch questions or hidden agendas.

Additional information will be introduced in the examination paper itself which candidates must take into account when answering the questions set.

Acquaint yourself thoroughly with the Case Study and be prepared to follow closely the instructions given to you on the examination day. To answer examination questions effectively candidates must adopt a report format.

The copying of pre-prepared "group" answers written by consultants/tutors is strictly forbidden and will be penalised by failure. The questions will demand analysis in the examination itself and individually composed answers are required to pass.

Candidate's Brief

You have been appointed as a Marketing Consultant to the Board of World Class International (WCI). WCI has recently been formed as a result of the merger of two companies. The company provides a range of services to many sectors of industry. The company has grown rapidly within the highly competitive sector of IT Services. This sector is fragmented and complicated, but growth rates have been impressive. The company has offices in three different locations around the world. It is now seeking to consolidate its position in the world market and grow into a substantial company. At the same time it needs to fully understand and grasp the new marketing opportunities offered by the merger, taking into account the technological shifts within e-commerce. The company is concerned about how to effectively communicate to the marketplace and develop the European market. Your name is Patrick Pearson and you have previously worked in the machine tool industry on business-to-business marketing. You were considered to be ideal for the current position. Based on an initial request, you have prepared the following report on the state of the company and the recent trends in the sector. At a later meeting, scheduled for 14th June 2002, you will be asked to elaborate on this report to the Board of Directors who will pose specific questions to you based on your current findings.

Important Notice

This case material is based on an actual organisation and existing conditions.

Candidates are strictly instructed NOT TO CONTACT World Class International (WCI) or any other companies in the industry. Additional information will be provided at the time of the examination. Further copies may be obtained from The Chartered Institute of Marketing, Moor Hall, Cookham, Maidenhead, Berkshire, SL6 9QH, UK.

World Class International (WCI)

Introduction

World Class International began its life in the UK in 1986 as JIT (Just-in-Time) Technology Ltd. Paul Collins, who had learnt lean manufacturing techniques at IBM and A. T. Kearney Inc., launched the company. Initially turnover was around £50,000, gained largely from consultancy fees. In 1989, Alistair J. Duncan, also from IBM, joined the company and became a 50% Equity Partner, forming WCI. As a result, the consulting services were broadened to cover manufacturing and service-based businesses. The main focus of the company's offering was operations improvement, utilising a range of techniques that integrated process, people and methodology. By 1989 revenue had risen to £1 million. The company continued to grow, reaching a turnover of £2.5 million by 1995. In 1998, David Cheesman, who had joined WCI in 1995, was made a Director and Equity Holder. From 1995 to 1999, WCI revenues grew to £11 million. Part of this growth was due to the company redirecting its energies from being technology led to being sales led, focused on three market areas (Life Sciences, TMT and Finance). The client list was by now quite prestigious, with 70% of business coming from retained clients. During this period an office was opened in Seattle, USA, initially to service Microsoft (WCI – USA). The office was later relocated to Atlanta, Georgia, USA, to service pharmaceutical and medical device clients. In 1997, an office was opened in Budapest, Hungary, to service Eastern European countries.

In 1998, the company adopted a policy of hiring only the best people, and to retain them through a combination of high remuneration, on the basis of results, and an open family-style culture. This policy resulted in the slogan 'People that make a difference' as a key marketing message. At this time WCI developed the ability to define IT strategies and solutions for its clients. The implementation of these strategies and solutions was subcontracted to another IT consulting firm. The company could see that it was giving the majority of its consulting revenues to competitive consulting firms. At the same time there were profound changes taking place in WCI's core business, based on supply chain management, customer relationship management and customer value management. These dramatic changes were driven by the emerging Internet-based technologies. The company needed to become stronger in the e-business arena, because otherwise it would be pushed out of the market.

In 2000, as a result of this necessity, 2GL Computing Services merged with WCI as a wholly-owned subsidiary of WCI Holdings Ltd., but operated as WCI Technologies Ltd. This merger meant that WCI could now become a 'full business solutions design and implementation provider', offering customer service, systems design and integration, customer value management, and post-implementation managed business services. The company structure is shown in Figure 1.

2

BPP PUBLISHING

Company Structure

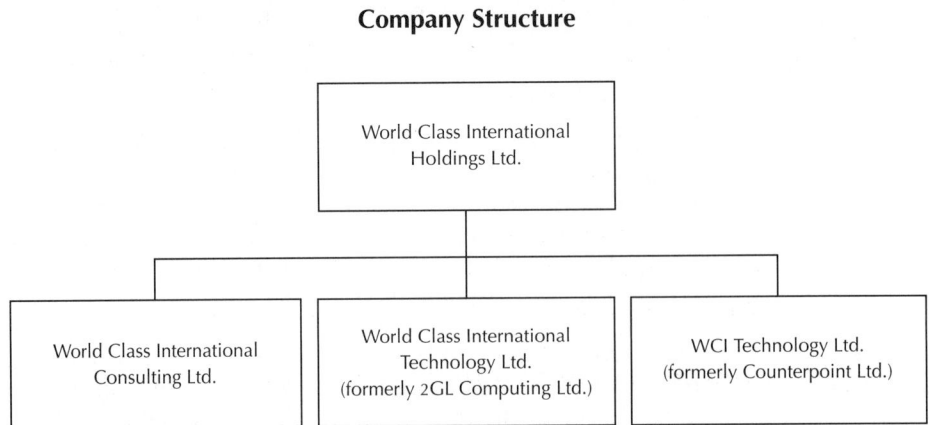

Figure 1.

There are three legal operating entities, managed within two distinct divisions of WCI, shown in Figure 2. These operate cohesively and provide a seamless, comprehensive service to clients. General services such as finance, marketing, communications, HR and sales, are provided centrally to the two key operating units.

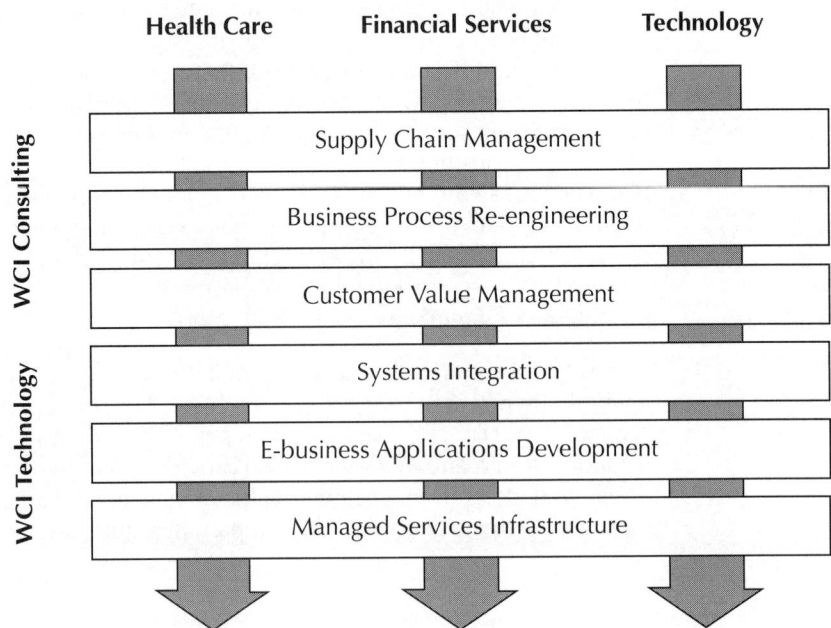

Figure 2.

The markets and main aspects of each of the key businesses are now detailed.

WCI Technology (formerly 2GL Computing Ltd. prior to the merger with WCI).

This company was formed in 1988 (by Simon Derrick and Carol Evans) in Southampton, as an accounting and networking solutions house for SME companies, based on IBM and Compaq platforms. Larger companies, such as Datacard and Pirelli, used the company as a supplier of a wide range of branded PC hardware, software and peripherals, as well as consulting services. The company expanded its sales force during the 1990s and also developed Novell networking expertise. It soon became a dominant player in the education market in the South of England by providing administrative schools networks. This was extended to curriculum development through a product called Classlink. The intellectual property rights for this software were eventually sold to Viglen PLC, who continue to develop and refine this award-winning school software.

In 1991, 2GL Health Care was formed as a subsidiary, in order to enable staff from former health authorities to continue their relationship with the National Health Service (NHS) by providing IT infrastructure and tailored software solutions. Initially Ashton Tate products were used, but then a strong relationship developed with Microsoft. In 2000, the company won a multi-million pound NHS Direct infrastructure and managed service contract as a partner of AXA Assistance.

By 1992, 2GL's corporate business to large enterprises needed its own focus and so it started to strengthen relationships with major IT companies. These relationships are shown in Figure 3.

2GL Business Relationships

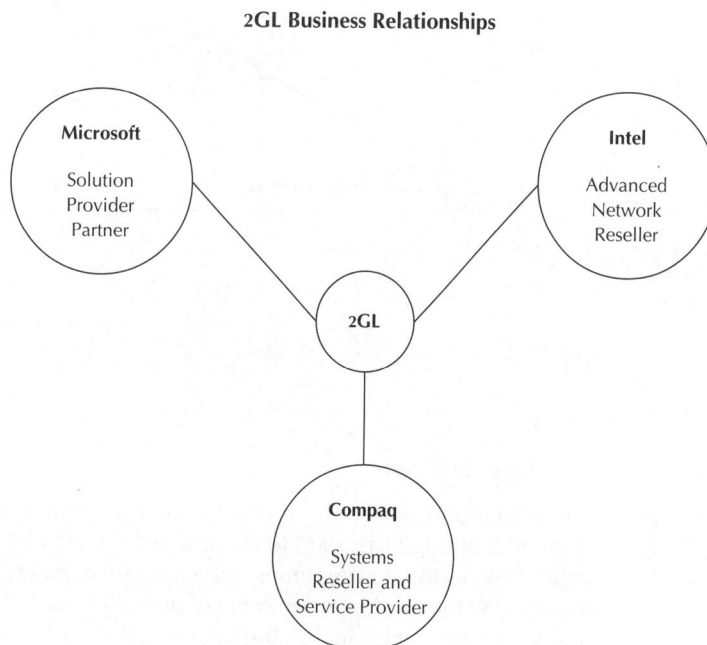

Figure 3.

These relationships enabled the company to achieve national credibility as a network infrastructure supplier and a support partner for some key companies such as Cisco Systems and Winterthur Life, a part of Credit Suisse First Boston. The Accounting Solutions Unit was sold in 1996 and a training division established. The company grew rapidly in 1997, and in 1998 the UK team was strengthened by the appointment of Andrew Gardner, the UK Managing Director of Seimens Computer Services, as Managing Director of 2GL. Dave Seddon then joined and became Deputy Managing Director in 1999. Simon Derrick continued as Chairman, with Carol Evans leading the consulting business. In 2000, the company acquired Counterpoint Consulting in Bristol, in order to strengthen its Systems Integration consulting arm and e-business Application Development.

Strategic analysis showed that in order to grow and develop its capabilities in Information Systems, as a result of the growth of the Internet, the company would need a suitable business partner. The merger with WCI was concluded in July 2000. The current company structure and business summary is given in Appendix 1.

World Class International Technology Ltd. Highlights

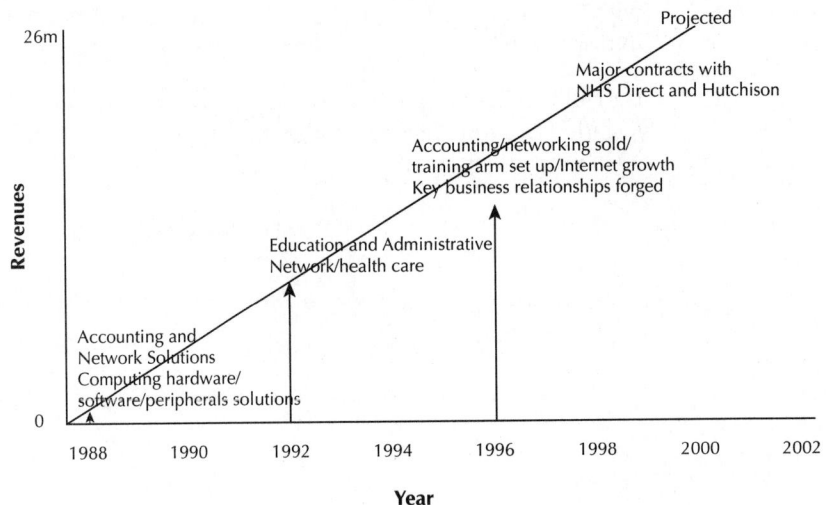

Figure 4.

Industry Sectors

The WCI group essentially serves the broad sector of management consulting. Five large accounting firms tend to dominate the world management consulting market. In addition to these companies, are companies that specialise along particular industry sectors, independent consultants and small firms. With the relentless march of information technology across all industry sectors, consulting firms are responding by incorporating IT capabilities into their skill set and by establishing partnerships with IT firms. Mergers and strategic alliances are also common. Trends show that IT firms have not only the ability to provide management consulting, but also the ability to implement these strategies.

5

Key Players

The key players in this sector come from various backgrounds, such as accounting, marketing or human resource management. The 'Big Five' accounting companies have been the largest players in the field so far. However, owing to legislation and controversy surrounding conflicts of interest when both auditing and consulting for the same firm, they have begun to either spin-off the consultancy divisions, or form joint ventures with IT companies (see Figure 5.). The traditional consulting firms generally offer strategic consulting at the top level in large organisations. These companies are shown in Figure 5. Boutique firms supply tailored solutions to sector-specific firms. Approximately 45% of all consultants are independent.

Management Consultancy/IT Services Evolution

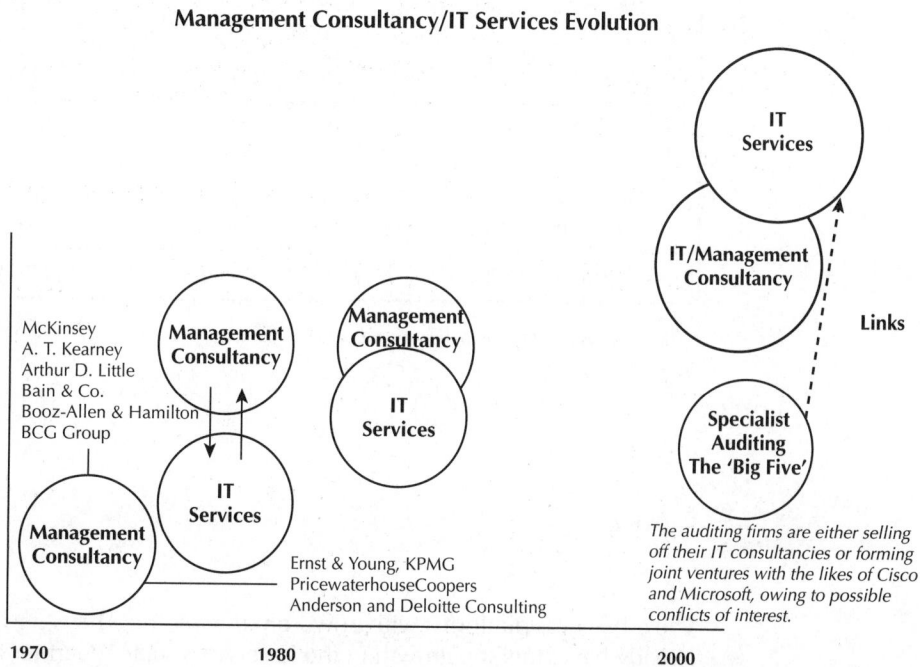

Figure 5.

It is likely that the worldwide management consultancy market will continue to grow, reaching over $110 billion by 2002. Between 1992 and 1996 the compound annual growth for strategy consulting was 18%, for information technology 16%, operations management saw 14% growth and human resources consulting grew by 10% (Kennedy Research Group). The IT sector is expected to outperform all sectors, having reached a 70% share of consulting.

IT Services Industry

The IT industry has been through a turbulent period over the last two years, with many stocks reaching record highs before plummeting to record lows as the predicted growth in e-business failed to materialise. However, as Figure 6. shows, the signs remain very good for growth in the business-to-business sector.

Warburg E-index – May 2000

E-index	UK	France	Spain	Germany	Sweden	US*
E-commerce revenue ($ billion)	3.6	2.38	0.58	4.78	0.72	26.3
% of Western e-commerce	19.96	13.2	3.22	26.53	3.99	146.0
% of Western Europe population	15.49	15.44	10.41	21.55	2.31	37.72
E-commerce revenues as % of GDP	1.26	0.83	0.49	1.13	1.51	1.43
B2B revenue ($ billion)	3.08	2.07	0.5	4.16	0.63	21.45
B2C revenue	0.52	0.31	0.08	0.62	0.09	4.85
M-commerce revenue	0.034	0.0311	0.022	0.036	0.008	0.157
% of Western Europe m-commerce	14.33	13.18	9.31	15.44	3.26	66.0
% of Western Europe B2B	0.0105	0.0097	0.0068	0.0113	0.0024	0.324

* These figures are relative to the whole European market.

Source: Financial Times

Figure 6.

The e-business platforms will grow from the existing IT systems that companies already have, fuelling growth in the IT services sector. Gartner Dataquest predicts that the worldwide IT services market is likely to reach US$603 billion by the end of 2002, growing by 8.9 per cent in 2001. As a result, the e-business consulting market is expected to grow from US$20 billion to US$80 billion by 2003. This growth is attracting interest from both consulting and traditional IT companies, showing the increasing convergence in these two areas (Figure 5.).

As a result of its merger, WCI has now truly become a 'one-stop shop' for potential clients. It offers a complete solution – from business strategy to network management and all the pieces in-between, ensuring that the Internet can become an effective and efficient business tool for companies. This makes WCI unique compared to many other organisations that may be either consultancy oriented or IT oriented. WCI can offer Internet web design, web site hosting, e-strategy, business process re-engineering, software design, supply chain management and a host of other services. WCI's unique selling proposition is Managed Services, encompassing all the key needs of a client. WCI's major competitors are A. T. Kearney, CTP, CGEY and IBM (see Appendix 5. for a list of the key competitors).

7

IT services incorporate Maintenance and Support, Development and Integration (of systems) and Strategic Planning. Most IT service companies operate in all three areas. The profitability of projects tends to increase when strategic planning is incorporated into the systems. The profit margins tend to be around 35-50% for strategic planning and 10-20% for hardware installation and operation. However, the demand for basic IT services is far greater than strategic services.

The worldwide IT services sector is highly fragmented, with few companies other than the 'Big Five' possessing important market shares. The largest concentration of IT service firms (49.8%) have between 2 and 4 employees and a turnover of less than $200,000. Medium-sized firms, with more than 25 employees, have the largest proportion of IT services work in the global marketplace. Figure 7. illustrates the key groupings on a global scale.

IT Service Firms Groupings

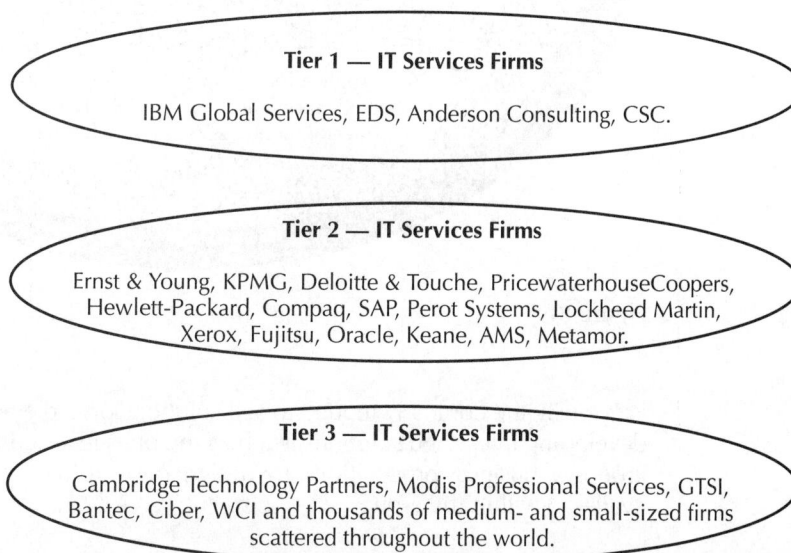

Tier 1 — IT Services Firms

IBM Global Services, EDS, Anderson Consulting, CSC.

Tier 2 — IT Services Firms

Ernst & Young, KPMG, Deloitte & Touche, PricewaterhouseCoopers, Hewlett-Packard, Compaq, SAP, Perot Systems, Lockheed Martin, Xerox, Fujitsu, Oracle, Keane, AMS, Metamor.

Tier 3 — IT Services Firms

Cambridge Technology Partners, Modis Professional Services, GTSI, Bantec, Ciber, WCI and thousands of medium- and small-sized firms scattered throughout the world.

Source: Deutsche Banc, Alex Brown, IT Services Sourcebook, 1st July, 1999

Figure 7.

Appendix 5. gives a breakdown of the key companies and their sizes.

WCI's Services

WCI offers a range of services to its clients. It combines expertise in process design, Internet technology and managed service capabilities. Businesses can therefore benefit from 'Building Better Businesses' on the web. The company feels that this is not about communications, but about trading more profitably using web technologies. The key areas of stock management, cost reduction and better service for customers are where WCI can enable businesses to be more successful in their served markets. WCI's key offerings are illustrated in Figure 8.

Key Product Groupings for WCI

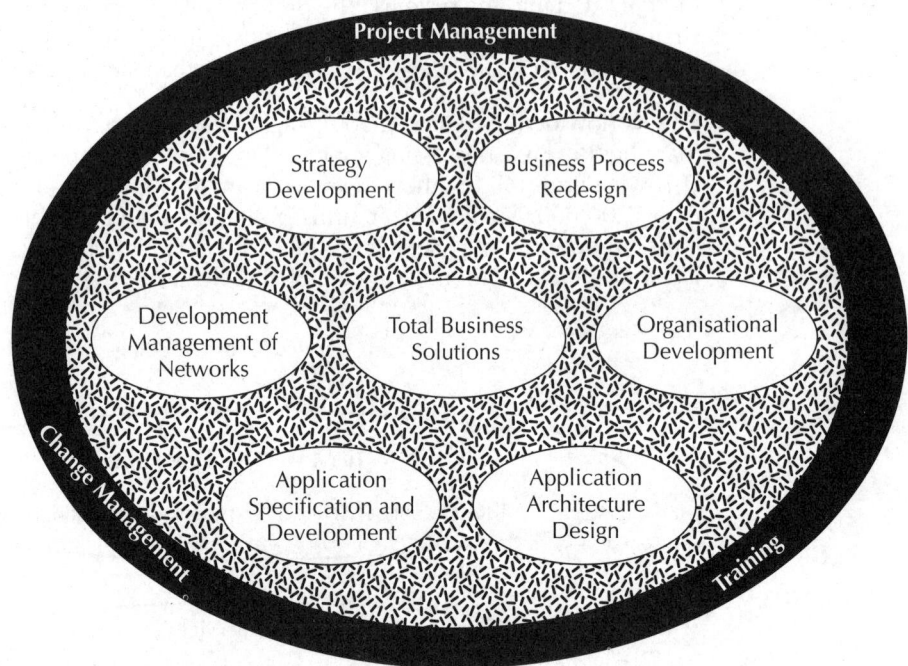

Figure 8.

Previously the company tended to sell solutions on a piecemeal basis, rather than developing integrated solutions, such as the ones featured in Figure 8. These groups of business propositions are designed to exploit the joint competencies available within the group.

E-business Strategy

This aspect of the company's offering concentrates on assisting companies to re-evaluate their business strategies in the web age. It enables them to look at new channels to market and the impact on their businesses through leveraging new technology. This type of strategic development focus may lead to:

- Integrating applications.
- Web-enabled legacy systems.
- Web-enabled processes that support the supply chain.
- Developing new routes to market and augmenting current ones.

Market growth in this area is high and the company has a low market share.

9

Selling Systems

WCI's combined experience in global supply chains, IT and Internet technology, enables the promise of e-commerce to be achieved. This experience allows products to be ordered online and delivered efficiently and speedily, utilising integrated processes. E-CRM (Customer Relationship Management) utilisation allows direct contact with customers and an understanding of their needs. WCI has a low market share in a high growth area.

Internal Systems

WCI offers waste-free, high-performance processes, which incorporate Internet technology – linking IT platforms and legacy systems together in order to ensure that integration is achieved throughout a business. The company has a good market share in a low growth area.

Purchasing

The company offers integration of all parts of the supply chain, in order to provide web-enabled advanced planning systems – working with manufacturing processes and suppliers. This helps to manage, and get closer, to real demand for products and services. In this high growth area the company has a low market share.

Lean Compliance

WCI Consulting derives 33% of its revenue from the Life Sciences sector, (pharmaceutical and medical device companies) offering lean compliance. Within the pharmaceutical sector, lean compliance is very important. The main area includes process optimisation for compulsory reporting (as required by regulatory bodies such as the Food and Drug Administration in the USA), for the drug approval process and supply chain management. WCI currently enjoys a unique niche hold in the areas of drug safety, coding and regulatory processes within the top 20 companies in the pharmaceutical industry. Recently a preferred partnership was formed with a US software company. This company's products, combined with WCI's operational and technology experience, can provide a complete solution for Internet linked processes between regulatory authorities, pharmaceutical companies and medical establishments (see Appendix 2. for details on the pharmaceutical industry). This is a high growth area and the company's share of the market is good.

A key growth sector within the pharmaceutical industry is bioinformatics, which is essentially cross-disciplinary and links all the strands of computing and molecular biology together, as shown in Figure 9. A key driver for this is the huge growth in genome data in the Life Sciences, both in the public and private sectors. At the same time, there is an increasing adoption of genomic strategies in drug target discovery; linking genomics and computational approaches down the drug discovery pipeline. However, accurate information is needed along supply chains before any new products go into manufacture. It is estimated that currently it costs about $500 million to bring a drug to market. This takes about 6-8 years, with the final phases taking 4-5 years. About 80% of drugs fail to get through clinical trials. These facts demonstrate the need for complex and sophisticated information systems within the biotechnology and pharmaceutical sectors.

10

Bioinformatics

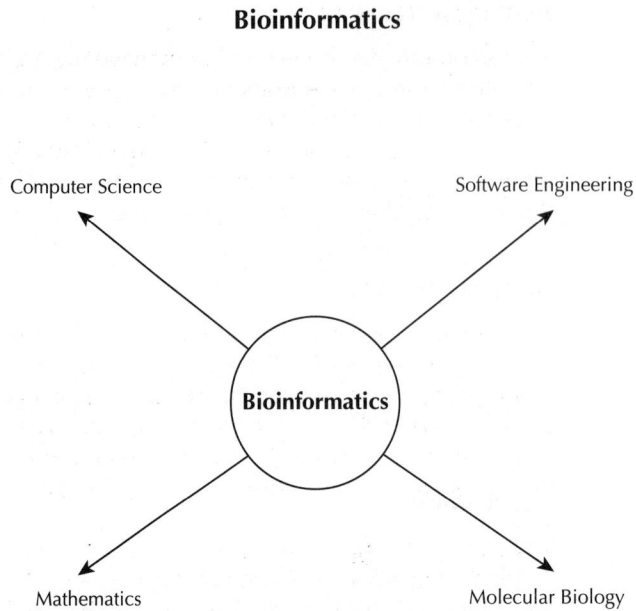

Figure 9.

E-software

This service offering includes a full range of software development services to create a digital business. Solutions often require a complex design, in order to incorporate issues of security, non-repudiation, scalability and application integration. This is a high growth area and the company's market share is low.

Infrastructure

The company offers a range of consulting expertise in networking systems infrastructure, combined with the ability to procure systems, install the software and add to a client's·new or existing networks. In order to improve implementation of infrastructures WCI provides both support and training. A 24-hour, 7-day support service and accredited training facilities are also available. This is a low growth area with the company taking a good share of the market.

Managed Services

This range of services offers solutions tailored to meet a customer's individual needs. These can vary from isolated services to complete IT operations, enabling clients to concentrate on their core business. The lease/purchase of hardware is also part of this service. This is a high growth market area, with the company taking a reasonable slice of the market. WCI currently manages IT resources for organisations such as the NHS, Volvo, W. H. Smith and Hutchison 3G.

Business Process Outsourcing

These are solutions developed to manage the non-core processes for clients. WCI can offer cost effectiveness, due to economies of scale and the increased process expertise on offer. Examples of process expertise offered are supply chain management, pharmaceutical drug safety and clinical trials. Again, this is a high growth area and the company's share is also growing rapidly (see Appendix 2. for details in the UK).

Industry Trends

The IT services industry continues to grow in size, as more corporations consider continual upgrades of their various complex systems, and also outsourcing such activities to companies such as WCI. Owing to technology and market pressures, companies have been forced to reinvent themselves in order to reach new markets and customers, whilst still retaining their old ones. According to Gartner Dataquest, the following trends are discernible:

- There is likely to be a growth in outsourcing the IT provision. The IT utility provisions may have reached maturity, and outsourcing services are likely to become an integral part of a service provider's portfolio.

- Companies are likely to look for more added value than just infrastructure and managed IT services.

- Globalisation and the advent of the Euro are powerful economic forces on the world economy. The IT services value chain has gone global, as companies go global and grapple with IT/Management issues.

- A clearer understanding of the impact of IT services on marketing measures. There is a growing need to develop marketing metrics linked to performance (see Appendix 2. for data on growth).

In addition to this, specific areas of application are also growing. One area is systems that provide market intelligence on a global basis. As companies become confident of their IT infrastructures on a global basis, they will be increasingly looking to access systems that can provide them with business intelligence. As technology develops further, business intelligence gathering will become a complex issue for most companies. Increasingly access to information is possible through hard-wired systems as well as wireless protocols. Mobile technology will have to be integrated within these intelligence-gathering systems.

Another important area of growth is Knowledge Management (KM). It is predicted that by 2005 services for KM will be around $12.6 billion (IDC report). Knowledge Management services include consulting, implementation, operation (outsourcing), maintenance and training. Increasingly corporations are beginning to realise that implementing a KM system is not merely a technical undertaking, it requires management endorsement and employee acceptance and buy-in. Increasingly systems are about people, processes and technology. Implementation of a system needs to be tailored to the specific needs of an organisation. In the 21st Century, organisations increasingly need to:

- Build knowledge capital and invest in efforts that create long-term competitive advantage, rather than short-term Return On Investment (ROI).

12

- Link knowledge areas by developing conceptual and transactional areas of internally contained knowledge, by connecting planning, research, marketing, e-business and customer relationship.

- Make sound business decisions based on knowledge.

An IT knowledge repository has many benefits, as shown in Figure 10.

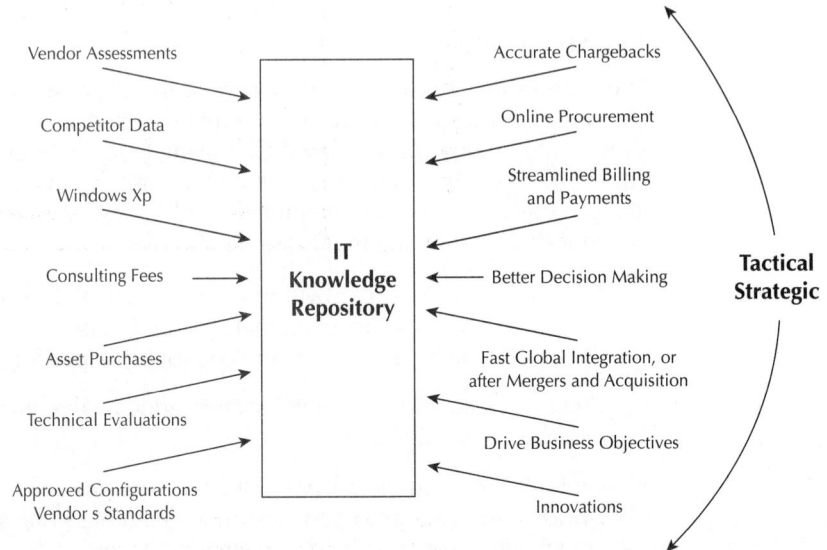

Figure 10.

This type of model is suitable for most businesses, especially those in the telecommunications and financial services markets. In general, linking company data to market information can lead to greater insights and better planning. Better planning can lead to better relationships with vendors and customers and help minimise surprises.

Digital Loyalty Networks – E-differentiated Supply Chain and Customer Management

In a survey undertaken by Deloitte Hoskins, 850 manufacturing executives in 35 countries were interviewed across Asia-Pacific, Europe, North America, Latin America and South Africa. They found that manufacturers who successfully link their Supply Chain Management (SCM) and Customer Relationship Management (CRM), to create loyalty networks, can generate significant competitive advantages.

Successful companies:

a.   Collaborate extensively with their supply chain partners (suppliers, distributors/retailers, and customers) and internally.

b.   Measure and exceed their goals for customer loyalty, and therefore excel at CRM, performing far better than most other companies analysed (see Figure 11.).

13

Digital Loyalty Network Quadrant

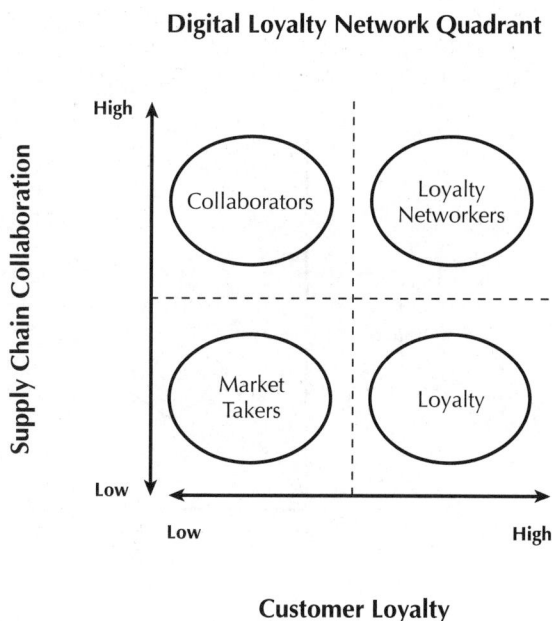

Figure 11.

The results were quite profound, and showed that Loyalty Networkers (companies that leverage their collaborative supply chains with a deep understanding of their loyal customers) were 54% more profitable than Market Takers (companies that perform below average on both supply chain collaboration and customer loyalty). Loyalty Networkers are also 19% more profitable than Loyalists (companies that have excelled in building customer loyalty but are not yet collaborating effectively with supply chain partners). The Internet technologies for supply chain management have now reached a stage where companies can create digital loyalty networks to profitably meet different customer needs with the appropriate supply chain capabilities. Businesses can therefore build e-collaboration, through improved supply chain collaboration across a network of suppliers and customers, and also build loyalty by differentiating (e-differentiation) the way they create value for every customer and segment.

The key changes in the coming years will be the challenge of integrating digital wireless communications into the e-business model. Figures 12. and 13. illustrate the rapidity with which mobile commerce is expected to grow. Lead times are increasingly shorter. Companies therefore will need effective IT services in the future, and providers that can incorporate all the new technologies seamlessly.

Current Diffusion Times

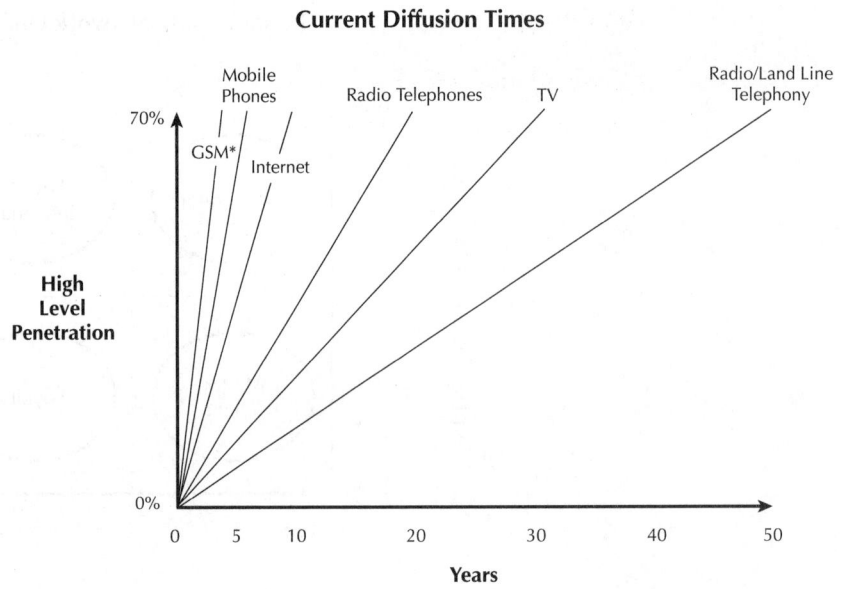

*GSM (Global System for Mobile Communications)

Figure 12.

Predicted Growth of M-commerce in Western Europe

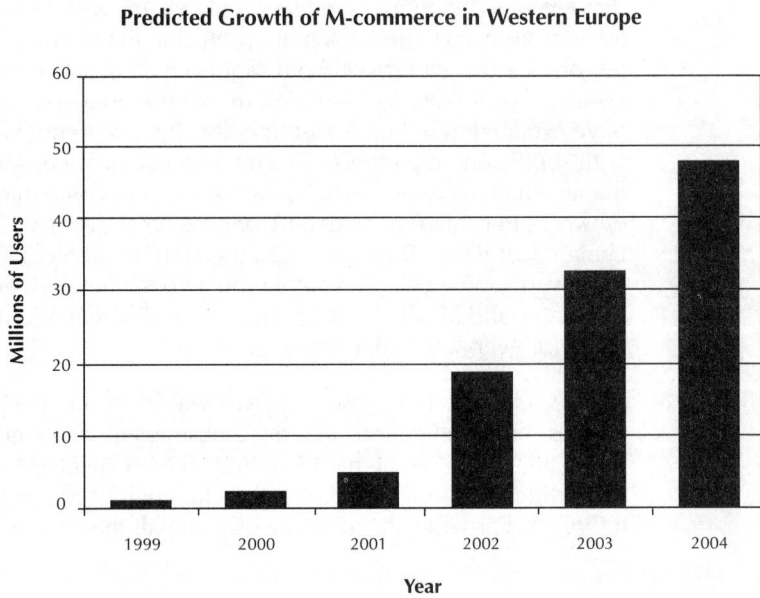

Figure 13.

Further analysis of the IT services sector is presented in Appendix 3.

Marketing Issues

The Served Market

The company operates within different industry sectors. These are:

a. Industrial

    The focus in this area is on web-enabled processes, re-engineering and managed services. The company's skills in world-class manufacturing are essential in this sector. The focus is now on global operators in manufacturing, rather than smaller companies.

b. FMCG

    This area of the market is not fully exploited by WCI. The company has skills in applying software development to planning and controlling operations in the branded food/drink market. WCI's expertise in supply chain management and web/digital strategies is quite important for companies operating in this sector.

c. Technology, Media and Telecoms (TMT) (see Appendix 1.)

    This area is currently an important revenue earner for the company, and works effectively by leveraging existing relationships with technology equipment suppliers for better client support in supply chain management.

d. Financial Services

    Managing a complex range of systems in the financial services area is quite a problem for most companies in this sector. This is especially so given the long history of the sector and the different legacy systems that exist. The sector is also becoming more interested in Customer Relationship Management. WCI currently has only a small number of clients in this area.

Rate of Return

The rate of return for the services varies according to the following Price/Earnings (P/E) ratios. This is shown below:

Business Process Outsourcing	40
Managed Services	25
Project Consulting (Technology and Business)	20
Hardware Resale	8

Stock market analysis shows that the P/E ratios of some companies involved in outsourcing are much higher than others. Table 1. illustrates this.

16

Price/Earnings Ratio

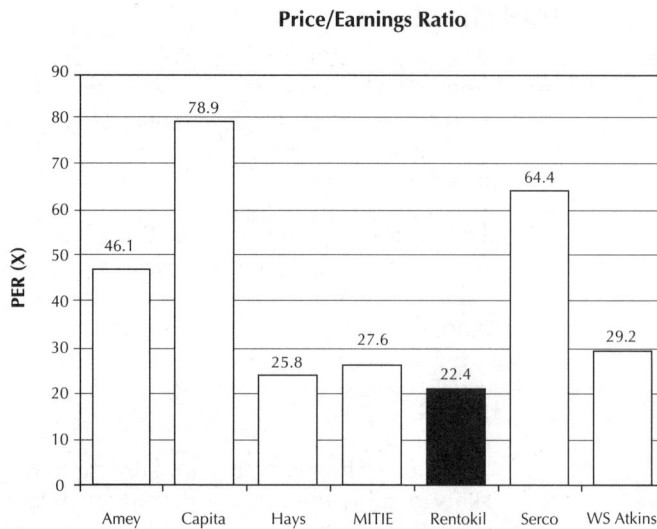

Source: Financial Times, 21st January, 2002
Source: Out of Report: HgCapital, Alumni Club, Business Services Sector Watch, January, 2002

Table 1.

	Share Price (p)	Market Value (£ Million)
AMEY	406	933
Capita	436	3,148
Hays	201	3,644
MITIE	147.5	457
Rentokil	265	5,393
Serco	386.5	1,509
WS Atkins	635	621

Source: Financial Times, 21st January, 2002
Source: Out of Report: HgCapital, Alumni Club, Business Services Sector Watch, January, 2002

Table 2.

WCI has found that it earns more regular revenues from outsourcing, as the contracts are long term and they help generate regular income. Approximately 56% of the FTSE have embraced the outsourcing of internal services. Companies outsource Business Processes (BPO) and Information and Communications Technology (ICT). The current level of outsourcing within the FTSE 100 is around £20 billion. ICT outsourcing is increasing. Outsourcing is changing from being merely IT Service to create a cost effective situation, to a strategic tool within the corporate setting. Companies have found that strategic outsourcing impacts positively on share value. In general, companies show a 5.3% premium in share value compared to the sector average. For further details on BPO and ICT in the UK see Appendix 2. The general world growth for IT services is also shown in Appendix 2., as are details of growth in Europe, the Middle East and Africa (EMEA).

17

Price

The company generally prices projects and contracts according to the market sectors they are dealing with. Pricing is complex, and very dependent on the perception of the company within each sector. WCI is a small company operating in a large fragmented market. As a brand it needs to be well established to command the highest fees. However, client satisfaction and loyalty can and do play a major role. Outsourcing contracts are generally long-term and are priced accordingly. They bring in regular revenue for several years.

Communications

The company currently spends in excess of £600,000 per annum on advertising and various brand-building activities. This is largely spent on the media, web site development, external events, corporate events, sponsorship, direct mail and sales and support. The company is currently reviewing the most effective way of spending this budget. The company produces a magazine called Management in Action (MiA). It contains topical case studies, thought-leadership articles, staff profiles, upcoming events and contact details (an example of this is provided in Appendix 3.). The company's current logo is illustrated below. The company's mission is to "help our clients become 'World Class' through excellence in process design, web technology and managed services." The company strives to inculcate this mission statement to its staff through the magazine and a sophisticated, well-developed Intranet facility. In a company that is heavily reliant on its staff, it is important that the brand personality is innovative and confident about the WCI philosophy. The company wants to position itself as being provocative and challenging, compared to its typical competitors in the IT services sector. To this end the brand has to be able to demonstrate the quality of the staff and the working environment.

18

Marketing and Human Resources

The company has a well-developed marketing structure, as shown in Appendix 1. A Marketing Co-ordinator covers each key business area. The company endeavours to have well-informed and motivated staff. The climate within the company is one of openness and transparency. Many of the staff work on client sites and rarely visit the WCI offices. The company practices what it preaches by utilising knowledge management and effective internal communications. The benefits of sharing knowledge are maintained through an Intranet, enabling employees to access product information, marketing materials, administration forms, contact details and a host of other information. A HTML newsletter is circulated to all WCI employees on a monthly basis. The newsletter 'What's Going On' provides information on current business, key projects, human resource and marketing issues, in addition to current news from all the international operations. Employee remuneration is based on a mixture of salary and commission. The company places an emphasis on skills development, as well as sales and business. The packages are competitive and staff are rewarded according to their skills and business generation. The company also has a share option scheme in place, so that all employees can benefit from the company's success.

Summary

WCI is at a crossroad in its development. Having recently integrated the various business offerings, it needs to consider how it will market itself strategically. A sales driven strategy has been successful in getting the company to its current financial position (see Appendix 4. for financial data). It competes in a highly fragmented market, but is a small- to medium-sized player within it (see Appendix 5. for a list of competitors). It has many competitors vying to offer similar services to customers, and it needs to build a distinguished brand. However, it appears that the company has specific niche market capabilities within the pharmaceutical and health markets. IT services are also faced with new challenges posed by mobile technologies. Nonetheless, this sector of the market is still growing rapidly. WCI's challenge is to continue growing, and to begin to challenge some of the bigger players within the sector by being innovative, and subtly shifting company focus from selling to strategic marketing with its new service offerings.

Appendix 1.

WCI Sectors of Business

Pharmaceuticals

WCI has helped many leading pharmaceutical companies strike a balance between cost and compliance in operational, development and regulatory processes.

Speed and compliance are the key to success in the pharmaceutical industry.

We create value for global leaders in the pharmaceutical industry by taking the principles of worldclass processes and the efficiencies of the web to create "lean" pharmaceutical companies. Reducing time to market, slashing development costs and consistently satisfying regulatory requirements. The result is our clients are striking an effective balance between cost and compliance in development, operational and regulatory processes.

Our services are focused in drug safety and regulatory affairs, research and development, data management, clinical trials and supply chain operations.

Our pharmaceutical team are drawn from a range of backgrounds in the industry including R&D, drug safety and manufacturing – some are qualified health care professionals. With a practical approach that delivers business results rather than reports, we work in partnership with client teams to deliver sustainable solutions at all levels, from global process integration to local performance improvements.

"With the growth in A&E volumes in excess of 23%, the old processes would not have handled the increasing case load and maintained compliance with the current headcount! We are delighted with the new processes and the WCI team", Dr Edmundo Muniz, Director Pharmacovigilance and Epidemiology, Eli Lilly.

Life Sciences

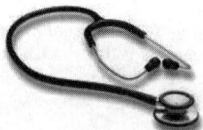

We're leaders in the Pharmaceutical and Health Care industries – 15 years of ground breaking experience.

In February 2001, a baby rhesus monkey called ANDi made the headlines. ANDi was the first primate to carry an alien gene – a gene that makes jellyfish glow green. The experiment intended to help scientists create transgenic monkeys that mimic diseases found in humans. The aim – to find cures for genetic diseases.

At the same time surgeons were experimenting with scalpels that use fibre optics to detect whether cells are cancerous whilst thousands of people were accessing the NHS Direct web site in the UK to gain medical assistance online. These examples illustrate the astonishing strides that have been made in Life Sciences since science took over from witch-craft.

WCI has been working in the Life Sciences industry for 15 years. Working with leading pharmaceutical companies, Pfizer to Bayer, GlaxoSmithKline to AstraZeneca, to improve research and development, drug safety and manufacturing. Our work for the NHS has positioned us as a lead supplier of technology and consulting solutions. We understand where the industry has come from and where it will be tomorrow, and our consulting and technology solutions will make the journey easier.

20

BPP PUBLISHING

Health Care

Our Health Care Team works in partnership with the NHS to meet the nations evolving health care needs.

Understanding the issues faced by the health care industry is essential. Patient care is critical and security and data protection vital. Legacy systems must be integrated with leading technology to deliver efficiencies and more than ever projects must be completed on time and within budget.

Our health care team has worked in partnership with the NHS since 1990. We deliver IT solutions that meet the evolving needs of the NHS from bespoke clinical software development to the design, roll-out and management of NHS networks providing national coverage.

Our technical and process expertise is coupled with an acute understanding of the NHS's operational practices. We work in conjunction with Health Service staff adopting an approach that 'fits' with the NHS, delivering solutions that gain 'buy in' at all levels.

We combine almost 100 man-years of NHS service with experience drawn from the pharmaceutical and hi-tech industries. We understand the NHS, taking an innovative approach to solutions that add value in the provision of patient care.

"It was a project with brutal timescales", says Andy Atkins, Account Manager for NHS Direct. "The first phase had to be completed in 3 months, to enable NHS Direct to achieve 100% coverage across England. This meant that within four months of winning the contract, we had to provide the network infrastructure, file servers, PCs and everything up to the desktop across five new sites and four existing locations".

Corporate

The economic climate is tough – are you ready to take advantage of the next boom?

Is the UK economy heading for a recession? Are we faring better than our European counterparts? Has consumers' spending moderated? The one thing we can be sure of is that the UK economy has definitely slowed down. During this uncertain climate businesses should be thinking aggressively rather than defensively and exploiting WCI's Lean Processes and web-based Lean Technology to maximise performance.

Our fresh approach to consulting and technology means helping your staff develop solutions that they enthusiastically own. Solutions that are flexible and easily adaptable to changes in the economic climate, ready to take advantage of the next upturn.

WCI works with many leading organisations in the UK and Ireland – Microsoft to Guinness, Volvo to Skandia. We've helped them achieve operational excellence by combining consulting insight with technology know-how.

WCI's services span business and technology consulting, software development, design and hardware procurement. Our unique combination of services enables us to create seamless organisations able to weather any economic storm.

Financial Services

Working with leading Financial Services businesses we ensure processes add real value to the customer and shareholder.

Amidst global consolidations, deregulation, fierce competition, volatile markets and changing customer expectations, financial services companies need to ensure their businesses are achieving the greatest efficiencies. Poor performance or failure to respond to market dynamics could result in profit or market share losses or worse a hostile takeover bid.

We tackle these issues. Excellently positioned to ensure your company's success, our team has experience in international financial businesses, innovative business environments and technology led organisations. The result is a team that provides the resource for your organisation to seize the opportunities presented by a dynamic industry.

Web technologies, streamlining processes and regulatory compliance are ways we help financial businesses reduce costs and improve service. Transforming internal operations to deliver excellence. We have the skills and proven track record to turn opportunities into differentiators and threats into competitive advantage.

"What I liked most was the experience of the WCI people and their focus on deliverables", Marc Adam, Managing Director – Financial Reporting, CSFB.

Technology, Media and Telecoms

We work with many leading FMCG companies to help them achieve excellence. We've even made Guinness flow faster!

The bubble burst, but the current twist in TMT companies' fortunes won't last. The growth of the Internet will revitalise company's futures and .NET will open new doorways of opportunity. To prepare for the next growth cycle TMT businesses should take advantage of the current economic blip.

We improve communications to make sure designers know as much about customers as the sales team, removing the need to forecast and guaranteeing information is available throughout the demand chain. We ensure customer's aspirations are met and the supply chain only produces what is required.

Our team is transforming companies' relationships with their customers by changing product sales to solutions-based business models; building customer loyalty, driving long-term revenue and protecting from economic troughs.

We have a wealth of knowledge and experience gained from leading TMT companies, FMCG businesses and successful dotcom start-ups. We've helped to create strong supply chain relationships which have delivered significant bottom line performance improvements. A team that can challenge your existing business model and implement lasting change.

"We are consistently looking for improvements across all aspects of our operations and are very open to change. We are embracing the innovation WCI helped to implement to stay at the forefront of our industry", Paul Nevin, Sales Director, Saturn.

Consumer Products

We manage your business processes using our consulting and technology experience to reduce cost, increase service and enable your management to concentrate on core business.

In today's competitive Consumer Product's marketplace, brands are not created and grown easily, quickly or without great expense. The equity created provides protection but, there are so many complex distractions and short-term performance targets that even the most diligent may fail to recognise undercurrents capable of changing their marketplace irrevocably. Squeezed profit margins, shortened lead-times, new distribution channels and increasingly fickle customers can revitalise or devastate the fortunes of FMCG companies.

WCI knows that before the benefits of a successful brand can be achieved the organisation must be functioning successfully. Combining our skills in business processes, supply chain, technology and industry experience we're expertly placed to help your company ensure its future success. Our team of consultants and technology experts provide vast industry knowledge gained from working with many leading consumer goods businesses. Our team's experience can help you stay ahead of industry trends and deliver improvements to the bottom line and shareholder.

The key to success in today's consumer market is to truly integrate business processes, technology and customers. Our team has the right mix of skills to make this happen; creating a competitive edge in an ultra-competitive market.

"Working with WCI has been a rewarding and revealing experience. Driving change usually needs expert analysis and creative solutions, both of which are key aspects of WCI's work. They also manage to combine this with a genuinely user-friendly approach", Bill Richards, Supply Chain Director, Fox's Biscuits.

Manufacturing

WCI combines exceptional manufacturing experience with the latest technologies to create better ways of working.

Industrial manufacturing still faces 'old economy' challenges of lead-time, demand, costs and margins. New product development costs are rising; responsiveness to customers is vital whilst inventories must be cut. Issues that have faced the sector for years, but the new economy provides an innovative approach to tackling them.

We can help you take advantage of the combination of worldclass manufacturing and technology integration. Our manufacturing experience is profound, with unparalleled experience implementing leading manufacturing processes in the aerospace, automotive and manufactured products industries.

We ensure clients improve margins whilst reducing inventories and time to market. Lean operations are essential and the digital economy presents new opportunities to collaborate with trading partners and service providers.

We lever technology to enhance the supply chain, integrating the flow of product and information to enable complete visibility, ensuring you can react faster and with more accuracy.

Our people have joined us from a range of manufacturing backgrounds. With expertise in supply chain integration, worldclass manufacturing and technology integration, our approach ensures results.

"The whole process is probably the most significant change and improvement project that Kelvin Hughes and our customers and shareholders have ever seen", Martin Jones, Managing Director, Kelvin Hughes.

23

Page 24 of World Class International

Client List

WCI works with the world's leading businesses.
From Microsoft to Cisco, Volvo to Pfizer.

Amtico	FLS Aerospace	Peachtree Railways
ANO Hutchison	Ford Motor Company	Pensions Management
AstraZeneca	Freemans	Pfizer
Avery Dennison		Pharmacia & Upjohn
	GKN	Pirelli
Bakony Muvek	GlaxoSmithKline	Portman
Barclays	Global One	Preussag
Bausch & Lomb	Guinness	
Bayer Pharmaceuticals		Raba
BBC	Hoffman La Roche	Rolls-Royce Aerospace
B-Braun Medical	HSBC	
Boehringer Ingelheim	Hutchison 3G	SAP
		Schwarz
Cable & Wireless	ICI Dulux	Skandia Life
Caradon	ING Barings	Smith & Nephew
Cisco	Invensys	Smiths Industries
Coats Viyella		Sonopress
Corel Corporation	Microsoft	South African Breweries
Covance	MMI	Symantec
Credit Swiss First Boston	Multimap.com	
		Tellabs
Dentsply	NHS Direct	
Dyno Nobel	Nortek	Volvo UK
	Northern Foods	
Eli Lilly		Wagon
Essef	Oakhill	Whitbread
Esselte Office Products		W. H. Smith
Everest		Winterthur Life
Exel		Wyeth Ayerst

WCI Business Services

We work with you to understand your company and business environment,
leveraging our knowledge of industry, processes and technology to create a
map for success.

Business Strategy

- **Development**
  We manage the business planning process, sharing our consulting and technology foresight to create winning solutions for your business.

- **Implementation**
  Once we've helped you create a vision for success our consultants and technology experts will assist you in implementing the plan, ensuring the vision becomes bottom line reality.

Business Transformation

Our methodology is to understand, simplify, automate and integrate. Creating waste-free high performance processes, streamlining activities to deliver sustainable business process improvement.

- **Supply Chain**
  We're experts at creating efficient global supply chains, which will take you closer to real demand. Integrating suppliers, distributors and retailers to ensure the seamless flow of product and information.

- **Customer Processes**
  We can help you create a customer-centric organisation using our customer contact map to highlight all interactions. We can improve visibility of customer value and implement processes that create loyalty and enhance shareholder value.

- **Business Processes**
  Combining excellence in process engineering and web technologies we're able to integrate systems to create lean, efficient processes, provide holistic data solutions, or e-commerce applications accessible via any Internet-capable machine.

Systems Architecture and Integration

Our excellence in consulting and technology enables us to link your business needs to technology solutions, creating lean organisations with built-in competitive advantage.

- **Web-enabled Processes**
  We've been creating web-enabled processes for 15 years, utilising our skills in process mapping, interface design and technology to create lean and robust digital solutions.

- **Software**
  We offer a full range of software development services, tackling the complex problems e-business solutions often require, dealing with issues caused by security, non-repudiation, scalability and application integration.

Infrastructure and Creative Solutions

From the installation of pre-configured hardware, user training or the realisation of creative solutions, we have the expertise to meet your needs.

- **Network Design and Build**
  We provide a range of consulting and technical expertise in networking and systems infrastructure. From the largest multi-site project, to one-day troubleshooting, the installation of pre-configured hardware or the management of complete projects, we work with you to identify the most appropriate skill set, matching the engineer to the task.

- **Training**
  We're a gold accredited partner for the Institute of IT Training and a Microsoft Office user specialist testing centre. We ensure all employees can successfully use the technology deployed across the organisation.

- **Hardware**
  With the assistance of our technology experts and online service – Procure, we make it easy to create a solution for your hardware and network needs.

- **Web Design**
  We transform business processes and web technologies into easy-to-use human interfaces, ensuring speed, navigation and simplicity to effectively link people to technology.

25

Managed Services and BPO

We manage your business processes using our consulting and technology experience to reduce cost, increase service and enable your management to concentrate on core business.

- **Customer Care Centre**
  Working on site or remotely we offer a complete call centre solution for your business based on our award-winning model. Providing helpdesk, procurement, asset management, hardware and network maintenance to an agreed service level agreement.

- **On/off Site Services IT Support**
  Our IT support service works to meet your business's needs. Providing either on or off site IT support, in-house or remote call centres, resident IT experts or roaming engineers, WCI is completely flexible to your needs.

- **Business Process Outsourcing**
  We provide the link between managed processes and your company, executing the outsource process, aligning and monitoring the daily activity of service providers and technologies to ensure your business's needs are met.

Type of Business:	Management consulting business/e-business Solution Provider.			

Sectors by Percentage of Revenue:	Life Sciences	10.8%	Systems Int. Solutions cons.	12.7%
	TMT (supply chain)	15.9%	Managed Customer Services	9.5%
	Supply chain (other)	2.7%	IT infrastructure	41.0%
	Financial Services	6.5%		

2000 Sales Estimates:	£37.3 million (US$56 million)

Number of Employees:	WCI Group Directors	4	Application Development	17
	Operations Directors	10	Commercial	9
	Sector Heads Principals	5	Sales	36
	Consultants – UK	47	Infrastructure staff	27
	Consultants – USA	17	Managed Services	48
	Marketing	6	S I Consultants	22
	Administration	12		
	Finance	4	**Total**	**270**
	Information Technology	3		
	HR	3		

Geographic Markets:	UK	69%
	European	21%
	USA	10%

Number of Active Accounts:	4 clients = 20% revenues	33 clients = 60% revenues
	13 clients = 40% revenues	55 clients = 70% revenues
	21 clients = 50% revenues	110 clients = 80% revenues

Major Customer (>2.5% of revenues):	Cisco Systems	6.5%	Pfizer	3.5%
	NHS Direct	5.5%	Winterthur Life	3%
	MSAS Logistics	4%	Bayer	3%
	Credit Suisse	4%	W. H. Smith	2.5%

Repeat Business:	Est. at 70% to 80% by management

Marketing/Promotions:	Web site – www.wcigroup.com Colour Brochures Advertising – Harvard Business Review etc., poster campaign in Dublin Airport – seminars – marketing promotions – hospitality events	Management In Action marketing magazine ... and other activities

Source: WCI

World Class International: Business Summary

Shareholder	Title of Owner
P. E. Collins	Chief Executive
A. J. Duncan	Ex Chairman, retired 1Q-2001
S. J. Derrick	New Group Chairman
D. R. Cheesman	WCI Consulting Direct
C. Evans	HR Director
J. Manning	IS Director
B. Ramsay	Director, Business Development
J. Tims	Group Finance Director
A. Gardner	CEO WCI Technology
D. Seddon	Ops Director, WCI Technology
Employees	Various

WCI Consulting Facilities	City, Country	% of Sales	Square Foot	Year Opened
Headquarters:	Denmead, UK	60%	5,000	1989
Branch:	Atlanta, USA	24%	3,692	1998
	Budapest, Hungary	16%	1,250	1997

WCI Technology Facilities	City, Country	% of Sales	Square Foot	Year Opened
Headquarters:	Southampton, UK	70%	13,500+	1997
Branch:	Bracknell, UK	22%	1,800	1999
	Bristol, UK	8%	3,000	1999

Source: WCI

28

Operations

Structure

Holding Board Structure

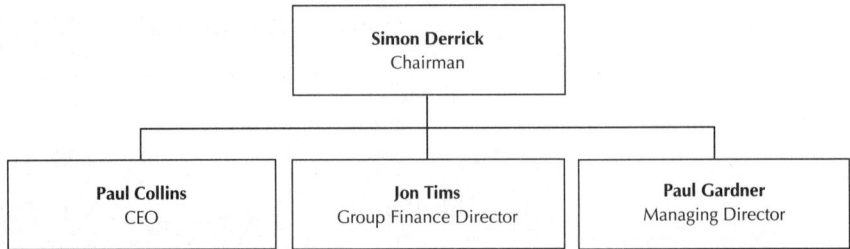

```
                    Simon Derrick
                      Chairman
```

Paul Collins	Jon Tims	Paul Gardner
CEO	Group Finance Director	Managing Director

Consulting Board Structure

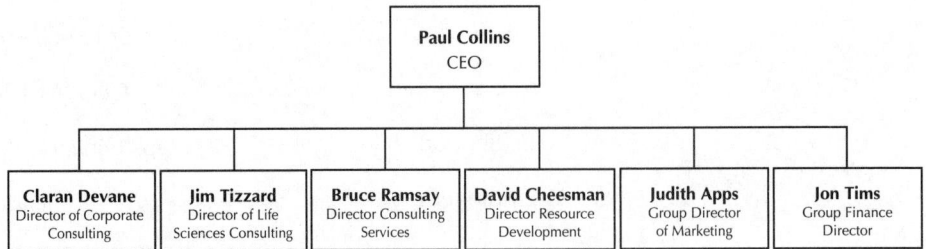

```
                    Paul Collins
                        CEO
```

Claran Devane	Jim Tizzard	Bruce Ramsay	David Cheesman	Judith Apps	Jon Tims
Director of Corporate Consulting	Director of Life Sciences Consulting	Director Consulting Services	Director Resource Development	Group Director of Marketing	Group Finance Director

Technology Board Structure

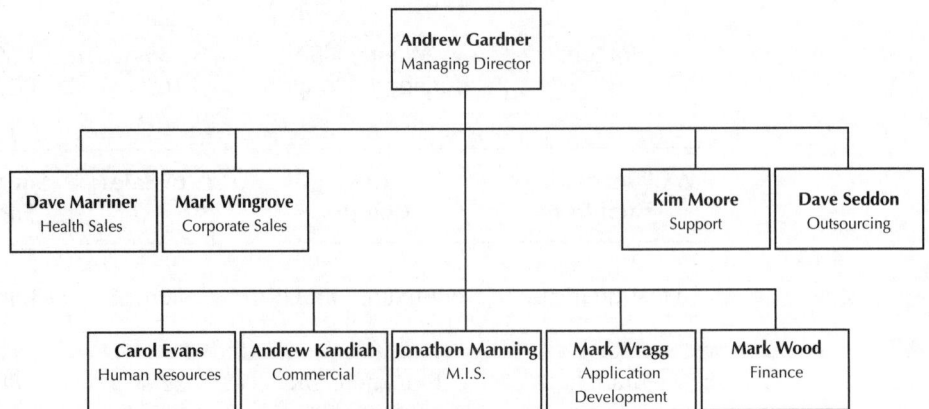

```
                  Andrew Gardner
                  Managing Director
```

Dave Marriner	Mark Wingrove		Kim Moore	Dave Seddon
Health Sales	Corporate Sales		Support	Outsourcing

Carol Evans	Andrew Kandiah	Jonathon Manning	Mark Wragg	Mark Wood
Human Resources	Commercial	M.I.S.	Application Development	Finance

Source: WCI

29

Page 30 of World Class International

Description of Vertical and Horizontal Structure

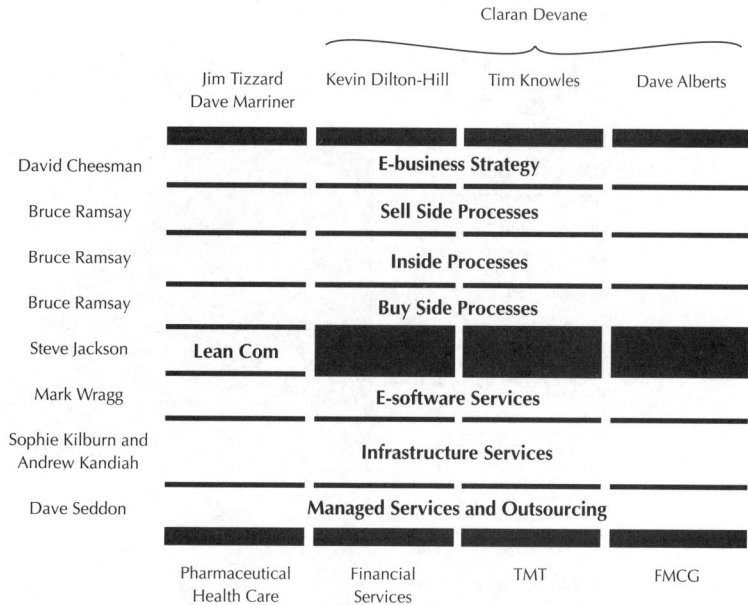

Claran Devane

	Jim Tizzard Dave Marriner	Kevin Dilton-Hill	Tim Knowles	Dave Alberts
David Cheesman		E-business Strategy		
Bruce Ramsay		Sell Side Processes		
Bruce Ramsay		Inside Processes		
Bruce Ramsay		Buy Side Processes		
Steve Jackson	Lean Com			
Mark Wragg		E-software Services		
Sophie Kilburn and Andrew Kandiah		Infrastructure Services		
Dave Seddon		Managed Services and Outsourcing		
	Pharmaceutical Health Care	Financial Services	TMT	FMCG

Marketing Structure

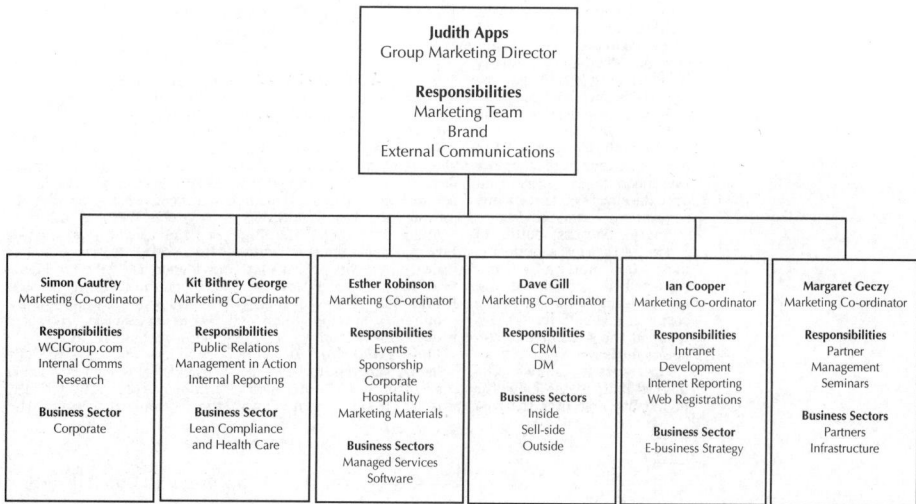

Judith Apps
Group Marketing Director

Responsibilities
Marketing Team
Brand
External Communications

Simon Gautrey Marketing Co-ordinator	**Kit Bithrey George** Marketing Co-ordinator	**Esther Robinson** Marketing Co-ordinator	**Dave Gill** Marketing Co-ordinator	**Ian Cooper** Marketing Co-ordinator	**Margaret Geczy** Marketing Co-ordinator
Responsibilities WCIGroup.com Internal Comms Research **Business Sector** Corporate	**Responsibilities** Public Relations Management in Action Internal Reporting **Business Sector** Lean Compliance and Health Care	**Responsibilities** Events Sponsorship Corporate Hospitality Marketing Materials **Business Sectors** Managed Services Software	**Responsibilities** CRM DM **Business Sectors** Inside Sell-side Outside	**Responsibilities** Intranet Development Internet Reporting Web Registrations **Business Sector** E-business Strategy	**Responsibilities** Partner Management Seminars **Business Sectors** Partners Infrastructure

Source: WCI

BPP PUBLISHING

Appendix 2.

Big Five fees rise as audits drop

Survey shows shift to non-audit work as accounting firms 'seriously challenged' in US

By Michael Peel

The Big Five accounting firms posted large rises in fee income from non-audit services for leading companies last year in spite of concerns that the growth could damage the quality of audits.

A survey published today by *Financial Director* magazine suggests audits became both quicker and more costly as the firms overcame pricing pressure suffered in the late 1990s.

The research comes amid a long-running debate over whether the integrity of audits is endangered by the Big Five's increasing focus on lucrative advisory work.

"The jury is still out," said Colin Reeves, director of the Review Board, which monitors regulation of the accounting profession. "Nevertheless, the figures do suggest that auditing is becoming a lower priority for the accountancy firms than non-audit services."

The *Financial Director* survey of FTSE-100 company annual reports found that the Big Five's income from non-audit work rose last year from £492.6m to £675m.

Total audit fees climbed 19.4 per cent, although the increase was a more modest 3.5 per cent once the effects of mergers and acquisitions were excluded.

Andrew Sawers, editor of *Financial Director*, said the figures for non-audit fees reflected a growth in tax advice owing to the increasing complexity of both the tax system and the structures of corporate deals.

The survey shows the marked shift in the emphasis of the Big Five over the past few years: audit fees accounted for 24.3 per cent of the firms' income last year, compared with 43.7 per cent in 1997.

The large firms have faced allegations in the US that the desire to win high-margin advisory contracts could damage the integrity of audits.

Andersen, one of the Big Five, has come under pressure for earning $27m (£18.6m) last year for non-audit work for Enron, the collapsed energy group – $2m more than it received for its audit.

The *Financial Director* research suggests the average time spent on FTSE-100 audits was 60 days last year, down from 61 in 2000 and 67 in 1997.

The audit times show far more variation by industry than by auditor. Andersen was responsible for both the fastest – the satellite operator British Sky Broadcasting, at 24 days – and the slowest – the advertising group WPP, at 124 days. For the second year running all the FTSE-100 were audited by a member of the Big Five – a consolidation that has caused some leading companies to express concerns about a lack of competition.

Average audit fees per £1m turnover of client companies climbed from £450 to £466, the second successive rise after a decline in 1999.

The Institute of Chartered Accountants in England and Wales, the main industry body, said the rising speed of audits was a sign of the increasing efficiency of companies rather than a reflection of hasty work by accountants.

John Collier, the institute's secretary-general, admitted the work of accounting firms in the US was being "very seriously challenged" but said allegations of conflicts of interest between audit and advisory services were unproven.

Rivals merge, Page 24
www.ft.com/accountancy

Accounting for growth

Total FTSE 100 non-audit fee income
£ million

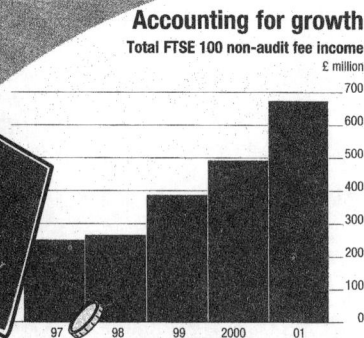

Biggest audit fees paid by FTSE 100 companies

Company	Auditors	Audit fees (£m)
HSBC	KPMG	17.2
Shell	KPMG/PwC	11.3
BP	Ernst & Young	10.0
Unilever	PwC	8.7
Anglo American	Deloitte & Touche	6.7
GlaxoSmithKline	PwC	6.3
British American Tobacco	PwC	6.0
BHP Billiton	KPMG/PwC	5.3
CGNU	Ernst & Young/PwC	4.9
Royal Bank of Scotland	Deloitte & Touche	4.9

Graphic by Lloyd Thatcher   Source: Financial Director

Source: Financial Times, Monday, 7th January 2002

FT/IT Review– 5th December, 2001

System Suppliers Face up to New Mood of Realism
by Andrew Fisher

Published: 3rd December, 2001 19:46GMT/Last Updated: 4th December, 2001 18:08GMT

Value for money is a concept that has often seemed alien to the IT industry – especially in the eyes of executives whose companies have paid vast sums for complex systems which fail to produce the promised advantages.

But with demand falling, profits dwindling and prospects uncertain – especially after the events of 11th September – companies are far less tolerant of investments which produce minimal or no returns. IT projects are expected to make significant and measurable contributions to performance.

"In these economically difficult times, companies are looking at investment in technology far more stringently," says Chris Dedicoat, Group Vice President for Europe at Cisco, the US network equipment company. *"They haven't stopped spending, but they're more cautious."*

Thus, there is far more emphasis on measuring results than during the 1990s phase of big ERP (Enterprise Resource Planning) projects, the pre-2000 IT spending spree to ward off millennium bug threats, and the infamous dotcom boom.

Sophisticated new software makes it possible to measure the effect of projects to an extent previously not possible. *"You shouldn't do IT projects because of generalised or vague future benefits,"* says Brent Habig, Head of US-based Tigris Consulting. *"If you can't calculate it, you probably should be critical of it."*

Such measurable benefits could be reduced inventory levels or lower purchase prices for materials. Mr Habig sees companies opting increasingly for smaller customised projects – often costing less than $500,000 – with specific goals, more easily measurable targets, and fairly short payback times.

It is also vital that IT is aligned much more closely to real business goals than in the past. *"IT is challenged to have a greater understanding of the business to succeed in the new environment,"* he adds. *"Fundamentally, it is a rewriting of the relationship between IT and business."*

Andy Tinlin, a Partner with KPMG Consulting, believes companies must be far clearer about what technology can and cannot do for them. This means greater awareness at board level about IT's benefits and drawbacks.

"It should be business driving the technology and not technology driving the business," he says. *"The next wave of technology adoption will be more considered, more enterprise-focused, and aligned very much to business objectives."*

This will be a sharp contrast to the way many companies have handled their IT strategies. A recent study by PA Consulting found that businesses were unhappy over returns on their IT spending.

"Many companies are frustrated by the practicalities and pressures on their IT resources and find that the impetus for delivering business benefits is frequently lost after the financial investment and immediate project deadlines are met," it said in the study, Increasing business value with Information Technology.

PA Consulting recommended that companies concentrate on three key principles: agree what drives value in the business, so that senior management can target opportunities for IT; agree who is responsible for realising the business value of IT; and drive all IT activities in pursuit of business value.

While the most advanced companies are now trying to do this, others are still struggling. PA Consulting found that only 40 per cent of executives surveyed in Europe, the US and Asia-Pacific had confidence in the business cases used to justify their companies' IT investments.

In addition, 72 per cent of respondents in PA Consulting's study believed visible success with IT was now far more important for the personal survival of the Chief Executive. "This view underlines the need for the CEO to take a personal lead in making the business value of IT visible on the board's agenda and in shareholder communication."

32

This means IT has to be regarded as an essential element in the business and not just as a separate investment. *"It is fundamental to how you create goods and services and how you create positive customer experiences,"* says Chris Formant, Chief Executive of Scient, the US digital business consultancy. *"It is not something you just delegate away."*

If IT is to be firmly embedded in companies' strategic thinking, CEOs must take a prominent role. *"This need not mean total involvement,"* says Tom Jones, a Partner with PwC Consulting. *"More important is the philosophy transmitted down to managers and board members about the importance of IT and how it relates to business benefits."*

This should help the complex process of ensuring that IT is tied firmly to business goals. Instead of following what other companies are doing, many are taking a more considered look at their IT investments and the rationale behind them.

"When you've got less money to invest, you target it better," Mr Jones adds. Much of this sharper focus is directed towards customers as the obvious source of increased revenues. Making it easier and more pleasant for people to deal with businesses through a variety of online and offline channels is central to many companies' ambitions.

"But simply putting in Customer Relationship Management (CRM) systems to improve links with customers is not enough," says Mr Formant. Companies should work out their real needs first by mapping in detail the ways people interact with the business through different channels.

He calls this approach Customer eXperience Management (CXM). Whatever the terms used, however, it is clear that businesses are becoming far more aware of the need to base decisions on hard numbers and analysis rather than imitation and intuition.

Unless they take this more methodical approach, they are unlikely to be well-placed to benefit from an eventual economic upturn. *"You need to know what development taps you can turn on first and where you can take cash and resources from,"* says Andy Jerram, Senior Vice President at United Management Technologies, the US consultancy.

Companies need to think hard about their priorities and whether these have changed in the light of the business downturn. By measuring the impact of information technology on crucial aspects of the business, executives can then make quick decisions when markets change.

They will then be able to use their IT weapons to outsmart rivals in the battle for future competitive advantage. Key themes in next year's series of FT-IT Reviews will highlight investment in IT business sectors, particularly the financial sector.

Source: FT.com (http://specials.ft.com/ftit/FT369G51RUC.html)

FT/IT Review – 5th December, 2001

Emerging World of Wider Industrial Collaboration
by Andrew Baxter

Published: 3rd December, 2001 20:48GMT/Last Updated: 4th December, 2001 18:08GMT

If vendors and consultants in the complex world of manufacturing IT have got it right, the next two or three years could be a time of far-reaching change in the way their big industrial customers approach the challenges of product development and manufacture.

The elements are in place, they say, for the fulfilment of a vision in which three-dimensional Computer-aided design (Cad) models and the product data associated with them become one of the key enabling tools in the creation of the extended digital enterprise.

33

The Internet will allow this digital information to be shared instantly and globally, among components suppliers, planners on the factory floor, the purchasing department and after-sales maintenance. Data will be used and re-used to further reduce development times and costs, and improve product quality and maintainability. This is the emerging, collaborative world of product life cycle management, or PLM.

"In the last 24 months, we have seen the beginning of a network-based revolution in the way products are designed, developed and manufactured," says Dick Brown, Chairman and Chief Executive of EDS.

The US IT services company is putting its money where its mouth is – in October it completed a $1.1 billion deal which combined its existing UGS subsidiary with rival SDRC to form EDS PLM Solutions. UGS and SDRC were two of the big names in design software and product data management software.

According to EDS, the total PLM market – covering everything from now well-established mechanical Cad software to newfangled web-based tools allowing non-engineers access to "lite" versions of 3D data – is estimated to be worth more than $17 billion this year.

The mechanical Cad market is seen as relatively mature – at least in western industrial countries – but still growing at single-digit rates. But the newer collaborative and visualisation tools, along with software that uses the 3D data to help companies plan factories and production digitally, are growing much faster. In fact, most observers believe the surface has barely been scratched.

Bernard Charles, President of France's Dassault Systemes, another of the big names in the sector, identifies three broad drivers underpinning the development of PLM.

First, companies that have been using digital mock-up software, to save time by reducing the need for physical mock-ups or prototypes, can now use the Internet as a communications vehicle, giving all their suppliers – today or in the future – access to the digital data. *"This is not well understood yet,"* says Mr Charles. *"It's seen as a new step, which will become an unstoppable wave."*

Secondly, he says, the Internet bubble of 1999 and early 2000 *"fed interest in start-up companies, such as online marketplaces. This generated an awareness at a very senior level that something was happening."* With the bursting of the bubble came the realisation that providing workable solutions would not be easy, and would take time.

Internet Opportunities

Thirdly, says Mr Charles, the Internet offers an unprecedented opportunity to make 3D digital data available to functions such as purchasing or maintenance departments which previously would never have benefited from them. United Airlines, for example, is using the French company's software to give maintenance staff online access to 3D design data.

However, despite the enticing vision which the IT vendors are projecting, turning the dream into reality is not a task that can be achieved overnight. The industry has to accept some of the blame for creating a characteristically confusing collection of more or less overlapping abbreviations – such as PLM, Collaborative Product Commerce (CPC), and collaborative Product Definition Management (cPDM).

"There is a lack of a common understanding about how to describe a complex situation," says Richard Harrison, Chief Executive of Massachusetts-based PTC, which along with Dassault Systemes (whose worldwide sales are handled by IBM) and the newly-formed EDS PLM Solutions makes up the big three in the product development software market.

PLM, however, is emerging as the most all-embracing description, reflecting the fact that the old boundaries between product development and production software are being blurred. Significantly, SAP, the leading vendor of Enterprise Resource Planning software (ERP), which is production oriented, is also using the PLM tag.

But there are other more fundamental obstacles, all of which are being addressed. One is confidentiality. *"The whole collaborative planning arena is fraught with the problem of trust,"* says Robin Tye, a Partner at PwC Consulting in London. *"(For manufacturers) it is very concerning if you are going to be as open as this demands."*

34

Geoff May, Technical Computing Manager at Sun Microsystems, agrees that implementation of CPC, as Sun calls it, is *"non-trivial. To get the full benefits an extensive evaluation of departmental structures and manufacturing processes, as well as supply chain communication, is required,"* he says. Top-level commitment is crucial, he adds, and data security is also an issue.

Mr Harrison believes that alerting companies to the importance of collaboration is *"not a missionary sale. Companies have always collaborated."* However, he says some of the initial implementations have been customised, 'Big Bang' solutions for large, early-adopter companies, and these solutions have lacked the maturity necessary to woo the mass market.

As a result, the implementation of PLM has been patchy so far. *"What we need is some good case studies,"* says Mr Tye at PwC Consulting. *"We're working with clients on several projects, but these are not quick – they are two- or three-year programmes involving aircraft parts, for example."*

Mr Charles at Dassault says the references are being built, although companies are approaching collaboration in many different ways. Some for example, are focusing initially on digital manufacturing – using visualisation tools to manage the production system – while others are starting by requiring suppliers to connect with portals and look at parts online.

Role models involving companies with widely-admired manufacturing and product development practices will clearly be important for the vendors to get their message across. An example is Toyota's emerging plans for a real-time virtual communication network in 3D, on which Dassault has been working.

Meanwhile, along with much of the rest of the IT industry, the PLM vendors are having to grapple with the after-effects of the 11th September terrorist attacks in the US and the subsequent US assault on Afghanistan.

Daratech, the Massachusetts-based IT analyst, has already revised downwards to $7.7 billion its forecast for the global PLM market this year (in discrete manufacturing, covering computer-aided design, manufacturing and engineering and product data management). It believes growth in 2002 is likely to slow further, due to continuing global recession – possibly compounded by the effects of terrorism and efforts to combat it – before reviving in 2003.

"Since 11th September, companies have been focusing on business continuity, IT back-up and securing against cyber-attack," says Bruce Jenkins, Executive Vice President at Daratech. And with fewer senior executives flying, PLM vendors are having to accept delays selling at enterprise level, where deals are larger, sales cycles longer and top-level decisions are required.

Industry leaders such as Mr Harrison at PTC admit there is a risk that the current political and economic situation could delay the fulfilment of their vision – turning what they see as a "must-have" solution into one that customers see as a "don't need quite yet" purchase.

But there is unanimity among vendors and observers about the strength of the mid- and long-term outlook. *"Manufacturing companies can't really survive and prosper by taking a purely defensive stance, they have to take the offensive, continually doing better the things they already do,"* says Mr Jenkins.

Mr Charles agrees – *"I think we are at the top of the list for investment to be done,"* he says. He points out that the industry is much less dependent on its customers' production volumes than on their product development programmes and continuing need for tools to promote innovation. *"I have not seen in the past six years so many new car projects as I have seen this year,"* he says.

Mr Harrison says the number of big deals has declined this year – *"people are not buying things they can't deploy in the next 12 months."* But even when times are slow, he notes, customers need to continue improving productivity in readiness for better times ahead.

Tentatively, both Mr Jenkins and Mr Harrison suggest recent events may even help sales of collaborative IT tools and infrastructure, by stimulating interest in web-based tools as an alternative to travel and face-to-face meetings.

If the ultimate benefits and significance of PLM remain unclear, the vision is becoming reality. As Mr Harrison puts it: *"(Customers) might not know what the end goal is, but they know they have to get going on something."*

Source: FT.com (http://specials.ft.com/ftit/FT35HQ41RUC.html)

35

FT – Understanding Supply Chain Management

Long Live the Revolution
By Vipul Agrawal and Morris Cohen

Published: 13th November, 2001 14:12GMT/Last Updated: 20th November, 2001 17:31GMT

Technological innovation opens the door to new business models, and such models eventually lead managers to develop new processes for matching demand with supply. As a result, changes occur in the supply chain that lead to major shifts in the competitive structure of industries.

Many argue that the effects of e-commerce on supply chain management typify this process and will overturn accepted business models. But to understand the effect of e-business, it is important to recognise that this is not the first time the supply chain has undergone a revolution. Changes at the turn of the 19th century formed the model for manufacturing and distribution throughout the 20th century. It is instructive to examine this revolution in more detail.

The First Revolution

Between 1870 and 1917, a massive reorganisation of the economies of developed nations took place. Before this, commerce had been characterised by small companies that operated within a limited geographic space and focused on a thin slice of the value chain. During this period these companies were replaced by large, vertically integrated corporations. Decisions about the allocation of resources that ensured the matching of supply with demand throughout the value chain were removed from the marketplace and placed in the hands of managers. The switch from market allocation to corporate allocation was based on a simple economic reality. The cost of allocation of resources within the company became lower than the cost of using the market. Those who recognised this fact developed business models that took advantage of the opportunity by expanding and integrating operations within the company. The primary areas where changes took place were in the production and distribution of goods – the supply chain. What were the technologies that enabled the movement to the "visible hand" to take place? Most important were the introduction of continental railroad and telegraph systems, and the arrival of high-speed, continuous-process production machinery. In developed countries, it became possible to ship goods and to communicate from coast to coast. For the first time, continental markets could be accessed, both for the supply of raw materials and the distribution of finished products. The scale and complexity of business increased, necessitating the invention of management skills such as scheduling, accounting and co-ordination across many interacting locations. Soon, mass distributors appeared. These companies used national rail networks to make fast, reliable, low-cost deliveries. Heavy use of such infrastructure gave them a high stock turnover for a high volume of goods. The successful distributors set up networks of retail chains and commodity dealerships and came to dominate their regional markets.

The success of mass distributors was based on "economies of speed" whereby a company internalised a high volume of market transactions. The increase in transaction volume led to high stock turnover, which in turn led to rapid cash flow. This cash flow then enabled companies to buy raw materials in large quantities at lower costs, with lower credit cost terms and, thus, to self-finance expansion. Moreover, the economies of speed supported the growth of market share because mass distributors were able to offer more variety at a lower cost to their consumers.

A second technological innovation was high-speed, continuous-process manufacturing equipment. This technology made the most of economies of scale. An example is the Bonsack machine, invented for making cigarettes. In 1881, Mr Duke of North Carolina acquired the first of these machines in the US. It was capable of producing 70,000 cigarettes a day (as opposed to a maximum of 3,000 a day for the manual rolling of cigars). Fifteen of these machines could saturate the entire US market. Consequently, Duke and his American Tobacco Company had to develop aggressive advertising techniques to persuade consumers to try this new product.

Process technology led to a new type of supply chain. National manufacturing corporations integrated with companies further down the chain to control distribution and marketing. These corporations also integrated with suppliers to manage the unprecedented flow of raw materials which was required to feed the newly mechanised processes.

Finally, networks of branch sales offices were built to handle the wholesaler function needed to co-ordinate distribution in regional markets. The first movers built empires by financing expansion internally, thus retaining ownership.

36

The resulting lower unit cost supported a larger market share and higher cash flow, and reduced the cost of capital. By 1917 the revolution was over and many industries in the US and Europe were controlled by large, integrated corporations.

The Second Revolution

Today, the Internet and B2B commerce are fuelling a second supply chain revolution. The seeds of this revolution were sown in the 1990s, the "golden age" of supply chain management. During this period, companies experimented with novel supply chain strategies. For example, under postponement, companies created finished products as close as possible to the point of customer demand. The success of these strategies was based on the introduction of mechanisms that reduced uncertainty and non-productive delays, enabled information to be shared and co-ordinated decision making throughout the supply chain.

Consider an ideal situation in which information, material flow, product attributes and decision making realise the full potential of e-commerce technologies. Information flows in this ideal world will be accurate, rich and instantaneous. Information, moreover, will be based on all supply chain transactions (retail to raw material) and will be visible throughout the chain. The Internet will reduce search costs to a minimum.

Goods will flow directly between suppliers and end customers, controlled by just-in-time shipment. In this environment, the cost of changing suppliers will be nil. Products will become more customised. Companies might also be able to develop economies of scale in production by adopting automated flexible manufacturing processes.

How realistic is this picture of the future? The technologies that can make it happen exist, along with the profit incentives for companies that can build such supply chains. The combination of unlimited information, computing power and capacity will make it possible for managers to match supply with demand on a global scale.

Innovative supply chain structures are rapidly emerging. These incorporate expanded access to "e-sources" of supply, which use web-based exchanges and hubs, interactive trading mechanisms and advanced optimisation and matching algorithms to link customers with suppliers for individual transactions. Thus, the dream of always providing the right product to the right customer at the right time and place, and at the right price, will very likely become a reality.

It is difficult to predict the final result of the second revolution, but companies are already adopting a range of new supply chain structures and competitive strategies. It is naive to think that one size will fit all or that any firm will restrict itself to a single structure for all of its transactions. Above all, new supply chains must provide diversity and flexibility. The structure of industry, however, will not remain static. As with the first supply chain revolution, the impact on corporate organisation and industry structure will be felt far beyond the present advances in supply chain management.

The history of the personal computer industry is a good illustration of this relationship. In the early 1980s IBM adopted a bold strategy for the design and production of this new product. It outsourced two key components, the operating system and the central processing unit, to Microsoft and Intel respectively. This "supply chain" decision was made at a time when most discounted the potential of the personal computer to overtake the mainframe as the dominant product.

When IBM made this decision, computers were highly integrated products produced in an industry that was essentially vertical. An IBM computer consisted of specialised components that could not be used in any competing product. The design, production, delivery and after-sales support of components, as well as the assembly of the final product, all took place in premises owned and managed by IBM. Other market leaders in the computer industry, such as DEC and Unisys, had similar structures.

IBM's seemingly innocuous outsourcing decisions coincided with a fundamental upheaval in the industry. IBM let Intel and Microsoft in. Product design shifted from integral (components are designed only for a specific product and assembled by a single company) to modular (components can be used in a variety of products and have standard interfaces). As a result, components could be supplied by different vendors; the industry moved from a vertical to a horizontal structure.

37

Another type of change in the supply chain occurred in the computer industry about ten years later. In the 1990s, Michael Dell began building computers to order in his college dormitory in Texas. Each customer could specify a configuration. This meant components could be procured and assembled by Dell with lower cost and shorter lead times than "make to stock" companies, because the product design was modular and the industry was horizontal. This simple supply chain strategy is known as the "Dell direct model". It is characterised by low inventory, high profit margins and a very high return on assets.

Since life cycles for computers are short, one of the major costs of storing components is obsolescence. The mass customisation process of the Dell model reduces this cost. Through its direct sales channel, Dell can shift a customer's demand to a configuration with a higher margin and better availability. It might present a choice between a rapid response for components that are in stock (and perhaps more expensive) and a delay for fulfilling the configuration initially requested with components that are unavailable but on order.

Dell's rapid response and lean asset base is supported by a supplier network that can place components at its assembly plants in Austin, Texas, within minutes of the order being made. These "revolver" distribution centres support just-in-time production. Dell's volume is sufficient inducement for most suppliers to absorb the capital costs and risks associated with supporting Dell's supply structure.

Recently Dell has shifted much of its sales to the Internet and these sales have risen to more than $30 million a day. Purchases made on the Internet have substantially higher margins and reduced costs. Customers make fewer telephone calls (one call, as opposed to five). The original call centre sales model also was limited due to the cost (in time) of providing information to customers. Sales staff have incentives to maximise the margin dollars earned per minute of contact time. They will thus act to conclude a sale with a choice that may not reflect the customer's willingness to pay for higher margin components. On the Internet, the indecisive customer can surf without limit and may end up buying a more expensive configuration.

What are the lessons we can learn from the PC industry? First, changes in the architecture of computers coincided with a shift in supply chain strategy and a reorganisation of the industry. Second, e-commerce can lead to lower costs, enhanced service and higher profit margins. The computer industry has already experienced the type of revolutionary change other industries are now going through.

Source: FT.com (http://specials.ft.com/scm/FT3H9RPQZTC.html)

FT – Understanding Supply Chain Management

Putting the Customer First
By Cindy Duffield

Published: 13th November, 2001 14:14GMT/Last Updated: 20th November, 2001 17:30GMT

Many companies excel either in the use of Supply Chain Management (SCM) techniques or in Customer Relationship Management (CRM), but few are able to integrate the two – a key target for modern manufacturers wishing to increase their competitiveness.

One approach to bringing the two areas together is the so-called "digital loyalty network", a phase coined by Deloitte & Touche Tohmatsu, the consultants.

Its goals are to implement a means of developing and delivering products via the most effective processes, and of extracting information from customer buying habits to concentrate sales and marketing efforts on those most profitable, most frequent and most loyal; differentiating the way in which each customer is treated.

The new approach recognises that tracking customers' behaviour and responding to their tastes and preferences requires more than it did in the past, when vendors and retailers relied mainly on analysing the content of shopping baskets. Customers can now access products from suppliers over the web, through call centres, interactive television and kiosks, as well as through traditional retail outlets. Meanwhile, at the back end, product sourcing, distribution and fulfilment have to be economically viable across multiple channels. For the data attainable from two such disparate systems to offer value, collaboration and integration are a must.

Several basic components are necessary for a digital loyalty network to function. Companies need to collect and analyse customer information, personalise their marketing efforts, and reflect the findings across the supply chain in real time.

Building profiles of customers is the fundamental asset on which the entire infrastructure depends, says Ed Brady, Principle of DiamondCluster, the Chicago-based digital strategy company.

"Suppliers must understand the motivations and interests of their most profitable customers to accurately identify opportunities to up-sell and cross-sell, doing it in a way that is unobtrusive and is perceived by the customer as a valued service," he says.

But building profiles is not straightforward given the cocktail of options available to customers. Not only can they choose and mix the multitude of different sales channels now available to them, but their choices of payment (credit card, partner's credit card, cash, for instance) makes it extremely difficult to accurately track their purchasing behaviour.

However, while suppliers are scurrying to capture as much information as possible on their customers, there is a growing trend among customers to resist their marketing tactics. In fact, customers are tuning out rather than tuning in, in response to the threat of information bombardment. As a result, new rules are being written.

For example, Permission Builders, developed by Bluparc, a UK-based software company, allows customers to choose the type of content they want to receive from suppliers, when it can be sent and to which devices. *"A bank customer might agree very narrow terms on how he or she wants to be contacted and the information that is acceptable. For example, fortnightly balances by Short Messaging Service (SMS),"* says Stewart Holness, founder of the company.

"Once trust between the two has been proven, the customer might extend the type of content he or she is willing to receive, agreeing to a quote when their insurance is due for renewal."

"The customer feels in control. The bank is building up a very accurate picture of needs and preferences which can be applied to both its customer relationship and supply chain infrastructures."

Lands' End, the US-based direct clothing company, is taking a similar stance, extending its already considerable efforts to develop relationships with its customers and reflecting their preferences in its supply chain. The company is planning to integrate historical purchases based on colours, sizes, price sensitivity and types of clothing purchased with customer-segmented emailed newsletters. Customers will opt to receive the emails on a frequency which they can determine, and will be sent relevant offers.

The business case for digital loyalty networks is a sound one. Without access to the same detailed, customer-specific information on value, requirements and cost, it will prove extremely difficult for competitors to distract customers.

The Deloitte research concludes that new products can be copied; functional aspects of an organisation – marketing, customer service and quality standards – can be mimicked. But duplicating how a company differentiates in real-time the way each customer and segment is served by a network of suppliers, logistics providers, vendors, manufacturers and distributors is almost impossible.

Businesses successful in an Internet-driven economy will at their core have an effective digital loyalty network. But for many, there remains a considerable distance to go.

Source: FT.com (http://specials.ft.com/scm/FT311MTQZTC.html)

FT/IT Review – 5th December, 2001/Supply Chain Collaboration

Viewpoint – An Important Role for Mobile Date Systems
By Martin Dunsby and Paul Lee

Published: 3rd December, 2001 20:34GMT/Last Updated: 6th December, 2001 10:40GMT

The success of organisations operating across a broad range of industry sectors depends on their ability to cut costs out of their supply chains. Now mobile data is the new weapon being deployed by leading-edge organisations to achieve that goal.

Yes many companies still remain unaware of the benefits that mobile can deliver today. This stems from a general disillusionment with mobile technology, driven by the delays and disappointments around Wireless application protocol (Wap) and third-generation (3G) telephony. But organisations need to look beyond this negative view if they are to avoid self-inflicting competitive disadvantage.

Mobile is one of the key technologies that can and will enhance the supply chain in the immediate term. But mobile is not confined to 3G or Universal Mobile Telecommunications System (UMTS). A suite of mobile and wireless technologies exists today that are stable, available and relevant for use in the supply chain.

These technologies are already having a positive impact on the supply chains of competitive organisations. They include mature technologies such as GSM, close proximity radio frequency tags, wireless LANs and the Global Positioning System, as well as emerging technologies that should become ubiquitous and dependable in 2002, such as Bluetooth and GPRS (a packet data based service available over GSM networks).

They can all have a positive impact on an organisation's supply chain.

According to recent research from Deloitte Consulting, several organisations that have developed mobile technology across their supply chain have enjoyed payback periods of under one year, while return on investment for some solutions is forecast at hundreds of per cent. And all this being realised without 3G.

Return on investment from mobilising the supply chain should be considered as a major incentive to deploy mobile and wireless technologies. The more agile and better-informed the supply chain is, the more productive it can be. The present uncertain economic climate should provide an additional spur to improve the supply chain. Mobile can be a tool both for increasing productivity and increasing revenues – even during an economic downturn.

The key to mobile's impact at the supply chain results from a faster flow of relevant information. The quicker staff have access to critical data, wherever they may be, the faster decisions can be taken. A mobile-powered supply chain can positively impact several key areas, including cost control, information accuracy, customer relationships and time to market.

- Impact on cost control: mobile can make an important contribution to cost control across the supply chain. As mobile improves the flow of information, approaches to supply chain management, including just-in-time delivery, are improved.

  This means that companies require smaller inventories. Communication between customers and suppliers is faster and more accurate, so stock holdings become more precise, leading to smaller stock levels and improved cash flows.

  Volkswagen, for example, found that its mobile data solution, based on Radio Frequency (RF) tags, allowed it to locate nearly finished vehicles far more quickly than the alternative – staff searching on foot. This allowed the company to accelerate the pace at which it could present brand new cars to customers at its flagship showroom in Germany. The information being communicated is tiny, but the solution was effective enough to pay for itself within a year.

- Impact on information accuracy: even in companies with sophisticated but non mobile-enabled supply chains, the usual technology underpinning the capture and validation of inventory is known by the systems all the time.

40

- Improved customer relationships: mobilising the supply chain improves customer relations through better flow of information. Improvements are principally achieved in the speed and accuracy of data. This would, for example, help a supplier provide informed, rapid and pro-active information to a customer requiring a delivery date and time.

  Monitoring a delivery vehicle's location through GPS, with co-ordinates being relayed from the truck via SMS, allows central co-ordinators to keep a running view of progress and any delays to the central schedule. Any more problems can be spotted quickly and customers alerted to the extent of the potential delay.

  For example RAC, the UK automotive services group, uses mobile data to reduce the time it takes to send its assessments of second-hand cars to their potential customers.

- Time to market: improved communication between all participants across the supply chain means faster time to market. Stock levels, product specifications, lead times and other key data can all be requested and provided more rapidly via mobile technologies.

  But time to market is not just about making existing processes faster, it is also about the pace of problem resolution. For example, time to market can be frustratingly prolonged as a result of mechanical failure. Mobile technology can speed the process made (through wireless LAN or Bluetooth access to technical databases); and new parts are specified and ordered (via a GSM-enabled PDA).

There are three steps that companies should observe when mobilising their supply chain:

- First, assess the supply chain and identify areas of weakness. Even in the most apparently technology penetrated companies, there usually remain several key bottlenecks within the supply chain.

- Second, evaluate which mobile and wireless technologies are relevant to us for addressing supply chain deficiencies. A range of technologies are available today, each of which has specific characteristics in the areas of price, bandwidth and device requirements.

- Third, calculate the potential return on investment and payback period from the solution. This calculation should include not only the immediate productivity benefits, but also secondary impacts, such as improvements in management information, customer relations and cash flow.

  The supply chain will be a key vehicle for competitive differentiation for the foreseeable future. Today's mobile technologies are already proving to be critical elements within that supply chain. Mobile-aware organisations have already seen rapid payback on their deployment, yet still too many organisations remain sceptical of mobile, or are mistakenly planning to defer deployment until 3G arrives.

Martin Dunsby is Global Wireless Initiative Leader, and Paul Lee Director of Mobile and Wireless Research, at Deloitte Consulting.

Source: FT.com (http://specials.ft.com/ftit/december2001/FT303Y41RUC.html)

41

BIA ANNUAL REVIEW 2001

UK Bioscience Facts and Figures 2000

BIA 14/15 Belgrave Square London SW1 8PS

Telephone: +44 (0) 20 7565 7190 Facsimile: +44 (0) 20 7565 7191

Email: admin@bioindustry.org Web: www.bioindustry.org

Public Spending on Biotech R&D

Data from Ernst & Young Eighth Annual European Life Sciences Report 2001

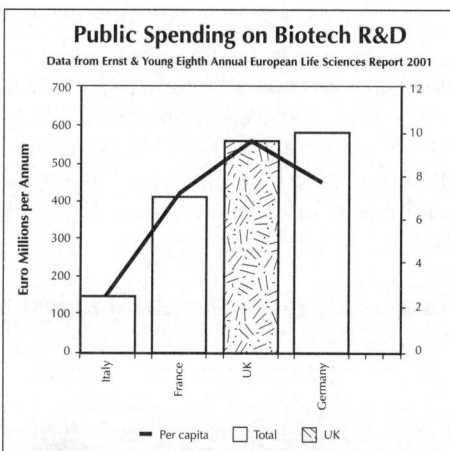

Per capita — Total — UK

Levels of Follow-on Investment in Europe

Data from BioCentury

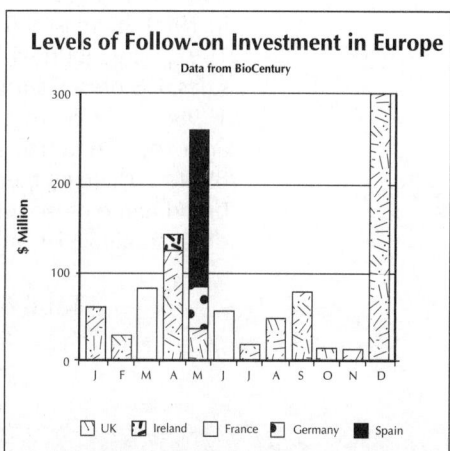

UK Ireland France Germany Spain

The Venture Capital of Europe

Data from the European Venture Capital Association

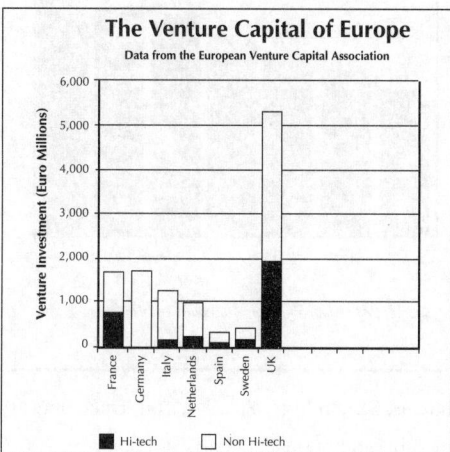

Hi-tech Non Hi-tech

Size and Number of European Biotechnology Companies

Data from Ernst & Young Eighth Annual European Life Sciences Report 2001

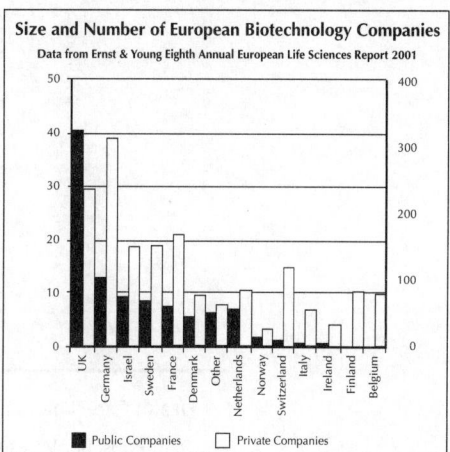

Public Companies Private Companies

Source: BIA Annual Review, 2001

42

The Pharmaceutical Industry

WCI Consulting derives 33% of its revenue from the Life Sciences sector (including pharmaceutical companies and medical device companies). Primary areas of concentration include process optimisation for mandated reporting and for the drug approval process and supply chain management. As such, events in the pharmaceutical industry will have a material impact on the business of WCI.

WCI has a unique niche hold in the area of drug safety, coding and regulatory processes within the top 20 companies in the pharmaceutical industry. A partnership has just been formed whereby WCI is the only preferred partner to a USA software company that has products that combined with WCI's operational and technology experiences can provide a complete solution for Internet linked processes between regulatory authorities, pharmaceutical companies and medical establishments providing a significant growth opportunity.

Pharmaceutical Industry Growth

Worldwide over-the-counter and prescription pharmaceutical sales will exceed $360 billion in 2000. Pharmaceutical sales increased about 8% from $330 billion in 1999, increased 5% from $315 billion in 1998, and 6% from $297 billion in 1997.[1] Ethical drugs, or prescription drugs, account for about 60% of total industry sales. US prescription drug sales accounted for about 35% of global retail sales in 1999. Total US prescription drug sales were estimated at $113 billion in 1999 and are expected to rise 10% per annum through 2002 with growth moderating to the 8% to 10% level thereafter (see table below).[2] Excluding over-the-counter drugs, brand name prescription drugs in 1999 totalled about $77 billion and generic drugs totaled $14 billion.[3]

Total Estimated US Pharmaceutical Industry Sales

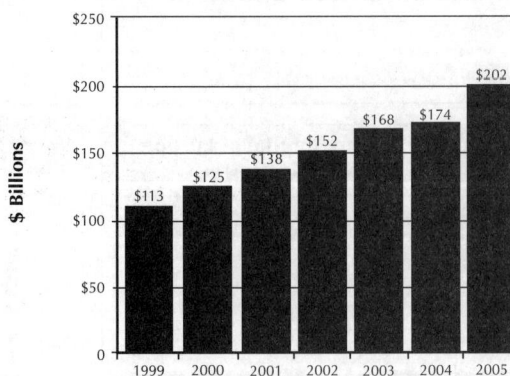

Source: IMS Health and Dain Rauscher Wessels, January 2000

---

[1] Health Care: Pharmaceuticals, S&P Industry Surveys, 16th December, 1999.

[2] Dain Rauscher Wessels, US-based pharmaceuticals, 10th January, 2000.

[3] Health Care: Pharmaceuticals, S&P Industry Surveys, 16th December, 1999.

43

Research and Development

Due to the implementation of the 1997 FDA Modernization Act, which increased the number of reviewers, the mean approval time for a new drug by the US FDA has been cut in half over the past 5-10 years. In 1996, 53 new drugs were approved, and in 1997, 39 new drugs and 10 new biologics were approved. Before 1996, an average of only 25 agents was approved annually. The FDA plans to implement an electronics submission and review system by 2002 to further speed up the review process.[4]

American pharmaceutical companies have over 1,000 new medications in development. Annual medical research expenditures have growth from $9.1 billion in 1987 to $17.3 billion in 1997. This increase in spending should continue into the next decade, reaching an estimated $24.0 billion in 2007.[5]

Drug and medical industry research and development divisions comprise 11.9% of total industry sales. Therefore, R&D not only contributes to product and industry advancement, but also contributes directly to overall industry sales at a much higher percent than any other US industry sectors.[6]

Worldwide Pharmaceutical Expenditures by US Companies for Research and Development

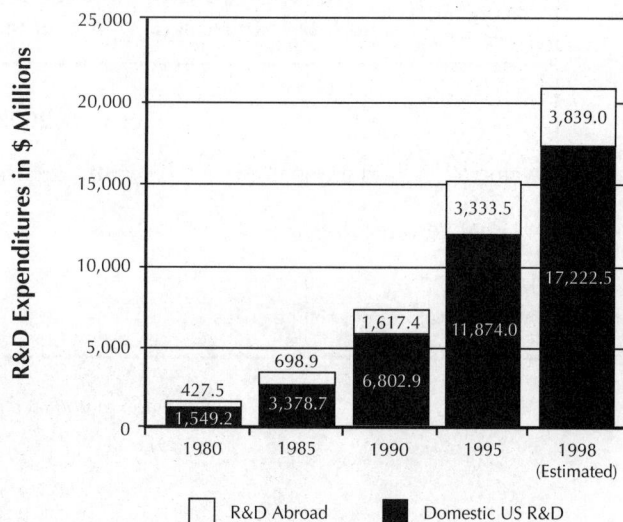

R&D Expenditures in $ Millions

	1980	1985	1990	1995	1998 (Estimated)
R&D Abroad	427.5	698.9	1,617.4	3,333.5	3,839.0
Domestic US R&D	1,549.2	3,378.7	6,802.9	11,874.0	17,222.5

R&D Abroad ☐   Domestic US R&D ■

---

4   PhRMA Industry Report, 1998, p. 17.

5   US Disposable Medical Supplies 2002, Freedonia Group, April, 1998.

6   PhRMA Industry Report, 1998, pp. 17-20.

Source: PhRMA Annual Survey, 1998

BPP PUBLISHING

Merger Activity

The global pharmaceutical industry has recently been characterised by large mergers. For example, Glaxo Wellcome and SmithKline Beecham have merged to form the world's largest pharmaceutical company. Among its pharmaceutical customers, Pfizer has recently won a hostile takeover bid to purchase Warner-Lambert – combined revenues of the merged entity will be US$28 billion. German-based Bayer is not currently involved in a merger, but is looking for acquisitions in the US. Hoffman-LaRoche is not currently planning any large acquisitions. Novartis, one of the world's largest pharmaceutical companies, was formed from the merger of Ciba-Geigy and Sandoz.

Although the number of major pharmaceutical firms has been reduced as a result of these mergers, IT services within WCI have already established a dedicated group with post-merger experience and methodology and anticipates significant consulting assignments over the next five years in the post-merger pharmaceutical industry.

Source: WCI

The Forecast UK Computer Services Market at Current Prices (£ Million at msp), 2001-2005

	2001	2002	2003	2004	2005
Value (£ Million at msp)	20,430	22,143	24,223	26,416	29,184
% change year-on-year	*7.8*	*8.4*	*9.4*	*9.1*	*10.5*

Key:
msp – manufacturer's selling prices

Information reproduced by the kind permission of Key Note Ltd.

Forecast Segmentation of the Computer Services Market at Current Prices (£ Million and %), 2001-2005					
	2001	**2002**	**2003**	**2004**	**2005**
Value (£ Million)					
Operational services	8,810	9,852	11,067	12,364	13,934
Professional services	6,579	7,025	7,634	8,353	9,212
Systems/solutions	4,221	4,525	4,872	5,146	5,590
Maintenance/support	820	741	650	553	447
Total	**20,430**	**22,143**	**24,223**	**26,416**	**29,183**
of which:					
Total outsourcing*	6,996	7,988	9,147	10,466	11,975
% of Total					
Operational services	43.1	44.5	45.7	46.8	47.7
Professional services	32.2	31.7	31.5	31.6	31.6
Systems/solutions	20.7	20.4	20.1	19.5	19.2
Maintenance/support	4.0	3.3	2.7	2.1	1.5
Total	**100.0**	**100.0****	**100.0**	**100.0**	**100.0**
of which:					
Total outsourcing*	34.2	36.1	37.8	39.6	41.0

Key:

msp – manufacturer's selling prices

* – operational outsourcing, applications management and processing

** – does not sum due to rounding

Information reproduced by the kind permission of Key Note Ltd.

Forecast Growth in Computer Services Revenue by Subsector at Current Prices (%), 2001-2005	
Applications management	76.9
Operational outsourcing	71.5
Education and training	57.3
Processing	52.9
Maintenance	45.5
Total market	42.8
Databases/VAS	36.4
Systems integration	34.7
Consultancy	34.3
Turnkey solutions/VAR	29.5
Systems development	24.3

Key:

VAS – Value-Added Services   VAR – Value-Added Reseller

Information reproduced by the kind permission of Key Note Ltd.

46

BPP PUBLISHING

IT Services Market Projections

The worldwide IT services* market will grow from $660.8 billion in 2000 to $1.344 trillion by 2005.

Service Lines	2000	2005
Transaction processing	5%	5%
Business Management	24%	26%
Consulting	7%	7%
Development and integration	23%	24%
Education and training	3%	3%
Hardware services	16%	10%
Management services	14%	17%
Software services	8%	8%

*   So far as the IT services itself goes, it represents 40.6% of the worldwide IT market (2000) rising to 45.2% by 2004 when the total value will be $2.55 trillion.

The Europe, Middle East and Africa (EMEA) market for IT services was $153.2 billion in 2000 and is expected to grow to $257.2 billion by 2005.

Source: Gartner Group

European Market

European Market IT spending was $412 billion in 2001. Despite the economic slowdown, Gartner forecasts overall growth of 6.6% for 2001-02. But 2002 will be a tough year for IT vendors, who will need guidance about exactly where this multi-faceted market will grow for the 13 verticals, from agriculture to transport, and across the 16 countries tracked in Western Europe.

Source: Excerpt from forthcoming Gartner Dataquest report, "European IT Market Trends 2000-05"

47

The UK plc

FTSE 100 Total Market Value £22.9 Billion
Distribution by Market Sector of BPO* and ICT**
Outsourced Services

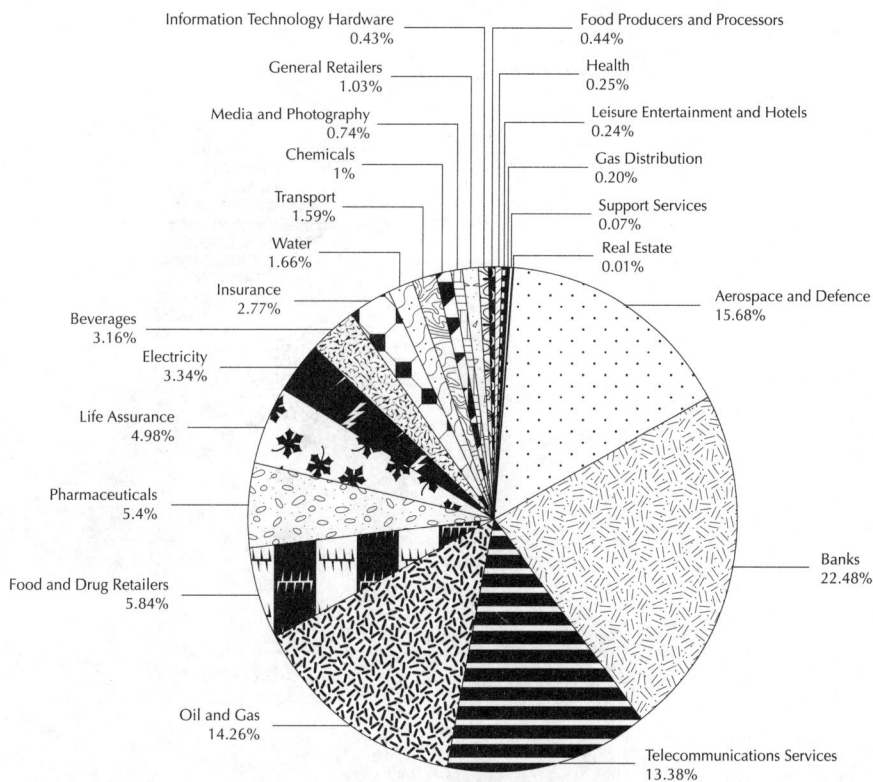

Information Technology Hardware
0.43%

General Retailers
1.03%

Media and Photography
0.74%

Chemicals
1%

Transport
1.59%

Water
1.66%

Insurance
2.77%

Beverages
3.16%

Electricity
3.34%

Life Assurance
4.98%

Pharmaceuticals
5.4%

Food and Drug Retailers
5.84%

Oil and Gas
14.26%

Food Producers and Processors
0.44%

Health
0.25%

Leisure Entertainment and Hotels
0.24%

Gas Distribution
0.20%

Support Services
0.07%

Real Estate
0.01%

Aerospace and Defence
15.68%

Banks
22.48%

Telecommunications Services
13.38%

*BPO = Business Process Outsourcing
**ICT = Information and Computer Technology

Source: www.cw360.com/outsourcingreport

Pie Chart 1.

The UK plc

FTSE 100 ICT* Outsourced Services Only
Total Market Value £17.08 Billion
Distribution by Market Sector

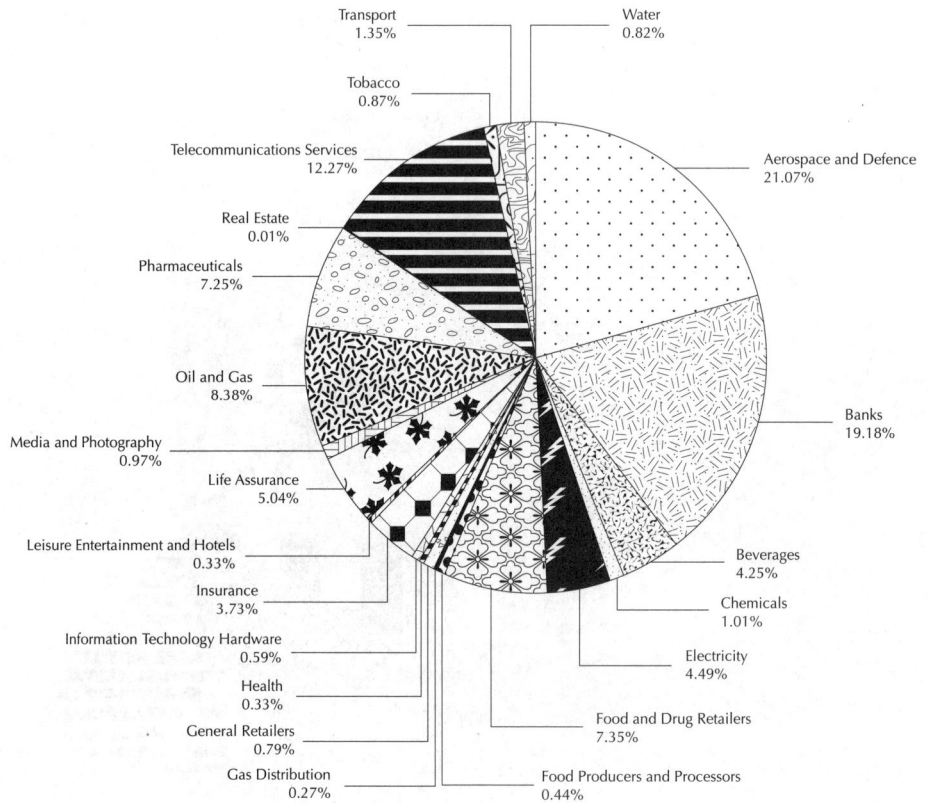

Transport
1.35%

Water
0.82%

Tobacco
0.87%

Telecommunications Services
12.27%

Aerospace and Defence
21.07%

Real Estate
0.01%

Pharmaceuticals
7.25%

Oil and Gas
8.38%

Banks
19.18%

Media and Photography
0.97%

Life Assurance
5.04%

Leisure Entertainment and Hotels
0.33%

Beverages
4.25%

Insurance
3.73%

Chemicals
1.01%

Information Technology Hardware
0.59%

Electricity
4.49%

Health
0.33%

General Retailers
0.79%

Food and Drug Retailers
7.35%

Gas Distribution
0.27%

Food Producers and Processors
0.44%

*ICT = Information and Computer Technology

Source: www.cw360.com/outsourcingreport

Pie Chart 2.

The UK plc

**FTSE 100 BPO* Services Only
Total Market Value £5.8 Billion
Distribution by Market Sector**

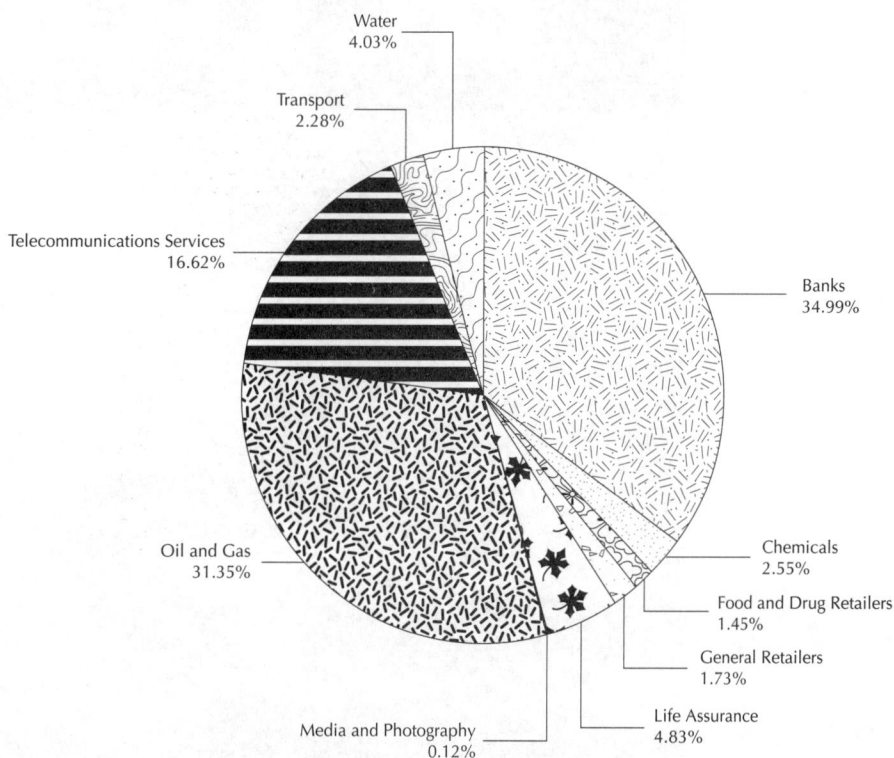

Water
4.03%

Transport
2.28%

Telecommunications Services
16.62%

Banks
34.99%

Oil and Gas
31.35%

Chemicals
2.55%

Food and Drug Retailers
1.45%

General Retailers
1.73%

Life Assurance
4.83%

Media and Photography
0.12%

*BPO = Business Process Outsourcing

Source: www.cw360.com/outsourcingreport

Pie Chart 3.

50

449 *BPP*

PUBLISHING

Appendix 3.

Source: Management in Action, WCI

WELCOME

PAUL COLLINS

PEOPLE THAT MAKE A DIFFERENCE

Welcome

Last October, World Class International merged its management consulting activities with computer services firm, 2GL. The new company of over 300 consulting and technology professionals can now offer a much broader range of services to new and existing clients across Europe and the USA.

It took both original companies 2 years to find a suitable partner to serve our clients better in this new millennium. We talked to many firms who had the requisite technical skills but were sadly lacking when it came to issues of ethics and culture. Putting client needs first and an equal respect for all our employees are values that underpinned both companies prior to the merger. Living those values during the past 6 months has produced a new organisation that is not only technically able but also refreshed, fit and enthusiastic about helping our clients face the challenges of the New Economy.

That's great for WCI, you might say, but what does that mean for us? Well, during this decade every business will be affected by the Internet. Massive opportunities exist for renewed operational effectiveness in every business process using web-based technology that will dwarf yesterday's BPR methods. Easier access to global markets via the web will challenge Market Strategy and offer both opportunities and threats. Faster, cheaper communications with suppliers, customers and partners will offer new ways of extracting value from the supply chain for all concerned. At WCI, we've assembled a team of professionals that can help your business take

advantage of these opportunities and avoid the threats. Our business and process skills have been creating shareholder and customer value in clients for over 15 years. Now we have the skills and experience to help you harness the Internet for sustained competitive advantage.

One generic impact of the web is the increased pace of change in business today. More and more companies are questioning whether they can continue to fight on all fronts, mastering all processes and technologies in order to compete effectively. WCI now has the capacity to manage technology-intensive processes for those clients who would like to release management time to concentrate on core activities. Inside this issue of Management in Action you can read about one example of technology outsourcing in the NHS where rapid growth in the roll-out of the new NHS Direct service was made possible by partnering with WCI and Axa Insurance, leaving the NHS to concentrate on managing the growth of core medical resources.

As always, I hope that you find this MIA issue of value and that it stimulates thought and, more importantly, ACTION! If you'd like us to share the load, don't hesitate to call. I look forward to talking with you . . .

Paul E. Collins
CHIEF EXECUTIVE

3

Source: Management in Action, WCI

52

World Class Capabilities

Many of you will have seen the IBM advert, where there's a management meeting taking place on a Sunday. Everyone's been called in because of problems with the e-commerce system. There's a general discussion about where the problem might be, and then the manager says 'well who's got overall responsibility for the system?' Everyone looks up rather sheepishly to say it's her.

Sadly for her the business world is becoming more and more dependent on Internet technologies, whilst at the same time these technologies are becoming more complex and more diverse. Managing that complexity may not be a core competence for many business managers. They need a Partner who has the skill and experience.

The last nine months has also seen the bubble burst on many dot com businesses, but many more of the established companies transforming their business models with new technologies and new routes to market. Again understanding what may be required or acquiring the skills to implement the new processes may not be something the traditional 'bricks and mortar' company has the time to do.

Against this background the merger of WCI and 2GL has created an organisation that has the capability to span all the skills required to go from creating an e-business strategy, through business process transformation, to designing and building a technology infrastructure and, if required, operating and taking responsibility for the new system. In WCI we have created an organisation that can take responsibility for delivering large and complex technology projects.

Increasingly these projects start with some Business Consulting requirements. However whether we start there or start further on in the cycle, we have built an organisation that has over 150 technical consultants. They can:

1. Design and build software applications, and design and build the architectures necessary to integrate new and legacy software.

2. Design and build the network architectures necessary to support the vast amounts of data flowing around these systems.

3. Operate and manage the server and PC networks once implemented to be highly available. If your customers can only order by using one of these systems any down time will be costing you money. WCI is establishing best practice in managing remote networks of PC's and Servers.

So the new WCI is a one-stop shop with the breadth of capability to help our clients with both their Consulting and Technology needs. The company is at a size where we have a growing, robust and stable base to support our clients for many years to come.

ANDREW GARDNER, MANAGING DIRECTOR

4

Source: Management in Action, WCI

Source: Management in Action, WCI

CASE STUDY

NHS DIRECT

clinical decision support system available worldwide".

WCI was a key member of the AXA led consortium which, last August, won the £70 million, seven-year contract to implement NHS Direct.

Viewed as one of the most significant National Health Service contracts for many years, WCI's responsibility is to deploy "a national technical architecture to support the most robust and technologically advanced clinical decision support system available worldwide," according to WCI's Director of Health Care, Dave Marriner.

NHS Direct is a 24-hour, seven day a week telephone helpline service which allows nurses to provide patients with confidential healthcare advice and information. It is one of the largest systems of its kind anywhere in the world - potentially serving the entire population of the UK.

Lead by Project Director Andy Atkins, WCI's brief is to design, implement and support the complete IT infrastructure as a managed service on behalf of the AXA Consortium at the 23 NHS Direct sites across England and Wales. Once fully implemented, an enquiry will be logged at any local call-centre and the patient's details are immediately available to every NHS Direct nurse no matter where the patient is calling from or where the nurse is located.

Working in partnership with the other members of the Consortium, WCI has also had to provide back-up and maintenance of the infrastructure, because, as Andy says, "we have to ensure not only that the system works - but that it doesn't fail."

With a fundamental design philosophy to provide a fully resilient 'no-single-point-of-failure' solution, WCI had to make use of leading technology. Taking full advantage of Compaq and Cisco infrastructure technology to leverage Microsoft's BackOffice 2000 platform, WCI could be sure of providing an infrastructure available 24 hours a day, 365 days a year.

The project centres around the deployment of NHS Direct's new Clinical Assessment System (CAS) software. The software adds value to the triage process by helping the on-line nurses to make their diagnoses.

"It was a project with brutal timescales," says Andy. The first phase had to be completed by December 2000, to enable NHS Direct to achieve 100% coverage across England. This meant that within four months of winning the contract, WCI had to provide the network infrastructure - file servers, PCs, and everything up to the desktop - across five new sites and four existing locations.

The second phase of the project, which is scheduled for completion in September 2001, involves the migration of all the other NHS Direct sites to CAS. This represents at least a further 1,000 workstations. This phase will also include the introduction of a fully disaster-tolerant national data repository across a number of data centres, the IT infrastructure of which will be managed by WCI.

One of the main reasons for the Consortium winning the contract, Dave says, is that "We were a good fit. We spoke the same language as the people at NHS Direct, and could talk to the NHS as peers - as members of the same team."

Dave himself has 26 years experience of working in and with the NHS, and 2GL, the Southampton-based healthcare computing company which merged with WCI in January 2001, had both the experience to know what the NHS needed, and the pool of high level skills necessary to carry it through.

More than 100 people from Southampton have been involved in implementing the project, says Dave, and "2GL has previously provided software and hardware applications to over 200 of the UK's 354 NHS Healthcare Trusts."

The NHS Direct service is predicted to grow significantly over the coming years, and it's IT network will also provide support for many other areas of the NHS, such as walk-in centres and Accident and Emergency departments.

WCI will therefore be playing a pivotal role in providing this vital national service.

One of the main reasons for winning the contract, Dave says, is that "We were a good fit. We spoke the same language as the people at NHS Direct, and could talk to the NHS as peers - as members of the same team."

DAVE
MARRINER

15

Source: Management in Action, WCI

Internal process transformation

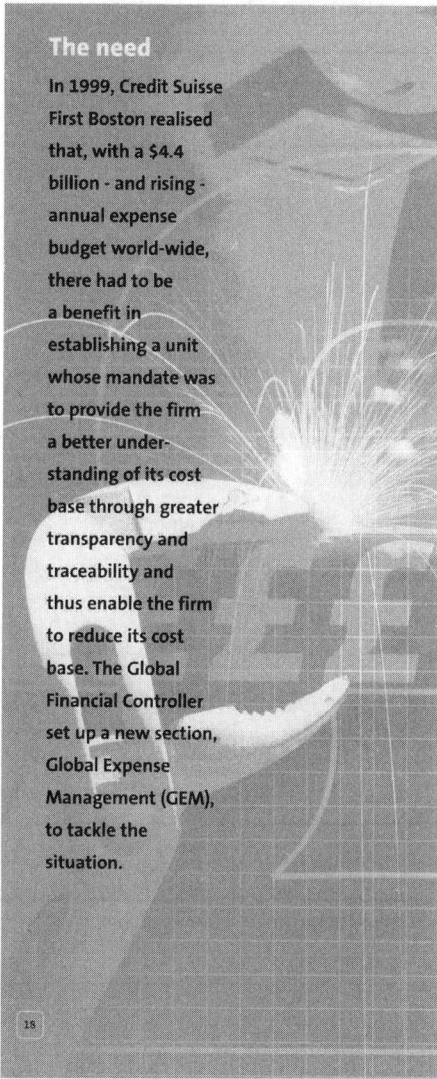

The need

In 1999, Credit Suisse First Boston realised that, with a $4.4 billion - and rising - annual expense budget world-wide, there had to be a benefit in establishing a unit whose mandate was to provide the firm a better under-standing of its cost base through greater transparency and traceability and thus enable the firm to reduce its cost base. The Global Financial Controller set up a new section, Global Expense Management (GEM), to tackle the situation.

Obstacles to improvement

The new team set out to add their value by analysing and interpreting the cost base but were quickly embroiled in fixing errors in their source data, producing reports and struggling to analyse accounts on a global basis. GEM's 'customers' around the world complained that figures were unreliable, reporting timelines poor and very little analysis and interpretation was performed. In short, GEM were not seen to be adding value to the firm. Many business units set up 'cottage industries' to cope, a tactic bound to exacerbate the cost base!

GEM's natural concentration on producing the numbers left them little time to identify root causes of errors or drivers of cost. Since inception GEM had battled to improve their situation - they had installed new reporting software, they had made a number of tactical changes to what they did, but they still had a long, long list of changes for their continuous improvement initiative. The problem seemed intractable: CSFB called in WCI. Marc Adam, CSFB's Managing Director responsible for financial reporting and analysis recalls "We asked WCI to help us identify and articulate to senior management the current state of affairs as well as to develop and implement solutions for us to achieve our goals".

The WCI approach

WCI broke down what GEM perceived to be a complex inter-related problem into 'bitesize chunks' and investigated each one to identify the issues in terms of GEM's strategic themes - control, service and efficiency. As part of a CSFB project team, some hard evidence was gathered to support the need for change:

- **Control** - Poor controls result in questionable monthly variances

- **Service** - The service the firm receives does not help them manage the cost base

- **Efficiency** - A large proportion of Expense Management resources add no value
  (Fig 1 - Source: WCI 2000)

Figure 1 - 70% of expense is non-value added

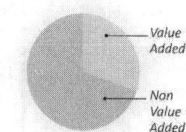

In WCI's experience, 75% of service industry costs add no value. Expense management is no exception.

Any step that is not essential to achieve the process objective using best practice is deemed non-value added.

These uncomfortable findings struck a chord with GEM's customers. A consensus for change was easily established. There would be two phases:

Firstly, fix the basics.
Putting right basic inadequacies (eliminating errors, speeding up the monthly expense reports and improving the quality of expense information) would have huge benefits quickly.
(Fig 2 - Source: WCI 2000)

Source: Management in Action, WCI

Appendix 4.

WCI Consulting
Historical Income Statements with Adjustment Details for the Fiscal Years ended 31st December (£000)

Schedule 1.

	Note	1997 Per Books	1997 Adj.	1997 Revised	1998 Per Books	1998 Adj.	1998 Revised	1999 Per Books	1999 Adj.	1999 Revised
Revenue UK		6,184	–	6,184	6,801	–	6,801	6,431	–	6,431
Revenue Hungary		0	–	0	421	–	421	1,670	–	1,670
Revenue USA		778	–	778	2,400	–	2,400	2,788	–	2,788
Total Sales		6,962	–	6,962	9,622	–	9,622	10,890	–	10,890
Total COGS	(1)	4,150	–	4,150	6,084	(260)	5,824	7,374	(301)	7,073
Total Gross Profit		2,812	–	2,812	3,538	260	3,798	3,516	301	3,817
Operating Expenses										
Administrative Expenses	(1)	2,288	(424)	1,864	2,615	(162)	2,453	2,961	(283)	2,678
Depreciation		183	–	183	263	–	263	295	–	295
Total Operating Expense		2,471	(424)	2,047	2,878	(162)	2,716	3,256	(283)	2,973
Other Expenses		0	–	0	0	–	0	0	–	0
EBIT		341	424	765	660	422	1,082	260	584	844
Interest	(2)	80	(80)	0	67	(67)	0	61	(61)	0
Pre-tax Income		262	504	765	593	489	1,082	198	645	844

Source: WCI

Notes and Adjustment Details to Schedule 1.

		1997	1998	1999
(1)	**Other COGS**			
	Costs related to closure of SA office	–	(260)	–
	One time Director costs	–	–	(301)
	Operating Expenses			
(1)	**Administrative Expenses**			
	Excess costs related to foreign office space	–	(4)	(71)
	Costs related to setup in USA and Hungary	(244)	(191)	(175)
	Adjust Management salaries to FMV	–	100	–
	Eliminate discretionary bonuses	(180)	(67)	(37)
(2)	**Adjustments to Interest Expenses**			
	Remove Interest as Analysis is Pre-debt	(80)	(67)	(61)

Source: WCI

57

WCI Technology
Historical Income Statements with Adjustment Details for the Fiscal Years ended 31st December (£000)

Schedule 2.

	Note	1997 Per Books	1997 Adj.	1997 Revised	1998 Per Books	1998 Adj.	1998 Revised	1999 Per Books	1999 Adj.	1999 Revised
Turnover		4,479	–	7,479	16,297	–	16,297	18,888	–	18,888
Cost of Sales		5,428	–	5,428	12,296	–	12,296	15,866	–	15,866
Gross Profit		2,051	–	2,051	4,001	–	4,001	3,022	–	3,022
Operating Expenses										
Administrative Expenses	(1)	1,781	(84)	1,697	3,357	(87)	3,271	2,305	–	2,305
Depreciation		156	–	156	97	–	97	140	–	140
Total Operating Expense		1,937	(84)	1,853	3,454	(87)	3,368	2,445	–	2,445
Disposal of business unit	(2)	27	(27)	0	0	–	0	0	–	0
Gain (Loss) on Sale (Operating)		15	–	15	5	–	5	0	–	0
Non-Operating Income	(3)	6	(6)	0	4	(4)	0	0	(6)	(6)
Other Expenses		0	–	0	0	–	0	0	–	0
EBIT		162	51	213	556	83	638	577	(6)	571
Interest	(4)	29	(29)	(0)	21	(21)	0	18	(23)	(5)
Pre-tax Income		133	80	213	535	104	638	559	17	576

Source: WCI

Notes and Adjustment Details to Schedule 2.		1997	1998	1999
(1)	**Operating Expenses** *Administrative Expenses* Eliminate non-recurring costs	(84)	(87)	–
(2)	**Adjustments to Other Operating Income** Eliminate gain on disposal of division	(27)	–	–
(3)	**Adjustments to Non-operating Income** Eliminate as non-operating	(6)	(4)	(6)
(4)	**Adjustments to Interest Expenses** Remove Interest as Analysis is Pre-debt	(29)	(21)	(23)

Source: WCI

WCI Group
Balance Sheets for the Period ended 1st October, 2000 (£000)

Current Assets

Cash (and cash equivalents)	79
Accounts Receivable	8,915
Stock and WIP	990
Prepayments	383
Total Current Assets	10,367
Fixed Assets – Net	1,814
Total Assets	12,181

Current Liabilities

Accounts Payable	3,845
Bank Loans	668
Social Security and other Taxes	1,110
Advances, Accrued Expenses	3,015
Deferred Income	898
Amounts due under finance leases	120
Loans from Directors	12
Total Current Liabilities	9,668
Bank Loans	49
Hire Purchase	131
Deferred Income Taxes	5
Total Liabilities	9,853
Stockholder's Equity	2,328
Total Liabilities and Equity	12,181

Source: WCI

Appendix 5.

No.	Company	£ Million	Employees	Services
1	3Com	200	11,500	4
2	Accenture	5,364	65,496	5
3	Adcore	*458	1,747	4
4	A. T. Kearney	100	5,300	9
5	Atlas Commerce	*52	200	1
6	Attenda	*31	120	1
7	Arthur Andersen	5,033	77,000	5
8	Axon	25	300	4
9	BSG	*62	240	6
10	BT	3,274	124,700	3
11	Cambridge Technology Partners	376	4,200	7
12	Canon	1,260	21,023	3
13	Cap Gemini Ernst & Young	2,760	39,626	7
14	Cisco	1,280	34,000	2
15	Clarus	5	192	3
16	Cluster	*124	475	4
17	CMG	606	8,656	4
18	Compaq	2,310	85,100	3
19	CompelSolve	288	1,200	3
20	Dell	1,090	39,000	1
21	Deloittes	3,000	28,600	5
22	DMR	540	9,000	6
23	Druid	109	*415	8
24	Easy Net	28	352	2
25	Egos	*21	80	1
26	Exodus	168	800	5
27	Fujitsu	29,700	18,800	6
28	Genuity	600	*2,285	2
29	IBM	52,500	307,401	8
30	InteBiz	3,600	18,000	1
31	Intel	10,535	70,200	1
32	Kana	8	350	2
33	Level 8	8	450	1
34	Logica	*2,152	8,200	1
35	Microsoft	13,700	39,170	1
36	Nortel Networks	13,300	76,600	3
37	NTL	950	20,000	2
38	Oracle	6,100	43,000	1
39	PricewaterhouseCoopers	*39,370	150,000	5
40	Siemens	1,987	443,000	3
41	Unisys	225	36,900	4
42	Vignette	*198	757	3
43	XO Communications	282	*1,074	3
44	Yantra	*65	250	1

N.B. *Denotes estimated figures based on the mean of the other competitors

Competitor Key:

1	–	9
Services not Similar		Services Similar

Source: WCI

BPP PUBLISHING

WCI Clients 2000

Client	Revenue £	Sector	Client	Revenue £	Sector
Cussons	4,375	FMCG	WILTSHIRE HEALTH AUTHORITY	38,840	Health
Waitrose	4,800	FMCG	SALISBURY HEALTH CARE NHS TRUST	38,955	Health
Avon	6,000	FMCG	ROYAL BOURNEMOUTH	41,757	Health
Bwise	17,625	FMCG	NORFOLK MENTAL HEALTH CARE NHS	44,524	Health
Green Isle	31,100	FMCG	PORTSMOUTH AND S.E. HANTS H.A.	45,237	Health
VITACRESS SALADS LTD	31,140	FMCG	WYETH LABORATORIES	46,392	Health
IMPERIAL TOBACCO LTD	36,575	FMCG	La Roche	51,702	Health
ALLDAYS STORES LTD	41,694	FMCG	THE ROYAL MARSDEN NHS TRUST	52,250	Health
Littlewoods	47,450	FMCG	Sola Lenses	53,750	Health
GUS	75,150	FMCG	Dentsply	54,907	Health
Devon Desserts	109,750	FMCG	HUNTLEIGH HYGEIA plc	56,103	Health
Fox's Biscuits	436,500	FMCG	Allergan Pharmaceuticals	62,162	Health
NAAFI	441,689	FMCG	FORT DODGE ANIMAL HEALTH LTD	62,601	Health
ESTÉE LAUDER COMPANIES LTD	463,906	FMCG	SHEFFIELD CHILDRENS HOSPITAL	62,646	Health
W. H. SMITH NEWS	1,428,088	FMCG	WORTHING PRIORITY CARE	68,217	Health
CIMA	5,100	FS	PORTSMOUTH HOSPITALS NHS TRUST	71,057	Health
Barclays	10,500	FS	SOUTHAMPTON COMMUNITY HEALTH	73,879	Health
FORTIS INSURANCE LTD	41,868	FS	ROYAL BROMPTON AND HAREFIELD NHS	79,459	Health
LOMBARD NETWORK SERVICES	44,506	FS	WYETH MANUFACTURING UK	86,637	Health
ING BARINGS FUTURES AND OPTs	52,384	FS	Inamed	90,090	Health
TOTAL ASSET FINANCE	39,108	FS	PORTSMOUTH HEALTH CARE NI IS	92,447	Health
DENPLAN LTD	94,582	FS	SOUTHAMPTON AND S.W. HANTS	96,313	Health
Railpen	99,900	FS	HAMPSHIRE AMBULANCE NHS TRUST	102,222	Health
Dow Corning	105,049	FS	SURREY AMBULANCE SERVICE	113,870	Health
INSURANCE ADVISORY SERVICES	230,926	FS	NEWCASTLE CITY HEALTH NHS	113,871	Health
BANCTEC UK LTD	394,607	FS	DORSET HEALTH CARE NHS TRUST	114,442	Health
PORTMAN BUILDING SOCIETY	523,175	FS	Bausch & Lomp	136,625	Health
WINTERTHUR SYSTEMS LEASING	910,000	FS	WESLEY JESSEN PBH LTD	139,273	Health
CSFB	1,500,000	FS	OXFORDSHIRE HEALTH AUTHORITY	140,292	Health
SKANDIA LIFE	1,832,524	FS	ISLE OF WHITE HEALTH CARE TRUST	146,548	Health
Ferring	1,300	Health	LODDON NHS TRUST	147,004	Health
Aviron	3,040	Health	PaperPak UK Ltd	154,110	Health
Immunex	23,649	Health	WEST SUFFOLK HOSPITAL	163,435	Health
NORTH SEFTON AND WEST LANCS	25,186	Health			
NORTHERN DEVON HEALTH CARE NHS	25,388	Health			
MARCHAM ROAD FAMILY HEALTH	29,901	Health			
Brent, Kensington, Chelsea	32,938	Health			
KING EDWARD VII HOSPITAL	35,159	Health			
SHROPSHIRE COMMUNITY AND MENTAL	37,925	Health			

Source: WCI

WCI Clients 2000

Client	Revenue £	Sector	Client	Revenue £	Sector
Horstmann	5,000	Industrial	GOODMANS LOUDSPEAKERS	65,712	Industrial
Smiths Industries	7,500	Industrial	BIFFA WASTE SERVICES LTD	66,165	Industrial
Wagon	8,020	Industrial	CIRCULAR DISTRIBUTORS LTD	72,272	Industrial
Betterware	12,000	Industrial	HAMPSHIRE PROBATION SERVICE	76,984	Industrial
Glanbia	12,000	Industrial	CHEWTON GLEN	76.995	Industrial
Plastic Card Co	16,500	Industrial	ARM LTD	77,098	Industrial
Park Sheet Metals	18,125	Industrial	COUNTRYSIDE PROPERTIES	86,355	Industrial
BURNETT SWAYNE – CHARTERED	25,150	Industrial	Screwfix	89,250	Industrial
HOTEL DU VIN (TUNBRIDGE WELLS)	25,986	Industrial	Kelvin Hughes	94,744	Industrial
SWAYTHLING HOUSING SOCIETY	26,136	Industrial	S. DANIELS	97,599	Industrial
TASC DIGITAL CONTROL SYSTEMS	27,385	Industrial	POSTAL SERVICES COMMISSION	102,497	Industrial
HAVANT INTERNATIONAL LTD	28,170	Industrial	Wards	108,700	Industrial
INTERNATIONAL COOLING GROUP	28,722	Industrial	NATIONWIDE REFRIDGERATION	130,902	Industrial
Hewetsons	31,250	Industrial	OFGEM – THE OFFICE OF GAS	131,856	Industrial
MPO	31,453	Industrial	Kingspan	140,750	Industrial
Soundcraft	33,000	Industrial	FIRE AND RESCUE SERVICES	144,995	Industrial
NORTHWEST AIRLINES INC	33,408	Industrial	AIR PARTNER PLC	145,138	Industrial
BKL Tenon	34,292	Industrial	Jarrold	153,088	Industrial
NEW THAMES PAPER COMPANY LTD	34,915	Industrial	PaperPak UK Ltd	154,110	Industrial
INTERPERTNER ASSISTANCE	34,986	Industrial	SOUTHAMPTON UNIVERSITY	155,537	Industrial
Rexam	35,800	Industrial	STENOAK ASSOC SERVICES PLC	208,241	Industrial
STREAMSERVE LTD	36,724	Industrial	TELINDUS K-NET LTD	216,964	Industrial
TY EUROPE LTD	37,233	Industrial	Avery	234,728	Industrial
Geest	38,750	Industrial	MMI	247,550	Industrial
VOSPER THORNYCROFT (UK) LTD	39,801	Industrial	NYK LINE (EUROPE) LTD	276,949	Industrial
Creedeck	39,900	Industrial	Hanson	297,350	Industrial
ZELLWEGER ANALYTICS LTD	40,160	Industrial	Oakhill	420,458	Industrial
SWEDISH MATCH	40,417	Industrial	Exel MSAS Global Logistics	549,830	Industrial
ACTIVE INTERNATIONAL LTD	44,835	Industrial	VOLVO CAR UK LTD	558,892	Industrial
BENCHMARK ADVISOR UK LTD	45,380	Industrial	MM GROUP LTD	795,173	Industrial
FOSTER WHEELER ENERGY LTD	46,222	Industrial	Oracle	9,000	TMT
Acco	48,075	Industrial	BBC	17,550	TMT
SALOMON TAYLOR MADE LTD	52,327	Industrial	Tellabs	21,000	TMT
SWATCH GROUP (UK) LTD	52,925	Industrial			
ASSOCIATED BRITISH PORTS	54,450	Industrial			
RED FUNNEL FERRIES/ABP	55,956	Industrial			
Roxspur	58,250	Industrial			
HOTEL DU VIN (WINCHESTER) LTD	58,326	Industrial			
Serck	60,096	Industrial			

Source: WCI

2 GUIDANCE NOTES FOR WORLD CLASS INTERNATIONAL (WCI)

> The following notes are intended to provide you with some insights to help you get started on WCI. Read them before starting your overview.

2.1 You should, by now have read the June 2002 examination Case Study – World Class International (WCI). You are probably wondering where to start, how you are going to cope and when you will find the time to undertake the necessary analysis. You might even already be wondering about the possible question areas – try not to. You need to complete the analysis first.

2.2 Before working through these guidance notes, do a scan read of the Case, if you haven't already done so. This will give you a context for the comments and observations that follow.

2.3 Senior Examiner Professor Ashok Ranchhod has again presented us with a challenging scenario from a dynamic sector, a successful and growing service company. You can be assured, that although the company size and sector are different from past Cases, comments and guidance offered in the past will remain equally valid and the skills and characteristics which are expected to be evident in a successful candidate remain unchanged. Emphasis is on the strategic rather than tactical in this paper and your ability to tackle decision-making in the exam room remains of critical importance. The analysis you undertake before the exam provides the foundation for your recommended strategies – but analysis alone will not get you a pass. Case exams emphasise a longer-term customer-oriented business strategy and the need for commercially credible proposals. You must be prepared to present these to the examiner in a professional way.

Tackling WCI

2.4 You do not have to have worked in IT or the consultancy sector to be able to tackle this successfully. Success in Case study depends on process – a process which can be applied across any sector and any organisation irrespective of its size or ownership or the geography of its target markets.

2.5 There is considerable material included in the case and it is normal for it to seem muddled at first. We have lots of numbers and data, as well as a range of articles and expert opinion about the sector. You must be clear what information you are going to extract before spending hours analysing and re-analysing data – try not to be put off by the extent of the data and the numbers we have.

2.6 From our perspective this looks to be one of the best 'marketing' Cases we have had for some time. Most organisations disguise product, customer value and profitability figures, making analysis and subsequent segmentation a matter of making assumptions. World Class International (WCI) appear to have been particularly generous in the data they have shared with us; of course we may find these numbers neither complete nor consistent when we come to analyse them.

2.7 Take your time and take care in the analysis and organisation of material. Do not be tempted to rush at the Case in an ad-hoc way. The key to examination success lies in thorough and well-planned analysis of the material and preparation for the examination questions. Take some time to get organised.

Establishing the Case Context

2.8 World Class International (WCI) may seem a daunting Case study when you first approach it. This is presented as a complex international business and you may find the Case information a bit difficult at first to read.

2.9 In fact, it is a fairly straightforward Consultancy services business but the individual 'products' they sell are in themselves complicated to grasp. They are helping people manage their value chain by lowering costs through improving processes or by adding value through improved customer service.

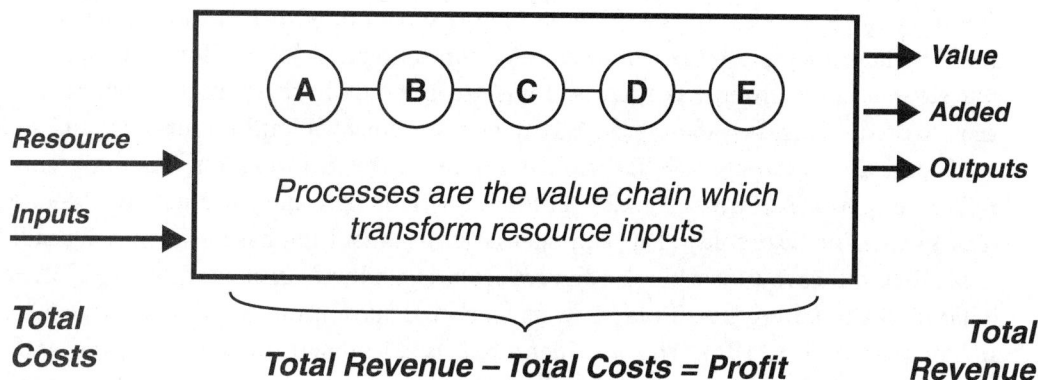

2.10 Remember that, fundamentally, all organisations are resource transformers which are judged by how much value they add in the 'transformation process' from inputs to outputs. Public and private sector firms face the same challenge, the main difference between them is what happens to the surplus.

2.11 WCI are in the business of helping clients understand, analyse and improve these processes. One of the enablers of improvement has been the 'e' capabilities and so 'e' strategies have become increasingly important as a solution they can offer their customers. Since merging with 2GL in 2000 (page 2, last paragraph) WCI can not only recommend strategies but provide the implementation as well (see figure 2, page 3).

2.12 As you work through the Case, you will find there are information gaps and anomalies – there always are. You need to identify them and decide what assumptions must be made and how best to handle them.

2.13 If you work steadily and logically through the Case, you will soon get a clear picture of what needs to be done and the challenges the company faces.

2.14 It should make for an interesting Case study. Take the information provided and work from that perspective. More detailed knowledge is not necessary: remember a Case study is simply a vehicle which allows the examiner to assess your ability to analyse and make decisions.

2.15 Note that it is an international business with offices in the USA and Hungary –it might be easy to lose sight of this international dimension as you work through the materials.

BPP
PUBLISHING

3 ABOUT THE COMPANY

3.1 WCI is a fairly young company, started in 1986 by its current CEO Paul Collins (page 1 and 29). It has grown steadily and by 1999 it had £11 million turnover and was looking for a partner, so it could increase its share of the client's wallet by offering implementation as well as Consultancy. The partner, now a wholly owned subsidiary, was 2GL Computing Services and according to the income statement (on page 58) for WCI Technology, it had income of almost £19 million in 1999. The two halves therefore must have created a £30 million company when they came together in 2000. By end the of 2000, they were forecasting sales of £37.3 million (see page 27) representing 25% growth approximately.

3.2 We seem to be working with 1999/2000 figures so can only make assumptions about 2002. At 25% share they might expect to achieve approximately £57m. However market growth has slowed, competition has increased and many sums have adjusted downwards market growth predictions. It is therefore likely to be less than a £50 million turnover and some 270 staff (page 27). Take care, firstly about the date of this information. The only clue is the reference to a sales estimate of £27.3m for 2000. This may suggest a date of 1999 – we can only guess. The Case study also suggests that only consulting has a presence abroad. If this is so, then we have to work some figures from consultant turnover only, eg USA market. That makes it a pretty small player in its market. Take a minute to look at page 60 and the list of competitors. IBM who are identified as a competitor, have 307,000 staff and a turnover of £52,500 m (note the 1-9 rating of how similar the services provided are to WCI's, you could use a positioning map to help locate the closest competition).

3.3 So, we have an SME service based business, identified in page 8 as a Tier 3 company but, again, note this was before the merger. It is hard to tell if WCI have now established themselves as Tier 2 – it seems unlikely.

3.4 You already have an outline of WCI's specialisms: improving business performance through the value chain. That means they can offer services and advise across the business spectrum, but it is not 'blue sky' thinking. Strategic planning, analysing and assessing opportunities, building brands or financial re-engineering – they are 'get your hands dirty' consultants who focus on making the business run better and so drive improved margins.

3.5 This fits well with the reported increase in demand from firms to measure improvements (page 32). Much of WCI's activity leads to specifically measurable improvements, less waste, less stock, faster frames to market etc.

A generic strategy for WCI?

3.6   So, a growing successful services business, but small in the context of its market, and certainly not a cost leader. WCI seems to have some successful niche activities, for example its work in life sciences (pages 20 and 43).

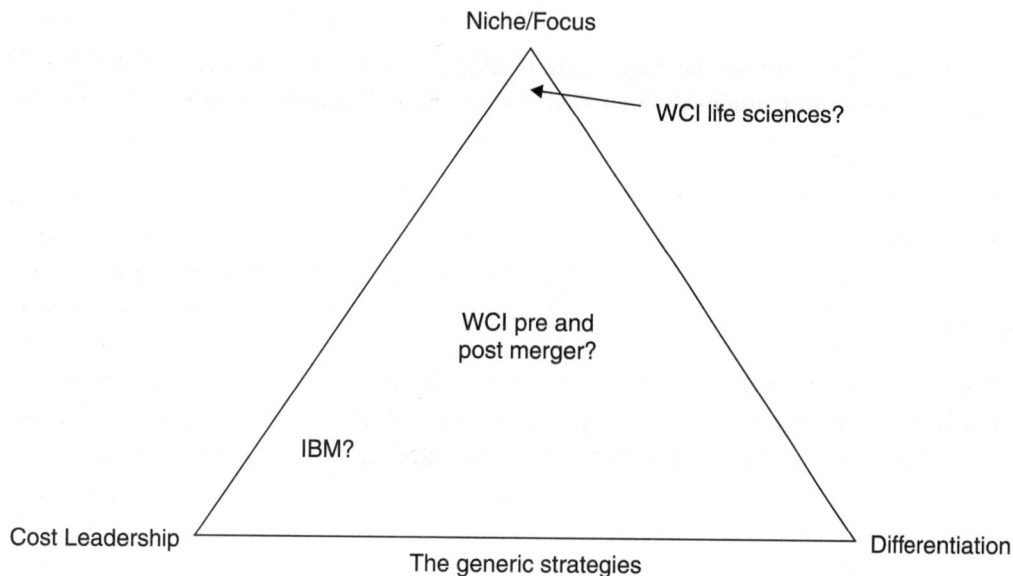

The generic strategies

3.7   On first review, WCI it looks like a company in danger of spreading itself too thinly. It sees many sales opportunities, but runs the risk of diluting its profile and ending up as a middle of the road player. Its position seems too diverse to be a credibly differentiated company, what precisely does it do **differently** to IBM or AT Kearney? Multi-niche may be a more appropriate description, but you will need to keep an open mind.

What PIMS tells us

3.8   Remember what the PIMS research tells you. Small niche players, (possibly both WCI and 2GL) are often profitable, so are the big players who can leverage scale economies and market impact from their size. The danger is the mid-size companies who fail to recognise that to succeed in competitive markets, when you are no longer as 'close' to your customer, you must be good at marketing. Differentiation (or customer-facing multi-niche strategies) will be critical to success.

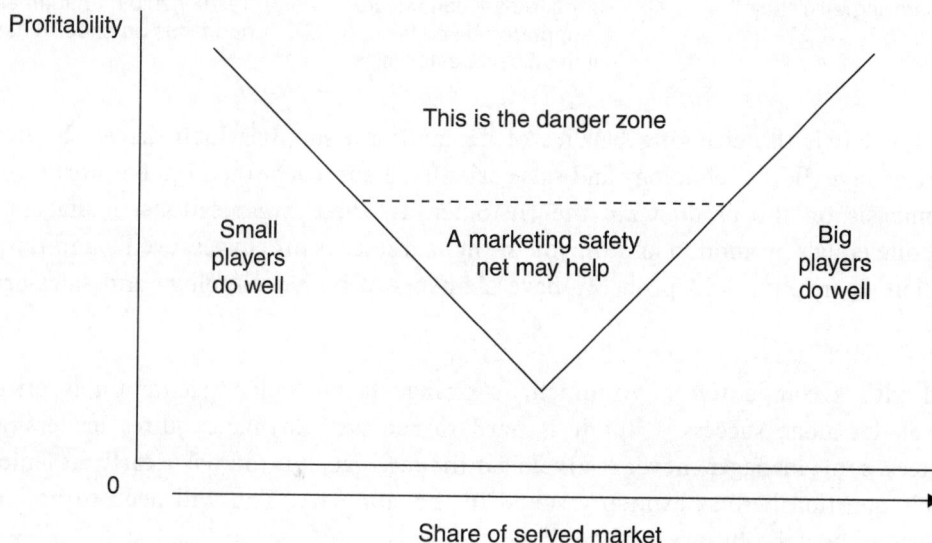

3.9 WCI has catapulted itself via the merger from a small to a bigger operation and so according to PIMS analysis, it will be in the downward slope of profitability. The challenge for you is, can you recommend a strategic marketing plan which will stop that slide? Apparently sales-driven, it will be easy for WCI to end up chasing revenue and market share with little awareness of deteriorating profitability....working harder not smarter is an easy trap to fall into.

3.10 Focus and selectivity are the heart of marketing activities and you need to be able to analyse opportunities and segments, which are attractive to the business in terms of:

- Profitability
- Potential
- Profile

Tutor note

3.11 You will almost certainly need to use a multi-factor matrix to help you assess products/markets and segments, possibly even countries to target. So, building up appropriate and relevant evaluation criteria will be important to you later on.

About the culture

3.12 It is always important not to take Case information or client briefings at face value. You need to look for evidence and make your own assessment.

3.13 We are told success for WCI has been because the company has shifted from a technology strategy to a sales driven strategy (pages 2 and 19).

Changing Culture

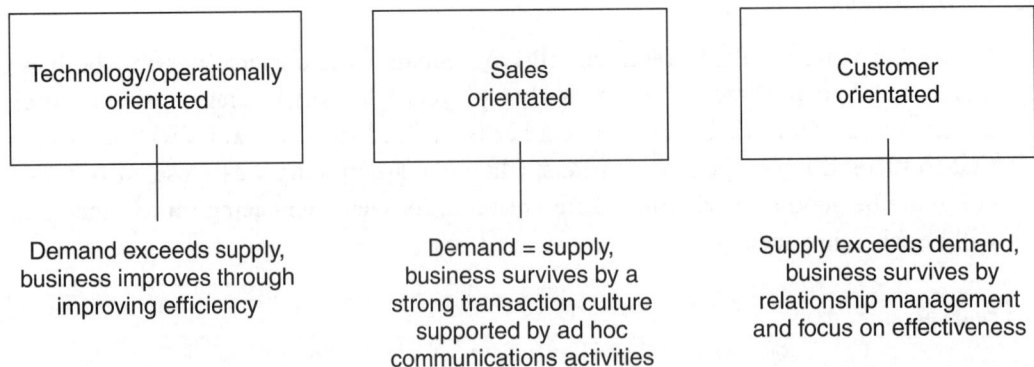

Technology/operationally orientated	Sales orientated	Customer orientated
Demand exceeds supply, business improves through improving efficiency	Demand = supply, business survives by a strong transaction culture supported by ad hoc communications activities	Supply exceeds demand, business survives by relationship management and focus on effectiveness

3.14 Remember, it is the changing balance of demand and supply which drives the need for culture change. Both technology and sales orientated approaches tend to be short term with an emphasis on the product *not* the customer. In these organisations, managers think marketing equals promotion and the job of the marketer is brochures, events and flowers in reception. In reality, WCI probably have elements of both technology and sales-oriented culture.

3.15 Faced with a competitive environment, a change to customer orientation is critical to survival, let alone success – but it is hard to achieve. Change requires leadership and resources, some managers never really do get the message, but there is clearly a theme and a possible question here as explicitly stated in the summary. You will need to be ready to recommend how the culture can/should be changed.

3.16   Putting what you do before the customer leaves the business vulnerable to more customer focused competitors. In an attempt to win and retain business, price not value, is the focus and margins are eroded – the market becomes commoditised.

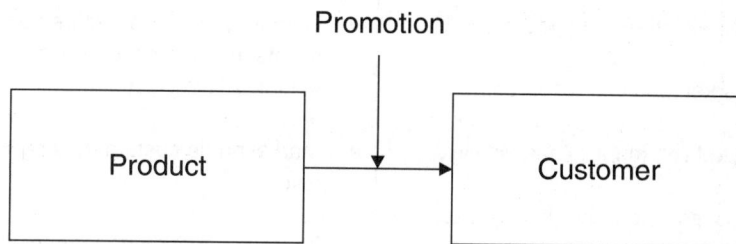

Promotion

```
┌─────────────┐                    ┌─────────────┐
│             │         ↓          │             │
│   Product   │──────────────────▶ │   Customer  │
│             │                    │             │
└─────────────┘                    └─────────────┘
```

Promotion is used only to support sales and so becomes ad hoc, often both inefficient and ineffective.

3.17   It is **market research,** not promotion, which characterises an effective customer focused business. We are told WCI spends £600,000 (page 18) on a menu of promotional activities, from advertising to events but there is no indication of serious market research activities.

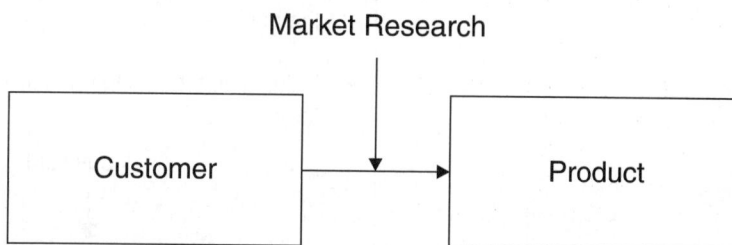

Market Research

```
┌─────────────┐                    ┌─────────────┐
│             │         ↓          │             │
│   Customer  │──────────────────▶ │   Product   │
│             │                    │             │
└─────────────┘                    └─────────────┘
```

3.18   One of the co-ordinators, Simon Gautrey (page 30), has been given research as just one of a number of areas of responsibility. We have no research findings done by the company. Much of the external information and industry data has been compiled from third party sources by the examiner.

Evidence of WCI culture

Sales focused	Customer focused
• Case says twice, 'it's sales focused'. • Limited or no market research resource. • A lack of integrated communications activity. • Some evidence of an 'opportunistic' approach to business development.	• Company seems structured around clients/markets *not* products, or at least a matrix structure is in place. • Marketing (ie customer) is represented at board level. • There is a marketing team of six and a budget of £600,000 on promotion. This is at the low end (1.5% of £40 million turnover) given growth ambitions but it is still in place. • The examples of corporate communication we have, the brochure (appendix 1 and newsletter Management in Action), are written in customer centric /benefit orientated terms and would demonstrate some clear marketing thinking in the business. • Valuing staff tends to result from the recognition that: Happy staff ↓ Happy customers ↓ Happy shareholders

3.19 You will need to collect your own evidence and make your mind up about the prevailing culture and how it may need to be tackled. Internal marketing and culture change programmes should be on your agenda, as well as theirs.

Your role

3.20 Your role is clear. You are Patrick Pearson, a recently appointed Marketing Consultant to the Board of Directors at World Class International (WCI). Less clear however, is what you are expected to deliver. It looks like elaborating on your initial brief, which focused on the state of the company and the recent trends in the sector.

3.21 The presentation will be to the Board of Directors and it is reasonable to expect some searching questions which focus on the concerns of the directors: business consolidation, business growth, opportunities, synergies created by the merger and more effective communication at home and abroad.

3.22 You will see as you work through the Case that the marketplace is very diverse and challenging, particularly in areas of segmentation, e commerce, products and communication. It looks like your meeting with the Board of Directors will give you the opportunity to make a good impression, demonstrating your powers of strategic analysis and creativity.

3.23 At the time of your meeting, you can expect to receive some additional information which you will need to analyse quickly and take account of when answering the questions. The examiners are *not* interested in either:

- Pre-prepared answers, which do not reflect the additional information; or

- Pages of analysis with no evidence of strategic direction, recommendations or decision making

3.24 As indicated, you might be asked to make recommendations on a number of areas and aspects of the Case, from positioning and brand building to segmentation, communication issues to strategic growth. The key issues and likely question areas will become more obvious as you work through your analysis. What is certain is that you will need to be prepared with for short, medium and long term recommendations. You can assume the emphasis will be on strategic, not tactical aspects of the business and that your exam success depends not only on the quality of your analysis and the credibility of your recommendations, but also on your effectiveness as a communicator.

What do you need to do?

3.25 You need to work through the analysis process rigorously to provide you with a solid foundation for any marketing or communications strategy questions which come up in the exam room.

3.26 You must respond **in the role** established by the brief. That means you work in role as Patrick Pearson the Marketing Consultant.

3.27 Your tone and language must be appropriate for dealing directly with the Board of Directors so you need to think as a senior marketer at a strategic level. These people are your colleagues. You have not worked with them before and will want to make a good impression. Your assessments must be clear and justified. Try to remain positive and constructive rather than damning and hyper-critical. Your recommendations must be realistic, particularly in terms of this company's resources and constraints of the market place.

3.28 You will need to convince the Board of Directors of the benefits any proposals may offer. They are interested in growth and the merger should have delivered synergies which may (or may not) now be evident. Merger is often a painful process. No two businesses are alike and the honeymoon period is likely to be over soon. 'Storming' is probably on the agenda and could lead to a loss of external focus. Strong leadership and vision will be key and we seem to have neither a clear vision or mission here.

3.29 You will need to be able to recommend a strategic marketing plan. Strategic marketing implies the customer orientation of the business plan. In other words, which products and which markets should WCI be selecting and prioritising? Selecting products and markets is clearly vital for this business and a process for doing so effectively could well be a question for you.

3.30 You might find it possible to develop a picture of the portfolio currently using a BCG matrix, to sort out the 'dogs' and 'cash cows' etc. The material from page 8-12 about WCI's services deems to lend itself to this, as we have an indication of market growth and WCI share (though not as real metrics, for the whole portfolio of products).

Tutor Note

3.31 Do take care to keep clear in your mind:

- What they sell (products and services), eg. e-software and business process software.
- Who they sell to (the markets), eg. fmcg and financial services (page 16).
- Where they operate (geography), eg. UK, Eastern Europe and USA.

As you work through the Case, sort material into its appropriate category.

4 OVERVIEW/FAMILIARISATION

Now you are ready to tackle the Case Study itself.

4.1 To do this thoroughly, you should allow about 4 hours of preparation time – there is a lot of information in this Case which needs sorting out. In particular we have general information mixed with company specific data – take care!

(a) If you have not already done so, read quickly through the Case once. You will probably find this easier to get to grips with if initially you do not worry about what you are going to be expected to do.

(b) Try to sort out the products and markets and the current activities and positioning of WCI in its various markets. Take it in a couple of short bursts if you start to get muddled. Sort out all the information on the industry/sector in general and then the specific information on the company.

(c) Do not just rely on what is written. Think about the business; try to picture it in your own mind.

(d) What do you know about the characteristics of marketing in the service sector? What are your views on these sort of products and your experiences as a customer?

(e) Forecasting, portfolio management, culture change and growth strategies are issues which could be on the Examiner's agenda and the brand development is important for long term market presence. Is there any real differential advantage in the WCI brand or offering currently?

(f) Who are the competitors and what external environmental factors are changing the market place? There are many.

(g) What factors will change buying behaviours and demand in the future and how should WCI keep in touch with the market? Research and information do look to be something of a black hole.

We are going to walk you through the Case page by page making any observations or comments as we come across the material. You can use these notes in conjunction with your overview analysis – we hope they help. Remember, the idea at this stage is to end up with information sorted under more useful headings so analysis will be easier.

Page	Comments

Page 2
- The history shows ambitious expansion including limited overseas activity.
- Forward looking HR strategies.
- Notice the core business in *paragraph 2* is defined around products not customers.
- E-business has become an expected skill for players in their sector not an augmented or differentiated offer.
- *Paragraph 3*. The merger is recent, keep your eyes open for pre and post 2000 information. How has doubling the business overnight changed things?

Page 3
Two distinct divisions still exist and this split is based on 'products' not customers, ie advising versus implementing. Does this cause client problems, no single points of contact etc? Are cross selling opportunities being maximised? If selling is a 'one stop solution', does it feel this way to clients? Remember, business units focused on what you tend to force an internal orientation.

Page 4
WCI Technology was formerly 2GL – so still a separate division, is synergy possible without integration or is this a conglomerate type structure?

Page 5
We have more detailed information about WCI Technology than WCI Consulting – it seem this implementation end of the spectrum may be more of the focus.

The merger was in line with industry trends again a 'one stop shop' appears to be expected, NOT augmented benefit.

Page 6
Some of the big players with finance parentage being effected by legal changes and demise of Andersen since Enron is a hole in a key competitor (note this is external to the Case but so much in the public domain its OK for you to know it).

Consulting is big business, WCI have a **very** small market share.

Page 7
Of course WCI are in business to business services and this table gives an indication of worldwide: the US is lucrative potentially; Eastern Europe is not a big part of the current market (but may have long term potential).

The last paragraph contradicts the earlier indication that trend is merger between consultancy and IT – here we see WCI is unique. Is it? Is it perceived to be? Does it influence buyer behaviour?

The key competitors are:

- AT Kearney* £100 million
- CTP £376 million
- CGEY £2,760 million
- IBM £52,500 million

* (Take care with the accuracy of this figure. The employee ratio suggests this could be a mistake.)

Page	Comments
Page 8	Profit margins will be useful later, 35% – 50% on strategic planning, 10 – 20% on installation, so there exists a high-volume lower-margin business in WCI Technology.
	The WCI portfolio of services runs from here to page 12. They do seem to be offering solutions not just services, which would again indicate some strategic marketing thinking in the business.
Page 10	1/3rd of WCI consulting's income (not total company revenue) comes from life sciences and lean compliance – however, this seems to be a core competence area. What other sectors have compliance issues and needs?
Page 11	Market share references are vague throughout this section and seem reasonable and good. However, this reflects how WCI defines the market. WCI is too small and spread too thin to be really significant anywhere – again 'niche' is an appropriate label.
Page 12	Trends are important in this business and case and with the cluster of articles provided in the appendices make you think some questions on forecasting scenario planning etc could be on the cards. Try plotting the different services on a generic life cycle. Knowledge management would be at the beginning and outsourced IT nearing the top half of growth curve. Remember it's not the size of a market opportunity but whether it is **still growing** which may be the best indicator of potential.
Page 13	Figure 10 is difficult to interpret. It is not company based knowledge management which is the 'hot topic' but seems limited to technical IT issues.
	What we know is, in the past the assets and resources of a business were tangible and WCI can help manage them.
	In the future, increasingly they will be intangible but capturing, storing and retrieving, knowledge and information will be critical to business success. This is a future possible arena?
Page 14	This chart shows WCI's client benefits if WCI help them develop integrated solutions.
Page 15	'M commerce'. Is this also an opportunity?
Page 16	Here we turn to the markets (not segments) served by WCI. Let us assume that pharmaceuticals are covered in industrial markets.
	Better margins to work with: if we have profitability by product (link these back to services, pages 8 – 12), this will help in any portfolio analysis.
Pages 16 – 17	Outsourcing looks like an attractive and still growing opportunity.
Page 17	56% of FTSE companies generating £20 billion outsourcing income.

Page	Comments

Page 18   Pricing seems to be based on an assessment of what the client can afford and competitor prices in the sector. This reference seems only to be related to pricing for outsourced projects but increased sophistication amongst buyers will, in future, make it harder for companies to have an opportunistic pricing strategy.

The £600,000 communication spend is presumably meant to build profile and to enable WCI to charge premium prices. Advertising without a meaningful differentiator is unlikely to be successful in an increasingly 'buyer's market'.

£600,000 may look generous, but is probably less than 1½% of turnover and is spread across a number of geographies and sectors. To have impact, it will need to be integrated around a clear corporate positioning and be very focused in execution. Any major growth initiatives would need additional marketing resource: remember for every 1% of revenue spent on marketing the gross profit margin goes down by 1%. The examiners will want you to demonstrate your understanding of this cause and effect relationship.

Page 19   Marketing and HR. It is interesting that the two are linked, only a few organisations have realised the benefits of an internally applied marketing approach, but in a consultancy business all the consultants are active marketers and sellers of the services. We have details of internal marketing going on, this will have been important in a successful merger. This would be an interesting question area for the examiner and would break new ground.

Read the summary again. Clues suggest what we need to do to help select product/markets and manage the change of culture.

Pages 20 – 26   This seems to be the company brochure – it looks professional and well done. It gives you further information on products and markets.

Page 27   Finally to some specific figures, you will need to assume a turnover of around £50 million? Perhaps higher if they have achieved 25% growth, then use the percentages and margin information to try and sort out what the company is making from what.

Revenue from the USA is small £4 million plus – what's it costing to have a presence in the US? Perhaps they need aggressive and focused activity to grow USA or withdraw presence. 17 consultants generate 10% of income (US). 47 consultants generate other 90%. Incomes per consultant look interesting.

Try creating customer bands based on average incomes. The top 4 brands = 5% of turnover each, at the other end 55 clients generate 10% income. Is this their maximum potential? What are the penetration strategies in place?

70% – 80% is repeat business, so each year there is a £8 – £12 million gap to equal last year's target.

Page	Comments

Page 27 cont.

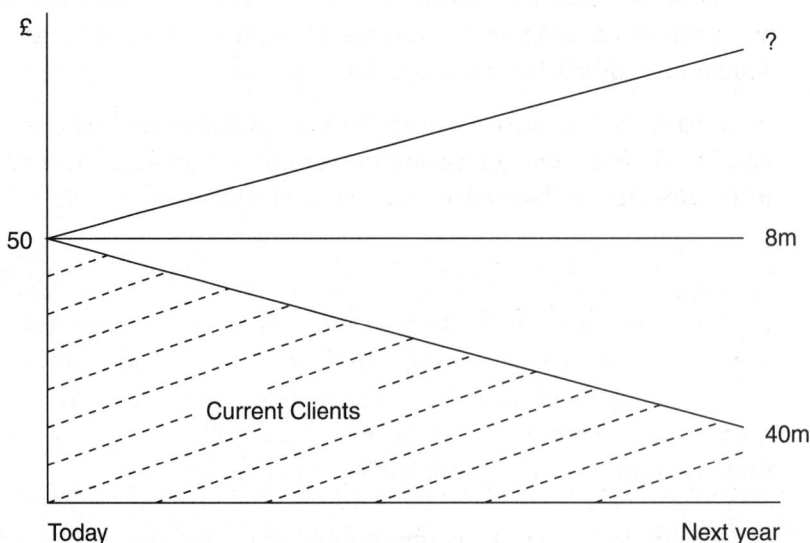

That leads to a thought about what sort of objectives the shareholders might expect – one would think quite bullish growth.

Page 28

We have a menu of communications activities.

You can have fun with this page looking at income by office space allocated per consultant etc. US consultants are given more space than their counterparts in the UK. Be careful here, you are looking at figures broken down by the 2 divisions. Furthermore, US land rental prices may be lower.

Page 29

The structure diagrams are interesting. Support services which should be pan-company are based in the **consulting** board structure, not holding or parent structure. That seems to leave no dedicated sales effort for consultancy and no line responsibility for marketing to WCI Technology sales. Are the strategies customer led or is this why the culture is described as sales driven?

Pages 31 – 42

Appendix 2 gives you lots of reading, pulls together information on emerging trends and problems. It offers an expert opinion that might help you build your PEST analysis and an opportunities and threats matrix.

Page 43

This page mixes WCI information and general market figures, so take care in using it.

Page 45

Another niche opportunity – is this now a competence after the merger?

Pages 46 – 47

Forecast information is always interesting. Where is the biggest growth? Objectives set in terms of retaining WCI's share, for example, outsourcing market would be a benchmark.

Page 51

Appendix 3 – a client newsletter, good quality and well done. It doesn't add much depth but some colour to your analysis.

Page	Comments

Pages 57 & 59 Take care with the numbers. They are pre-merger and post merger and you need to add them together to get totals. Also, we have profit and loss accounts for two companies and a balance sheet for the combined companies. This makes it difficult or impossible to do some ratios.

Remember you are not supposed to be an accountant. Look at the big picture. How profitable is the business? Can we afford to expand? Remember capacity, not just customers, are needed to build a business.

Page 61 – 62 At a client and sector level you can look at revenues billed in 2000, remember 70-80% will be repeat buyers.

A summary

4.2 The comments above should help you to clarify the picture. A dynamic company, recently doubled in size through merger, provides a 'one stop shop' for business improvement services to a number of sectors. Whilst a medium sized player in size (because many consultants are individuals working alone), compared with key competitors the company is a small operation, trying to compete in the big league. WCI has expanded geographically as well as by developing new products through the strategy of merger with 2GL.

The sales driven strategy may explain the sense of a business spreading itself too thin rather than focusing and growing profile and share in clearly defined niche segments, where clearly they have potential.

4.3 The future looks challenging.

- Customers are becoming increasingly sophisticated and demanding. They want measurable benefits.

- Increased competition and the danger of commoditisation.

- New 'products' needed and will require developing.

- Maintaining share in rapidly growing markets will need significant resources – including attracting the right consultants.

- The company must tackle the internal culture change and whilst the pieces are in place the internal attitude and structural changes will still be upsetting.

- They can not succeed if they try to be all things to all people.

5 YOUR INVIEW ANALYSIS

5.1 **By the end of the first step, you should have familiarised yourself thoroughly with the case.**

5.2 Take a further sheet of paper and use this to record information about the role you must adopt and make key notes about the interests and expectations of both **the marketing team** and the **WCI Board** and its stakeholders.

5.3   Keep a separate note of information gaps, there are plenty and this will help you later if there is a research question and there could be.

Tips

- Do not be tempted at this stage to make decisions and/or jump to conclusions. Collect all the information and analyse it carefully before you start changing things.

- Try not to work in a mechanistic way as though this was an academic exercise; play your part.

- What questions would you ask?

- What extra information would you want if you were in this role?

- Take care with the appendices, check years and currencies (some data is in $'s).

5.4   You should now have a clear picture of your role and what you are expected to do. Re-read the candidate's brief. You will also have a much fuller picture of the challenges and opportunities faced by WCI.

Starting your Inview Analysis

5.5   Working from your overview analysis, set up an indexed section in your working file for all the key areas which need detailed study. Your aim is to extract all the relevant information from the Case.

5.6   Use charts, graphs, ratios, matrices and diagrams to help you assimilate the information. An environmental audit (PEST analysis) will help you to identify macro environmental issues, whilst a situational analysis will bring together the corporate strengths and weaknesses. Together this will provide the foundation for a business or corporate SWOT analysis, you will find there are gaps, but try and give the various factors identified a weighting to indicate their relative importance.

5.7   **You should try to construct a market map.**

In this case, you will find it easiest if you start by sorting all the information about the market and then looking at the company.

- What business are WCI in?
- Who buys their products and why?
- Who are the competitors?
- What are the possible bases for adding value?

5.8   With the information available, complete what you can. You have limited information to let you know about buyers priorities or buying behaviour, but sort out what you can.

- Next, try to sort out the big picture. What do we know about WCI's performance and reputation? Do we know who the closest competitors are and how they are positioned?

- What seems to be happening in this market? What are the environmental changes? Work through your PEST analysis. You will need to make assumptions about this from your own knowledge. Porter's Five Forces could be particularly helpful. Use ours as a starting point.

Take time to look at customer profiles, current and potential approaches to segmentation, remember industry sector and size are not always reflective of buyer behaviour.

Porter's Five Forces

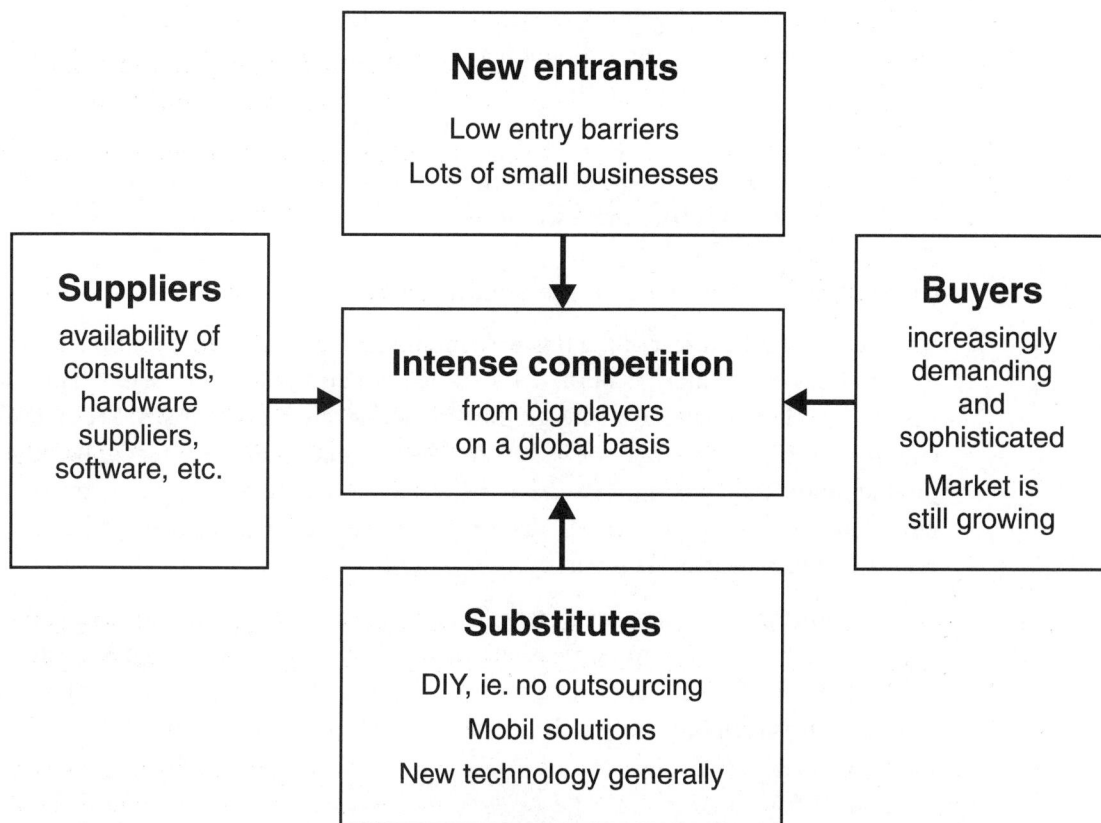

```
                        ┌─────────────────────────┐
                        │      New entrants        │
                        │    Low entry barriers    │
                        │  Lots of small businesses │
                        └─────────────────────────┘
                                    │
                                    ▼
┌──────────────────┐    ┌─────────────────────────┐    ┌──────────────────┐
│    Suppliers     │    │   Intense competition    │    │      Buyers      │
│   availability of │───▶│     from big players     │◀───│   increasingly   │
│   consultants,    │    │     on a global basis    │    │    demanding     │
│   hardware        │    │                          │    │      and         │
│   suppliers,      │    │                          │    │  sophisticated   │
│   software, etc.  │    │                          │    │   Market is      │
└──────────────────┘    └─────────────────────────┘    │  still growing   │
                                    ▲                    └──────────────────┘
                        ┌─────────────────────────┐
                        │      Substitutes         │
                        │  DIY, ie. no outsourcing │
                        │     Mobil solutions      │
                        │  New technology generally │
                        └─────────────────────────┘
```

5.9 This is your special area of expertise so make sure you have these consumer insights to hand.

(a) Having sorted through the key external issues and factors collect together everything you know about internal strengths and weaknesses. Sort out the marketing mix. What are the key issues? What has worked and what hasn't? We have some information about the pricing and promotion. What about the sales activities, problems and challenges? What about customer service?

(b) Then try and step back to the corporate level. What are the capabilities and capacity of the business? What do we know about profitability, finances, people, operations, sales and marketing, corporate culture and information systems?

5.10 Your brief is not specific in terms of time frames. Recent cases have tended to take a longer term view of strategy and marketing planning, but remember the examiner could ask for a plan just for one year ahead.

Keep focused on what you have to do – a competitive strategy and a strategic marketing plan will be critical to maximise the potential performance of what should continue to be a growing business. An international strategy and positioning of the WCI business is needed, probably as a niche player in a number of markets.

5.11 Identify what information you can from the data and check if anything can be gleaned by relating information from one part of the material to another. See what can be done with what information you have.

Action Plan 2

You should now undertake a detailed internal and external analysis (Case steps 2 and 3) for WCI.

6 POSITION ANALYSIS

6.1 Only now can you begin to pull all the strands together and clarify the current position of the business. Our preferred technique for doing this audit of 'where are we now?' is to use the **SWOT framework** – in this case you may have already done some of this work, but you will need an audit of the corporate and marketing activities. These may not be complete, or very detailed, but it is essential that you do not get them confused.

(a) The **Corporate Position** – strengths and weaknesses, covers internal controllables like people, finance, infrastructure, capacity, supplies, etc and the opportunities and threats the uncontrollable PEST factors (political, economic, technology and culture) plus the competitors. The micro market – customer analysis.

(b) The **Marketing Position** of the business including – the internal controllable strengths and weaknesses, an analysis of the 7 P's of the marketing mix and the opportunities and threats which you will be able to classify using an Ansoff matrix. These are the opportunities that you may be asked to identify and evaluate. Remember that such product/market opportunities arise because of changes in the external macro environment which you have already examined eg the growth in demand for knowledge management systems.

(c) A **communications audit** separately for this Case – you might be tempted to pull together an audit of communications issues, strengths and weaknesses as well as external environmental considerations likely to impact on future communications strategies. It is thin but likely to be an issue – WCI must build a profile in their chosen markets.

6.2 It is likely that you will undertake several of these SWOT exercises to pull all the strands together, but it is vitally important not to mix general management issues with the marketing picture. This will lead to confusion of the real issues and can result in you muddling your recommendations in the exam room. You need to be clear when you are advising the management team about the marketing aspects of a 'market' development strategy to achieve a given objective, e.g. penetration of the life science market, or the communications strategy for repositioning the brand.

6.3 Take time to identify the critical success factors, key issues and business implications – remember these provide clues for the questions.

7 FROM ANALYSIS TO DECISION

7.1 You will now be ready to move on to Case steps 5 – 10. Think about what needs to be done and what the issues are.

7.2 *Strategic Marketing Issues*

(a) What business should WCI be in? What international strategy or philosophy should they adopt? Should the current products and markets be rationalised?

(b) How should the company develop its brand and what should be done to build that brand?

7.3 *Operational Marketing Plans*

(a) What is an appropriate marketing strategy for each selected corporate strategy?

(b) Your analysis stage will have answered the question 'What business are they in now?'. Now you need to address the question 'What business should they be in?'.

(c) Next, consider the objectives – management expectations are not specific but what would be realistic objectives? Is 30% profit margin on a £60 million turnover by 2005 realistic? This is still a growth market, but margins are under pressure and it is showing some evidence of maturing. What can this company realistically sustain? You will need to be confident that you can deliver these objectives if your proposals are to come over as credible.

(d) Establish realistic, clear, objectives quantified over time. You will need to express these in terms of revenues, average client numbers or activities and projects. Armed with these you can now move off in a number of directions.

(e) The Examiner may ask you to indicate what your views are about the potential growth targets for the business and advise on a marketing strategy to achieve it. It may be that you will be expected to address the challenge of improving the performance of any new services, or to develop a strategy for gaining market share in America.

(f) Remember, this is a marketing management examination. You are expected to demonstrate your appreciation of other functions and how they inter-relate with marketing, but most emphasis will be on marketing and communication strategy – but you must be aware of the financial implications of your recommendations. Show the examiner you are not afraid of the numbers.

(g) It is quite likely that you will get at least one question on a specific and more tactical aspect of the Case Study, so this can be the final element of your preparation. Such a question may be about the management information you recommend as necessary for the future plan attracting the best staff to feed growth or change the culture. In effect, you are simply trying to 'question spot'. As your familiarity with the Case increases, areas which need attention will become obvious. Make a note of them as they occur to you.

8   TEMPLATES TO HELP DECISION MAKING

Use the following templates and reminders to help you work through the decision stages for WCI.

8.1   Vision, mission and objectives: where is the business going?

WCI: a vision

Write a vision here

WCI: a mission

Write a mission here

8.2   WCI: establishing a planning gap: fill in this template

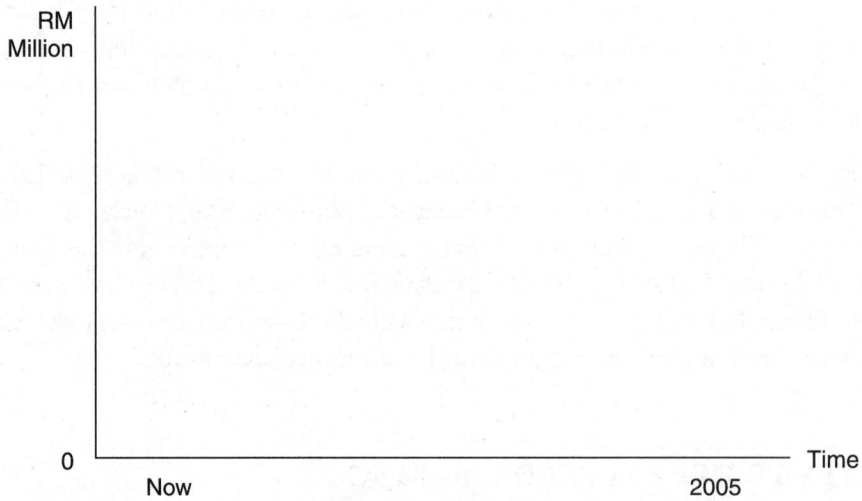

RM
Million

0

Now   2005   Time

8.3   Determining business strategy

What are the options for WCI? Note them down

PRODUCTS

	Existing	New
Existing		
New		

MARKETS

8.4   Which products and which markets?

Evaluating and selecting strategies. With WCI, we may need to evaluate the existing portfolio of products or select new ones, choose business strategies or market segments.

Note some evaluation criteria for WCI	Note some customer criteria to assess WCI's competitive advantage

BPP PUBLISHING

You will need to show your completed decision matrix.

Attractive to the segment

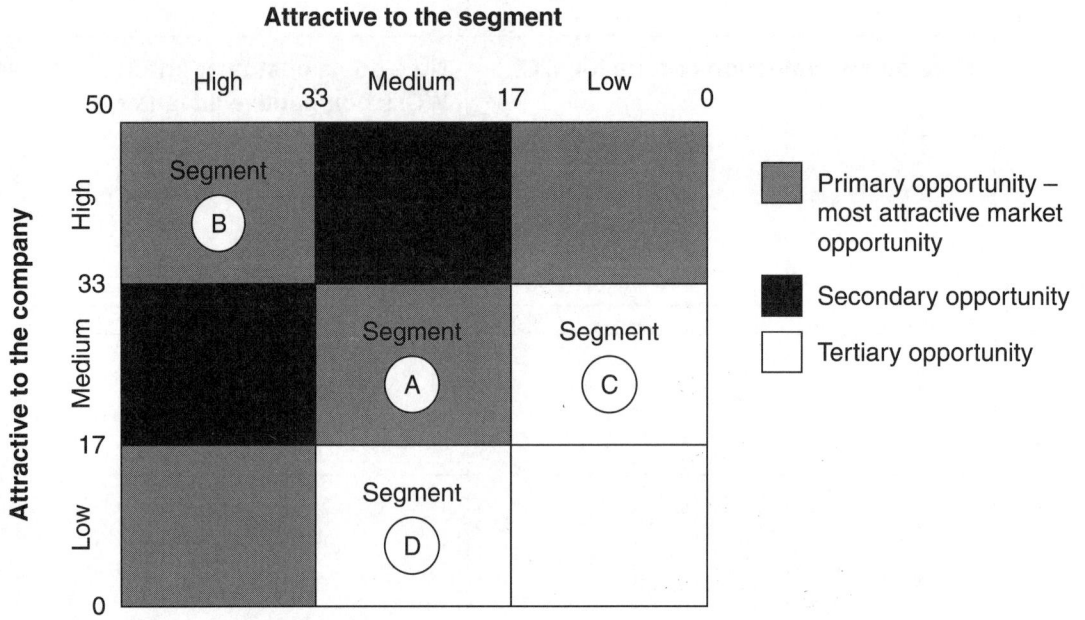

Attractive to the segment

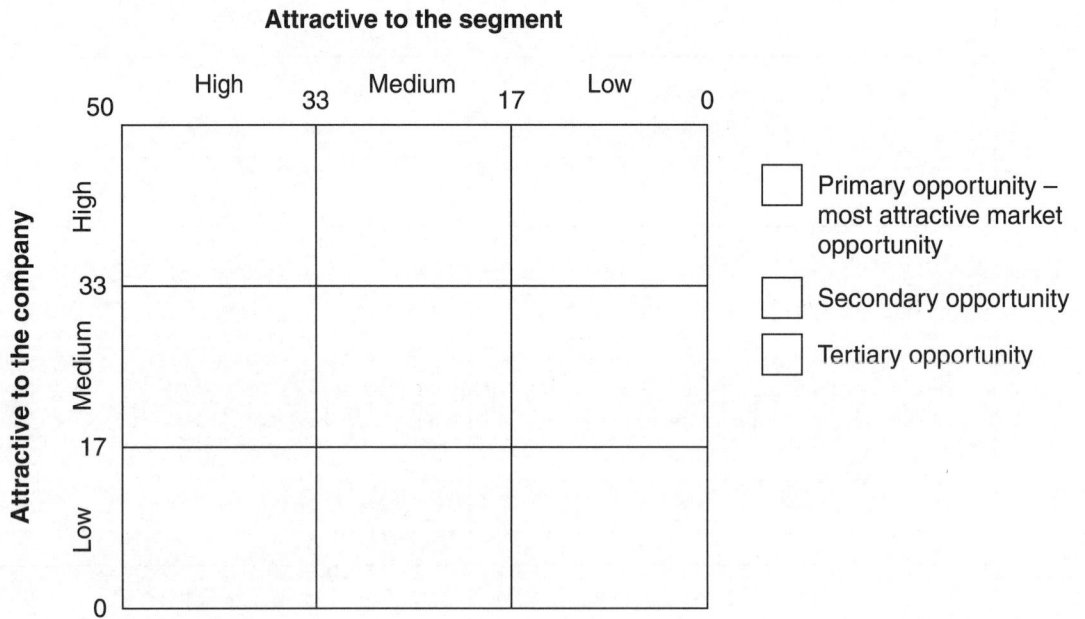

8.5 Establish a **competitive position** and brand development strategy for WCI.

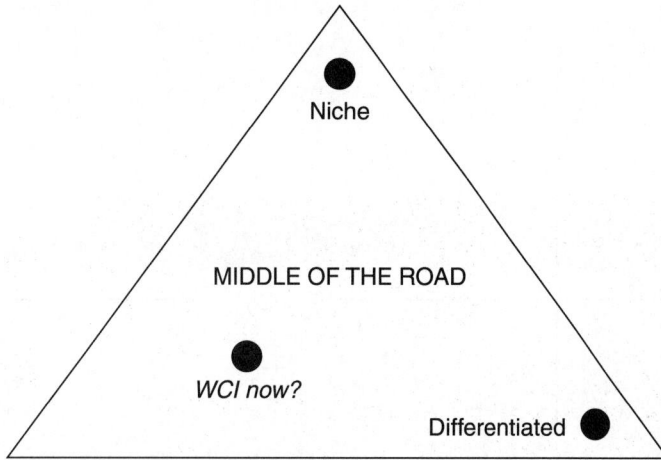

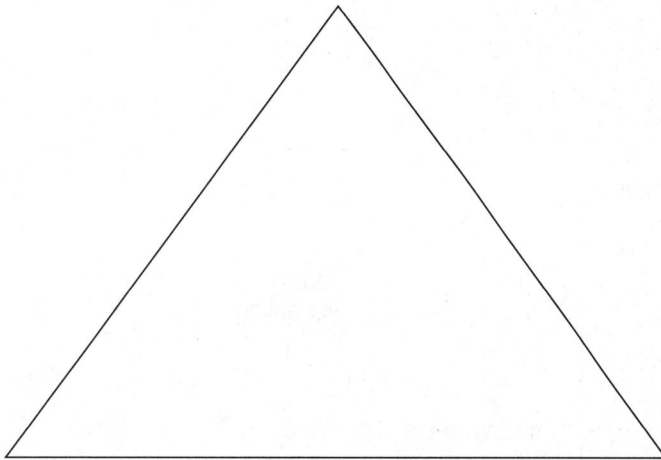

Current positioning

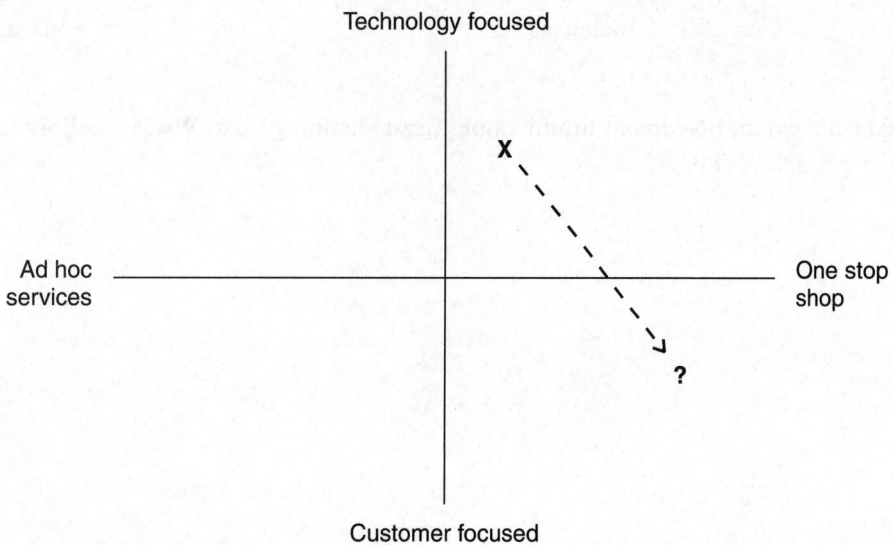

How should the company position itself?

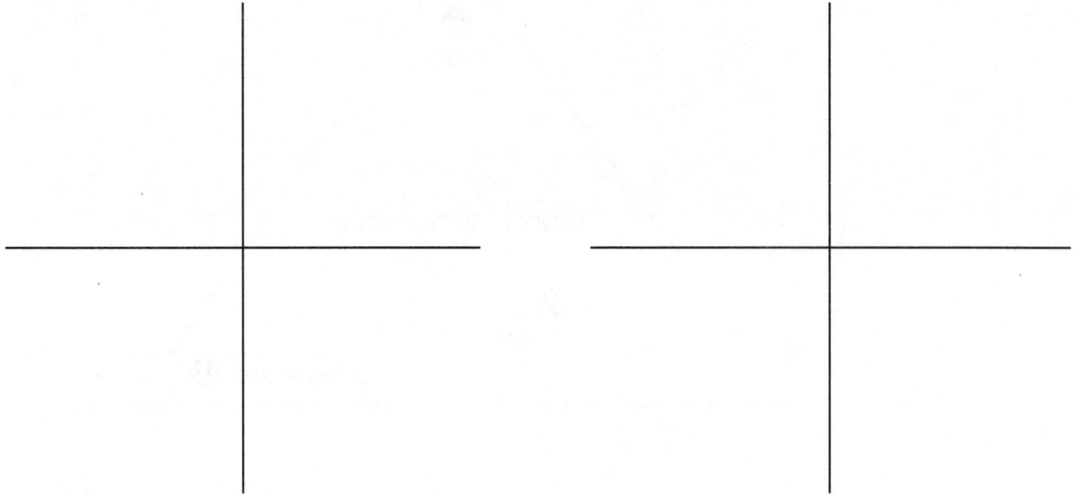

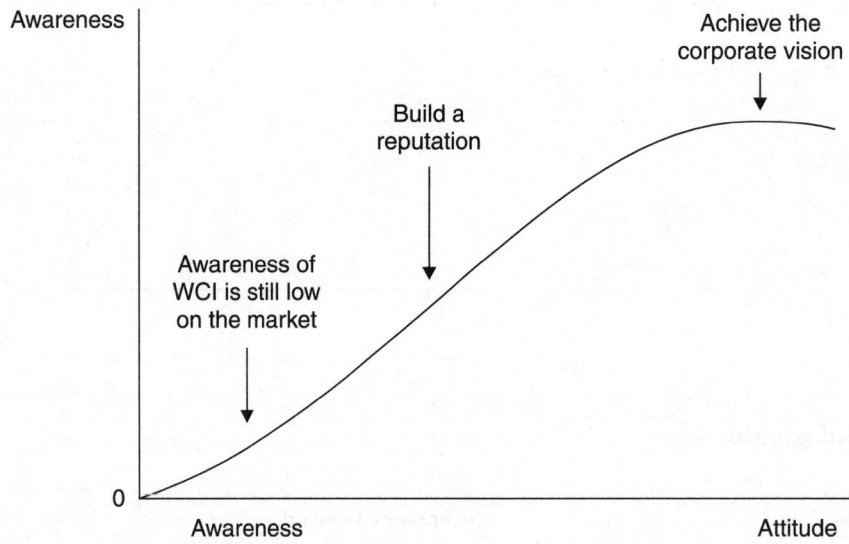

To what extent do current brand values need changing? Can WCIS credibly use its brand to differentiate its offer?

8.6   Communications actions

8.7   Stakeholder communication issues

8.8   **A question of segmentation**

How should this market be segmented?

If all companies use the same basis for segmenting the market, gaining a sustainable, competitive advantage becomes very difficult.

8.9   WCI's positioning and targeting

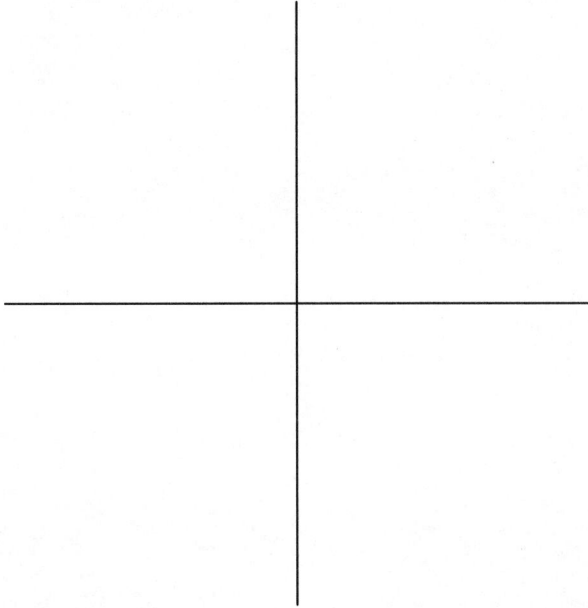

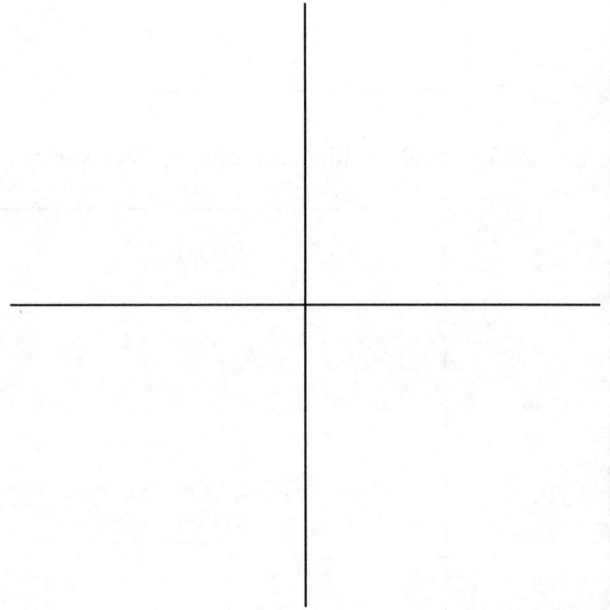

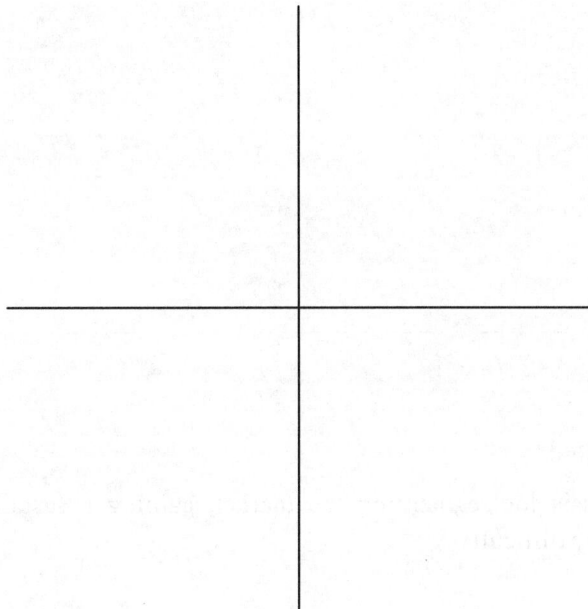

The marketing mix – which targeting strategy is appropriate?

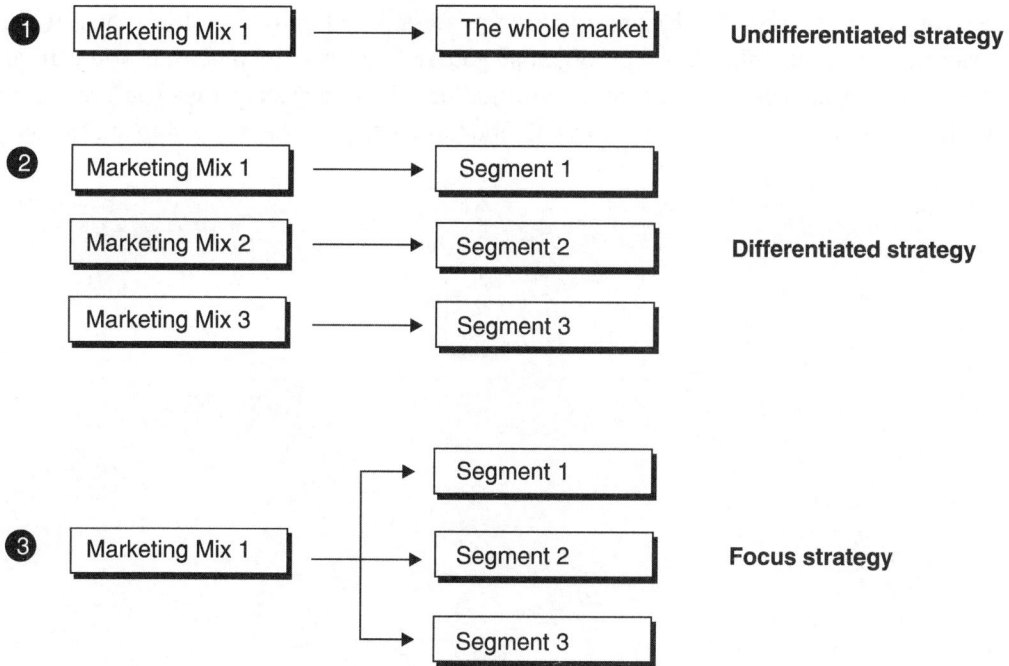

① Marketing Mix 1 ⟶ The whole market → **Undifferentiated strategy**

② Marketing Mix 1 ⟶ Segment 1

Marketing Mix 2 ⟶ Segment 2 → **Differentiated strategy**

Marketing Mix 3 ⟶ Segment 3

③ Marketing Mix 1 ⟶ Segment 1

Segment 2 → **Focus strategy**

Segment 3

Your plans must convince the examiner that you could implement them, so touch base with all the Ps and remember the importance of controls.

	International	Domestic
Product		
Price		
Promotion		
Place		
Service		

Control issues		
Information		
Budget		
Timetable		

9 YOUR DECISION FILE

9.1 As you work through the decision making process, build your Case file as you will for the examination. Remember how you organise yourself and use the materials you can take into the exam – a key element of exam technique. Establish a system that you are comfortable with and use this final exam paper as an opportunity to practise using your materials.

20

The World Class International Exam

Chapter Topic List

Introduction

In this chapter you will:

- Work the World Class International case under exam conditions (allow 3 hours)

- Have the opportunity to review student sample answers to the exam

- Consider tutor comments and examiner feedback for World Class International

1   THE EXAM

Tutor Tip

WCI exam paper and sample answers

In this chapter, you will have another opportunity to tackle the actual exam paper under exam conditions, no matter how much or little of the analysis you have completed.

Independently, we would strongly advise you to take the time out to tackle an actual paper.

To be of value, you really need to do this under exam conditions.

Once you have prepared yourself, make the time to tackle the paper, ideally in:

- An undisturbed environment
- A single three hour sitting

If that is **not** possible, tackle it in two or three timed sessions. Do **not** cheat and give yourself any longer: managing time is one of the biggest obstacles to case success and the more prepared you are, the harder it is to fit everything in.

For City of Daugavpils, we offered you very detailed preparatory guidance. For WCI, we have offered a shorter section on guidance, but this is supplemented by the two sample scripts, with the examiner's comments, showing how you could have earned marks and giving you an insight into the examiner's perspective.

By the end of this chapter, you will have:

- Seen the WCI question paper and considered the additional information

- Undertaken WCI as a practice exam paper

- Reviewed your own exam technique and approach

- Considered two sample scripts as a comparison for your own work and to show you what others were able to achieve in the exam room

- Seen the examiner's comments about this paper

The Chartered
Institute of marketing

Diploma
in Marketing

Strategic Marketing Management: Analysis & Decision

9.54: Strategic Marketing Management: Analysis & Decision

Time: 14.00 – 17.00

Date: 14th June, 2002

3 Hours Duration

This paper requires you to make a practical and reasoned evaluation of the problems and opportunities you have identified from the previously circulated case material. From your analysis you are required to prepare a report in accordance with the situation below. Graphing sheets and ledger analysis paper are available from the invigilators, together with continuation sheets if required. These must be identified by your candidate number and fastened in the prescribed fashion within the back cover of your answer book for collection at the end of the examination.

Read the questions carefully and answer the actual questions as specified. Check the mark allocation to questions and allocate your time accordingly. Candidates must attempt ALL parts. Candidates should adopt a report format; those who do not will be penalised.

BPP
PUBLISHING

World Class International (WCI)

Examination Paper

Additional Information

WCI has been comfortably meetings its growth targets, in spite of the downturn in the stock markets around the world. The United Kingdom has held firm and continued to succeed as a result of government support for the health sector. In January 2002, several countries in Europe abandoned their own currencies and adopted the Euro including major countries such as Germany, France, Italy and Spain. WCI has not had a presence in this market, and part of its deliberations are about size, effectiveness and branding in order to enter the European market.

Examination Questions

As the appointed Consultant you have been asked to prepare a report answering the following questions:

Question 1.

Prepare a five year strategic marketing plan for WCI, after carefully analysing the company's current competitive position.

(40 marks)

Question 2.

Develop a communication plan for the company, within its given budget, and justify the key media that you would use to enhance its brand image.

(The communication plan should take into consideration the business-to-business nature of the company.)

(30 marks)

Question 3.

Given the company's strengths in some sectors, develop a European entry strategy for its services.

(30 marks)

(100 marks in total)

Note the distribution of marks and allocate your time accordingly.

2   THE EXAMINER'S REVIEW OF THE QUESTIONS

Overview

2.1   This case is about a fast growing SME within the IT Services sector. The company is made up of various areas related to IT Services. The company has grown both organically and through acquisitions over the last five years. The company competes effectively with larger companies and has an impressive range of clientele. IT services are growing at a rapid rate throughout the world. The sector is highly competitive and very fragmented. The company is faced with a bewildering array of choices with regards to its future. The company is now actively involved in building its brand and moving into new services and markets. The company's main market is business–to-business. This raises issues about developing the best marketing strategies to match client needs. The markets and sector specific presence is discussed at length in the case. The case also covers possible areas of growth led by technological change. This one of the few cases covering a relatively new services sector within the general IT Sector. This case has no personalised comments, is factual and contains no 'red-herrings'. Nonetheless, as usual, there is the problem of an extensive range of detailed information. There is a need to develop clear and concise insights into the key issues involved in developing a strategy.

New Information on the day of the examination

NEW INFORMATION

WCI has been comfortably meeting its growth targets, in spite of the downturn in the stock markets around the world. The United Kingdom, however has held firm and continued to succeed as a result of government support for the Health Sector. In January 2002, several countries in Europe abandoned their own currencies and adopted the Euro. The major countries such as Germany, France, Italy and Spain are now trading in Euros. WCI has not had a presence in this market and part of its deliberations is about size, effectiveness and branding in order to enter the European market.

2.2   **Key issues facing WCI**

(a)   The company is essentially an SME and it needs to grow to a reasonable size to challenge its main competitors.

(b)   The nature of the IT service market is constantly changing.

(c)   Challenges are being posed by the growth of e-commerce and m-commerce.

(d)   The company is heavily dependent on the pharmaceutical sector.

(e)   Companies are getting more sophisticated in their needs, demanding more value added services.

(f)   The company needs to globalise as quickly as its clients globalise.

(g)   With the recent merger, the company has to establish a clear brand image.

(h)   The company has grown on the back of a range of consultants who are linked to the company, so marketing instead of selling becomes an important priority.

(i)   Moving steadily towards m-commerce platforms.

(j)   The company needs to develop the outsourcing market substantially.

(k)   Developing focused and targeted marketing for local/national/international clientele.

(l)   Current climate where the Nasdaq and the Techmarket have fallen substantially. This makes it difficult to consider a float.

(m) The company has a good asset base.

(n) Utilising the marketing budget effectively.

(o) The company needs to consider whether its marketing budget is sufficiently large for building an important brand.

(p) How to best group its product market sectors and develop sub brands.

(q) Helping companies develop digital loyalty networks.

(r) Business management and development and integration show the highest growth rates for the future. These areas need to be considered carefully.

(s) Managing growth and keeping the internal culture dynamic.

(t) Considering the Pareto Rule when segmenting clients groupings.

(u) Taking advantage of the changes taking place within the large auditing firms.

(v) Developing a CRM strategy.

The Answers

2.3 This case is reasonably straightforward and does not contain many surprises. There is also a large amount of data concerning market sectors and market spread. It is important, therefore that the following issues are considered.

1 The application of theory

2 The amount of International marketing theory/ application that the students can apply to the case. The amount of communication theory that they can also apply.

3 The candidates should be thinking strategically not tactically

4 The answers given must be realistic and practical.

5 A degree of innovation and lateral thinking should be rewarded.

6 It is important that the questions are answered within the given context.

7 The additional information highlights the dilemma the company faces in terms of its image. Should it be known as an important company, which straddles America and the UK, or should it be better known in Europe?

Question 1: Prepare a five-year strategic marketing plan for WCI, after carefully analysing the company's current competitive position. *(40 Marks)*

2.4 This question requires students to use many of the strategic planning models used by marketers. Candidates will then need to consider the following.

(a) Consider the objectives that they wish to set WCI City for the next five years.

(b) Candidates need to consider the product market sectors that the company is operating in with appropriate segmentation.

(c) Consider whether the company should be looking for a listing within five years.

(d) In the longer term consider how the budget could be increased through EC grants.

(e) Is their mission in line with current strategies or should it change?

(f) Address, in the short and long term, its reliance on the Pharmaceutical market.

(g) The board needs to consider the key markets in which it wants to grow.

(h) How can the company get better known in the business world, especially when it is competing with major brand names such as IBM?

(i) Should the company have only one headquarter in the UK, to show that it is an integrated company?

(j) Should the company start to tackle the growing biotechnology market?

(k) Matching the company strengths to the potential growth areas shown in Appendix 2.

(m) Models such as Porter, Ansoff, BCG, GEC, Shell Directional and GAP could be used in the analysis of the case. Especially as general market shares of the various services are given. Also a good competitor analysis could be undertaken.

		Relative market share		
		Low	Medium	High
Market structure	Concentration	• Sales: likely to decline rapidly • Action: retreat from market, divest or liquidate	• Sales: likely to stagnate • Action: milk product to finance other areas	• Sales: modest growth • Action: dominate market, or market segment, harvest profits and look for potential acquisitions
	Fragmentation	• Sales: likely to reach peak • Action: find profitable market segment	• Sales: Average growth • Action: differentiate product to gain advantage from revenue side	• Sales; likely to grow rapidly • Action: ride the experience curve, use cost advantages to increase market share
	Perfect competition	• Sales: growth through imitation • Action: Follow the leaders	• Sales: growth through imitation or innovation • Action: gain market share fast	• Sales: growth through innovation. • Action: exploit technical advantages

This could be used to develop the service/market strategies for WCI. This could be used in conjunction with the GE Matrix using the information given in the case. A matrix plotting similarity of service against company size will help to position WCI in relation to its competitors.

(n) What are the constraints to the given strategy? What is a market-led strategy for the company? What would be a realistic marketing budget?

(p) How should the organization chart be redeveloped to create and maintain an emphasis on marketing?

(q) Developing the role for the Internet.

2.5   Points in a strategic plan:

> 1)   Set corporate objectives
>
> 2)   Identify target markets
>
> 3)   Set marketing objectives
>
> 4)   Develop marketing strategy and tactics
>
> 5)   Organise control systems

2.6   **Given the points above, the best answers will show a clear grasp of the following.**

> 1.   A good analysis of the current position
>
> 2.   The development of a strategic plan with fully developed implementation strategies
>
> 3.   A good justification of the strategies to be adopted
>
> For pilot study centres, fifteen marks will be allocated for the prepared material. The mark allocations for the questions received from the pilot centres are shown in brackets.

Question 2: Develop a communication plan for the company, within its given budget and justify the key media that you would use to enhance its brand image. (The communication plan should take into consideration the business-to-business nature of the company.)

(30 Marks)

2.7   Some key factors that should be analysed and assessed are as follows.

(a)   The company has an interesting name, but it needs to convey a meaning.

(b)   The general marketing communications budget is given.

(c)   The company has to develop a brand that can compete with the larger companies.

(d)   Consideration of how much should be allocated to internal brand building activities.

(e)   The importance of credible communications with the press and having a sustained public relations exercise with national and international media.

(f)   Expanding capabilities on the Net.

(g)   Looking at the various activities within the marketing structure and developing sub-plans for each product/market sector.

(h)   Slicing the budget for media/PR/Events/advertising /in-house magazine promotion/ sponsorship.

(i)   Although a timespan is not indicated, candidates who take both a short-term and then a long-term view to mirror Question 1 should be rewarded.

(j)   How can web marketing be integrated with the rest of the offerings?

(k)   As the company grows, integrated marketing will become more and more important.

(l) Candidates need to understand that the company operates in a B2B market and TV advertising may not be appropriate. However indirect TV advertising through billboards on sports events such as cricket or football may be appropriate.

(m) Considering budgets and constraints for communications.

Horizontal co-ordination (across countries)

	High	Low
High	Globally integrated strategies	Multidomestic integrated strategy
Low	Global but non-integrated strategy	Multidomestic non-integrated strategy

Vertical co-ordination (across disciplines)

The above could be used as a typology for looking at a globally integrated marketing communication strategy. These and any other relevant points should be taken into consideration.

Finally the students should consider how these factors could be seamlessly linked up with the strategies that the company has developed.

2.8 **A good answer will take into account the following:**

(a) Sensible development of a marketing communications plan
(b) Links with the overall strategy

Question 3: Given the company's strengths in some sectors, develop a European entry strategy for its services. *(30 Marks)*

2.9 This question offers a range of interesting options to students. The company is generally locked into the UK and USA markets; yet a sizeable proportion of its business emanates from Europe. The key issues to consider are the growth of the European market and the way in which a company such as WCI could establish a strong presence.

2.10 There are some points to consider before embarking on a European presence.

(a) Establishing a brand image in Europe.

(b) The European market is huge, but complex and fragmented.

(c) The WCI brand is not a global brand.

(d) For a UK based company what sort of European strategies would be most effective?

(e) What are the product service matches between the UK and Europe?

(f) Which European country would be the most appropriate for an entry?

(g) What is the most appropriate strategy for the company? Is to be geocentric, ethnocentric or polycentric?

(h)   The above has an impact on the entry method chosen.

(i)   Good market research prior to entry.

2.11   In each country, WCI has an opportunity to work through intermediaries, own salesforce or by acquisition. Each of these strategic alternatives has its own set of problems.

(a)   If the company attempts to develop its own salesforce, it will need to carefully budget the costs related to such an operation and set important targets. The advantage may lie in recruiting staff that understand the local issues involved.

(b)   Working through intermediaries can also work well if they are committed to the mission of the company. This route may pose difficulties, owing to the fact that this is a complex services company and intermediaries may not easily understand the complexities involved.

(c)   If the company attempts entry through acquisitions it would have to raise a substantial amount of money and then this should be justified by a reasonable ROI. Good candidates may be able to show that Guardian IT followed such a strategy and this proved to be disastrous for the company.

(d)   Another possible strategy may be for the company to set up its own offices in the best growth market and exploit its possibilities. Within one or two years this could be repeated through Europe. WCI could also extend its operations through current multinational contacts, especially in Germany and France.

2.12   The company has an excellent website, tailoring this to the differing European audiences may be a useful first step.

2.13   Some key issues are:

(a)   Awareness of the key International marketing issues surrounding the company
(b)   Developing an appropriate European strategy discussing possible options

2.14   As usual, it is important to demonstrate coherence, strategic thinking, justification and detail featuring in the answers. The case is quite long and there is considerable amount of data so that candidates should be able to fashion a range of interesting answers. The case should elicit some interesting answers, which may be dependent on the different regions of the world. Creativity and innovation should be rewarded.

Sample scripts

2.15   The following two answers in Sections 3 and 4 have been chosen to illustrate reasonable answers to the questions set. They are by no means definitive answers, but they show differing and valid approaches to developing strategies. All the answers could have benefited from different approaches, analyses and detail. This is pointed out in the comments. The given answers should be compared and contrasted with the ideas offered in the Senior Examiner's marking scheme.

3   SAMPLE SCRIPT 1

BPP Note. The wording and structure are as presented by the student.

Script 1: Question 1

Report

To: **Board of Directors**
From: Patrick Pearson, Marketing Consultant
Subject: Five year strategic marketing plan for WCI
Date: 14th June 2002

Summary

1.   Introduction – including competitor analysis
2.   Market overview
3.   Situational analysis
4.   SWOT Analysis
5.   Where does WCI want to go?
6.   Marketing strategy
7.   Marketing tactics
8.   Implementation and control

1   Introduction

1.1   WCI Company history

WCI specialises in offering a complete business solution in the field of IT consultancy to sectors from pharmaceutical and life sciences to finance and FMCG. Over the years the company has developed its product portfolio, most recently from the merger with 2GL Computing Services. This merger was extremely well placed and executed and both companies are now totally integrated. Having all the necessary skills available in house to offer a full service solution, gives WCI a competitive edge in the market. WCI also has strong market advantage as a result of the policy launched in 1998 of only employing the best people in the industry. Originally technology led WCI has moved away from this to be sales led and is currently trying to develop a marketing focus. In addition to its impressive growth in the UK, WCI has also expanded overseas, with one office in Atlanta to service pharmaceutical and medical device clients and another office opened in Budapest, Hungary to service Eastern Europe. Despite extensive research, I have been able to trace relatively little information about this office and would like to discuss this at our forthcoming meeting.

1.2   Why is this plan needed?

WCI has grown rapidly over the past ten years and is making growth targets in spite of the downturn in stock markets in other countries. I do however feel there are four particular areas worthy of consideration in this plan.

1.2.1   The IT Consultancy Market – Competitive Analysis

WCI is a relatively small player in a large fragmented market. Its main threats are from the Big 5 accountancy firms such as KPMG, Ernst and Young and PWC, most of which have now set up specialist IT divisions and from mergers of smaller IT consultancy companies. Most of these companies only employ between 2 and 4 people and nearly half of them have a turnover of less than $200,000.   Many of these companies do not provide a full service offering, specialising in certain consultancy aspects. The world-wide IT consultancy market is expected to reach over $110 billion by 2002, illustrating the potential for WCI to gain market share.

1.2.2   Market Sectors

WCI currently has customers in a wide range of market sectors including healthcare, pharmaceuticals, FMCG, manufacturing, TMT and Finance, with 70-80% client retention WCI has the potential to develop existing clients as well as developing new ones.

1.2.3 Trading Overseas

WCI clearly has the potential to expand overseas due to market demand and its connections with major international players. Please refer to my European entry strategy for further details.

1.2.4 Communication

WCI clearly needs to assess the way it spends its budget in this area. Please refer to my .communications plan for further details.

2 Market Overview

ICT consulting is increasing, particularly amongst FTSE 100 companies who are seeking a one-stop shop. Clients are more conscious of how they spend their money and want to see value in their IT improvements. There has also been increased interest in lean compliance and new technology areas such as m-commerce, KM, e-CRM, e-purchasing etc.

2.1 Market Sectors

There is expected to be significant growth in the following sections over the next five years.

(a) Pharmaceutical
     The total US pharmaceutical industry sales were estimated at $113 billion in 1999 and are expected to reach $202bn by 2005. More IT work has been created as a result of the reduction in the time taken to approve new drugs, an increase in product development and by the increased number of mergers.

(b) Financial services
     Mergers have also become increasingly common in this sector. Due to strong competition there is also a focus towards e-CRM.

(c) Healthcare
     In the UK significant resources are being invested in this sector by the government to develop ICT within the NHS.

3 Situational Analysis

3.1 Pest Analysis

This analysis has raised the following points for WCI

Political

(a) The need to be aware of legal issues relating to data protection and security developments in all countries in which WCI operates
(b) The need to thoroughly research political and economic situations in any overseas markets which ECI chooses to enter.
(c) The need to assess methods of working with government organisations.
(d) WCI also needs to research potential political barriers which the company may face as a result of the UK not being a member of the Euro

Economic

(a) Potential for growth in ICT, particularly within the sector of e-business.
(b) There are a large number of mergers and acquisitions taking place within IT, but also within the target markets of finance and pharmaceuticals.
(c) The Euro has brought stability in interest rates and more consistency exchange rates.

Social

(a) There is significant growth in outsourcing in IT services
(b) There is a demand to obtain value for money.
(c) There is also a demand to make use of new technologies i.e. m-commerce

Technological

(a) Significant growth in new technologies, m-commerce in W. Europe is expected to grow from 1 million users in 1999 to 48 million users in 2004.
(b) Within the key market of pharmaceuticals, the speed research and development is increasing
(c) There is increasing requirement for cross-platform comparability.

3.2 The microenvironment-Porter's 5 Forces

1 The threat of new entrants

The IT services industry is heavily fragmented. New companies area attracted due to high growth rates and profitability and minimal; outlay. Smaller companies need to differentiate as they cannot effectively compete with the economies of scale of the Big 5. This may, in time dissuade new entrants.

2 The threat of substitutes

New products and services are constantly being developed. Many products are however incompatible and may dissuade companies who wish to upgrade their systems.

3 The bargaining power of customers

Customers are becoming more demanding and focused. They want services completed with shorter lead times, but are becoming increasingly focused on long term ROI. They are restricted due to the high cost of switching suppliers.

4 The bargaining power of suppliers

WCI has strong power due to its relationship with high tech companies such as Microsoft, Intel, Compaq.

5 Competitive Rivalry

Competition is intense, smaller companies are being forced to differentiate or become the subject of merger/alliance.

3.3 Analysis of Existing Marketing Operations

3.3.1 Product

WCI aims to be a 'full business solutions design and implementation provider', providing a one-stop-shop management and IT service.

BCG Matrix

MARKET GROWTH

		High	Low
MARKET SHARE	*High*	Lean Compliance Managed Services	e-business/software selling systems Purchasing Knowledge Management M-Commerce
	Low	Internal systems Infrasrtucture	

WCI's cash cows are currently in maturity/decline and the company should look to develop other products such as m-commerce to continue funding.

3.3.2 Price

WCI has a complex pricing policy. The company cannot command the highest prices due to the weaknesses of its brand.

3.3.3 Place

Services are supplied direct to the customer with much work taking place on the client's premises.

3.3.4 Promotion

WCI currently spends more than £600,000 a year on marketing, including media, website development, events, direct mail etc. Internal marketing is strong as is expertise within the marketing department. Branding, is however weak.

3.3.5 People

Key to the success of a service business such as WCI is the company's marketing message: 'people that make a difference'. This really helps to motivate staff.

3.3.6 Physical evidence

The appropriate company image should be promoted through the appearance of people, offices and literature.

3.3.7 Processes

Work is managed through 2 divisions WCI Technology and WCI Consulting, but a seamless service is given to the customer.

3.4 Positioning Strategy

The company does not have a clear positioning strategy at present and offers a range of services to a range of market segments. By changing its focus to niche marketing, WCI would be able to differentiate and compete more effectively in the areas in which it has strengths.

4 SWOT Analysis

4.1 Strengths

- Ability to offer full business solution
- High customer retention
- Diverse client portfolio
- Ability to manage mergers
- Strengths in niche areas e.g. lean compliance, pharmaceuticals.

4.2 Weaknesses

- Small player in a fragmented industry
- Weak branding and logo
- Sales led
- Few clients with growth access of FS and FMCG

4.3 Opportunities

- Sell more to existing customers
- Expand in particular market niches overseas
- Exploit the demand for lean compliance
- Exploit the profitability within the BPO sector
- Gain market share in new biotechnology areas
- Work with companies who have recently merged

4.4 Threats

- **Big 5/other large companies move into market niches**
- **Smaller competitors merge to compete effectively**

5 Where does WCI want to be?

5.1 Mission

WCI's mission is to 'help our clients become 'World-Class', through excellence in process design, web technology and managed services.'

5.2 Corporate objectives

(1) To achieve a 45% gross profit margin in WCI Consulting by 2006 and a 35% gross profit margin for WCI Technology by 2007. Despite meeting targets, profit margins have been steadily falling over the past few years, reaching 35% in 1999 for WCI Consulting and 19% for WCI Technology.

(2)   To Increase group revenue to £55 million by 2007.
(in 1999) combined division revenue is approx £30million).

(3)   To increase European market to 4.5 % of turnover by 2005

Justification

- Growth in the IT services market
- Potential for growth in Europe
- Brand awareness and credibility is currently having a negative effect in some market sectors

5.3. **Marketing Objectives**

(1)   To increase brand awareness in the UK industrial market to 50% of all companies in current market segments by 2003.

(2)   To develop relationships with existing customers to increase new sales to these customers by 50% BY 2005.

(3)   To gain a 30% market share in lean compliance in the French and German pharmaceutical markets by 2005.

(4)   To gain a 15% share in the m-commerce market in the UK by 2007.

Justification

- **Negative current effect of brand awareness**

- **Existing customers cost less service ⟶ increased profits. Many large customers currently only give a small percentage of business to WCI.**

- **High potential for growth in France and Germany (Biotech, R&D-€400 million in France, €500 million in Germany - significant growth in m-commerce. Currently there are 1m users and the 2004 projection indicates 48m users.**

6   **Marketing Strategy**

Porter's Generic Strategies

Cost Leadership

With a turnover of approximately £30m and 270 employees, WCI should not strive to be the lowest cost producer in the industry. In trying to compete with larger companies, WCI has seen a market decline in profit margins since 1997.

Differentiation

WCI is able to differentiate itself through the quality of service offered by its people, the complete business solution offered and the ability to provide areas of expertise, for example in pharmaceuticals.

Focus

WCI should combine its differentiation strategy with a focus strategy. Its current client base is too wide and the company can more advantage from focusing on a niche.

Ansoff's Matrix

Ansoff's matrix shows how the marketing objectives could be formulated to achieve strategies.

Ansoff's Matrix

PRODUCT

	Existing	New
Existing MARKET	**MARKET PENETRATION** Increase brand awareness Increase sales to existing Customers	**PRODUCT DEVELOPMENT** e-business/software selling systems Purchasing Knowledge Management M-Commerce
New	**MARKET DEVELOPMENT** Increase brand awareness Develop share in lean Compliance in French and German Pharmaceuticals Market	**DIVERSIFICATION**

Diversification should be avoided as this would carry too high a risk for WCI as it already has a diverse customer and product portfolio.

7 **Marketing Tactics**

7.1 **Market Penetration**

Objective 1-Increase brand awareness in the UK industrial market by 50% in comparison to all companies in the current market segments by 2003.

(a) **Product**
Research current customer perception. Use information to build branding strategy.

(b) **Price**
Effective branding will allow WCI to command higher prices.

(c) **Place**
Continue with current distribution channels.

(d) **Promotion-profile strategy**
Please refer to the communications plan

(e) **People**
Appoint member of the marketing team as a brand manager

(d) **Physical Evidence-Profile strategy**
    1   Change logo to improve corporate image
    2   Redesign literature

(g) **Processes**- make sure processes are consistent with a revised brand image.
Objective 2.- Develop relationships with existing customers and increase sales by 50% by 2005.

(h) **Product**
    1   Carry out an audit of products being sold. Identify complimentary products to be sold.
    2   Segment the product offering

(i) **Price**
Review the pricing strategy- do not alienate the current customers

(j) **Place**
Obtain contracts through existing clients.

BPP PUBLISHING

       (k)   **Promotion-see communications plan**

       (l)   **People**
           Assign key account managers.

       (m)   **Physical evidence**
           Re-inforce image/brand

       (n)   **Processes**
           Ensure system integration for customers purchasing new services.

7.2 Market Development

    1   Objective 3- Gain a 30% market share in lean compliance in the French and German pharmaceutical markets by 2005.
        See European entry strategy.

       (a)   **New Products**
           Objective 4-Gain a 15% market share in the m-commerce market in the UK by 2007.

       (b)   **Product**
           Carry out market research

       (c)   **Price**
           Combine with the branding strategy to command a premium price.

       (d)   **Place**
           Distribute via current channels

       (e)   **Promotion—communications plan**

       (f)   **People**
           Train a specialist within the marketing team to provide m-commerce.

       (g)   **Physical Evidence**
           Develop new promotional literature to sell this product and spend around £12,000.

       (h)   **Processes**
           Develop products that meet customer needs

8 Conrea

8.1 Implementation and Control

       (a)   Initial measures
- A member of the marketing team should be responsible for the development of each strategy.
- Performance targets should be set for the marketing team
- Advertising/PR- check the number of responses
- Direct mail-check the number of responses
- Telemarketing/exhibitions-meetings set up for sales people
- Website: assess the number of hits

       (b)   Key performance indicators should be set for the sales team and the targets should be monitored and re-assessed.

Gantt Chart

STRATEGY	2002	2003	2004	2005	2006	2007
Market penetration Brand awareness Research Logo redesign/internal Marketing Specific Advertising						
Market Development Market Research Set up satellite offices Advertising						
Product Development Research Develop product Develop literature Product launch						

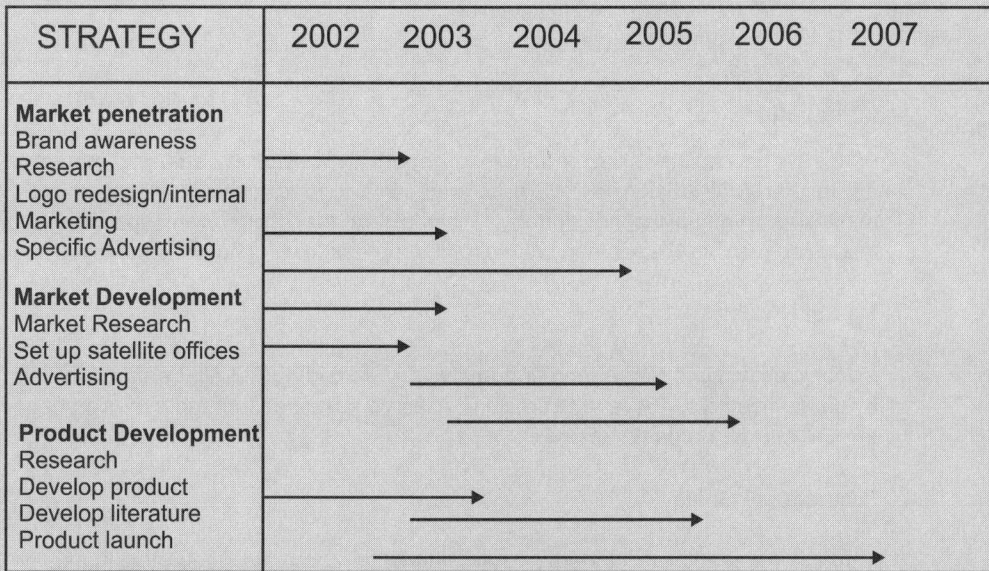

8.2 **Contingency plans**

1   Enter less competitive overseas pharmaceutical markets e.g. Italy

2   Attract new clients with existing market segments

3   Consider developing other new technologies eg eCRM within the financial services sector

I look forward to discussing these strategies at our forthcoming meeting.

Examiner's comments

This is a well- organised question with a good analysis of the current company situation. The strategies to be adopted are laid out well. However the candidate has not fully utilised all the available information. Strategies need to be supported by detail. Also worthy of consideration would have been customer relationship strategies.

BPP PUBLISHING

Script 1: Question 2

To: **The Board of Directors WCI**
From: Patrick Pearson, Marketing Consultant
Subject: Marketing Communications
Date: 14th June 2002

Introduction

Further to the points raised in my initial report and within my strategic marketing plan, I am aware that WCI is keen to review its marketing communications budget of £600,000 and its marketing communications strategy. I am aware that the current spend is over the entire marketing mix, but I have been unable to find a breakdown of how this money is spent.

Market Research

I would recommend that a thorough analysis is carried out, of all the media activity undertaken by our competitors. Above-the-line activity can be assessed through a media agency, but below-the-line may be harder to assess.

Promotional Goals

Through my marketing strategy, I have identified corporate goals and marketing goals. WCI wants to increase business with existing customers, increase profitability, and use its foothold in the niche pharmaceuticals market to develop the sector in France and Germany. At the same time the company needs to develop new technology products in the area of m-commerce.

Current promotional activity has been successful to some extent as targets for growth have been achieved. Internal marketing has been a particularly successful part of the marketing communications as employees are kept informed and motivated by an intranet and HTML newsletter. I recommend that these activities should be continued as they are working well.

4   Promotional strategy

Profile strategy

One area in which WCI has however been weak is that of brand and corporate image. This has prevented the company from changing premium prices for what is undoubtedly an excellent level of service and has had a negative effect on profit margins as WCI struggles to compete with it's larger competitors. The company logo also lacks clarity and does not tell the customer what to expect from WCI. I would therefore recommend that as one of the earliest objectives in its strategic plan that WCI adopts a profile strategy to raise its corporate image.

4.2   Pull Strategy

WCI currently supplies its services directly to B2B customers without using any intermediaries. It is therefore using a pull strategy to attract these customers, rather than a push strategy, which is often associated with a B2B business using agents and distribution. I would recommend that WCI continues to develop this in conjunction with the profile strategy outlined above.

5   Communications Mix

5.1   Profile Strategy

Initially the WCI logo should be redesigned to reflect the forward thinking company mission statement. I would estimate this to cost approximately £8,000. All corporate literature should also be redesigned to match the new corporate image, at an approximate cost of £30,000. The new branding strategy should be promoted internally at a cost of £5,000.

Once all this has been successfully achieved, I would recommend the following:

(a) Advertising in trade titles within key market sectors such as pharmaceuticals. A burst campaign should be used to gain initial high awareness of the brand and the presence should be maintained with a drip campaign. –cost £50,000

(b) Public Relations –in key trade titles. This is a cheap way of building the brand with the credible backing of opinion formers, such as editors and industry leaders.-cost £10,000

(c) Corporate Events- These should be used as a re-branding platform for new and existing clients-cost £20,000

(d) Direct Mail leaflets- These should be sent out to new and existing customers to reinforce brand values and to try to get customers to book a free systems evaluation audit- £10,000

(e) Development of company website- £30,000

5.2 Pull strategy

This profile strategy should be followed by a pull strategy which allows WCI to target its other marketing objectives, specific to the market areas and product development. Activities in this strategy would be directed at market segments, rather than being aimed at the broader objective of building the brand.

5.2.1 Develop relationships with existing customers

(1) Advertising in trade magazines within the market sectors which these customers currently read e.g. Manufacturing Week -£20,000

(2) Direct Mail-to inform clients of all the services provided. They may currently be unaware of many of them-£5,000

(3) Telemarketing-to follow up direct mail campaign. This will allow WCI to focus more closely on customer needs-£5,000

(4) Corporate events-to inform customers of new services-£10,000

(5) Personal selling to Industrial customers

5.2.2 Gain Market Share in the French and German market specialising in Lean Compliance in Pharmaceuticals

(1) Advertising in pharmaceutical publications in France and Germany. I would recommend the use of a local advertising agency to overcome cultural differences-£50,000

(2) Corporate Events for foreign subsidiaries of current UK customers- £45,000

(3) Trade exhibitions/Conferences-perhaps arrange for a speaker to conduct a seminar on lean compliance-£50,000

5.2.3 Develop the M-Commerce Market

(1) Advertising campaign in the titles within the marketing sector-e.g. Marketing Week, new technology titles. This should be a BURST campaign, followed by a DRIP campaign to maintain awareness-£10,000

(2) Direct Mail to existing customers to inform them of the new product launch-£10,000

(3) Promote product launch on the company website-similar customers ate likely to be interested in new technology- £20,000

Additional Budget costs

I would recommend that an additional £40,000 should be allocated to the budget for incidental costs. This would allow WCI to reduce its current marketing budget from £600,000 to £450,000 (not including staff costs).

6   **Implementation and Control**

All marketing communication effectiveness should be regularly reviewed and assessed.

Methods of doing this should include:
Advertising/PR- The number of responses to media enquiries
Direct Mail – number of responses received
Telemarketing/Corporate Events/Exhibitions-numbers of meetings arranged
Website- Number of hits

I hope that this information has been of interest and look forward to discussing it with you.

Regards

Patrick Pearson

Examiner's comments

This question has been answered in detail and covers all the key areas of B2B communications. More detail on an integrated communication strategy would have helped. The candidate could also have developed more of a discussion on brand values and brand awareness as this is a key factor in WCI's future growth.

Script 1: Question 3

To: Board of directors
            Patrick Pearson , Marketing consultants
Subject: European entry strategy
Date: 14th June 02

Introduction

Further to my marketing strategy this report will discuss the proposed entry strategy into the French and German markets for WCI.

Should WCI market abroad?

My research to date has indicated that there is clearly a potential in Europe for the services which WCI has been so successful in the UK, USA, and Eastern Europe. With the advert of the Euro, trading in Europe should become easier, although the UK's decision to delay membership may put us at a disadvantage initially many of WCI's current customers such as Volvo, Avon and Estee Lauder currently have operations abroad offering an initial point of contract.

Which markets should be entered?

The pharmaceutical sector (including life sciences) currently generates 33% of revenue for WCI. The company has built up a great deal of expertise and contracts within this field. There is huge potential for growth within this sector due to the reduction in time taken for drug reviews and the increase in the amount of the product development. Growth has also been encouraged due to the large number of mergers within the industry, WCI has already established a post merger group to deal with this WCI's particular strength is in lean compliance within this industry and I feel that although the company's ultimate aim is to offer a full service business, I feel that this would be no ambitious when entering a new market. It should therefore be used to gain a foothold within the market.

As strong economies with high levels of spending on biotech R+D (400E million France 2000) (500E million Germany 2000) I would suggest that WCI should initially target these markets, after conducting a comprehensive review of present activity.

Due to cultural differences in the ways of working/lifestyle I do not feel that WCI should attempt to operate this business as export marketing. The marketing objective to gain a 30% market share in learn compliance in the French and German pharmaceutical market by 2005 is ambitious and is being supported by a significant level of investment. I would therefore suggest a multinational marketing strategy. An office has already been established in E Europe and satellite offices should be set up in France and Germany. These should be staffed by foreign nationals, who already have knowledge of the market and contracts within the appropriate industry. This will give WCI a foothold in the market and many foreign clients prefer to deal with their own nationality setting up offices ie from home will also reduce travelling costs as the business grows. Care should however be taken to train these naïve sales people carefully to ensure that they project the correct corporate image. This could be achieved by extension of the existing internal marketing and by setting up training causes. These people must not feel isolated and should be integrated within the culture of WCI.

As a result of this need for close integration and the need to reflect the people aspect of WCI as a service business, selling through distributors or agents would not be a suitable distribution channel.

The marketing mix to achieve objectives product

The product needs of the customers in these markets should be thoroughly researched. It is likely that a standardisation approach although cheaper cannot be adopted due to system incompatibility and that products will need to be adapted clients should initially be sold loan compliance and then other products should be cross sold as the market develops.

Price

Extensive research also needs to be carried out into market pricing in these two countries. It should also be remembered that the WCI brand will not be developed at all in these sectors so premium prices may not be able to be charged.

Place

As previously mentioned naïve sales people should be recruited they will know the culture and are likely to have contract. Additional contracts could be obtained through UK pharmaceutical contacts.

Promotion – Pull strategy / Profile strategy

Although in the medium term this will be a pull strategy, in the short term it could be argued that the need to promote the brand within the European market could from part of the overall company profile branding strategy. By building up a brand in these countries, pricing can be increased.

Pull strategy activities include-

(1) Advertising in pharmaceutical publications in France and Germany. Media may not be as diverse as in the UK and a local advertising agency should be used to overcome any cultural differences. It is unlikely that the UK based advertising would be interpreted in the same way by the French and German £50,000

(2) Corporate events – again these should be organised by nationals to ensure that they are suited to local trust £45,000.

(3) Trade exhibitions /conferences - £50,000 these are popular in overseas markets and will gain credibility from local opinion formers.

People

Use foreign nationals to portray the marketing message. It is likely that a differentiation approach will need to be adopted to target these markets.

Physical evidence

Staff and the literature given out must project the correct corporate image, as well as fitting in with local culture and tastes.

Processes

The post merger group, which has been successful in the UK should be used to look for new business. If any work for European clients is carried out in the UK, seamless approach should be given to the customer.

Other considerations

In addition to the 7ps which are so important to a service business, WCI should also carefully research the costs of entry into these markets and any barriers to entry, for example competition reluctance to use foreign companies etc. barriers to exit.

Implementation and control

As with the entry into any market, it is essential for WCI to review the marketing strategies and objectives for the French and German pharmaceutical markets. It may be necessary to take the decision to withdraw from these markets due to market conditions or to adapt the European marketing mix to be used in another country e.g. Italy.

I hope that this is of interests and look forward to further discussion

Regards

Patrick Pearson

Examiner's comments

In this question, the candidate has taken a broad brush approach. The use of the Harrel and Keifer model would have made sense in terms of country attractiveness. Market entry strategies also have to be based on strengths within sectors and this should have been discussed more.

4 SAMPLE SCRIPT 2

BPP note. The wording and structure of this script are as presented by the student

---

Script 2: Question 1

Report
To: The Board, WCI
From: Patrick Pearson, Consultant.

1. Current competitive position and 5 year strategic marketing plan.
2. Communications plan
3. European entry strategy.

Note:

- All page numbers given refer to page numbers in the case.
- Parts of relevant models only are used, for brevity.
- Assumptions will be stated and examples from other industries used if necessary.

1 WCI current competitive position

(a)

- The IT consultancy and outsourcing market is large ($110 billion estimated revenues by 2002-p.7), complex and constantly changing.

- WCI is a small player in a fragmented market with intense competition. However the 'Big 5' and IBM hold considerable market power.

- WCI's 'one stop shop' capabilities and lean process skills could act as a differentiator but WCI could be overwhelmed if it spreads itself too thinly.

- The company has not developed a clear brand or position- it has a broad portfolio of products and markets and unclear direction.

- Customer loyalty is relatively low for an industry reliant on long relationships for profitability.

We move on from the competitive analysis to look at WCI itself and the opportunities it faces.

WCI is solvent but profitability has decreased (net-4.5% average in 1999) also there are areas of duplication on the board and the number of offices.

WCI faces opportunities for growth in the US and in Europe following the advent of the Euro, in sectors such as pharmaceuticals, which offer scope for our products – cost saving lean processes and outsourcing, or products for bio informatics.

Trends such as the growth in outsourcing web technologies, the strategic role of IT and customer needs for added value are in line with WCI strengths.

Key areas:

- WCI must focus efforts on certain markets to keep up with the pace of change

- Formal marketing planning with clear segmentation and targeting will aid market selection, guide mix strategies and improve focus on key customer relationships

- Strong brand development is needed.

- Market entry strategies are required across Europe.

- The company structure and product portfolio must be streamlined to market target market and improve profitability and efficiency/effectiveness.

(b)   In the light of there aims a strong mission statement is proposed to motivate staff, communicate to state holders and customers and guide marketing strategy;

'WCI seek to offer total web based IT solutions to the health, pharmaceutical and consumer/ food manufacturing industries, building lean businesses and adding value for our customers while protecting our main asset- people'

(c)   Corporate objectives

- These show WCI's aims for growths and financial performance;

- To grow turnover at 50% pa over 5 years, reaching £174 million by 2007.

- To enter key European market taking advantage of the opportunities and cost benefits created by the Euro.

- To improve grows profitability from 34% to 40% by 2007

- Assumption; 2002 turnover 23.3m.

(d)   From these objectives from the marketing objectives and thus the basis of our strategy for brand and market entry.

- To penetrate and increase loyalty in existing health network, consumer and pharmaceutical market (US&UK) achieving 10% share of pharmaceutical IT outstanding in 5 years.

- To enter the French German and Spanish market for consumer and pharmaceutical manufacture over 5 years.

- To achieve brand awareness in all target market sectors of 20% in yr 1, 50% by years 3 and 90% by year.

(e)   To satisfy these market, WCI must define its generic approach, which will determine competitive strategy and guide mix programmes. The 3 generic strategies are shown with the current and projected position for WCI:

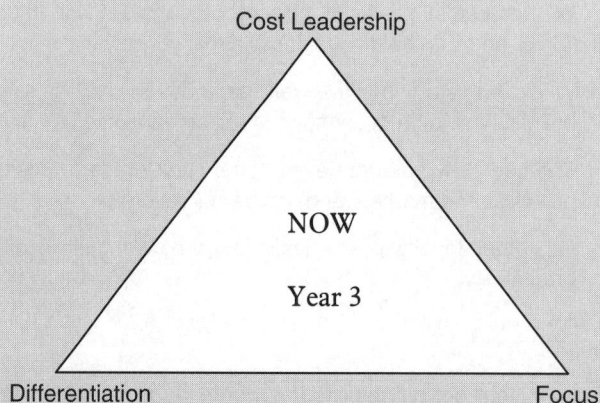

Cost Leadership

NOW

Year 3

Differentiation   Focus

Justification:

WCI must focus effort on familiarity with key sectors (see segmentation) because the IT market is too large and fast moving to stay with the current market spread (pp61-2).

WCI will focus on segment where it has experience, relationships and core competence, providing close relationships and a tailored offer.

WCI will differentiate via it strong band (see brand strategy in part) it streamlined total offer (see 'product') and it expertise.

(f)   Segmentation, targeting, positioning.

These are critical to a successful strategy.

Segmentation bases appropriate to b2b;

- SIC code eg pharmaceutical drug development
- Size of industry eg >1000 employees
- Geographical location

Hence, Bayer in Germany is a target.

Target segment	Rationale
Pharmaceutical companies in Europe and US	• Existing experience • Refs: Bayer, Pfizer Growth market (p43)
Health provider: Networks across Europe	• NHS experience • Web competencies • Health/human position (see below)
Food and cosmetics: Manufacture	Regulated, as per pharmaceuticals (FDA). With lean capabilities References: Fox's biscuits

We will reduce focus on TMT, finance and 'other' manufacturing – we need to focus, and have either fewer customers in these segments.

Positioning

In a large complex market WCI require a strong position in customers' minds relative to the competition. This will support the generic strategy of focus/differentiation

Variables

Product teachers :	One stop shop
Price/quality:	Added value
User:	See segmentation; 'health and people – care positioning'

(g)   The **GE model markets investment options to market sectors:**

- Sector attractiveness: market size, growth, growth in consultancy & IT outstanding growth, profitability (eg strategy consulting over infrastructure services) and competition;

- WCI strengths: sector experience, customer references (NHS –p21) product range and brand strength.

GE Matrix
Sector attractiveness

	High	Medium	Low
High	Lean processes strategy and managed services for targeted segments - Invest for growth	Infrastructure services (cash cow)	
Medium	E-bsuiness for 4 target segments - Invest for growth	General manufacturing (wrong position) Harvest/DIvest	
Low	Mobile Technologies NPD needed - Invest for growth	Financial services - low TMT experience - complex sector - selectively invest	

(WCI STRENGTHS)

BPP PUBLISHING

(h)   The Ansoff matrix shows our growth options.

Ansoff Matrix

PRODUCT

Existing Products   *New Products*

	MARKET PENETRATION	NEW PRODUCT DEVELOPMENT
Existing MARKETS	Of 4 key segments in the US/UK - increase loyalty - streamline product offer - CRM - Brand awareness	Mobile technologies for our target segments in the UK and US
New	MARKET DEVELOPMENT - Germany - France - Spain - (see place and part3 - market entry)	

The GE matrix underpins our segmentation and guides our mix strategy. The Ansoff matrix guides market entry, NPD and mix strategies.

(i)   **Competitive Strategy**

WCI cannot meet big players 'head on' as it lacks the resource to take on IBM for example. It should, therefore, follow a niche strategy serving its chosen markets well- eg with lean processes tailored to cosmetic manufacture.

A bypass strategy can be followed, building specialist IT capabilities in the 4 segments which will help to build barriers around WCI-using customer relationship and key account management tools (CRM/KAM) to collect data on customers and tailor new offers such as m-technologies to suit their needs.

(j)   **The marketing mix**

The extended service mix is necessary in WCI's people based business.

Product

Integrated total offer, yet tailored to each individual customer within a sector or the general business environment.

Core: 'better leaner businesses'

Actual product: 'all IT needs, right from the customer value chain through to the strategy and supply chain management, incorporating internal processes and e-commerce.

Augmented product : 24/7 web access to help and advice, KAM, on-site IT experts, full after sales service.

Investment is to be made in a parallel NPD process e.g. for mobile technologies, such as drug data for pharmaceutical representatives.

Place

Exclusive distribution from WCI offices, one per market. Direct sales force and KAM to build customer relationships.

See also part 2: communications

Part 3: European entry strategy

Pricing

The added value position points to a premium price strategy, however, a more market based approach may be taken for new market entry (penetration pricing). The need for customers to outsource and use IT strategically to create an efficient value chain makes them less price sensitive for the IT solution itself, if precisely tailored to their needs.

People

People are WCI's brand ambassadors. They must be selected carefully, well trained for sales, IT or KAM expertise and motivated with bonuses e.g. for customer retention.

Brand building will attract the best staff. We must inculcate the brand values throughout the company (see brand strategy).

Locals will be used in the new markets (see part 3-market entry)

Process

Partnership with software suppliers and other consultants; Intel, Compaq, Dell and Microsoft for supply and local consultants in new markets. The need for KAM and an excellent NPD process has been mentioned. However, the main thrust here is the customer facing processes:

* A good website with clear links
* Key account management
* Access to service personnel around the clock

Promotions

See part 3 for promotional plan.

Physical evidence: see branding in part 2

(k) **Budget**

The historical budget is £600,000, but is being reviewed. The benchmark for best practice marketing organisations is around 5% of turnover, this also fits the objective and task approach, bearing in mind, the needs of the marketing plan.

A larger marketing department is needed, restructured to include:

* Country managers

* Functional IT (product managers)

* Business development managers for each target segment and the cost of these and the Key Account Managers has been taken into account.

Marketing will need a budget for greater planning and research responsibilities.

Sales turnover			*Marketing budget*
Year			
1	(2002-3)	£34.5m	£1.8m
2	(2003-4)	£51.75m	£2.7m
3	(2004-5)	£77.6m	£4m
4	(2005-6)	£116.4	£6m
5	(2006-7)	£174.6m	£9m

This budget is ample for all activities and also for support for overseas growth and penetration.

Breakdown for marketing in £'000

	Year				
Activity	1	2	3	4	5
Salaries	300	450			
Salesforce & key account managers	900	1350			
Marketing planning	75	112			
Research	50	75			
MKIS	50	75			
CRM database	50	75			
Marketing Communications	(300)	(450)			
Internet Development	50	75			
Partnership Building	75	112			
PR/sponsorship	45	68			
Internal marketing	30	45			
Promotions	100	150			
Contingency	75	112			
Total	1800	2700			

The increase in marketing will be funded by increased turnover and profitability

- The streamlined product approach
- Efficient country/product/business manager structure
- Improved customer retention via CRM and branding

Timescale and action plan

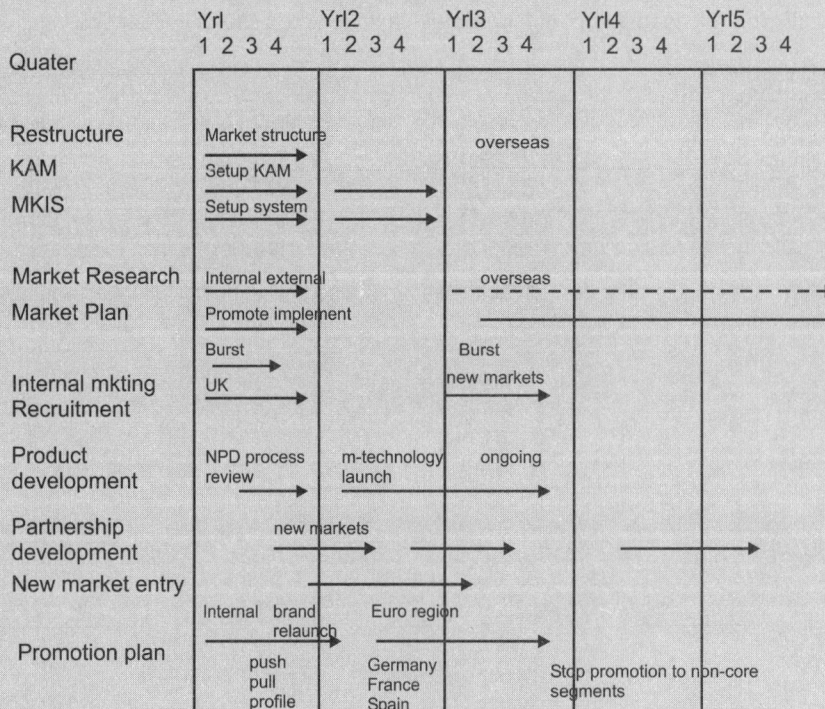

(l)   **Measurement and Control**

- The marketing structure and KAM proposals have been described
- A comprehensive MKIS must be set up including :
  - Market intelligence (trends/competitors)
  - Internal records (customer details and satisfaction linked to CRM database
  - Decision support e.g. BERI index forecasts
  - Marketing research e.g. for brand awareness, and cross cultural analysis of new markets

Marketing Metrics

These are useful measures of the success of the strategy:

- New customers per month, customer retention ratios
- New channel relationships
- Lead generation/order ratio
- Sales and turnover increase
- Brand awareness
- Number of new products
- % income from new products
- Customer satisfaction ratings
- Size of repeat orders
- Relationship duration
- Proportion of earnings from target vs. non-target segments year –on-year
- Market share increase in new markets

These measures link to the marketing objectives of new product introduction, new market entry, market penetration and brand building.

The rest of the strategies continue in the next sections.

Examiner's comments

This question is very comprehensively answered and there are some good analyses to back up the arguments. The candidate has also discussed how the success of the strategies could be assessed, by using marketing metrics. Some more analysis of the detail given in the appendices would have helped.

Script 2: Question 2

Communications plan

WCI needs to develop a distinctive brand to support its competitive approach and position (described in part 1); to communicate its streamlined product offer, superior value and focus on its target markets.

A strong brand will:

- Allow premium pricing.
- Facilitate the launch of new products such as mobile technologies

WCI must build awareness of the brand and comprehension of its focus on the four target market segments, to aid current market penetration and new entry into Germany, France, Spain and other European countries.

WCI has both internal and external stakeholders to consider.

- Competitors to whom to signal its position
- Internal employees who must cope with structural change and growth.

BPP PUBLISHING

- Possible new market partners, not least, customers in target segments.

In B2B markets, rational, promotional messages work best-IT solutions are 'high involvement' items of capital expenditure.

The organisational decision making unit must be considered including IT directors (deciders) finance directors (financiers) and IT experts (users/influencers).

Promotional tools can create awareness but a direct sales force must close sales.

Key Account managers are a major conduit for communications: relationship marketing is key as WCI gains much income from long-term contracts.

With these factors in mind, the Promotional objectives are to:

- Create a united coherent brand from the merged companies, understood by key internal markets within one year

- To create awareness of the WCI brand among key influencers in existing markets, reaching 90% by year 5.

- To create awareness in new markets of 25% after year 2 and 50% by year 5

- To have reached the target positioning in customers' minds by the end of year 4

These communications based objectives also link to the company sales turnover objectives, basically supporting them.

Key message

We are the one-stop shop for lean IT solutions in the web age for your market sector-we add value for customers via innovation and our employees.

Strategy

Push-opening channels to market via partnerships and KAM

Pull - creating awareness and conviction of our brand & position among key decision makers in our target markets

Profile-communicating our brand identity to all stakeholders

Internal marketing-creating internal support for change and embedding brand values.

All strategies to be underpinned by our brand strategy.

Tools and tactics

'Push'

Creating partnerships with independent consultants in new target markets using a rebranded website and visiting IT exhibitions in key markets. Joining trade missions and using trade press advertising. The direct sales force should be used to build contacts and relationships.

'Pull'

Advertising in trade magazines for IT but also target segments e.g. drug development press.

Re-branded website with good links to customers, industry sectors and IT portals.

Attendance at key IT and customer industry exhibitions.

Direct Mail- using 'Management-in-Action' by sending it to well researched targets e.g. food manufacturers and IT managers. The magazine should include case studies needed in the industry to understand IT strategy and solutions (p.333 and 35 of the case)

Company literature

Written around target segments rather than products. These should be rebranded and should be downloadable from the Net. It should also contain direct salesforce activities.

Profile

- Press releases and technical articles for the trade press to build 'niche' status
- Hospitality for key customers heads
  Eg board members who influence IT strategy (see p.32 of the case)

- Seminars eg 'tying IT to business goals'

Brand Strategy

An umbrella 'WCI' brand should remain the first choice as it works best for service offers where the whole packaged offer is important, it also suits our one-stop shop capabilities, and is a good platform for building partnerships. The brand can be illustrated by describing its core, possible extension areas and 'no-go' areas. Any new product development must build on this core, and strengthen the relevance of the brand to staff and customer segments.

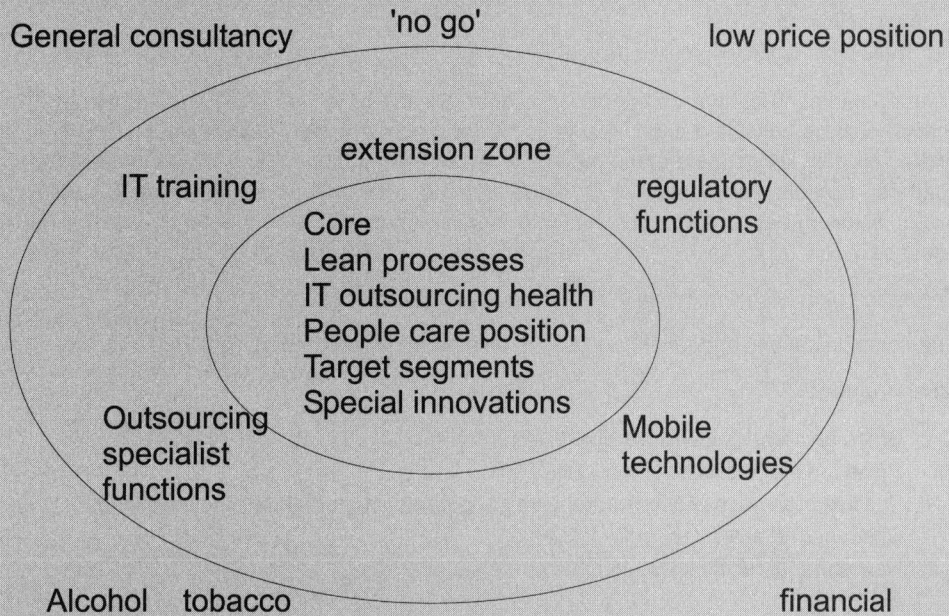

General consultancy   'no go'   low price position

extension zone

IT training   regulatory
functions

Core
Lean processes
IT outsourcing health
People care position
Target segments
Special innovations

Outsourcing
specialist
functions   Mobile
technologies

Alcohol   tobacco   financial

The brand staircase shown illustrates the planned progress of the brand over five years

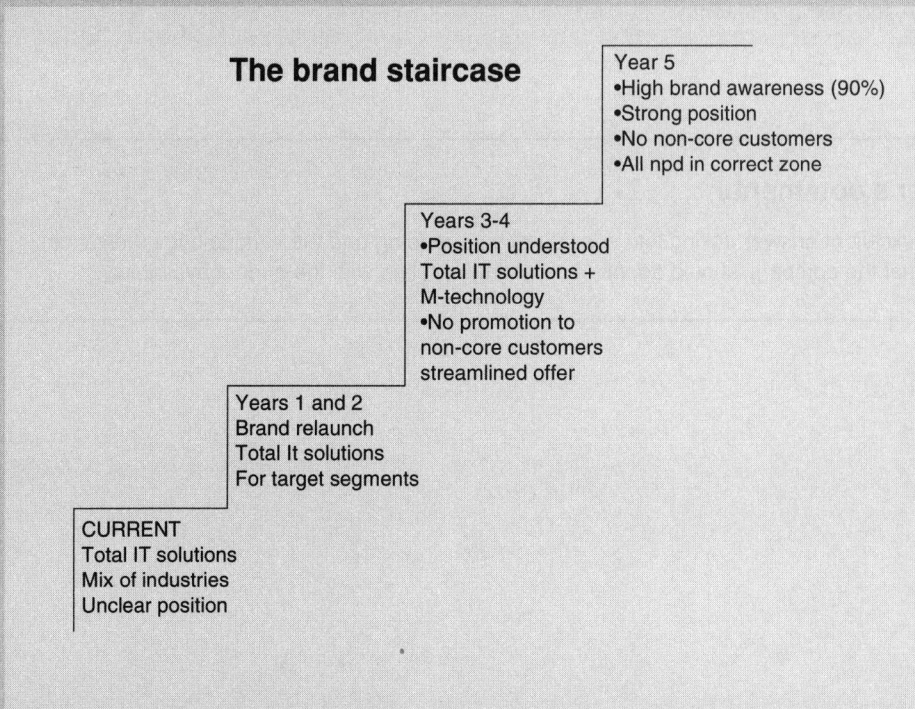

The brand staircase

Year 5
- High brand awareness (90%)
- Strong position
- No non-core customers
- All npd in correct zone

Years 3-4
- Position understood
Total IT solutions +
M-technology
- No promotion to
non-core customers
streamlined offer

Years 1 and 2
Brand relaunch
Total It solutions
For target segments

CURRENT
Total IT solutions
Mix of industries
Unclear position

Brand awareness research will be required using telephone questionnaires and focus group input from key customers. A brand relaunch is required in year 1 with a logo redesign to show the 'people/health/medical' position and application across all points of customer contact such as the website, literature, MiA magazine and correspondence, also in reception areas (physical evidence).

Ongoing research will be required will be required to measure brand awareness and associations (perhaps using Likert scales for attitudinal research). This could be by post, on the telephone or the internet.

Together all these steps will help to build brand equity:

- awareness
- associations
- help with new market penetration

Internal marketing cannot be ignored; the staff are the brand as WCI is so people and skills based. Staff should be consulted and involved in the rebrand exercise. They should also be sold the concept of the new company structure and the expanded role of marketing. The intranet should be used to keep scattered consultants aware of all changes and successes. Good customer service training should be given, including best practice guidelines for service quality. Customer retention will be rewarded using bonuses.

The action plan is shown in part 1 (I) showing actions and timescales.

The communications budget of £300,000 is also broken down in part 1(k).

Measurement

- Brand awareness levels (re-objectives)
- Press coverage and column inches
- Positive brand associations among key segments, customer satisfaction ratings
- Customer referrals secured
- New channel relationships in new markets
- Staff retention
- Website hits
- Catalogues requested
- Sales leads/order conversion rates.

Summary

The communications plan will thus contribute to the marketing objectives of brand building, customer retention and new market entry.

Examiner's comments

This as an excellent answer, taking into consideration, branding and the various communications strategies that the company should adopt. The costing is in line with the budget availability.

Script 2: Question 3

WCI has major opportunities ahead for growth in Europe. The pharmaceutical sector is growing rapidly (p. 43 case) and has plans to grow in Germany and Austria.

Companies to focus on include Bayer and Roche.

The consumer food and manufacturing sector is also growing and targeting transactional segments across Europe-for example, the Germany retailer Aldi is expanding across Europe causing food and FMCG manufacturers to follow them. Unilever operates across Europe and seeks partners for outsourcing who are also spread across its markets.

WCI's markets are multinational and WCI needs to mirror this in its efforts.

In fact the advent of the Euro, together with the transnational operation of these MNE's makes much of Europe a potential single market for WCI, reducing the complexity for transactions.

Our web capabilities will allow us to access customers across Europe. Thus we should access 'strategically equivalent segments' based on target industries across Europe in Germany, Spain, Italy and France, mainly in the four target segments identified in part 1 of this report. Firstly WCI needs to research the target markets in question for:

(a) **Size**

Based on MNE activity of our four target sectors

(b) **Accessibility**

The reduction in barriers across Europe makes this much easier, plus we can create a virtual network right across the market, linking consultants and service IT personnel to our main offices.

(c) **Risk**

The BERI index of O (risky) to 4(not risky) could be used

PESTLE Analysis

This should also be carried out, and competitors analysis e.g. there are particular legal requirements we should take note of, when designing IT solutions for the food and pharmaceutical sectors in Germany, as opposed to UK regulations.

Which competitors eg CTP, are also active in these markets and what are their strategies?

Cross-cultural analysis is also important, particularly for service organisations involving face to face direct selling. The differences involve high and low context cultures, or differences based on Hofstede's cultural dimensions. German customers tend to be lower-context aware than Spanish customers, for instance, according to Hofstede.

Research sources can include: Chambers of Commerce, The DTI, The Internet, www.WTI.com

The markets will be chosen according to the analysis described: We assume, Germany, Spain and France, initially and then the new entries will be based on the success in these key markets.

To achieve the scale and turnover WCI wishes to achieve, it will need to research partnerships in the target markets. Independent consultants (and 45% of consultants are independent, according to the case), could provide a good route. They know their own markets and would be familiar with the culture of doing business and building relationships.

WCI could research partnerships on the Internet, via the trade press or by joining trade missions. The WCI website should link to key IT recruitment sites for Europe. The partnerships would work by WCI providing full support, training and the total product package to the consultants who are selected. Brand and company inculcation would be required and legal contracts need to be outlined.

In larger markets such as Germany, WCI should consider the acquisition of total consultancies.

A WCI office is required in each market as a base for local personnel, although most support would be provided via the Intranet. The closure of extra UK offices (there are 4) could fund the opening of a new office in Germany.

The Internet site and company literature must be translated into the languages of the target markets. English is an international business language, but translation shows a 'polycentric' concessionary approach, demonstrating market commitment.

Another market entry option is to consider a joint venture, focused on a specific industry, using a similar sized JV partner such as Druid.

BPP PUBLISHING

The involvement in the markets would thus show a balance between growing organically (too slow) and retaining involvement with and closeness to the markets. The strong WCI culture and its focus on caring for its consultants will help it to spread internationally.

The product offer will need to be adapted to suit the legal and technical features of each market. Promotion and people are linked. We will use local sales people and KA managers although UK expatriates will help start-ups.

Pricing will need to take account of market forces in each market. This is a problem because although the Euro is Europe-wide, cost differences still exist between markets, for example, in terms of wages.

Distribution strategy

The use of partnerships and local key account managers has been described.

The brand building strategy described in part 2 of the report is essential for building the brand equity and recognition across IT and customer markets. It will thus facilitate market entry as customers will choose what they recognise. International trade magazines and exhibitions will be a key tool.

Timings and actions are important. The activity plan and timescales chart shown in part 1, includes international market research, partnership development and overseas market entry-please refer back to part 1.

International control is made complex by geographical distances and cultural distances. WCI should maintain contact with its subsidiary offices using video-conferencing facilities. Sales targets should be clearly set out, taking account of the different economic conditions in different countries.

Conclusion

This entire report provides a cohesive plan for WCI over the next few years. Good attention to monitoring and control, market sensing and new product development, together with a brand and target market focus should ensure growth and success.

Examiner's comments

A practical solution for WCI. The candidate has taken account of the cultural problems that the company may face in different European countries. Some models justifying the entry strategies would have been helpful.

Part D
Exam notes

21

Exam Preparation

Chapter Topic List

1	Exam technique
2	Report format

1 EXAM TECHNIQUE

1.1 You have probably already sat successfully a number of CIM examinations, and the general tips on exam technique all remain equally valid. The following notes will provide you with the opportunity to remind yourself of best exam practice to ensure you do not throw away a case study through poor presentation or exam technique.

1.2 **Get organised**

Make sure you have space and materials e.g. files, dividers etc so you can get down to organizing your notes and analysis as soon as the case comes.

> **Tutor Tip**
>
> You may have found the idea of having blank templates of key models helpful. If you have Ansoff, PLC, market maps etc. you can simply add the case detail to these as you come across them.

1.3 **Developing an exam timetable**

You are now ready to make your final exam preparations. You should already have planned to make time available for the case study preparation. Use the attached timetable to help you plan your case preparation.

BPP PUBLISHING

Step	Timing
Case Step 1 Read and overview case	
Case Step 2 Complete internal inview analysis	
Case Step 3 Complete external inview analysis	
Case Step 4 Prioritise and identify critical success factors	
Case Step 5 Establishing the strategic direction	
Case Step 6 Consider the business implications	
Case Step 7 Develop marketing strategies	
Case Step 8 Develop marketing tactics	
Case Step 9 Develop controls	
Case Step 10 Organise your exam file	

2 REPORT FORMAT

2.1 You **must** work in report format for this paper.

You **must** answer the questions in the order set.

Report format requires the following:

- Title and contents page

- Numbered sections and sub-sections

  Treat Q1 as Section 1
  Treat Q2 as Section 2
  Treat Q3 as Section 3

- Use bullet points rather than a, b, c or numbering

- Include diagrams and tables within your content

- Add that white space and colour to highlight your work

2.2 You will only convince the examiners if your approach is clear and decisive with your assessment and recommendations justified.

BPP PUBLISHING

Tutor note

2.3 We know it is tempting to prepare your answers in detail and rehearse them before the exam but you **must not do so**. You must be able to incorporate the **last minute** information provided in the exam, into your analysis and recommendations. Do take time to think through the implications of this last minute information on your plans and make sure it is **highlighted** in your responses. The examiner will be impressed if he feels you are flexible and responsive to changing conditions.

Tips

2.4 Keep your presentation notes brief and structure your decision.

(a) Prepare key notes pages as prompts for any question area which might come up (make sure you add relevant numbers, using specific data which will help demonstrate your command of the material).

(b) Have a broad outline structure for tackling any identified question.

(c) Prepare your portfolio of pictures and models which you can use to justify and illustrate your answers. Produce these in black felt tip, one per page so that lines can be traced onto your answer book to scale etc. You will find this saves precious minutes in the exam room, which you will welcome.

2.5 Time management will be critical and you will not be able to have a minute over your allocated time - the responsibility to manage that time against the marks allocated is yours. Think about adding a first page in your decision file so it forces you to look at the mark allocations and plan a finish time for each question accordingly.

Marks

Question 1	finished by	......
Question 2	finished by	......
Question 3	finished by	5 p.m.
	180 minutes	100

Exam Briefing and Tutorials

If you are working alone and independently on the case, you may be glad of some final help and advice. Angela and Juanita working through Tactics for Exam Success (www.tacticsforexamsuccess.co.uk) produce case guidance notes, final briefings and offer workshops and one to one tutorials for Case.

To find out availability and prices, please contact them on 020 8313 9317.

BPP PUBLISHING

CIM Order

To BPP Publishing Ltd, Aldine Place, London W12 8AA

Tel: 020 8740 2211. Fax: 020 8740 1184
email: publishing@bpp.com
online: www.bpp.com

Mr/Mrs/Ms (Full name)

Daytime delivery address

Postcode

Date of exam (month/year)

Daytime Tel

POSTAGE & PACKING

Study Texts

	First	Each extra	
UK	£3.00	£2.00	£
Europe*	£5.00	£4.00	£
Rest of world	£20.00	£10.00	£

Kits/Success Tapes

	First	Each extra	
UK	£2.00	£1.00	£
Europe*	£2.50	£1.00	£
Rest of world	£15.00	£8.00	£

Grand Total (Cheques to *BPP Publishing*) I enclose

a cheque for (incl. Postage) £

Or charge to Access/Visa/Switch

Card Number

Expiry date   Start Date

Issue Number (Switch Only)

Signature

	8/02 Texts	9/02 Kits	Success Tapes (old syllabus)
STAGE 1 NEW SYLLABUS			
1 Marketing Fundamentals	£18.95 ☐	£9.95 ☐	£12.95 ☐
2 Marketing Environment	£18.95 ☐	£9.95 ☐	£12.95 ☐
3 Customer Communications	£18.95 ☐	£9.95 ☐	£12.95 ☐
4 Marketing in Practice	£18.95 ☐	£9.95 ☐	£12.95 ☐
ADVANCED CERTIFICATE OLD SYLLABUS *			
5 The Marketing Customer Interface	£18.95 ☐	£9.95 ☐	£12.95 ☐
6 Management Information for Marketing Decisions	£18.95 ☐	£9.95 ☐	£12.95 ☐
7 Effective Management for Marketing	£18.95 ☐	£9.95 ☐	£12.95 ☐
8 Marketing Operations	£18.95 ☐	£9.95 ☐	£12.95 ☐
DIPLOMA OLD SYLLABUS *			
9 Integrated Marketing Communications	£18.95 ☐	£9.95 ☐	£12.95 ☐
10 International Marketing Strategy	£18.95 ☐	£9.95 ☐	£12.95 ☐
11 Strategic Marketing Management: Planning and Control	£18.95 ☐	£9.95 ☐	£12.95 ☐
12 Strategic Marketing Management: Analysis and Decision (9/02)	£25.95 ☐	N/A	N/A

* Texts and kits for remaining new syllabus items will be available in the spring and summer of 2003.

SUBTOTAL £

We aim to deliver to all UK addresses inside 5 working days. A signature will be required. Orders to all EU addresses should be delivered within 6 working days.

All other orders to overseas addresses should be delivered within 8 working days.

* Europe includes the Republic of Ireland and the Channel Islands.

REVIEW FORM & FREE PRIZE DRAW

All original review forms from the entire BPP range, completed with genuine comments, will be entered into one of two draws on 31 January 2003 and 30 July 2003. The names on the first four forms picked out on each occasion will be sent a cheque for £50.

Name: _____ Address: _____

_____

_____

How have you used this Text?
(Tick one box only)

☐ Self study (book only)

☐ On a course: college_____

☐ With BPP Home Study package

☐ Other _____

Why did you decide to purchase this Text?
(Tick one box only)

☐ Have used BPP Texts in the past

☐ Recommendation by friend/colleague

☐ Recommendation by a lecturer at college

☐ Saw advertising in journals

☐ Saw website

☐ Other _____

During the past six months do you recall seeing/receiving any of the following?
(Tick as many boxes as are relevant)

☐ Our advertisement in the *Marketing Success*

☐ Our advertisement in *Marketing Business*

☐ Our brochure with a letter through the post

☐ Our brochure with *Marketing Business*

☐ Saw website

Which (if any) aspects of our advertising do you find useful?
(Tick as many boxes as are relevant)

☐ Prices and publication dates of new editions

☐ Information on product content

☐ Facility to order books off-the-page

☐ None of the above

Have you used the companion Success Tape for this subject?　　☐ Yes　　☐ No

Your ratings, comments and suggestions would be appreciated on the following areas.

	Very useful	Useful	Not useful
Introductory section			
Part A	☐	☐	☐
Biocatalytsts	☐	☐	☐
Daugavpils	☐	☐	☐
WC1	☐	☐	☐

	Excellent	Good	Adequate	Poor
Overall opinion of this Text	☐	☐	☐	☐

Please note any further comments and suggestions/errors on the reverse of this page.

✂ **Please return to: Kate Machattie, BPP Publishing Ltd, FREEPOST, London, W12 8BR**

REVIEW FORM & FREE PRIZE DRAW (continued)

Please note any further comments and suggestions/errors below.

FREE PRIZE DRAW RULES

1   Closing date for 31 January 2003 draw is 31 December 2002. Closing date for 31 July 2003 draw is 30 June 2003.

2   Restricted to entries with UK and Eire addresses only. BPP employees, their families and business associates are excluded.

3   No purchase necessary. Entry forms are available upon request from BPP Publishing. No more than one entry per title, per person. Draw restricted to persons aged 16 and over.

4   Winners will be notified by post and receive their cheques not later than 6 weeks after the relevant draw date. List of winners will be supplied on request.

5   The decision of the promoter in all matters is final and binding. No correspondence will be entered into.